# Now Read This II

# Genreflecting Advisory Series

Diana Tixier Herald, Series Editor

*Genreflecting: A Guide to Reading Interests in Genre Fiction,* 5th Edition
By Diana Tixier Herald

*Teen Genreflecting*
By Diana Tixier Herald

*Romance Fiction: A Guide to the Genre*
By Kristin Ramsdell

*Fluent in Fantasy: A Guide to Reading Interests*
By Diana Tixier Herald

*Now Read This: A Guide to Mainstream Fiction, 1978–1998*
By Nancy Pearl with assistance from Martha Knappe and Chris Higashi

*Now Read This II: A Guide to Mainstream Fiction, 1990–2001*
By Nancy Pearl

*Hooked on Horror: A Guide to Reading Interests in Horror Fiction*
By Anthony J. Fonseca and June Michele Pulliam

*Junior Genreflecting: A Guide to Good Reads and Series Fiction for Children*
By Bridget Dealy Volz, Cheryl Perkins Scheer, and Lynda Blackburn Welborn

*Christian Fiction: A Guide to the Genre*
By John Mort

*Strictly Science Fiction: A Guide to Reading Interests*
By Diana Tixier Herald and Bonnie Kunzel

# Now Read This II

## A Guide to Mainstream Fiction, 1990–2001

**Nancy Pearl**

2002
Libraries Unlimited
A Division of Greenwood Publishing Group, Inc.
Greenwood Village, Colorado

LIBRARIES UNLIMITED
A Division of Greenwood Publishing Group, Inc.
7730 East Belleview Avenue, Suite A200
Greenwood Village, CO 80111
1-800-237-6124
www.lu.com

**Library of Congress Cataloging-in-Publication Data from *Now Read This***

Pearl, Nancy.
    Now read this : a guide to mainstream fiction, 1978-1998 / Nancy
Pearl, with the assistance of Martha Knappe and Chris Higashi ; foreword
by Joyce G. Saricks.
    xvii, 432 p., 19x26 cm.
    Annotated list of 1000 books categorized by setting, story,
characterization, or language.
    Includes bibliographical references and index.
    ISBN 1-56308-659-X
    1. Fiction--20th century Bibliography. 2. Fiction--20th century--
Stories, plots, etc.--Indexes.  3. Best books.  I. Knappe, Martha.
II. Higashi, Chris.  III. Title.
Z5916.P43  1999
[PN3503]
016.80883'04--dc21                                          99-015280
                                                                 CIP

*Now Read This II*
ISBN 1-56308-867-3

# Contents

Acknowledgments..................................................................vii
Introduction .........................................................................ix
Mainstream Fiction Today ....................................................xvii

Chapter 1: Setting..................................................................1
Chapter 2: Story ...................................................................23
Chapter 3: Characters ...........................................................67
Chapter 4: Language .............................................................145

    Appendix A: How to Create a Dynamic Book Club...............165
    Appendix B: Book Awards ............................................169
    Appendix C: Bridges to Genre Fiction...............................171

    Author/Title Index.....................................................175
    Subject Index...........................................................209
    Author/Title Index from *Now Read This*............................253

# Acknowledgments

Libraries Unlimited is grateful to NoveList (of EBSCO Publishing) for their permission to adapt and use images from their program throughout the Genreflecting Advisory Series.

My thanks to all the readers who contributed to *Now Read This II*: Jennifer Baker, Gloria Gehrman, Chris Higashi, Barbara Ittner, Martha Knappe, Jan Lawrence, Marnie Webb, David Wright, and Neal Wyatt.

I apologize in advance if I have inadvertently left anyone off this list. I want to especially thank my editor at Libraries Unlimited, Barbara Ittner, without whom neither *Now Read This* nor *Now Read This II* would have come into being. Once again, I'd like to thank Paul Feavel, who manipulated the data and tolerated all my dumb questions with humor and grace. And lastly, enormous thanks go to my husband, Joe, who arranges his life so that my reading life is possible.

# Introduction

## The Timeless Allure of Fiction

If you are a dedicated fiction reader, you already know that the pleasures and rewards of reading fiction are plentiful. By simply opening a book, you enter the world of a novel where you may meet fascinating characters or travel to familiar or exotic locales and times. In this fictional world, you may also revel in the unfolding of a compelling story or bask in the elegance or power of the story's language. By reading fiction, you can learn; you can gain insights; you may even be spiritually nourished. You also experience a special intimacy in sharing the vision and interior world of another individual—the author.

But one of the most enduring joys of reading a novel is that it can lead to a seemingly unlimited number of other books, both fiction and nonfiction. Good novels, novels that we deeply enjoy, stimulate and direct such curiosity, such wandering. It is this wandering—exploring the various direct paths and indirect byways that come to mind as a novel is read—that makes reading fiction such an exciting adventure. By entering the world of a single novel, we find we have also entered a universe of fiction.

Those of us who are in the business of guiding readers in these wanderings (e.g., librarians, bookstore personnel) are fortunate to be able to share our love of reading and recommend specific books to others who share our passion for fiction. But it is often challenging to know how to satisfy our own cravings for fiction; and it's even more difficult to help others choose books that they will enjoy. Unless we know someone who shares or understands our reading taste and can actually recommend another book, the curiosity and expansion of interests brought about by a good novel can easily wander astray, become lost, or be discouraged. That is because reading recommendations tend to be highly personal—it's easy to recommend to a reader a book that *you* loved without fully appreciating the likes and dislikes of the other reader.

For genre readers, the process of finding and recommending fiction is not so difficult. The publishing industry supports the categorization of fiction into genres—mystery, romance, horror/suspense, and so on. There are journals, Web sites, and even bookstores devoted to specific genres. There are also genre guides that further explain and categorize genre titles by subgenre and theme, according to reading preferences. For example, the classic genre guide, Diana Tixier Herald's *Genreflecting*, now in its fifth edition (Libraries Unlimited, 2000), organizes more than 6,000 genre fiction titles into more than 100 genres, subgenres, and themes.

But with mainstream (or literary) fiction, there are no simple formulas, no foolproof guides. Certainly mainstream novels may have genre elements (e.g., historical, adventure). For example, Lisa Carey's *In the Country of the Young* has an element of fantasy that is central to its plot—the ghost of a little girl who died a hundred years ago reappears in the present. But Carey firmly grounds her novel in the real world, and we would not classify her as a writer of fantasy—nor would we, as readers' advisors, shelve her book in the fantasy section of the fiction shelves. She and many other writers who use magic realism simply use fantasy to further illuminate character, setting, or plot. Fantasy becomes a tool to help bring the novel to life, but it is not the point of the novel. In the same way, Suzanne Berne's *A Crime in the Neighborhood* revolves around the murder of a 12-year-old boy. Yet the focus of the novel is not on what happened, who the murderer was, or how the crime could be solved, but rather on the effect of the murder on the main character—how it, along with other events, shaped her life.

Similarly, there are many novels that take place during particular major events in the twentieth century, such as Michael Ondaatje's *Anil's Ghost* or Lan Cao's *Monkey Bridge*. What makes these books mainstream rather than genre novels? First of all, the development of the characters and their motivations are determined by the larger events surrounding them, but the books are not about those events per se. The authors are less interested in presenting an accurate historical account than they are in exploring a particular character's response to these events. Thus, in *Anil's Ghost*, Anil, the main character, returns to Sri Lanka at the time of the tripartite Civil War. Ondaatje draws our attention not to the specific events of the war, but to how Anil's life will be altered by her experiences there.

So these books, although they contain elements of a genre, are not genre fiction. Instead, their common bond is that they realistically explore aspects of the human experience—love, death, illness, aging, and fear, and the moral and ethical choices people make throughout a lifetime. (Mainstream fiction is also referred to as *literary fiction*, although that term often puts readers off, as they interpret it as being fiction that is dense and difficult to read, or is written in an experimental style.)

We often say that a mainstream novel "transcends its genre," that is, it may make use of some or many of the characteristics of the genre in its plot, but it tweaks those characteristics enough so that novel moves beyond the strict confines of genre novels. It may use the techniques of genre fiction, but it will likely bend or break the rules. A good example of an author whose novels consistently transcend their genre is Jonathan Lethem. Lethem plays fast and loose with the science fiction genre in *As She Climbed Across the Table* and the mystery genre in *Motherless Brooklyn*, so that although the former deals with a black hole named Lack (and the physicist who falls in love with it), and the latter is about the search for a murderer, neither one is strictly genre fiction. Instead, the conventions of each genre are worked into plots that explore relationships and life experiences.

## The Appeals Approach

"Can you recommend a good book?" is one of the most challenging questions that librarians and booksellers face. And answering that question can be one of the most rewarding aspects of library work and of the book business. In their book *Readers' Advisory Service in the Public Library* (2d ed., American Library Association, 1997), Joyce G. Saricks and Nancy Brown articulate a theory of why readers might enjoy books that seem, at first glance, to be radically different from one another. Their theory involves what they call "appeal characteristics," by which they mean those elements in books that make patrons enjoy them. Readers enjoy books not because of their specific themes or plot details—when is the last time someone asked for a good book about a young child caught between her scientist father and a lovingly eccentric mother who is going off the deep end into madness?—but because they are taken with the characters, or because the setting transports them to a different time and/or place, or because the writing is so beautiful that they savor every sentence, or because the story was so engrossing that it seemed as though the pages turned over by themselves.

*Now Read This II* and its predecessor *Now Read This* (Libraries Unlimited, 1999) are based on an appeal-characteristics approach to literature, with adaptations and additions dictated by our experience in advising readers. The two volumes are designed to facilitate the process of finding something else to read and easily guide readers from one book to another along the meandering and ever-enlarging path of their own interests, encouraging the idiosyncratic and informal education that recreational reading can be. Both guides focus on contemporary mainstream fiction—that is, books set in the twentieth or twenty-first centuries. *Now Read This II* encompasses mainstream novels published between 1990 and 2001.

*Now Read This* and its companion *Now Read This II* differ from other readers' guides because they focus on mainstream fiction and because they use the appeal-characteristics approach. Appeal characteristics speak directly to why a person may like or dislike particular books. Because it is frequently not the subject of a novel that determines whether or not a reader enjoys the book, readers' advisory tools that are purely subject-driven limit the possibility that readers will discover some other book they will enjoy reading. It is the elusive "feeling" a reader gets from a certain novel that is reflected in the appeal characteristics.

Of course, virtually all novels have characters, a setting in place and/or time, a story, and make use of language, but most are driven by one (or two) of these features. That is, one characteristic of the book is more apparent, or important, than the others. It's the rare novel that has more than two of the major appeal characteristics, but many readers would argue (quite convincingly!) that Pat Conroy's *The Prince of Tides*, Cormac McCarthy's *All the Pretty Horses*, and Larry McMurtry's *Lonesome Dove* appeal on all four characteristics. The more appeal characteristics that a book has, the wider its readership and popularity will be, because more people will be drawn to it. Different readers will access the novel through different appeal characteristics (and, in essence, each will read a different book).

To understand how to use appeal characteristics in readers' advisory work, it is necessary to understand the four major characteristics as we have applied them to mainstream novels.

In a book with **Setting** as its major appeal characteristic, the setting is essential to understanding character, conflict, or theme. The novel is very much specific to its location in time or place. In some novels, the setting functions almost as another character. When we describe such a book we invariably start off by saying where the book takes place: "Port William, Kentucky, is home to Jayber Crow, resident philosopher, grave digger, lifelong bachelor, and the town's only barber" is one way of describing Wendell Berry's *Jayber Crow*. About James Buchan's *The Persian Bride*, we might say, "When he arrives in Isfahan, Iran, in 1974, 18-year-old Englishman John Pitt falls in love with 17-year-old Shirin; their love is challenged by the terrible events following the Iranian revolution and the war with Iraq." There's a good chance that any reader who fell in love with the descriptions of Port William, Kentucky, the setting of Berry's novel, will also fall under the spell of Buchan's magnificent picture of Iran before and during the revolution that toppled the shah. (Incidentally, as might be gathered from these descriptions, character is a strong secondary appeal of both books.)

**Setting** also refers to the time period in which the book is set. Keith Maillard's *Gloria* strongly evokes the 1950s in the choices it lays out for its eponymous heroine. Gloria would have found her life far different if she came of age in the 1960s or the 1970s, when women's lives were far less constrained than they were in the period in which Maillard sets his book.

Some other examples of novels in which setting is the major appeal characteristic are Colum McCann's *This Side of Brightness*, Steven Millhauser's *Martin Dressler: The Tale of an American Dreamer*, and Pankaj Mishra's *The Romantics*.

In a book with **Story** as the major appeal, the plot dominates the novel. The reader is eager to turn the pages of the book to find out what happens or becomes enrapt with the complexity and surprising twists of the story. A description of the book will stress the events of the novel. In talking about Susan Merrell's *A Member of the Family*, we will most likely describe the novel in terms of what happens: The adoption of a Romanian orphan shatters the adopting family in ways nobody could have foreseen. In talking about Deirdre McNamer's *My Russian*, any description of the book will begin with the plot: Francesca Woodbridge uses a planned trip to Greece as an opportunity to change her life—without her husband and children. The stories can be as dissimilar as that of a child who believes she hears the voice of God (Jodi Picoult's *Keeping Faith*) to a creative writing teacher whose life is changed when a student accuses him of sexual harassment (Francine Prose's *Blue Angel*). Plot-driven novels can deal with difficult subjects, as in Kerri Sakamoto's *The Electrical Field*, in which events from the past continue to haunt the life of Japanese Canadian Asako Saito, or they can treat their subjects humorously, as in Matthew Sharpe's *Nothing Is Terrible*, in which Mary White falls in love with her sixth-grade teacher and the two decamp to Manhattan to live together.

In a novel with **Characters** as the major appeal, the characters are three-dimensional and seem to step off the page. In describing this type of novel we talk first about the people in them. Two character-driven novels are John Irving's *A Widow for One Year* and Hans-Ulrich Treichel's *Lost*. Characters can be children (Susan Richard Shreve's *Plum & Jaggers*) or adults (Colm Toibin's *The Blackwater Lightship*). They can enjoy relatively happy lives (Carol Shields's *Larry's Party*) or find themselves undergoing many difficulties (Judy Troy's *From the Black Hills*). What sets these novels apart from those with **Story** as the primary appeal is that we are more interested in the people than in what happens to them.

Of course, language underlies all writing. Without language we would not have the novel with three-dimensional characters, or a beautifully pictured setting, or a fast-paced, enjoyable story. But in a novel with **Language** as the major appeal characteristic, the quality of the writing is what makes the novel stand out. The author's use of language is evocative, unusual, thought-provoking, or poetic. The writing style can be as poetic and complex as that used by Sebastian Barry in *The Whereabouts of Eneas McNulty*, as powerful and energetic as Roddy Doyle's *A Star Called Henry*, or as mysteriously elliptical as Michael Ondaatje's *Anil's Ghost*. Despite the different styles of writing in each of these novels, it is impossible to talk about them without commenting on the way each of their authors makes use of language. Novels with **Language** as a major appeal characteristic often make us look at the world in a different way. As we experience the voice of the author, we find ourselves inside the mind of an elderly woman (Margaret Atwood's *The Blind Assassin*) or a young man in love (James Buchan's *The Persian Bride*). We can look at the world through the eyes of a South African teacher (J. M. Coetzee's *Disgrace*) or a contender in a bodybuilding competition (Harry Crews's *Body*).

There are many variations of appeals within these four areas (e.g., pacing, tone) as well as other areas of appeal (e.g., happy endings) and of rejection (e.g., size of book), as Professor Catherine Ross discovered in her research (Shearer, 2001). But given too many specifics and options, readers can be as overwhelmed as when they are given none at all. Thus, we have chosen to organize the books here under major appeal factors and create access to other attributes through the indexes.

As those of us—librarians and avid readers—who read and annotated for *Now Read This II* attempted to identify the major appeal of each book we read, we realized that the best way to decide what appeal a particular book has was to imagine describing it to a friend. As we thought about the description we would give, we asked ourselves the following questions: What would we emphasize in this description? Is it the setting, the rich description and establishment of a time or place? The story the book tells? The development of compelling, three-dimensional characters? The writer's use of language? In most cases, there was instant agreement; in some cases, spirited e-mail and verbal discussions took place before a consensus was reached. Despite our care in assigning appeal characteristics, we recognize that these are, in the end, somewhat subjective assignments. One person's character-driven novel might be viewed by a different reader as emphasizing setting or language. Rest assured, however, that these appeal characteristics represent the best thinking among the contributors to this book.

Sometimes it is the subject of a novel that draws a reader to a particular book. Often readers are interested in the complexities of family relationships, or the particular dynamics that occur between mothers and daughters, or novels set in the American Southwest. For the benefit of those readers, subject headings have been assigned to each of the more than 500 novels included in *Now Read This II*. Among these subject headings, we have identified novels that contain significant genre elements, such as mystery or romance. In addition, in Appendix C you will find lists of titles that bridge mainstream with genre fiction.

## The Selection Process

*Now Read This II* describes more than 500 titles, with more than 400 new to this volume. The remaining titles first appeared in *Now Read This*. Many of the carryover entries have been updated with new recommendations in the "Now try" sections. The two volumes are designed to be used as companions. As mentioned above, *Now Read This II* includes mainstream novels published between 1990 and 2001. Because readers of mainstream fiction tend to be very interested in reading award-winning fiction, we have included novels selected by the American Library Association's Notable Book Council from 1990 to 2000. Also included are books that have received the Pulitzer Prize, the National Book Award, the National Book Critics Circle Award, and the Booker Prize, as well as somewhat lesser known literary awards, including the Betty Trask Award, the Whitbread Award, the Orange Prize, and the IMPAC/Dublin Award. Oprah's Book Club selections are included as well. (More information about these awards can be found in Appendix B.)

Finally, we added some titles that were not award winners but that we thought should have been! These are books we loved and wanted to recommend for the pleasure of other readers.

# The Arrangement of the Book

*Now Read This II* is arranged in four sections, corresponding to the four appeal characteristics: setting, story, characters, and language. Books in each section are arranged alphabetically by the author's last name.

Each entry in *Now Read This II* begins with the book's author, title, publisher, date of publication, and number of pages in the book. Bibliographic information was taken from the OCLC FirstSearch database. When a book is a translation, the original language is noted along with the name of the translator. ISBNs are not given because of their volatility—in other words, they change when the books are, for example, issued in paperback or large-print editions, or when rights are sold.

Bibliographic information is followed by a brief summary of the plot, secondary appeal characteristic (if applicable), and subject headings. Novels that are especially good for discussion are noted with an icon "Book Groups," and novels that would appeal to young adults are noted by "YA." (See Appendix A for help in selecting good books for a discussion group.)

In the section of each entry called "Now try," you'll find suggestions for further reading. This section broadens the scope of *Now Read This II* considerably because a large percentage of the titles that are mentioned in "Now try" do not themselves have main entries. Included in this section are both fiction (including short stories) and nonfiction.

Following the four main sections are three appendixes (one on book groups, one on book awards, and one on genre links), an author/title index, and a subject index for this book. To further enhance the usefulness of both books, a combined author/title index from *Now Read This* is reproduced in this volume.

# What Else Is New in *Now Read This II*?

Several new features have been added to this book. "YA" denotes a book that is particularly good for young adult readers. To the subject line, we have added terms to describe books that share elements with genre fiction, and an appendix offers lists of these "genre bridges." We have added more titles and a greater diversity of genres to "Now try"— including more short story collections, nonfiction titles, and even poetry. There are also many "see also" references in the subject index, which will make searching for similar titles easier— when you look up "Love Stories" you will find a reminder that you may want to check out books under the subject of "Love Affairs." We have also added a new section on fiction trends and an additional appendix on creating and maintaining a well-functioning book group.

# How to Use This Book

By making use of *Now Read This* and *Now Read This II*, you will find that appeal characteristics link novels that may on the surface appear to be completely dissimilar. Understanding novels in terms of their appeal is a different way of choosing good books to read and may at first glance seem difficult to apply. Actually, it's quite easy. If you are looking for read-alikes, look first within a common primary appeal feature. This can be done by checking the index for the title that has already been read. If the book is not included in the index, ask your reader (or yourself) to describe the book. Is the description focused on the characters in the novel? The writing style? The plot? The setting? Your description will give you all the clues you need to identify the appeal characteristics of that book. Then go to that section in *Now Read This* and *Now Read This II* and browse through the entries, looking for a plot description that sounds interesting to you or your reader. You can also look for commonalities in secondary appeals, subject, or genre links.

To find titles with genre links, check the subject line. Novels where there is a mystery aspect to the story include "Mystery" as one of the subjects. Likewise, genre links to historical fiction have "Historical Setting" in the subject line; links to fantasy can be found by checking titles with "Magic Realism" in the subject line. For links with romance, look for the key words "Love Stories." Lists of titles that have strong genre elements can be found in Appendix C at the back of this book. In addition to those mentioned, you'll find suspense, horror, and gentle reads.

Sometimes, this is not enough. Anyone who has ever recommended a book to someone knows that it is impossible to guarantee that someone will enjoy a particular book, even if the appeal characteristics are a perfect match. Readers' advisors are acutely aware of this. The confounding variable—the issue that makes choosing books for yourself or others so challenging—is how much of a book's appeal is dependent on the mood of the reader. I know that in my own reading I lean heavily toward books whose appeal characteristics are either **Language** or **Characters**. What happens in a book, or where it is set, is far less important to me than to whom the events happen. I love to stop in the middle of a paragraph in a novel and savor the words that an author has written or the images he or she has conjured up. I enjoy looking into the lives of characters, sometimes living vicariously through their experiences. I normally pounce eagerly on every new Michael Ondaatje, Anne Tyler, or John Irving novel. Yet even with my strong predilection for these sorts of novels, I find that sometimes I want to read a novel that doesn't make demands on my mind, that doesn't explore deep issues, that doesn't deal with heart-wrenching events. Often I don't even know that I feel that way until I find myself beginning novel after novel, finding nothing satisfying enough to make me want to continue reading. Then I realize that it's time to browse through the **Story** sections of *Now Read This* and *Now Read This II* to find novels that meet that particular need. Later, when my mood has changed, I find that I can easily go back to those books that I had rejected in favor of a lighter read.

Those of us who have worked on these books, who have incorporated using appeal characteristics in our own book selection and in our readers' advisory work, are convinced of the efficacy of this way of thinking about and recommending books. It helps us successfully navigate ourselves and our patrons through the world of fiction.

I hope you will find *Now Read This* and *Now Read This II* useful, whether you are an individual looking for something good to read, a librarian doing readers' advisory service, or a member of a book group trying to select good titles for discussion. As you read through these books, be prepared to jot down dozens of titles. And enjoy!

# To Find Out More

More information on mainstream fiction (including frequently updated recommendations) is now available on the Genreflecting.com Web site. Questions and comments on books and mainstream fiction can be sent to me via the "Ask the Experts" feature of this site.

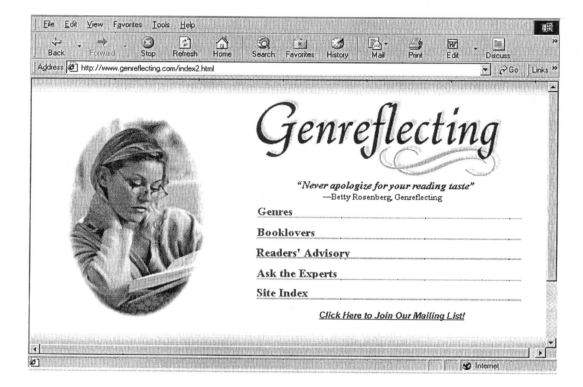

# Mainstream Fiction Today

## Publishing Trends

*Tumultuous* might be the best term to describe the state of the publishing world today. At the end of the twentieth century and the beginning of the twenty-first, the publishing world, and more specifically the world of mainstream fiction, saw enormous changes. Publishers merged, acquired, sold, and went defunct. Many of the major publishing companies were bought by large media corporations—Bertelsmann bought Random House and its associated companies (Vintage, Knopf, Crown, Harmony, Villard); Holtzbrinck purchased Farrar, Straus and Giroux; St. Martin's Press, HarperCollins, and Morrow were purchased by Rupert Murdoch's group, News Corp.; and Viacom bought Simon & Schuster. In addition, there was a consolidation of formerly independent publishing companies—Bantam, Dell, Doubleday became part of the Random House family, and Scribner became part of the Simon & Schuster group.

To book lovers and those who work with them, these changes looked ominous. Readers, writers, librarians, and booksellers feared that fewer mid-list fiction titles would be published. Mid-list fiction can be understood as those books that will never make it to the bestseller list but that are still worthy (or, perhaps, more worthy!) of being published and read. This fear was magnified in 1997 when HarperCollins canceled a number of contracts with authors whose books—both fiction and nonfiction—they believed would not be profitable enough in the current publishing climate.

In spite of these ominous signs and our dark forebodings, what we saw during these years was an outpouring of fine fiction published by a wide variety of presses. Many novels perceived by large commercial houses to be less than bestsellers found homes in small or independent presses. During the 1990s MacMurray & Beck, a small Colorado publishing house, published some wonderful novels by authors Frederick Reuss (*Horace Afoot* and *Henry of Atlantic City*), Rick Collignon (*Perdido*), and Patricia Henley (*Hummingbird House*), among others. Henley's novel was a finalist for the National Book Award, while Reuss's *Henry of Atlantic City* was named an ALA (American Library Association) Notable Book. Algonquin Books of Chapel Hill in North Carolina consistently published entertaining fiction, ranging from William Baldwin's *The Fennel Family Papers* to Carrie Brown's *Lamb in Love*, Frederick Dillen's *Fool*, and Daniel Wallace's *Ray in Reverse*. Permanent Press in New York State brought out Nicole Bokat's *Redeeming Eve*. Steerforth Press in Vermont published Nancy Huston's award-winning *The Mark of the Angel*. Both *The Lost Glass Plates of Wilfred Eng* by Thomas Orton and *Breakfast with Scot* by Michael Downing came from Counterpoint Press in Washington, D.C. Moyer Bell in Rhode Island brought out Shena Mackay's *The Artist's Widow*. Fjord Press in Seattle published Nancy Rawles's *Love Like Gumbo*. And the tiny publishing house Red Crane Books in New Mexico issued Keith Egawa's first novel, *Madchild Running*.

In addition, commercial publishers both large and small continued to publish good fiction. Atlantic Monthly Press published *The Sound of One Hand Clapping*, Richard Flanagan's painful novel of family relationships in 1950s Tasmania. Houghton Mifflin brought out Elizabeth Gilbert's delightful first novel *Stern Men* and Ward Just's *A Dangerous Friend*. Pantheon added to its luster as a publisher of serious, literary fiction by publishing Ha Jin's *Waiting* (which went on to win a National Book Award as well as being selected as an ALA Notable Book) and Hans-Ulrich Treichel's black comedy *Lost*. Riverhead, part of the Putnam Group, brought out such diverse mainstream novels as J. Robert Lennon's *The Funnies* and Danzy Senna's *Caucasia*.

## A New Genre Is Born

In terms of the type of fiction being published, it's interesting to note that another fiction genre began to flourish in recent years. "Near novels," or books made up of a series of interconnected short stories in which characters either overlap or similar themes are explored, became ubiquitous on library and bookstore shelves. Of course, the differences between a "near novel" and a novel are fluid. One way to tell a novel from a "near novel" is that in the latter, each chapter could stand alone (and frequently has been published as a short story). The chapters of a conventional novel, on the other hand, are much more interdependent on one another. Yet, at the same time, reading the stories or chapters in a "near novel" as a unit significantly deepens their impact. Some examples of these "near novels" include Julie Hecht's *Do the Windows Open?*, Melissa Banks's *The Girls' Guide to Hunting and Fishing*, Julia Alvarez's *How the Garcia Girls Lost Their Accents*, Sylvia Foley's *Life in the Air Ocean: Stories*, Allegra Goodman's *The Family Markowitz*, Nance Van Winckel's *Quake*, Bob Wake's *Caffeine and Other Stories*, Bliss Broyard's *My Father Dancing*, and Justin Cronin's *Mary and O'Neil*.

## More Multiculturalism

A recent trend that has continued is the appreciation for literature exploring other cultures and countries, including the immigrant experience, living as a hyphenated American, Native Americans in the United States, and life in other countries. Although smaller and independent presses published many of these novels, the large trade houses also saw the commercial value of books by such authors as Louise Erdrich, Gus Lee, Terry McMillan, Barbara Kingsolver, and Amy Tan. Some examples of multicultural fiction include Thomas King's *Truth and Bright Water* (Native American), Bino Realuyo's *The Umbrella Country* (Philippines), Nancy Rawles's *Love Like Gumbo* (Mexico/Creole), and Lucinda Roy's *The Hotel Alleluia* (Sierra Leone).

## Online Bookstores

Another business phenomenon that changed the book industry at the end of the millennium was the growth of online bookstores, especially Amazon.com. So-called brick-and-mortar bookstores, even independent stores, quickly caught the wave and worked to establish their online presence. What intrigues users isn't so much that they can look up and instantly order books off the Internet 24 hours a day; rather, it is the add-ons that are offered—the reviews reprinted from a variety of sources, including *Kirkus*, *Publishers Weekly*, and *Booklist*, and the comments of other readers. Here is an opportunity to discover what other readers thought of the book that you just finished reading and in turn to share your thoughts with them.

## Book Clubs and Oprah

While readers have flocked to online bookstores and listservs to express their opinions about books, traditional book clubs have sprouted up in libraries, churches, neighborhoods, and online. The growth of these book clubs over the past decade has been exponential.

In 1996 Oprah Winfrey began adding a book discussion component to her popular television show. The initial selection for discussion was Jacquelyn Mitchard's first novel, *The Deep End of the Ocean*. This book leaped to the top of the bestseller list, and libraries all over the country bought many additional copies to meet the unexpected demand. Other Oprah choices included Pearl Cleage's *What Looks Like Crazy on an Ordinary Day*, Wally Lamb's *She's Come Undone*, Ernest Gaines's *A Lesson Before Dying,* Joyce Carol Oates's *We Were the Mulvaneys*, and Bernhard Schlink's *The Reader*—all novels in which the major appeal characteristic is characters. While it's clear that being chosen as an "Oprah book" guarantees that the book will become a bestseller, what is not so clear—yet—is the effect that being chosen has on other books by the author. Oprah's Book Club readers tend to read what Oprah recommends, but there has been no indication that they will then seek out and read the author's earlier or later titles as well. Certainly the many fans who made *The Deep End of the Ocean* a bestseller did not seek out and purchase Mitchard's second novel, *The Most Wanted.*

# The Future of Books and Reading

What does the future hold for books and readers? It's pretty safe to say that we'll continue to get strong books from small and independent presses, that multicultural literature will continue to be an important part of publishing, and that book clubs will continue to grow in number. Unfortunately, our crystal ball is too cloudy to predict the future of online bookstores, or whether Oprah will continue to be a force in the world of publishing.

# Chapter 1
## Setting

### Ackerman, Marianne
#### Jump
McArthur. 2000. 349 pp.

Freelance journalist Myra Grant struggles with her ex-husband's nervous breakdown and her near-adult children's decisions to live independent lives, all the while keeping a close eye on the political fervor surrounding the vote over independence for Quebec in 1995.

**Subjects**  Beckett, Samuel • Canada • Canadian Authors • First Novels • Journalists • Montreal, Canada • Quebec, Canada • Single Mothers • Teenagers • Theater

**Now try**  Ackerman is the author of numerous plays, including "L'Affaire Tartuffe," "Celeste," and "Venus of Dublin." Samuel Beckett's influence and writings also form part of the plot in James McManus's *Going to the Sun*.

### Alcalá, Kathleen
#### The Flower in the Skull
Harcourt Brace. 1998. 180 pp.

From late-nineteenth-century Mexico to late-twentieth-century Los Angeles, three generations of women gradually come to understand themselves and their cultural identity.

**2d Appeal**  Story                                                                                   Book Groups 📖

**Subjects**  Family Relationships • Immigrants and Refugees • Latino Authors • Latinos in America • Los Angeles, California • Mexican American Authors • Mexico • Multigenerational Novels • Political Fiction • Tucson, Arizona

**Now try**  *The Flower in the Skull* is the second volume of a trilogy that begins with *Spirits of the Ordinary* and concludes with *Treasures in Heaven*. Alcalá is also the author of *Mrs. Vargas and the Dead Naturalist*. Another novel that explores the coming together of the American and Latino cultures is *The Tortilla Curtain* by T. Coraghessan Boyle. For a look at Chinese assimilation into Anglo culture during the same time period, try *Disappearing Moon Café* by Sky Lee.

## Alvarez, Julia
### In the Time of the Butterflies
Algonquin Books of Chapel Hill. 1994. 325 pp.

During the oppressive Trujillo regime in the Dominican Republic, Patria, Minerva, Maria Theresa, and Dede struggle to be strong women, loving wives, dedicated mothers, and revolutionary *compañeras.*

**2d Appeal**   Characters                                             Book Groups 📖

**Subjects**   ALA Notable Books • Dominican Authors • Dominican Republic • Family Relationships • Historical Setting • Latino Authors • Latinos • Political Fiction • Political Unrest • Sisters

**Now try**   In addition to several novels and books of poetry, Alvarez is the author of ***Something to Declare***, a collection of essays. Montserrat Fontes's ***Dreams of the Centaur***, Lawrence Thornton's ***Imagining Argentina***, James Buchan's ***The Persian Bride***, and Omar Rivabella's ***Requiem for a Woman's Soul*** are all novels about life under a politically repressive government.

## Amidon, Stephen
### The New City
Doubleday. 2000. 416 pp.

In the early 1970s in suburban Maryland, plans for building Newton, an ideal community free from crime, racial tension, and urban blight, go disastrously awry when white lawyer and developer Austin Swope and black construction boss Earl Wooten find themselves competing for the same job—as their high-school-age sons, formerly best friends, are drifting apart.

**2d Appeal**   Story                                                    Book Groups 📖

**Subjects**   1970s • Business and Businessmen • Fathers and Sons • Maryland • Race Relations • Racism • Teenage Boys • Teenagers • Vietnam Veterans

**Now try**   Amidon is also the author of the novels ***Thirst*** and ***The Primitive***. This tragedy of good intentions gone wrong is reminiscent in theme to Mary Doria Russell's ***The Sparrow*** and Ward Just's ***A Dangerous Friend***.

## Anderson-Dargatz, Gail
### A Recipe for Bees
Harmony Books. 2000. 305 pp.

Augusta Olsen looks back on a rugged and difficult life on a farm in British Columbia— a life as multifaceted as her beehives, and sometimes as sweet as the honey found within them.

**2d Appeal**   Characters                                             Book Groups 📖

**Subjects**   Aging • Bees and Beekeeping • British Columbia, Canada • Canada • Canadian Authors • Family Relationships • Farms and Farm Life • Male/Female Relationships

**Now try**   Anderson-Dargatz's first novel was ***A Cure for Death by Lightning***. Other novels about feisty Canadian women are Margaret Laurence's ***The Stone Angel***, Elizabeth Hay's ***A Student of Weather***, and Constance Beresford-Howe's ***The Book of Eve***.

## Bail, Murray
### Eucalyptus
Farrar, Straus and Giroux. 1998. 255 pp.

Ellen's suitors must correctly identify each one of the hundreds of species of eucalyptus on her father's plantation in order to win her hand in marriage.

**2d Appeal**   Characters                                             Book Groups 📖

**Subjects**  Australia • Australian Authors • Botany • Fathers and Daughters •
Male/Female Relationships • New South Wales, Australia • Trees

**Now try**  Other books by Bail include *Homesickness* and *Holden's Performance*.
*Eucalyptus* won the Commonwealth Writers Prize for Best Book. Other
novels that share with *Eucalyptus* a sense of magic are Alexander
Baricco's *Ocean Sea* and Lisa Carey's *In the Country of the Young*.

## Bainbridge, Beryl
### The Birthday Boys
Carroll & Graf. 1991. 189 pp.

Five members of the doomed 1912 Scott expedition to the Antarctic recount, at
first with naïve optimism and then poignant despair, their progressively disastrous
trek to the ends of the Earth.

**2d Appeal**  Characters                                    Book Groups 📖

**Subjects**  ALA Notable Books • Antarctica • Biographical Fiction • British Authors • Death and Dying • Explorers and Explorations • Historical Setting
• Men's Friendships • South Pole

**Now try**  Bainbridge's other novels include *An Awfully Big Adventure* and *Master
Georgie*. *The Cage* by Audrey Schulman and *Antarctic Navigation* by Elizabeth Arthur are two novels in which female heroines risk their lives in search
of adventure. Just as the Antarctic is a character in Bainbridge's novel, the settings of E. Annie Proulx's *The Shipping News* and Howard Norman's *The
Bird Artist* are characters in those novels. Other loosely fictionalized real people are found in Jane Mendelsohn's *I Was Amelia Earhart*, Tomas Eloy
Martinez's *Santa Evita*, Jay Cantor's *The Death of Che Guevara*, Judith
Farr's *I Never Came to You in White*, and Don DeLillo's *Libra*. Another po-
lar expedition, although in this case to the North Pole, is described in Andrea
Barrett's novel *The Voyage of the Narwhal*.

## Baker, Kevin
### Dreamland
HarperCollins. 1999. 519 pp.

Swaggering toughs, abused garment workers, corrupt politicos, and an opportu-
nistic dwarf grope toward the garish, incandescent promise of Coney Island amidst the
indifferent brutality of New York, circa 1910.

**2d Appeal**  Story

**Subjects**  1910s • Amusement Parks • Brooklyn, New York • Coney Island •
Dwarfs • First Novels • Freud, Sigmund • Gangsters • Historical Setting •
Immigrants and Refugees • Jews and Judaism • Organized Crime •
Rags-to-Riches Story • Triangle Shirtwaist Factory Fire

**Now try**  Baker's nightmarish cityscape recalls E. L. Doctorow's *Ragtime* and *The
Waterworks*, crossed with the in-your-face perversity of Harry Crew's *The
Mulching of America*. Nathanael West's *The Day of the Locust* shares
Baker's jaundiced tone, as do T. Coraghessan Boyle's *Without a Hero* and
*World's End*, and *Martin Dressler: The Tale of an American Dreamer* by
Steven Millhauser. John Dos Passos's *The 42nd Parallel, 1919*, and *The Big
Money* (which comprise his USA trilogy) explore a similar terrain as Baker
with similar immediacy, as do William Kennedy's Albany Cycle (*Legs,
Ironweed, Billy Phelan's Greatest Game*, and others). Those intrigued by
the Freud/Jung subplot may enjoy D. M. Thomas's *Eating Pavlova*.

## Bedford, Simi
### Yoruba Girl Dancing
Viking. 1991. 185 pp.

At the age of six, Remi is sent from her grandparents' loving home in Lagos, Nigeria, to attend a boarding school in England, where she is the only African student.

**2d Appeal**   Characters

**Subjects**   Coming-of-Age • England • First Novels • Grandparents • Humorous Fiction • Immigrants and Refugees • Lagos, Nigeria • Nigeria • Nigerian Authors • Private Schools • Women's Friendships

**Now try**   Other novels with Nigerian settings include *Mister Johnson* by Joyce Cary, *I Saw the Sky Catch Fire* by T. Obinkaram Echewa, *The Bride Price* by Buchi Emecheta, and *Song of Enchantment* by Ben Okri. School-age girls are the central characters of Colette's *Claudine at School*, Madeleine L'Engle's *The Small Rain*, and Muriel Spark's *The Prime of Miss Jean Brodie*.

## Bennett, Ronan
### The Catastrophist
Simon & Schuster. 1999. 336 pp.

Irish novelist James Gillespie arrives in the Congo in 1959 to win back his former lover Ines, an Italian reporter who is a follower of Patrice Lumumba.

**2d Appeal**   Characters                                          Book Groups 📖

**Subjects**   1950s • Africa • Belgian Congo • Congo • Expatriates • Historical Setting • Irish Authors • Journalists • Love Affairs • Lumumba, Patrice

**Now try**   This is Bennett's third novel, but his first to be published in the United States. Other novels that combine a love story with a political thriller are Graham Greene's *The Human Factor* and James Buchan's *The Persian Bride*. Another novel set in the Congo during the same time period is Barbara Kingsolver's *The Poisonwood Bible*. Both Michela Wrong's *In the Footsteps of Mr. Kurtz: Living on the Brink of Disaster in Mobutu's Congo* and *King Leopold's Ghost: A Story of Greed, Terror, and Heroism in Colonial Africa* by Adam Hochschild are excellent background reading and will extend the pleasure of Bennett's book.

## Berry, Wendell
### Jayber Crow
Counterpoint Press. 2000. 384 pp.

Jayber Crow, one-time ministerial student, is now a philosopher, a grave digger, a lifelong bachelor, and Port William, Kentucky's only barber.

**2d Appeal**   Characters                                          Book Groups 📖

**Subjects**   Friendship • Kentucky • Men's Lives • Small-Town Life

**Now try**   Among Berry's other books (which include fiction, nonfiction, and poetry) are *Nathan Coulter: A Novel, What Are People For?* (a collection of essays), *Fidelity: Five Stories*, and *A World Lost*. Port William is the community whose residents Berry has written about in other works of fiction, including *The Wild Birds: Six Stories of the Port William Membership*. Other works of literature in which place and character come together are Thornton Wilder's "Our Town" and Edgar Lee Masters's *Spoon River Anthology*. Other novels set in Kentucky include *In Country* by Bobbie Ann Mason and Susan M. Dodd's *No Earthly Notion*.

## Buchan, James
### The Persian Bride
Houghton Mifflin. 2000. 352 pp.

After arriving in Isfahan, Iran, in 1974, 18-year-old Englishman John Pitt falls in love with 17-year-old Shirin, daughter of a general in the shah's army; but their love is threatened by the terrible events following the Iranian revolution and the subsequent war with Iraq.

| 2d Appeal | Language | Book Groups 📖 |
|---|---|---|

**Subjects** British Authors • Expatriates • Iran • Love Stories • Male/Female Relationships • Middle East • Violence • War

**Now try** Buchan is also the author of *A Parish of Rich Women* and *High Latitudes*. His novel *Heart's Journey in Winter* won the Guardian Prize for Fiction. Another love affair played out against a backdrop of war and violence is Marianne Wiggins's *Eveless Eden*.

## Camus, Albert
### The First Man
Knopf. 1995. 325 pp.

At age 40, Jacques Cormery leaves France for Algeria to search for information about his father, who died in World War I when Jacques was an infant. Translated from the French by David Hapgood.

**2d Appeal** Language

**Subjects** Africa • ALA Notable Books • Algeria • French Authors • Novels in Translation • Single Mothers

**Now try** This, Camus's last (and unfinished) novel, contains some of the same themes that can be found in his earlier books, such as *The Stranger*, *The Fall*, and *The Plague*. Claire Messud's *The Last Life* and Thomas Givon's *Running Through the Tall Grass* are also set in Algeria.

## Chamoiseau, Patrick
### Chronicle of the Seven Sorrows
University of Nebraska Press. 1999. 226 pp.

The marketplace of colonial Martinique bursts with colorful fruits and vegetables, along with folklore and stories of vagabonds, lovers, voodoo, colonialism, and human ingenuity. Translated from the French and Creole by Linda Coverdale.

| 2d Appeal | Language | Book Groups 📖 |
|---|---|---|

**Subjects** Caribbean • Caribbean Authors • Colonialism • Creole Culture • Creoles • Folktales • Magic Realism • Martinique • Novels in Translation

**Now try** Chamoiseau's *Texaco* deals with many of the same themes as this novel. Salman Rushdie's *The Ground Beneath Her Feet* similarly traces the lives of many colorful characters living in a colonial culture. Paule Marshall's *Praisesong for the Widow* deals with immersion into the magic of Creole culture and the power of personal folklore.

## Choy, Wayson
### The Jade Peony
Picador USA. 1997. 238 pp.

Jook-Liang, Jung-Sum, and Sek-Lung, three children of an immigrant Chinese family living in Vancouver, Canada, in the 1940s, are torn between the ways of old China that their parents expect and their own desire to be true Canadians.

| 2d Appeal | Characters | Book Groups 📖 |
|---|---|---|

**Subjects**　ALA Notable Books • Asian Canadians • Boxing • Brothers and Sisters • Canadian Authors • Chinese Canadians • Family Relationships • First Novels • Immigrants and Refugees • Vancouver, Canada • World War II

**Now try**　A nonfiction book about Chinese Canadians is Denise Chong's *The Concubine's Children*. Like Jung-Sum in this novel, the main character in Gus Lee's *China Boy* gains acceptance and self-respect by learning to box, as does the main character in Bryce Courtenay's *The Power of One* (although Courtenay's novel is set in South Africa).

## Currie, Sheldon
### The Glace Bay Miners' Museum
Breton Books. 1995. 130 pp.

The relationship between bagpipe-playing Neil Currie and Margaret MacNeil, whose father and brother have been killed in the Cape Breton coal mines, is played out against a backdrop of an isolated company town.

**Subjects**　Canada • Canadian Authors • Cape Breton Island, Canada • Labor Unions • Mental Illness • Mines and Mining • Nova Scotia, Canada

**Now try**　Currie is also the author of *The Company Store*, another story of the hard life of laborers. Ann-Marie MacDonald's *Fall on Your Knees* also takes place on Cape Breton Island. Nova Scotia Province is the setting for Angela Davis-Gardner's *Felice*, Howard Norman's *The Museum Guard*, D. R. MacDonald's *Cape Breton Road*, and Thomas H. Raddall's *Hangman's Beach*. Other novels about labor unrest in North American mining towns include Denise Giardina's *Storming Heaven*, Robert Houston's *Bisbee '17*, Donald McCaig's *The Butte Pola*, and Mary Lee Settle's *The Scapegoat*.

## Davis, Claire
### Winter Range
Picador USA. 2000. 262 pp.

Trouble between Sheriff Ike Parsons and rancher Chas Stubblefield (who is in love with Parsons's wife Pattiann) comes to a head during a ferocious Montana winter.

**2d Appeal**　Story

**Subjects**　Farms and Farm Life • First Novels • Male/Female Relationships • Marriage • Montana • Policemen • Revenge • Sheriffs • Small-Town Life

**Now try**　Linda Hasselstrom's memoir *Feels Like Far: A Rancher's Life on the Great Plains* also describes the perils and beauty of relying on the land for survival, as does Jonathan Raban's *Bad Land: An American Romance*. Other novels that explore the Montana landscape include Thomas Savage's *The Corner of Rife and Pacific*, Ivan Doig's *Bucking the Sun*, Deirdre McNamer's *One Sweet Quarrel*, and Michael Dorris's *A Yellow Raft in Blue Water*.

## Ferré, Rosario
### The House on the Lagoon
Farrar, Straus and Giroux. 1995. 407 pp.

As Isabel Montfort Mendizabal writes her family's history and reviews her own life, her husband adds his own version of events, so that together they describe over 70 years of Puerto Rican history.

**2d Appeal**　Characters

**Subjects**  Caribbean • Caribbean Authors • Colonialism • Family Relationships • Family Secrets • Husbands and Wives • Latino Authors • Latinos • Multigenerational Novels • Puerto Rican Authors • Puerto Rico

**Now try**  Ferré's other novels available in English include *Eccentric Neighborhoods*, *Sweet Diamond Dust*, and *The Youngest Doll*. Other stories of Puerto Rico include *Caribe* by Evangeline Blanco, *Ballad of Another Time* by José Luis Gonzalez, and *True and False Romances* by Ana Lydia Vega. Ferré's Latin family saga is reminiscent of Isabel Allende's *The House of the Spirits*, Sylvia Lopez-Medina's *Cantora*, and Alicia Yánez Cossío's *Bruna and Her Sisters in the Sleeping City*.

## Foden, Giles
### The Last King of Scotland
Knopf. 1998. 335 pp.

Seeking a little adventure in a rural medical outpost in Uganda, Nicholas Garrigan winds up as the personal physician for Idi Amin during the last deranged days of his regime.

**2d Appeal**  Characters                                      Book Groups 📖

**Subjects**  1970s • Africa • Amin, Idi • British Authors • Doctors and Patients • First Novels • Historical Setting • Scotland • Uganda

**Now try**  Foden is also the author of *Ladysmith*, set in South Africa at the end of the nineteenth century. Other novels that demonstrate the rift between native African cultures and circumstances and those of Western "civilizers" include Chinua Achebe's *Things Fall Apart*, William Boyd's *A Good Man in Africa*, Richard Dooling's *White Man's Grave*, and Barbara Kingsolver's *The Poisonwood Bible*. *The Last King of Scotland* won the Whitbread Prize for First Novel and the Somerset Maugham Award.

## Foran, Charles
### Butterfly Lovers
HarperCollins. 1996. 308 pp.

David, a divorced man coming to terms with his epilepsy, his uncaring mother, and the deterioration of his AIDS-stricken best friend, abandons his unfulfilling life in Montreal to teach English in post–Tiananmen Square Beijing.

**Subjects**  AIDS • Canada • Canadian Authors • China • Communism • Epilepsy • First Novels • Men's Friendships • Men's Lives • Middle-Aged Men • Mothers and Sons • Teachers

**Now try**  Foran also wrote *Sketches in Winter*, a nonfiction account of the Tiananmen Square massacre. *Butterfly Lovers* appears to be highly autobiographical, not unlike Martha McPhee's *Bright Angel Time* and Reeve Lindbergh's *The Names of the Mountains*. Peter Hessler's *River Town: Two Years on the Yangtze* is a nonfiction account of the author's experiences teaching in a small town in China.

## Galvin, James
### Fencing the Sky
Henry Holt. 1999. 258 pp.

In the mountains on the border of Colorado and Wyoming, three longtime friends find their lives changed when one of the three kills a land developer and tries to escape in the rugged wilderness.

**Subjects**  American West • Colorado • Cowboys • Men's Friendships • Murder • Wyoming

**Now try**  Galvin is also the author of *The Meadow*. J. Robert Lennon's *On the Night Plain* also does a beautiful job of evoking the landscape of the West. Richard Flanagan's *The Sound of One Hand Clapping* is another novel in which the author alternates between past and present in telling his story.

# Galvin, James
## The Meadow                                                    Henry Holt. 1992. 230 pp.

The author describes 100 years in the life of a Colorado mountain meadow as viewed by the settlers, ranchers, and their descendants who were possessed by its beauty.

**Subjects**  Aging • ALA Notable Books • American West • Colorado • Cowboys • First Novels • Friendship

**Now try**  Galvin is also a poet, whose many books include *Resurrection Update: Collected Poems 1975–1997*. Molly Gloss's *The Jump-Off Creek*, Glendon Swarthout's *The Homesman*, Craig Lesley's *Winterkill*, and Ivan Doig's *This House of Sky* all describe a sense of both isolation and community in the western United States. *Plains Song, for Female Voices* by Wright Morris and John Thorndike's *The Potato Baron* are both novels in which landscape shapes character.

# Gemmell, Nikki
## Alice Springs                                                    Viking. 1999. 260 pp.

When Snip's grandmother dies and leaves her a note that says "hunt him down," Snip takes a journey to the Australian outback, her father, and the past.

**Subjects**  Aboriginals • Art and Artists • Australia • Australian Authors • Family Relationships • Fathers and Daughters • Male/Female Relationships • Mothers and Daughters

**Now try**  Gemmell also wrote the novel *Shiver*. Other novels set in remote Australian towns include Janette Turner Hospital's *Oyster* and Richard Flanagan's *The Sound of One Hand Clapping*. Another novel that presents both sides of a relationship is Stephanie Gertler's *Jimmy's Girl*.

# Healy, Dermot
## A Goat's Song                                                    Viking. 1995. 407 pp.

Jack Ferris tells the sad and haunting story of his lost love Catherine Adams through both his memories of overcoming alcoholism and her family's involvement with Ireland's religious wars.

**2d Appeal**  Characters                                          Book Groups 📖

**Subjects**  Alcoholics and Alcoholism • Ireland • Irish Authors • Love Stories • Political Fiction • Religious Wars

**Now try**  Healy is also the author of the memoir *The Bend for Home* and the novel *Sudden Times*. *The Woman Who Walked into Doors* by Roddy Doyle presents the same hard look at the battle to recover from both drinking and a broken life. Other novels about the religious warfare in Ireland include Deirdre Madden's *One by One in the Darkness*, Roddy Doyle's *A Star Called Henry*, Patrick McCabe's *Breakfast on Pluto*, Geoffrey Beattie's *Corner Boys*, and Thomas Flanagan's *The End of the Hunt*.

## Henley, Patricia
### Hummingbird House

MacMurray & Beck. 1999. 326 pp.

After two decades of working among Central American peasants, nurse-midwife Kate Banner decides to return home to Indiana but finds herself derailed in Guatemala when she befriends eight-year-old Marta, whose brother has disappeared, and falls in love with Father Dixie Ryan, a radical priest.

**2d Appeal**  Characters                                          Book Groups 📖

**Subjects**  Central America • Expatriates • First Novels • Guatemala • Ministers, Priests, Rabbis • Nurses • Political Fiction • Political Prisoners • Political Unrest

**Now try**  Henley is also the author of two collections of stories: *Friday Night at Silver Star* and *The Secret of Cartwheels*. Another novel in which people get caught up in the political life of another country is Barbara Kingsolver's *The Poisonwood Bible*.

## Huo, T. C.
### Land of Smiles

Plume. 2000. 215 pp.

Boontakorn, a 14-year-old Laotian boy, tells of his experiences in a refugee camp in Thailand, and later in California, as he and his father try to live normal lives following the upheavals of the Vietnam War.

**Subjects**  1970s • Asia • Asians in America • California • Death of a Parent • Fathers and Sons • Immigrants and Refugees • Laos • Laotian Authors • Southeast Asia • Thailand • Vietnam War

**Now try**  Huo is also the author of *A Thousand Wings*. Other fiction about Southeast Asian refugees includes Robert Olen Butler's *A Good Scent from a Strange Mountain* and Mary Gardner's *Boat People*. *Land of Smiles* won the Asian Pacific American Award for Literature in 2001.

## Huston, Nancy
### The Mark of the Angel

Steerforth Press. 1999. 222 pp.

A young German woman who lost her innocence in World War II comes to Paris in 1957 and marries an aristocratic musician, but she can only regain her soul through her relationship with a Hungarian Jewish refugee.

**2d Appeal**  Characters                                          Book Groups 📖

**Subjects**  1950s • Adultery • Algeria • Canadian Authors • Colonialism • France • French Authors • Immigrants and Refugees • Music and Musicians • World War II

**Now try**  Born in Canada, but living and writing in France for the last 25 years, Huston has won various literary awards in both countries. Her other novels available in English include *The Goldberg Variations*, *Instruments of Darkness*, and *Plainsong*. Paris in the dozen or so years after the end of World War II provides the setting for Arthur Koestler's *The Age of Longing*, Piers Paul Read's *Polonaise*, and Boris Vian's *Mood Indigo*. Other novels dealing with the effects of French colonialism in Algeria include Albert Camus's *The First Man*, Robert Irwin's *Mysteries of Algiers*, Djanet Lachmet's *Lallia*, Claire Messud's *The Last Life*, and Brian Moore's *The Magician's Wife*.

## Jennings, Kate
### Snake
Ecco Press. 1996. 157 pp.

Irene and Rex try to make a life on 800 acres of isolated Australian farmland, but Irene needs more than her two children and garden to keep herself alive.

**2d Appeal**   Characters

**Subjects**   Adultery • Australia • Australian Authors • Farms and Farm Life • First Novels • Husbands and Wives • Marriage

**Now try**   Jennings also published a collection of stories, *Women Falling Down in the Street*. The difficult life of a farmer or rancher is described in Edna Ferber's *Giant*, Miles Franklin's *Up the Country*, Wallace Stegner's *The Big Rock Candy Mountain*, Mildred Walker's *Winter Wheat*, and Patrick White's *The Tree of Man*.

## Johnson, Diane
### Le Mariage
Dutton. 2000. 322 pp.

The impending marriage of American freelance reporter Tim Nolinger to French antiques dealer Anne-Sophie d'Argel occasions many different people to assess their lives, especially the former movie star Clara Holly; her husband, film director Serge Cray; and gallant man-about-Paris Antoine de Persand.

**2d Appeal**   Characters

**Subjects**   Adultery • Comedy of Manners • France • Love Affairs • Marriage • Paris, France

**Now try**   Johnson is also the author of *Le Divorce* (which shares some characters with *Le Mariage*), *The Shadow Knows*, and *Loving Hands at Home*. Henry James's *The Ambassadors*, *Portrait of a Lady*, and *Daisy Miller*, although far different in tone from Johnson's novel, also deal with the collision between European and American sensibilities, as do Lily King's *The Pleasing Hour* and Katherine Weber's *Objects in Mirror Are Closer Than They Appear*.

## Johnston, Wayne
### The Colony of Unrequited Dreams
Doubleday. 1999. 562 pp.

Joe Smallwood, the first premier of the Province of Newfoundland, and Shelagh Fielding, his one true love, take turns telling the story of their lifelong, yet always difficult and complicated, relationship.

**2d Appeal**   Story                                                                    Book Groups 📖

**Subjects**   ALA Notable Books • Biographical Fiction • Canada • Canadian Authors • Historical Setting • Male/Female Relationships • Newfoundland, Canada • Novels with Multiple Viewpoints • Rags-to-Riches Story

**Now try**   Johnston is the author of four novels, including *The Divine Ryans*, and the memoir *Baltimore's Mansion*. Johnston's style—and the way he describes his characters—bring to mind the novels of John Irving (*The 158-Pound Marriage*, among others). Johnston's tale of Joe Smallwood and the large cast of colorful characters with which he's surrounded bring to mind *David Copperfield* by Charles Dickens. Another complicated and long-term relationship is described in Mark Winegardner's *Crooked River Burning*.

## Julavits, Heidi

### The Mineral Palace
G.P. Putnam's Sons. 2000. 325 pp.

Bena Jonssen's move to Pueblo, Colorado, in 1934, with her philandering physician-husband Ted, is marked by her worry about their newborn son and the town's secrets she begins to uncover as a reporter for the local paper.

**2d Appeal**   Characters                                    Book Groups 📖

**Subjects**   1930s • American West • Colorado • First Novels • Husbands and Wives • Prostitutes • Small-Town Life

**Now try**   Other novels set in Colorado include *Stygo* by Laura Hendrie and Kent Haruf's *The Tie That Binds* and *Plainsong*. A woman struggling for independence is the subject of Wallace Stegner's *Angle of Repose*, Molly Gloss's *The Jump-off Creek* and *Wild Life*, and Kate Wheeler's *When Mountains Walked*.

## Koch, Christopher

### Highways to a War
Viking. 1995. 469 pp.

When combat photographer Michael Langford disappears, his oldest friend Raymond tries to puzzle out the reasons Langford chose to cross the border and risk his life in war-torn Cambodia.

**2d Appeal**   Story                                         Book Groups 📖

**Subjects**   1970s • Asia • Australian Authors • Cambodia • Journalists • Men's Friendships • Photography and Photographers • Southeast Asia • Vietnam War

**Now try**   Koch is also the author of *The Year of Living Dangerously*, a novel about foreign journalists in Indonesia. *Highways to a War* is a novel about the pull of Asia and the desire to penetrate its mysteries, a theme also present in Graham Greene's *The Quiet American* and Ward Just's *A Dangerous Friend*. Marianne Wiggins's *Eveless Eden* is another novel about a war correspondent and a photojournalist. *Highways to a War* won the Miles Franklin Award.

## Libera, Antoni

### Madame
Farrar, Straus and Giroux. 2000. 439 pp.

The unnamed narrator recounts his journey from adolescence to adulthood in postwar Soviet-dominated Poland, including his experiences starting a jazz band, taking part in a theater group, and falling in love with his stern and demanding French teacher, who does not reciprocate his affection. Translated from the Polish by Agnieszka Kolakowska.

**2d Appeal**   Characters

**Subjects**   Coming-of-Age • Communism • Eastern Europe • Eastern European Authors • Eastern Europeans • First Novels • Novels in Translation • Older Women/Younger Men • Poland • Political Fiction • Teenage Boys

**Now try**   Eastern Europe during the cold-war period is also the setting for Nina Fitzpatrick's *The Loves of Faustyna*, Norman Manea's *The Black Envelope*, and Herta Müller's *The Land of Green Plums*. Young men entranced with older women can also be found in Rose Tremain's *The Way I Found Her* and *Snakebite Sonnet* by Max Phillips.

## Macfarlane, David
### Summer Gone
Crown. 2000. 266 pp.

Bay Newling, divorced and estranged from his son, tries to understand the losses in his life through his memories of summers past.

**2d Appeal**    Language                                                    Book Groups 📖

**Subjects**    Canada • Canadian Authors • Canoeing • Divorce • Fathers and Sons • First Novels • Ontario, Canada • Wilderness

**Now try**    Macfarlane also wrote *Danger Tree*, a memoir. *How It Was for Me*, a collection of stories by Andew Sean Greer, mines the memories of childhood and the facets of loss in much the same way that Macfarlane does. Macfarlane's treatment of time and memory is reminiscent of Dermont Healy's *A Goat Song*. Wallace Stegner's *Crossing to Safety* explores with the same quiet intensity the toll living takes on two couples.

## Maillard, Keith
### Gloria
Soho Press. 1993. 643 pp.

In the summer after her college graduation in 1957, Gloria Cotter, having grown up in a wealthy family in a small town in West Virginia, tries to balance her family's expectations against her love of literature and her desire to go to graduate school.

**2d Appeal**    Story

**Subjects**    1950s • Canadian Authors • Coming-of-Age • Mothers and Daughters • Older Men/Younger Women • Upper Classes • West Virginia

**Now try**    Other works of fiction by Maillard include *Hazard Zone* and *Light in the Company of Women*. *Gloria* was short-listed for Canada's Governor General's Literary Award. Other novels that convey an era and the coming-of-age of the main character as beautifully as *Gloria* does include Herman Wouk's *Marjorie Morningstar*, Mona Simpson's *Off Keck Road*, and Mary McCarthy's *The Group*. The upper-class society that Maillard describes is similar to the setting for many of John O'Hara's novels and short stories, including *Elizabeth Appleton*.

## McCann, Colum
### This Side of Brightness
Metropolitan Books. 1998. 292 pp.

Dual narratives tell the stories of Treefrog (born Clarence Nathan Walker), who lives in the train tunnels under New York in 1991 and his grandfather Nathan Walker, a sandhog and survivor of a tunnel construction blowout in 1916.

**2d Appeal**    Characters                                                Book Groups 📖

**Subjects**    African Americans • Construction Accidents • Homelessness • Interracial Relationships • Irish Authors • New York • Race Relations • Tunnels

**Now try**    McCann is also the author of *Songdogs*, another novel that intertwines present and past. A similar, fact-based tunnel accident is mentioned in E. L. Doctorow's *Ragtime*. Other novels about homelessness include Nicola Barker's *Wide Open*, Tim McLaurin's *Cured by Fire*, and Shena Mackay's *Dunedin*. A good memoir about being homeless is Lars Eighner's *Travels with Lizbeth*.

## Millhauser, Steven

### Martin Dressler:
### The Tale of an American Dreamer
Random House. 1996. 293 pp.

As New York City rushes headlong to embrace the twentieth century, young entrepreneur Martin Dressler rises from bellhop to builder of dream palaces, only to lose himself in the process.

**2d Appeal** Language        Book Groups 📖

**Subjects**   Architects and Architecture • Business and Businessmen • Historical Setting • New York • Pulitzer Prize Winners • Rags-to-Riches Story

**Now try**   Among Millhauser's other works of fiction are *The Knife Thrower and Other Stories* and *Edwin Mullhouse: The Life and Death of an American Writer, 1943–1954*, which is a satirical look at biographies. The main characters in Penelope Lively's *City of the Mind*, Richard Rayner's *The Cloud Sketcher*, and Ayn Rand's *The Fountainhead* are architects.

## Mishra, Pankaj

### The Romantics
Random House. 2000. 260 pp.

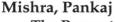

East and West collide with none-too-happy results when Samar, a young and naïve Indian intellectual living in Benares, meets the worldly expatriate friends of his neighbor Miss West, an Englishwoman, and falls in love with the beautiful Frenchwoman, Catherine.

**2d Appeal** Language        Book Groups 📖

**Subjects**   Benares, India • Coming-of-Age • Cultural Identity • Expatriates • First Novels • India • Indian Authors

**Now try**   Kazuo Ishiguro in *The Remains of the Day* and other novels, and Chang-rae Lee in *A Gesture Life*, also write of the interior lives of their characters. Other novels in which the setting functions almost as another character are E. Annie Proulx's *The Shipping News*, Howard Norman's *The Bird Artist*, and Samantha Gillison's *The Undiscovered Country*. Although Mishra's novel shares none of Salman Rushdie's hyperkinetic language and magic realism (as found in *The Moor's Last Sigh* and *Midnight's Children*), through their descriptions both men allow the reader to experience the sights, sounds, and smells of India.

## Mones, Nicole

### Lost in Translation
Delacorte. 1998. 370 pp.

Estranged from her high-powered father, expatriate Alice Mannegan is hired to act as a translator for two archaeologists who have come to China looking for the remains of Peking Man.

**2d Appeal** Story        Book Groups 📖

**Subjects**   Archaeologists and Archaeology • China • Expatriates • Fathers and Daughters • First Novels • Love Affairs • Politics

**Now try**   A good nonfiction account of Peking Man is *Dragon Bones: The Story of Peking Man* by Penny van Oosterzee. A good overview of contemporary China is *China Wakes: The Struggle for the Soul of a Rising*

*Power* by Nicholas D. Kristoff and Sheryl Wudunn. A fictional view of the difficulties of ordinary life in modern China can be found in Ha Jin's *The Bridegroom*, a collection of stories, as well as his novel *Waiting*. Another expatriate is the main character of *Rules of the Wild* by Francesca Marciano.

## Nordan, Lewis
### Music of the Swamp
Algonquin Books of Chapel Hill. 1991. 191 pp.

In the southern-fried heart of Arrow Catcher, Mississippi, adolescent Sugar Mecklin learns to deal with dead bodies popping up in unlikely places as well as with his parents' dying marriage.

**2d Appeal**   Characters                                             Book Groups 📖

**Subjects**   ALA Notable Books • Alcoholics and Alcoholism • American South • Coming-of-Age • Mississippi • Small-Town Life • Southern Authors • Teenage Boys

**Now try**   In William McPherson's *Testing the Current* another adolescent boy observes the failure of his parents' marriage. The Mississippi Delta setting of Nordan's books is also the setting of *The River Is Home* and *Angel City* by Patrick D. Smith, Larry Brown's *Fay* and his *Big Bad Love*, and William Faulkner's *As I Lay Dying* and *Absalom, Absalom* (among others). Both Carson McCullers's *The Member of the Wedding* and William Faulkner's *The Reivers* are coming-of-age stories.

## Payne, Peggy
### Sister India
Riverhead Books. 2001. 275 pp.

Guests arriving at the Saraswati Guest House in Varanasi are shocked when they find proprietor Madame Natraja, an obese, surly, white woman in a sari, and become her captives when Hindu-Muslim clashes lead to a citywide curfew.

**2d Appeal**   Story                                                   Book Groups 📖

**Subjects**   Benares, India • Boardinghouses • British Authors • Culture Clash • Eccentrics and Eccentricities • First Novels • India

**Now try**   Another novel set in Benares with a cast of both Indians and non-Indians is *The Romantics* by Pankaj Mishra. Other novels about Hindu-Muslim religious wars include Rohinton Mistry's *A Fine Balance*, *Cracking India* by Bapsi Sidhwa, and Salman Rushdie's *Midnight's Children*.

## Popham, Melinda Worth
### Skywater
Graywolf. 1990. 206 pp.

An aging husband and wife observe a band of coyotes that, faced with a diminishing water supply, set out across the southwestern desert in search of the mythical "source of all water."

**Subjects**   Aging • ALA Notable Books • American Southwest • Animals • Ecofiction • First Novels • Wildlife

**Now try**   The children's book *Rabbit Hill* by Robert Lawson is also about the relationships between people, animals, and the land they share. The classic novel told from an animal's point of view is *Watership Down* by Richard Adams. Other books about the Desert Southwest include Edward Abbey's *Desert Solitaire* and *Desert Images*, and Richard Shelton's *Going Back to Bisbee*. Craig Childs's *Crossing Paths: Encounters with Animals in the Wild* has an interesting chapter on coyotes.

## Proulx, E. Annie
### The Shipping News
Scribner. 1993. 337 pp.

An awkward newspaperman named Quoyle, his two daughters, and his aunt try to reclaim their lives in a small Newfoundland fishing town.

**2d Appeal**   Language                                    Book Groups 📖

   **Subjects**   ALA Notable Books • Canada • Family Relationships • Journalists • Love Stories • National Book Award Winners • Newfoundland, Canada • Pulitzer Prize Winners • Small-Town Life

   **Now try**   Proulx's other books include *Postcards*, *Close Range: Wyoming Stories*, and *Accordion Crimes*. Other novels with a strong sense of place are Howard Norman's *The Bird Artist*, Shena Mackay's *The Orchard on Fire*, and *The Funeral Makers* and other Mattagash novels by Cathie Pelletier. *The Shipping News* shares its darkly comic vision and quirky characters with Lewis Nordan's novels *The Sharpshooter Blues* and *Wolf Whistle*. Another novel set in Newfoundland is Patrick Kavanagh's *Gaff Topsails*.

## Rice, Ben
### 🆈🅰 Pobby and Dingan
Knopf. 2000. 94 pp.

When Kellyanne Williamson's imaginary friends go missing, her skeptical brother Ashmol organizes the entire opal-mining settlement of Lightning Ridge, Australia, into a rescue party.

**2d Appeal**   Characters                                  Book Groups 📖

   **Subjects**   Australia • British Authors • Brothers and Sisters • Childhood • First Novels • Imaginary Friends

   **Now try**   Peter Carey's *Illywacker* and *The Fat Man in History: Stories* are both whimsical fiction, as is Tom Gilling's *The Sooterkin*, Italo Calvino's *The Baron in the Trees*, and Gabriel Garcia Marquez's *Innocent Erendira and Other Stories* and *Leaf Storm and Other Stories*. *Pobby and Dingan* won the Somerset Maugham Award.

## Roberts, Karen
### The Flower Boy
Random House. 2000. 322 pp.

With the 1935 birth of Rose Lizzie, his mother's employee's daughter, life for four-year-old Chandi on a tea plantation in Ceylon changes forever.

**2d Appeal**   Characters                                  Book Groups 📖

   **Subjects**   Ceylon • Coming-of-Age • First Novels • Interracial Relationships • Sri Lanka • Sri Lankan Authors

   **Now try**   Roberts's writing style is not the exuberant, overheated prose of Arundhati Roy's *The God of Small Things*, but rather the restrained style of her fellow Sri Lankan writer Michael Ondaatje in *Anil's Ghost*, and Kazuo Ishiguro's *The Remains of the Day*, although Roberts's novel is not nearly as elliptical as either of the other two novels. Another young boy trying to make sense of his world—also the world of Sri Lanka, albeit some decades later—is the young main character in Shyam Selvadurai's *Funny Boy*.

## Salzman, Mark
### Lying Awake
Knopf. 2000. 181 pp.

When the doctor tells Sister John of the Cross that her blinding headaches (and perhaps her intense mystical visions of God that have led to her becoming a successful poet) are caused by a tumor, she must decide whether or not to have it removed.

**2d Appeal**  Characters
Book Groups 📖

**Subjects**  Carmelites • Convents • Illness • Nuns • Poets and Poetry

**Now try**  Salzman is also the author of the novel *The Soloist* and two memoirs: *Iron and Silk* and *Lost in Place: Growing Up Absurd in Suburbia*. Another novel that focuses on the smallest details of a person's experiences is Kazuo Ishiguro's *The Remains of the Day*.

## Schulman, Audrey
### The Cage
Algonquin Books of Chapel Hill. 1994. 228 pp.

When the cage Beryl is using to protect herself while she photographs bears in the Arctic fails to keep her safe, she has to rely on both her mental and physical strengths in order to survive.

Book Groups 📖

**Subjects**  ALA Notable Books • Arctic • First Novels • Photography and Photographers

**Now try**  Other novels by Schulman include *Swimming with Jonah* and *A House Named Brazil*. Barbara Quick's *Northern Edge* and *Antarctic Navigation* by Elizabeth Arthur are both novels in which the protagonists need to find strength to survive in difficult situations. A nonfiction account of an adventure gone terribly wrong is Jon Krakauer's *Into Thin Air: A Personal Account of the Mt. Everest Disaster*.

## Selvadurai, Shyam
### Cinnamon Gardens
Hyperion. 1999. 357 pp.

In upper-class 1920s Columbo, Ceylon, 22-year-old Annalukshmi, a teacher, resists her father's attempts to broker an arranged marriage, while her uncle Balendran, under the thumb of an even more domineering father, struggles to deny and hide his desire for men.

**2d Appeal**  Story
Book Groups 📖

**Subjects**  1920s • Ceylon • Gay Men • Indian Authors • Male/Female Relationships • Sri Lanka • Upper Classes

**Now try**  Other fiction set in Ceylon (now Sri Lanka) include Karen Roberts's *The Flower Boy*, *Monkfish Moon* by Romesh Gunesekera, Ambalavaner Sivanandan's *When Memory Dies*, and *Anil's Ghost* by Michael Ondaatje.

## Selvadurai, Shyam
### Funny Boy
Morrow. 1994. 310 pp.

As the Sinhalese and Tamil forces clash violently in Sri Lanka in the 1970s and 1980s, a young and sensitive Tamil boy struggles with his emerging homosexuality and the impact it has both on him and his family.

**2d Appeal**  Characters
Book Groups 📖

**Subjects**  1970s • 1980s • ALA Notable Books • Coming-of-Age • First Novels • Gay Teenagers • Indian Authors • Race Relations • Sri Lanka • Violence

**Now try**   Other books about race relations in the Indian subcontinent following the establishment of Pakistan in 1947 include Rohinton Mistry's *Such a Long Journey* and *A Fine Balance*. The violence in Sri Lanka is also the subject of Michael Ondaatje's *Anil's Ghost*. *Funny Boy* received the Lambda Literary Award.

## Simecka, Martin M.
### The Year of the Frog
Simon & Schuster. 1993. 247 pp.

In the politically repressive environment of 1980s Czechoslovakia, young intellectual Milan muddles through a succession of menial jobs and falls in love with Tania, an aristocratic student, as he comes to an understanding of life, love, and death. Translated from the Czechoslovakian by Peter Petro.

**2d Appeal**   Characters                                   Book Groups 📖

**Subjects**   1980s • Coming-of-Age • Communism • Czechoslovakia • Czechoslovakian Authors • Eastern Europe • Eastern European Authors • Eastern Europeans • First Novels • Novels in Translation • Political Fiction

**Now try**   Tibor Fischer's *Under the Frog*, set in Hungary, Antoni Libera's *Madame*, set in Poland, Herta Müller's *The Land of Green Plums*, set in Romania, and Ivan Klima's *Judge on Trial* (also set in Czechoslovakia) are all about life in Eastern Europe under politically repressive governments.

## Singh, Jacquelin
### Home to India
Permanent Press. 1997. 217 pp.

When American Helen falls in love with Tej Singh and moves to a small village in the Punjab with him, she must make peace with the fact that Tej has another wife.

**2d Appeal**   Story                                        Book Groups 📖

**Subjects**   Bigamy and Bigamists • Family Relationships • First Novels • Husbands and Wives • India • Intermarriage • Sikhs • Triangles

**Now try**   Another novel about a woman who struggles with her situation as a foreigner (in this case, English) and being her Indian husband's wife number two is Nayantara Sahgal's *Rich Like Us*.

## Smiley, Jane
### A Thousand Acres
Knopf. 1991. 317 pp.

A midwestern farm family copes with long-buried memories of a father's abuse, disagreements among the three sisters and their husbands and lovers, cancer, and pollution of the land.

**2d Appeal**   Characters                                   Book Groups 📖

**Subjects**   ALA Notable Books • Cancer • Family Relationships • Farms and Farm Life • Fathers and Daughters • Iowa • National Book Critics Circle Award Winners • Pulitzer Prize Winners • Sexual Abuse • Sisters

**Now try**   Smiley is a versatile writer whose books range from *Moo*, a satire of academia, to *Duplicate Keys*, a mystery, to *The Age of Grief*, a collection of stories and novellas, and a historical novel, *The All-True Travels and Adventures of Lidie Newton*. Jane Hamilton's *A Map of the World* is frequently compared to *A Thousand Acres*, due to their farm settings and heavy-duty plots. Richard Powers's *Gain* is also about a woman who develops cancer as a result of pollution.

## Smith, Jane S.

### Fool's Gold
Zoland Books. 2000. 340 pp.

When ecofeminist art historian Vivian and her photographer-husband Richard Hart decide to sublet their Manhattan apartment and spend six months in Provence, they are totally unprepared for all that France has in store for them.

**2d Appeal**   Characters

**Subjects**   Art Historians • Brothers and Sisters • First Novels • France • Humorous Fiction • Photography and Photographers • Provence, France • Satirical Fiction

**Now try**   Smith is also the author of *Patenting the Sun: Polio and the Salk Vaccine* and *Elsie de Wolfe: A Life in the High Style*. Less satirical (and nonfiction) accounts of time spent in Provence can be found in Peter Mayle's *A Year in Provence* and its sequels. Mayle's warm fictional homage to the area is *Hotel Pastis*, which takes place in a Provence that wouldn't be unfamiliar to Smith's characters. Gustaf Sobin's *The Fly-Truffler*, although also set in Provence, shares only the setting with Smith's book—it is a magical love story.

## Soueif, Ahdaf

### The Map of Love
Bloomsbury. 1999. 529 pp.

Cousins Amal and Isabel use the contents of an inherited tin trunk to piece together a 100-year-old story about Anna, an Englishwoman who scandalized the British colonials by marrying a prominent Egyptian.

**2d Appeal**   Characters                                          Book Groups 📖

**Subjects**   Arab Authors • Colonialism • Egypt • Egyptian Authors • Intermarriage • Love Stories • Middle East • Muslim/Christian Marriage • Muslims

**Now try**   Soueif is also the author of the novel *In the Eye of the Sun*. Other fiction of Middle Eastern or Muslim women include Hanan al-Shayk's *Women of Sand and Myrrh* and Alifa Rifaat's *Distant View of a Minaret*. Egyptian Nobel Prize winner Naguib Mahfouz is best known by American readers for his Cairo trilogy, which begins with *Palace Walk*. Americans in the Middle East is the subject of Hilary Mantel's *Eight Months on Ghazzah Street* and Diane Johnson's *Persian Nights*. Geraldine Brooks has written an enlightening nonfiction book about the area, *Nine Parts of Desire: The Hidden World of Islamic Women*.

## Stillman, Whit

### The Last Days of Disco with Cocktails at Petrossian Afterwards
Farrar, Straus and Giroux. 1998. 339 pp.

Junior adman Jimmy Steinway is hired to turn the movie *The Last Days of Disco*—the story of bright young things in the Manhattan club scene in the 1980s—into a novel.

**2d Appeal**   Characters

**Subjects**   1980s • Disco • First Novels • Humorous Fiction • Male/Female Relationships • New York • Upper Classes

**Now try**   Another novel set among the upper classes in Manhattan in the 1980s is Caitlin Macy's *Fundamentals of Play*, although there is no humor to be found in Macy's book. The characters in Stillman's novel first appeared in a film called *The Last Days of Disco*.

## Tuck, Lily

### Siam: Or The Woman Who Shot a Man Overlook Press. 1999. 192 pp.

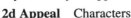

In 1967, newly married Claire arrives in Bangkok with her husband James, an engineer who builds airstrips for American bombers; in Thailand she discovers the difficulties—large and small—of communicating across cultures and becomes obsessed with discovering what happened to Jim Thompson, a wealthy American who mysteriously disappeared in Thailand.

**2d Appeal**   Characters Book Groups 📖

**Subjects**   Culture Clash • Husbands and Wives • Murder • Southeast Asia • Thailand

**Now try**   Tuck is also the author of *Interviewing Matisse or The Woman Who Died Standing Up* and *The Woman Who Walked on Water*. The issues of miscommunication and culture shock that Tuck explores are also found in Hilary Mantel's *A Change of Climate* and *Eight Months on Ghazzah Street*. Ward Just's *A Dangerous Friend* is another novel about an American becoming involved in the politics of Southeast Asia just as the Vietnam War is beginning to heat up.

## Watson, Larry

### 🆈🅰 Montana 1948 Milkweed. 1993. 175 pp.

Twelve-year-old David Hayden grows up very quickly when he learns that his war-hero uncle, the town's doctor, is about to be arrested for rape by the town's sheriff, David's father.

**2d Appeal**   Characters Book Groups 📖

**Subjects**   ALA Notable Books • American West • Brothers • Coming-of-Age • Family Relationships • Fathers and Sons • Montana • Sexual Abuse

**Now try**   Watson also wrote *Justice*, which is a prequel to *Montana 1948*, as well as *White Crosses*, another tale set in Bentrock, Montana. Norman Maclean's *A River Runs Through It* is a lyrical account of shattering events affecting a group of Montanans. *The Edge of the Crazies* by Jamie Harrison is a mystery set in a well-evoked small town in Montana.

## Wells, Ken

### Meely LaBauve Random House. 2000. 244 pp.

Fifteen-year-old Emile LaBauve, more commonly known as Meely, finds his life changed in a series of encounters with the school bully Junior Guidry, his gang, and his dangerous uncle—a policeman.

**2d Appeal**   Characters

**Subjects**   Alcoholics and Alcoholism • American South • Cajuns • Coming-of-Age • Fathers and Sons • First Novels • Interracial Relationships • Southern Authors • Teenage Boys

**Now try**   Other fiction about Cajuns includes Ernest J. Gaines's *Catherine Cormier* and *A Gathering of Old Men*, Diane Glancy's *The Only Piece of Furniture in the House*, the two long stories published as *Marshland Brace* by Chris Segura, and the detective fiction of James Lee Burke (including *Black Cherry Blues* and *Cimarron Rose*, among others). There is danger, violence, and deprivation in Meely's southern countryside as there is in Larry Brown's novels *Joe* and *Fay*, Pete Dexter's *The Paperboy*, Lewis Nordan's *Music of the Swamp* and *The Sharpshooter Blues*, Robert McCammon's *Boy's Life*, and Chris Offutt's *The Blood Brother*.

## Wheeler, Kate
### When Mountains Walked                                    Houghton Mifflin. 2000. 375 pp.

When Maggie Goodwin and her husband Carson go to a small, isolated village in Peru to run the local health clinic, Maggie discovers that many of her grandmother's experiences traveling around the world with her seismologist husband parallel her own.

**2d Appeal**   Characters                                   Book Groups 📖

**Subjects**   Adultery • First Novels • Husbands and Wives • Love Affairs • Marriage • Peru • Revolution and Revolutionaries • Women's Lives

**Now try**   Wheeler is the author of a collection of stories, *Not Where I Started From*. Wheeler's novel is similar in tone and plot to Wallace Stegner's *Angle of Repose*. The parallel experiences of two women in a foreign land are also the subject of *Heat and Dust* by Ruth Prawer Jhabvala. In 1996, *Granta Magazine* named Wheeler one of the "20 Best Young American Novelists."

## Wolfe, Swain
### The Lake Dreams the Sky                                  Cliff Street Books. 1998. 334 pp.

Boston businesswoman Liz returns to her roots to visit her grandmother in rural Montana and begins to unravel the legendary love affair between post–World War II drifter and painter Cody and waitress Rose Red Crows.

**2d Appeal**   Characters                                   Book Groups 📖

**Subjects**   American Indians • American West • Art and Artists • Interracial Relationships • Love Stories • Mental Illness • Montana • Psychiatric Hospitals

**Now try**   Wolfe's first book was a fantasy, *The Woman Who Lives in the Earth*. Other books featuring American Indian characters in Montana include Michael Dorris's *A Yellow Raft in Blue Water*, Larry Watson's *Montana 1948*, James Welch's *Winter in the Blood*, Colin Stuart's *Shoot an Arrow to Stop the Wind*, and the Gabriel Du Pre mysteries (*Notches* and *Wolf, No Wolf*, among others) by Peter Bowen. Other books about male mental patients include Ken Kesey's *One Flew Over the Cuckoo's Nest* and Thomas King's *Green Grass, Running Water*.

## Wolk, Lauren
### Those Who Favor Fire                                     Random House. 1998. 374 pp.

Rachel's love affair with the man known only as Joe takes place in Belle Haven, Pennsylvania, a town whose beauty is belied by the dangerous fires burning in the abandoned coal mine beneath it.

**2d Appeal**   Characters                                   Book Groups 📖

**Subjects**   American Northeast • First Novels • Love Stories • Male/Female Relationships • Mines and Mining • Pennsylvania • Small-Town Life

**Now try**   Another novel of a Pennsylvania coal mine on fire is James Finney Boylan's *The Constellations*. Sheldon Currie's *The Glace Bay Miners' Museum* takes place in a coal-mining town on Cape Breton Island, Canada, while Denise Giardina's *Storming Heaven* takes place in a coal-mining town in West Virginia. Small-town life in the eastern United States is explored in Beatriz Rivera's *Midnight Sandwiches at the Mariposa Express*, Richard Russo's *Empire Falls*, John Gardner's *Nickel Mountain*, and Cathie Pelletier's novels about Mattagash, Maine, including *The Weight of Water* and *Once Upon a Time on the Banks*.

## Yamashita, Karen Tei
### Brazil-Maru
Coffee House Press. 1992. 248 pp.

In 1925, a boatload of Japanese Christians lands in Sao Paulo to start a settlement in the jungle; once there, the emerging leaders and their passions for painting, baseball, and chicken and egg raising take their isolated community past the grudgingly acknowledged Japanese defeat in 1945 to a more modern time.

Book Groups 📖

**Subjects**   Adultery • Asian American Authors • Baseball • Brazil • Communal Living • Family Relationships • Farms and Farm Life • Immigrants and Refugees • Japan • Japanese American Authors

**Now try**   Yamashita's other fiction includes the surreal and futuristic *Through the Arc of the Rain Forest* and *Tropic of Orange*. One of the characters in *Brazil-Maru* is a charismatic, egocentric, conniving visionary, not unlike principal characters in Robert Stone's *Damascus Gate*, Paul Theroux's *The Mosquito Coast*, and John Updike's *S*. Other novels about Japanese settling outside of Japan and their relationships with their mother country include Deborah Iida's *Middle Son*, Joy Kogawa's *Obasan*, Lydia Minatoya's *The Strangeness of Beauty*, Milton Mirayama's *Plantation Boy*, and Yoshiko Uchida's *Picture Bride*.

## Yánez Cossío, Alicia
### Bruna and Her Sisters in the Sleeping City
Northwestern University Press. 1999. 228 pp.

The Catovil family, with their ghosts and their eccentric history, occupy an imposing, rambling house in an isolated mountain-ringed town subject to the winds of lassitude, gossip, and narrow-mindedness. Translated from the Spanish by Kenneth J. A. Wishnia.

**2d Appeal**   Language

**Subjects**   Eccentrics and Eccentricities • Ecuadorian Authors • Latino Authors • Latinos • Magic Realism • Multigenerational Novels • Novels in Translation • Small-Town Life

**Now try**   Although this novel was originally published in 1971, its 1999 publication marks the first of Yánez Cossío's novels to be available in English. She is in the tradition of other Latin American magic realists such as

Kathleen Alcalá (*Mrs. Vargas and the Dead Naturalist*), Jorge Luis Borges (*Ficciones* and *The Book of Sand*), José Donoso (*A House in the Country*), and Laura Esquivel (*Like Water for Chocolate*). Other magical houses are settings for Isabel Allende's *The House of the Spirits*, Carol Orlock's *The Hedge, the Ribbon*, and Lane Von Herzen's *The Unfastened Heart*.

## Zelitch, Simone

### Louisa
G.P. Putnam's Sons. 2000. 377 pp.

In 1949, Holocaust survivor (and chain-smoker) feisty Nora and her gentile daughter-in-law Louisa arrive in Israel, hoping to find Nora's beloved cousin Bela, who, it seems, may not want to be found.

**2d Appeal**   Characters                                     Book Groups 📖

**Subjects**   1940s • Daughters-in-Law • Holocaust • Hungary • Israel • Jews and Judaism • Male/Female Relationships • Middle East • Mothers-in-Law • Palestine • World War II • Zionism

**Now try**   Zelitch is also the author of the novel *The Confession of Jack Straw*. The building of the state of Israel is also the subject of Leon Uris's classic novel *Exodus* and Linda Grant's *When I Lived in Modern Times*. Other novels set in Israel include Meyer Levin's *The Settlers* and *The Harvest* and Amos Oz's *Panther in the Basement*. Another novel about Hungarian Jews before and during World War II is Janos Nyiri's *Battlefields and Playgrounds*.

# Chapter 2

## Story

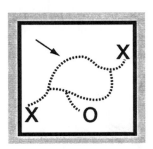

## Ackerman, Karl
### Dear Will
Scribner. 2000. 314 pp.

When literary agent Will Gerard receives a letter from a young woman who may or may not be his biological daughter, it not only reminds him of his past, but also complicates his relationship with the woman of his dreams Annie Leonard, who is herself eager to have a child.

**2d Appeal** Characters

**Subjects** Comedy of Manners • Fathers and Daughters • Literary Agents • Love Stories • Male/Female Relationships • Single Men

**Now try** Ackerman's first novel was ***The Patron Saint of Unmarried Women***. Like Stephen McCauley (***The Easy Way Out***) and Elinor Lipman (***The Inn at Lake Devine***), Ackerman fills his books with intelligence, good humor, and a nice sense of how real people respond to the situations in which they find themselves. Another novel exploring male-female relationships with a light touch is Josie Lloyd and Emlyn Rees's ***Come Together***.

## Agee, Jonis
### The Weight of Dreams
Viking. 1999. 389 pp.

Ty Bonte believed that he had put his troubled past behind him when, after a night spent drinking with his best friend Harney Rivers (a night that led to a warrant for Ty's arrest), he left his abusive father and the cattle ranch in the Nebraska foothills. When Harney reenters his life years later, Ty learns that he will always be haunted by the past unless he goes home to face it down.

**Subjects** American Midwest • Child Abuse • Dysfunctional Families • Fathers and Sons • Juvenile Delinquents • Kansas • Nebraska • Violence

**Now try** Agee is also the author of ***South of Resurrection*** and ***Taking the Wall: Stories***. Her message in this novel, that forgiveness is redemptive, is also the theme of Laura Hendrie's ***Remember Me***.

## Ansa, Tina McElroy
### The Hand I Fan With
Doubleday. 1996. 462 pp.

Lena spends her life catering to the needs of others in Mulberry, Georgia, but when she and her best friend conjure up the perfect man, Lena learns a romantic and life-affirming lesson.

**Subjects** African American Authors • African Americans • American South • Georgia • Ghosts • Male/Female Relationships • Romance • Small-Town Life

**Now try** This is the sequel to *Baby of the Family*. Other novels with a similar breezy style include Terry McMillan's *A Day Late and a Dollar Short* and Helen Fielding's *Bridget Jones's Diary*. Other romances with a ghostly twist include Elswyth Thane's *Tryst*, Margot Livesey's *Eva Moves the Furniture*, and Lisa Carey's *In the Country of the Young*.

## Auerbach, Jessica
### Catch Your Breath
G.P. Putnam's Sons. 1996. 247 pp.

Separated from her husband, still grieving over the death of her infant child from Sudden Infant Death Syndrome, and trying to deal with her son Jason's increasingly severe asthma attacks, Rosie Sloan's life is rocked by accusations of child abuse.

**Subjects** Asthma • Child Abuse • Death of a Child • Single Mothers

**Now try** Auerbach is also the author of *Sleep, Baby, Sleep* and *Painting on Glass*. Another family stunned by accusations of child abuse is found in Jane Hamilton's *A Map of the World*.

## Averill, Thomas Fox
### Secrets of the Tsil Café
BlueHen Books. 2001. 304 pp.

Wes Hingler has to find his own way in life and the world of food—somewhere between his father's Tsil Café, with its Mexican menu, and his mother Maria's catering company, Bueno AppeTito.

**2d Appeal** Characters

**Subjects** Cafés and Restaurants • Coming-of-Age • Cooking • Culture Clash • Family Relationships • First Novels

**Now try** Other books focusing on food and cooking include *Bread Alone* by Judith Ryan Hendricks, Billie Letts's *The Honk and Holler Opening Soon*, and *World of Pies* by Karen Stolz. Another book in which children must balance between the different cultures of their parents is Marie Arana's memoir, *American Chica: Two Worlds, One Childhood*.

## Becker, Laney Katz
### Dear Stranger, Dearest Friend
Morrow. 2000. 304 pp.

When she is diagnosed with breast cancer, Lara turns to a chat room for help and becomes friends with Susan, a cancer survivor.

**Subjects** Cancer • Epistolary Novels • First Novels • Illness • Terminal Illness • Women's Friendships

**Now try** Two other novels about women's friendships in the face of cancer are *The Saving Graces* by Patricia Gaffney and *Talk Before Sleep* by Elizabeth Berg.

## Berg, Elizabeth
**YA Durable Goods**                    Random House. 1993. 192 pp.

Still grieving over the death of her mother, 12-year-old Katie writes poetry and tries to endure the physical abuse she suffers at the hands of her violent father.

Book Groups 📖

**Subjects**    1960s • Child Abuse • Coming-of-Age • Death of a Parent • Fathers and Daughters • First Novels • Sisters

**Now try**    Berg is also the author of *Talk Before Sleep*, *Joy School* (which continues Katie's story), *Never Change*, and *Range of Motion*. Other resilient teenagers are Frankie in Carson McCullers's *The Member of the Wedding*, the eponymous heroine of Kaye Gibbons's *Ellen Foster*, and Bone, in *Bastard Out of Carolina* by Dorothy Allison.

## Berg, Elizabeth
**Until the Real Thing Comes Along**                    Random House. 1999. 241 pp.

Patty Hansen always wanted to get married, have several children, and live in a big, comfortable house, but as she makes her way through her 30s, she realizes that unless she prevails on her best friend whom she's loved since childhood (the decidedly homosexual Ethan Gaines) to father her child, it's unlikely her dreams will ever come true.

**Subjects**    Gay Men • Single Mothers • Single Women

**Now try**    Berg is also the author of *Talk Before Sleep*, *The Pull of the Moon*, and *Range of Motion*, among other novels. The plot of this novel—woman loves gay man—is also the plot of Stephen McCauley's *The Object of My Affection* and Susan Isaacs's *Lily White*.

## Bingham, Kate
**Mummy's Legs**                    Simon & Schuster. 2000. 207 pp.

From the time she is a child, Sarah's life is defined by the demands that her emotionally volatile mother Catherine places on her, and her own futile attempts to make Catherine happy.

**Subjects**    British Authors • Depression • First Novels • Mothers and Daughters

**Now try**    Other difficult and emotionally disturbed mothers can be found in Susanna Moore's *My Old Sweetheart*, Jenny Offill's *Last Things*, and Diana O'Hehir's *I Wish This War Were Over*.

## Bledsoe, Lucy Jane
**Working Parts**                    Seal Press. 1997. 208 pp.

Twenty-seven-year-old Lori Taylor has a lot going for her—a new girlfriend, a job as a bicycle mechanic, and good friends—but she finally must face the fact that she is unable to read.

Book Groups 📖

**Subjects**    First Novels • Illiteracy • Lesbians • Literacy • Women's Friendships

**Now try**    Bledsoe is also the author of a collection of stories, *Sweat*. *Life Is So Good* by George Dawson and Richard Glaubman is a true—and moving—account of a man who did not learn to read until he was close to 100 years old. *Working Parts* won a Gay, Lesbian and Bisexual Book Award from the ALA. Another winner is Emma Donoghue's *Hood*. Kristin McCloy's *Some Girls* and Elizabeth Stark's *Shy Girl* both recount lesbian love affairs.

## Bohjalian, Chris

### Midwives

Harmony Books. 1997. 312 pp.

Vermont midwife Sibyl Danforth stands trial in court and among her friends and neighbors after the suspicious death of one of her patients.

Book Groups 📖

**Subjects**    Midwives • Mothers and Daughters • New England • Oprah Winfrey Selection • Trials • Vermont

**Now try**    Bohjalian is also the author of *The Law of Similars* and *Trans-Sister Radio*. Other novels about women who become the focus of controversy in their communities include Joanne Harris's *Chocolat* and Penelope Fitzgerald's *The Bookshop*. Books about the struggle between traditional medicine and the medical community include Anne Fadiman's *The Spirit Catches You and You Fall Down* (nonfiction) and John Irving's novel *The Cider House Rules*.

## Bokat, Nicole

### Redeeming Eve

Permanent Press. 2000. 264 pp.

Eve's attempt to live an ordered life like the heroines of her beloved Jane Austen (the subject of her unfinished dissertation) is thwarted when she falls in love with Hart, gets married, and has a daughter.

**Subjects**    Austen, Jane • First Novels • Infertility • Jews and Judaism • Male/Female Relationships • Mothers and Daughters

**Now try**    Other novels about mothers overwhelming their daughters are Rebecca Wells's *The Divine Secrets of the Ya-Ya Sisterhood* and *Then She Found Me* by Elinor Lipman.

## Bromell, Henry

### Little America

Knopf. 2001. 395 pp.

History professor Terry Hooper sets out to discover exactly what happened in Kurash, a small country in the Middle East, where his father was the CIA station chief and advisor to the young king.

**2d Appeal**    Characters

**Subjects**    1950s • CIA • Cold War • Fathers and Sons • Middle East • Political Fiction

**Now try**    Bromell won the Houghton Mifflin Literary Award for *The Slightest Distance*, his first novel. Like Mark Winegardner in *Crooked River Burning*, Bromell mixes real people and invented characters to fine effect. Other political novels include Ward Just's *The American Ambassador* and Graham Greene's *The Human Factor*.

## Brown, Rosellen
### Before and After
Farrar, Straus and Giroux. 1992. 354 pp.

The parents of a New Hampshire teenager who killed his girlfriend are forced to examine their own relationship as well as the moral principles they hold dear.

**2d Appeal**   Characters                                               Book Groups 📖

**Subjects**   ALA Notable Books • Death of a Child • Family Relationships • Murder • New England • New Hampshire • Teenage Boys

**Now try**   Among Brown's other novels are *Tender Mercies* and *The Autobiography of My Mother*. Nadine Gordimer's *The House Gun* is another novel that explores the effect on a family when the son is accused of murder. The well-drawn family relationships found in Brown's novel can also be found in Sue Miller's *Inventing the Abbotts, and Other Stories* (as well as in her novels) and Chris Bohjalian's *Midwives*.

## Brown, Rosellen
### Half a Heart
Farrar, Straus and Giroux. 2000. 402 pp.

One legacy of Miriam Vener's experiences as a civil rights activist in the 1960s is the daughter she left to be raised by the African American father of the child; now, after 18 years of no contact with either father or daughter, living a comfortably affluent life in Houston, Texas, Miriam finally reconnects with Veronica and must reassess the choices she made years before.

Book Groups 📖

**Subjects**   Biracial Characters • Civil Rights • Interracial Relationships • Mothers and Daughters • Upper Classes

**Now try**   Brown is also the author of the novels *The Autobiography of My Mother*, *Tender Mercies*, and *Civil Rights*. Novels about the lives of biracial children include Danzy Senna's *Caucasia* and Annie Waters's *Glimmer*. Rebecca Walker explores the same topic in *Black, White and Jewish: Autobiography of a Shifting Self*.

## Cahill, Michael
### 🆈🅰 A Nixon Man
St. Martin's Press. 1998. 234 pp.

Eleven-year-old Jack Costello relates the events of the turbulent year of 1972, when his parents decide that his sister Macie needs to live in a group home for mentally retarded teenagers, the Watergate hearings begin, his parents' marriage further deteriorates, and Jack learns some hard truths about the past.

**Subjects**   1960s • 1970s • Brothers and Sisters • Coming-of-Age • Developmental Disabilities • Family Relationships • Family Secrets • First Novels

**Now try**   *A Nixon Man* won the Pirate's Alley Faulkner Award for best new novel. Other novels about adolescent boys include *Thumbsucker* by Walter Kirn, *The Catcher in the Rye* by J. D. Salinger, *The Secret Diaries of Adrian Mole* by Sue Townsend, and Bruce Robinson's *The Peculiar Memories of Thomas Penman*.

## Castillo, Ana
### Peel My Love Like an Onion
Doubleday. 1999. 213 pp.

Carmen "La Coja" has overcome polio to become a talented flamenco dancer, but she cannot overcome her love for Manolo, the young gypsy dancer who deserted her.

**2d Appeal**   Characters                                                      Book Groups 📖

**Subjects**   American Midwest • Chicago, Illinois • Dancers and Dancing • Gypsies • Latino Authors • Latinos • Latinos in America • Love Affairs • Mexican American Authors • Mexican Americans • Physical Disabilities • Polio

**Now try**   Castillo's other books include *So Far from God*, a novel, and *Loverboys: Stories*. Denise Chavez's *Face of an Angel* also tells the story of the unhappy love life of a Mexican American woman struggling to make a living.

## Cheever, Benjamin
### The Plagiarist
Atheneum. 1992. 322 pp.

Arthur, the son of an alcoholic famous writer, leaves his suburban newspaper job to take a position at a magazine very much like *Reader's Digest*, and as he makes his way to the upper echelons of the company, he discovers aspects of himself that will change his life.

**2d Appeal**   Characters

**Subjects**   Alcoholics and Alcoholism • Business and Businessmen • Fathers and Sons • First Novels • Writers and Writing

**Now try**   Cheever is also the author of *The Partisan*, which is another iteration of the son-of-a-famous-father plot, as well as *Selling Ben Cheever: Back to Square One in a Service Economy*, an account of his life in the world of work. *The Plagiarist*, an autobiographical novel, should be read in conjunction with Scott Donaldson's *John Cheever*, the biography of Cheever's father, as well as *The Journals of John Cheever*. Susan Cheever's *Home Before Dark* is a biography of her father. Another novel about (and by) a child of a famous novelist is Sarah Gaddis's *Swallow Hard*.

## Chernoff, Maxine
### A Boy in Winter
Crown. 1999. 241 pp.

Nancy Horvath's affair with Frank Nova, the man next door, comes to a horrible end when her 11-year-old son Danny accidentally kills Frank's 10-year-old son Eddie.

Book Groups 📖

**Subjects**   Accidental Death • Adultery • Death of a Child • Love Affairs • Mothers and Sons • Murder • Novels with Multiple Viewpoints

**Now try**   Chernoff is also the author of the novels *Bop* and *American Heaven*. In *Evening News* Marly Swick also deals with the accidental death of a child at the hands of another child.

## Chiaverini, Jennifer
### The Quilter's Apprentice
Simon & Schuster. 1999. 271 pp.

When Sarah McClure takes quilting lessons from her difficult boss Mrs. Compson, both women learn lessons about forgiveness and familial love.

**Subjects**   Elderly Women • First Novels • Pennsylvania • Quilting • Women's Friendships

**Now try**   The main characters in Chiaverini's first novel also appear in ***Round Robin*** and ***The Cross-Country Quilters***. Other novels whose plots include quilting are ***Happenstance*** by Carol Shields and Whitney Otto's ***How to Make an American Quilt***.

## Clark, Robert

### Mr. White's Confession
Picador USA. 1998. 341 pp.

In 1939, an odd, isolated, memory-impaired clerk suspected of murder and the abandoned, grizzled homicide detective who puts him in prison seek salvation in their different experiences.

Book Groups 📖

**Subjects**   1930s • Minnesota • Murder • Mystery • Older Men/Younger Women • Policemen • Psychological Fiction • Sex Crimes • St. Paul, Minnesota

**Now try**   Clark's other novels include ***In the Deep Midwinter*** and ***Love Among the Ruins***. Although ***Mr. White's Confession*** won the 1999 Edgar Award for Best Novel, it is far more than a simple whodunit, as are these other award-winning mysteries: Joseph Kanon's ***Los Alamos***, Barbara Vine's ***A Dark-Adapted Eye***, and Minette Walters's ***The Sculptress***. Other psychological novels in which a crime occurs include Frederick Busch's ***Girls***, William Trevor's ***Felicia's Journey***, and John Lanchester's ***The Debt to Pleasure***.

## Cobbold, Marika

### Frozen Music
HarperCollins. 1999. 378 pp.

Children of best friends, although they grew up in different countries, Esther and Linus find their romantic relationship threatened when Esther's muckraking articles derail a planned architectural project of Linus's.

**Subjects**   Architects and Architecture • British Authors • Journalists • Love Stories • Sweden • Writers and Writing

**Now try**   Cobbold's other novels include ***Guppies for Tea***, ***The Purveyor of Enchantment***, and ***A Rival Creation***. Esther's painfully humorous search for true love is reminiscent of the heroine of Helen Fielding's ***Bridget Jones's Diary***.

## Coomer, Joe

### Beachcombing for a Shipwrecked God
Graywolf. 1995. 245 pp.

Three women—all suffering from very different personal problems—find the strength of friendship on a shared yacht moored in Portsmouth, New Hampshire.

Book Groups 📖

**Subjects**   Abusive Relationships • Archaeologists and Archaeology • Art and Artists • Boats and Boating • New England • New Hampshire • Overweight Women • Stroke Patients • Women's Friendships

**Now try**   Other novels by Coomer include ***Decatur Road***, ***The Loop***, and ***Apologizing to Dogs***. His nonfiction includes the nautical ***Sailing in a Spoonful of Water***. Other novels in which boats are an important part of the plot include John Casey's ***Spartina***, Pam Conrad's ***Pumpkin Moon***, Susan Kenney's ***Sailing***, and Robert Stone's ***Outerbridge Reach***. Other

novels in which women's friendships span a variety of ages, adding to the diversity and strength of their bond, include E. M. Broner's *A Weave of Women*, Lori Marie Carlson's *The Sunday Tertulia*, Gloria Naylor's *The Women of Brewster Place*, and Nancy Thayer's *Three Women at the Water's Edge*.

## Coyle, Beverly
### In Troubled Waters
Ticknor & Fields. 1993. 324 pp.

When Lois returns to her father's Florida home with her husband Paul (who is in the early stages of Alzheimer's), the extended family must deal with painful memories and the present reality of racial prejudice.

**2d Appeal**   Characters                                              Book Groups 📖

**Subjects**   ALA Notable Books • Alzheimer's Disease • American South • Child Abuse • Family Relationships • Florida • Racism • Southern Authors

**Now try**   Coyle's other novels include *Taken In* and *The Kneeling Bus*. Another novel about a family member suffering from Alzheimer's is Michael Ignatieff's *Scar Tissue*.

## Craze, Galaxy
### By the Shore
Atlantic Monthly Press. 1999. 231 pp.

The arrival of two visitors—a handsome writer and May's reckless father—to the seaside bed-and-breakfast that May and her young mother run kindles May's understanding of both her mother and herself.

**2d Appeal**   Setting

**Subjects**   1970s • British Authors • Fathers and Daughters • First Novels • Hippies • London, England • Mothers and Daughters • Single Mothers

**Now try**   Other novels about a daughter of a bohemian mother searching for her father include *The Saskiad* by Brian Hall and Liza Nelson's *Playing Botticelli*.

## Davenport, Kiana
### Song of the Exile
Ballantine Books. 1999. 360 pp.

Keo and Sunny, growing up in Hawaii prior to World War II, find their love threatened when war breaks out and Sunny is captured and forced to serve as a "comfort woman" for the Japanese troops in Rabaul.

**2d Appeal**   Characters                                              Book Groups 📖

**Subjects**   Hawaii • Historical Setting • Love Affairs • Male/Female Relationships • Music and Musicians • Prisoners of War • World War II

**Now try**   Davenport is also the author of *The Shark Dialogues*. Other novels about "comfort women" include Chang-rae Lee's *A Gesture Life* and Nora Okja Keller's *Comfort Woman*.

## Dawson, Carol
### The Mother-in-Law Diaries
Algonquin Books of Chapel Hill. 1999. 284 pp.

Upon hearing of her son's recent marriage (making her a mother-in-law), Lulu reviews her own four marriages and her intense connections to the women who were her own mothers-in-law.

**Subjects**   Daughters-in-Law • Male/Female Relationships • Marriage • Mothers and Sons • Mothers-in-Law

**Now try** Dawson is also the author of *Body of Knowledge*, *The Waking Spell*, and *Meeting the Minotaur*. Another novel written in diary format is Lee Smith's *Fair and Tender Ladies*. *Esperanza's Book of Saints* by María Escandón is also the story of a search for identity written in a light tone.

## Dimmick, Barbara
### In the Presence of Horses
Doubleday. 1998. 343 pp.

Running from the pain of losing her beloved sister, Natalie ends up working on a Pennsylvania horse farm, whose owner Pierce is also in the grip of sorrow.

**Subjects** Death of a Sibling • First Novels • Grief • Horses • Love Stories • Pennsylvania • Sisters

**Now try** Other novels about the intricate and intimate relationships between people and horses include Nicholas Evans's *The Horse Whisperer* and Jane Smiley's *Horse Heaven*.

## Egawa, Keith
### Madchild Running
Red Crane Books. 1999. 222 pp.

Levi, a young social worker in Seattle, Washington, tries to help one of his charges, a poetry-writing teen named Nicki.

**Subjects** American Indian Authors • American Indians • First Novels • Pacific Northwest • Seattle, Washington • Suicide • Teenage Girls

**Now try** Other American Indian authors include Sherman Alexie (his novel *Indian Killer* is also set in Seattle), Michael Dorris (*A Yellow Raft in Blue Water*), and James Welch (*Fools Crow* and *The Heartsong of Charging Elk*).

## Emshwiller, Carol
### Leaping Man Hill
Mercury House. 1999. 221 pp.

On a California ranch in 1915, a young woman hired to take care of a mute boy struggles to find a place in the hierarchy and heart of a troubled and unstable family.

**Subjects** 1910s • Abusive Relationships • American West • California • Cowboys • Family Relationships • Historical Setting • Love Stories • Mental Illness • World War I

**Now try** *Leaping Man Hill* is the sequel to *Ledoyt*, which focuses on other members of this ranching clan. Emshwiller is also the author of *The Start of the End of It All* and *Joy in Our Cause*, two collections of stories. Another look at the effects of World War I on a Western family can be found in Thomas Savage's *The Corner of Rife and Pacific*.

## Escandón, María Amparo
### Esperanza's Box of Saints
Scribner. 1999. 254 pp.

After the vision of San Judas Tadeo tells her that her daughter Blanca is alive, Esperanza boxes up the mementos of her faith and goes in search of her daughter through the seamy sides of Tijuana and Los Angeles.

**Subjects** Death of a Child • First Novels • Latino Authors • Latinos • Latinos in America • Magic Realism • Mexican Authors • Mothers and Daughters • Tijuana, Mexico

**Now try** Other books about Mexican American women include Denise Chavez's *Face of an Angel* and Sylvia Lopez-Medina's *Cantora*. Lane Von Herzen's *The Unfastened Heart* is another high-spirited, charming novel.

## Evans, Nicholas
### The Loop
Delacorte. 1998. 434 pp.

The U.S. government's decision to introduce wolves back into the western United States brings Buck Calder, a powerful Montana rancher, into conflict with Helen Ross, a beautiful young biologist, who also happens to fall in love with Calder's son Luke.

**Subjects** American West • Biologists • Conservation • Love Stories • Male/Female Relationships • Montana • Ranchers • Wolves

**Now try** Evans is the author of *The Horse Whisperer*. Other novels about wildlife and wildlife conservation include *Skywater* by Melinda Worth Popham, Fred Bodsworth's *Last of the Curlews*, and Anastasia Hobbet's *Pleasure of Believing*.

## Faulks, Sebastian
### Charlotte Gray
Random House. 1998. 399 pp.

Recruited to become a courier for secret British shipments to the French Resistance in the countryside of Vichy, France, Charlotte decides to stay on after her first mission in order to look for her missing lover, a pilot who didn't return from a bombing raid.

Book Groups 📖

**Subjects** 1940s • Art and Artists • British Authors • England • Fathers and Daughters • Fathers and Sons • France • Historical Setting • Love Stories • World War II

**Now try** Faulks's earlier novels (including *Birdsong* and *The Girl at the Lion d'Or*) also deal with the effects of the world wars on Europeans. Other novels about the German occupation of France are Alan Furst's *The World at Night*, Jean Rouaud's *The World More or Less*, Jean-Paul Sartre's *Troubled Sleep*, and *Sandman* and other St.-Cyr/Kohler crime novels by J. Robert Janes. Other wartime love stories include Jonathan Hull's *Losing Julia*, Sebastien Japrisot's *A Very Long Engagement*, and Michael Ondaatje's *The English Patient*.

## Fforde, Katie
### Life Skills
St. Martin's Press. 1999. 343 pp.

After she breaks off her engagement and loses her job, 30-something Julia Fairfax takes a job as a cook on an English canal boat, only to find herself knee-deep in difficult guests, health inspectors, and both new and old boyfriends.

**Subjects** Boats and Boating • British Authors • England • Humorous Fiction • Love Stories • Single Women

**Now try** Fforde's novel *Stately Pursuits* is another of her trademark fast-moving and humorous romances. In her manless state, Julia might be compared to the heroine of Helen Fielding's *Bridget Jones's Diary*, but she whines far less than Bridget does. Another young woman who answers a newspaper ad and finds her life taking different directions than she anticipated is the main character in Rachel Cusk's *The Country Life*.

## Finnamore, Suzanne
### Otherwise Engaged
Knopf. 1999. 209 pp.

At age 36, Eve has finally gotten engaged to Michael, but their yearlong engagement threatens to derail the happy couple.

**Subjects** California • First Novels • Humorous Fiction • Male/Female Relationships

**Now try** Finnamore is the author of *The Zygote Chronicles*, also a novel. Other humorous novels about male-female relationships include Jane Shapiro's *The Dangerous Husband* and Laura Zigman's *Animal Husbandry*.

## Fitch, Janet
### White Oleander
Little, Brown. 1999. 390 pp.

Life in a series of foster homes teaches Astrid how to survive, but she must still work out her difficult relationship with her mother Ingrid, a poet who is sent to prison for life for killing the man who abandoned her.

Book Groups 📖

**Subjects** First Novels • Foster Children • Mothers and Daughters • Murder • Oprah Winfrey Selection • Poets and Poetry • Women in Prison

**Now try** Other novels about young adults living in foster homes are *Martha Calhoun* by Richard Babcock and *Ellen Foster* by Kaye Gibbons.

## Flanagan, Richard
### The Sound of One Hand Clapping
Atlantic Monthly Press. 2000. 425 pp.

Now 38, pregnant and unmarried, Sonja Buloh returns to her childhood home in Tasmania to confront her abusive father and learn the truth about her mother, who disappeared when Sonja was three.

Book Groups 📖

**Subjects** Abusive Relationships • Alcoholics and Alcoholism • Australia • Australian Authors • Child Abuse • Dysfunctional Families • Fathers and Daughters • Immigrants and Refugees • Mothers Deserting Their Families • Tasmania • Working Classes

**Now try** Flanagan's novel won the Australian Booksellers' Book of the Year Award. He is also the author of the novel *Death of a River Guide*. *English Passengers* by Matthew Kneale is a novel about Tasmania's history. Children deal with parental abuse in *The House Tibet* by Georgia Savage.

## Frayn, Michael
### Headlong
Metropolitan Books. 1999. 342 pp.

Philosopher Martin Clay's hunch that a painting owned by his neighbor Tony Churt is a long-lost masterpiece by the Flemish artist Brueghel, and his attempts to wrest the work from Churt involve him in a madcap chase through European history, the contemporary art world, and his own larcenous heart.

**Subjects** Art and Artists • British Authors • Brueghel, Pieter • Husbands and Wives • Satirical Fiction

**Now try**    Other works by Frayn include a play, "Noises Off," and the novels *The Trick of It* and *A Landing on the Sun*. Martin's attemps to justify his own behavior have less serious consequences than the main characters have in Scott Smith's *A Simple Plan*. *Headlong* was short-listed for the Booker Prize.

## Freeman, Charlotte McGuinn
### Place Last Seen
Picador USA. 2000. 294 pp.

Maggie Baker, a six-year-old with Down Syndrome, disappears while playing hide-and-seek with her older brother Luke while the family is hiking in the Desolation Wilderness of the Sierra Nevadas.

**2d Appeal**    Characters

**Subjects**    American West • Down Syndrome • Family Relationships • First Novels • Mothers and Daughters • Search-and-Rescue Teams

**Now try**    Other domestic disaster novels include *The Deep End of the Ocean* by Jacquelyn Mitchard, *Evening News* by Marly Swick, and *A Boy in Winter* by Maxine Chernoff.

## Fromm, Pete
### How All This Started
Picador USA. 2000. 305 pp.

Abilene's manic dreams to turn her younger brother Austin into a pitching phenomenon even greater than the legendary Nolan Ryan come close to destroying both of them.

**2d Appeal**    Characters                                                       Book Groups ▢

**Subjects**    Baseball • Brothers and Sisters • First Novels • Manic Depression • Mental Illness • Texas

**Now try**    From is the author of several short story collections, including *Dry Rain* and *Night Swimming*, as well as the memoir *Indian Creek Chronicles*. Another novel about a family obsessed with baseball is David James Duncan's *The Brothers K*. Larry McMurtry's *The Last Picture Show* is also set in a dying town in west Texas. Other novels with manic-depressive characters include Ron Faust's *Fugitive Moon* (also with a baseball background) and Kaye Gibbons's *Sights Unseen*.

## Gadol, Peter
### Light at Dusk
Picador USA. 2000. 277 pp.

When his ex-lover Will Law resurfaces after an absence of several years, Pedro begins to reexamine the different paths their lives took—his into art history, Will's into diplomacy.

**Subjects**    Diplomacy • Gay Men • Immigrants and Refugees • Kidnapping • Men's Friendships • Paris, France

**Now try**    Gadol is also the author of *The Mystery Roast* and *Closer to the Sun*. James Buchan's *The Persian Bride* is an even darker novel about people caught up in the whirlwind of history.

## Gaffney, Patricia
### The Saving Graces
HarperCollins. 1999. 394 pp.

For 10 years, four friends—Lee, Rudy, Emma, and Isabel—have supported each other during the joys and crises in their lives, but they are forced to come up with new emotional resources when Isabel is diagnosed with rapidly metastasizing breast cancer.

**2d Appeal**   Characters                                    Book Groups 📖

**Subjects**   Cancer • Death and Dying • Infertility • Terminal Illness • Women's Friendships

**Now try**   Gaffney is also the author of *Forever and Ever* and *To Have and to Hold*. Other novels about women's friendships in the face of cancer are Elizabeth Berg's *Talk Before Sleep* and Abby Frucht's *Life Before Death*.

## Ganesan, Indira
### Inheritance
Knopf. 1998. 193 pp.

Fifteen-year-old Sonil, in frail health, has come to recover in her beloved grandmother's house on the fictional Indian island of Pi; there she gossips with her cousin Jani, falls in love for the first time (with an American twice her age), and tries to forgive her mother, who abandoned her as a baby.

**2d Appeal**   Characters

**Subjects**   Family Secrets • India • Indian Authors • Love Affairs • Mothers and Daughters • Mothers Deserting Their Families • Older Men/Younger Women • Teenage Girls

**Now try**   Ganesan set her first novel, *The Journey*, on the same island of Pi. Chitra Banerjee Divakaruni's *Sister of My Heart*, set in Calcutta, is also about teenaged girls and family secrets. Other novels that explore a difficult mother-daughter relationship include Elizabeth Strout's *Amy and Isabelle*, Mona Simpson's *Anywhere But Here*, and Marly Swick's *Paper Wings*.

## Ghosh, Amitav
### The Glass Palace
Random House. 2001. 474 pp.

Colonial Burma, India, and Malaya during a century of turbulent history from the British Raj to the present form the backdrop for this multigenerational saga of Rajkumar, once a poor Indian boy, and now a wealthy teak trader, and lovely Dolly, former child maid to the royal family of Burma.

**2d Appeal**   Setting

**Subjects**   Burma • Colonialism • Family Relationships • Historical Setting • India • Indian Authors • Love Stories • Malaya • Multigenerational Novels • Rags-to-Riches Story

**Now try**   Other novels by Ghosh include *The Shadow Lines* and *The Calcutta Chromosome: A Novel of Fevers, Delirium and Discovery*. Other expansive novels set in the same parts of the world include *The Singapore Grip* by J. G. Farrell and *The Raj Quartet* by Paul Scott.

## Giardina, Denise
### Saints and Villains
W.W. Norton. 1998. 487 pp.

The German theologian Dietrich Bonhoeffer grows up in Berlin, studies in depression–era New York City, returns to Germany in hopes of convincing church leaders of the growing Nazi evil, and is imprisoned after participating in a failed plot to assassinate Hitler.

**Subjects** Biographical Fiction • Bonhoeffer, Dietrich • Concentration Camps • Germany • Historical Setting • Moral/Ethical Dilemmas • Nazis • Political Prisoners • Theologians and Theology • World War II

**Now try** Giardina also covers epic territory in her other works, including *Storming Heaven*, *Good King Harry*, and *The Unquiet Earth*. Thomas Keneally's *Schindler's List* tells the story of another German who clandestinely resisted the Nazis. A good biography of Bonhoeffer is Renate Wind's *Dietrich Bonhoeffer: A Spoke in the Wheel*.

## Gilson, Chris
### Crazy for Cornelia
Warner Books. 2000. 345 pp.

Kevin Doyle, reluctant doorman at a posh Manhattan apartment house, finds himself falling for seemingly ditzy debutante Cornelia Lord, whose interest in coronas and Nikola Tesla lands her in a psychiatric hospital.

**Subjects** Business and Businessmen • First Novels • Humorous Fiction • Love Stories • New York • Psychiatric Hospitals • Tesla, Nikola • Upper Classes

**Now try** Other lighthearted, feel-good novels include Jane Heller's *Princess Charming*, Jennifer Weiner's *Good in Bed*, Mameve Medwed's *Mail*, and Laura Zigman's *Dating Big Bird*.

## Godwin, Gail
### Evensong
Ballantine Books. 1999. 405 pp.

Episcopal priest Margaret Bonner and her husband Adrian find their comfortable, but not particularly happy, lives rocked by a visit from a mysterious man, a planned protest march, and an unhappy student at the school where Adrian works.

Book Groups 📖

**Subjects** American South • Husbands and Wives • Marriage • Ministers, Priests, Rabbis • North Carolina • Small-Town Life • Teenage Boys

**Now try** Margaret's childhood is described in Godwin's novel *Father Melancholy's Daughter*. Godwin is also the author of *Violet Clay*, *The Odd Woman*, and *A Mother and Two Daughters*. Margaret's struggles to live a spiritually satisfying life in the last years of the twentieth century are reminiscent of the poet Louise Glück's works, including *The Wild Iris* and *Vita Nova*. Another priest caught up in questions of faith is the main character in Mary Doria Russell's *The Sparrow*.

## Goldberg, Myla
### Bee Season
Doubleday. 2000. 275 pp.

When nine-year-old Eliza Naumann—who has always been out of step with her brilliant parents and older brother—begins winning one spelling bee after another (her school, district, and state), her success sets off a series of events that shake the family to its roots.

**2d Appeal** Characters
Book Groups 📖

**Subjects** Brothers and Sisters • Coming-of-Age • Fathers and Daughters • First Novels • Gifted Children • Husbands and Wives • Jews and Judaism • Kleptomania

**Now try** Eliza's decision to take responsibility for her own actions is similar to the decisions made by the main character in *The Saskiad* by Brian Hall.

## Goldman, Judy
### The Slow Way Back

Morrow. 1999. 274 pp.

When her aunt unexpectedly sends Thea some old letters written by her grand-mother, Thea finally understands her family's history and the secrets that have created chasms of misunderstanding among them.

**Subjects**   American South • Family Secrets • First Novels • Intermarriage • Jews and Judaism • North Carolina • Sisters

**Now try**   Another novel in which long-suppressed secrets are revealed is Fannie Flagg's *Welcome to the World, Baby Girl!* Small-town Jewish life is also explored in *The Jew Store*, a memoir by Stella Suberman, and Tova Mirvis's *The Ladies Auxiliary*.

## Griffith, Patricia Browning
### The World Around Midnight

G.P. Putnam's Sons. 1991. 254 pp.

The death of her father brings Dinah Reynolds back to Midnight, Texas, to take over as editor of the town's weekly paper, all the while coping with news of her husband's infidelity and the appearance in Midnight of her old boyfriend.

**Subjects**   Adultery • ALA Notable Books • American West • First Novels • Humorous Fiction • Husbands and Wives • Journalists • Male/Female Relationships • Small-Town Life • Texas

**Now try**   Griffith also wrote *Supporting the Sky*, a novel about the tribulations of a divorced mother in Washington, D.C. Other novels set in contemporary Texas include Janis Arnold's *Daughters of Memory* and Larry McMurtry's *Duane's Depressed*.

## Gutcheon, Beth
### More Than You Know

Morrow. 2000. 269 pp.

Two mother-daughter relationships, two love stories, and two centuries come together in Dundee, Maine, during the 1920s, when Hannah Gray and Conary Crocker confront a malevolent spirit.

**Subjects**   Ghosts • Husbands and Wives • Love Stories • Maine • Mothers and Daughters • Murder • New England

**Now try**   Beth Gutcheon is also the author of *Domestic Pleasures*, *Saying Grace*, and *Five Fortunes*. In *More Than You Know*, she has written a classic ghost story in the grand tradition of Henry James's *The Turn of the Screw*. Gutcheon's novel also has plot similarities to *The Weight of Water* by Anita Shreve. For a different type of ghost story (told from the ghost's point of view), try Abby Frucht's *Polly's Ghost*.

## Hagy, Alyson
### Keeneland

Simon & Schuster. 2000. 270 pp.

Kerry Connelly goes back to her home racetrack to try to recuperate from a money-losing, abusive husband whose schemes have killed a horse.

**Subjects**   Abusive Relationships • Equestrians • First Novels • Horse Racing • Horses • Husbands and Wives • Kentucky

Now try    Hagy has also published three collections of short stories, including *Graveyard of the Atlantic*, *Madonna on Her Back*, and *Hardware River Stories*. Other equine novels include *Horse Heaven* by Jane Smiley and Barbara Dimmock's *In the Presence of Horses*. A good nonfiction book for horse lovers is *Seabiscuit: An American Legend* by Laura Hillenbrand.

## Hamill, Pete
### Snow in August                                           Little, Brown. 1997. 327 pp.

In 1940s Brooklyn an unusual friendship develops between Michael Devlin, an Irish Catholic teenager, and an elderly rabbi from Prague.

Subjects    1940s • Anti-Semitism • Brooklyn, New York • Friendship • Golems • Jews and Judaism • Ministers, Priests, Rabbis • Teenage Boys

Now try    Among his other books, Hamill also wrote the memoir *A Drinking Life* and *Loving Women: A Novel of the Fifties*. Golems also play a part in Michael Chabon's *The Amazing Adventures of Kavalier & Clay* and *Watch Your Mouth* by David Handler. Another unlikely friendship that develops in Brooklyn in the 1940s is found in Steve Kluger's *Last Days of Summer*. Jewish life after the Holocaust is explored in Chaim Potok's *My Name Is Asher Lev*, *The Chosen*, and other novels.

## Harris, E. Lynn
### Not a Day Goes By                                        Doubleday. 2000. 271 pp.

Wealth, fame, sex, and glamour define the lives of Basil (a retired football player who has become a sports agent) and Yancey (a budding Broadway diva), as they attempt to succeed both in their relationship and their sometimes conflicting careers.

Subjects    Actors and Acting • African American Authors • African Americans • Love Affairs • Male/Female Relationships • Sports

Now try    Harris is also the author of *Abide with Me* and *If This World Were Mine*. Other novels written by African American men about love, sex, and relationships include Eric Jerome Dickey's *Liar's Game* and *Milk in My Coffee*, and Omar Tyree's *For the Love of Money* and *Single Man*.

## Hegi, Ursula
### The Salt Dancers                                Simon & Schuster. 1995. 235 pp.

At 41, pregnant and unmarried, Julia returns to her childhood home to confront her father and brother with her memories of their shared and troubled past.

Book Groups 📖

Subjects    Architects and Architecture • Career Women • Family Relationships • Fathers and Daughters • Single Women

Now try    Hegi is also the author of *Hotel of the Saints: Stories*, *Floating in My Mother's Palm*, *The Vision of Emma Blau*, and *Stones from the River*. Another pregnant and unmarried daughter returns home to face her painful past in Julie Schumacher's *The Body Is Water*.

## Hendricks, Judith Ryan

### Bread Alone
Morrow. 2001. 358 pp.

After her husband leaves her, Wynter Morrison moves to Seattle from California and begins to remake herself through her work at a local bakery.

**Subjects**   Bakeries • Cooking • First Novels • Love Stories • Seattle, Washington • Women's Friendships

**Now try**   Other novels that prominently feature food and cooking include Jayne Ann Krentz's *Trust Me* and Laura Esquivel's *Like Water for Chocolate*.

## Hoffman, Alice

### Blue Diary
G.P. Putnam's Sons. 2001. 303 pp.

When, after 13 years of idyllic marriage, Ethan is arrested for the rape and murder of a teenage girl 15 years earlier, Jorie has to face the reality that her beloved husband is a stranger.

**2d Appeal**   Characters

**Subjects**   Cancer • Family Relationships • Family Secrets • Husbands and Wives • Marriage • Mothers and Sons • Sisters • Women's Friendships

**Now try**   Among Hoffman's many other novels are *The River King* and *At Risk*. In *Prodigal Summer*, Barbara Kingsolver also writes beautifully of the world of nature. Another family that must face a crisis brought on by murder is found in Rosellen Brown's *Before and After*.

## Hood, Ann

### Ruby
Picador USA. 1998. 225 pp.

Trying to get over the unexpected death of her husband, Livia befriends Ruby, a pregnant 15-year-old who doesn't seem capable of taking care of her own baby—a baby that Livia wants desperately to adopt.

**2d Appeal**   Characters                                    Book Groups

**Subjects**   Adoption • Death of a Spouse • Pregnancy • Single Mothers • Teenage Girls • Widows • Women's Friendships

**Now try**   Hood is also the author of *Somewhere Off the Coast of Maine* and *Something Blue*, as well as other novels. *Plainsong* by Kent Haruf and *Marchlands* by Karla Kuban are other novels about pregnant teenagers.

## Hyde, Catherine Ryan

### Pay It Forward
Simon & Schuster. 1999. 288 pp.

Twelve-year-old Trevor McKinney unleashes a national phenomenon when he promotes his social studies project—to do a "good deed" for three people who must then do good deeds for three others, and so on.

**Subjects**   Death and Dying • Disfigurement • Love Stories • Mothers and Sons • Vietnam War • Violence

**Now try**   Hyde is also the author of *Funerals for Horses* and *Earthquake Weather*. This warmhearted novel is a modern-day variation on the theme presented in Lloyd Douglas's *Magnificent Obsession*. Readers may also be reminded of Winston Groom's novel (and later, movie) *Forrest Gump*. The altruism of a young man is the subject of John Irving's *A Prayer for Owen Meany*.

## Iida, Deborah
### Middle Son
Algonquin Books of Chapel Hill. 1996. 228 pp.

His mother's approaching death forces Spencer to recall the accidental drowning of his older brother Taizo at age 12, and the effect the tragedy had on the entire Fujii family.

**Subjects**  ALA Notable Books • Asian Americans • Asians in America • Brothers • Death of a Child • First Novels • Hawaii • Japan • Japanese Americans

**Now try**  Graham Salisbury's *Blue Skin of the Sea* is another novel about how tragedy shaped a family's life. Hawaii's plantations are also the setting of Lois-Ann Yamanaka's *Wild Meat and the Bully Burgers*.

## Jenkins, Amy
### Honeymoon: A Romantic Rampage
Little, Brown. 2000. 282 pp.

While on her honeymoon, Honey runs into the man she spent an evening with seven years earlier, never saw again, and has always told friends was the love of her life.

**Subjects**  Adultery • British Authors • First Novels • Male/Female Relationships • Marriage • Single Women

**Now try**  Other novels about young Brits and their relationships include Helen Fielding's *Bridget Jones's Diary* and *Bridget Jones: The Edge of Reason*, Isabel Wolff's *Trials of Tiffany Trott* and *Making Minty Malone*, and Anna Maxted's *Getting Over It*.

## Joe, Yolanda
### This Just In...
Doubleday. 2000. 281 pp.

Five women—four black and one white—who work together in the newsroom at a Chicago television station battle corporate chicanery, racism, and sexism while still trying to remain friends.

**Subjects**  African American Authors • African Americans • American Midwest • Chicago, Illinois • Racism • Sexism • Television • Women's Friendships

**Now try**  Joe also wrote the novels *He Say, She Say* and *Bebe's by Golly Wow!* Another novel set in a television newsroom is David Haynes's *Live at Five*. Other breezy novels about the lives of black women include Terry McMillan's *A Day Late and a Dollar Short* and Karen E. Quinones Miller's *Satin Doll*.

## Johnson, Wayne
### Don't Think Twice
Harmony Books. 1999. 291 pp.

Paul Two Persons must face his troubled marriage, his ties to the Chippewa reservation, and a business cartel as he struggles to save his hotel, his land, and his life.

**2d Appeal**  Setting

**Subjects**  American Indians • Death of a Child • Minnesota • Mystery • Ojibwa Indians • Resorts

**Now try**    Paul Two Persons is the central character in Wayne Johnson's *Six Crooked Highways*. The novels of Nevada Barr (*Deep South*, *Liberty Falling*; and others) share the same tightly controlled writing and mix of hard-edge tension with a compelling sense of place.

## Kafka, Kimberly
### True North

Dutton. 2000. 273 pp.

Alaskan bush pilot Bailey Lockhart finds herself embroiled in tribal politics and heartache when she purchases a piece of land surrounded by thousands of acres owned by the Native American Ingalik tribe.

**2d Appeal**    Setting

**Subjects**    Alaska • American Indians • First Novels • Interracial Relationships • Love Stories • Mental Retardation • Pilots • Property Disputes • Single Women • Sisters • Violence

**Now try**    Kafka's novel has some of the tension and Arctic flavor of Audrey Schulman's *The Cage*. Other novels set in Alaska include mysteries by Dana Stabenow (*A Cold Day for Murder* and *Hunter's Moon* are two good ones), Sue Henry (*Murder on the Iditarod Trail* and *Death Takes Passage*, among others), and John Straley (*The Curious Eat Themselves* and *The Angels Will Not Care*). For a real-life picture of the Alaskan wilderness experience, try Farley Mowat's *Never Cry Wolf*. Property disputes are also the subject of Jane Smiley's *A Thousand Acres* and Andre Dubus III's *House of Sand and Fog*.

## Kalpakian, Laura
### Steps and Exes

Bard. 1999. 321 pp.

Her daughter's desire for a lavish engagement party (à la Martha Stewart) brings together the far-flung group of people (ex-lovers, their children, their new spouses, etc.) that aging hippie Celia Henry has collected in her devotion to maintaining the unfettered bonds of relationships.

**Subjects**    Family Relationships • Love Affairs • Male/Female Relationships

**Now try**    Kalpakian is also the author of *The Delinquent Virgin*, a collection of stories, and the novels *Graced Land* and *Beggars and Choosers*, among other works of fiction. Lynne Sharon Schwartz's *In the Family Way* is another charming novel that offers new understandings of what makes a family.

## Kay, Terry
### Taking Lottie Home

Morrow. 2000. 294 pp.

Two ex-baseball players fall in love with Lottie: Foster Lanier, whose leg was amputated as the result of a baseball injury, will marry Lottie and father her son, while young and idealistic Ben Phelps will be the one to take Lottie home.

**2d Appeal**    Characters

**Subjects**    1900s • American South • Baseball • Male/Female Relationships • Small-Town Life • Southern Authors

**Now try**   Kay's other novels include *To Dance with the White Dog*, *Shadow Song*, and *The Runaway*. Kay's nostalgia and affection for small-town southern life brings to mind the novels of Ferrol Sams, including *Run with the Horsemen* and *The Whisper of the River*.

## Kirchner, Bharti
### Sharmila's Book
Dutton. 1999. 296 pp.

Thoroughly Americanized Sharmila (whose parents emigrated from India years before) allows herself to be the bride in an arranged marriage in India and discovers that her new husband's family is filled with secrets.

**Subjects**   Family Secrets • India • Male/Female Relationships • Marriage

**Now try**   Kirchner is also the author of the novel *Shiva Dancing*. She has also written several cookbooks, including *The Bold Vegetarian: 150 Innovative International Recipes*. Other novels about contemporary life in India include Chitra Banerjee Divakaruni's *Sister of My Heart* and *Mistress of Spices*.

## Kirn, Walter
### Thumbsucker
Broadway Books. 1999. 300 pp.

Though hypnosis helps teenager Justin Cobb stop sucking his thumb, it can't quite smooth his way through the difficulties of adolescence.

**Subjects**   Coming-of-Age • Fathers and Sons • Humorous Fiction • Mormons • Obsessive-Compulsive Disorder • Teenage Boys • Thumb Sucking

**Now try**   Kirn's other novels include *Up in the Air*, *She Needed Me*, and *My Hard Bargain*. Other novels about adolescent boys include J. D. Salinger's *The Catcher in the Rye*, John Keegan's *Clearwater Summer*, and Russell Banks's *Rule of the Bone*, although none of them has any of the humor so prevalent in Kirn's novel. Tobias Wolff's memoir, *This Boy's Life*, is a wonderful account of growing up in a difficult family situation.

## Kohler, Sheila
### Cracks
Zoland Books. 1999. 165 pp.

A group of women reunite after 40 years to help raise money for their old boarding school and relive the events leading up to the disappearance of Fiamma Coronna, the foreign student who was one of their teammates on the swim team.

**2d Appeal**   Characters

**Subjects**   Friendship • Private Schools • South Africa • South African Authors • Teenage Girls • Violence

**Now try**   Kohler is also the author of *The House on R Street*, *One Girl: A Novel in Stories*, and *The Perfect Place*. Other novels told from the point of view of a group of people that are narrated in one voice include Jeffrey Eugenides's *The Virgin Suicides* and Tova Mirvis's *The Ladies Auxiliary*. A mysterious disappearance is at the heart of Joan Lindsay's novel *Picnic at Hanging Rock* (which was also made into an excellent movie). The relationship of the group of girls to their teacher Miss G parallels the relationship Miss Brodie has with her special students in Muriel Spark's *The Prime of Miss Jean Brodie*.

## Lamar, Jake
### The Last Integrationist
Crown. 1996. 344 pp.

It's 2008, and amidst a circus of racial controversy and conspiracy, Melvin ("Hang 'Em High Hutch") Hutchinson, conservative politician and first black attorney general of the United States, aims for the White House, but his success is tempered by the death of his daughter and threatened by a secret in his past.

    **Subjects**   African American Authors • African Americans • Art and Artists • First Novels • Interracial Relationships • Law and Lawyers • Political Fiction • Race Relations

    **Now try**   Lamar is also the author of the memoir *Bourgeois Blues* and the novel *Close to the Bone*, which explores interracial relationships against the backdrop of the O. J. Simpson trial. Other provocative political page-turners are Sherman Alexie's *Indian Killer*, Tom Wolfe's *The Bonfire of the Vanities*, and Richard Condon's *The Manchurian Candidate*. *Negrophobia: An Urban Parable* by Darius James, *Erasure* by Percival Everett, and *High Cotton* by Darryl Pinckney are daring satires on America's racial divide.

## Landvik, Lorna
### The Tall Pine Polka
Ballantine Books. 1999. 440 pp.

The diverse population of Tall Pine, Minnesota, is delighted to share in the fame garnered by Fenny Ness when she is discovered by a Hollywood writer and hired to play the lead in a romantic comedy to be filmed in their hometown.

    **Subjects**   American Midwest • Love Stories • Minnesota • Motion Picture Industry • Small-Town Life • Women's Friendships

    **Now try**   Landvik's other novels include *Your Oasis at Flame Lake*, *Welcome to the Great Mysterious*, and *Patty Jane's House of Curl*. Another Minnesota town filled with endearing characters is described in the humorous books of Garrison Keillor, including *Lake Wobegon Days*.

## Lattany, Kristin Hunter
### Do Unto Others
One World. 2000. 265 pp.

When African Americans Zena and her husband Lucius give a young woman from Africa a temporary home, Zena finds that both her beliefs and romantic notions may be misconceptions after all.

    **2d Appeal**   Characters

    **Subjects**   African American Authors • African Americans • Africans • Family Relationships

    **Now try**   Lattany is also the author of the novel *Kinfolks*. Another novel in which a woman is challenged to rethink her life's goals and her belief systems is Benilde Little's *The Itch*.

## Laurimore, Jill
### Going to Pot
Thomas Dunne Books. 1999. 338 pp.

As Little Watling Hall slowly collapses around them, Fliss and Ivor Harley-Wright devise a scheme to save the family home by selling their sole valuable asset, the Harley-Wright collection of Commemorative Drinking Vessels, to a rich and eccentric American businessman.

      **Subjects**    British Authors • Culture Clash • England • Family Relationships • First Novels • Humorous Fiction

      **Now try**    For another humorous take on dilapidated country homes, try Katie Fforde's *Stately Pursuits*. Both Susan Orlean's *The Orchid Thief* (nonfiction) and Michael Palin's *Hemingway's Chair* (fiction) are humorous looks at obsessive collecting.

## Lewis, Sara
### The Answer Is Yes
Harcourt Brace. 1998. 274 pp.

Just when it seems that Jenny's life has hit rock bottom—her marriage is unfulfilling, she is stymied in her search for her birth mother, and she's been downsized from her bank job—she discovers The Institute for Affirmation, an adult education center where everything is possible.

      **Subjects**    Actors and Acting • Adoption • American West • Humorous Fiction • Husbands and Wives • San Diego, California • Science and Scientists • Theater

      **Now try**    Other books by Lewis include *But I Love You Anyway*, *Heart Conditions*, and *Trying to Smile and Other Stories*. Another novel with the same light and affirming tone is Sherwood Kiraly's *Big Babies*. Other novels about adoptees and their birth parents include Elinor Lipman's *Then She Found Me*, Frederick Busch's *Long Way from Home*, and Laurie Alberts's *Lost Daughters*.

## Long, David
### The Daughters of Simon Lamoreaux
Scribner. 2000. 270 pp.

Miles Fanning thought he had successfully recovered from the traumatic event of his adolescence—the never-solved disappearance of his high school girlfriend Carly—but when Carly's sister contacts Miles almost a quarter of a century later, he realizes that the past is still haunting him.

      **Subjects**    Adultery • Fathers and Daughters • Mystery • Sisters • Unsolved Crimes

      **Now try**    Long's other books include a collection of stories, *Blue Spruce*, and the novel *The Falling Boy*, which is also about a man involved with two sisters. Other novels about the effects of a disappearance on those left behind are *The Odd Sea* by Frederick Reiken and Scott Spencer's *Waking the Dead*.

## Mailer, Norris Church
### Windchill Summer
Random House. 2000. 395 pp.

Cherry Marshall's 21st year is marked by the arrival into her life of a Vietnam veteran and the mysterious death of Carlene, a young single mother.

      **Subjects**    1960s • Arkansas • Coming-of-Age • First Novels • Single Mothers • Small-Town Life • Vietnam War • Working Classes

      **Now try**    Another coming-of-age novel set against the background of the Vietnam War is Bobbie Ann Mason's *In Country*.

## Marino, Anne N.
### The Collapsible World
W.W. Norton. 2000. 171 pp.

When her mother disappears, Lillie's life is further complicated by problems surrounding her drug-abusing physician-father and the sudden illness of her employer.

      **Subjects**    American West • Drugs and Drug Abuse • Fathers and Daughters • First Novels • Maps • San Francisco, California • Sisters

**Now try**   This novel has the same tone and setting as *Jumping the Green* by Leslie Schwartz, in which the main character becomes increasingly self-destructive as a result of a family crisis.

## Mark, Andrew
### Falling Bodies
G.P. Putnam's Sons. 1999. 259 pp.

When his wife and two young children are killed by a drunk driver, Jackson Tate believes he will never find happiness again, until he meets Livvy, whose sorrow over her own difficulties seems as great as Jackson's own.

**Subjects**   Alcoholics and Alcoholism • Alzheimer's Disease • Death of a Child • Death of a Spouse • First Novels • Love Stories • Maine • Science and Scientists

**Now try**   David R. Slavitt's *Lives of the Saints* is another novel about how a man deals with the deaths of his wife and child, although in Slavitt's case the appeal of the novel is language, not story.

## Martin, Emer
### More Bread or I'll Appear
Houghton Mifflin. 1999. 271 pp.

Twenty-eight-year-old Keelin, the youngest and most stable of her siblings, searches for her older sister Aisling on a journey that takes her through Japan, New York, Hawaii, and Honduras.

**Subjects**   Brothers and Sisters • Eating Disorders • Expatriates • Family Relationships • Ireland • Irish Authors • Mental Illness • Mothers and Daughters

**Now try**   Martin's first novel, *Breakfast in Babylon*, also deals with Irish drifters in precarious living situations. Other novels that combine black humor with a grim view of Irish life include J. P. Donleavy's *The Ginger Man*, Roddy Doyle's Rabbitte family trilogy (*The Commitments*, *The Snapper*, and *The Van*), and Patrick McCabe's *Breakfast on Pluto*. Another sibling tracking down an older sister is found in Jennifer Egan's *The Invisible Circus*, although there is no humor—even black—in Egan's novel.

## Matson, Suzanne
### The Hunger Moon
W.W. Norton. 1997. 252 pp.

When Renata takes her newborn son and moves across the country to Boston, she finds herself involved in the lives of Eleanor, a 78-year-old widow, and June, a young dancer whom Eleanor hires to care for her.

**Subjects**   Ballet Dancers • Boston, Massachusetts • Dancing and Dancers • Eating Disorders • First Novels • New England • Single Mothers • Waitresses • Women's Friendships

**Now try**   Matson is also the author of two books of poetry (*Sea Level* and *Durable Goods*) and the novel *A Trick of Nature*. Another novel about the friendship between two very different women is Agnes Rossi's *Split Skirt*. In Ann Patchett's *The Patron Saint of Liars*, the main character also leaves town without telling her baby's father that she is pregnant.

## Matson, Suzanne
### A Trick of Nature
W.W. Norton. 2000. 252 pp.

Greg Goodman's placid suburban life as a husband, father, and high school football coach is thrown into disarray when one of his players is hit by lightning, he has a brief affair with an old acquaintance, and his wife moves out of their home.

**Subjects**   Adultery • Drugs and Drug Abuse • Family Relationships • Football Coaches • Husbands and Wives • Love Affairs • Mothers Deserting Their Families • Twins

**Now try**   Matson is also the author of *The Hunger Moon*. Sue Miller's *While I Was Gone* is another novel about a family reevaluating their relationships to one another. Gretel Ehrlich's *A Match to the Heart* is a nonfiction account of her experiences after being hit by lightning. Other novels about football coaches include John Ed Bradley's *The Best There Ever Was* and Nanci Kincaid's *Balls* (although these are both about college football).

## McMurtry, Larry
### Duane's Depressed
Simon & Schuster. 1999. 431 pp.

At age 62, oilman Duane believes that his life isn't worth living and starts searching for ways to make it meaningful, all of which totally mystifies his friends and family.

**2d Appeal**   Characters

**Subjects**   American West • Depression • Humorous Fiction • Men's Lives • Middle-Aged Men • Midlife Crisis • Texas

**Now try**   Duane is also a character in McMurtry's *Texasville* and *The Last Picture Show*. Other novels about men struggling with middle-aged angst include Richard Russo's *Straight Man*, Francine Prose's *Blue Angel*, and Michael Chabon's *Wonder Boys*.

## McNamer, Deirdre
### My Russian
Houghton Mifflin. 1999. 278 pp.

Francesca Woodbridge uses a planned trip to Greece as an opportunity to live the sort of life—sans husband and family—that she always thought she wanted.

Book Groups 📖

**Subjects**   Adultery • Husbands and Wives • Marriage • Midlife Crisis • Mothers Deserting Their Families

**Now try**   McNamer is also the author of *Rima in the Weeds* and *One Sweet Quarrel*. Other novels about women who find themselves in the midst of a midlife crisis include Elizabeth Berg's *The Pull of the Moon* and Anne Tyler's *Ladder of Years*.

## Medwed, Mameve
### Host Family
Warner Books. 2000. 309 pp.

Throughout the 20 years they've been married, Daisy and Henry Lewis have hosted international students in their home, but now their son is off to college and Henry decides he has fallen in love with a young French student.

**Subjects**   Adultery • Cambridge, Massachusetts • Fathers and Daughters • Marriage • Mothers and Sons • New England • Science and Scientists

**Now try**   Medwed is also the author of *Mail*. Other novels displaying a similar wit and warmth include Elinor Lipman's *Isabel's Bed* and Stephen McCauley's *The Easy Way Out*. Anne Bernays's *Professor Romeo* also takes place in Cambridge.

## Merrell, Susan
### A Member of the Family

HarperCollins. 2000. 350 pp.

When Deborah and Chris Latham adopt 18-month-old Michael, an orphan from Romania, their dreams of a happy family life are shattered by Michael's increasingly violent behavior both in school and at home.

Book Groups 📖

**Subjects**   Adoption • Family Relationships • Fathers and Sons • First Novels • Mothers and Sons • Orphans • Romania

**Now try**   The experiences of Romanian orphans are also described in Marianne Wiggins's *Eveless Eden*.

## Mirvis, Tova
### The Ladies Auxiliary
W.W. Norton. 1999. 311 pp.

Members of the Orthodox Jewish community in Memphis, Tennessee, find their comfortable lives challenged by the arrival of convert Batsheva Jacobs, who brings spirit and innovation to the traditional practices and becomes a favorite of the community's teenaged girls.

**Subjects**   First Novels • Jews and Judaism • Memphis, Tennessee • Single Women • Tennessee

**Now try**   Other novels set in tight-knit Orthodox Jewish comunities include Allegra Goodman's *Kaaterskill Falls* and Pearl Abraham's *The Romance Reader*. Judy Goldman also writes about Jewish life in *The Slow Way Back*.

## Moran, Thomas
### Water, Carry Me
Riverhead Books. 2000. 269 pp.

Medical student Una Moss falls in love with architectural draftsman Aidan Ferrell against the backdrop of the political troubles in Northern Ireland.

**2d Appeal**   Characters

Book Groups 📖

**Subjects**   Grandparents • Ireland • Male/Female Relationships • Orphans • Political Fiction • Violence

**Now try**   Moran's other novels include *The Man in the Box* and *The World I Made for Her*. In both tone and subject matter, *Water, Carry Me* brings to mind Katherine Weber's *The Music Lesson*. Other novels about the conflict between Protestants and Catholics in Ireland include Roddy Doyle's *A Star Called Henry* and Patrick McCabe's *Breakfast on Pluto*.

## Morris, Mary

### Acts of God

Picador USA. 2000. 244 pp.

When Tess Winsterstone unwillingly returns home for her 30th high school reunion, she is forced to confront the unhappiness of her past, including her father's betrayal and an unresolved relationship with an old friend.

**Subjects**   1950s • 1980s • Business and Businessmen • Insurance Agents • Love Affairs • Reunions • Single Mothers

**Now try**   Morris is also the author of the novels *House Arrest* and *The Night Sky*. Another novel about growing up in the 1950s is Keith Maillard's *Gloria*.

## Mort, John

### Soldier in Paradise

Southern Methodist University Press. 1999. 180 pp.

Jimmy Patrick ("Irish") Donnelly's life after he returns to the United States from Vietnam is as dismal as it was in country.

**2d Appeal**   Characters                                             Book Groups 📖

**Subjects**   1960s • First Novels • Florida • Men's Friendships • Vietnam War

**Now try**   Mort has published two works of short fiction: *Tanks* and *The Walnut King and Other Stories*. Another powerful work about the Vietnam War told through the eyes of a soldier is Tim O'Brien's *The Things They Carried*. The aftermath of the war is portrayed from a different but equally sensitive perspective in Bobbie Ann Mason's *In Country*. Readers who appreciate Mort's honesty and his straight language about complex issues may also enjoy the classic works of Ernest Hemingway dealing with past wars—*A Farewell to Arms* (World War I) and *For Whom the Bell Tolls* (the Spanish civil war). *Soldier in Paradise* won the ALA's 2000 Bill Boyd Award, honoring the best fiction set in a period when the United States was at war.

## Murphy, Yannick

### The Sea of Trees

Houghton Mifflin. 1997. 227 pp.

Ten-year-old Tian's experiences during and immediately after World War II begin with life in a Japanese prison camp with her French mother, followed by a move to Tian's father's home in China, but when mother and daughter move back to Vietnam, they find themselves caught in the escalating violence between the French and the Vietnamese.

**2d Appeal**   Setting                                               Book Groups 📖

**Subjects**   China • Coming-of-Age • First Novels • Immigrants and Refugees • Indochina • Mothers and Daughters • Vietnam • World War II

**Now try**   J. G. Ballard's *Empire of the Sun* is also about a child's experiences during World War II; both it and *The Sea of Trees* show the devastation war wreaks on everyone, even noncombatants.

## Nelson, Liza

### Playing Botticelli

G.P. Putnam's Sons. 2000. 279 pp.

Sixteen-year-old Dylan runs away from her mother Godiva Blue (born Judy Blitch) to find the father she's never known.

Book Groups 📖

**Subjects**  Art and Artists • Coming-of-Age • First Novels • Florida • Mothers and Daughters • New Mexico • Runaways • Single Mothers • Teenage Girls

**Now try**  Other daughters searching for the fathers they never knew can be found in Mona Simpson's *The Lost Father* and Brian Hall's *The Saskiad*.

## O'Brien, Tim
### Tomcat in Love
Broadway Books. 1998. 347 pp.

Thomas Chippering, a professor of linguistics, has two obsessions: to win back his wife Lorna Sue and to have sex with every woman he meets.

**Subjects**  Adultery • College Professors • Humorous Fiction • Male/Female Relationships • Men's Lives • Minnesota

**Now try**  O'Brien's other books include *If I Die in a Combat Zone*, *In the Lake of the Woods*, and *The Things They Carried*. Another novel in which the reader develops a love-hate relationship with the main character is *A Confederacy of Dunces* by John Kennedy Toole. In *The Tomcat's Wife and Other Stories*, Carol Bly offers a woman's perspective on a man like Thomas Chippering.

## Orlock, Carol
### The Hedge, the Ribbon
Broken Moon Press. 1993. 254 pp.

An unnamed narrator regularly visits an aged, homebound woman living in a large house surrounded by an increasingly impenetrable hedge and tells her stories of a neighborhood in the small town of Millford where there is a certain magic in everyday lives.

**Subjects**  Art and Artists • Eccentrics and Eccentricities • Elderly Women • Family Relationships • Magic Realism • Small-Town Life

**Now try**  Orlock is also the author of *The Goddess Letters*, which is imagined correspondence between Persephone and her mother Demeter. Other books celebrating small-town life and the people who live there include Garrison Keillor's *Lake Wobegon Days*, W. P. Kinsella's stories of the Ermineskin Reserve (*Dance Me Outside*, *Brother Frank's Gospel Hour*, and others), and Stephen Leacock's *Sunshine Sketches of a Little Town*. The magical, fairy-tale elements found here, where odd happenings are commonplace, can also be found in Max Beerbohm's *Zuleika Dobson*, Truman Capote's *The Grass Harp*, Angela Carter's *Nights at the Circus*, William Kotzwinkle's *Fata Morgana*, James Purdy's *Malcolm*, and the novels of Alice Hoffman, including *Practical Magic* and *Illumination Night*.

## Orton, Thomas
### The Lost Glass Plates of Wilfred Eng
Counterpoint Press. 1999. 245 pp.

Down on his luck, Seattle art dealer and historian Robert Armour discovers glass-plate negatives that could resurrect his career and personal life or destroy them.

**Subjects**  Art and Artists • First Novels • Life Choices • Male/Female Relationships • Seattle, Washington

**Now try**   Other novels where the middle-aged main character is facing a crisis in his life include Joe Coomer's *The Loop*, *Nobody's Fool* by Richard Russo, and *Continental Drift* by Russell Banks.

## Peck, Richard
### London Holiday
Viking. 1998. 254 pp.

Three high school friends whose lives, almost two decades later, have taken them down different paths, find that a trip to London opens up opportunities for each that they never would have expected.

**Subjects**   Antiques • England • London, England • Middle-Aged Women • Women's Friendships

**Now try**   Richard Peck's other novels for adults include *Amanda/Miranda* and *This Family of Women*. Peck's adept storytelling will appeal to fans of Hilma Wolitzer (*Tunnel of Love* and others) and Joanna Trollope (*Marrying the Mistress* and others).

## Perez, Loida Maritza
### Geographies of Home
Viking. 1999. 321 pp.

Iliana's attempt to escape her smothering family in New York City by going to college in upstate New York proves futile, as she is drawn back into the complicated and troubling lives of her brothers and sisters.

**Subjects**   Brothers and Sisters • Dominican Authors • Family Relationships • First Novels • Latino Authors • Latinos • Latinos in America • New York • Rape • Seventh-Day Adventists

**Now try**   Another novel in which Seventh-Day Adventists play a major role is David James Duncan's *The Brothers K*. Julia Alvarez (*Yo!* and *How the Garcia Girls Lost Their Accents*) is another Dominican author, but there the similarity ends. Alvarez's characters, unlike Perez's, are from the upper class. Sara Maitland's *Ancestral Truths* is also about a young woman thrust into the complicated brother-and-sister dynamics of her family.

## Perrotta, Tom
### 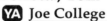 Joe College
St. Martin's Press. 2000. 306 pp.

Danny's life as a college student at Yale is complicated by his relationships with two women, his feelings of inadequacy stemming from his working-class background, and his need to suddenly take over his father's business driving a lunch truck called the Roach Coach to New Jersey businesses.

**Subjects**   1980s • College Students • Fathers and Sons • Humorous Fiction • Working Classes

**Now try**   Perrotta is also the author of *Bad Haircut: Stories of the '70s*, *Election*, and *The Wishbones*. Perrotta's is one of the few humorous novels dealing with life as a college student.

## Picoult, Jody
### Keeping Faith
Morrow. 1999. 422 pp.

When her seven-year-old daughter Faith insists that God is speaking to her, Mariah takes her to a psychiatrist, but when Faith develops stigmata and displays the ability to heal people miraculously, everyone involved, from family to the media to religious leaders and religious debunkers, begins to suspect that Faith actually may be hearing the word of God.

Book Groups 📖

| | |
|---|---|
| **Subjects** | Adultery • Custody Battles • Divorce • Mothers and Daughters • Religion |
| **Now try** | Picoult is also the author of, among other novels, *The Pact* and *Picture Perfect*. Both Ron Hansen's *Mariette in Ecstasy* and Mark Salzman's *Lying Awake* explore possibly true, or possibly bogus, religious experiences. Other nasty custody battles can be found in Sue Miller's *The Good Mother* and Carol Muske-Dukes's *Saving St. Germ*. |

## Power, Susan
### The Grass Dancer
G.P. Putnam's Sons. 1994. 300 pp.

Like an archaeological dig, the lives of Sioux Indians on a North Dakota reservation are uncovered a layer at a time, moving backward to show how the past has influenced the present.

Book Groups 📖

| | |
|---|---|
| **Subjects** | ALA Notable Books • American Indian Authors • American Indians • Coming-of-Age • First Novels • Magic Realism • North Dakota • Sioux Indians |
| **Now try** | Another novel in which the past is slowly uncovered is *First Light* by Charles Baxter. American Indian life is also explored in Thomas King's *Truth and Bright Water*, Leslie Marmon Silko's *Garden in the Dunes*, *The Sharpest Sight* by Louis Owens, and Sherman Alexie's *The Toughest Indian in the World*. |

## Preston, Caroline
### Jackie by Josie
Scribner. 1997. 314 pp.

Events in her own life are thrown into perspective when Josie Trask takes a job researching the life of Jacqueline Kennedy Onassis for a celebrity biography.

| | |
|---|---|
| **Subjects** | First Novels • Marriage • Onassis, Jacqueline Kennedy • Writers and Writing |
| **Now try** | Preston's second novel is *Lucy Crocker 2.0*. Rebecca Goldstein's *The Mind-Body Problem* and *Rameau's Niece* by Cathleen Schine are both about the difficulty women have being married to men considered to be much more intelligent than they themselves are. Josie's voice in this novel is similar to the voice of the main characters in Luanne Rice's *Crazy in Love* and Susan Trott's *Crane Spreads Wings: A Bigamist's Story*. |

## Prose, Francine
### Blue Angel

HarperCollins. 2000. 314 pp.

Long unable to write his own novel, Swenson, a creative-writing teacher at a third-rate college in Vermont, is thrilled when one of his students, the body-pierced and tattooed Angela Argo, shows a definite talent for writing—until she accuses him of sexual harassment.

Book Groups 📖

**Subjects**   College Professors • Sexual Harassment • Vermont • Writers and Writing

**Now try**   Prose is also the author of *Hunters and Gatherers*, *Bigfoot Dreams*, and *Guided Tours of Hell*, among other works of fiction. Another novel dealing with an accusation of sexual harassment is J. M. Coetzee's *Disgrace*, although Coetzee's novel has a far more serious tone. The way that Swenson deludes himself into believing what he wants to believe is similar to the behavior of the main character in Michael Frayn's *Headlong*. Other novels about sexual harassment include Ellen Akins's *Hometown Brew* and Anne Bernays's *Professor Romeo*.

## Rawles, Nancy
### Love Like Gumbo

Fjord Press. 1997. 266 pp.

Twenty-year-old Grace Broussard struggles to reconcile her ties and obligations to her large (and overpowering) Creole family in 1978 in South Central Los Angeles and her growing love for a young Mexican woman.

**2d Appeal**   Setting

**Subjects**   Creoles • Family Relationships • First Novels • Interracial Relationships • Lesbians • Los Angeles, California

**Now try**   Lesbian relationships are also explored in Julia Darling's *Crocodile Soup* and Emma Donoghue's *Hood*. Family dynamics are the subject of Julia Alvarez's *Yo!* and *How the Garcia Girls Lost Their Accents*, as well as J. Robert Lennon's *The Funnies*.

## Ray, Jeanne
### Julie and Romeo

Random House. 2000. 192 pp.

Although their rival florist-shop-owning families have feuded with one another since they were children, Julie (now 60 and divorced) and Romeo (also 60, a widower) fall in love, only to be greeted with shocked anger by children, parents, and Julie's ex-husband.

**Subjects**   Family Feuds • First Novels • Florists • Love Stories • Massachusetts • Seniors

**Now try**   This lighthearted novel is by the mother of author Ann Patchett (*The Patron Saint of Liars* and other novels). Another entertaining novel in which the main character is a florist is Elinor Lipman's *The Way Men Act*. Other novels about two people falling in love well past their youth are *Love in the Middle Ages* by Helen Barolini and *Harry and Catherine* by Frederick Busch.

## Reardon, Lisa

### Blameless
Random House. 2000. 323 pp.

After discovering the body of a dead girl and being forced to testify at the subsequent murder trial of the child's mother, Mary Culpepper discovers that she may not be as blameless in the significant events of her life as she once assumed.

**Subjects**   Adultery • Child Abuse • Michigan • Murder • Sisters • Small-Town Life

**Now try**   Reardon is also author of the novel *Billy Dead*. Another novel in which the main character is forced to reassess the past is Pat Barker's *Border Crossing*.

## Reed, Kit

### @expectations
Forge. 2000. 256 pp.

Jenny's real life, living in little Brevert, South Carolina, with a loving but exasperating husand and two difficult stepchildren, pales in comparison to her experiences online and her virtual love affair with Reverdy.

**Subjects**   Computers • Husbands and Wives • Internet • Love Affairs • Stepfamilies

**Now try**   Among Kit Reed's other novels are *At War As Children*, *J. Eden*, and *Seven for the Apocalypse*. Other novels about online relationships are *Dear Stranger, Dearest Friend* by Laney Katz Becker and Sylvia Brownrigg's *The Metaphysical Touch*.

## Reynolds, Marjorie

### The Civil Wars of Jonah Moran
Morrow. 1999. 288 pp.

Jessica Moran's lifelong habit of taking care of her younger brother, always regarded as "different" by the people of the small logging town in Washington State where they live, leads her to defend him when he is accused of an arson fire that killed three men—even if by doing so she is forced to interact with her high school boyfriend Callum Luke, a member of the Bureau of Alcohol, Tobacco, and Firearms, who is sent to investigate the fire.

**Subjects**   Arson • Asperger's Syndrome • Brothers and Sisters • Mothers and Daughters • Pacific Northwest • Small-Town Life • Washington

**Now try**   Reynolds is also the author of *The Starlite Drive-In*. Another overbearing mother is found in Molly Giles's *Iron Shoes*.

## Ridgway, Keith

### The Long Falling
Houghton Mifflin. 1998. 305 pp.

When her physically abusive husband is killed in a hit-and-run accident, Grace Quinn believes her troubles are over, until she discovers to her horror that both a policeman and a newspaper reporter know the identity of the car's driver.

**Subjects**   Abortion • Abusive Relationships • Child Abuse • Death of a Child • Death of a Spouse • Dublin, Ireland • First Novels • Gay Men • Ireland • Irish Authors • Mothers and Sons • Murder

**Now try**   Another Irish novel about domestic abuse is Roddy Doyle's *The Woman Who Walked into Doors*. One of the subplots of Ridgway's novel is about a young Irish woman seeking an abortion; Irish writer Edna O'Brien wrote about the same issue in *Down by the River*.

## Rinaldi, Nicholas
### The Jukebox Queen of Malta
Simon & Schuster. 1999. 368 pp.

When Rocco Raven is sent to Malta to work as the radio operator for the American liaison team during World War II, he falls in love with Melita, a young Maltese woman who delivers the jukeboxes her cousin has fashioned from wreckage caused by the German bombing raids.

**Subjects**    1940s • Love Stories • Malta • World War II

**Now try**    Rinaldi is also the author of the novel *Bridge Fall Down* and three collections of poetry. Malta during World War II is also the setting of Joanna Trollope's novel (written as Caroline Harvey) *The Brass Dolphin*. Other love stories set against the chaos and losses of war include Louis de Berniere's *Corelli's Mandolin* and Michael Ondaatje's *The English Patient* (although Rinaldi's novel does not have the poetic language of Ondaatje's).

## Rizzuto, Rahna Reiko
### Why She Left Us
HarperCollins. 1999. 295 pp.

Four of Emi Okada's relatives—her son Eric, her daughter Mariko, her mother Kaori, and her brother Jack—take turns telling the story of Emi's life, in an attempt to finally understand how she could have dishonored the family and abandoned her son.

Book Groups 📖

**Subjects**    Asian American Authors • Asian Americans • Asians in America • First Novels • Internment Camps • Japanese American Authors • Japanese Americans • Mothers and Sons • Mothers Deserting Their Families • Novels with Multiple Viewpoints

**Now try**    Other novels about the internment of Japanese Americans during World War II include David Guterson's *Snow Falling on Cedars*, Stewart Ikeda's *What the Scarecrow Said*, and Kerri Sakamoto's *The Electrical Field*. Another novel told in four different voices is Russell Banks's *The Sweet Hereafter*.

## Robbins, Tom
### Fierce Invalids Home from Hot Climates
Bantam. 2000. 415 pp.

Switters, a CIA errand boy, monkey-wrench advocate, student of *Finnegan's Wake*, and the cursee of a pyramid-headed Amazonian shaman, makes his way from Seattle to South America to Syria.

**Subjects**    Amazon • CIA • Convents • Curses • Humorous Fiction • Nuns • Pacific Northwest • Parrots • Prophecy • Seattle, Washington • South America • Syria

**Now try**    "Lingo jockey" Robbins also demonstrates his talent for wacky writing and keen sociopolitical observation in many novels including *Half Asleep in Frog Pajamas* and *Jitterbug Perfume*. Other novels with a streak of capitalist sabotage include Edward Abbey's *The Monkey Wrench Gang* and William Eastlake's *Dancers in the Scalp House*. Kurt Vonnegut used a similar frame of unconventionality in such books as *Player Piano* and *Cat's Cradle*.

## Robinson, Roxana
### This Is My Daughter
Random House. 1998. 416 pp.

Peter Chatfield and Emma Goodwin's marriage founders due to the difficult relationship between their respective daughters, Amanda and Tess.

|        |                                                                 |
|--------|-----------------------------------------------------------------|
| **Subjects** | Fathers and Daughters • Husbands and Wives • Mothers and Daughters • Remarriage • Sisters • Stepfamilies |
| **Now try**  | Robinson is also the author of *Asking for Love and Other Stories* and *Summer Light*. Other novels that describe the problems associated with blended, or step families include Paul Estaver's *His Third, Her Second* and Robert Boswell's *Mystery Ride*. |

## Rosenfeld, Lucinda
### What She Saw...
Random House. 2000. 304 pp.

Phoebe Fine details her experiences with 15 different men, from the boy who gave her her first kiss at age 10 to her college professor–lover and the men she meets in New York's singles scene.

|        |                                                                 |
|--------|-----------------------------------------------------------------|
| **Subjects** | Coming-of-Age • First Novels • Male/Female Relationships • New York • Single Women |
| **Now try**  | Other women looking for men can be found in Candace Bushnell's *Four Blondes*, Jennifer Weiner's *Good in Bed*, and Anna Maxted's *Getting Over It*. |

## Ross, Ann B.
### Miss Julia Speaks Her Mind
Morrow. 1999. 273 pp.

Miss Julia Springer is totally stunned when Hazel Marie Puckett arrives on her doorstep and announces that the father of Little Lloyd, her nine-year-old son, is Miss Julia's late husband, the fine, upstanding banker Lloyd Springer.

|        |                                                                 |
|--------|-----------------------------------------------------------------|
| **Subjects** | American South • First Novels • Humorous Fiction • North Carolina • Small-Town Life • Widows |
| **Now try**  | Miss Julia's adventures continue in *Miss Julia Takes Over*. The light humor of this novel, as well as its small-town setting, is similar to that found in Jan Karon's *At Home in Mitford* and others in her Mitford series, as well as Clyde Edgerton's *The Floatplane Notebooks*. |

## Roy, Lucinda
### The Hotel Alleluia
HarperCollins. 2000. 357 pp.

When Joan Plum comes to West Africa to find her half sister Ursuline, the two become involved in the political upheavals in revolution-torn Sierra Leone.

Book Groups 📖

|        |                                                                 |
|--------|-----------------------------------------------------------------|
| **Subjects** | Africa • Biracial Characters • Political Fiction • Sierra Leone • Sisters • West Africa |
| **Now try**  | Roy's first novel was *Lady Moses*. Other novels set in Africa with political overtones are Barbara Kingsolver's *The Poisonwood Bible* and Julian Pierce's *Speak Rwanda*. Mary Lee Settle's *Celebration* is another novel concerned with issues of love, death, and forgiveness. |

## Rubio, Gwyn Hyman
### Icy Sparks
Viking. 1998. 352 pp.

Growing up in a small Kentucky town, Icy Sparks does not realize that her own weird mannerisms and strange behavior—which set her apart from the rest of the community—are caused by Tourette's syndrome.

| Subjects | Appalachia • Family Relationships • First Novels • Kentucky • Oprah Winfrey Selection • Small-Town Life • Tourette's Syndrome |
| --- | --- |
| Now try | Another novel in which the main character suffers from Tourette's syndrome is Jonathan Lethem's *Motherless Brooklyn*. A good nonfiction account of a man's lifelong experiences with Tourette's is Lowell Handler's *Twitch and Shout: A Touretter's Tale*. |

## Sakamoto, Kerri
### The Electrical Field
W.W. Norton. 1998. 305 pp.

Thirty years after her family was interned in a camp for Japanese Canadians, Asako Saito finds the past brought vividly to the present when a beautiful woman is found murdered.

Book Groups 📖

| Subjects | Brothers and Sisters • Canada • Canadian Authors • Fathers and Daughters • First Novels • Internment Camps • Japanese Canadians • Murder |
| --- | --- |
| Now try | Another novel dealing with a daughter who is forced to care for her father and brother is Susan Dodd's *No Earthly Notion*. Stewart David Ikeda's *What the Scarecrow Said* is about a man's life following his release from an internment camp during World War II. |

## Schroeder, Joan Vannorsdall
### The Hearts of Soldiers
DK Publishing. 1999. 312 pp.

The accidental death of Hannah, her younger—and favorite—daughter, sharpens the divide between Allison and her minister-husband Jeremy, especially after Allison becomes involved with the reclusive Vietnam veteran who lives next door.

| 2d Appeal | Setting | Book Groups 📖 |
| --- | --- | --- |
| Subjects | Death of a Child • Death of a Sibling • Family Relationships • Gettysburg, Pennsylvania • Love Affairs • Vietnam Veterans | |
| Now try | Schroeder is also the author of the novel *Solitary Lives*. Like Toni Volk in *Maybe in Missoula* and Jodi Picoult in *Mercy*, Schroeder examines the lives of her characters with warmth and concern. | |

## Scott, Joanna C.
### The Lucky Gourd Shop
MacMurray & Beck. 2000. 290 pp.

Abandoned as a child outside a gourd shop in postwar South Korea, Mi Sook's difficult marriage to Kun Soo leads her to give up her three children for adoption by an American family.

Book Groups 📖

| Subjects | Adoption • First Novels • Korea • Korean Americans • South Korea |
| --- | --- |
| Now try | A nice complement to this novel is *Birth Mother*, a collection of Scott's poems that provides context and background for her novel. Other novels about South Korea include Susan Choi's *The Foreign Student* and *Memories of My Ghost Brother* by Heinz Insu Fenkl. A good nonfiction account of the experiences faced by adoptees is Susan Soon-Keum Cox's *Voices from Another Place: A Collection of Works from a Generation Born in Korea and Adopted to Other Countries*. |

## See, Carolyn

### The Handyman

Random House. 1999. 220 pp.

While searching for his artistic vision, 28-year-old painter Bob Hampton spends a summer as a handyman in Los Angeles, mending, fixing, and cleaning up other people's lives.

**2d Appeal**   Characters

**Subjects**   Art and Artists • Los Angeles, California • Single Men

**Now try**   See is also the author of ***Making History*** and ***Golden Days***. Other winning novels in which the main character helps improve the lives of others include Thornton Wilder's ***Theophilus North*** and Lane Von Herzen's ***The Unfastened Heart***.

## Sharpe, Matthew

### Nothing Is Terrible
Villard. 2000. 269 pp.

Orphaned at her parents' death, and left alone by the unexpected death of her twin brother, Mary White falls in love with her sixth-grade teacher, and the two decamp to Manhattan to live together.

Book Groups 📖

**Subjects**   Coming-of-Age • First Novels • Humorous Fiction • Lesbians • New York • Orphans • Teachers

**Now try**   Sharpe is also the author of a story collection, ***Stories from the Tube***. ***The Extra Man*** by Jonathan Ames is another novel that is surprising, humorous, and unexpectedly tender.

## Shea, Suzanne Strempek

### Lily of the Valley
Pocket Books. 1999. 279 pp.

While less than successful artist Lily Wilk is painting a family portrait for the richest woman in town, she discovers that there is more than one way to define what a family is.

**Subjects**   Art and Artists • Family Relationships • Stepfamilies

**Now try**   Shea is also the author of ***Selling the Lite of Heaven*** and ***Hoopi Shoopi Donna***. New definitions of family are explored in Laura Kalpakian's ***Steps and Exes*** and Lynn Sharon Schwartz's ***In the Family Way: An Urban Comedy***.

## Sherwood, Ben

### The Man Who Ate the 747
Bantam. 2000. 262 pp.

J. J. Smith, who works for the Book of Records, investigates the rumor that Wally Chubb ate a 747 airplane to prove his love for Willa Wyatt.

**Subjects**   First Novels • Humorous Fiction • Love Stories • Male/Female Relationships • Nebraska

**Now try**   Fannie Flagg's *Welcome to the World, Baby Girl!* has a similarly light tone.

## Shiner, Lewis
### Say Goodbye
St. Martin's Press. 1999. 245 pp.

A biographer who is more than half in love with his subject tells the story of the swift rise and equally swift fall of singer and songwriter Laurie Moss, as she tries to make a name for herself in the world of popular music.

**2d Appeal**   Setting

**Subjects**   Love Affairs • Male/Female Relationships • Music and Musicians • Rock and Roll

**Now try**   Shiner is also the author of the novels *Glimpses*, *Deserted Cities of the Heart*, and *Slam*. He writes about music for the periodicals *Crawdaddy!*, *The Mississippi Review*, and *The Village Voice*. The absolute realism of this novel—the way it describes the unglamorous life of struggling bands—is similar to the story told in Richard Currey's *Lost Highway*.

## Shreve, Anita
### The Pilot's Wife
Little, Brown. 1998. 293 pp.

When the plane Jack Lyons is flying explodes on a return flight from England, his wife Kathryn discovers aspects of her husband's life that force her to confront the past and reassess the present.

Book Groups 📖

**Subjects**   Adultery • Bigamy and Bigamists • Death of a Spouse • Male/Female Relationships • Marriage • Oprah Winfrey Selection • Pilots

**Now try**   Shreve is also the author of *The Last Time They Met*, *The Weight of Water*, and *Fortune's Rocks*. Another novel about secrets revealed after a plane crash is Warren Adler's *Random Hearts*.

## Shreve, Anita
### Where or When
Harcourt Brace. 1993. 240 pp.

Charles and Sian met at a summer camp when they were both 14; 31 years later, both now married to other people, they meet again and discover they are still in love with one another.

Book Groups 📖

**Subjects**   Adultery • Business and Businessmen • Husbands and Wives • Love Affairs

**Now try**   Shreve is also the author of *Eden Close*, *Resistance*, *Strange Fits of Passion*, and *The Last Time They Met*, among other novels. The almost obsessive love that Charles feels for Sian is mirrored in Scott Spencer's *Endless Love*, although the protagonists in that novel are much younger. Shreve tells the story by alternating viewpoints between Charles and Sian; a similar technique can be found in Carol Shields's *Happenstance*.

## Singer, Katie
### The Wholeness of a Broken Heart
Riverhead Books. 1999. 369 pp.

When Hannah Felber's relationship with her mother changes from intense closeness to inexplicable coldness and separation, the voices of her female ancestors observe and guide her to wholeness.

**2d Appeal**   Characters

**Subjects**   Family Relationships • First Novels • Jews and Judaism • Mothers and Daughters • Sexual Abuse • Single Women

**Now try**   Other difficult mothers—and the impact they have on their daughters—can be found in Jenny Offill's *Last Things*, Marly Swick's *Paper Wings*, and Mona Simpson's *Anywhere But Here*. Another mother-daughter relationship that changes from intense closeness to inexplicable coldness can be found in Elizabeth Strout's *Amy and Isabelle*.

## Slater, Dashka
### The Wishing Box

Chronicle Books. 2000. 311 pp.

When 30-year-old Julie and her sister Lisa fashion a wishing box to bring their father—who left the the family more than 20 years before—home, they can't imagine how their lives will be changed as a result.

**Subjects**   Fathers and Daughters • Fathers Deserting Their Families • First Novels • Magic Realism • Single Mothers • Sisters

**Now try**   Another novel that includes both the fantastical and the real is Nancy Willard's *Things Invisible to See*.

## Stegner, Lynn
### Undertow

Baskerville. 1993. 367 pp.

Anne, a marine biologist working in the San Juan Islands in Washington State, discovers she is pregnant by her married lover and is forced to face her own childhood of neglect and sexual abuse.

Book Groups 📖

**Subjects**   Adultery • Child Abuse • First Novels • Love Affairs • Male/Female Relationships • Pacific Northwest • Science and Scientists • Sexual Abuse • Washington • Women Scientists

**Now try**   Stegner also wrote *Fata Morgana* and *Pipers at the Gates of Dawn: A Triptych*. The protagonist of Julie Schumacher's novel, *The Body Is Water*, is another pregnant woman looking back on her unhappy childhood.

## Swanson, Eric
### The Boy in the Lake

St. Martin's Press. 1999. 197 pp.

When one of his young patients commits suicide and his grandmother dies, social worker Christian Fowler uses his trip to settle his grandmother's affairs in his boyhood home in central Ohio to try to understand a traumatic childhood event.

**Subjects**   Friendship • Gay Men • Grandparents • Ohio • Psychiatrists, Psychoanalysts, Psychotherapists • Suicide • Teenage Boys • Teenagers

**Now try**   Swanson is also the author of the novel *The Greenhouse Effect*. The effects of a suicide on those friends and family left behind are explored in *The Bubble Reputation* by Cathie Pelletier and David Madden's *The Suicide's Wife*.

## Swick, Marly
### Evening News
Little, Brown. 1999. 356 pp.

Nine-year-old Teddy accidentally shoots and kills his half sister, two-year-old Trina, and the event forever changes not only Teddy, but also the relationship between his mother Gizelle and his stepfather.

Book Groups 📖

**Subjects**   Accidental Death • California • Death of a Child • Husbands and Wives • Mothers and Sons • Murder

**Now try**   Swick's first novel was *Paper Wings*. Other domestic novels include Sue Miller's *The Good Mother* and Jane Hamilton's *A Map of the World*. Another novel about a young boy who must try to forgive himself for a childhood murder is Maxine Chernoff's *A Boy in Winter*.

## Tan, Amy
### The Bonesetter's Daughter
G.P. Putnam's Sons. 2001. 353 pp.

With her mother LuLing suffering from Alzheimer's disease, Ruth learns the full story of LuLing's early life in China when she finally reads her mother's old journals.

**2d Appeal**   Characters                                                  Book Groups 📖

**Subjects**   Alzheimer's Disease • Asian American Authors • Asian Americans • Asians in America • China • Chinese Americans • Chinese American Authors • Family Relationships • Family Secrets • Mothers and Daughters

**Now try**   Tan is also the author of *The Kitchen God's Wife*, *The Joy Luck Club*, and *The Hundred Secret Senses*. Another novel about adult children dealing with their parents' Alzheimer's disease is Michael Ignatieff's *Scar Tissue*. Another novel about life in China is Gu Hua's *Virgin Widows*. Other novels about Chinese Americans include Fae Myenne Ng's *Bone*, *China Boy* by Gus Lee, and Shawn Wong's *American Knees*.

## Tan, Amy
### The Kitchen God's Wife
G.P. Putnam's Sons. 1991. 415 pp.

Many years after she left China to live in California, Winnie Louie finally tells her daughter Pearl the details of her life in China in the 1930s and 1940s.

**2d Appeal**   Characters                                                  Book Groups 📖

**Subjects**   ALA Notable Books • Asian American Authors • Asian Americans • Asians in America • California • China • Chinese American Authors • Chinese Americans • Culture Clash • Family Relationships • Family Secrets • Mothers and Daughters • World War II

**Now try**   Tan is also the author of *The Hundred Secret Senses*, *The Bonesetter's Daughter*, and *The Joy Luck Club*. Other books about Chinese families who have moved to America include Fae Myenne Ng's novel *Bone* and Lisa See's story of her family, *On Gold Mountain: The Hundred-Year Odyssey of a Chinese-American Family*.

## Townsend, Sue
### Adrian Mole: The Cappuccino Years
Soho Press. 1999. 390 pp.

Adrian, now 30, copes with being a single father, the news of his mother's adultery, his father's misery, and his ongoing love for Dr. Pandora Braithwaite, now a Member of Parliament.

**Subjects**   British Authors • Culinary Arts • Diaries • Fathers and Sons • Humorous Fiction • Mothers and Sons • Politics • Single Fathers

**Now try**   Townsend introduced Adrian Mole at age 13 in 1985 in *The Secret Diaries of Adrian Mole*. Her other books include *The Queen and I* and *Adrian Mole: The Lost Years*. Another humorous novel about the travails of unrequited love is *The Man Who Ate the 747* by Ben Sherwood.

## Tremain, Rose
### The Way I Found Her
Farrar, Straus and Giroux. 1998. 358 pp.

Thirteen-year-old Lewis Little accompanies his mother Alice to Paris, where she will spend the summer translating the latest medieval romance by bestselling Russian novelist Valentina Gavrilovich; when Valentina disappears, Lewis, besotted, sets out to find her, with both touching and tragic results.

**2d Appeal**   Characters   Book Groups 📖

**Subjects**   British Authors • Coming-of-Age • Kidnapping • Mothers and Sons • Obsessive Love • Older Women/Younger Men • Paris, France • Writers and Writing

**Now try**   Rose Tremain is the author of seven novels, including *Sacred Country* and *Restoration*. Herman Raucher's *Summer of '42* is another novel whose teenage protagonist leaves behind childhood and innocence in the course of his friendship with an older woman. Max Phillips's *Snakebite Sonnet*, Bernhard Schlink's *The Reader*, and Antoni Libera's *Madame* are also about young men obsessed with older women.

## Trigiani, Adriana
### Big Stone Gap
Random House. 2000. 272 pp.

When spinster Ave Maria Mulligan, Big Stone Gap's pharmacist, finds out that the man she thought was her father was, in fact, not her father at all, the discovery sends her on a quest to learn who she really is, which eventually leads to two marriage proposals.

**2d Appeal**   Characters

**Subjects**   1970s • Eccentrics and Eccentricities • First Novels • Humorous Fiction • Male/Female Relationships • Pharmacists • Small-Town Life • Virginia

**Now try**   Lorna Landvik's *Your Oasis on Flame Lake*, *Patty Jane's House of Curl*, and *The Tall Pine Polka* are also humorous novels. The sequel to this book is *Big Cherry Holler*.

## Trobaugh, Augusta
### Resting in the Bosom of the Lamb
Baker Books. 1999. 229 pp.

Of the four elderly women who spend all their time together, only Pet, an African American who has worked for Miss Cora, Wynona, and Lauralee's family all her life, knows the secret that unites their family with hers.

**Subjects**    African Americans • Elderly Women • Family Secrets • Southern Authors • Women's Friendships

**Now try**    Trobaugh's first novel was *Praise Jerusalem!* Other contemporary novels about the South in which race and ancestors play an important part are Nancy Peacock's *Home Across the Road* and Hamilton Basso's *The View from Pompey's Head*. Many of the themes that Trobaugh touches on in her novel are also explored in Henry Wiencek's *The Hairstons: An American Family in Black and White*, a nonfiction account of a southern family from the Revolutionary War to the present.

## Trollope, Joanna
### A Passionate Man
Berkley Books. 2000. 295 pp.

When Archie's beloved father dies shortly after his unexpected marriage to Marina, a beautiful and wealthy widow, it shakes the foundations of Archie's own marriage to Liza.

**Subjects**    Adultery • British Authors • Death of a Parent • Doctors and Patients • Fathers and Sons • Husbands and Wives • Love Affairs

**Now try**    Trollope's other enjoyable novels include *The Men and the Girls*, *The Rector's Wife*, and *A Spanish Lover*. She also writes historical novels under the name of Caroline Harvey, including *Legacy of Love* and *The Brass Dolphin*. Trollope's affection for her characters and her ability to tell a good story are reminiscent of the books of Maeve Binchy (*Circle of Friends* and *Tara Road*).

## Tsukiyama, Gail
### The Language of Threads
St. Martin's Press. 1999. 276 pp.

In the 1930s, Pei, a silk worker from rural China, arrives in Hong Kong to make a new life for herself and orphan Ji Shen, but the Japanese occupation of Hong Kong tears apart their new home with Mrs. Finch, a British expatriate.

**2d Appeal**    Setting
Book Groups 📖

**Subjects**    1930s • Asian American Authors • China • Chinese American Authors • Friendship • Hong Kong • Internment Camps • Japanese American Authors

**Now try**    *The Language of Threads* is a sequel to *Women of the Silk*. Tsukiyama is also the author of the novels *The Samurai's Garden* and *Night of Many Dreams*. Another novel detailing life in internment camps is Kerri Sakamoto's *The Electrical Field*.

## Veciana-Suarez, Ana
### The Chin Kiss King
Farrar, Straus and Giroux. 1997. 311 pp.

Maribel's well-organized life is shattered with the birth of Victor, her "big heart brave heart bird-boy," while her relationships with her mother and grandmother stretch almost to the breaking point.

**2d Appeal**    Characters
Book Groups 📖

| | |
|---|---|
| **Subjects** | Birth Defects • Cuba • Family Relationships • First Novels • Florida • Latino Authors • Latinos • Latinos in America • Magic Realism • Mothers and Daughters • Multigenerational Novels • Premature Babies |
| **Now try** | Other novels with a Cuban backdrop include Christine Bell's *The Perez Family*, Cristina Garcia's *The Aguero Sisters* and *Dreaming in Cuban*, and Oscar Hijuelos's *The Fourteen Sisters of Emilio Montez O'Brien*. Premature babies are important to the plots in Carrie Brown's *The Hatbox Baby*, Rosemary Kay's *Saul*, and Linda Raymond's *Rocking the Babies*. |

## Wallace, Daniel

### Ray in Reverse
Algonquin Books of Chapel Hill. 2000. 225 pp.

As he sits in Heaven in his Last Words Group, Ray looks back over the past 50 years, remembering the best and worst moments of a not-very-unusual life.

Book Groups 📖

| | |
|---|---|
| **Subjects** | Adultery • Fathers and Sons • Humorous Fiction • Marriage |
| **Now try** | Wallace is also the author of the novel *Big Fish*. Ray's life is presented backward, somewhat like an archaeological dig, so that the present becomes clearer the more the past is uncovered. Other novels that take a similar approach are Susan Power's *The Grass Dancer* and Jim Crace's *Being Dead*. |

## Welter, John

### Night of the Avenging Blowfish:
### A Novel of Covert Operations, Love,
### and Luncheon Meat
Algonquin Books of Chapel Hill. 1994. 313 pp.

Doyle Coldiron, a lonely Secret Service agent dealing with the ironies of White House service, is prepared to annihilate assassins who never actually materialize; instead, he plans for phantom baseball games against the CIA, defends the chef's preparation of a Spam (and cat food) state dinner, and longs for the lovely but married Natalie.

| | |
|---|---|
| **Subjects** | Humorous Fiction • Loneliness • Male/Female Relationships • Political Fiction • Satirical Fiction • Single Men • Washington, D.C. |
| **Now try** | Welter's literary lunacy is also well demonstrated in his novels *Begin to Exit Here* and *I Want to Buy a Vowel*. The comedic and sly one-liners that Welter offers are reminiscent of Douglas Adams's *The Hitchhiker's Guide to the Galaxy* (and others in the series), Robert Coover's *Ghost Town* and *The Universal Baseball Association, Inc., J. Henry Waugh, Prop.*, S. J. Perelman's *Chicken Inspector No. 23* and *Vinegar Puss*, and Max Shulman's *Rally Round the Flag, Boys!* For a heady dose of political satire try Joseph Heller's classic novel *Catch 22* as well as his *Good as Gold*, Ishmael Reed's *The Terrible Twos* and *Japanese by Spring*, Kurt Vonnegut's *Jailbird*, and Leonard Wibberley's *The Mouse That Roared* and its sequels. |

## Wesley, Valerie Wilson
### Ain't Nobody's Business If I Do
Avon Books. 1999. 323 pp.

When her husband Hutch walks out on her after 10 years of marriage, Eva discovers that even though change is often frightening, it's not always a bad thing.

Book Groups 📖

**Subjects**   Adultery • African American Authors • African Americans • Art and Artists • Gay Men • Husbands and Wives

**Now try**   Wesley is also the author of a series of mysteries featuring private eye Tamara Hayle, including *Easier to Kill* and *No Hiding Place*. Another novel about a professional African American man who is confused about the kind of life he wants to live is found in Omar Tyree's *A Do Right Man*.

## Wolitzer, Meg
### Friends for Life
Crown. 1994. 213 pp.

As they approach the age of 30, three professional women who have been inseparable since fifth grade face choices that threaten their friendship.

**Subjects**   1980s • 1990s • Career Women • Women's Friendships

**Now try**   Wolitzer also wrote *This Is Your Life* and *Hidden Pictures*. Alice Adams's *Families and Survivors* and Marianne Fredriksson's *Two Women* both explore female friendships.

## Zabor, Rafi
### The Bear Comes Home
W.W. Norton. 1997. 480 pp.

When a saxophone-playing, mystically inclined bear gets his big break as a jazz artist, all sorts of things begin to happen in his life—a recording contract, fame, and love.

**2d Appeal**   Language

**Subjects**   First Novels • Humorous Fiction • Jazz • Magic Realism • Music and Musicians

**Now try**   Another tongue-in-cheek novel about the development of an artist is Steven Millhauser's *Edwin Mullhouse: The Life and Death of an American Writer, 1943–1954*. Dorothy Baker's *Young Man with a Horn* is a novel about a jazz musician, as is Jack Fuller's *The Best of Jackson Payne*. A bear is the main character in William Kotzwinkle's *The Bear Went Over the Mountain*. *The Bear Comes Home* won a PEN/Faulkner Award.

## Zadoorian, Michael
### Second Hand
W.W. Norton. 2000. 270 pp.

Richard, aka "Junk," is reasonably contented with his life buying merchandise at garage sales and selling it at his secondhand store, Satori Junk, until he meets Theresa (another junk lover) and must go through his parents' possessions after his mother dies.

**Subjects**   American Midwest • Animals • Antiques • Detroit, Michigan • Euthanasia • First Novels • Love Stories

**Now try**   Another novel set around the world of junk and junk collecting is Joe Coomer's *Apologizing to Dogs*. The sweet relationship between Junk and Theresa is reminiscent of the relationships in Elinor Lipman's *The Inn at Lake Devine*.

## Zigman, Laura

### Dating Big Bird

Dial Press. 2000. 246 pp.

Thirty-five-year-old Ellen, besotted with her toddler niece and realizing that her biological time clock is ticking away, tries to decide whether or not to stay in a hopeless relationship with a man who doesn't want children or to have a baby on her own.

**Subjects**  Aunts • Career Women • New York • Single Mothers • Single Women • Sisters

**Now try**  Zigman's first novel was ***Animal Husbandry***. Elizabeth Berg's ***Until the Real Thing Comes Along*** is another novel about a single woman whose desire to have a child leads her to make an unusual decision.

# Chapter 3

## Characters

### Adams, Glenda
#### Longleg
Cane Hill Press. 1992. 339 pp.

At age 10, William Badger lives with his crippled father and manic mother—his fondest wish is for a boy-size mannequin that could be his friend; as an adult, he spends his time selling pens and pencils in Sydney, hanging out with radicals in Brussels, and driving a tourist bus in London, but his fondest wish has not changed.

**Subjects**  Australia • Australian Authors • Boys' Lives • Family Relationships • Mental Illness • Mothers and Sons • Psychological Fiction • Sydney, Australia

**Now try**  Adams's other books include *Games of the Strong*, *The Tempest of Clemenza*, and *Dancing on Coral*, which won the Miles Franklin Award. Other novels about families in Australia include Thea Astley's *It's Raining in Mango*, Patrick White's *The Tree of Man*, and Tim Winton's *Cloudstreet*. Other novels about troubled relationships between mothers and sons include Ann Beattie's *Chilly Scenes of Winter*, Ivy Compton-Burnett's *Mother and Son*, Timothy Findley's *The Piano Man's Daughter*, and Joyce Carol Oates's *Expensive People*.

### Alvarez, Julia
#### How the Garcia Girls Lost Their Accents
Algonquin Books of Chapel Hill. 1991. 290 pp.

Uprooted from their family home in the Dominican Republic, the four Garcia sisters arrive in New York City in 1960 to find a life far different from the genteel existence of maids, manicures, and extended family they left behind.

Book Groups 📖

**Subjects**  Acculturation • ALA Notable Books • Dominican Authors • Family Relationships • First Novels • Latino Authors • Latinos • Latinos in America • Sisters

**Now try**    Alvarez has also published books of poetry, including *The Other Side*, *Home-coming*, and *The Housekeeping Book*, as well as several other novels, including *In the Time of the Butterflies* and *Yo!* (Yolanda, one of the characters in *How the Garcia Girls Lost Their Accents*, is the main character in *Yo!*) Eva Hoffman's memoir about adjusting to life in a different culture is *Lost in Translation: A Life in a New Language*. Lore Segal's *Her First American* is a fictional account of the same process. Maxine Chernoff's *American Heaven* is about a recent Polish immigrant who works as a nurse-companion to an aging jazz musician.

## Alvarez, Julia
### Yo! Algonquin Books of Chapel Hill. 1997. 309 pp.

Yolanda Garcia's life is seen through the eyes of the friends, lovers, and family members who know her best.

Book Groups 📖

**Subjects**    ALA Notable Books • Dominican Authors • Family Relationships • Latino Authors • Latinos • Latinos in America • Sisters

**Now try**    Yolanda Garcia also appears in Alvarez's *How the Garcia Girls Lost Their Accents*. The different ways a person's life can be interpreted is the subject of Carol Shields's *Swann*. Other books about Latino families include *The House on Mango Street* by Sandra Cisneros, *Bless Me, Ultima* by Rudolfo Anaya, and *Rain of Gold* by Victor Villasenor.

## Anderson, Barbara
### Portrait of the Artist's Wife W.W. Norton. 1993. 308 pp.

Sarah becomes a painter despite many setbacks, including her marriage to a well-known writer, her years as a young wife and mother in difficult circumstances, and her difficulty in finding a teacher.

Book Groups 📖

**Subjects**    Adultery • Art and Artists • Family Relationships • Marriage • Mothers and Daughters • New Zealand • New Zealand Authors • Women Artists • Writers and Writing

**Now try**    In addition to collections of short stories, Anderson's fiction includes *All the Nice Girls* and *Long Hot Summer*. The lives of women artists are the focus of Anna Banti's *Artemisia*, Emily Hahn's *Purple Passage: A Novel About a Lady Both Famous and Infamous*, Shena Mackay's *The Artist's Widow*, and Alma Luz Villanueva's *The Ultraviolet Sky*. Life in New Zealand is also explored in Damien Wilkins's *The Miserables*, Keri Hulme's *The Bone People*, Janet Frame's *Owls Do Cry*, and Sue Reidy's *The Visitation*.

## Anderson, Scott
### Triage Scribner. 1998. 235 pp.

Returning to New York from his latest assignment as a war photographer, Mark finds it impossible to overcome the memories of events in Kurdistan, including the disappearance of his best friend Colin—until he meets Joaquin, his girlfriend Elena's grandfather, who has his own secrets left over from his experiences in Spain after the Spanish civil war.

Book Groups 📖

**Subjects**   ALA Notable Books • First Novels • Grandparents • Kurdistan • New York • Photography and Photographers • Spain • Spanish Civil War

**Now try**   Anderson is also the author of the biography *The Man Who Tried to Save the World: The Dangerous Life and Mysterious Disappearance of Fred Cuny*. Other novels about war photographers include Marianne Wiggins's *Eveless Eden*, Christopher Koch's *Highways to a War*, and Philip Caputo's *DelCorso's Gallery*.

## Antunes, Antonio Lobo
### The Natural Order of Things
 Grove Press. 2000. 288 pp.

The lives of two families over three generations are inextricably woven into the history of modern Portugal. Translated from the Portuguese by Richard Zenith.

Book Groups

**Subjects**   Family Relationships • Multigenerational Novels • Novels in Translation • Portugal • Portuguese Authors

**Now try**   This is the second novel in Antunes's Benfica trilogy, following *The Act of the Damned*. The author's demanding style and exhilarating use of language bring to mind the novels of fellow Portuguese novelist Jose Saramago (*Blindness* and *The History of the Siege of Lisbon*), as well as Salman Rushdie's *The Moor's Last Sigh* and Gabriel Garcia Marquez's *Love in the Time of Cholera* and *One Hundred Years of Solitude*.

## Appachana, Anjana
### Listening Now
Random House. 1998. 518 pp.

In Delhi, Padma builds a new life for herself and her daughter Mallika, earns the love and loyalty of her neighbors Anu and Madhu, and has her secrets slowly revealed as she, her mother, sister, daughter, and good friends tell their own version of events.

Book Groups 📖

**Subjects**   Delhi, India • Family Secrets • First Novels • India • Indian Authors • Mothers and Daughters • Women's Friendships

**Now try**   Appachana is also the author of *Incantations and Other Stories*. Family secrets are also revealed in Ann Marie MacDonald's *Fall On Your Knees* and Kate Atkinson's *Behind the Scenes at the Museum*.

## Astley, Thea
### The Slow Natives
G.P. Putnam's Sons. 1993. 223 pp.

Bernard, his wife Iris, and their teenage son Keith punish themselves and each other with rebelliousness, infidelity, and anger, until events force them all into the beginnings of reconciliation.

**Subjects**   Adultery • Australia • Australian Authors • Child Abuse • Dysfunctional Families • Family Relationships • Fathers and Sons • Teenage Boys • Teenagers

**Now try**    Astley is also the author of *Reaching Tin River* and *Vanishing Points*. Other novels about difficult family relationships include Jessica Auerbach's *Catch Your Breath*, Rick Moody's *The Ice Storm*, and Dorothy Allison's *Bastard Out of Carolina*.

## Atkinson, Kate
### Behind the Scenes at the Museum
Picador USA. 1995. 332 pp.

The secrets of four generations of her Yorkshire, England, family are slowly uncovered by Ruby Lennox, who along the way also discovers the truth about her own life.

**2d Appeal**    Story                                                            Book Groups 📖

**Subjects**    ALA Notable Books • British Authors • Family Relationships • Family Secrets • First Novels • Humorous Fiction • Multigenerational Novels

**Now try**    Atkinson also wrote *Human Croquet* and *Emotionally Weird*. Secrets being slowly uncovered is the main theme of Arundhati Roy's *The God of Small Things*. The family relationships in Atkinson's book are reminiscent of those found in Tim Winton's *Cloudstreet*. *Behind the Scenes at the Museum* won the Whitbread Prize.

## Atkinson, Kate
### Emotionally Weird
Picador USA. 2000. 346 pp.

On a remote island in the Hebrides, Effie tells the woman who may or may not be her mother about her experiences as a college student at Dundee University, where she spends her time trying to figure out how to dump her boyfriend Star Trek Bob, elude the faculty demanding her overdue papers, and avoid being caught up in various complicated shenanigans.

**2d Appeal**    Story

**Subjects**    1970s • Academia • British Authors • College Students • Dysfunctional Families • Hebrides • Humorous Fiction • Mothers and Daughters • Postmodern Fiction • Scotland

**Now try**    College English departments are fertile fields for foolery, as can be seen in Malcolm Bradbury's *Eating People Is Wrong*, Robert Grudin's *Book: A Novel*, Alan Isler's *Kraven Images*, and John L'Heureux's *The Handmaid of Desire* (although these are all told from the point of view of the faculty, not the students). Atkinson's novel has an unorthodox structure, including, as it does, samples of students' novel-writing assignments and the frame of Effie's own family's story. Other authors who don't follow the rules in their fiction include John Irving (*The Water-Method Man*), Connie Willis (*Passage*), Helen DeWitt (*The Last Samurai*), Tom Robbins (*Another Roadside Attraction*, *Skinny Legs and All*), Carol Shields (*Swann*), Muriel Spark (*Loitering with Intent*, *Reality and Dreams*), and Ronald Sukenick (*Blown Away*, *Doggy Bag*).

## Auster, Paul
### Leviathan
Viking. 1992. 275 pp.

Novelist Peter Aaron races to record the life of his recently deceased friend Sachs—a writer turned political terrorist—before the FBI and the press can misrepresent his friend's career and intentions.

**2d Appeal**    Language                                                         Book Groups 📖

Subjects    ALA Notable Books • Men's Friendships • Moral/Ethical Dilemmas • Poets and Poetry • Terrorists and Terrorism • Writers and Writing

Now try    Auster's other works of fiction include *Mr. Vertigo* and *The New York Trilogy*. The novels of Don DeLillo (*The Names*, *Ratner's Star*, and others), like those of Auster, encourage readers to look at the world in different ways. The title of this novel comes from Thomas Hobbes's *Leviathan*, which would be worth reading just to see what light it sheds (or doesn't shed) on this novel. Like Auster's works, the novels of Siri Hustved, including *The Enchantment of Lily Dahl* and *The Blindfold*, also describe a slightly off-key world.

## Auster, Paul
### Timbuktu
Henry Holt. 1999. 181 pp.

When his owner and best friend, itinerant poet and sometime schizophrenic Willy G. Christmas, becomes mortally ill, Mr. Bones recalls their life together and wonders if dogs can ever ascend into Willy's version of Heaven, Timbuktu.

2d Appeal    Language

Subjects    Dogs • Eccentrics and Eccentricities • Mental Illness • Poets and Poetry • Writers and Writing

Now try    Auster is the author of many works of fiction, including *The Music of Chance* as well as a memoir, *Hand to Mouth*. Another novel narrated by a dog is John Berger's *King*. Mr. Bones and his life with Willy bring to mind the memoir *Travels with Lizbeth* by Lars Eighner.

## Bacon, Charlotte
### Lost Geography
Farrar, Straus and Giroux. 2000. 288 pp.

Four generations of women find themselves compelled by love (for spouses, for parents, for the men they meet) to find their own places in a world beset by the vicissitudes of fate and fortune.

2d Appeal    Language                                                    Book Groups 📖

Subjects    Brothers and Sisters • Canada • Death of a Parent • Farms and Farm Life • First Novels • France • Mothers and Daughters • Multigenerational Novels • Saskatchewan, Canada • Women's Lives

Now try    Bacon is also the author of *A Private State: Stories*. Other novels that chart the lives of women with sympathy are Deirdre McNamer's *One Sweet Quarrel*, Kaye Gibbons's *Charms for the Easy Life*, and Carol Shields's *The Stone Diaries*.

## Bailey, Paul
### Kitty and Virgil
Overlook Press. 2000. 280 pp.

Kitty Crozier and Virgil Florescu meet and fall in love in London, but their relationship is complicated by Virgil's memories of his difficult father and growing up in Romania during the corrupt Ceausescu regime.

Subjects    London, England • Love Affairs • Love Stories • Poets and Poetry • Political Fiction • Romania • Writers and Writing

**Now try**    Bailey is also the author of the novels *At the Jerusalem* and *Gabriel's Lament*, as well as the memoir *An Immaculate Mistake*. Other novels about life in Romania under the Ceausescus include Marianne Wiggins's *Eveless Eden*, Herta Müller's *The Land of Green Plums*, and Norman Manea's *The Black Envelope*.

## Baldwin, William

### The Fennel Family Papers                    Algonquin Books of Chapel Hill. 1996. 284 pp.

Paul Danvers hopes to further his small-time academic career by exploiting his relationship with Ginny, one of the infamous Dog Tooth Shoal Fennels, whose eccentric family offers Paul not historical insight but adventures that are comic, ghostly, and thrilling.

**2d Appeal**    Story

**Subjects**    Academia • American South • Eccentrics and Eccentricities • Family Secrets • Lighthouses • South Carolina

**Now try**    Baldwin is also the author of *The Hard to Catch Mercy*. Other academic satires include Malcolm Bradbury's *Eating People Is Wrong*, David Lodge's *Nice Work* and *Small World*, Jon Hassler's novels of Rookery State College, including *Rookery Blues* and *The Dean's List*, Michael Malone's *Foolscap*, James Hynes's *The Lecturer's Tale*, Jane Smiley's *Moo*, and Richard Russo's *Straight Man*. Eccentric families play important roles in Cathie Pelletier's stories of Mattagash, Maine, starting with *The Funeral Makers*, Fred Chappell's *I Am One of You Forever*, and James Wilcox's novels of Tula Springs, Louisiana, including *Modern Baptists* and *North Gladiola*.

## Banks, Russell

### The Sweet Hereafter                    HarperCollins. 1991. 257 pp.

After a tragic schoolbus accident, the residents of a small town in upstate New York react in different ways to their loss and to the attorney who encourages them "to channel their rage" in a lawsuit.

**2d Appeal**    Setting                    Book Groups 📖

**Subjects**    ALA Notable Books • Death of a Child • Grief • New York • Novels with Multiple Viewpoints • Sexual Abuse • Small-Town Life

**Now try**    Banks is also the author of *Hamilton Stark* and *Family Life*, among other novels. Other novels that dwell on the effects a tragedy has on a family are Rosellen Brown's *Before and After* and Chris Bohjalian's *Past the Bleachers*. The setting of this novel—New York State in the winter—is similar to the setting of Frederick Busch's *Girls*. Banks tells this story from the point of view—and in the voices of—four different people, all affected differently by the tragedy; John Burnham Schwartz uses a similar technique in *Reservation Road*.

## Barker, Pat

### Another World                    Farrar, Straus and Giroux. 1999. 277 pp.

Nick is torn between his responsibilities to his wife, children, and stepchildren and the needs of Geordie, his dying grandfather, who is still haunted by his memories of World War I.

**2d Appeal**    Story                    Book Groups 📖

**Subjects**    British Authors • England • Family Relationships • Grandparents • Husbands and Wives • Stepfamilies • World War I

**Now try**    Barker is also the author of *Union Street*, *Border Crossing*, and *Blow Your House Down*. Other books that movingly and effectively describe the carnage of World War I include Barker's trilogy, composed of *Regeneration*, *The Eye in the Door*, and *The Ghost Road*, as well as Patricia Anthony's *Flanders*, and Erich Maria Remarque's *All Quiet on the Western Front*.

## Barkley, Brad
### Money, Love

W.W. Norton. 2000. 336 pp.

Gabe Strickland is caught between his mother Gladys, who yearns for stability, and his father Roman, the ultimate salesman, who is always on the lookout for easy money, whether it's selling cleaning supplies or lawn chairs or undertaking a tour through the southern states with an exhibit called "Death Cars of the Stars."

**Subjects**    1970s • American South • Coming-of-Age • Family Relationships • First Novels • Humorous Fiction • North Carolina • Southern Authors

**Now try**    Barkley's writing style, southern setting, and over-the-top plot bring to mind Michael Malone's *Handling Sin*.

## Barnes, Julian
### England, England

Knopf. 1999. 275 pp.

Egomaniacal Sir Jack Pitman plans to develop a theme park on the Isle of Wight, whose subject is none other than English history, so visitors will be able to meet the royal family, tour Stonehenge, and attend the beheading of Charles I, all in one day.

**2d Appeal**    Setting

**Subjects**    British Authors • Career Women • England • Humorous Fiction • Isle of Wight • Satirical Fiction

**Now try**    Barnes is also the author of *Talking It Over*, *Love, Etc.*, *Metroland*, and *Flaubert's Parrot*, among other novels. Other satirical novels include Percival Everett's *Erasure* and Martin Amis's *Dead Babies*.

## Barry, Lynda
### Cruddy: An Illustrated Novel

Simon & Schuster. 1999. 305 pp.

In 1971, 16-year-old Roberta Rohbeson writes down her experiences of five years before, when she and her father embarked on a nightmare car trip, punctuated by arson, murder, and betrayals.

**2d Appeal**    Story

**Subjects**    1960s • Crime • Drugs and Drug Abuse • Fathers and Daughters • Suicide • Teenage Girls

**Now try**    Barry, a cartoonist as well as a novelist, is also the author of *The Good Times Are Killing Me*. Other novels that describe a difficult teenage life include *Push* by Ramona Lofton (Sapphire) and Sister Souljah's *The Coldest Winter Ever*.

## Bausch, Robert
### A Hole in the Earth
Harcourt Brace. 2000. 368 pp.

Henry Porter's 39th summer is marked by two life-changing events: his teenaged daughter (whom he has seen only rarely since her mother divorced him more than a decade before) comes to live with him, and his girlfriend announces that she is pregnant.

**Subjects**    Baltimore, Maryland • Fathers and Daughters • Gamblers and Gambling • Male/Female Relationships • Single Fathers

**Now try**    Bausch is also the author of the novels *The Lives of Riley Chance* and *Almighty Me*, as well as the short story collection *The White Rooster & Other Stories*. Another complicated relationship between two no-longer-young lovers is the subject of Frederick Busch's *Harry and Catherine*, while *Gambler's Rose* by G. W. Hawkes is about a family whose love of gambling has changed their lives (and not always for the worse).

## Baxter, Charles
### The Feast of Love
Pantheon. 2000. 320 pp.

A writer named Charles Baxter gets some advice from a neighbor named Bradley about the kind of novel Baxter should write: a series of interviews with people Bradley knows (and Bradley himself) about their experiences—happy, sad, and in between—with love.

**Subjects**    Adultery • American Midwest • Ann Arbor, Michigan • Love Stories • Male/Female Relationships • Michigan • Teenage Love • Teenagers • Writers and Writing

**Now try**    Baxter's other works of fiction include *Harmony of the World*, *Believers*, and *Through the Safety Net*. Different kinds of love are explored in Jayne Anne Phillips's *MotherKind*, *Polly's Ghost* by Abby Frucht, Wallace Stegner's *Crossing to Safety*, and, of course, Shakespeare's "A Midsummer Night's Dream," which Baxter has very loosely adapted for this novel. Another author whose novels are set in Ann Arbor, Michigan, is Nancy Willard (*Sister Water* and *Things Invisible to See*).

## Beard, Richard
### Damascus
Arcade Publishing. 1999. 310 pp.

Spencer and Hazel, a pair of lovers who are destined (perhaps) for years of happiness together, a 10-year-old girl, an aging agoraphobic, and a deranged Japanese student who is destined (perhaps) for years of happiness with Hazel find their lives converging on November 1, 1993.

**2d Appeal**    Story

**Subjects**    Agoraphobia • British Authors • Humorous Fiction • London, England • Love Affairs • Mental Illness • Obsession

**Now try**    Beard also wrote *X20: A Novel of (Not) Smoking*. Beard's semicomic novel displays his fondness for his characters, as does Carol Shields's *The Republic of Love* and Connie Willis's *Bellwether*. Like Alan Lightman's *Einstein's Dreams*, Beard demonstrates how time may behave differently from what is expected.

## Bell, Christine
### The Perez Family 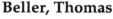 W.W. Norton. 1990. 256 pp.

In Miami, after the Marielito boat lift, former political prisoner Juan Raul Perez finds himself with two families: a long-suffering wife and daughter who have waited 20 years for him, and an artificial family consisting of a vivacious wife, a loony father, and a petty-criminal son, all acquired to make it easier to emigrate to the United States.

Book Groups 📖

**Subjects** ALA Notable Books • Bigamists and Bigamy • Cuba • Culture Clash • Immigrants and Refugees • Latinos • Latinos in America • Marriage • Miami, Florida

**Now try** Bell's other books include *The Seven Year Atomic Make-Over Guide and Other Stories* and *Saint. The Death of Che Guevara* by Jay Cantor is a remarkable novel about Castro's closest friend during the Cuban Revolution. Both *Dreaming in Cuban* and *The Aguero Sisters* by Cristina Garcia are about families divided by the Cuban Revolution. Life in Castro's prisons is graphically described in Armando Valladares's *Against All Hope: A Memoir of Life in Castro's Prisons*.

## Beller, Thomas
### The Sleep-Over Artist W.W. Norton. 2000. 256 pp.

Alex Fader relates the stories of his relationship with members of the female sex, from his adolescence on New York City's Upper West Side, to his love affair as an adult with an older woman in London.

**Subjects** Male/Female Relationships • Mothers and Sons • New York • Older Women/Younger Men • Single Men

**Now try** Alex Fader is also the main character in Beller's *Seduction Theory*. Young New Yorkers at work and play are also the subjects of Caitlin Macy's *The Fundamentals of Play*. Alex's wry tone is reminiscent of the voice of the main character in Jonathan Ames's *The Extra Man*, another novel set in Manhattan.

## Bender, Aimee
### An Invisible Sign of My Own Doubleday. 2000. 242 pp.

Twenty-year-old Mona Gray, who teaches mathematics to a second-grade class in her hometown, is haunted both by her father's strange and unclassifiable illness and her own compulsion to give up everything she's good at doing.

**Subjects** Fathers and Daughters • First Novels • Illness • Love Stories • Mathematics • Teachers

**Now try** Bender is the author of *The Girl in the Flammable Skirt*, a collection of stories. Another novel in which mathematics plays a role is Apostolos Doxiados's *Uncle Petros and Goldbach's Conjecture*. A far different type of math teacher than Mona is found in Elizabeth Strout's *Amy and Isabelle*. Bender's sister Karen also had a first novel published in 2000, entitled *Like Normal People*.

## Bender, Karen
### Like Normal People
Houghton Mifflin. 2000. 288 pp.

Octogenarian Ella, who has spent her life caring for her retarded daughter Lena, has always tried to be an equally good mother to her second, "normal" daughter Vivien.

Book Groups 📖

| | |
|---|---|
| **Subjects** | Developmental Disabilities • Family Relationships • First Novels • Los Angeles, California • Mental Retardation • Sisters |
| **Now try** | Other novels with mentally retarded characters include Colleen McCullough's *Tim*, Tim Parks's *Goodness*, and Bret Lott's *Jewel*. Karen Bender's sister Aimee also published a first novel in 2000, entitled *An Invisible Sign of My Own*. |

## Berne, Suzanne
### A Crime in the Neighborhood
Algonquin Books of Chapel Hill. 1997. 285 pp.

Marsha Eberhardt remembers back to the Watergate summer of 1972, when not only was her parents' marriage disintegrating, but the body of a local 12-year-old boy was found quite near their suburban Washington, D.C., home.

Book Groups 📖

| | |
|---|---|
| **Subjects** | 1970s • Adultery • Coming-of-Age • Death of a Child • First Novels • Murder • Suburbia • Washington, D.C. |
| **Now try** | Another novel in which a child's personal experiences are conflated with a death in the neighborhood is *Snow Angels* by Stewart O'Nan. Children dealing with family crises can be found in Bruce Duffy's *Last Comes the Egg* and Karin Cook's *What Girls Learn*. *A Crime in the Neighborhood* won the Orange Prize. |

## Betts, Doris
### Souls Raised from the Dead
Knopf. 1994. 339 pp.

When 10-year-old Mary Grace Thompson is diagnosed with kidney disease, her estranged parents try to overcome their anger and hostility with one another and come to terms with the impending loss of their daughter.

**2d Appeal**   Story
Book Groups 📖

| | |
|---|---|
| **Subjects** | ALA Notable Books • American South • Death of a Child • Divorce • Fathers and Daughters • Male/Female Relationships • Mothers and Daughters • North Carolina • Southern Authors • Terminal Illness |
| **Now try** | Betts's other works of fiction include *The Sharp Teeth of Love* and *Heading West*, as well as collections of short stories. Other novels about the loss of children include Lorene Cary's *The Price of a Child*, Russell Banks's *The Sweet Hereafter*, Jo-Ann Mapson's *Shadow Ranch*, *Points of Light* by Linda Gray Sexton, *The Tin Can Tree* by Anne Tyler, *Girls* by Frederick Busch, and *At Risk* by Alice Hoffman. |

## Binding, Tim
### Lying with the Enemy
Carroll & Graf. 1998. 360 pp.

On the German-occupied island of Guernsey during World War II, the death of a beautiful young woman brings together in an uneasy alliance the two men who loved her: a Nazi officer and a local policeman.

Book Groups 📖

Subjects    British Authors • Fathers and Daughters • Grief • Guernsey • Historical Setting • Love Affairs • Men's Friendships • Murder • Nazis • World War II

Now try    Binding's other novels include *A Perfect Execution* and *In the Kingdom of Air*. *Lying with the Enemy* combines the characteristics of a World War II thriller (like Jack Higgins's *Cold Harbour* and *The Eagle Has Landed*) with a thoughtful, character-driven story of love, betrayal, and loss, as Michael Ondaatje does in *The English Patient*. Louis de Bernieres's *Corelli's Mandolin* also shares with Binding's novel an island setting, Nazi occupiers, and a poignant love story.

## Boyd, William
### Armadillo

Knopf. 1998. 337 pp.

Lorimer Black, born Milomre Blocj, an insurance adjuster, a student of style, and an insomniac, finds his settled life unhinged by his passion for a face seen in a passing car, a family crisis, and an arson case that seems to have a number of suspicious and career-ending possibilities.

2d Appeal    Story

Subjects    Arson • British Authors • Business and Businessmen • England • Gypsies • Immigrants and Refugees • Insomnia • Insurance Investigations • London, England

Now try    Other works by Boyd include *Blue Afternoon*, *Brazzaville Beach*, and *A Good Man in Africa*. Odd plot twists and engaging, unusual characters are present in the works of Peter Dickinson, such as *The Glass-Sided Ants' Nest* and *The Yellow Room Conspiracy*. The Eastern European–Gypsy element is also memorable in Robertson Davies's The Cornish trilogy (*The Rebel Angels*, *What's Bred in the Bone*, and *The Lyre of Orpheus*).

## Boyle, T. Coraghessan
### East Is East

Viking. 1990. 364 pp.

Able-bodied seaman Hiro Tanaka jumps ship off the coast of Georgia and lands in the middle of floundering writer Ruth Dershowitz's life.

Book Groups 📖

Subjects    ALA Notable Books • Asian Americans • Asians in America • Culture Clash • Georgia • Interracial Relationships • Japanese Americans • Male/Female Relationships • Racism • Sailors and Sailing • Writers and Writing

Now try    Other books by Boyle include *World's End*, *A Friend of the Earth*, *Riven Rock*, *Budding Prospects*, and *Water Music*. Pete Dexter's *Paris Trout* is also about racism in Georgia.

## Brookner, Anita
### Falling Slowly

Random House. 1998. 227 pp.

Two middle-aged sisters—Beatrice, a classical pianist at the end of her career, and Miriam, a translator of French texts—lead isolated, lonely lives, searching for love while at the same time valuing their independence.

2d Appeal    Language

Book Groups 📖

**Subjects**    British Authors • Loneliness • Love Affairs • Male/Female Relationships • Single Men • Single Women • Sisters

**Now try**    *Falling Slowly* is Brookner's 18th novel. *Hotel du Lac*, for which she won the Booker Prize, is also about women living repressed and solitary lives. Barbara Pym's novels—particularly *Excellent Women* and *Jane and Prudence*—also describe the lives of educated and independent women, but their tone is far less claustrophobic than *Falling Slowly*. Another insightful novel about the lives of sisters is Elizabeth Hay's *A Student of Weather*.

## Brown, Carrie
### The Hatbox Baby                                    Algonquin Books of Chapel Hill. 2000. 348 pp.

At Chicago's 1933 Century of Progress Exhibition, fan-dancer Caroline and her cousin St. Louis become involved with an abandoned baby and Dr. Leo Hoffman, who funds his research on premature babies by means of a very popular baby incubator exhibit.

**Subjects**    1930s • Abandoned Children • Chicago, Illinois • Doctors and Patients • Dwarfs • Historical Setting • Premature Babies • World's Fairs

**Now try**    Brown is also the author of *Rose's Garden* and *Lamb in Love*. The characters in Robert Levandoski's *Going to Chicago* are on the road to the same Chicago World's Fair; trips to other early-twentieth-century world's fairs are the backdrop for Miles Beller's *Dream of Venus*, E. L. Doctorow's *World's Fair*, and Thomas Wolfe's *The Lost Boy*. Neonatology is also a key element in Linda Raymond's *Rocking the Babies* and Ana Veciana-Suarez's *The Chin Kiss King*.

## Brown, Carrie
### Lamb in Love                                        Algonquin Books of Chapel Hill. 1999. 336 pp.

On the night of the moon landing in 1969, which happens to be his 55th birthday, postmaster and lifetime bachelor Norris Lamb unexpectedly falls in love with middle-aged spinster Vida Stephen, who works as a nanny for the son of the town's richest man, a retarded boy she has raised from babyhood.

Book Groups 📖

**Subjects**    1960s • Eccentrics and Eccentricities • England • Love Stories • Mental Retardation • Single Men • Single Women • Small-Town Life

**Now try**    Brown is also the author of *Rose's Garden* and *The Hatbox Baby*. Another eccentric man who finds his life changed unexpectedly is the main character in Frederick Reuss's *Horace Afoot*. The sweetness of this novel is similar to that found in Jon Cohen's *The Man in the Window* and Chet Raymo's *The Dork of Cork*.

## Brown, Larry
### Joe                                                 Algonquin Books of Chapel Hill. 1991. 345 pp.

Deep in the backwoods of Mississippi, 15-year-old migrant Gary Jones strikes up an unlikely friendship with hard-drinking, hard-living Joe Ransom.

**2d Appeal**    Language                                    Book Groups 📖

**Subjects**    ALA Notable Books • Alcoholics and Alcoholism • American South • Dysfunctional Families • Men's Friendships • Mississippi • Poverty • Southern Authors

**Now try**    Brown also wrote *Father and Son* and *Dirty Work*. Brown's dark and gritty novel is reminiscent of the novels of Pete Dexter (*The Paperboy*, and others), Harry

Crews (*A Feast of Snakes*, *Body*, and others), Cormac McCarthy (*Blood Meridian*, *All the Pretty Horses*, and others), and Jim Thompson (*The Grifters*, and others). A minor character in *Joe* becomes the major character in Brown's novel *Fay*.

## Budhos, Marina
### The Professor of Light

G.P. Putnam's Sons. 1999. 254 pp.

During one of their regular summer vacations in England, Meggie Singh watches helplessly as her mother becomes more depressed than ever, and her father, a philosophy professor who emigrated from Guyana years before, becomes more and more obsessed with understanding the nature of light.

> **Subjects**    Dysfunctional Families • Guyana • Immigrants and Refugees • Intermarriage • Obsession • Philosophy • Physics • Science and Scientists

> **Now try**    Budhos is also the author of *The House of Waiting* (a novel) and *Remix: Conversations with Immigrant Teenagers*. Philosophy also plays a part in Rebecca Goldstein's *The Mind-Body Problem* and Lynne Sharon Schwartz's *Disturbances in the Field*. Physics is the background for Jonathan Lethem's *As She Climbed Across the Table* and *Einstein's Dreams* by Alan Lightman.

## Burnard, Bonnie
### A Good House
Henry Holt. 2000. 309 pp.

Three generations of the Chambers family live out their ordinary lives in their small Canadian hometown near London, Ontario.

> **2d Appeal**    Setting                                Book Groups 📖

> **Subjects**    Brothers and Sisters • Canada • Canadian Authors • Death of a Parent • Death of a Sibling • Family Relationships • First Novels • Multigenerational Novels • Small-Town Life

> **Now try**    Burnard's novel won the Giller Prize. Her other books include two collections of stories: *Casino & Other Stories* and *Women of Influence*. Other novels by Canadian authors about small-town life include David Bergen's *A Year of Lesser* and Sandra Birdsell's *The Chrome Suite*. In her loving and detailed descriptions of the lives of men and women, adults and children, Burnard's novel is reminiscent of *The Stone Diaries* and *Larry's Party* by Carol Shields.

## Byatt, A. S.
### Possession
Random House. 1990. 555 pp.

In the process of studying the lives of two Victorian poets, postdoctoral student Roland Mitchell and Dr. Maud Bailey meet and fall in love.

> **2d Appeal**    Language                              Book Groups 📖

> **Subjects**    ALA Notable Books • Booker Prize Winners • British Authors • College Professors • College Students • Love Stories • Poets and Poetry • Research Novels • Writers and Writing

> **Now try**    Byatt's other novels include *The Biographer's Tale*, *Still Life*, and *Babel Tower*. John Fowles (*The Magus*, and others), Margaret Drabble

(Byatt's sister and the author of *The Needle's Eye*, and other novels), and Iris Murdoch (*The Italian Girl*, *Under the Net*, and others) are all formidably intelligent writers who can also tell a good story. (Byatt has also written extensively about Murdoch's novels.) Other novels about literary scholars include Cathleen Schine's *Rameau's Niece*, *Hallucinating Foucault* by Patricia Duncker, Lindsay Clarke's *The Chymical Wedding*, and Jane Urquhart's *Changing Heaven*. Valerie Townsend Bayer's *City of Childhood* is another novel within a novel.

## Cameron, Peter
### The Weekend
Farrar, Straus and Giroux. 1994. 241 pp.

On the first anniversary of his brother Tony's death from AIDS, John and his wife Marian host a weekend get-together for Tony's old lover Lyle, who unexpectedly brings along his new friend Robert.

Book Groups 📖

**Subjects**   AIDS • Brothers • Family Relationships • Friendship • Gay Men • Upper Classes

**Now try**   Cameron's earlier novel, *Leap Year*, is a bit less intense than *The Weekend*. E. M. Forster in both *Maurice* and *Howards End* shows a similar compassion for his characters. F. Scott Fitzgerald's *The Great Gatsby* also eloquently portrays a life of privilege and inherited wealth.

## Cao, Lan
### Monkey Bridge
Viking. 1997. 260 pp.

Not until she reads her mother's secret journal and discovers the long-hidden secrets of her family's past in South Vietnam does teenager Mai Nguyen understand why her mother is having such a difficult time adjusting to a new life in suburban Washington, D.C., in 1978.

Book Groups 📖

**Subjects**   Asian American Authors • Asian Americans • Asians in America • Family Secrets • First Novels • Immigrants and Refugees • Mothers and Daughters • South Vietnam • Vietnam War • Vietnamese Authors • Washington, D.C.

**Now try**   The importance of understanding the past is also the theme of Alan Brown's *Audrey Hepburn's Neck*, Seamus Deane's *Reading in the Dark*, and Nora Okja Keller's *Comfort Woman*. Cao mixes myths and legends into her narrative in much the same way Maxine Hong Kingston did in *The Woman Warrior*. Robert Olen Butler's *A Good Scent from a Strange Mountain* is about Vietnamese immigrants in Louisiana; Mary Gardner's *Boat People* is about the immigrant experience in Texas.

## Carrington, Roslyn
### A Thirst for Rain
Kensington. 1999. 200 pp.

The loves and losses of each character—from Myra, the hard-working single mother expecting her second child, to Odile, her defiant, pregnant teenaged daughter, to Jacob, the once-great stick fighter living next door—intertwine, leading to dangerous consequences for everyone in a rural Trinidad neighborhood.

**Subjects**   Caribbean • Caribbean Authors • Family Relationships • First Novels • Male/Female Relationships • Mothers and Daughters • Teenage Girls • Teenage Pregnancy • Trinidad • Trinidadian Authors

**Now try**   Lisa Carey's *The Mermaids Singing* and Elizabeth Strout's *Amy and Isabelle* also deal with troubled mother-daughter relationships. *Ruby* by Ann Hood explores the situation that arises between a widow yearning for a child and a pregnant teenager who are brought together by unlikely circumstance. Earl Lovelace (*The Dragon Can't Dance*, and others) is another Trinidadian novelist. V. S. Naipaul's *Fireflies* and *The Chip-Chip Gatherers* are both set in semirural Trinidad.

## Carter, Dori
### Beautiful Wasps Having Sex                    Morrow. 2000. 320 pp.

When Frankie Jordan (almost 40, about to be divorced, unable to finish the movie script she's writing) meets her agent's secretary Jonathan Prince (24, handsome, intelligent, ambitious, and a fan of Frankie's writing), she believes her life is about to take a turn for the better.

**2d Appeal**   Setting

**Subjects**   Career Women • First Novels • Hollywood • Jews and Judaism • Motion Picture Industry • Older Women/Younger Men • Writers and Writing

**Now try**   Budd Schulberg's *What Makes Sammy Run* is another Hollywood novel about ambition and friendship in Tinsel Town. Other Hollywood novels include Nathanael West's *The Day of the Locust* and Carey Cameron's *Daddy Boy*.

## Cartwright, Justin
### Leading the Cheers                    Carroll & Graf. 1999. 246 pp.

When Dan Silas leaves his London home to attend his 30-year reunion in the small town where he spent his senior year in high school, he is greeted with the news that his then-girlfriend Gloria believes that Dan is the father of her daughter (conceived on their senior trip back east) and that his friend Gary Beaner believes that he is really Pale Eagle, a Shawnee Indian who died in 1813 during the Battle of Detroit.

**Subjects**   American Indians • British Authors • Male/Female Relationships • Reunions • Satirical Fiction

**Now try**   Cartwright is also the author of *Masai Dreaming*, *Look at It This Way*, and other novels. *Leading the Cheers* won the Whitbread Award. Other novels that fold American Indian history into their plots are Thomas Perry's novels about Jane Whitefield, including *Dance for the Dead* and *Vanishing Act*, and Paul Bryers's *The Prayer of the Bone*.

## Casey, John
### The Half-Life of Happiness                    Knopf. 1998. 513 pp.

North Carolina attorney Mike and filmmaker Joss Reardon's seemingly perfect life turns upside down when she leaves him for a woman and he decides to run for Congress.

Book Groups 📖

**Subjects**   Family Relationships • Fathers and Daughters • Lesbians • Marriage • North Carolina • Politics • Suicide

**Now try**   Casey is also the author of *Spartina*, a National Book Award winner. Other novels about crises in men's lives include Richard Russo's

*Straight Man*, Russell Banks's *Continental Drift*, David Gates's *Preston Falls*, and *Larry's Party* by Carol Shields.

## Chabon, Michael
### The Amazing Adventures of Kavalier & Clay      Random House. 2000. 639 pp.

Joseph Kavalier, newly arrived in America after escaping Prague in the 1940s, and his cousin, Brooklyn-born-and-bred Sammy Clay, together create a superhero, the Escapist, for the brand-new (and booming) comic-book market.

| | | |
|---|---|---|
| **2d Appeal** | Story | Book Groups 📖 |

**Subjects**   1940s • ALA Notable Books • Brooklyn, New York • Comic Books • Cousins • Gay Men • Golems • Holocaust • Jews and Judaism • Pulitzer Prize Winners

**Now try**   Chabon is also the author of *The Mysteries of Pittsburgh*, *A Model World and Other Stories*, *Werewolves in Their Youth*, and *Wonder Boys*. Other novels about the comics include Tom DeHaven's *Derby Dugan's Depression Funnies* and J. Robert Lennon's *The Funnies*. David James Duncan's *The Brothers K* also explores the often contradictory, frequently difficult relationship between family members. Another book that also touches on the mythical golem is Marge Piercy's *He, She and It*. *Understanding Comes* by Scott McCloud is must reading for any comics lover.

## Ciresi, Rita
### Pink Slip      Delacorte. 1999. 353 pp.

When Lisa leaves her dead-end job in the New York publishing world for a position at a prestigious company, it gives her the opportunity to start writing a satirical novel about corporate life and to fall in love with her boss—the buttoned-up, secretive, and unobtainable Eben Strauss.

**Subjects**   Career Women • Italian Americans • Love Affairs • Male/Female Relationships • Single Women • Writers and Writing

**Now try**   Ciresi is also the author of *Blue Italian*, *Sometimes I Dream in Italian*, and *Mother Rocket: Stories*. Ciresi's fondness for her characters brings to mind the novels of Elinor Lipman, especially *The Way Men Act*, in which the main character also falls in love with someone seemingly unavailable.

## Clark, Martin
### The Many Aspects of Mobile Home Living      Knopf. 2000. 345 pp.

When Ruth Esther English, an unusual used-car saleswoman, asks North Carolina judge Evers Wheeling to dismiss a drug charge against her younger brother, she involves Wheeling in a series of events that offer him the opportunity to make something of his life.

**Subjects**   American South • Drugs and Drug Abuse • First Novels • Humorous Fiction • Interracial Relationships • Law and Lawyers • Magic Realism • North Carolina • Southern Authors

**Now try**   Michael Malone's *Handling Sin* is another novel filled with wacky characters, outlandish escapades, and writing that makes you laugh aloud.

## Cohen, Matt
### Elizabeth and After
Picador USA. 2000. 370 pp.

In a small town in Ontario, Elizabeth McKelvey affects the lives of several men (her husband, lover, and son); this influence lasts for decades after her death and alters personalities, characters, and destinies.

Book Groups 📖

**Subjects**  Canada • Canadian Authors • Death of a Parent • Death of a Spouse • Family Relationships • Husbands and Wives • Mothers and Sons • Small-Town Life

**Now try**  Other novels set in small Canadian towns include Alice Munro's *Lives of Girls and Women*, Sandra Birdsell's *Agassiz: A Novel in Stories*, David Bergen's *A Year of Lesser*, and W. O. Mitchell's *Who Has Seen the Wind*. Cohen's novel won Canada's Governor General's Literary Award for Fiction in 1999.

## Colwin, Laurie
### Goodbye Without Leaving
Poseidon Press. 1990. 253 pp.

Despite having a wonderful husband and a delightful son, Geraldine Colsehares Miller wonders whether she will ever find the true happiness she had as the only white backup singer to Vernon and Ruby Shakely and the Shakettes.

**Subjects**  Adultery • Husbands and Wives • Music and Musicians • New York • Rock and Roll

**Now try**  Among Colwin's other novels are *Family Happiness* and *A Big Storm Knocked It Over*. She is also the author of several short story collections and two cooking memoirs, *Home Cooking* and *More Home Cooking: A Writer Returns to the Kitchen*. Colwin's writing style is uniquely her own, but Susan Trott comes close in *Crane Spreads Wings: A Bigamist's Story*, as does Leslie Brenner in *Greetings from the Golden State*.

## Combs, Maxine
### The Inner Life of Objects
Calyx Books. 1999. 179 pp.

The Zoetic Society, devoted to investigating the paranormal, brings together five people—the 59-year-old director Opal Kirschbaum, who still wonders if she made the right career choice; Poppy, a single mother who is reading lots of books about women's issues; Geneva, who has a Ph.D. in English but no boyfriend in sight; Sol, Opal's artist husband; and Abel Moore, a psychic whose predictions are right about a third of the time.

**Subjects**  Cancer • Husbands and Wives • Paranormal Phenomena • Psychics • Single Mothers

**Now try**  Combs is also the author of *Handbook of the Strange*, *The Foam of Perilous Seas*, and *Swimming Out of the Collective Unconscious*. Rhian Ellis's *After Life* is also about paranormal phenomena.

## Conrad, James
### Making Love to the Minor Poets of Chicago
St. Martin's Press. 2000. 436 pp.

Various university and literary types become involved in the machinations of Vivian Reape, a successful and powerful poet, as she schemes to have a poet included in a project to warn people away from a nuclear waste dump for the next 10,000 years.

**Subjects**   Academia • Chicago, Illinois • College Professors • First Novels • Male/Female Relationships • Poets and Poetry • Writers and Writing

**Now try**   Other novels exploring the absurdities of academic life include *Pearl's Progress* by James Kaplan, Richard Russo's *Straight Man*, David Lodge's *Changing Places* and *Small World*, Jane Smiley's *Moo*, and Mary McCarthy's *The Groves of Academe*.

## Coomer, Joe
### Apologizing to Dogs
Scribner. 1999. 287 pp.

For Aura (owner of Aura's Silver Matching Service), Effie (owner of Effie's Little Corner of Europe), Mr. Haygood (Toys for Big Boys), Mazelle (Mazelle's Rare and Medium Rare Books), and other owners of the antique stores along Worth Avenue in Fort Worth, Texas, a violent thunderstorm forces past secrets into the open and changes everyone's future—some for the better and some for the worse.

**Subjects**   American West • Antiques • Dogs • Eccentrics and Eccentricities • Family Secrets • Fort Worth, Texas • Love Stories

**Now try**   Coomer's other novels include *The Loop* and *Beachcombing for a Shipwrecked God*. Coomer shows great affection for the large cast of eccentrics that he has created, as does Lorna Landvik in her novels *The Tall Pine Polka*, *Patty Jane's House of Curl*, and *Your Oasis on Flame Lake* and Frederick Reuss's *Horace Afoot*.

## Cusk, Rachel
### The Country Life
Picador USA. 1999. 341 pp.

When 20-ish Stella Benson decides to leave her home in London and accept a job in rural Sussex as an au pair to Martin, the disabled son of Piers and Pamela Madden, she soon learns that she has absolutely no aptitude for the country life.

Book Groups 📖

**Subjects**   ALA Notable Books • British Authors • Humorous Fiction • Physical Disabilities • Satirical Fiction • Sussex, England

**Now try**   Cusk's first novel, *Saving Agnes*, won the Whitbread Prize for Best Novel in 1993. *The Country Life* is an homage to Stella Gibbons's very funny novel *Cold Comfort Farm*.

## Darling, Julia
### Crocodile Soup
Ecco Press. 2000. 350 pp.

Gert spends her days as a museum curator courting Eva, another museum employee, and remembering her bizarre childhood with an absent father (gone to Africa to run the family's crocodile farm), a self-absorbed mother, and her telepathic, obsessive twin Frank.

**Subjects**   British Authors • Dysfunctional Families • First Novels • Lesbians • Museums • Obsession • Twins

**Now try**   Darling's novel shares a humorous sensibility with Kate Atkinson's *Behind the Scenes at the Museum* and Jeanette Winterson's *Oranges Are Not the Only Fruit*.

## Davies, Stevie
### Four Dreamers and Emily
St. Martin's Press. 1997. 258 pp.

An Emily Brontë conference in the English countryside brings together an ailing widower, a prudish spinster, a harried English professor, and an overweight waitress; while each hopes to uncover secrets about their beloved but mysterious Emily, the weekend quickly becomes more about self-discovery.

**Subjects**   Academia • British Authors • Brontë, Emily • England • Humorous Fiction • Male/Female Relationships • Single Women

**Now try**   Davies is also the author of *Boy Blue*. A. S. Byatt's *Possession* and *The Matisse Stories*, while much less overtly funny, are also witty, character-driven novels with a passionate appreciation of literature and art. Other satires of academia include Jane Smiley's *Moo* and David Lodge's *Small World*.

## Davis, Kathryn
### The Walking Tour
Houghton Mifflin. 1999. 264 pp.

The death of her artist-mother years before on a walking tour in Wales still preoccupies Susan; using her mother's letters, a journal written by her mother's best friend, and transcripts from the negligence trial that followed, Susan attempts to understand just what occurred.

**2d Appeal**   Language

**Subjects**   Art and Artists • Death of a Parent • Husbands and Wives • Mothers and Daughters • Mystery • Wales

**Now try**   Davis is also the author of *The Girl Who Trod on a Loaf* and *Hell*. Davis's novels are not easy to read, but they reward the persevering reader with the quality of their writing and the inventiveness of their plots, not unlike the novels of Jeanette Winterson (*Oranges Are Not the Only Fruit*, and others) and Barbara Gowdy (*The White Bone* and *Mister Sandman*).

## D'Erasmo, Stacey
### Tea
Algonquin Books of Chapel Hill. 2000. 317 pp.

The suicide of Isabel Gold's mother when she was a child has colored the rest of Isabel's life, affecting her relationships with her father and sister, and with her lover Thea.

**Subjects**   Death of a Parent • First Novels • Jews and Judaism • Lesbians • Sisters • Suicide

**Now try**   Hope Edelman's *Motherless Daughters: The Legacy of Loss* is a sensitive nonfiction exploration of the effects a mother's early death has on her daughter. *Housekeeping* by Marilynne Robinson, Karin Cook's *What Girls Learn*, Kelly Dwyer's *The Tracks of Angels*, and Sheila Ballantyne's *Imaginary Crimes* are all novels about the lives of girls after the deaths of their mothers.

## Derbyshire, John
### Seeing Calvin Coolidge in a Dream
St. Martin's Press. 1996. 273 pp.

Chai, a former Red Guard in China who now lives in suburban New York with his wife and daughter, develops an obsession with Calvin Coolidge, the long-dead 30th president of the United States; when he learns that his first love is living near Boston, he dreams of rekindling their love affair—and it takes both his wife Ding and the former president to keep Chai on the straight and narrow.

**2d Appeal**   Story                                                Book Groups 📖

**Subjects**   British Authors • Business and Businessmen • China • Coolidge, Calvin • First Novels • Husbands and Wives • Obsession • Red Guards

**Now try**   This funny and poignant novel brings to mind both Jon Cohen's *The Man in the Window* and John Welter's *I Want to Buy a Vowel*.

## Desai, Anita
### Fasting, Feasting
Houghton Mifflin. 2000. 227 pp.

After two humiliating, failed arranged marriages, Uma, the unattractive older daughter in a middle-class Indian family, now caters to her demanding parents' every need; meanwhile, her younger brother Arun struggles to adapt to his new life at college in Massachusetts.

**2d Appeal**   Setting                                              Book Groups 📖

**Subjects**   Brothers and Sisters • Family Relationships • India • Indian Authors

**Now try**   *Fasting, Feasting* was short-listed for the Booker Prize, as were Desai's *Clear Light of Day* and *In Custody*. Bharti Kirchner's *Sharmila's Book* is another novel about an arranged marriage in India—this time between an American woman and an Indian man.

## DeWitt, Helen
### The Last Samurai
Hyperion. 2000. 530 pp.

Working from the various clues his mother Sybilla lets fall, Ludo, a child prodigy, tries to discover the identity of his father, all the while watching and rewatching with Sybilla Akira Kurosawa's film *The Seven Samurai*.

**2d Appeal**   Language                                             Book Groups 📖

**Subjects**   ALA Notable Books • Child Prodigies • First Novels • Geniuses • Gifted Children • London, England • Mothers and Sons • Movies • Single Mothers

**Now try**   Other child prodigies can be found in *Saving St. Germ* by Carol Muske-Dukes, Bernice Ruben's *Madame Sousatzka*, Mark Salzman's *The Soloist*, and Stephen Millhauser's *Edwin Mullhouse: The Life and Death of an American Writer, 1943–1954*. Another most unusual child is the main character in Suneeta Peres da Costa's *Homework*.

## Dillen, Frederick
### Fool
Algonquin Books of Chapel Hill. 1999. 302 pp.

After losing all his money and status and sent to jail as a punishment for securities fraud, Barnaby Griswold leaves his upscale New York life to move to Oklahoma City and take care of his former mother-in-law.

**Subjects**    Divorce • Elderly Women • Entrepeneurs • Fathers and Sons • Investment Advisors • Middle-Aged Men • Midlife Crisis • Oklahoma

**Now try**    Dillen is also the author of the novel *Hero*. Richard Russo's *Straight Man* is another warmly humorous and wise novel about a man in the midst of a midlife crisis.

## Divakaruni, Chitra

### Sister of My Heart
Doubleday. 1999. 322 pp.

Cousins Sudha and Anju were born in Calcutta the same day that their fathers died under mysterious circumstances; despite their arranged marriages, and the different twists and turns their lives take, their fates remain intertwined.

**2d Appeal**    Setting

**Subjects**    Calcutta, India • Cousins • Family Secrets • India • Indian Authors • Love Stories

**Now try**    Divakaruni is also the author of *The Mistress of Spices*, *The Unknown Errors of Their Lives*, and *Arranged Marriage*, a collection of short stories and *The Vine of Desire*, which continues the story of Sudha and Anju. Both of Bharti Kirchner's novels (*Sharmila's Book* and *Shiva Dancing*) are plot-driven novels set in a well-described India.

## Donoghue, Emma

### Hood
HarperCollins. 1995. 309 pp.

After Cara's unexpected death at the age of 30, her lover Penelope remembers the 14 years they spent together, from their meeting as schoolgirls in Catholic school to the present.

**Subjects**    Death and Dying • Ireland • Irish Authors • Lesbians • Women's Friendships

**Now try**    Donoghue is also the author of the novels *Slammerkin* and *Stir-fry*. Other novels about lesbian relationships include Jean Swallow's *Leave a Light on for Me* and Stacey D'Ersamo's *Tea*.

## Downing, Michael

### Breakfast with Scot
Counterpoint Press. 1999. 194 pp.

When Ed and Sam learn that they have been named as guardians of an 11-year-old boy, they have no idea of how much Scot's arrival will change their lives.

**Subjects**    Adoption • Gay Men • Men's Friendships • Orphans

**Now try**    Downing's other novels include *Perfect Agreement* and *A Narrow Time*. The author's warm feelings for all his characters are also found in Caroline Preston's *Jackie by Josie* and Mark O'Donnell's *Getting Over Homer*.

## Downs, Robert C. S.

### The Fifth Season
Counterpoint Press. 2000. 246 pp.

Sixty-year-old Ted Neely's visit to his aging and increasingly ill parents force both him and his father to try to mend their stormy relationship.

Book Groups 📖

**Subjects**    Aging • Alzheimer's Disease • Brothers • Cancer • Elderly Men • Elderly Women • Fathers and Sons • Florida • Mothers and Sons

**Now try**   Downs is also the author of *Living Together*, *Country Dying*, and *Peoples*. Other novels about adult children dealing with aging parents include Michael Ignatieff's *Scar Tissue* and Molly Giles's *Iron Shoes*.

## Doyle, Roddy
### A Star Called Henry
Viking. 1999. 343 pp.

Henry Smart grows up impoverished in the slums of Dublin, takes part in the 1916 Easter Uprising, and becomes an assassin for the IRA.

**2d Appeal**   Language                                                Book Groups 📖

**Subjects**   ALA Notable Books • Coming-of-Age • Dublin, Ireland • Ireland • Irish Authors • Irish Republican Army • Lower Classes • Murder • Poverty • Terrorists and Terrorism

**Now try**   Doyle's other novels include *Paddy Clarke Ha-Ha-Ha* and *The Snapper*. *A Star Called Henry* is the first book in The Last Roundup trilogy. It is interesting to compare Henry's childhood to that described in Frank McCourt's memoir *Angela's Ashes*. Another novel about the Irish Republican Army, set during the same time period, is Thomas Flanagan's *The End of the Hunt*.

## Doyle, Roddy
### The Van
Viking. 1992. 311 pp.

Jimmy Rabbitte Sr. is miserable until he and his best friend Bimbo set off in a van to sell fish-and-chips around Dublin.

**2d Appeal**   Setting

**Subjects**   Business and Businessmen • Dublin, Ireland • Entrepreneurs • Family Relationships • Humorous Fiction • Ireland • Irish Authors • Men's Friendships

**Now try**   *The Van* is the third book in Doyle's Barrytown trilogy, which also includes *The Commitments* and *The Snapper*. Another warm and humorous family trilogy set in Ireland is Brendan O'Carroll's *The Mammy*, *The Chisellers*, and *The Granny*.

## Doyle, Roddy
### The Woman Who Walked into Doors
Viking. 1996. 226 pp.

Thirty-nine-year-old housewife Paula Spencer suffers through almost constant domestic violence while wrestling with her twin demons of alcoholism and a continuing physical attraction to the man who abuses her, her husband Charlo.

**2d Appeal**   Language                                                Book Groups 📖

**Subjects**   Abusive Relationships • ALA Notable Books • Alcoholics and Alcoholism • Domestic Violence • Husbands and Wives • Ireland • Irish Authors

**Now try**   Doyle's other novels include *The Commitments*, *The Snapper*, and *The Van*. *The Woman Who Walked into Doors* is Doyle's only novel told in a woman's voice. Other novels of domestic abuse include Susan Brownmiller's *Waverly Place* and *Picture Perfect* by Jodi Picoult.

## Drury, Tom
### The End of Vandalism
Houghton Mifflin. 1994. 321 pp.

Life in Grouse County, Iowa, is described mainly through the eyes of Sheriff Dan Norman, his wife Louise, and Louise's ex-husband Tiny, a plumber and a thief.

**2d Appeal**  Setting

**Subjects**  Abandoned Children • ALA Notable Books • American Midwest • Iowa • Marriage • Sheriffs • Small-Town Life • Triangles

**Now try**  Drury is also the author of ***The Black Brook*** and ***Hunts in Dreams***. Frederick Busch's ***Harry and Catherine*** is another novel about two men in love with the same woman. Peter Hedges's ***An Ocean in Iowa*** is also set in Iowa. Another novel in which an abandoned baby is important to the plot is Margot Livesey's ***Criminals***. In 1996, *Granta Magazine* named Drury one of the "20 Best Young American Novelists."

## Dubus, Andre, III
### House of Sand and Fog
W.W. Norton. 1999. 365 pp.

When Behrani, once a colonel in the shah's air force, but now an exile in the United States who works at humiliating and low-paying jobs to support his wife and son in the style in which they had lived in Iran, purchases a house, he sets in motion a series of events involving the house's previous owner and her married lover—events that will end happily for no one.

Book Groups 📖

**Subjects**  Adultery • ALA Notable Books • California • Culture Clash • Drugs and Drug Abuse • Iran • Kidnapping • Murder • Novels with Multiple Viewpoints • Oprah Winfrey Selection • Property Disputes

**Now try**  Dubus is also the author of another novel, ***Bluesman***, and ***The Cage Keeper and Other Stories***. T. Coraghessan Boyle's ***The Tortilla Curtain*** is another novel in which a sense of doom plays itself out in the lives of the characters.

## Duncan, David James
### The Brothers K
Doubleday. 1992. 635 pp.

The Chance family is united by their love of baseball and nearly destroyed by Mrs. Chance's fanatical devotion to the Seventh-Day Adventist Church.

Book Groups 📖

**Subjects**  1960s • 1970s • ALA Notable Books • Baseball • Brothers • Brothers and Sisters • Family Relationships • Pacific Northwest • Religion • Religious Extremism • Vietnam War

**Now try**  Duncan also wrote ***The River Why*** and ***River Teeth: Stories and Writing***. Baseball plays a central role in the plot of Nancy Willard's ***Things Invisible to See***, Steve Kluger's ***Last Days of Summer***, and Pete Fromm's ***How All This Started***. Other novels in which plot, characters, and writing all come together beautifully to fashion a novel that the reader hates to finish are Michael Malone's ***Dingley Falls*** and Pat Conroy's ***The Prince of Tides***. Ken Kesey's novel ***Sometimes a Great Notion*** also gives a good sense of life in the Northwest.

## Dunmore, Helen
### With Your Crooked Heart
Atlantic Monthly Press. 1999. 249 pp.

The lives of Paul, a successful property developer, Louise, his faded, alcoholic wife, and Johnnie, his criminally minded and irresponsible brother, intersect in their relationships to Paul and Louise's daughter Anna.

Book Groups 📖

**Subjects**   Adultery • Alcoholics and Alcoholism • British Authors • Brothers • Business and Businessmen • Divorce • Family Relationships • Stepfamilies

**Now try**   Dunmore won the Orange Prize for *A Spell of Winter*. Her other novels of psychological insight include *Talking to the Dead* and *Your Blue-Eyed Boy*. Convoluted family relationships are at the heart of Robert Boswell's *Mystery Ride*, Elizabeth Bowen's *The Death of the Heart*, John Casey's *The Half-Life of Happiness*, and Craig Lesley's *The Sky Fisherman*. The ill effects of brotherly love are demonstrated in Martin Amis's *Success*, Donald Antrim's *The Hundred Brothers*, William Boyd's *An Ice Cream War*, and Larry Woiwode's *Born Brothers*.

## Dwyer, Kelly
### Self-Portrait with Ghosts
G.P. Putnam's Sons. 1999. 254 pp.

When Luke kills himself after years of suffering from debilitating depression, it forces his sisters, his mother, and his niece to finally face the anger and hurt that has divided the family for so long.

Book Groups 📖

**Subjects**   Brothers and Sisters • Depression • Dysfunctional Families • Family Relationships • Mental Illness • Novels with Multiple Viewpoints • Suicide • Uncles

**Now try**   Dwyer is also the author of the novel *The Tracks of Angels*. The emotional suffering of a would-be suicide that Dwyer describes so well is also the subject of Kay Redfield Jamison's *Night Falls Fast: Understanding Suicide* and *An Unquiet Mind*, which explores her own struggles with depression. Ellen Gilchrist's *The Anna Papers* and Cathie Pelletier's *The Bubble Reputation* are also about the effects of suicide on the survivors.

## Earley, Tony
### Jim the Boy
Little, Brown. 2000. 227 pp.

Jim Glass's 11th year, spent in Aliceville, North Carolina, is filled with new friendships in a new school building, new lessons learned from and wonders revealed by his bachelor uncles and his mother, and the growing realization that there is a broader world outside his small town.

Book Groups 📖

**Subjects**   1930s • American South • Boys' Lives • Coming-of-Age • Family Relationships • First Novels • Mothers and Sons • North Carolina • Small-Town Life • Southern Authors • Uncles • Widows

**Now try**   Earley is also the author of a collection of stories, *Here We Are in Paradise*, where Jim Glass first appears. The warm family relationships in this novel bring to mind Bonnie Burnard's *A Good House*, Ivan Doig's *English Creek*, Kent Haruf's *Plainsong*, and Richard Llewellyn's *How Green Was My Valley*. Other storytellers of the southern mountains include Fred Chappell (*I Am One of You*

*Forever*), Clyde Edgerton (***Walking Across Egypt***), Jessie Stuart (***Hie to the Hunters***), Robert Morgan (***Gap Creek***), Lee Smith (***Oral History***), and John Ehle (***The Journey of August King***).

## Ellis, Alice Thomas
### The 27th Kingdom
Moyer Bell. 1999. 159 pp.

In 1954 London, the insular existence of Irina, a cosmopolitan Russian émigré, and Kyril, her smugly precious nephew, is shattered when a beautiful young postulant from the West Indies comes to live with them at their boardinghouse.

Book Groups 📖

**Subjects** British Authors • Good vs. Evil • Humorous Fiction • London, England • Magic Realism • Mothers and Sons • Nuns • West Indians • Widows

**Now try** Ellis also wrote ***The Summer House: A Trilogy***. Her spare, slyly humorous style is reminiscent of Barbara Pym's ***Some Tame Gazelle*** and ***No Fond Return of Love***, but Ellis's novels are edgier and include a touch of the fantastical.

## Evans, Elizabeth
### Carter Clay
HarperFlamingo. 1999. 404 pp.

Carter Clay's attempts to make amends for a disaster he caused—while he was driving drunk, he plowed into a family standing by the side of the road, leaving Joe Alitz dead, Katherine Alitz alive but brain damaged, and their teenaged daughter Jersey paralyzed—leads him to become a caretaker for the two survivors.

Book Groups 📖

**Subjects** Alcoholics and Alcoholism • Car Accidents • Death of a Parent • Drunk Driving • Physical Disabilities • Teenage Girls • Teenagers • Vietnam Veterans

**Now try** Evans's other novels include ***Rowing in Eden*** and ***The Blue Hour***. Another harrowing novel about good intentions leading to terrible results is Mary Doria Russell's ***The Sparrow***.

## Findley, Timothy
### The Piano Man's Daughter
Crown. 1995. 461 pp.

Charlie Kilworth reconstructs the life of his mother Lily, the piano man's daughter, who—because of her inherited "spells"—is cast out of her family, kept away from society, sent away to school, and never stops running from the shadows that pursue her.

**2d Appeal** Story

Book Groups 📖

**Subjects** Canadian Authors • Epilepsy • Historical Setting • Mental Illness • Mothers and Daughters • Mothers and Sons • Multigenerational Novels • Ontario, Canada

**Now try** Among Findley's many novels are ***The Last of the Crazy People***, ***The Wars***, and ***Famous Last Words***. Other novels involving children dealing with mentally ill mothers include ***A Star Called Henry*** by Roddy Doyle, ***Sights Unseen*** by Kaye Gibbons, ***In Another Country*** by Susan Kenney, ***The Butcher Boy*** by Patrick McCabe, and ***My Old Sweetheart*** by Susanna Moore.

## Findley, Timothy
### Pilgrim
HarperCollins. 2000. 486 pp.

In 1912, Pilgrim is delivered to Carl Jung's clinic in Zurich after another successful suicide attempt and another successful revivification. Is Pilgrim immortal, having inhabited many personalities, or merely disturbed?

**2d Appeal**   Story                                                    Book Groups 📖

**Subjects**   Canadian Authors • Historical Setting • Immortality • Jung, Carl • Mental Illness • Psychiatric Hospitals • Psychiatrists, Psychoanalysts, Psychotherapists • Suicide

**Now try**   Findley often weaves historical and literary figures into his fiction, as seen in his novels *Not Wanted on the Voyage* and *Headhunter*. Other novels populated with real people include E. L. Doctorow's *Ragtime* and *Billy Bathgate*, *The Old Gringo* by Carlos Fuentes, *Nevermore* by William Hjortsberg, and *Los Alamos* by Joseph Kanon. Novels using upper-class psychiatric hospitals as a frame include T. Coraghessan Boyle's *Riven Rock*, Robertson Davies's *The Manticore*, Mark Helprin's *Memoir from Antproof Case*, and Roderick MacLeish's *The First Book of Eppe*.

## Fitzgerald, Penelope
### Human Voices
Houghton Mifflin. 1999. 143 pp.

During the 1940s, the drama of World War II is rivaled by what's happening to the staff working for the BBC, where love, birth, human follies, and various crises are unfolding behind the scenes.

**Subjects**   British Authors • Comedy of Manners • Humorous Fiction • London, England • Radio Stations • World War II

**Now try**   Fitzgerald's other novels include *The Bookshop*, *Offshore* (for which she won the Booker Prize), and *The Blue Flower*. Mary Wesley's *Part of the Furniture*, also set in World War II London and Muriel Spark's *A Far Cry from Kensington* are also witty explorations of their characters' lives.

## Ford, Richard
### Independence Day
Knopf. 1995. 451 pp.

New Jersey real estate agent Frank Bascombe's plans for a trip to the Basketball Hall of Fame with his troubled teenage son go awry.

**2d Appeal**   Language                                                 Book Groups 📖

**Subjects**   Business and Businessmen • Fathers and Sons • Middle-Aged Men • Midlife Crisis • Pulitzer Prize Winners

**Now try**   In addition to *The Sportswriter*, in which Frank Bascombe is introduced, Ford's other books include *Women with Men: Three Long Short Stories* and *Wildfire*. Like Ford, John Updike, in his series of books about Rabbit Angstrom (*Rabbit, Run*, and others), evokes the angst of aging men. Bascombe's ennui and depression are similar to Binx Bolling's in Walker Percy's *The Moviegoer*. *Independence Day* also won a PEN/Faulkner Award.

## Frucht, Abby

### Polly's Ghost

Scribner. 2000. 362 pp.

Even after she dies giving birth to her seventh child Tip, Polly Baymiller continues to try to protect him from loneliness, sorrow, and the everyday aches and pains of growing up.

**Subjects**    Death of a Parent • Ghosts • Mothers and Sons

**Now try**    Frucht's other novels include *Are You Mine?* and *Life Before Death.* Another novel in which a mother's love is tested by extreme circumstances is Maxine Chernoff's *A Boy in Winter.* Ghosts also form part of the plot in Lisa Carey's *In the Country of the Young.*

## Gaines, Ernest

### A Lesson Before Dying

Knopf. 1993. 256 pp.

University-educated, agnostic, African American Grant Wiggins is coerced by an overbearing aunt to impart pride, knowledge, and religion to her best friend's godson Jefferson, a young man sentenced to die in the electric chair for a crime he didn't commit.

**2d Appeal**    Language                                    Book Groups 📖

**Subjects**    1940s • African American Authors • African Americans • ALA Notable Books • American South • Friendship • Louisiana • Men's Friendships • National Book Critics Circle Award Winners • Oprah Winfrey Selection • Racism

**Now try**    Gaines's other books include *The Autobiography of Miss Jane Pittman* and *A Gathering of Old Men.* Another novel that packs a similar emotional punch is Ernest Hill's *A Life for a Life.* Other books set in Mississippi are William Faulkner's *As I Lay Dying* and Eudora Welty's *The Optimist's Daughter.* The poignancy of the diary Jefferson keeps while he is in prison is also found in the diary described in Daniel Keyes's *Flowers for Algernon.*

## Gale, Patrick

### Tree Surgery for Beginners

Faber. 1999. 275 pp.

Murder suspect Lawrence Frost, usually happiest living among trees, tries self-transplantation to help get his life back together after his family deserts him.

**Subjects**    Adultery • British Authors • California • Murder • Older Women/Younger Men • Psychological Fiction • Tree Surgeons • Trees

**Now try**    Several of Gale's other novels have farcical or satirical elements, including *Kansas in August*, *Facing the Tank*, and *Little Bits of Baby.* Plot twists involving coincidences as well as the California setting are reminiscent of Armistead Maupin's *Tales of the City* and its sequels. (Gale also wrote a biography of Maupin.) Other stories that begin with murder but are decidedly comedic are Mark Childress's *Crazy in Alabama* and Sue Townsend's *Rebuilding Coventry.*

## Gardner, Mary
### Milkweed
Papier-Maché Press. 1993. 307 pp.

Susan, who grew up an orphan on the prairies of North Dakota, shocks her family and neighbors when she leaves her husband's farm to open a boardinghouse in town.

Book Groups 📖

**Subjects**    Eccentrics and Eccentricities • Minnesota • Mothers and Daughters • North Dakota • Orphans • Single Mothers • Women's Lives

**Now try**    Gardner is also the author of the novels *Keeping Warm* and *Boat People*. Susan's frustrations and spirit are similar to those of Susan, the main character in Wallace Stegner's *Angle of Repose*, and Edna Pontellier, the heroine of Kate Chopin's *The Awakening*. Other novels about a woman's difficult life include Kent Haruf's *The Tie That Binds* and Carol Shields's *The Stone Diaries*.

## Gates, David
### Preston Falls
Knopf. 1998. 337 pp.

Doug Willis takes a leave of absence from his unfulfilling job in public relations and goes to his family's vacation home in Preston Falls, a small town in upstate New York, where his dissatisfaction and distaste for the life he's been leading cause him to make decisions that will affect his family.

Book Groups 📖

**Subjects**    Cocaine • Drugs and Drug Abuse • Fathers Deserting Their Families • Marriage • Middle-Aged Men • Midlife Crisis • New York

**Now try**    Gates is also the author of a novel, *Jernigan*, and a collection of stories, *The Wonders of the Invisible World*. Other men suffering from middle-aged angst can be found in *Rabbit, Run* by John Updike and Richard Ford's *Independence Day*.

## George, Anne Carroll
### This One and Magic Life
Avon Books. 1999. 276 pp.

After the death of Artie Sullivan, her family gathers in Mobile Bay, Alabama, and tries to find peace with her passing, with the lives they have all led, and with each other.

**Subjects**    Alabama • American South • Art and Artists • Family Relationships • Southern Authors • Twins

**Now try**    George also writes the Southern Sisters mystery series; some of the titles include *Murder Makes Waves* and *Murder Runs in the Family*. Gail Godwin writes about family dynamics in *A Southern Family*. *Cakewalk* by Lee Smith shares the joyful sense of all things southern, while *Souls Raised from the Dead* by Doris Betts also depicts a southern family confronting death.

## Gilbert, Elizabeth
### Stern Men
Houghton Mifflin. 2000. 289 pp.

After she graduates from the New Hampshire boarding school where she's spent her high school years, 18-year-old Ruth Thomas returns home to Fort Niles Island, off the coast of Maine, to live with her lobsterman father, visit with her eccentric friends, and decide what she wants to do with her life.

Book Groups 📖

**Subjects**   Eccentrics and Eccentricities • First Novels • Fishing • Maine • Teenage Girls

**Now try**   Gilbert is also the author of *Pilgrims*, a collection of short stories. Gilbert's novel has the same high spirits and quirky characters that are found in John Irving's novels (*The Cider House Rules* and *The World According to Garp*, among others). Cathie Pelletier is another novelist whose books (*The Funeral Makers* and *Once Upon a Time on the Banks*, among others), set in Maine, are filled with eccentric characters.

## Giles, Molly
### Iron Shoes
Simon & Schuster. 2000. 239 pp.

Nothing is going right for Kay Sorensen: Her glamorous (and nasty) mother is dying, her emotionally cold father keeps her at arm's length, and her marriage is falling apart.

**Subjects**   California • Coming-of-Age • Fathers and Daughters • Husbands and Wives • Illness • Mothers and Daughters • Terminal Illness

**Now try**   Giles is also the author of two collections of stories: *Rough Translations* and *Creek Walk and Other Stories*. Other novelists who combine tragedy and comedy in their work include Lewis Nordan (*The Sharpshooter Blues*) and Hilary Mantel (*Every Day Is Mother's Day* and *Vacant Possession*).

## Golding, Michael
### Benjamin's Gift
Warner Books. 1999. 299 pp.

In 1930, Jean Pierre Michel Chernovsky—still fabulously wealthy despite the depression—adopts Benjamin, a young boy orphaned by the double suicide of his parents, and learns that the youngster has the power to magically transport himself from one place to another—through both the past and present.

Book Groups 📖

**Subjects**   Coming-of-Age • Magic Realism • Older Women/Younger Men • Orphans

**Now try**   Golding is also the author of *Simple Prayers*. Magic realism is also woven into Isabel Allende's *The House of the Spirits* and *Eva Luna*, Lawrence Thornton's *Imagining Argentina*, and Abby Frucht's *Polly's Ghost*.

## Goldman, Francisco
### The Ordinary Seaman
Atlantic Monthly Press. 1997. 387 pp.

A group of Central Americans discover that the cargo ship they were recruited to man is a burned-out ex-Japanese freighter owned by a couple of deadly incompetents, and at the same time they realize that they are trapped on the ship by their lack of English and money and by the gangs on the Brooklyn waterfront.

**2d Appeal**   Setting                                                              Book Groups 📖

**Subjects**   Boats and Boating • Central America • Gangs • Immigrants and Refugees • Latinos in America • Political Fiction • Working Classes

**Now try**   Goldman's first novel, *The Long Night of White Chickens*, deals with the ugly politics of Guatemala during the time of the death squads, as does Patricia Henley's ***Hummingbird House***. Other intense political novels include Ward Just's ***A Dangerous Friend***, James Buchan's ***The Persian Bride***, and Graham Greene's ***The Honorary Consul*** and ***The Power and the Glory***.

## Govrin, Michal
### The Name
Riverhead Books. 1998. 375 pp.

Amalia, troubled daughter of Holocaust survivors, gives up a promising career as a photographer in New York to live as an Orthodox Jew in Jerusalem. Translated from the Hebrew by Barbara Harshav.

**2d Appeal**   Setting                                   Book Groups 📖

**Subjects**   First Novels • Holocaust • Israel • Israeli Authors • Jerusalem, Israel • Jews and Judaism • Novels in Translation • Photography and Photographers • Religion

**Now try**   Simone Zelitch's ***Louisa*** also weaves together the present and the past in its account of the lasting effects of the Holocaust.

## Gowdy, Barbara
### Mister Sandman
Steerforth Press. 1997. 268 pp.

A quirky middle-class family copes with raising the oldest daughter's illegitimate child, a strange, silent girl with remarkable musical talent, who becomes the repository for the family's secrets and deceptions.

Book Groups 📖

**Subjects**   Canadian Authors • Eccentrics and Eccentricities • Family Relationships • Family Secrets • Gay Men • Lesbians • Music and Musicians

**Now try**   Gowdy also wrote ***Through the Green Valley*** and ***The White Bone***. ***Even Cowgirls Get the Blues*** by Tom Robbins also centers around a character who can be termed a "freak." Tim Winton's ***Cloudstreet*** portrays relationships in a family filled with quirky characters.

## Graver, Elizabeth
### The Honey Thief
Hyperion. 1999. 263 pp.

Pre-teen Eva, living unhappily in a small town in upstate New York where her mother Miriam has moved them in the hope that it will nip her daughter's kleptomania in the bud, finds her life changing for the better when she meets Burl, a former lawyer and now beekeeper, who is living alone and raising bees on his grandparents' farm.

Book Groups 📖

**Subjects**   Bees and Beekeeping • Kleptomania • Mental Illness • Mothers and Daughters • New York • Single Men • Single Mothers

**Now try**   Graver is also the author of ***The Unravelling*** and ***Have You Seen Me? A Recipe for Bees*** by Gail Anderson-Dargatz is another novel in which bees and beekeeping also play an important part.

## Griesemer, John

### No One Thinks of Greenland Picador USA. 2001. 310 pp.

When Corporal Rudy Spruance is sent to an army base in Qanggatarsa, Greenland, as its public information officer, he begins to uncover some of its secrets and is forced to make difficult choices about the people he's come to love.

**2d Appeal** Story                                    Book Groups 📖

**Subjects** First Novels • Greenland • Korean War • Love Stories • Military Hospitals • Soldiers • U.S. Army

**Now try** The affecting and understated quirkiness of the plot and characters is reminiscent of *Horace Afoot* and *Henry of Atlantic City* by Frederick Reuss, *Biggest Elvis* by P. F. Kluge, and *The Man in the Window* by Jon Cohen.

**3**

## Grimsley, Jim

### Comfort and Joy Algonquin Books of Chapel Hill. 1999. 291 pp.

Dr. Ford McKinney had a hard enough time admitting to himself that he was attracted to hospital administrator Dan Crell, but even more difficult is telling his southern aristocrat parents, whose lifelong expectations have been that Ford will return to Savannah, marry, and have children.

Book Groups 📖

**Subjects** Coming Out • Family Relationships • Gay Men • Georgia • Love Stories

**Now try** Grimsley is also the author of *My Drowning*, as well as *Winter Birds*, which is about Dan Crell's childhood. Other novels about gays and lesbians coming out to their family and friends include Brian Bouldrey's *Genius of Desire*, Peter Lefcourt's *The Dreyfus Affair: A Love Story*, and David Leavitt's *The Lost Language of Cranes*.

## Grimsley, Jim

### My Drowning Algonquin Books of Chapel Hill. 1997. 58 pp.

Ellen Tote's triumphant survival of the abuse, neglect, and poverty of her North Carolina childhood is undermined by two recurring dreams.

Book Groups 📖

**Subjects** Alcoholics and Alcoholism • American South • Brothers and Sisters • Child Abuse • Male/Female Relationships • North Carolina • Poverty • Suicide

**Now try** Grimsley also wrote *The Winter Birds* and *Dream Boy*, his debut novel about young homosexual love and child abuse. Dorothy Allison's *Bastard Out of Carolina* and Alice Walker's *The Color Purple* both show the effects of abuse and neglect on the lives of women.

## Hall, Sands

### Catching Heaven Ballantine Books. 2000. 374 pp.

Sisters Maud and Lizzie—whose lives have taken very different turns—find themselves dealing with crises in their lives involving careers, relationships, and family ties.

Book Groups 📖

**Subjects**   Actors and Acting • American Southwest • Art and Artists • First Novels • Love Affairs • New Mexico • Single Mothers • Sisters

**Now try**   Other novels about sisters include Libby Schmais's *The Perfect Elizabeth*, Jo-Ann Mapson's *The Wilder Sisters* (also set in New Mexico), and Karen Karbo's *The Diamond Lane*. Other novels that take place in New Mexico include Robert Boswell's *American Owned Love* and Rick Collignon's *Perdido*.

## Hamilton, Jane
### The Short History of a Prince                    Random House. 1998. 349 pp.

During his adolescence, Walter must come to terms with his growing realization that he is gay, as well as with the death of his older brother.

**2d Appeal**   Story                                    Book Groups 📖

**Subjects**   Ballet Dancers • Brothers • Coming Out • Dancers and Dancing • Death of a Sibling • Gay Men • Gay Teenagers

**Now try**   Hamilton is also the author of *The Book of Ruth* and *A Map of the World*. Other young men struggling to understand their sexuality can be found in Michael Cunningham's *A Home at the End of the World* and Ben Neihart's *Hey, Joe*.

## Harris, Joanne
### Chocolat                                          Viking. 1999. 242 pp.

Newly arrived in a small French town, Vianne Rocher opens a confectionary, serving up a sympathetic ear and, always, the perfect piece of chocolate.

**Subjects**   Chocolate • Culinary Arts • France • Gypsies • Small-Town Life

**Now try**   Harris is also the author of *Blackberry Wine*, set in the same French village where *Chocolat* takes place. Other novels in which food plays an important part are *Like Water for Chocolate* by Laura Esquivel, *Bread Alone* by Judith Ryan Hendricks, and *The Priest Fainted* by Catherine Temma Davidson.

## Harrison, Jim
### The Road Home                              Atlantic Monthly Press. 1998. 446 pp.

Over a period of nearly a century, four generations of the Northridge family endure difficulties of family relationships, struggles with racism, and coming to terms with death and dying.

**2d Appeal**   Setting                                  Book Groups 📖

**Subjects**   Adoption • American Indians • Death and Dying • Family Relationships • Lakota Sioux Indians • Mothers and Sons • Multigenerational Novels • Novels with Multiple Viewpoints

**Now try**   This novel completes the story begun in *Dalva*, when the book's namesake begins to search for the son she gave up for adoption. Harrison's other books include *Legends of the Fall* and *Julip*. Another novel told from multiple points of view is *English Passengers* by Matthew Kneale. Kiana Davenport's *Shark Dialogues* is another multigenerational novel.

## Harrison, Kathryn
### Thicker Than Water
Random House. 1991. 271 pp.

A young woman raised by her grandparents struggles to understand her distant, unloving mother and her confusing relationship with her father.

Book Groups 📖

**Subjects**   Coming-of-Age • Eating Disorders • Family Relationships • First Novels • Grandparents • Incest • Mothers Deserting Their Families

**Now try**   Harrison is also the author of the novels *Poison*, *Exposure*, and *The Binding Chair: A Visit from the Foot Emancipation Society*. Her memoir, *The Kiss*, is an account of her consensual affair with her father. Other novels that deal with father-daughter incest include Jane Smiley's *A Thousand Acres* and Ann-Marie MacDonald's *Fall On Your Knees*.

**3**

## Haruf, Kent
### Plainsong
Knopf. 1999. 301 pp.

In the prairie town of Holt, Colorado, Bobby and Ike Guthrie try to understand why their mother is acting strangely; meanwhile, their father Tom, a high school teacher, faces the reality of raising his sons alone; a pregnant teenager is thrown out of her house by her angry mother; and the McPherons, two lifelong bachelors, find that there is room for more in their lives than raising cattle.

Book Groups 📖

**Subjects**   American West • Bachelors • Brothers • Colorado • Mothers Deserting Their Families • Small-Town Life • Teachers • Teenage Girls • Teenage Pregnancy

**Now try**   Haruf's first novel was *The Tie That Binds*. The harsh realities of life described in such stark detail in Haruf's novel can also be found in J. Robert Lennon's *On the Night Plain* and Karla Kuban's *Marchlands*.

## Hawkes, G. W.
### Gambler's Rose
MacMurray & Beck. 2000. 231 pp.

When Charlie Halloran (son, grandson, and great-grandson of card sharks) meets mathematician Lia O'Donel, he decides he has to give up gambling—but not before his father ropes him into one last high-stakes game.

**Subjects**   Boats and Boating • Brothers • Fathers and Sons • Gamblers and Gambling • Love Stories • Mathematics

**Now try**   Hawkes's other novels include *Surveyor* and *Semaphore*. Gamblers are the main characters in Robert Bausch's *A Hole in the Earth*, Jim Nelson's *Compulsive*, and Frederick Barthelme's *Bob the Gambler*.

## Haynes, David
### **YA** Right by My Side
New Rivers Press. 1993. 181 pp.

Teenager Marshall Field Finney tries to make the best of a bad time when his mother runs off to find herself and Marshall is left behind with his hard-drinking father.

**Subjects**   African American Authors • African Americans • Alcoholics and Alcoholism • Coming-of-Age • Fathers and Sons • First Novels • Mothers and

Sons • Mothers Deserting Their Families • Race Relations • St. Louis, Missouri • Teenage Boys • Teenagers

**Now try**    Haynes also wrote *Live at Five* and *All American Dream Dolls*. Another teenager trying to make sense of changes in her world is Willie Tarrant in Thulani Davis's *1959*.

## Heller, Zoe
### Everything You Know                                    Knopf. 2000. 203 pp.

While recuperating in Mexico from a heart attack, Willy Muller finds his past intruding into his present as he works on a screenplay about his wife's suspicious death and reads the journal his daughter Sadie kept before she committed suicide.

**Subjects**    Death of a Child • Death of a Parent • Death of a Spouse • First Novels • Mexico • Suicide • Writers and Writing

**Now try**    Willy's narrative voice is reminiscent of the voice of the main character in Steve Tesich's *Karoo* and Mark Helprin's hero in *Memoir from Antproof Case*.

## Hendrie, Laura
### Remember Me                                    Henry Holt. 1999. 373 pp.

In the small town of Queduro, New Mexico, 29-year-old Rose Devonic is an outcast—disliked by the townspeople for her independence and sharp intelligence—so when her landlord and only friend, elderly bachelor Birdie, has a stroke and his older sister threatens to sell the motel where Rose has been living, she is forced to reassess her position in Queduro, her assumptions about the past, and her plans for the future.

**2d Appeal**    Setting                                    Book Groups 📖

**Subjects**    Alzheimer's Disease • American Southwest • Bachelors • Embroidery • New Mexico • Small-Town Life • Stroke Patients

**Now try**    Hendrie's first novel, *Stygo*, set in a small Colorado town, was a nominee for a PEN/Hemingway Award. Two other novels set in small New Mexico towns are Antonya Nelson's *Nobody's Girl* and Rick Collignon's *Perdido*.

## Hijuelos, Oscar
### Empress of the Splendid Season                        HarperFlamingo. 1999. 342 pp.

Lydia Espana comes to New York in the 1940s with high hopes of love and success; she marries and raises a family, only to find herself a widowed cleaning lady in Harlem, far from her wealthy roots in pre-Castro Cuba.

Book Groups 📖

**Subjects**    Cuba • Cuban Authors • Family Relationships • Latino Authors • Latinos • Latinos in America • New York • Widows

**Now try**    Hijuelos won the Pulitzer Prize for his novel *The Mambo Kings Play Songs of Love*. He also wrote *Our House in the Last World*. Other almost-larger-than-life characters can be found in Gabriel Garcia Marquez's *Love in the Time of Cholera*. Other novels about a cleaning woman (although totally different in tone and setting) are Paul Gallico's *Mrs. 'Arris Goes to Paris* and its sequels. Cristina Garcia, author of *The Aguero Sisters*, is another Cuban author.

## Hillmer, Timothy
### The Hookmen
University Press of Colorado. 1994. 244 pp.

To earn a living while caring for his alcoholic father, Roy Cruz takes a job with the Forest Service recovering drowned bodies from the Kern River.

Book Groups 📖

**Subjects**   Alcoholics and Alcoholism • American West • Colorado • Coming-of-Age • Fathers and Sons • First Novels • Park Rangers

**Now try**   Hillmer's novel won the Colorado Fiction Award. Another work of fiction centered on water is Norman Maclean's *A River Runs Through It, and Other Stories*. Joe Coomer's *The Loop* also features a man with an unusual job.

## Hobbie, Douglas
### This Time Last Year
Henry Holt. 1998. 324 pp.

During a summer spent apart from his wife, and mourning the death of his daughter, Henry Ash discovers that the best way to honor the dead is to live life to the fullest.

Book Groups 📖

**Subjects**   Death and Dying • Death of a Child • Middle-Aged Men • Vermont

**Now try**   Hobbie is also the author of *The Day*, *Being Brett*, and *Boomfell*. Other novels about middle-aged men trying to understand their lives include the equally somber *The Sportswriter* and *Independence Day* by Richard Ford, David Gates's *Preston Falls*, as well as the far more humorous *Straight Man* by Richard Russo.

## Hoffman, Alice
### Illumination Night
G.P. Putnam's Sons. 1992. 224 pp.

Andre and Vonny's marriage is threatened by a lack of money and their teenaged neighbor's obsession with Andre.

**2d Appeal**   Language                                    Book Groups 📖

**Subjects**   ALA Notable Books • American Northeast • Magic Realism • Marriage • Martha's Vineyard, Massachusetts • New England • Obsessive Love • Older Men/Younger Women • Teenage Girls

**Now try**   Ann Patchett's novels, *Taft*, *The Patron Saint of Liars*, and *The Magician's Assistant*, are similar in tone to Hoffman's books. Other novels set on Martha's Vineyard include Anne Rivers Siddons's *Up Island* and Dorothy West's *The Wedding*.

## Hoffman, Alice
### The River King
G.P. Putnam's Sons. 2000. 324 pp.

The drowning or suicide of Gus, a new (and unpopular) student at an exclusive prep school in Haddan, Massachusetts, prompts an investigation that threatens to reveal some of the school's darkest secrets.

Book Groups 📖

| | |
|---|---|
| **Subjects** | American Northeast • Ghosts • Love Stories • Massachusetts • New England • Policemen • Private Schools • Small-Town Life • Suicide • Teachers • Teenage Boys • Teenagers |
| **Now try** | Hoffman's novels generally deal with both the mundane and the magical, as in *Practical Magic* and *Turtle Moon*. Other novelists who spin equally haunting tales include Amy Herrick (*At the Sign of the Naked Waiter*) and Michael Grant Jaffe (*Skateaway*). Novels that use the claustrophobic world of private schools for their settings include Thomas H. Cook's *The Chatham School Affair*, Robert Cormier's *The Chocolate War*, and Jacquie Gordon's *Flanders Point*. |

## Hornby, Nick
### About a Boy
Riverhead Books. 1998. 307 pp.

Will Freeman pretends that he is a single father so that he can meet single mothers, but instead of true love, he finds very depressed Fiona and her 12-year-old son Marcus, who is as uncool and square as Will is cool and hip.

| | |
|---|---|
| **2d Appeal** | Story |
| **Subjects** | ALA Notable Books • British Authors • Depression • Humorous Fiction • London, England • Single Men • Single Mothers • Single Women • Teenage Boys |
| **Now try** | Hornby's other novels include *High Fidelity* and *How to Be Good*. He is also the author of *Fever Pitch*, a memoir. Other bittersweet novels about boys include Steve Kluger's *Last Days of Summer* and Michael Downing's *Breakfast with Scot*. |

## Howard, Maureen
### A Lover's Almanac
Viking. 1998. 270 pp.

The lives of two pairs of lovers—one pair in their 30s and one in their 70s—are interwoven with bits of history, astrology, art, technology, and excerpts from the *Old Farmers' Almanac*.

| | |
|---|---|
| **2d Appeal** | Language |
| **Subjects** | Art and Artists • Elderly Men • Elderly Women • Love Affairs • Millennium • New York • Orphans |
| **Now try** | Howard's other novels include *Natural History* and *Expensive Habits*. Like Maureen Howard, Iris Murdoch (*Jackson's Dilemma*, *The Book and the Brotherhood*) is another erudite, intelligent novelist. The wittiness of Howard's novel is reminiscent of Robertson Davies's *The Rebel Angels*. |

## Huddle, David
### The Story of a Million Years
Houghton Mifflin. 1999. 189 pp.

When 15-year-old Marcy has a secret affair with Robert, her mother's best friend's husband, the repercussions are felt for decades afterward in the lives of Marcy, her husband, and their closest friends, as well as Robert and his wife Suzanne.

Book Groups 📖

| | |
|---|---|
| **Subjects** | Adultery • First Novels • Husbands and Wives • Love Affairs • Novels with Multiple Viewpoints • Older Men/Younger Women |
| **Now try** | Huddle's other books include three short story collections: *Tenorman*, *Intimates*, and *Only the Little Bone*. Other novels told from multiple points of view include Stephen Dixon's *Interstate*, John Burnham Schwartz's *Reservation Road*, and Russell Banks's *The Sweet Hereafter*. |

## Huffey, Rhoda
### The Hallelujah Side
Delphinium Books. 1999. 262 pp.

Roxanne Fish battles her family (social misfits one and all) and their Assemblies of God fundamentalism on her spiritual quest for truth and her adolescent need for independence.

**Subjects**    1950s • American Midwest • Coming-of-Age • First Novels • Humorous Fiction • Iowa • Religion • Religious Extremism • Teenage Girls • Teenagers

**Now try**    Other novels narrated in the voice of a young girl are Meera Syal's *Anita and Me*, Lisa Shea's *Hula*, Esther Freud's *Hideous Kinky*, and Martha McPhee's *Bright Angel Time*. Other novels about religious fundamentalism include Sheri Reynolds's *The Rapture of Canaan* and David James Duncan's *The Brothers K*.

## Hull, Jonathan
### Losing Julia
Delacorte. 2000. 358 pp.

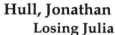

During his experiences in the trenches in France during World War I and the final stages of his life in a nursing home, Patrick Delaney finds comfort in his close friendships and dark humor, and is filled with longing for Julia.

Book Groups 📖

**Subjects**    Aging • Death and Dying • Elderly Men • First Novels • France • Historical Setting • Love Stories • Nursing Homes • World War I

**Now try**    Other novels that deal with the battle lines in France during World War I are Sebastien Japrisot's *A Very Long Engagement*, Australian author David Malouf's *The Bread of Time to Come*, Sebastian Faulks's *Birdsong*, and Erich Maria Remarque's *All Quiet on the Western Front*. Nursing home settings are central to Manuel Puig's *Eternal Curse on the Reader of These Pages* and Marika Cobbold's *Guppies for Tea*.

## Irving, John
### A Widow for One Year
Random House. 1998. 537 pp.

Thirty-seven years in the life of Ruth Cole—from her unusual and unhappy childhood as the daughter of a famous writer to her development as a novelist, and her life as a wife and widow.

Book Groups 📖

**Subjects**    Adultery • Fathers and Daughters • Male/Female Relationships • Older Women/Younger Men • Widows • Women's Lives • Writers and Writing

**Now try**    Irving is also the author of *The World According to Garp*, *The Hotel New Hampshire*, *The Cider House Rules*, *The Fourth Hand*, and other novels. Although the characters are the main appeal of all of Irving's novels, his plots are like Charles Dickens's (*Bleak House*, and others) in their complications and intricacies. In addition, Irving shares with Dickens the ability to mix pathos and humor.

## Ishiguro, Kazuo
### The Unconsoled
Knopf. 1995. 535 pp.

Arriving in an unnamed and imaginary European city, presumably to give a piano recital, Ryder constantly confronts the uneasy feelings that he should know more than he does and that people expect more of him than he can give.

**2d Appeal**    Language                                              Book Groups 📖

    **Subjects**    ALA Notable Books • British Authors • Japanese Authors • Male/Female Relationships • Music and Musicians

    **Now try**    This, Ishiguro's fourth novel following *The Remains of the Day*, *A Pale View of the Hills*, etc., is suffused with an uncomfortable, dreamlike quality that is strongly reminiscent of the works of Franz Kafka (*The Trial*). Although Ryder is unfamiliar with the variety of people he meets, they all seem to know him, much like the situation in which Alice finds herself in Lewis Carroll's *Alice in Wonderland*.

## Ishiguro, Kazuo
### When We Were Orphans
Knopf. 2000. 335 pp.

After the mysterious disappearance of his parents in post–World War I Shanghai, Christopher Banks is sent to live in England where he grows up to become a famous detective; the ultimate test of his skills comes when he returns to Shanghai in the 1930s to discover what happened to his mother and father.

Book Groups 📖

    **Subjects**    1930s • British Authors • China • Detectives • England • Japanese Authors • Loss of a Parent • Memory • Mystery • Shanghai, China

    **Now try**    Ishiguro is also the author of *A Pale View of the Hills*, *An Artist of the Floating World*, and *The Remains of the Day*. Other novels that illuminate life in China between the wars include J. G. Ballard's *Empire of the Sun* and Lisa Huang Fleischman's *Dream of the Walled City*.

## Jaffe, Michael Grant
### Skateaway
Farrar, Straus and Giroux. 1999. 260 pp.

Clem, Garrett, and Sam grow up in the shadow of their father's mental illness and their fear of what might happen as a result of their mother's job as a doctor in an abortion clinic.

Book Groups 📖

    **Subjects**    Abortion • American Midwest • Brothers and Sisters • Doctors and Patients • Family Relationships • Hockey • Mental Illness • Ohio

    **Now try**    Jaffe is also the author of the novel *Dance Real Slow*. Other brothers and sisters forced to cope with a difficult mother can be found in David James Duncan's *The Brothers K*.

## Janowitz, Tama
### A Certain Age
Doubleday. 1999. 317 pp.

In a short time, and through no real fault of her own, 32-year-old Florence Collins, desperate to find a wealthy husband, finds herself accused of killing a friend's daughter and sleeping with the same friend's husband, investing in a nonexistent restaurant, and winding up homeless in Manhattan.

**Subjects**   1990s • Adultery • Homelessness • Male/Female Relationships • New York • Satirical Fiction • Single Women

**Now try**   Janowitz's other novels include *Slaves of New York*, *The Male Cross-Dresser Support Group*, *A Cannibal in Manhattan*, and *American Dad*. Another novel of conspicuous consumption is Tom Wolfe's *The Bonfire of the Vanities*. Candace Bushnell's *Four Blondes* and Helen Fielding's *Bridget Jones: The Edge of Reason* are other novels about relationships and finding satisfactory partners.

# Kay, Jackie
## Trumpet
Pantheon. 1998. 278 pp.

Race and gender issues are explored in the life of (black) trumpet player Joss Moody, whose death reveals that he was really a woman, and who is mourned by his loving (white) wife, his angry and hurt adopted son, and a series of friends upon whom he left a lasting impression.

**2d Appeal**   Language                                        Book Groups 📖

**Subjects**   1950s • England • First Novels • Gender Roles • Interracial Relationships • Jazz • Music and Musicians • Racism • Scottish Authors

**Now try**   This first novel is based on the true story of Billy Tipton, a jazz musician who was only discovered to be a woman upon "his" death. A good biography of him is Diane Wood Middlebrook's *Suits Me: The Double Life of Billy Tipton*. Women disguised as men are featured in Isabel Allende's *Daughter of Fortune*, Sena Jeter Naslund's *Ahab's Wife*, and Susan Richards Shreve's *Daughters of the New World*. Transgender issues are dealt with in Patrick McCabe's *Breakfast on Pluto*, Chris Bohjalian's *Trans-Sister Radio*, and Rose Tremain's *Sacred Country*. Interracial marriage is the subject of *The Wedding* by Dorothy West. Dorothy Baker's *Young Man with a Horn*, Richard Hill's *Riding Solo with the Golden Horde*, and Rafi Zabor's *The Bear Comes Home* all explore the lives of jazz musicians.

# Kim, Patti
## YA A Cab Called Reliable
St. Martin's Press. 1997. 156 pp.

When Ahn Joo Cho is nine years old, a cab called Reliable carries away her mother and younger brother, leaving Ahn Joo and her father to make a life together as best they can.

Book Groups 📖

**Subjects**   Asian American Authors • Asian Americans • Asians in America • Fathers and Daughters • First Novels • Korean American Authors • Korean Americans • Mothers Deserting Their Families

**Now try**   Another novel about a mother who takes one child with her and leaves another behind when she moves away from home is Rahna Reiko Rizzuto's *Why She Left Us*.

## King, Lily
### The Pleasing Hour
Atlantic Monthly Press. 1999. 237 pp.

After giving up her illegitimate baby to her married older sister, 19-year-old Rosie leaves her New Hampshire home for a job as an au pair with the Tivots, a glamorous French family who live on a houseboat in Paris, where she immediately becomes enmeshed in the family dynamics.

**2d Appeal**   Story                                                             Book Groups 📖

**Subjects**   Adultery • Au Pairs • Family Relationships • First Novels • France • Single Women • Sisters

**Now try**   Although the tone of Diane Johnson's *Le Divorce* is much different from King's, it too contrasts American and French views of love and marriage. Other novels about au pairs include *Do Try to Speak as We Do* by Marjorie Leet Ford and Rachel Cusk's *The Country Life*.

## King, Thomas
### 🆈🅰 Truth and Bright Water
Atlantic Monthly Press. 1999. 266 pp.

Teenager Tecumseh's summer is filled with mysteries and wonderment: why his cousin Lum must suffer his father's beatings with no one to help him; why his aunt Cassie has returned home; what project Monroe Swimmer, the town's most famous native son has planned; and whether Tecumseh's parents will get back together.

**2d Appeal**   Setting                                                           Book Groups 📖

**Subjects**   Abusive Relationships • ALA Notable Books • American Indian Authors • American Indians • Child Abuse • Coming-of-Age • Dogs • Fathers and Sons • Montana • Small-Town Life • Teenage Boys • Teenagers

**Now try**   King is also the author of *Green Grass, Running Water*, which takes place in a small town not far from *Truth and Bright Water*. Both Sherman Alexie (*Reservation Blues* and *The Lone Ranger and Tonto Fistfight in Heaven*) and Susan Power (*The Grass Dancer*) are American Indian writers whose works are set on American Indian reservations. Another coming-of-age novel is John Grisham's *A Painted House*.

## Kingsolver, Barbara
### Animal Dreams
HarperCollins. 1990. 342 pp.

Cosima Noline returns to her hometown of Grace, Arizona, to teach biology at the local high school and learns her own lessons about love, family, and the past.

**2d Appeal**   Setting                                                           Book Groups 📖

**Subjects**   ALA Notable Books • Alzheimer's Disease • Arizona • Ecofiction • Family Secrets • Fathers and Daughters • Love Stories • Sisters • Small-Town Life

**Now try**   Among Kingsolver's other books are *The Poisonwood Bible* and *Pigs in Heaven*. The well-evoked southwestern setting of this novel can also be found in *Going Back to Bisbee* by Richard Shelton, as he describes a trip he takes through Arizona's desert.

## Kingsolver, Barbara
### The Poisonwood Bible
HarperFlamingo. 1998. 546 pp.

The wife and four daughters of evangelical Baptist minister Nathan Price take turns telling the story of the family's experiences when they moved to the Congo in 1959.

**2d Appeal**   Setting                                      Book Groups 📖

**Subjects**   Africa • Congo • Death of a Child • Family Relationships • Fathers and Daughters • Ministers, Priests, Rabbis • Mothers and Daughters • Novels with Multiple Viewpoints • Oprah Winfrey Selection • Political Fiction • Sisters

**Now try**   Kingsolver's other novels include *The Bean Trees* and *Pigs in Heaven*. Other political fiction set in Africa includes Julian Pierce's *Speak Rwanda*, Giles Foden's *The Last King of Scotland*, and Ronan Bennett's *The Catastrophist*. Adam Hochschild's *King Leopold's Ghost* is a good work of nonfiction to read in conjunction with Kingsolver's novel, as it provides the context for the situation in which the Price family find themselves.

## Klima, Ivan
### Judge on Trial
Knopf. 1993. 549 pp.

In 1968, Adam Kindl is designated as the judge in a murder trial in Prague, but as the trial progresses he begins to realize the government has actually put him on trial as a test of his loyalty to the Communist Party. Translated from the Czechoslovakian by A. G. Brian.

**2d Appeal**   Setting                                      Book Groups 📖

**Subjects**   ALA Notable Books • Communism • Concentration Camps • Czechoslovakia • Czechoslovakian Authors • Eastern Europe • Eastern European Authors • Novels in Translation • Political Fiction

**Now try**   Klima is also the author of *Love and Garbage*, *The Ultimate Intimacy*, *No Saints or Angels*, and *My Golden Trades*. Milan Kundera's *The Book of Laughter and Forgetting* combines the personal with the political. *A Desert in Bohemia* by Jill Paton Walsh describes the experiences of a group of people in a fictionalized Czechoslovakia during and after World War II.

## Kluger, Steve
### 🆈🅰 Last Days of Summer
Bard. 1998. 353 pp.

In the years leading up to World War II, Joey Margolis finds a difficult childhood made easier by his sometimes stormy, but always loving, relationship with Charlie Banks, third baseman for the New York Giants.

**2d Appeal**   Story

**Subjects**   1940s • Baseball • Brooklyn, New York • Epistolary Novels • First Novels • Friendship • Jews and Judaism • World War II

**Now try**   Kluger is also the author of *Yank, the Army Weekly: World War II from the Guys Who Brought You Victory* and a play, "Bullpen: A Late Inning Comedy." This poignant and funny novel has the same sweetness that can be found in Frederick Reuss's *Henry of Atlantic City* and Jon Cohen's *The Man in the Window*.

## Kowalski, William
### Eddie's Bastard
HarperCollins. 1999. 367 pp.

William Amos Mann IV (Billy) tells the story of his life from the time his grandfather finds him lying in a basket on the doorstep with a note that says "Eddie's Bastard," up until his father's death almost two decades later; along the way, Billy also shares stories about the rip-roaring lives of his father, grandfather, and great-grandfather.

**2d Appeal**   Story

**Subjects**   Coming-of-Age • First Novels • Grandparents • New York • Orphans

**Now try**   Kowalski is also the author of *Somewhere South of Here*. *Eddie's Bastard* is similar in its enthusiasm, narrative voice, and numerous subplots to the novels of John Irving (*The World According to Garp*) and Larry Baker's *The Flamingo Rising*.

## Lasser, Scott
### Battle Creek
Rob Weisbach Books. 1999. 265 pp.

Gil Davison, whose volunteer job coaching an amateur baseball team is far more important than anything else in his life, hopes that his dying father will live to see Gil's team win the national championship and finally give his approval to Gil's love of baseball.

**Subjects**   Baseball • Fathers and Sons • First Novels • Men's Friendships • Michigan

**Now try**   Other novels in which baseball plays an important part are Steve Kluger's *Last Days of Summer*, Nancy Willard's *Things Invisible to See*, and David James Duncan's *The Brothers K*, although Lasser's writing style is much more laconic and spare than the others. Three classic baseball novels are Bernard Malamud's *The Natural*, Robert Coover's *The Universal Baseball Association, Inc., J. Henry Waugh, Prop.*, and Mark Harris's *Bang the Drum Slowly*.

## Lee, Chang-Rae
### A Gesture Life
Riverhead Books. 1999. 356 pp.

Franklin "Doc" Hata's melancholy and repressed life running a surgical supply store and raising an adopted daughter in a wealthy New York suburb is shaped by his experiences as a medic in the Japanese army during World War II.

**2d Appeal**   Language                                    Book Groups 📖

**Subjects**   Adoption • ALA Notable Books • Asian American Authors • Asian Americans • Asians in America • Comfort Women • Korean American Authors • Korean-Japanese Relations • Single Mothers • Suburbia • World War II

**Now try**   Lee is also the author of *Native Speaker*, another ALA Notable Book. Other novels about the experience of "comfort women" during World War II include Nora Okja Keller's *Comfort Woman*, *Audrey Hepburn's Neck* by Alan Brown, and *Song of the Exile* by Kiana Davenport. The repressed nature of Hata's character is similar to the narrator of Kazuo Ishiguro's *The Remains of the Day*.

## Lee, Chang-Rae
### Native Speaker
G.P. Putnam's Sons. 1995. 324 pp.

Korean American Henry Park is hired to spy on politician John Kwang at the same time that he is trying to recover from the death of his son and his wife's decision to leave him.

**2d Appeal**   Language                                    Book Groups 📖

**Subjects**   ALA Notable Books • Asian American Authors • Asian Americans • Asians in America • Death of a Child • Fathers and Sons • First Novels • Husbands and Wives • Korean American Authors • Korean Americans

**Now try**   Like Lee's novel, both David Mamet's play, "Oleanna," and Eva Hoffman's memoir, *Lost in Translation: A Life in a New Language*, describe how language shapes our thoughts and behavior. David Carkeet's *Double Negative* is a much less serious look at the same topic.

## Lee, Helen Elaine
### Water Marked
Scribner. 1999. 319 pp.

Sunday Owens returns to the town of her birth and her estranged sister Delta so that the two can finally try to understand their father's life and death.

**2d Appeal**   Setting

**Subjects**   African American Authors • African Americans • Family Relationships • Fathers Deserting Their Families • Sisters • Small-Town Life

**Now try**   Lee's first novel was *The Serpent's Gift*. Other novels about African American families include Connie Porter's *All-Bright Court* and Dorothy West's *The Wedding*.

## Leebron, Fred
### Six Figures
Knopf. 2000. 224 pp.

When fund-raising professional Warren Lutz is accused of viciously attacking his wife Megan with a hammer, he, as well as the couple's friends and relatives, try to understand how he could do such a thing—if, indeed, he did it.

Book Groups 📖

**Subjects**   American South • Amnesia • Charlotte, North Carolina • First Novels • Husbands and Wives • North Carolina • Violence

**Now try**   Another husband who may or may not have assaulted his wife is found in Tim O'Brien's *In the Lake of the Woods*.

## Lennon, J. Robert
### The Funnies
Riverhead Books. 1999. 301 pp.

When wildly successful cartoonist Carl Mix dies, he leaves his comic strip to his wildly unsuccessful artist-son Tim, on the condition that Tim can convince the syndicators he can carry on his father's work.

**Subjects**   Brothers and Sisters • Cartoons and Cartooning • Comics • Dysfunctional Families • Family Relationships

**Now try**   Lennon is also the author of the novel *The Light of Falling Stars* and *On the Night Plain*. Another novel about the comics is Michael Chabon's *The Amazing Adventures of Kavalier & Clay*. The wry style of this novel is similar to that of Richard Russo's *Straight Man*.

## Lennox, Judith
### Some Old Lover's Ghost
Quill. 1999. 479 pp.

As Rebecca Bennett writes the biography of Dame Tilda Franklin, the loves, dreams, and tragedies of both women's lives are revealed.

**2d Appeal**   Setting

**Subjects**   British Authors • Death of a Child • England • Love Stories • Orphans • Research Novels • World War II • Writers and Writing

**Now try**   Other novels by Lennox include *The Secret Years* and *Till the Day Goes Down*. *Plainsong* by Kent Haruf shares the same quiet revelations of lives being lived as fully as they can, while Gail Godwin's *Father Melancholy's Daughter* and *The Journey Home* by Olaf Olafsson have similarly strong female characters searching for lives of their own. Joanna Trollope's novels, including *The Rector's Wife*, share a similar pace with Lennox's novel.

## Lesley, Craig
### The Sky Fisherman
Houghton Mifflin. 1995. 304 pp.

When Culver Martin and his mother return to the small town of Gateway, Culver begins to question the circumstances surrounding the death of his father, who was lost while fishing with Culver's Uncle Jake, a fishing guide, compatriot of the bull-throwing backroom boys, and a local hero loved by the whole tightly knit community.

**2d Appeal**   Setting                                                      Book Groups 📖

**Subjects**   1950s • American Indians • Coming-of-Age • Fishing • Mothers and Sons • Pacific Northwest • Small-Town Life

**Now try**   Lesley's earlier novels *Winterkill* and *River Song* also mix Northwest settings with indigenous characters and culture. Other writers who present the lure of outdoor life in the Pacific Northwest include Robin Cody (*Ricochet River*), Norman Maclean (*A River Runs Through It*), and David James Duncan (*The River Why*). Western storytellers with a slightly laconic tone but a surprisingly extravagant turn of phrase include Sherman Alexie (*The Lone Ranger and Tonto Fistfight in Heaven*), Ivan Doig (*This House of Sky*, *Dancing at the Rascal Fair*, and others), Anna Linzer (*Ghost Dancing*), David Long (*Blue Spruce*), and Larry Watson (*Montana 1948*).

## Leslie, Diane
### 🆈 Fleur de Leigh's Life of Crime
Simon & Schuster. 1999. 301 pp.

Growing up in Hollywood is not much fun for poor-little-rich-girl Fleur—she is cursed with self-centered parents, and a group of incompetent nannies, including an escapee from a mental hospital.

**Subjects**   1950s • California • Dysfunctional Families • First Novels • Hollywood • Humorous Fiction

**Now try**   Fleur is a resilient and resourceful little girl who is not unlike the main character in Patty Dann's ***Mermaids***, although Dann's is a more serious novel. The bittersweet humor of Leslie's novel can also be found in Carrie Fisher's ***Postcards from the Edge***, another story of growing up in Hollywood.

## Lipman, Elinor

**YA** The Inn at Lake Devine                                    Random House. 1998. 253 pp.

As a young teenager, Natalie Marx was stunned by the anti-Semitism her family encountered when they tried to stay at the Inn at Lake Devine; as an adult, Natalie finds her fate intertwined with that of the Berry family, owners of the inn.

**2d Appeal**   Story

**Subjects**   Anti-Semitism • Jews and Judaism • Love Stories • Male/Female Relationships • Resorts

**Now try**   Lipman is also the author of the novels ***The Dearly Departed***, ***The Way Men Act***, ***Isabel's Bed***, ***The Ladies' Man***, and ***Then She Found Me***. The sweetness and humor found in all of Lipman's novels can also be appreciated in Stephen McCauley's ***The Object of My Affection*** and ***The Easy Way Out***.

## Lively, Penelope

Spiderweb                                    HarperFlamingo. 1998. 218 pp.

When anthropologist Stella Brentwood retires to Somerset, England, she must finally decide if she wants to become part of the community there, or else continue to live her life as an observer.

Book Groups 📖

**Subjects**   Anthropologists and Anthropology • British Authors • England • Single Women • Women's Lives

**Now try**   Lively's other books include ***Moon Tiger*** and ***According to Mark***. Other British novelists who write with the same quiet authority about women living solitary lives are Anita Brookner (***The Debut***, ***Undue Influence***) and Barbara Pym (***Quartet in Autumn***, ***Excellent Women***).

## Livesey, Margot

The Missing World                                    Knopf. 2000. 325 pp.

Hazel's amnesia after an accident leaves her without memory of the previous three years—which gives her ex-lover Jonathan an opportunity to win her back through deceiving her about the state of their relationship when the accident occurred.

Book Groups 📖

**Subjects**   Actors and Acting • Amnesia • London, England • Male/Female Relationships • Scottish Authors

**Now try**   Livesey is also the author of the novels ***Eva Moves the Furniture***, ***Criminals***, and ***Homework***. Livesey's novels—with their emphasis on characters placed in often difficult or ambiguous situations—can be compared to Graham Swift's ***Waterland*** and Ward Just's ***A Dangerous Friend***.

## Mackay, Shena
### The Artist's Widow
Moyer Bell. 1999. 151 pp.

When well-known artist John Crane dies, he leaves his paintings to his wife Lyris, also an artist, who must now deal with the slighty batty friends, relatives, and friends of relatives who make demands on her and her legacy.

**Subjects** Art and Artists • Death of a Spouse • Eccentrics and Eccentricities • Scottish Authors • Widows • Women Artists

**Now try** Mackay is also the author of *The Orchard on Fire* and *A Bowl of Cherries*. Novels about artists include Joyce Cary's *The Horse's Mouth*, Fernanda Eberstadt's *When the Sons of Heaven Meet the Daughters of the Earth*, Jane Urquhart's *The Underpainter*, and Salman Rushdie's *The Moor's Last Sigh*.

## Macy, Caitlin
### Fundamentals of Play
Random House. 2000. 289 pp.

George Lenhart observes his friends—his wealthy Dartmouth roommate Chatland Wethers and lower-class Harry Lombardi, Dartmouth dropout turned successful venture capitalist—as they vie for the heart of Kate Goodenow, the woman George knows is unattainable for himself.

**2d Appeal** Setting

**Subjects** 1980s • Business and Businessmen • First Novels • Lower Classes • Male/Female Relationships • Men's Friendships • New York • Upper Classes

**Now try** Reading Macy's novel brings to mind the milieu of F. Scott Fitzgerald's *The Great Gatsby*, and Kate Goodenow is not unlike Daisy Buchanan, while George Lenhart resembles Nick Carraway, Fitzgerald's narrator. Other novels set in Manhattan in the 1980s include Jay McInerney's *Brightness Falls* and Tom Wolfe's *The Bonfire of the Vanities*.

## Maitland, Sara
### Ancestral Truths
Henry Holt. 1994. 295 pp.

Clare is unable to remember what happened when she and her abusive lover were mountain climbing in Zimbabwe—all she knows is that David is missing and that her right hand has been amputated.

**2d Appeal** Language        Book Groups 📖

**Subjects** Abusive Relationships • ALA Notable Books • Amnesia • British Authors • Deafness • Family Relationships • Middle-Aged Women • Mystery • Physical Disabilities

**Now try** Maitland's other novels include *Daughter of Jerusalem* and *Three Times Table*, the latter about a day in the life of three generations of women living in a house in London. Cees Nooteboom's *The Following Story* also deals with amnesia. Marianne Wiggins's novel *Almost Heaven* is also about a woman who is unable to remember the events surrounding a terrible accident.

## Malone, Michael
### Foolscap
Little, Brown. 1991. 392 pp.

Theo Ryan, a professor of theater studies, finds his life in turmoil when he becomes the biographer of a hard-living, hard-loving, hard-drinking playwright.

**2d Appeal**   Story

**Subjects**   Academia • ALA Notable Books • Humorous Fiction • Male/Female Relationships • North Carolina • Research Novels • Writers and Writing

**Now try**   Malone's other novels include three character-driven mysteries, *Time's Witness*, *First Lady*, and *Uncivil Seasons*, and a much darker novel, *Dingley Falls*. Richard Russo's *Straight Man* shares some of the same exhilarating writing that is found in *Foolscap*.

## Mapson, Jo-Ann
### The Wilder Sisters
HarperFlamingo. 1999. 364 pp.

At 35 Lily returns home to her family's New Mexico farm to understand the direction her life has taken and discovers that her older sister Rose is also trying to cope with huge changes in her own life.

**2d Appeal**   Story

**Subjects**   Alcoholics and Alcoholism • American Southwest • New Mexico • Sisters • Widows

**Now try**   Mapson's other novels include *Blue Rodeo*, *Shadow Ranch*, *Hank and Chloe*, and *Loving Chloe*. Another novel about sisters that is set in New Mexico is Sands Hall's *Catching Heaven*.

## Martin, Valerie
### Italian Fever
Knopf. 1999. 259 pp.

When her employer DV, a second-rate novelist, dies unexpectedly, 30-ish Lucy Stark goes to Italy to handle the funeral arrangements and ship back his possessions, but instead she catches a dreadful case of the flu, embarks on a passionate love affair with a married man, and perhaps meets up with DV's ghost, all of which force her to rethink her view of herself as being plain, practical, and utterly reliable.

**2d Appeal**   Setting

**Subjects**   Ghosts • Italy • Love Affairs • Single Women • Writers and Writing

**Now try**   Martin's other novels include *The Great Divorce* and *Mary Reilly*. Other women who travel to Europe and discover they are not quite the person they always thought they were can be found in Diane Johnson's *Le Divorce* and *Le Mariage* and Lily King's *The Pleasing Hour*.

## McCabe, Patrick
### Breakfast on Pluto
HarperFlamingo. 1998. 202 pp.

In the midst of trying to find "Mr. Dark and Brooding," Patrick "Pussy" Braden, a transvestite prostitute, faces consequences of Ireland's religious strife.

**2d Appeal**   Language                                    Book Groups 📖

**Subjects**   1970s • Ireland • Irish Authors • Prostitutes and Prostitution • Religious Extremism • Sexual Identity • Transvestites

**Now try**    Other novels by McCabe include *The Butcher Boy* and *The Dead School*. The character in contemporary fiction who comes closest to Pussy's concerns about dress, dating, and finding the right man is Bridget Jones, the heroine of Helen Fielding's *Bridget Jones's Diary*. Jonathan Ames's novel *The Extra Man* is also about transvestites.

## McCabe, Patrick
### The Butcher Boy
Fromm International. 1993. 215 pp.

Disarmingly boisterous Francie Brady narrates his own troubled childhood in 1960s Ireland, a journey from grubby street kid to pathetic monster.

**2d Appeal**    Language                                                    Book Groups 📖

**Subjects**    1960s • Coming-of-Age • Ireland • Irish Authors • Murder • Sociopaths • Teenage Boys • Violence • Working Classes

**Now try**    McCabe is also the author of *The Dead School* and *Breakfast on Pluto*. Another novel about a pathetic monster is William Trevor's *Felicia's Journey*. A true monster of a human being can be found in Joyce Carol Oates's *Zombie*. Other novels with the same emotional ring as McCabe's book include Alan Sillitoe's *The Loneliness of the Long Distance Runner*, Anthony Burgess's *A Clockwork Orange*, *Acts of Revision* by Martyn Bedford, and *The History of Luminous Motion* by Scott Bradford. *The Butcher Boy* was short-listed for the 1992 Booker Prize.

## McCafferty, Jane
### One Heart
HarperCollins. 1999. 291 pp.

Sisters Gladys and Ivy struggle to understand the deaths of Gladys's children, the love they both have for Gladys's ex-husband James, and their own challenging relationship.

Book Groups 📖

**Subjects**    Death of a Child • First Novels • Love Affairs • Sisters

**Now try**    McCafferty is also the author of *Director of the World*, a short story collection that won the 1992 Drue Heinz Literature Prize. The insight McCafferty brings to complicated family relationships and the compromises people are forced to make in the face of love and sorrow are also found in Elizabeth Strout's *Amy and Isabelle*. Another novel about two sisters in love with the same man is Elizabeth Hay's *A Student of Weather*.

## McCauley, Stephen
### The Man of the House
Simon & Schuster. 1996. 287 pp.

Adult education teacher Clyde Carmichael finds his life turned upside down by his difficult father, his roommate's ex-lover Louise, Louise's young son, and their engaging stray dog.

**Subjects**    Cambridge, Massachusetts • Dogs • Friendship • Gay Men • Single Mothers • Teachers

**Now try**    McCauley's other novels include *The Object of My Affection* and *The Easy Way Out*. McCauley's fondness for his characters brings to mind Elinor Lipman's novels *The Inn at Lake Devine*, *Isabel's Bed*, *The Way Men Act*, and others, as well as Mark O'Donnell's *Getting Over Homer*.

## McEwan, Ian
### Amsterdam
N.A. Talese. 1999. 193 pp.

After Molly Lane's painful and lingering death, two of her many former lovers make a pact to assist each other in dying if the right circumstances arise—but they neglect to define the circumstances.

Book Groups 📖

**Subjects**    Booker Prize Winners • British Authors • Composers • Journalists • Men's Friendships • Music and Musicians

**Now try**    McEwan's other novels include *Black Dogs*, *Enduring Love*, and *The Innocent*. Another novel about a composer is Bernard MacLaverty's *Grace Notes*. E. L. Doctorow's *The Waterworks* is also about a newspaper editor investigating political corruption. Francine Prose writes humorously about tabloid journalism in *Bigfoot Dreams*.

## McEwen, Todd
### Arithmetic
Jonathan Cape. 1998. 184 pp.

In 1960s Orange County, California, Joe Lake's life is defined by his experiences in kindergarten, his difficulty understanding arithmetic, his best friend Fard, his love of the science books by Dr. Herbert S. Zim, boy scouts, and his addiction to cartoons.

**Subjects**    1960s • Boys' Lives • California • Coming-of-Age • Humorous Fiction

**Now try**    McEwen is the author of *Fisher's Hornpipe* and *McX: A Romance of the Dour*. Another novel about the life of a boy around Joe's age is *An Ocean in Iowa* by Peter Hedges, although Hedges's novel does not have the humor of McEwen's.

## McGhee, Alison
### Shadow Baby
Harmony Books. 2000. 243 pp.

Eleven-year-old Clara winter (she prefers to spell her last name with a lowercase *w*) searches for the truth about her grandfather and her father (both of whom she's never met), as well as her twin sister, who died at birth.

**2d Appeal**    Story                                                    Book Groups 📖

**Subjects**    Coming-of-Age • Mothers and Daughters • New York • Single Mothers • Twins

**Now try**    McGhee's first novel was *Rainlight*. Another novel about a missing twin is Kate Atkinson's *Behind the Scenes at the Museum*. The charm of this novel is Clara's voice—bright, curious, and fully knowledgable about the power of storytelling. Other novelists who convey the same sense in the life of a young girl include Karin Cook (*What Girls Learn*), Esther Freud (*Hideous Kinky*), and Patty Dann (*Mermaids*).

## McKinney-Whetstone, Diane
### Tempest Rising
Morrow. 1998. 280 pp.

When their parents' successful business fails in Philadelphia in 1985, three sisters are sent to live with foster caregiver Mae and her daughter Ramona, unexpectedly giving Mae a second chance to rebuild her relationship with Ramona.

Book Groups 📖

**Subjects**   1960s • African American Authors • African Americans • Child Abuse • Family Relationships • Foster Children • Mothers and Daughters • Philadelphia, Pennsylvania • Sisters

**Now try**   Among McKinney-Whetstone's other novels are *Tumbling* and *Blues Dancing*. The experience of a young woman in foster care is also explored in Janet Fitch's novel *White Oleander* and Richard Babcock's *Martha Calhoun*.

## McNally, T. M.
### Almost Home
Scribner. 1998. 235 pp.

Teenagers Patrick and Elizabeth's love for one another develops against a backdrop of easy drugs and troubled families.

**2d Appeal**   Story

**Subjects**   1970s • Alcoholics and Alcoholism • Arizona • Brothers and Sisters • Death of a Parent • Drugs and Drug Abuse • First Novels • Teenage Boys • Teenage Girls • Teenage Love • Teenagers

**Now try**   McNally is also the author of *Low Flying Aircraft* and *Until Your Heart Stops*, two short story collections. The tone of this novel is similar to that of David James Duncan's *The Brothers K* and Scott Spencer's *Endless Love* (although it lacks the claustrophobic feel of the latter). The relationship between Patrick and his older sister Caroline brings to mind the relationship described between the brother and sister in David Shields's *Dead Languages*.

## Messud, Claire
### The Last Life
Harcourt Brace. 1999. 352 pp.

Now an adult living in the United States, Sagesse LaBasse looks back on her French Algerian family's experiences as hoteliers in France, trying to understand how quickly their lives fell apart after her grandfather shot some teenagers who he felt were making too much noise in the hotel's pool.

Book Groups 📖

**Subjects**   Algeria • Dysfunctional Families • France • Suicide • Teenage Girls

**Now try**   Messud's first novel was *When the World Was Steady*; she is also the author of *The Hunters: Two Short Novels*. Other novels set in Algeria include Albert Camus's *The First Man* and Assia Djebar's *So Vast the Prison*.

## Miller, Sue
### Family Pictures
Harper & Row. 1990. 389 pp.

With the birth of their third child, an autistic boy, Lainie and David's marriage slowly and inexorably comes to an end.

**2d Appeal**    Story                                    Book Groups 📖

   **Subjects**    ALA Notable Books • Autism • Brothers and Sisters • Dysfunctional Families • Marriage • Mothers and Sons

   **Now try**    Miller's other books include *The Good Mother* and *For Love*. *Saving St. Germ* by Carol Muske-Dukes and Frederick Busch's *Girls* are both about marriages in trouble over issues relating to children.

## Miller, Sue
### While I Was Gone
Knopf. 1999. 265 pp.

Middle-aged Joey Becker, normally happy in her roles as wife, mother, and veterinarian, suddenly finds herself terribly dissatisfied with the status quo when Eli Mayhew, a man she knew a quarter century before, reenters her life.

**2d Appeal**    Story                                    Book Groups 📖

   **Subjects**    Adultery • Family Relationships • Husbands and Wives • Marriage • Murder • Oprah Winfrey Selection • Veterinarians

   **Now try**    Miller's other novels include *The World Below* and *The Distinguished Guest*. Lynne Sharon Schwartz's *Disturbances in the Field* is another thoughtful novel about marriage and the ease with which a good life can come to a crashing end.

## Mills, Magnus
### All Quiet on the Orient Express
Arcade Publishing. 1999. 211 pp.

When a young man agrees to stay on a few days as a handyman after a holiday in England's Lake District, one task after another seems to bind him more firmly to the campground and the somewhat sinister employer he keeps planning to leave.

**2d Appeal**    Language

   **Subjects**    Black Humor • England • Humorous Fiction • Scottish Authors • Single Men • Small-Town Life

   **Now try**    Mills's first novel is *The Restraint of Beasts*. Another novel with the same sort of mild black humor is Hans-Ulrich Treichel's *Lost*.

## Mills, Magnus
### The Restraint of Beasts
Arcade Publishing. 1998. 214 pp.

Fence builders and champion slackers Tam and Richie travel from their home in Scotland to England on a job with their ineffective English foreman, leaving in their wake a dead man, saggy fences, and work undone.

   **Subjects**    Black Humor • First Novels • Humorous Fiction • Laborers • Scotland • Scottish Authors • Working Classes

**Now try**   Mills is also the author of ***Three to See the King*** and ***All Quiet on the Orient Express***, another novel filled with sly, unsettling humor. ***The Restraint of Beasts*** was short-listed for both the Whitbread Award and the Booker Prize in Great Britain.

## Mootoo, Shani
### Cereus Blooms at Night
Grove Press. 1998. 249 pp.

As the gender-bending Nurse Tyler gains the trust of his seemingly insane ward Mala, he begins to unravel the tragic secrets of her past.

**2d Appeal**   Setting                                                                                      Book Groups 📖

**Subjects**   Canadian Authors • Child Abuse • Elderly Women • First Novels • Gay Men • Gender Roles • Incest • India • Lesbians • Mothers Deserting Their Families • Nurses • Sexual Identity

**Now try**   Mootoo's writing style and tone are very similar to Isabel Allende's (***Eva Luna***, and others). The struggle the characters in Mootoo's novel have with gender roles and identity recall the characters in Jeanette Winterson's novels ***The Passion*** and ***Written on the Body***, as well as Dinitia Smith's ***The Illusionist***, David Ebershoff's ***The Danish Girl***, and Rose Tremain's ***Sacred Country***. Another novel about child abuse and incest is Georgia Savage's ***The House Tibet***. Mootoo's novel was a finalist for both the Giller Prize and the Ethel Wilson Fiction Prize, as well as being short-listed for the Chapters/Books in Canada First Novels Award.

## Morris, Mary McGarry
### A Dangerous Woman
Viking. 1991. 358 pp.

A longtime social outcast, novelist-vagabond Martha Horgan finds that her relationship with Colin Mackey both confuses and hurts her, but eventually drives her to attempt to take control of her life.

Book Groups 📖

**Subjects**   ALA Notable Books • Sexual Abuse • Small-Town Life • Vermont • Writers and Writing

**Now try**   ***Suspicious River*** by Laura Kasischke also details the life of a woman on the fringes of life. Dorothy Allison's ***Cavedweller*** is the story of an outsider who returns to her hometown and tries to make a place for herself.

## Morris, Mary McGarry
### Fiona Range
Viking. 2000. 418 pp.

Thirty-year-old Fiona Range, who is the town's (and her family's) bad girl—she describes herself as "a magnet for trouble"—tries to put her life in order, but, instead, falls in love with her cousin's fiancé.

**2d Appeal**   Story

**Subjects**   Adultery • Cousins • Family Secrets • Mothers Deserting Their Families • Single Women

**Now try**   Morris is also the author of ***Vanished***, a National Book Award nominee, and ***Songs in Ordinary Time***. Family secrets are also slowly revealed in Ann-Marie MacDonald's ***Fall On Your Knees*** and John Gregory Brown's ***Decorations in a Ruined Cemetery***.

## Mosley, Walter
### Always Outnumbered, Always Outgunned
W.W. Norton. 1998. 208 pp.

After 27 years in prison for a double murder, Socrates Fortlow grinds out a precarious life in Watts, battling his own and others' demons, and shaping a life of dignity with his rock-breaking hands.

Book Groups 📖

**Subjects**   African American Authors • African Americans • Ghetto Life • Homelessness • Los Angeles, California • Moral/Ethical Dilemmas • Murder • Poverty

**Now try**   The story of Socrates Fortlow is continued in *Walkin' the Dog*, while Mosley's *RL's Dream* depicts—with the same spare beauty—the daily struggles of the disenfranchised. John Edgar Wideman's *Brothers and Keepers*, *Philadelphia Fire*, and *All Stories Are True*, James Baldwin's *If Beale Street Could Talk*, and James Agee's *Let Us Now Praise Famous Men* all sound the painful majesty in hard and brutal lives.

## Murray, Yxta Maya
### What It Takes to Get to Vegas
Grove Press. 1999. 308 pp.

Rita Zapata, Queen of the Street Fighters in East Los Angeles, sees a rising young boxer as her ticket to recognition and respect in the neighborhood, but the curse of the Zapata women may be too much to overcome.

**Subjects**   Boxing • Coming-of-Age • Latinos • Latinos in America • Los Angeles, California • Mexican Americans • Mothers and Daughters • Sisters

**Now try**   Murray's first novel, *Locas*, deals with Mexican girl gangs in Los Angeles. Other novels spiced with Latina vitality include Julia Alvarez's *How the Garcia Girls Lost Their Accents* and *Yo!*, Sandra Benitez's *Bitter Grounds*, Ana Castillo's *So Far from God*, and Ana Veciana-Suarez's *The Chin Kiss King*. Boxing is an important element in the young lives of the main characters of Gus Lee's *China Boy* and Bryce Courtenay's *The Power of One*, and it forms part of the plot of some of Thom Jones's stories in *The Pugilist at Rest*, Deirdre McNamer's *One Sweet Quarrel*, Joyce Carol Oates's *You Must Remember This*, and Budd Schulberg's *The Harder They Fall*.

## Nahai, Gina B.
### Moonlight on the Avenue of Faith
Harcourt Brace. 1999. 376 pp.

When Lili is five years old, her mother Roxanna the Angel, believing she can escape her destiny, leaves her home in the Jewish community of Tehran and disappears; not until Lili is 18 does she learn what happened that night when she watched her mother seemingly grow wings and fly away.

**2d Appeal**   Setting                                           Book Groups 📖

**Subjects**   Ghetto Life • Immigrants and Refugees • Iran • Jews and Judaism • Los Angeles, California • Magic Realism • Mothers and Daughters • Mothers Deserting Their Families

**Now try**   Nahai's first novel was *Cry of the Peacock*, in which she also described the life of Jews in Iran. The magic realism Nahai employs is reminiscent of Isabel Allende's (e.g., *The House of the Spirits*) and Salman Rushdie's (e.g., *Midnight's Children*). Nahai has indicated that she is most influenced by the writings of Oriana Fallaci (*A Man*, *Letter to a Child Never Born*, and others). Another view of Jewish life in Iran is Dorit Rabinyan's *Persian Brides*, which is set at the beginning of the twentieth century.

## Naylor, Gloria
### Bailey's Café                                                    Harcourt Brace. 1992. 229 pp.

A small restaurant caters to a varied group of outcasts, misfits, and the walking wounded, each with a different and difficult story to tell.

**2d Appeal**   Language                                                          Book Groups 📖

**Subjects**   1940s • African American Authors • African Americans • ALA Notable Books • Cafés and Restaurants • Magic Realism

**Now try**   Naylor also wrote *The Women of Brewster Place* and *Linden Hills*. Gita Mehta's *A River Sutra* also uses the technique of having many characters tell their individual stories. Alice Hoffman's *Turtle Moon* also has a hint of magic realism. Other novels in which a café functions as part of the plot include Carson McCullers's *The Ballad of the Sad Café*, Fannie Flagg's *Fried Green Tomatoes at the Whistle Stop Cafe*, *Midnight Sandwiches at the Mariposa Express* by Beatriz Rivera, and *Buster Midnight's Cafe* by Sandra Dallas. *The Serpent's Gift* by Helen Elaine Lee and *Tumbling* by Diane McKinney-Whetstone are other portraits of African American community life.

## Nelson, Antonya
### Living to Tell                                                      Scribner. 2000. 317 pp.

The Mabie family of Wichita, Kansas, tries to adjust to the return of 33-year-old Winston, who has spent the previous five years in prison for the killing of his grandmother in a drunk-driving accident.

                                                                       Book Groups 📖

**Subjects**   ALA Notable Books • Brothers and Sisters • Cancer • Car Accidents • Drunk Driving • Family Relationships • Kansas • Sisters • Wichita, Kansas

**Now try**   Nelson's other books include *Talking in Bed*, *Nobody's Girl*, and *Family Terrorists*. Nelson's sense of both the strength and tenuous nature of family relationships brings to mind the novels of Anne Tyler, particularly *Dinner at the Homesick Restaurant* and *Searching for Caleb*.

## Nicholson, Geoff
### Female Ruins                                                    Overlook Press. 2000. 221 pp.

Kelly Howell, drifting through her 30s as a mini-cab driver in London, is still conflicted about her dead father, a fabulous architectural theorist who apparently built no buildings at all.

**Subjects**   Architects and Architecture • British Authors • Fathers and Daughters • London, England • Love Affairs

**Now try**   Among Nicholson's many other novels are *Bleeding London* (which was shortlisted for the Whitbread Prize) and *Flesh Guitar*. Architects are also the main characters in Penelope Lively's *City of the Mind*, Ayn Rand's *The Fountainhead*, Louis Begley's *As Max Saw It*, Richard Rayner's *The Cloud Sketcher*, and Henrik Ibsen's *The Masterbuilder*.

## Nordan, Lewis
### The Sharpshooter Blues
Algonquin Books of Chapel Hill. 1995. 291 pp.

When the two "lovely children" who try to rob the William Tell Grocery in the Mississippi Delta town of Arrow Catcher get shot and killed in the process, sweet and simple Hydro Raney decides to remove himself from the pain of it all.

**2d Appeal**   Setting                                     Book Groups 📖

**Subjects**   ALA Notable Books • American South • Black Humor • Fathers and Sons • Mississippi • Murder • Small-Town Life • Southern Authors

**Now try**   Nordan's other books include *Lightning Song* and *Boy with Loaded Gun: A Memoir*. Other novelists who mix tragic and comic elements in their novels include Pat Conroy in *The Prince of Tides*, John Irving in *A Widow for One Year*, and Steve Tesich in *Karoo*.

## O'Brien, Tim
### In the Lake of the Woods
Houghton Mifflin. 1994. 306 pp.

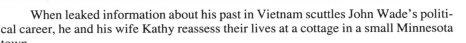

When leaked information about his past in Vietnam scuttles John Wade's political career, he and his wife Kathy reassess their lives at a cottage in a small Minnesota town.

**2d Appeal**   Story                                     Book Groups 📖

**Subjects**   ALA Notable Books • Marriage • Midlife Crisis • Minnesota • Mystery • Vietnam Veterans • Vietnam War

**Now try**   Other novels by O'Brien include *The Nuclear Age* and *Going After Cacciato*. *Seven Moves* by Carol Anshaw is another novel about a disappearance and how it affects those left behind. James McManus's *Going to the Sun* and Jon Cohen's *The Man in the Window* also have somewhat ambiguous endings.

## O'Dell, Tawni
### Back Roads
Viking. 2000. 338 pp.

With his mother in jail for murdering his father, 19-year-old Harley Altmyer finds his life is difficult enough raising his three younger sisters, but when he falls in love with Callie Mercer, the mother of his youngest sister's best friend, he sets into motion events that will change the lives of everyone he loves.

Book Groups 📖

**Subjects**   Dysfunctional Families • First Novels • Murder • Older Women/Younger Men • Oprah Winfrey Selection • Teenage Boys

**Now try**   Other teenagers caught up in difficult situations can be found in Tom McNeal's *Goodnight, Nebraska* and Janet Fitch's *White Oleander*.

## Offill, Jenny
### 🆈🅰 Last Things
Farrar, Straus and Giroux. 1999. 263 pp.

Eight-year-old Grace Davitt finds herself increasingly caught between her scientist father, who has a rational answer for everything, and a lovingly eccentric mother who is going mad.

Book Groups 📖

**Subjects**    First Novels • Mental Illness • Ornithologists • Road Novels • Science and Scientists • Vermont

**Now try**    Other novels that describe the world through the eyes of a child include Esther Freud's *Hideous Kinky*, Shena Mackay's *The Orchard on Fire*, and *An Ocean in Iowa* by Peter Hedges.

## Olafsson, Olaf
### The Journey Home                                              Pantheon. 2000. 296 pp.

As Disa, a cook in England, journeys home to Iceland, she remembers how she struggled to forge an independent life.

**2d Appeal**    Language                                              Book Groups 📖

**Subjects**    Coming-of-Age • Cooks • Culinary Arts • England • Iceland • Icelandic Authors • Terminal Illness • Women's Lives • World War II

**Now try**    Olafsson is also the author of the novel *Absolution*. *The Hours* by Michael Cunningham also weaves the past and present, time and place with exquisitely controlled language.

## O'Nan, Stewart
### 🆈🅰 Snow Angels                                              Doubleday. 1994. 305 pp.

Fifteen-year-old Arthur Parkinson faces two tragedies: the end of his parents' marriage and the murder of his beloved childhood babysitter.

Book Groups 📖

**Subjects**    ALA Notable Books • Divorce • First Novels • Murder • Pennsylvania • Teenage Boys

**Now try**    Other books by O'Nan include *The Circus Fire* (nonfiction), *Everyday People*, *A Prayer for the Dying*, and *In the Walled City*. *Hotel Paradise* by Martha Grimes is another novel in which a crime propels the coming-of-age of the main character. In William Maxwell's *So Long, See You Tomorrow*, a young man tries to understand the deaths of three people close to him. In 1996, *Granta Magazine* named O'Nan one of the "20 Best Young American Novelists."

## Ondaatje, Michael
### The English Patient                                              Random House. 1992. 307 pp.

In a bomb-damaged villa near Florence, Italy, as World War II draws to a close, a young nurse devotedly tends a mysterious "English" patient, a nameless burn victim haunted by his own memories of passion, betrayal, and rescue.

**2d Appeal**    Language                                              Book Groups 📖

**Subjects**    ALA Notable Books • Booker Prize Winners • Canadian Authors • Italy • Male/Female Relationships • North Africa • World War II

**Now try**    Ondaatje also wrote a memoir, *Running in the Family* (an ALA Notable Book), and three books of poetry that echo the themes of this novel. The heartbreak that runs throughout Ondaatje's novel can also be found in Anne Michaels's *Fugitive Pieces* and *Corelli's Mandolin* by Louis de Bernieres. Penelope Lively's *Moon Tiger* shares the North African setting with Ondaatje's novel. J. L. Carr's *A Month in the Country* is another novel that describes the effects of war on its survivors. Jim Crace's *Arcadia* is also written in vividly poetic prose. *The English Patient* won Canada's Governor General's Literary Award.

## Parks, Tim
### Goodness
Grove Weidenfeld. 1991. 185 pp.

Son of a murdered missionary and a mother who is an incurable optimist, George's attempt to escape his family and live a good life is challenged by his wife's unhappiness, which is exacerbated by the birth of their profoundly deformed and retarded daughter.

Book Groups 📖

**Subjects**   Adultery • ALA Notable Books • Black Humor • British Authors • Husbands and Wives • Physical Disabilities

**Now try**   Parks's other novels include *Tongues of Flame* (about the difficult life of an Anglican vicar), *Family Planning* (about a group of family members preoccupied with their own problems), and *Loving Roger* (about love and murder). Parks's worldview is shared by Kingsley Amis in *Lucky Jim*.

## Patchett, Ann
### The Patron Saint of Liars
Houghton Mifflin. 1992. 336 pp.

Rose embarks on a life filled with lies after she deserts her husband and ends up in a home for unwed mothers.

Book Groups 📖

**Subjects**   ALA Notable Books • First Novels • Kentucky • Male/Female Relationships • Nuns • Single Mothers

**Now try**   Patchett's other novels include *Taft* and *Bel Canto*. *The Sweetheart Season* by Karen Joy Fowler is another novel that raises the question of whether the narrator is reliable in the story she tells. Susan Pope's *Catching the Light* is also about a single mother keeping her baby.

## Pelletier, Cathie
### The Bubble Reputation
Crown. 1993. 290 pp.

When Rosemary's lover of eight years commits suicide while on a trip to London, only her eccentric family and a visit from her college roommate help her regain her own desire to live without William.

Book Groups 📖

**Subjects**   Art and Artists • Eccentrics and Eccentricities • Family Relationships • Gay Men • Maine • Mothers and Daughters • Sisters • Suicide

**Now try**   Pelletier is the author of *The Weight of Winter* and *Beaming Sunny Home*, among other novels. (She also writes under the name of K. C. McKinnon.) Other novels about the effects of suicide on those left behind include Kelly Dwyer's *Self-Portrait with Ghosts* and Madison Smartt Bell's *The Year of Silence*.

## Perrotta, Tom
### 🆈🄰 The Wishbones
G.P. Putnam's Sons. 1997. 290 pp.

When 31-year-old, guitar-playing, wedding-band-member Dave Raymond pops the question to the woman he's been dating—on and off—for the the last 15 years, he discovers just how ambivalent to marriage he is.

**2d Appeal**    Story

**Subjects**    1990s • ALA Notable Books • First Novels • Humorous Fiction • Love Affairs • Male/Female Relationships • Music and Musicians • Rock and Roll

**Now try**    Richard Russo's *Straight Man* has the same laugh-out-loud quality as this novel. *Jack Frusciante Has Left the Band* by Enrico Brizzi and *The Commitments* by Roddy Doyle are both entertaining novels about love and rock and roll.

## Phillips, Jayne Anne
### MotherKind
Knopf. 2000. 295 pp.

Single-mother Kate must balance the needs of her newborn son and those of her terminally ill mother, who has come to spend her final months of life with Kate.

**Subjects**    Cancer • Mothers and Daughters • Single Mothers • Terminal Illness

**Now try**    Phillips is also the author of the novels *Machine Dreams* and *Shelter*. Other novels dealing with the death of a parent include Karin Cook's *What Girls Learn* and Michael Ignatieff's *Scar Tissue*.

## Porter, Connie
### All-Bright Court
Houghton Mifflin. 1991. 224 pp.

The harsh realities of life over two decades confront the Taylor family after the promise of jobs and opportunity has drawn them from Mississippi north to a housing development adjacent to the mills outside Buffalo, New York.

Book Groups 📖

**Subjects**    African American Authors • African Americans • ALA Notable Books • Buffalo, New York • Family Relationships • First Novels • Housing Projects

**Now try**    The attitudes of Porter's black characters to whites is similar to the attitudes seen in Toni Morrison's characters in *Paradise*. Morrison's *Jazz* is also about African Americans who migrated north for a better life.

## Puertolas, Soledad
### Bordeaux
University of Nebraska Press. 1998. 143 pp.

Three marginally related characters struggle with isolation, self-knowledge, and melancholy expectations of love. Translated from the Spanish by Francesca Gonzalez-Arias.

**Subjects**    Career Women • Elderly Women • France • Latino Authors • Latinos • Loneliness • Novels in Translation • Single Men • Spanish Authors

**Now try**    Although he has written many novels and short stories, this is Puertolas's first novel to be translated into English. Novels about an earlier Spain include Emilia Pardo Bazan's *The House of Ulloa*, Victor Catala's *Solitude*, Merce Rodoreda's *The Time of the Doves* and *Camellia Street*, as well as the suspense novels of Arturo Pérez-Reverte (*The Club Dumas* and *The Flanders Panel* ). Other authors who describe their characters at points of quiet frustration in their lives include

Beryl Bainbridge (*A Quiet Life*, *The Dressmaker*), Anita Brookner (*Hotel du Lac*, *Brief Lives*), Gail Godwin (*Father Melancholy's Daughter*), Penelope Lively (*Moon Tiger*, *Perfect Happiness*), and Barbara Pym (*Excellent Women*, *Jane and Prudence*).

## Realuyo, Bino A.
### The Umbrella Country
Ballantine Books. 1999. 298 pp.

Living in poverty under martial law in the Philippines in the 1970s, Gringo must cope with his brother's obsession with dressing up as a girl, his father's violence, and his mother's emotional distance from her children.

**2d Appeal**   Setting                                    Book Groups 📖

**Subjects**   1970s • Asian American Authors • Coming-of-Age • Family Relationships • Fathers and Sons • Filipino American Authors • Filipino Authors • First Novels • Gay Teenagers • Manila, Philippines • Philippines • Teenage Boys

**Now try**   Two other novels set in the Philippines are Jessica Hagedorn's *Dogeaters* and Linda Ty-Casper's *DreamEden*. Other coming-of-age novels include Graham Salisbury's *Blue Skin of the Sea* and Ardashir Vakel's *Beach Boy*.

## Reiken, Frederick
### The Lost Legends of New Jersey
Harcourt Brace. 2000. 320 pp.

When Anthony Rubin's mother abandons her family (in the wake of her discovery of her husband's adultery), Anthony finds that his only solace in the resulting upheaval is his deepening friendship with Juliette Dimiglio, his next-door neighbor, whom he hopes to rescue from an abusive boyfriend, and a growing bond with his grandfather.

**Subjects**   1980s • Adultery • Family Relationships • Grandparents • Hockey • Mothers Deserting Their Families • New Jersey • Suicide • Teenage Boys • Teenage Girls • Teenagers

**Now try**   Reiken is also the author of *The Odd Sea*. Other sensitive novels about teenage boys include Enrico Brizzi's *Jack Frusciante Has Left the Band* and John Keegan's *Clearwater Summer*.

## Reuss, Frederick
### Henry of Atlantic City
MacMurray & Beck. 1999. 249 pp.

When his father, formerly chief of security at Caesar's Palace in Atlantic City, New Jersey, abandons him, six-year-old Henry relies on his photographic memory and the writings of the Gnostics—the heretical sect popular in the centuries after the death of Christ—to help him understand what is happening in his life.

**2d Appeal**   Story                                    Book Groups 📖

**Subjects**   Adoption • ALA Notable Books • Coming-of-Age • Fathers and Sons • Fathers Deserting Their Families • Gnosticism • New Jersey

**Now try**   Reuss's first novel, *Horace Afoot*, is blessed with an equally inventive plot and captivating main character. Another little boy, almost exactly Henry's age, who is also trying his best to understand the changes in his family and his world, can be found in Peter Hedges's *An Ocean in Iowa*.

## Richards, Elizabeth
### Rescue
Pocket Books. 1999. 276 pp.

When her teenaged stepson comes to live with Paige Austin and her husband, she finds that his presence eases her unhappiness about the death of her beloved father and her inability to conceive a child, yet at the same time it complicates her marriage.

**2d Appeal**    Story

**Subjects**    Family Relationships • Infertility • Juvenile Delinquents • Stepfamilies • Stepmothers • Teenage Boys

**Now try**    Richards is also the author of *Every Day*. The realistic dialogue and well-paced story brings to mind the novels of Judith Guest (*Ordinary People* and *Errands*) and Jacquelyn Mitchard (*The Deep End of the Ocean* and *A Theory of Relativity*).

## Robinson, Eden
### Monkey Beach
Houghton Mifflin. 2000. 384 pp.

When she learns that her younger brother Jimmy is lost at sea, 19-year-old Lisamarie Michelle Hill remembers incidents from her childhood and how she struggled to live in both the Western world and the world of her Haisla ancestors.

**2d Appeal**    Setting                                                    Book Groups 📖

**Subjects**    British Columbia, Canada • Brothers and Sisters • Canadian Authors • Canadian Indians • Coming-of-Age • Death of a Sibling • Family Relationships • First Novels • First Peoples • Grandparents • Haisla Indians

**Now try**    Robinson is also the author of the short story collection *Traplines*. Other novels that combine the spirit and real worlds are *Leaving Tabasco* by Carmen Bullosa and Nancy Willard's *Things Invisible to See*.

## Roth, Philip
### The Human Stain
Houghton Mifflin. 2000. 361 pp.

Coleman Silk, professor of classics at Athena College, is forced into retirement after a statement he makes is wrongly interpreted as a racial slur.

Book Groups 📖

**Subjects**    Academia • African Americans • College Professors • Racism • Sexism

**Now try**    Roth is the author of numerous other novels, including *Sabbath's Theater*, *My Life as a Man*, and *American Pastoral*. Another novel about a college professor dismissed from his position for questionable reasons is Michael Downing's *Perfect Agreement*, while the main character in J. M. Coetzee's *Disgrace* is dismissed from his academic appointment for sexual harassment.

## Roth, Philip
### I Married a Communist
Houghton Mifflin. 1998. 323 pp.

When his wife denounces him publicly for being a communist, Ira Ringold, well-known radio star, finds his career ruined and his life in disarray.

Book Groups 📖

**Subjects**    1950s • ALA Notable Books • Communism • Husbands and Wives

**Now try**    Roth's recurring character (and alter-ego) Nathan Zuckerman relates this tale, and appears as well in Roth's novels *Zuckerman Unbound*, *The Counterlife*, *The Ghost Writer*, and *The Prague Orgy*. Other novels about communism in the United States include Chaim Potok's *Davita's Harp*, Howard Fast's *The Pledge*, and Mark Lapin's *Pledge of Allegiance*.

## Russo, Richard
### Empire Falls
Knopf. 2001. 483 pp.

Miles Roby, proprietor of a greasy spoon in Empire Falls, New York, cannot bring himself to force any issue to its conclusion, including his desire to buy the restaurant, his feelings about his ex-wife's new husband, his daughter's odd new boyfriend, or the antics of his irascible father.

**2d Appeal**    Setting    Book Groups 📖

**Subjects**    Brothers and Sisters • Cafés and Restaurants • Fathers and Daughters • Father and Sons • Husbands and Wives • New York • Small-Town Life • Teenage Boys • Teenage Girls • Teenagers • Working Classes

**Now try**    Russo is also the author of *Straight Man*, *The Risk Pool*, and *Mohawk*. The same sense of a dying town and its inhabitants is conveyed in Rhian Ellis's *After Life*. Another totally uncontrollable father can be found in Michael Malone's *Handling Sin*.

## Russo, Richard
### Nobody's Fool
Random House. 1993. 549 pp.

Sully, a sometime construction worker in a small town in upstate New York who is down on his luck, still manages to keep from going completely under by helping out, or hindering when it's called for, the people who make up his community.

Book Groups 📖

**Subjects**    ALA Notable Books • Family Relationships • Humorous Fiction • Men's Friendships • New York • Single Men • Small-Town Life

**Now try**    Other books by Russo include *Straight Man*, *Empire Falls*, *The Risk Pool*, and *Mohawk*. Other books about men dealing with life in their own unique ways include Carol Shields's *Larry's Party*, the husband's half of the tale in Shields's *Happenstance*, and *Love Warps the Mind a Little* by John Dufresne.

## Salamanca, J. R.
### That Summer's Trance
Welcome Rain. 2000. 430 pp.

Ben Oakshaw and his wife Priscilla invite Ben's old lover and fellow drama student for a visit at their summer home on the Outer Banks, with disastrous results.

Book Groups 📖

**Subjects**    Actors and Acting • Adultery •American South • Husbands and Wives • Love Affairs • Marriage • North Carolina

**Now try**    Salamanca also wrote the novels *Lilith*, *Southern Light*, and *A Sea Change*. The return of a lover into one's life is also explored in Bernhard Schlink's *The Reader*.

## Schmais, Libby
### The Perfect Elizabeth: A Tale of Two Sisters                    St. Martin's Press. 2000. 240 pp.

Thirty-something Eliza Ferber finds her life barely tolerable (her boyfriend is unwilling to get married; she can't quite see that her future lies in walking dogs for a living) as her sister Bette's life takes a turn for the better when she falls in love with the ideal man.

**Subjects**    Actors and Acting • First Novels • New York • Sisters

**Now try**    The light tone of this novel is similar to that found in Diane Johnson's *Le Divorce*, Jennifer Weiner's *Good in Bed*, and Suzanne Finnamore's *Otherwise Engaged*.

## Schumacher, Julie
### The Body Is Water                                           Soho Press. 1995. 262 pp.

Pregnant, unmarried, and wondering what to do with her life, Jane Haus returns to her father's run-down house on the New Jersey shore and realizes that she needs to understand the past before she can deal with the future.

**2d Appeal**    Language                                        Book Groups 📖

**Subjects**    ALA Notable Books • Fathers and Daughters • First Novels • Mothers Deserting Their Families • New Jersey • Single Women • Sisters

**Now try**    Schumacher is also the author of *An Explanation for Chaos*, a collection of stories. The complicated relationship between Jane and her sister Bea is similar to the relationship of the sisters in Gail Godwin's *A Mother and Two Daughters*.

## Schwartz, Leslie
### Jumping the Green                                       Simon & Schuster. 1999. 270 pp.

The death of her sister Esther sends talented sculptor Louise Goldblum into the orbit of sexy and dangerous Zeke Heirholm, a photographer whose ideas of pleasure include inflicting pain.

**2d Appeal**    Story

**Subjects**    Art and Artists • Brothers and Sisters • Death of a Sibling • Family Relationships • First Novels • Love Affairs • San Francisco, California • Sisters

**Now try**    *Jumping the Green* won the James Jones Literary Society Award for best first novel. Another eccentric, though somewhat less self-destructive, family can be found in *The Funnies* by J. Robert Lennon. Louise will bring to mind the main characters in Susanna Moore's *In the Cut* and Kathryn Harrison's *Exposure*.

## Schwartz, Lynne Sharon
### In the Family Way                                            Morrow. 1999. 352 pp.

Psychotherapist Roy and his ex-wife Bea, a caterer, live in the apartment building owned by Bea's octogenarian mother Anna, along with various children, spouses, ex-spouses, and lovers.

**Subjects**    Divorce • Elderly Women • Husbands and Wives • Love Affairs • New York • Psychiatrists, Psychoanalysts, Psychotherapists

**Now try**    Other novels by Schwartz include *Disturbances in the Field* (a much darker novel), *Rough Strife*, and *Falling*. This witty comedy of manners is similar in tone to Diane Johnson's *Le Divorce* and *Le Mariage*. Another novel about new definitions of family is Laura Kalpakian's *Steps and Exes*.

## Schweighardt, Joan
### Virtual Silence
Permanent Press. 1995. 176 pp.

When her friend Bev is killed, Ginny retreats into silence, believing that it is the only way to deal with a violent world.

**Subjects**   Coming-of-Age • Friendship • New Jersey • Teenage Girls • Teenagers • Violence

**Now try**   Schweighardt is also the author of the novels *Island* and *Homebodies*. Other novels that consider various levels of criminal behavior include Jane Hamilton's *Disobedience* and Margot Livesey's *Criminals*.

## Scott, Joanna
### Make Believe
Little, Brown. 2000. 246 pp.

Three-year-old Bo becomes the object of a custody battle between his two very different sets of grandparents after his teenage mother dies in an automobile accident.

**2d Appeal**   Language                                             Book Groups 📖

**Subjects**   Custody Battles • Grandparents • Interracial Relationships • Novels with Multiple Viewpoints

**Now try**   Scott is also the author of the novels *The Manikin*, *Arrogance*, and *Fading, My Parmacheene Belle*, among other writings. Child custody is the subject of Carol Muske-Duke's *Saving St. Germ*, Jacquelyn Mitchard's *A Theory of Relativity*, and Sue Miller's *The Good Mother*.

## Senna, Danzy
### Caucasia
Riverhead Books. 1998. 353 pp.

Birdie takes after her white, New England–bred mother, while her sister Cole resembles her father, a black intellectual. When her father leaves her mother, he takes Cole with him, and both sisters separately struggle to make sense of their mixed heritage.

Book Groups 📖

**Subjects**   1970s • Biracial Characters • Coming-of-Age • Family Relationships • First Novels • Interracial Relationships • Sisters

**Now try**   Hettie Jones's *How I Became Hettie Jones*, a memoir written by the former wife of Amiri Baraka, essentially tells the same story from the point of view of Birdie and Cole's white mother. Another novel about a biracial child is Rosellen Brown's *Half a Heart*.

## Sharma, Akhil
### An Obedient Father
Farrar, Straus and Giroux. 2000. 282 pp.

Drunk one night, widower Ram Karan, a corrupt civil servant who lives with his widowed daughter Anita and granddaughter Asha in a Delhi slum, indulges himself in a sexual act; when his daughter Anita discovers what has occurred, it unleashes all of her repressed hatred of her father for his unspeakable behavior toward her 20 years before.

Book Groups 📖

**Subjects**   Family Relationships • Fathers and Daughters • First Novels • Incest • India • Indian Authors • Pedophilia • Political Fiction

**Now try**    Another unsympathetic but not totally despicable character (although he is unsympathetic for very different reasons) is found in David Gates's **Preston Falls**. Other novels set in India include Vikram Seth's **A Suitable Boy**, Anita Rau Badami's **The Hero's Walk**, and Pankaj Mishra's **The Romantics**.

## Sharp, Paula
### I Loved You All
Hyperion. 2000. 370 pp.

When Penny's mother enters an alcohol treatment center for the summer, Penny and her older sister Mahalia are left to the care and persuasion of right-wing fundamentalist and anti-abortion crusader Isabel Flood.

**2d Appeal**    Story                                                        Book Groups 📖

**Subjects**    Abortion • Alcoholics and Alcoholism • Dysfunctional Families • Mothers and Daughters • Religious Extremism • Sisters

**Now try**    Sharp is also the author of **Crows Over a Wheatfield**. Other novels that explore the dynamics of family life include David James Duncan's **The Brothers K**, Kate Atkinson's **Behind the Scenes at the Museum**, and Rhoda Huffey's **Hallelujah Side**.

## Sherrill, Steven
### The Minotaur Takes a Cigarette Break
John F. Blair. 2000. 313 pp.

Five thousand years tend to mellow even the fiercest monster, and the Minotaur—known as M to his friends—lives a simple life in Lucky-U Mobile Home Estates, driving his Vega to his chef's job at the rib joint across from a defunct Holiday Inn, and yearning (but only in a totally wholesome way) for waitress Kelly.

Book Groups 📖

**Subjects**    Cafés and Restaurants • Cooks • Culinary Arts • First Novels • Mythological Creatures • North Carolina • Southern Authors

**Now try**    The everyday problems of a monstrous/mythological personage can also be studied in John Barth's **Chimera**, Robert Coover's **Pinocchio in Venice**, John Gardner's **Grendel**, and Rachel Ingall's **Mrs. Caliban**. The everyday activities in a busy restaurant are also a major part of Fannie Flagg's **Fried Green Tomatoes at the Whistle Stop Cafe**, Anthony Powell's **Casanova's Chinese Restaurant**, Zadie Smith's **White Teeth**, and Lane Von Herzen's **Copper Crown**.

## Shields, Carol
### Larry's Party
Viking. 1997. 339 pp.

Larry Weller's life between 1977 and 1997 is shaped by his relationships with women and his growing interest in designing garden mazes.

**2d Appeal**    Story                                                        Book Groups 📖

**Subjects**    Coming-of-Age • Gardens and Gardening • Male/Female Relationships • Marriage • Mazes • Men's Lives • Middle-Aged Men • Winnipeg, Canada

**Now try**    Other middle-aged men coming of age can be found in Richard Ford's **The Sportswriter** and **Independence Day**.

## Shields, Carol, and Blanche Howard
### A Celibate Season
Penguin. 1999. 226 pp.

During their 10-month separation, attorney Jocelyn and her architect-husband Charles find the strengths and weaknesses of their marriage revealed in the letters they exchange.

Book Groups 📖

| | |
|---|---|
| **Subjects** | Architects and Architecture • Canada • Epistolary Novels • Husbands and Wives • Law and Lawyers • Marriage |
| **Now try** | Shields also wrote *Happenstance*, another novel that describes a marriage from the point of view of both the husband and wife. Anita Shreve in *Where or When* also uses this technique to tell the story of a relationship. |

## Shreve, Susan Richards
### Plum & Jaggers
Farrar, Straus and Giroux. 2000. 228 pp.

Years after he and his three younger siblings were orphaned by a terrorist bombing in Italy, Sam McWilliams turns that experience (and his obsessive need to protect his brother and sisters) into a series of comedy sketches.

| | |
|---|---|
| **2d Appeal** | Story |
| **Subjects** | Actors and Acting • Brothers and Sisters • Death of a Parent • Orphans • Television • Terrorists and Terrorism |
| **Now try** | Shreve is also the author of the novels *The Train Home* and *The Visiting Physician*. Other lives disrupted by terrorism can be found in Philip Roth's *American Pastoral*, Graham Greene's *The Comedians*, Robert Hellenga's *The Fall of a Sparrow*, David Malouf's *Child's Play*, and Ward Just's *The American Ambassador*. Orphans are the central characters of John Dufresne's *Louisiana Power and Light* and Jonathan Lethem's *Motherless Brooklyn*. |

## Smiley, Jane
### Horse Heaven
Knopf. 2000. 561 pp.

Multiple characters (human, equine, and canine) romp madly through the rich, sordid, sad, and euphoric world of horse racing.

| | |
|---|---|
| **Subjects** | Equestrians • Horse Racing • Horses • Humorous Fiction • Satirical Fiction |
| **Now try** | Jane Smiley is also the author of *The Age of Grief*, *Barn Blind*, and *Ordinary Love and Good Will*. Alyson Hagy's *Keeneland* also mixes a variety of strong characters around the world of horse racing. |

## Smiley, Jane
### Moo
Knopf. 1995. 414 pp.

At the midwestern university affectionately nicknamed Moo U, members of the administration and faculty are their normal eccentric selves, even as a secret experimental project involving a large hog named Earl Butz is underway.

| | |
|---|---|
| **2d Appeal** | Setting |
| **Subjects** | Academia • College Professors • Eccentrics and Eccentricities • Humorous Fiction • Male/Female Relationships • Satirical Fiction |

Now try  Smiley's other novels include *The Greenlanders* and *Duplicate Keys*. Other satires of academia include David Lodge's *Changing Places* and Randall Jarrell's *Pictures from an Institution*.

## Spencer, Scott
### The Rich Man's Table
Knopf. 1998. 271 pp.

Billy Rothchild is obsessed with getting to know the man he believes is his father—rock legend Luke Fairchild—and to have Luke acknowledge that Billy is his son.

Book Groups 📖

Subjects  Coming-of-Age • Fathers and Sons • Music and Musicians
Now try  Spencer is also the author of the novels *Waking the Dead*, *Men in Black*, and *Endless Love*. Billy's father is loosely based on folk music legend Bob Dylan, and Dylan's own novel, *Tarantula*, makes a good companion read. Although the tone of Angela Carter's *Wise Children* is satirical and witty (which Spencer's novel is not), it is also about twin girls trying to get their elusive father to acknowledge them.

## St. John, Madeleine
### A Stairway to Paradise
Carroll & Graf. 1999. 185 pp.

When journalist Alex meets Barbara, who has been hired to care for his children while he and his wife are away from home, he finds his marriage of convenience more and more inconvenient, yet he can't quite bring himself to abandon his children.

Subjects  Adultery • British Authors • Love Affairs • Triangles
Now try  St. John's other novels include *The Essence of the Thing*, *A Pure Clear Light*, and *The Women in Black*. Another novel about two men and the woman they both love, marked by the same sort of witty dialogue and ironic tone, is Julian Barnes's *Talking It Over*. St. John's novel is less densely written than Iris Murdoch's *A Fairly Honourable Defeat*, although St. John shows the same deep insight into human behavior.

## Stollman, Aryeh
### The Far Euphrates
Riverhead Books. 1997. 206 pp.

Alexander, a rabbi's son growing up in Windsor, Ontario, during the 1950s and 1960s, is deeply affected by secrets having their origin in Hitler's concentration camps.

Book Groups 📖

Subjects  ALA Notable Books • Canada • Coming-of-Age • Family Secrets • First Novels • Holocaust • Jews and Judaism • Ontario, Canada • World War II
Now try  The moral questions raised by this novel are the same sort that Chaim Potok explores in *The Chosen* and *The Promise*. *The Sparrow* by Mary Doria Russell is also concerned with questions of faith, forgiveness, and belief. Mordecai Richler's *Joshua Then and Now* is another novel about a young man coming of age in Canada.

## Strout, Elizabeth
### Amy and Isabelle

Random House. 1998. 303 pp.

When Isabelle Goodrow discovers that her daughter Amy has been having an affair with her high school mathematics teacher, the former close relationship between mother and daughter is stretched to the breaking point.

**2d Appeal**   Story  Book Groups 📖

**Subjects**   First Novels • Illegitimate Children • Mothers and Daughters • New England • Older Men/Younger Women • Small-Town Life • Teenage Girls

**Now try**   Katie Singer's *The Wholeness of a Broken Heart* is another novel in which the loving relationship between a mother and daughter is suddenly changed. Like Anne Tyler (*The Clock Winder*, and other novels) and Alice Munro (*The Moons of Jupiter*, and other books), Strout sympathetically examines the often difficult emotional states of her characters.

## Sullivan, Faith
### What a Woman Must Do

Random House. 2000. 205 pp.

Bess—about to go off to college in the fall—becomes involved with a married man; and her great-aunt Katie and cousin Harriet, who raised her after the death of her parents, find themselves torn between memories of the past and the demands and desires of the present.

**Subjects**   1950s • Aunts • Cousins • Family Relationships • Love Affairs • Minnesota • Orphans • Teenage Girls

**Now try**   Sullivan is also the author of the novels *The Cape Ann* and *The Empress of One*. Another novel of a young woman involved with a married man is Elizabeth Strout's *Amy and Isabelle*.

## Suri, Manil
### The Death of Vishnu

W.W. Norton. 2001. 295 pp.

Vishnu lies dying and dreaming on the first-floor landing of the Bombay apartment where he has been the houseboy, while the neighbors argue over ghee and water and who will pay the ambulance to take him away.

**2d Appeal**   Story

**Subjects**   Bombay, India • Death and Dying • First Novels • Hindus • India • Indian Authors • Muslims

**Now try**   Both Rohinton Mistry in *A Fine Balance* and Peggy Payne in *Sister India* convey the deep distrust and hatred that exist in contemporary India between Hindus and Muslims. Iris Murdoch's *Bruno's Dream* is another novel about a man in the process of dying.

## Swift, Graham
### Last Orders

Knopf. 1996. 295 pp.

Driving from London to scatter their friend Jack's ashes along the English coast, Vic, Ray, Lenny, and Jack's son Vince look back on their intertwined lives with humor and wonder.

**2d Appeal**   Language   Book Groups 📖

Subjects   ALA Notable Books • Booker Prize Winners • British Authors • Men's Friend-ships • Men's Lives • World War II

Now try   Swift also wrote *Learning to Swim and Other Stories* and *Waterland*. Another novel about a group of old friends traveling together is Bob Greene's *All Summer Long*. In addition to its other honors, *Last Orders* also won the James Tait Black Award.

## Tarloff, Erik
### The Man Who Wrote the Book
Crown. 2000. 308 pp.

Nebbishy itinerant professor Ezra Gordon gets out of a rut and into hot water when he anonymously authors *Every Inch a Lady*, a blockbuster pornographic novel.

Subjects   Academia • College Professors • Humorous Fiction • Pornography • Sex and Sex-uality • Writers and Writing

Now try   Tarloff is also the author of *Face-Time: A Novel*. Other witty novels whose themes touch on those of Tarloff's novel include Michael Chabon's *Wonder Boys*, Anne Bernays's *Professor Romeo*, *Changing Places* and *Small World* by David Lodge, Philip Roth's *Portnoy's Complaint*, *Erasure* by Percival Everett, and *The Russian Girl* by Kingsley Amis.

## Theroux, Marcel
### A Stranger in the Earth
Harcourt Brace. 1998. 279 pp.

When 22-year-old Horace Littlefair leaves the country to work in London at his great-uncle's newspaper, he becomes involved in a series of events involving a broken netsuke, illegal immigrants, killer Scrabble games, nightclubs, corruption, gardening, and the fate of the urban fox.

Subjects   Eccentrics and Eccentricities • England • First Novels • Humorous Fiction • Jour-nalists • London, England • Newspapers

Now try   Theroux is also the author of *The Confessions of Mycroft Holmes: A Paper Chase*. Another novel about a young man who comes to London to make his for-tune is Henry Fielding's *Tom Jones*. The tone of Theroux's novel brings to mind Magnus Mills's *Restraint of Beasts* and *All Quiet on the Orient Express*.

## Thornton, Lawrence
### Naming the Spirits
Doubleday. 1995. 257 pp.

When she arrives at the home of a couple whose daughter is among the Disappeared in Ar-gentina (victims of the political repression) in order to carry the final testimony of 11 missing people, Teresa is unable to speak.

2d Appeal   Language                                          Book Groups 📖

Subjects   1970s • Argentina • Genocide • Magic Realism • Political Fiction • Political Un-rest • South America

Now try   This novel is the third in a trilogy that includes *Imagining Argentina* and *Tales from the Blue Archives*. Other novels set in Argentina include *The Long Night of Francisco Sanctis* by Humberto Constantini and *The Story of the Night* by Colm Toibin. Other political novels set in Latin America include *In the Time of the Butterflies* by Julia Alvarez and *Hummingbird House* by Patricia Henley.

## Toibin, Colm
### The Blackwater Lightship
Scribner. 2000. 273 pp.

Declan, in the last stages of AIDS, comes to stay at his grandmother's seaside cottage, which provides an opportunity for his sister, mother, and grandmother to reassess their long estrangement from one another and Declan.

Book Groups 📖

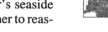

**Subjects**    AIDS • Brothers and Sisters • Family Relationships • Gay Men • Ireland • Irish Authors • Mothers and Daughters

**Now try**    Like his previous novels *The South* and *The Heather Blazing*, *The Blackwater Lightship* was short-listed for the Booker Prize. His novel *The Story of the Night* also deals with AIDS. AIDS becomes a catalyst for an exploration of family, community, and roots in Peter Cameron's *The Weekend*, William Carpenter's *A Keeper of Sheep*, Nisa Donnelly's *The Love Songs of Phoenix Bay*, and Geoff Ryman's *Was*. Mother's and daughter's reassess their relationships and approach reconciliation in Michael Dorris's *A Yellow Raft in Blue Water*, Gail Godwin's *A Mother and Two Daughters*, Lydia Minatoya's *The Strangeness of Beauty*, Amy Tan's *The Kitchen God's Wife*, and Ursula Hegi's *The Salt Dancers*.

## Treichel, Hans-Ulrich
### Lost
Pantheon. 1999. 136 pp.

When his parents decide they are going to find their young son who disappeared during World War II, the eight-year-old narrator realizes that despite his parents' grief, he doesn't really want his older brother back. Translated from the German by Carol Brown Janeway.

**2d Appeal**    Setting                                              Book Groups 📖

**Subjects**    Black Humor • Brothers • First Novels • German Authors • Germany • Humorous Fiction • Novels in Translation

**Now try**    Treichel is the author of several books of poetry and prose, but this is his first book to be published in the United States. The bizarre experiences of the narrator and his parents at the Institute of Forensic Anthropology are reminiscent of the blackly comic novels of Franz Kafka (*The Trial*, and others). This view of the world through the eyes of a little boy is similar in tone (a combination of wisdom and befuddlement) to *Henry of Atlantic City* by Frederick Reuss. Janeway also translated Bernhard Schlink's *The Reader*.

## Troy, Judy
### From the Black Hills
Random House. 1999. 283 pp.

Eighteen-year-old Mike Newlin's life changes forever when his father disappears after being accused of killing the young woman who works in his office.

Book Groups 📖

**Subjects**    Fathers and Sons • Murder • Older Women/Younger Men • Small-Town Life • South Dakota • Teenage Boys

**Now try**   Troy is also the author of the novel *West of Venus* and *Mourning Doves: Stories*. In *Girls*, Frederick Busch shares Troy's talent for exploring the emotional consequences of a tragic event on the lives of survivors.

## Tyler, Anne
### Back When We Were Grownups
*Knopf. 2001. 273 pp.*

At age 53, Rebecca—widowed in her 20s, now mother, stepmother, grandmother, and caregiver for her aging uncle-in-law—finds herself reexamining choices she has made, including jilting her college sweetheart.

**2d Appeal**   Story                                                   Book Groups 📖

**Subjects**   Aging • Baltimore, Maryland • Family Relationships • Male/Female Relationships • Marriage • Mother and Daughters • Stepmothers • Widows

**Now try**   Tyler's other novels include *Saint Maybe* and *Ladder of Years*, among many others. Other novels about examining the past and coming-of-age later in life include Jessica Anderson's *Tirra Lirra by the River*, Pagan Kennedy's *Spinsters*, and Stanley Elkin's *Mrs. Ted Bliss*.

## Unsworth, Barry
### Losing Nelson
*N.A. Talese. 1999. 338 pp.*

Historian and would-be biographer Charles Cleasby spends his days and nights reliving the events of Admiral Horatio Nelson's life (even reenacting Nelson's naval battles using model ships) and, to help with the book, engages a sensible, kindhearted secretary who doesn't share Cleasby's high regard for his subject.

**2d Appeal**   Language                                                Book Groups 📖

**Subjects**   British Authors • England • Mothers Deserting Their Families • Nelson, Horatio • Obsessive Love

**Now try**   Unsworth's other novels include *Morality Play* and *Sacred Hunger*, for which he won the Booker Prize. Other novels about Horatio Nelson include Nigel Foxell's *Loving Emma* and Susan Sontag's *The Volcano Lover*. Other novels that look at history through fiction include William Styron's *The Confessions of Nat Turner* and Beryl Bainbridge's *Master Georgie*.

## Urquhart, Jane
### The Underpainter
*Viking. 1997. 340 pp.*

Seventy-five-year-old Austin Fraser reflects on his life as a painter, in which his total absorption into his art has caused him to carelessly (and cruelly) destroy the lives of his two closest friends.

**2d Appeal**   Language                                                Book Groups 📖

**Subjects**   Art and Artists • Canadian Authors • Elderly Men • Men's Friendships • Men's Lives

**Now try**   Urquhart's other novels include *Changing Heaven* and *Away*. *What's Bred in the Bone* by Robertson Davies and Chaim Potok's *My Name Is Asher Lev* each offer a view of a painter's life. Merle Miller's *A Gay and Melancholy Sound* is another novel about a man who willfully damages the lives of those who love him. *The Underpainter* won Canada's Governor General's Award.

## Vanderhaeghe, Guy
### The Englishman's Boy
Picador USA. 1998. 333 pp.

Hollywood writer Harry Vincent is recruited by the reclusive and obsessive mogul of Best Chance Pictures to locate and write the supposedly epic story of old-time cowboy bit player Shorty McAdoo.

Book Groups 📖

**Subjects**   1920s • 1980s • American Indians • Canada • Canadian Authors • Cowboys • Elderly Men • Hollywood • Massacres • Saskatchewan, Canada

**Now try**   In addition to collections of short stories, Vanderhaeghe has also written novels of some dark, antiheroic characters: *My Present Danger* and *Homesick*. Another epic tale of an antihero is Peter Carey's *True History of the Kelly Gang*. Early Hollywood is classically depicted in Nathanael West's *The Day of the Locust*, as well as F. Scott Fitzgerald's *The Last Tycoon*, Peter Lovesey's *Keystone*, and Budd Schulberg's *What Makes Sammy Run* and *The Disenchanted*. Compare the settings of the Canadian West in George Bowering's *Shoot!*, Margaret Craven's *I Heard the Owl Call My Name*, Benedict Freedman's *Mrs. Mike*, Wallace Stegner's *The Big Rock Candy Mountain*, and Thomas Wharton's *Icefields*. *The Englishman's Boy* won Canada's Governor General's Literary Award.

## Vargas Llosa, Mario
### The Notebooks of Don Rigoberto
Farrar, Straus and Giroux. 1998. 259 pp.

Fantasy and reality are intermingled in the experiences of a wealthy Peruvian businessman, his beautiful estranged wife, and his son, a golden-haired youth obsessed with the art of Egon Schiele. Translated from the Spanish by Edith Grossman.

**2d Appeal**   Language            Book Groups 📖

**Subjects**   Art and Artists • Erotica • Love Affairs • Magic Realism • Novels in Translation • Peru • Peruvian Authors • Schiele, Egon • South America • South American Authors

**Now try**   Vargas Llosa's earlier novel, *In Praise of the Stepmother*, introduces the characters in *The Notebooks of Don Rigoberto*. Among Vargas Llosa's other novels are *Aunt Julia and the Scriptwriter* and *The Real Life of Alejandro Mayta*. Milan Kundera's *Slowness* also explores a man's sexual fantasies. Another novel of literary erotica is *Vox* by Nicholson Baker. Joanna Scott's *Arrogance* is a novel about the artist Egon Schiele.

## Warner, Sharon Oard
### Deep in the Heart
Dial Press. 2000. 392 pp.

When 40-year-old Hannah Solace becomes pregnant for the first time and decides not to have the child, her choice puts her in conflict not only with her husband Carl, but also with a charismatic young minister who is rallying his church members to stage a protest at the local abortion clinic.

Book Groups 📖

**Subjects**  Abortion • American Southwest • Austin, Texas • First Novels • Husbands and Wives • Marriage • Teenage Girls • Texas

**Now try**  Another novel about a woman's decision to have an abortion and the impact it has on a marriage is *Are You Mine?* by Abby Frucht. Walter Kirn's *She Needed Me* is a less serious novel about a man and woman who meet at an abortion clinic: She is there to have an abortion and he is there as one of the protesters.

## Weber, Katharine
### The Music Lesson
Crown. 1998. 178 pp.

When she falls in love with her distant cousin Mickey O'Driscoll, art historian Patricia Dolan unwittingly becomes involved with a splinter group of the Irish Republican Army.

Book Groups 📖

**Subjects**  Art and Artists • Ireland • Irish Republican Army • Love Affairs • Murder • Religious Extremism • Vermeer, Johannes

**Now try**  Weber is also the author of *Objects in Mirror Are Closer Than They Appear*. Other books in which paintings by the artist Vermeer play a role are Susan Vreeland's *Girl in Hyacinth Blue* and Tracy Chevalier's *Girl with a Pearl Earring*. James Hynes's *The Wild Colonial Boy* is another novel in which a naïve American unwittingly aids the Irish Republican Army in its fight for an independent Ireland.

## Wesley, Mary
### An Imaginative Experience
Viking Penguin. 1995. 222 pp.

When recently widowed Julia Piper pulls the emergency brake on her commuter train to save an upended sheep, she catches the eye of mild divorcee Sylvester Wykes and playboy-birdwatcher Maurice Benson.

**Subjects**  British Authors • Car Accidents • Humorous Fiction • London, England • Male/Female Relationships • Widows

**Now try**  Among Wesley's other novels are *Jumping the Queue* (in which the plot also concerns the results of a kindly and impulsive action) and *Part of the Furniture*. Other writers who explore male-female relationships with humor include Muriel Spark (*Loitering with Intent* and *Territorial Rights*) and Penelope Fitzgerald (*Gate of Angels*).

## Whitehead, Colson
### The Intuitionist
Anchor Books. 1999. 255 pp.

When an elevator that Lila Mae Watson has certified as safe crashes, the animosity simmering between the Empiricist and the Intuitionist factions of the Department of Elevator Inspectors shifts into active violence.

**2d Appeal**  Language

Book Groups 📖

**Subjects**  African American Authors • African Americans • Elevators • First Novels • Race Relations • Racism

**Now try**  Other novels that stretch the boundaries of contemporary fiction are Jonathan Lethem's *Motherless Brooklyn* and *As She Climbed Across the Table*. Like Toni Morrison's *The Bluest Eye*, Whitehead's novel explores America's racial divide in well-written prose.

## Whitehead, Colson
### John Henry Days
Doubleday. 2001. 389 pp.

J, a journalist who specializes in attending press junkets, travels to West Virginia for the celebration surrounding the release of a stamp commemorating the life of the mythical John Henry.

**2d Appeal**  Language                                Book Groups 📖

**Subjects**  African American Authors • African Americans • Henry, John • Journalists • Race Relations • Racism

**Now try**  Whitehead's first novel was ***The Intuitionist***. Other novels concerning race relations include ***Live at Five*** by David Haynes and Julius Lester's ***Do Lord Remember Me***. Whitehead's solid narrative style brings to mind Richard Russo's ***Empire Falls***, although the subject matter of the novels is very different.

## Wideman, John Edgar
### Two Cities
Houghton Mifflin. 1998. 242 pp.

The lives of three people intertwine against a backdrop of urban decay: a mid-30s woman who has lost two sons to gang violence and her husband to AIDS in prison; the older man she meets who makes her think about the possibility of happiness again; and the elderly boarder, a photographer, who has his own set of stories to reveal.

**2d Appeal**  Language

**Subjects**  African American Authors • African Americans • Death of a Child • Death of a Spouse • Ghetto Life • Grief • Mothers and Sons • Older Men/Younger Women • Philadelphia, Pennsylvania • Pittsburgh, Pennsylvania • Pennsylvania

**Now try**  This novel incorporates images of the 1985 bombing of the group MOVE in Philadelphia, which Wideman also wrote about in the Pen/Faulkner Award–winning ***Philadelphia Fire***; his ***Sent for You Yesterday*** won the PEN/Faulkner Award as well. Other novels dealing with the everyday heroics of living in the battle zones and ordinary neighborhoods of America's older inner cities include Sandra Cisneros's ***The House on Mango Street***, Diane McKinney-Whetstone's ***Tumbling***, Walter Mosley's ***Always Outnumbered, Always Outgunned*** and ***RL's Dream***, Gloria Naylor's ***The Women of Brewster Place***, Ann Petry's ***The Street***, and April Sinclair's ***Coffee Will Make You Black***.

## Wiggins, Marianne
### Eveless Eden
HarperCollins. 1995. 337 pp.

Foreign correspondent Noah John's love affair with a photojournalist is compromised and complicated by the appearance of a sinister British spy who is also an official in the Romanian government.

**2d Appeal**  Language                                Book Groups 📖

**Subjects**  ALA Notable Books • Eastern Europe • Foreign Correspondents • Journalists • Love Stories • Photography and Photographers • Romania

**Now try**   Among Wiggins's other novels are *John Dollar* and *Almost Heaven*. The spy novels of Len Deighton (*Berlin Game*, and others) and John le Carré (*The Constant Gardener*, and others) come the closest to the intensity of Wiggins's novel.

## Williams, Joy
### The Quick & the Dead
Knopf. 2000. 307 pp.

In a surreally pictured present-day Arizona, three teenage girls become friends and help one another discover the difference between the living and the dead.

**2d Appeal**   Language                                                    Book Groups 📖

**Subjects**   ALA Notable Books • Arizona • Death of a Parent • Friendship • Ghosts • Magic Realism • Teenage Girls

**Now try**   Other novels by Williams include *The Changeling*, *Breaking and Entering*, and *State of Grace*, as well as collections of short stories. Richard Powers's *Three Farmers on Their Way to a Dance* is another fiercely intelligent novel, although it lacks the humor with which Williams imbues her writing. Another novel about a troubled teenage girl is Lynda Barry's *Cruddy*.

## Williamson, Eric Miles
### East Bay Grease
Picador USA. 1999. 248 pp.

A tough kid in a tough family in a tough town, T-Bird Murphy's trumpet is the one note of purity in a young life marked by violence and revenge.

**Subjects**   California • Coming-of-Age • Dysfunctional Families • Fathers and Sons • First Novels • Jazz • Juvenile Delinquents • Music and Musicians • Oakland, California • Teenage Boys

**Now try**   Other books about kids with whom you wouldn't want your children hanging out include Anthony Burgess's *A Clockwork Orange* and Willard Motley's *Let No Man Write My Epitaph*. Other novels about young musicians include Richard Hill's *Riding Solo with the Golden Horde* and Enrico Brizzi's *Jack Frusciante Has Left the Band*.

## Willis, Sarah
### Some Things That Stay
Farrar, Straus and Giroux. 2000. 275 pp.

Fifteen-year-old Tamara hates the fact that her artist-father moves the family all over the United States in his search for landscapes to paint, but more important issues come to the fore when her mother is diagnosed with tuberculosis.

**Subjects**   1950s • Art and Artists • Brothers and Sisters • Coming-of-Age • First Novels • Religion • Teenage Girls • Tuberculosis

**Now try**   Karin Cook's *What Girls Learn* is another novel about a teenager facing her mother's imminent death.

## Winegardner, Mark
### Crooked River Burning
Harcourt Brace. 2001. 561 pp.

The love between blue-collar David Zielinsky and blue blood Anne O'Connor develops against events in the city where they both grow up: Cleveland, Ohio.

**2d Appeal**   Setting                                                    Book Groups 📖

**Subjects** American Midwest • Cleveland, Ohio • Fathers and Sons • Male/Female Relationships • Ohio • Upper Classes • Working Classes

**Now try** Winegardner is also the author of *The Veracruz Blues*. John Dos Passos's USA trilogy (*The Big Money*, *The 42nd Parallel*, and *1919*) also uses the technique of incorporating real people into a fictional tale.

## Winterson, Jeannette
### Written on the Body
Knopf. 1993. 190 pp.

A narrator of undisclosed gender describes a passionate relationship with a married woman.

**2d Appeal** Language Book Groups

**Subjects** Adultery • British Authors • Cancer • Love Affairs

**Now try** Winterson's other novels include *Oranges Are Not the Only Fruit*, *The Passion*, *The Powerbook*, and *Sexing the Cherry*. Two other novels with characters of undisclosed gender include Rose Macaulay's *The Towers of Trebizond* and Sarah Caudwell's *Thus Was Adonis Murdered*.

## Winton, Tim
### The Riders
Scribner. 1995. 377 pp.

When Fred Scully's wife disappears, he and his seven-year-old daughter Billie try desperately to understand why Jennifer left them, and where she has gone.

**2d Appeal** Story Book Groups

**Subjects** Australian Authors • Fathers and Daughters • Mothers Deserting Their Families • Obsessive Love

**Now try** *The Riders* was short-listed for the Booker Prize. Winton's other novels include *Cloudstreet*, *That Eye*, *The Sky*, and *Blueback*. Another novel about a man's search for the woman he loves is Scott Spencer's *Waking the Dead*.

## Wright, Bil
### Sunday You Learn How to Box
Scribner. 2000. 220 pp.

Louis Bowman is struggling to grow up in the projects of Stratfield, Connecticut, trying not to get beaten up, jeered at, taken advantage of, or otherwise ostracized—unsuccessfully.

Book Groups

**Subjects** African American Authors • African Americans • Child Abuse • Coming-of-Age • Connecticut • First Novels • Ghetto Life • Housing Projects • Mothers and Sons • Sexual Identity • Stepfamilies

**Now try** Other novels set in public housing or urban slums include Ramona (Sapphire) Lofton's *Push*, Connie Porter's *All-Bright Court*, and Richard Price's *Clockers*. Isolated, outsider teens coming-of-age are the main characters in Gus Lee's *China Boy*, Ben Neihart's *Hey, Joe*, Daniel Vilmure's *Toby's Lie*, Shay Youngblood's *Soul Kiss*, and Lois-Ann Yamanaka's *Wild Meat and the Bully Burgers*.

## Yamanaka, Lois-Ann
### Blu's Hanging
Farrar, Straus and Giroux. 1997. 260 pp.

Three young Japanese children deal with the grief of losing their mother while learning how to cope with the perverse adult world of their impoverished community on a Hawaiian island.

Book Groups 📖

**Subjects**   ALA Notable Books • Asian American Authors • Asian Americans • Brothers and Sisters • Death of a Parent • Hawaii • Japanese American Authors • Orphans

**Now try**   Yamanaka's first novel was *Wild Meat and the Bully Burgers*. *Comfort Woman* by Nora Okja Keller and *My Old Sweetheart* by Susanna Moore are both novels about girls growing up in Hawaii with emotionally ill mothers.

## Yarbrough, Steve
### The Oxygen Man
MacMurray & Beck. 1999. 280 pp.

Brother and sister Ned and Daze Rose have shared their family house for over 20 years as adults, separated by guilt and silent accusation: Ned enthralled by his rich, vicious high school buddies; Daze afraid of turning into her libidinous mother.

Book Groups 📖

**Subjects**   1970s • American South • Brothers and Sisters • Dysfunctional Families • First Novels • Fish Farming • Mississippi • Murder • Southern Authors

**Now try**   Yarbrough has published three collections of stories, including *Veneer* and *Mississippi History*. This novel, like Larry Brown's *Father and Son*, Pete Dexter's *The Paperboy*, Robert McCammon's *Boy's Life*, and Lewis Nordan's *The Sharpshooter Blues*, is in the southern gothic tradition of fiction. The brother and sister relationship in *The Oxygen Man* is similar to those in John Gardner's *October Light* and Joyce Carol Oates's *Angel of Light*.

## Yglesias, Helen
### The Girls
Delphinium Books. 1999. 213 pp.

When Jenny, the youngest (at 80) of four sisters, comes to Miami to stay with Flora (age 85) so that the two can look after the affairs of Naomi (age 90), who is about to have a second surgery for cancer, and Eva (age 95), who is having a bad reaction to her latest medication, she discovers that even the indignities of aging and approaching death do not erase the tensions and jealousies of childhood.

**Subjects**   Aging • Death and Dying • Elderly Women • Florida • Miami, Florida • Sisters

**Now try**   Yglesias is also the author of the novels *How She Died* and *Family Feeling*. Both Elizabeth Taylor's *Mrs. Palfrey at the Claremont* and *The Diaries of Jane Somers* by Doris Lessing describe the lives of elderly women. The memoirs of Doris Grumbach, particularly *Extra Innings: A Memoir*, and May Sarton, especially *Endgame: A Journal of the Seventy-Ninth Year*, are also good companion reads to Yglesias's novel.

## Yoshikawa, Mako
### One Hundred and One Ways
Bantam. 1999. 278 pp.

Twenty-nine-year-old Kiki Takehashi, a graduate student in English, accepts a marriage proposal from lawyer-boyfriend Eric but is haunted by the ghost of her true love Philip, who died in an avalanche in Nepal; she sorts out her feelings by imagining conversations with her grandmother, a former geisha.

Book Groups 📖

**Subjects** Asian American Authors • Asian Americans • First Novels • Ghosts • Interracial Relationships • Japanese American Authors • Japanese Americans • Male/Female Relationships • Multigenerational Novels

**Now try** *A Bridge Between Us* by Julie Shikeguni is another novel about Japanese American mothers and daughters. Arthur Golden's *Memoirs of a Geisha* is a novel about a renowned geisha. Other novels about three generations of women in one family include Kaye Gibbons's *Charms for the Easy Life* and Isabel Allende's *The House of the Spirits*. Another novel about a young woman dealing with the death of her lover is James McManus's *Going to the Sun*.

## Zeidner, Lisa
### Layover
Random House. 1999. 267 pp.

After the death of her only child and her discovery of her husband's infidelity, Claire finds herself seeking clandestine sexual adventures in anonymous hotel rooms on her regular business trips around the country.

**Subjects** Adultery • Death of a Child • Grief • Husbands and Wives • Sexual Adventures

**Now try** Zeidner is also the author of *Customs* and *Limited Partnerhsips*, both novels of subversive wit. Other books that deal with the loss of a child include Alice Thomas Ellis's *Birds of the Air* and Denis Johnson's *The Name of the World*. Elizabeth Berg's main character in *The Pull of the Moon* also gives into the lure of another life.

# Chapter 4

# Language

## Amis, Martin
### Night Train
Harmony Books. 1998. 175 pp.

Hard-boiled lady cop Mike Hoolihan grapples with an existential mystery in the apparent suicide of the brainy and beautiful Jennifer Rockwell, a girl with everything to live for.

**Subjects**    British Authors • Crime • Death and Dying • Mystery • Policewomen • Suicide

**Now try**    Amis also explores suicide in his novels ***London Fields*** and ***Money***. Other mysteries that transcend the genre are Paul Auster's ***New York Trilogy***, ***A Philosophical Investigation*** by Phillip Kerr, Robert Grudin's ***Book***, and Jonathan Lethem's ***Motherless Brooklyn***. Amis's novel is also reminiscent of ***Bullet Park*** by John Cheever.

## Atwood, Margaret
### The Blind Assassin
Random House. 2000. 521 pp.

Now in her 80s, Iris Chase Griffen looks back over a life filled with disappointments—the early death of her mother, an unsatisfactory marriage, a difficult relationship with her daughter—and the love that sustained her.

**2d Appeal**    Characters Book Groups 📖

**Subjects**    ALA Notable Books • Booker Prize Winners • Canada • Canadian Authors • Elderly Women • Love Affairs • Sisters • Women's Lives

**Now try**    Atwood is also the author of ***Lady Oracle***, ***The Robber Bride***, and ***Cat's Eye***, among many other novels and short story collections. The layered story-within-a-story structure is also used in Kate Atkinson's ***Emotionally Weird***, Ellen Gilchrist's ***The Anna Papers***, MacDonald Harris's ***Hemingway's Suitcase***, Lawrence Norfolk's ***Lempriere's Dictionary***, and Carol Shields's ***Swann***. Elderly women narrate their life stories in distinctive voices in Jessica Anderson's ***Tirra Lirra by the River***, Angela Carter's ***Wise Children***, Margaret Laurence's ***The Stone Angel***, and Penelope Lively's ***Moon Tiger***.

## Azzopardi, Trezza

### The Hiding Place
Atlantic Monthly Press. 2000. 288 pp.

Dolores Gauci, growing up in Cardiff, Wales, relates the story of her unhappy, poverty-stricken family, which includes her gambler-father, her tired, exasperated mother, and her four older sisters, each of whom have their own stories to tell.

Book Groups 📖

**Subjects**   1960s • Dysfunctional Families • Fathers and Daughters • First Novels • Gamblers and Gambling • Immigrants and Refugees • Mothers and Daughters • Poverty • Sisters • Wales • Women's Lives

**Now try**   Although its descriptions of poverty, disease, and family dysfunction bring to mind Frank McCourt's *Angela's Ashes*, the tone of Azzopardi's first novel, and its first-person child narrator, is more reminiscent of Kate Atkinson's *Behind the Scenes at the Museum*. *The Hiding Place* was short-listed for the Booker Prize.

## Barry, Nicholas

### The Whereabouts of Eneas McNulty
Viking. 1998. 308 pp.

A seemingly simple decision to earn his living as a policeman for the Royal Irish Constabulary changes the course of Eneas McNulty's life, forcing him to flee his home and family and spend years living in fear and isolation.

**2d Appeal**   Setting
Book Groups 📖

**Subjects**   Friendship • Historical Setting • Ireland • Irish Authors • Irish Republican Army • Religious Extremism • Violence

**Now try**   Barry is also a poet and the author of two plays, "Our Lady of Sligo" and "The Steward of Christendom." Roddy Doyle's *A Star Called Henry* tells a similar story—set around the same time as Barry's novel—about a young man on the Irish Republican Army's side of "The Troubles" in Ireland. Patrick McCabe's *Breakfast on Pluto* is another novel about a young man caught up in Ireland's sectarian violence. *The Long Falling* by Keith Ridgway is about an Irish family shunned by their tight-knit community in much the same way as was Eneas McNulty.

## Bradley, James

### Wrack
Henry Holt. 1999. 352 pp.

While archaeologist David Norfolk is searching in the remote desert sands of New South Wales, Australia, for the wreck of a Portuguese ship used by explorers in the fifteenth and sixteenth centuries, a long-buried body of a man is discovered, and Kurt Seligmann, a scarred and dying recluse, seems to hold the answers to the mysteries of both the whereabouts of the ship and the identification of the body.

**2d Appeal**   Setting

**Subjects**   Archaeologists and Archaeology • Australia • Australian Authors • Elderly Men • First Novels • Love Affairs

**Now try**   Bradley's novel, like Michael Ondaatje's *The English Patient*, is both beautifully written and moves back and forth in time to explore a love affair's beginning and end.

## Bush, Catherine
### The Rules of Engagement
Farrar, Straus and Giroux. 2000. 302 pp.

After two men fought a duel over her, Arcadia Hearne fled Toronto for London where she now works as a researcher at the Center for Contemporary War Studies; when she falls in love with Amir, an Iranian refugee, she is forced to confront her beliefs and her past.

Book Groups 📖

**Subjects**   Canada • Duels • Immigrants and Refugees • Iran • London, England • Love Affairs • Political Fiction • Toronto, Canada

**Now try**   Bush is also the author of *Minus Time*. Other novels of love affairs set against the violence of the contemporary world include Marianne Wiggins's *Eveless Eden* and James Buchan's *The Persian Bride*. The intelligence of the main character and the tone of the novel bring to mind the novels of Margaret Atwood, especially *Life Before Man* and *Cat's Eye*.

## Carey, Lisa
### In the Country of the Young
Morrow. 2000. 290 pp.

When the ghost of a little girl who died a hundred years ago takes refuge in Oisin's house on an island off the coast of Maine, the reclusive artist finds his life changed forever.

**2d Appeal**   Characters                                    Book Groups 📖

**Subjects**   Art and Artists • Brothers and Sisters • Child Prodigies • Geniuses • Ghosts • Gifted Children • Ireland • Magic Realism • Maine • Twins

**Now try**   Carey is also the author of the novel *The Mermaids Singing*. Another novel set on an island off the Maine coast (athough the two books are otherwise dissimilar) is *Stern Men* by Elizabeth Gilbert. The beautiful writing and tone of Carey's novel are similar to those of Alessandro Baricco's *Ocean Sea*.

## Carey, Lisa
### The Mermaids Singing
Avon Books. 1998. 257 pp.

The voices of three generations of women are brought together when 15-year-old Grainne returns to her grandmother's seaside village in Ireland and attempts to make sense of the choices that devastated her family.

**2d Appeal**   Setting                                       Book Groups 📖

**Subjects**   First Novels • Ireland • Irish Mythology • Male/Female Relationships • Mothers and Daughters

**Now try**   Other novels that explore the difficult terrain of mother-daughter relationships include *A Thirst for Rain* by Roslyn Carrington and *Solar Storms* by Linda Hogan. Another novel set in Ireland with a strong female character is Walter Keady's *Mary McGreevy*. The lyrical writing and Irish mythology found in Carey's book are also present in Niall Williams's *Four Letters of Love*.

## Coetzee, J. M.
### Age of Iron
Random House. 1990. 198 pp.

As Mrs. Curren, a retired white classics professor, lies dying of cancer, she writes to her daughter in the United States about her illness and the sickness in South Africa's political system of apartheid.

**2d Appeal**  Setting                                                   Book Groups  📖

**Subjects**  Africa • ALA Notable Books • Apartheid • Cancer • College Professors • Death and Dying • Epistolary Novels • Mothers and Daughters • South Africa • South African Authors

**Now try**  Included among Coetzee's other novels are *Waiting for the Barbarians* and *In the Heart of the Country*. His spare writing style is similar to that of Aharon Appelfeld's novels *Badenheim, 1939* and *Unto the Soul*. Andre Brink's *Imaginings of Sand* is also about a dying elderly white South African woman trying to understand her own and her country's past.

## Coetzee, J. M.
### Disgrace
Viking. 1999. 220 pp.

After aging Cape Town professor David Lurie loses his job and his reputation, he seeks refuge on his daughter's farm where a shocking act of violence forces him to reevaluate his life and struggle toward redemption.

**2d Appeal**  Setting                                                   Book Groups  📖

**Subjects**  Africa • ALA Notable Books • Apartheid • Booker Prize Winners • Cape Town, South Africa • College Professors • Farms and Farm Life • Fathers and Daughters • Older Men/Younger Women • Rape • South Africa • South African Authors • Veterinarians • Violence

**Now try**  Coetzee also won the Booker Prize for *Life & Times of Michael K*. Another novel that forces the reader to read between the lines is Michael Ondaatje's *Anil's Ghost*.

## Crace, Jim
### Being Dead
Farrar, Straus and Giroux. 2000. 193 pp.

Thirty years of married life slowly unravel as zoologists Joseph and Celice lie moldering on a secluded beach, murdered by a stranger.

**2d Appeal**  Story

**Subjects**  ALA Notable Books • British Authors • Death and Dying • England • Marriage • Murder • National Book Critics Circle Award • Science and Scientists • Violence • Zoology and Zoologists

**Now try**  Crace is also the author of the equally imaginative novels *Arcadia, Quarantine* (in which Crace applies his naturalistic scalpel to the story of Christ's temptation in the desert) and *The Gift of Stones*. Another novel that plays itself out backward is *Ray in Reverse* by Daniel Wallace. Martin Amis's *Night Train*, Leo Tolstoy's *The Death of Ivan Ilych*, Iris Murdoch's *Bruno's Dream*, and Louis Begley's *Mistler's Exit* are all cool, stylish meditations on how we die. William Trevor (*Death in Summer* and *Felicia's Journey*) and John Lanchester (*Mr. Philips*) share Crace's compassionate but unsparing eye.

## Crews, Harry

### Body
Poseidon Press. 1990. 240 pp.

Backwoods belle Dorothy Turnipseed tortures herself into the sculpted androgyny of Shereel Dupont, contender in the Ms. Cosmos bodybuilding competition.

**Subjects**   Black Humor • Body Image • Bodybuilding • Humorous Fiction • Satirical Fiction • Sex and Sexuality • Southern Authors

**Now try**   Crews is also the author of the novels *All We Need of Hell*, *Feast of Snakes*, and *The Knockout Artist*. *The Spirit Cabinet* by Paul Quarrington and *The Road to Wellville* by T. Coraghessan Boyle both have fun with health fanatics and the cult of the body. Barry Hannah's fiction (*The Tennis Handsome* and *Bat Out of Hell*) approaches the demonic comedic fury of Crews's novels.

## Cunningham, Michael

### The Hours
Farrar, Straus and Giroux. 1998. 229 pp.

The lives of three women are examined in interconnected chapters: a fictionalized Virginia Woolf, just as she is planning the book that became *Mrs. Dalloway*; a young woman with her husband and son in Los Angeles right after World War II; and a middle-aged New Yorker, who is planning a party for a close friend, an award-winning poet who is dying of AIDS.

**2d Appeal**   Characters                                          Book Groups 📖

**Subjects**   ALA Notable Books • Mothers and Sons • Pulitzer Prize Winners • Women's Lives • Woolf, Virginia • Writers and Writing

**Now try**   Among Cunningham's other novels are *Flesh and Blood* and *A Home at the End of the World*. Although the reader need not be familiar with Virginia Woolf's novel *Mrs. Dalloway* in order to enjoy Cunningham's book, reading it will certainly enhance the pleasure of *The Hours*. In its attention to the smallest details of the lives of its characters, *The Hours* is similar to Susan Minot's *Evening*.

## Deane, Seamus

### Reading in the Dark
Knopf. 1997. 245 pp.

The political upheavals in Northern Ireland provide a backdrop to the life of the narrator, who tries to puzzle out the nature of love, the effects of violence, and the secrets his family carries.

**2d Appeal**   Setting                                               Book Groups 📖

**Subjects**   ALA Notable Books • Coming-of-Age • Family Relationships • Family Secrets • First Novels • Ireland • Irish Authors

**Now try**   The writings of Isaac Babel (*Collected Stories*), although set in a different time and place, offer the same sense of how history can affect family relationships. Another good evocation of childhood can be found in Tim Pears's *In the Place of Fallen Leaves*. Deane's novel was a finalist for the 1996 Booker Prize and won the Guardian Prize for fiction.

## DeLillo, Don

### Underworld
Scribner. 1997. 827 pp.

Historical figures (J. Edgar Hoover, Frank Sinatra, and Jackie Gleason, among others) and assorted fictional characters make their way through 50 years of history against a backdrop of the Cold War and American culture.

**2d Appeal**  Story

**Subjects**  Baseball • Cold War • Male/Female Relationships • Political Fiction • Postmodern Fiction

**Now try**  Among DeLillo's other novels exploring aspects of American culture are *End Zone*, *Libra*, and *White Noise*. Both E. L. Doctorow (*Ragtime*) and Mark Winegardner (*Crooked River Burning*) combine historical figures and fictional characters in their novels.

## Dexter, Pete

### The Paperboy
Random House. 1995. 307 pp.

Jack James looks back on his brother Ward's fall from fame with sorrow and regret.

Book Groups 📖

**Subjects**  ALA Notable Books • American South • Brothers • Fathers and Sons • Florida • Violence • Writers and Writing

**Now try**  Dexter's other books include *Brotherly Love*, *God's Pocket*, and *Deadwood*. Interesting relationships between brothers are found in Adrian Louis's *Skins* and Russell Banks's *Affliction*.

## Emerson, Gloria

### Loving Graham Greene
Random House. 2000. 176 pp.

In 1992, wealthy and eccentric Molly Benson and two friends travel to Algeria to try to give support to writers and journalists whose lives are threatened by Islamic fundamentalists.

**2d Appeal**  Setting
Book Groups 📖

**Subjects**  1990s • Algeria • First Novels • Greene, Graham • Political Fiction • Upper Classes

**Now try**  Emerson is also the author of two nonfiction books: *Gaza: A Year in the Intifada* and *Winners & Losers*, which explores the war in Vietnam and its effects on Americans. Other novels about innocents abroad include Ward Just's *A Dangerous Friend* and Mary Doria Russell's *The Sparrow*. Two other novels set in Algeria are Claire Messud's *The Last Life* and Albert Camus's *The First Man*.

## Eugenides, Jeffrey

### The Virgin Suicides
Farrar, Straus and Giroux. 1993. 249 pp.

The narrators, a group of men who write in one voice, try to make sense of the defining event of their adolescence—the deaths by suicide of their friends, the five beautiful Lisbon sisters.

**2d Appeal**  Characters
Book Groups 📖

**Subjects**  ALA Notable Books • First Novels • Men's Friendships • Suicide • Teenage Boys • Teenage Girls • Teenagers

**Now try**  *That Night* by Alice McDermott also describes a neighborhood watching events play out. Suicide and its effects on the people left behind is the subject of Yukio Mishima's *Spring Snow*, Kate Chopin's *The Awakening*, and William Faulkner's *The Sound and the Fury*. In 1996, *Granta Magazine* named Eugenides one of the "20 Best Young American Novelists."

## Gaddis, William
### A Frolic of His Own
Poseidon Press. 1994. 586 pp.

A series of lawsuits, including Oscar Crease's suit against a Hollywood director for plagiarism, Oscar himself being sued for plagiarizing from Eugene O'Neill's "Mourning Becomes Electra," Oscar's attempts to decide whom to sue in order to recover damages for injuries suffered when his car ran over his foot while he was trying to hot-wire it, and a dog's death in an outdoor sculpture, all provide much work for the legal profession.

**Subjects**  Humorous Fiction • Law and Lawyers • National Book Award Winners • Postmodern Fiction • Satirical Fiction

**Now try**  Gaddis's first novel was *The Recognitions*, followed by *JR* and *Carpenter's Gothic*. Another darkly humorous look at the legal profession and an endless lawsuit can be found in Charles Dickens's *Bleak House*. Gaddis and his contemporary Thomas Pynchon (*Gravity's Rainbow*, and others) are both leading innovators in the world of twentieth-century American fiction, and both owe a debt of gratitude to James Joyce (*Ulysses*, and others).

## Gunesekera, Romesh
### The Reef
New Press. 1995. 190 pp.

Triton, a young Sri Lankan, is brought up in the household of Mr. Salgado, a marine biologist, and learns from him not only how to cook, but how best to live.

**Subjects**  Coming-of-Age • Cooks • Culinary Arts • First Novels • Sri Lanka

**Now try**  Gunesekera is also the author of a collection of short stories, *Monkfish Moon*. *The Reef* was short-listed for the Booker Prize. It is most similar in tone to Kazuo Ishiguro's *The Remains of the Day* and Michael Ondaatje's *Anil's Ghost*: The authors leave much unsaid in telling their stories. The lush descriptions of the countryside are reminiscent of *The Undiscovered Country* by Samantha Gillison. Shyam Selvadurai also writes about Sri Lanka in his novels *Funny Boy* and *Cinnamon Gardens*. Another domestic novel set against political upheaval is Arundhati Roy's *The God of Small Things*.

## Guterson, David
### East of the Mountains
Harcourt Brace. 1999. 279 pp.

Dr. Ben Givens, a solitary widower diagnosed with terminal cancer, sets out on a hunting trip during which he plans to take his own life to spare himself a long and painful death and his family the burden of his care.

Book Groups 📖

| | |
|---|---|
| **Subjects** | Brothers • Cancer • Dogs • Family Relationships • Illness • Love Stories • Marriage • Pacific Northwest • Terminal Illness • Washington • Widowers |
| **Now try** | Guterson's first novel was ***Snow Falling on Cedars***, which won the PEN/Faulkner Award. Jim Harrison's ***The Road Home*** evokes a similar connection to the land and nature. Richard Flanagan's ***The Sound of One Hand Clapping*** also uses flashbacks to show how the past influences the present. |

# Helprin, Mark
## Memoir from Antproof Case
Harcourt Brace. 1995. 514 pp.

Eighty-year-old Oscar, coming to the end of a full life that has been dominated by his hatred of coffee, recounts the adventures that brought him to where he is, including his experiences as a fighter pilot in World War II, a bank robber and murderer, his stay in an exclusive Swiss insane asylum, and years spent as a successful businessman.

| | | |
|---|---|---|
| **2d Appeal** | Characters | Book Groups 📖 |

| | |
|---|---|
| **Subjects** | Business and Businessmen • Coffee • Death of a Parent • Elderly Men • Men's Lives • Psychiatric Hospitals |
| **Now try** | Helprin's other novels include ***A Soldier of the Great War*** and ***A City in Winter***. Like Salman Rushdie in ***The Moor's Last Sigh***, Helprin comes up with such bizarre plots that it's impossible to imagine that anyone could imagine them. Another novel in which coffee plays an important part is Peter Gadol's ***Mystery Roast***. |

# Hoffman, Alice
## Seventh Heaven
G.P. Putnam's Sons. 1990. 256 pp.

When Nora Silk moves into a house on Hemlock Street in suburban Long Island, New York, her arrival triggers changes in the lives of many of her neighbors.

Book Groups 📖

| | |
|---|---|
| **Subjects** | 1950s • ALA Notable Books • Long Island, New York • Male/Female Relationships • Older Women/Younger Men • Suburbia |
| **Now try** | Hoffman also wrote ***Practical Magic***, ***The Drowning Season***, and ***Angel Landing***, among many other novels. Nora Silk is similar to the main character Justine in Anne Tyler's ***Searching for Caleb***. Other novels that describe a relationship between an older woman and a younger man are Colleen McCullough's ***Tim***, Dianne Highbridge's ***A Much Younger Man***, and David Martin's ***The Crying Heart Tattoo***. |

# Hoffman, Alice
## Turtle Moon
G.P. Putnam's Sons. 1992. 255 pp.

In Verity, Florida, where anything can happen during the month of May, single mother Lucy Rossen and policeman Julian Nash revisit their shattered pasts as they attempt to solve a murder involving a troubled adolescent.

| | | |
|---|---|---|
| **2d Appeal** | Characters | Book Groups 📖 |

| | |
|---|---|
| **Subjects** | ALA Notable Books • Divorce • Florida • Juvenile Delinquents • Love Stories • Magic Realism • Murder • Mystery • Single Mothers • Teenage Boys |

**Now try**    Hoffman is also the author of ***Blue Diary*** and ***The River King***. Another interesting picture of a troubled adolescent can be found in Jo-Ann Mapson's ***Blue Rodeo***. ***Boy's Life*** by Robert McCammon also combines a murder mystery with magic realism.

## Hogan, Linda
### Solar Storms
Scribner. 1995. 351 pp.

Seventeen-year-old Angel, looking for answers about the scars on her face and her empty past, returns to the Minnesota village of her birth and becomes an integral part in the unfolding story of five generations of American Indian women.

**2d Appeal**    Characters                                   Book Groups 📖

**Subjects**    American Indian Authors • American Indians • Coming-of-Age • Family Relationships • Minnesota • Multigenerational Novels • Women's Friendships

**Now try**    Linda Hogan's other novels include ***Mean Spirit*** and ***Power***. Her other works include ***Woman Who Watches Over the World: A Native Memoir*** and ***Book of Medicines: Poems***. The connections Hogan makes between women and nature are similar to those made by Terry Tempest Williams in her memoir, ***Refuge: An Unnatural History of Family and Place***. Susan Power's ***The Grass Dancer*** is another novel about American Indians written in similar lyrical language.

## Ignatieff, Michael
### Scar Tissue
Farrar, Straus and Giroux. 1994. 199 pp.

A professor of philosophy mourns the slow and terrible descent of his mother into senility as a result of Alzheimer's disease and discovers that modern medicine is as powerless as philosophy to help him comprehend what is happening.

Book Groups 📖

**Subjects**    ALA Notable Books • Alzheimer's Disease • Brothers • Death of a Parent • Mothers and Sons • Philosophy

**Now try**    Among Ignatieff's other books are ***The Russian Album***, ***Isaiah Berlin: A Life*** and ***Asya: A Novel***. Beverly Coyle's ***In Troubled Waters*** includes a character suffering from Alzheimer's disease. ***A Time to Dance*** by Walter Sullivan shows the effects of Alzheimer's from inside the mind of the person suffering from it. Andrew Solomon's ***A Stone Boat*** also deals with the close relationship between a son and his dying mother. The lack of consolation that philosophy offers in a time of tragedy is also revealed in Lynne Sharon Schwartz's ***Disturbances in the Field***.

## Jin, Ha
### Waiting
Pantheon. 1999. 308 pp.

A Chinese doctor in the Revolutionary army, trapped in a loveless marriage, wishes to divorce his wife and marry the nurse he loves, but Communist Party functionaries look upon divorce with deep suspicion, and for 17 years, his wife refuses to go along with his wishes.

**2d Appeal**    Setting                                      Book Groups 📖

| | |
|---|---|
| **Subjects** | ALA Notable Books • Asian Authors • Asians • China • Chinese Authors • Doctors and Patients • Male/Female Relationships • National Book Award Winners • Nurses |
| **Now try** | Ha Jin's other books include two volumes of poetry, a novel, *In the Pond*, as well as *Ocean of Words: Army Stories*, *Under the Red Flag: Stories*, and *The Bridegroom: Stories*. "Doc" Hata in Chang-rae Lee's *A Gesture Life* is also a man who discovers he doesn't know how to love. |

## Johnson, Denis
### The Name of the World
HarperCollins. 2000. 129 pp.

Mike Reed withdrew from the world when his wife and daughter were killed in an automobile accident, but meeting college student Flower Cannon (a performance artist, stripper, painter, caterer's assistant, and cellist) leads him to take tentative steps back into the land of the living.

Book Groups 📖

| | |
|---|---|
| **Subjects** | Academia • College Professors • Death of a Child • Death of a Spouse • Older Men/Younger Women |
| **Now try** | Johnson also wrote *Fiskadoro*, *Jesus' Son*, and *Angels*, as well as other books of fiction and poetry. Another college professor who finds it nearly impossible to rebound from the death of his wife and child is found in David R. Slavitt's *Lives of the Saints*. |

## Jones, Gayl
### The Healing
Beacon Press. 1998. 283 pp.

Harlan Jane Eagleton traces the story of her life from her grandmother's beauty shop in Louisville, Kentucky, to rock star manager to faith healer.

Book Groups 📖

| | |
|---|---|
| **Subjects** | African American Authors • African Americans • Faith Healing • Love Affairs • Music and Musicians • Racism |
| **Now try** | Jones is also the author of *Mosquito* and *Corregidora*, among other books. Another novel written in the vernacular is *I Been in Sorrow's Kitchen and Licked Out All the Pots* by Susan Straight. Readers who appreciate the language and politics of Jones's novel may also enjoy Amiri Baraka's *6 Persons*, as well as the more performance-oriented *Negrophobia: An Urban Parable* by Darius James and "Venus," a play by Suzan-Lori Parks. *The Color Purple* and *The Temple of My Familiar* by Alice Walker offer a softer, more emotional take on the same topics. |

## Jones, Gayl
### Mosquito
Beacon Press. 1999. 616 pp.

In her travels through southwest border towns, independent trucker Sojourner Jane Nadine Johnson (aka Mosquito) encounters a pregnant Mexican woman and ends up getting involved in the Sanctuary Movement and finding romance.

| | | |
|---|---|---|
| **2d Appeal** | Characters | Book Groups 📖 |
| **Subjects** | African American Authors • African Americans • American Southwest • Feminism • Immigrants and Refugees • Texas • Truck Drivers • Women's Friendships | |

**Now try**    Jones is also the author of ***Eva's Man*** and ***White Rat***, among other titles. Readers who enjoy Jones's use of the vernacular and her radical politics and humor will enjoy the work of Ishmael Reed, particularly ***Mumbo Jumbo***. Alice Walker offers an intimate exploration of African American feminist issues in ***The Color Purple***. Marge Piercy (***Woman at the Edge of Time*** and ***Vida***, among others) also deals with political and feminist issues.

## Just, Ward
### A Dangerous Friend
Houghton Mifflin. 1999. 256 pp.

When Sydney Parade arrives in South Vietnam in 1965 and becomes involved in the rescue of a captured American pilot, his actions endanger the lives and well-being of both friends and acquaintances.

**2d Appeal**    Setting    Book Groups 📖

**Subjects**    ALA Notable Books • Friendship • Political Fiction • Southeast Asia • Vietnam

**Now try**    Just is also the author of ***The American Ambassador***, ***The Congressman Who Loved Flaubert, and Other Washington Stories***, and ***Echo House***, among many other works of fiction. Just's novel has echoes of Graham Greene's ***The Quiet American*** in both its setting and its subject matter: The naïveté of an individual parallels the naïveté of the United States in its relationship with the Vietnamese. Another novel that explores the reverberations from the involvement of the United States in Southeast Asia is Lily Tuck's ***Siam: Or The Woman Who Shot a Man***.

## Kurzweil, Allen
### The Grand Complication
Hyperion. 2001. 359 pp.

When reference librarian Alexander Short is asked by the mysterious bibliophile and aesthete Henry James Jesson II to research the whereabouts of a watch supposedly made for Marie Antoinette, Alex finds his life in disarray and his marriage in trouble.

**2d Appeal**    Story

**Subjects**    Bibliophiles • Husbands and Wives • Librarians • Mystery • New York • Watches

**Now try**    Kurzweil's first novel is ***A Case of Curiosities***, which is set in the late eighteenth century. Other novels filled with erudition and wordplay include Umberto Eco's ***The Name of the Rose*** and ***The Island of the Day Before*** and Iain Pears's ***An Instance of the Fingerpost***.

## Lethem, Jonathan
### Motherless Brooklyn
Doubleday. 1999. 311 pp.

The fact that he suffers from Tourette's syndrome does not prevent Lionel Essrog (aka The Human Freakshow) from trying to discover the person who murdered small-time hoodlum Frank Minna, the man who rescued Lionel from the Brooklyn orphanage where he grew up.

**2d Appeal**    Characters    Book Groups 📖

    **Subjects**  ALA Notable Books • Brooklyn, New York • Detectives • Murder • Mystery • Orphans • Tourette's Syndrome

    **Now try**  Lethem's other genre-defying novels include *Amnesia Moon* and *Girl in Landscape*. Icy Sparks, the eponymous heroine of Gwyn Hyman Rubio's novel, also has Tourette's syndrome.

## MacLaverty, Bernard
### Grace Notes
W.W. Norton. 1997. 276 pp.

    When Catherine McKenna returns home to Belfast for her father's funeral, memories of her childhood growing up Roman Catholic in Protestant Ireland with a family that didn't appreciate her musical talent nearly overwhelm her.

    **2d Appeal**  Characters        Book Groups 📖

    **Subjects**  Alcoholics and Alcoholism • Composers • Ireland • Mothers and Daughters • Music and Musicians • Postpartum Depression • Scottish Authors

    **Now try**  MacLaverty's earlier novel, *Cal*, also deals with Catholics in Protestant Northern Ireland. Other novels with musical themes include Ian McEwan's *Amsterdam*, Mark Salzman's *The Soloist*, Ellen Hunnicutt's *Suite for Calliope*, and Mary Ann Taylor-Hall's *Come and Go, Molly Snow*. Male writers effectively writing female characters include Roddy Doyle in *The Woman Who Walked into Doors*, Norman Rush in *Mating*, and William Boyd in *Brazzaville Beach*.

## Marcom, Micheline Aharonian
### Three Apples Fell from Heaven
Riverhead Books. 2001. 270 pp.

    The horrific story of the Armenian genocide is told in changing, interweaving voices.

    **2d Appeal**  Setting

    **Subjects**  Armenia • First Novels • Genocide • Novels with Multiple Viewpoints

    **Now try**  *Fugitive Pieces* by Anne Michaels is written in the same poetic language and style. Another novel that loops back and forth in time is *The Moor's Last Sigh* by Salman Rushdie. Peter Balakian's *Black Dog of Fate: A Memoir* is also about the Armenian genocide and its lasting effects on Armenian families in the United States.

## Mattison, Alice
### The Book Borrower
Morrow. 1999. 278 pp.

    Toby Ruben and Deborah Laidlaw meet as young mothers in 1975, and over the next 20 years they discuss their children, their marriages, God, death, teaching, and the whereabouts of a book Deborah let Toby borrow when they first became friends.

    **2d Appeal**  Characters

    **Subjects**  Anarchists • Art and Artists • Death and Dying • Women's Friendships

    **Now try**  Mattison's other novels include *Hilda and Pearl* and *Men Giving Money, Women Yelling: Stories*. Both Mattison's writing style and the way her characters speak bring to mind the fiction of Grace Paley, including *Later the Same Day* and *Enormous Changes at the Last Minute: Stories*.

## McCarthy, Cormac
### All the Pretty Horses
Knopf. 1992. 301 pp.

In the 1930s, two teenaged boys go south to Mexico for an adventure, but their experiences turn them into men.

Book Groups 📖

**Subjects**   1930s • ALA Notable Books • Coming-of-Age • Mexico • National Book Award Winners • National Book Critics Circle Award Winners • Teenage Boys

**Now try**   This is the first book in The Border trilogy, followed by *The Crossing* and *Cities of the Plain*. Other books by McCarthy include *Blood Meridian* and *Suttree*. The violence endemic to McCarthy's novels is also a characteristic of the novels of Ian McEwan, including *The Cement Garden* and *Amsterdam*.

## McDermott, Alice
### Charming Billy
Farrar, Straus and Giroux. 1998. 280 pp.

When his friends and family gather to toast Billy Lynch at his wake, they speak of his prodigious drinking, his good humor, his great charm, and the woman he was supposed to marry who went back to Ireland after they were engaged and never returned to him.

**2d Appeal**   Characters

Book Groups 📖

**Subjects**   ALA Notable Books • Alcoholics and Alcoholism • Irish Americans • National Book Award Winners

**Now try**   McDermott's other novels include *At Weddings and Wakes* and *That Night*. Another author who writes about Irish American family life is Mary Gordon (*The Other Side*).

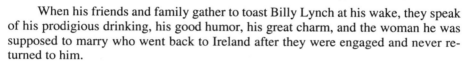

## Minot, Eliza
### The Tiny One
Knopf. 1999. 257 pp.

Thinking about the death of her mother in a car accident a few days before, eight-year-old Via relives, in every detail, that awful day.

Book Groups 📖

**Subjects**   Brothers and Sisters • Death of a Parent • First Novels • Massachusetts

**Now try**   Susan Minot, Eliza's older sister, wrote about a similar occurrence in her novel *Monkeys*.

## Minot, Susan
### Evening
Knopf. 1998. 264 pp.

Now 65 and dying of cancer, Ann Lord looks back over her life and remembers a weekend 40 years before when she met the love of her life—a passion that has remained constant through three marriages and the raising of five children.

**2d Appeal**   Characters

Book Groups 📖

**Subjects**   Cancer • Death and Dying • Love Affairs • Upper Classes

**Now try**  Minot's other novels include *Monkeys* and *Folly*. Other authors who, like Minot, make use of the details of their characters' lives to make them real for their readers are Virginia Woolf (in *Mrs. Dalloway* and *To the Lighthouse*) and Michael Cunningham's *The Hours*. Another novel in which the elderly main character re-lives the most important event of her life is Susan Stonich's *These Granite Islands*.

## Mistry, Rohinton
### A Fine Balance
Knopf. 1996. 603 pp.

Two lower-caste tailors, an upper-caste widow, and a student all form an unlikely alliance while sharing a cramped apartment during a state of emergency in India in 1975.

**2d Appeal**  Setting                                                    Book Groups 📖

**Subjects**  1970s • ALA Notable Books • Canadian Authors • Family Relationships • Friendship • India • Indian Authors • Oprah Winfrey Selection • Violence

**Now try**  Mistry also wrote *Swimming Lessons & Other Stories* and *Tales from Firozsha Baag*. Mistry's epic tales are not unlike those of Leo Tolstoy's (*Anna Karenina* and *War and Peace*) in their scope and vision. Caste plays an important part in Arundhati Roy's novel *The God of Small Things*. Mistry's harrowing novel has unexpected touches of humor, much like the fiction of Lewis Nordan (*Wolf Whistle* and *The Sharpshooter Blues*, among others). *A Fine Balance* won both the Giller Prize and Canada's Governor General's Literary Award.

## Mistry, Rohinton
### Such a Long Journey
Knopf. 1991. 339 pp.

Gustad Noble, a devout Parsi, strives to do the right thing for his family and friends, but he finds himself involved in the political corruption of Indira Gandhi's government, with terrible results.

**2d Appeal**  Setting                                                    Book Groups 📖

**Subjects**  Canadian Authors • Family Relationships • First Novels • Friendship • India • Indian Authors

**Now try**  *Such a Long Journey* received Canada's Governor General's Award and was short-listed for the Booker Prize. Mistry's blend of humor and tragedy, as well as his playful use of language, is reminiscent of Salman Rushdie's writing in, for example, *Midnight's Children* and *The Moor's Last Sigh*.

## Morrison, Toni
### Jazz
Knopf. 1992. 229 pp.

The rhythms of 1920s Harlem punctuate this nonlinear novel of the urban black experience and a marriage gone bad.

Book Groups 📖

**Subjects**  1920s • Adultery • African American Authors • African Americans • ALA Notable Books • Harlem • Jazz • Love Stories • Male/Female Relationships • New York

**Now try**  Among Morrison's other novels are *Sula*, *Beloved*, and *The Bluest Eye*. *Jonah's Gourd Vine* by Zora Neale Hurston is another view of the black experience. Both David Lewis's *When Harlem Was in Vogue* and Ann Douglas's *Terrible Honesty:*

***Mongrel Manhattan in the 1920s*** are about the New York world where Morrison's characters live. Connie Porter's ***All-Bright Court*** is another novel about African Americans who migrated to the north in search of a better life.

## Morrison, Toni

### Paradise

Knopf. 1998. 318 pp.

Violence erupts between the men of Ruby, a small, all-black town in rural Oklahoma that was founded by descendants of freed slaves, and residents of a nearby town.

Book Groups 📖

**Subjects**   African American Authors • African Americans • Oklahoma • Oprah Winfrey Selection • Small-Town Life • Violence

**Now try**   *Paradise* is Morrison's first novel since she won the Nobel Prize for Literature. Her other novels include ***The Bluest Eye***, ***Jazz***, and ***Beloved***. Another novel partially set in a small, all-black town in Oklahoma is Rilla Askew's ***Fire in Beulah***.

## Murakami, Haruki

### The Wind-Up Bird Chronicle

Knopf. 1997. 613 pp.

When his wife mysteriously disappears, Toru Okada sets out to search for her, encountering along the way a variety of bizarre people and events, all linked by the memory of a massacre in 1939 of Japanese troops by the Soviet army at Nomonhan, on the Manchurian border. Translated from the Japanese by Jay Rubin.

Book Groups 📖

**Subjects**   ALA Notable Books • Asia • Asian Authors • Eccentrics and Eccentricities • Husbands and Wives • Japan • Japanese Authors • Novels in Translation • Political Fiction • World War II

**Now try**   Murakami is also the author of ***South of the Border, West of the Sun***, ***A Wild Sheep Chase***, and ***Hard-Boiled Wonderland and the End of the World***. The main character in Kazuo Ishiguro's ***The Unconsoled*** also drifts through events that may be real or may be simply hallucinations.

## Nordan, Lewis

### Wolf Whistle

Algonquin Books of Chapel Hill. 1993. 290 pp.

In this tragicomic version of the real-life 1955 murder of a black teenager who had dared to whistle at a white woman, the lost souls of Arrow Catcher, Mississippi, grapple with their differing levels of complicity in the crime as well as the true meaning of evil.

**2d Appeal**   Setting

**Subjects**   ALA Notable Books • American South • Black Humor • Magic Realism • Mississippi • Murder • Racism • Southern Authors

**Now try**   Some of the same characters from ***Wolf Whistle*** also appear in Nordan's ***Music of the Swamp***. Nordan's southern blend of humor and pathos can be found in William Baldwin's ***The Hard to Catch Mercy***.

## Norman, Howard
### The Bird Artist
Farrar, Straus and Giroux. 1994. 289 pp.

Fabian Vas is known for three things in Witless Bay, Newfoundland: his moderate success as an artist, his longtime affair with the wild and irreverent Margaret, and the murder of a local lighthouse keeper.

**2d Appeal**  Characters                                               Book Groups 📖

**Subjects**  Adultery • ALA Notable Books • Art and Artists • Birds • Canada • Love Stories • Male/Female Relationships • Mothers and Sons • Murder • Newfoundland, Canada • Small-Town Life

**Now try**  Both of Norman's other novels, *The Northern Lights* and *The Museum Guard*, display the same economy of writing as *The Bird Artist*. Another novel set in Newfoundland is E. Annie Proulx's *The Shipping News*.

## Ondaatje, Michael
### Anil's Ghost
Knopf. 2000. 311 pp.

Anil Tissera returns to her home in Sri Lanka on behalf of a human rights organization to investigate the many murders being committed in the ongoing ethnic, religious, and political violence.

**2d Appeal**  Setting                                                  Book Groups 📖

**Subjects**  ALA Notable Books • Brothers • Canadian Authors • Doctors and Patients • Forensics • Murder • Political Fiction • Sri Lanka • Violence

**Now try**  Ondaatje is also the author of *Coming Through Slaughter* and *In the Skin of a Lion*, as well as several books of poems. Another political novel that is nearly as understated as Ondaatje's is Lawrence Thornton's *Imagining Argentina*. Other political novels are Patricia Henley's *Hummingbird House* and Barbara Kingsolver's *The Poisonwood Bible*. *Anil's Ghost* won the 2000 Kiriyama Pacific Rim Book Prize, as well as two Canadian awards: the Giller Prize and the Governor General's Literary Award for fiction.

## Powers, Richard
### Plowing the Dark
Farrar, Straus and Giroux. 2000. 415 pp.

Adie Klarpol leaves her unsatisfying job in New York to join a group of virtual reality researchers in the Pacific Northwest as their resident artist; at the same time, Taimur Martin, an American teacher in Lebanon, is kidnapped by Islamic fundamentalists.

**Subjects**  Art and Artists • Kidnapping • Pacific Northwest • Postmodern Fiction • Religious Extremism • Seattle, Washington • Teachers • Violence • Virtual Reality • Washington

**Now try**  Powers is also the author of *Gain*, *Three Farmers on Their Way to a Dance*, *Galatea 2.2*, and *The Gold Bug Variations*, among other novels. Another author of relentlessly intelligent novels is Don DeLillo (*Underworld*, *White Noise*, and *Libra* are three of his best).

## Price, Reynolds
### The Promise of Rest
Scribner. 1995. 353 pp.

Although Duke University professor Hutch Mayfield and his wife Ann have recently separated, they come together once again to care for their son Wade, who is dying from AIDS.

**2d Appeal**  Characters                                               Book Groups 📖

**Subjects**   AIDS • Death and Dying • Family Relationships • Fathers and Sons • Gay Men • Illness • Mothers and Sons • Terminal Illness

**Now try**   *The Promise of Rest* concludes Price's Mayfield family trilogy, which includes *The Surface of Earth* and *The Source of Light*. Mark Doty's memoir *Heaven's Coast* is also about caring for someone dying of AIDS. Many of the characters in Alan Gurganus's *Plays Well with Others* live with the knowledge that their closest friends and lovers are dying of AIDS.

## Rush, Norman

### Mating

Knopf. 1991. 496 pp.

The unnamed narrator, an anthropologist, pursues utopian scientist Nelson Denoon across the Kalahari to his experimental, self-sustaining, matriarchal community, where she hopes to gain acceptance and love.

**2d Appeal**   Characters Book Groups 📖

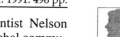

**Subjects**   Africa • Botswana • First Novels • Love Stories • Male/Female Relationships • National Book Award Winners • Science and Scientists • Utopian Novels

**Now try**   Rush's first book, *Whites*, a collection of stories, was an ALA Notable Book. (The heroine of *Mating* first appeared as a character in a short story in *Whites*.) Another novel written by a man in the voice of a strong, very smart heroine whose determination and dogged pursuit of a goal lead to precarious situations is Peter Hoeg's *Smilla's Sense of Snow*. A satirical look at a matriarchal society in action can be found in Francine Prose's *Hunters and Gatherers*.

## Rushdie, Salman

### The Ground Beneath Her Feet

Henry Holt. 1999. 575 pp.

The myth of Orpheus and Eurydice is retold in the epic of Ormus Cama and Vina Apsara, two rock-and-roll idols from Bombay whose fantastic lives take them from India to London to New York and beyond, on a wave of twentieth-century popular culture.

**2d Appeal**   Characters Book Groups 📖

**Subjects**   India • Indian Authors • Love Affairs • Music and Musicians • Mythology • Rock and Roll

**Now try**   Rushdie is also the author of *Fury*, *Shame*, *Midnight's Children*, and *Haroun and the Sea of Stories*, all of which display his love of language and talent for fantastical writing. Another epic parody of popular culture is David Foster Wallace's *Infinite Jest*. Don DeLillo's *Great Jones Street* is an erudite, tongue-in-cheek look at the life of a rock star. The scope, tone, Bombay setting, and multiple characters in Rushdie's novel bring to mind John Irving's novel *A Son of the Circus*.

## Rushdie, Salman
### The Moor's Last Sigh
Pantheon. 1996. 435 pp.

Moraes "Moor" Zogoiby describes his colorful family and their spicy life in Cochin, filled with failed relationships, early deaths, betrayals, passion, a hunger for power, and the seductions of art.

Book Groups 📖

**Subjects**   Art and Artists • Family Relationships • India • Indian Authors • Men's Lives • Multigenerational Novels

**Now try**   Rushdie's breathtaking use of language is similar to Gabriel Garcia Marquez's (*Chronicle of a Death Foretold*), Jose Saramago's (*The Stone Raft*), and Alexander Theroux's (*D'Arconville's Cat*).

## Shields, Carol
### The Stone Diaries
Viking. 1993. 361 pp.

The long and "ordinary" life of Daisy Stone Goodwill unfolds in bittersweet detail through a collage of narrative, letters, newspaper clippings, and multiple voices.

Book Groups 📖

**Subjects**   Canada • Family Relationships • National Book Critics Circle Award Winners • Pulitzer Prize Winners • Women's Lives

**Now try**   Shields is also the author of *Swann*, *The Box Garden*, *Various Miracles*, and *Small Ceremonies*, among other works of fiction. Both *Kate Vaiden* and *Roxanna Slade* by Reynolds Price are about the lives of strong women.

## Smith, Zadie
### White Teeth
Random House. 2000. 448 pp.

The families of unlikely best friends—working-class Englishman Archibald Jones, his Jamaican wife Clara, and their daughter Irie, and Samad Iqbal, a Bengali Muslim waiter, his wife Alsana, and twin sons Millat and Magid—intertwine in contemporary London, a city filled with a bewildering array of ethnicities, religions, cultures, and beliefs.

**2d Appeal**   Characters

Book Groups 📖

**Subjects**   ALA Notable Books • Biracial Characters • British Authors • First Novels • Husbands and Wives • London, England • Men's Friendships • Multigenerational Novels • Twins

**Now try**   Smith's exuberant writing brings to mind Salman Rushdie's *The Moor's Last Sigh*. Smith's novel won the Whitbread First Novel Award, the Orange Prize, and the Guardian First Book Award.

## Trevor, William
### Felicia's Journey
Viking. 1995. 213 pp.

A pregnant young Irish girl flees a family shamed by her situation and vainly seeks her lover in England, only to fall into the path of a deceptively mild-mannered serial killer—or maybe a worse fate.

**2d Appeal**   Characters

Book Groups 📖

**Subjects**   Family Relationships • Ireland • Irish Authors • Pregnancy • Serial Killers • Sexual Abuse

**Now try**   Trevor's other books include *The Children of Dynmouth*, *The Collected Stories*, *Fools of Fortune*, and *Excursions in the Real World: Memoirs*. *Zombie* by Joyce Carol Oates is another novel about a serial killer. Roddy Doyle's *The Snapper* is a much more humorous novel about an Irish girl's unwanted pregnancy. Like Felicia in Trevor's novel, the main character in William Faulkner's *Light in August* is also searching for the father of her child. *Felicia's Journey* won the Whitbread Prize.

# Updike, John
## Rabbit at Rest

Knopf. 1990. 512 pp.

After suffering from a heart attack while saving his granddaughter from drowning, 55-year-old Harry (Rabbit) Angstrom struggles to find reasons to live in an America ridden with drugs, crime, and AIDS.

**2d Appeal**   Characters

Book Groups 📖

**Subjects**   Drugs and Drug Abuse • Family Relationships • Grandparents • Male/Female Relationships • Middle-Aged Men • National Book Critics Circle Award Winners • Pulitzer Prize Winners

**Now try**   Rabbit's passage through life is chronicled in Updike's *Rabbit, Run*, *Rabbit Redux*, *Rabbit Is Rich*, and *Rabbit at Rest*. Another exploration of a man's life is found in *Larry's Party* by Carol Shields.

# Appendix A: How to Create a Dynamic Book Club

Book clubs are not a new idea in the United States. The Great Books Reading and Discussion programs have been popular with adult readers since their inception in 1947. What *is* new is a widespread interest in developing reading communities in a variety of shapes and formats. The Washington Center for the Book at the Seattle Public Library annually presents "If All of Seattle Read the Same Book," in which book groups throughout the Puget Sound area read and discuss the same book, then come together over three days to meet and talk to the author. Interested readers can join in a book discussion group online (a good one is The Washington Post Book Club—Live [http://www.washingtonpost.com/wp-srv/liveonline/ books/bookclub. htm]). Special interest reading groups online can be found at www. Readinggroupsonline.com. Readers can watch Oprah's Book Club on television, or they can participate in National Public Radio's once-a-month Book Club of the Air. There are book groups that meet at public libraries, at bookstores, and at literary and community centers. Or you can start a book club of your own that meets at the homes of friends and neighbors. Check on the Internet for listservs and other book club information.

Although there are many people who find that reading is a totally pleasurable solitary activity and have no desire to talk about what they read in a structured setting, the growing popularity of book groups makes it clear that many readers find that their appreciation, pleasure, and understanding of a book is broadened and deepened through discussion.

Although *Now Read This* and *Now Read This II* are not guides to setting up and running a book group (I've included a brief list of such guides at the end of this appendix), they can help in selecting books for your group. Nearly every book included in *Now Read This* and *Now Read This II* is a fine choice for a book discussion, but the ones designated "Book Groups" make for an especially interesting discussion.

That being said, here are some of the more basic issues to keep in mind when you're beginning, or reinvigorating, a book group.

## Choosing a Book to Read

Those who have been part of an unsuccessful book group will agree that choosing the right books to discuss is one of the most difficult (and enjoyable) aspects of a successful book club.

There are several issues to keep in mind when you're choosing books for your group. It's important to realize that not every member of a group is going to like every book that's discussed. Book groups are based on the premise that reading likes and dislikes are idiosyncratic. Everyone in a group may read exactly the same book, with identical covers and identical pagination, but, in fact, each member is reading a different book. Each person brings to their reading of a book a unique history with a unique set of memories and influences. Each person is in a different place in his or her life when reading the book. And all of those differences—as subtle or as obvious as they might be—greatly influence how and why certain people may like or dislike any particular book. Keep in mind that these differences are often what make for an exciting discussion!

People often wonder what makes a good book for a discussion. Although it's true that sometimes a book that one group finds totally stimulating is a total dud for another group, in general there are books that lead to good discussions and books that don't.

I find it helpful to think of book discussions this way: When you're talking about a book, what you're really talking about is everything that the author hasn't said; in effect, all that white space on the printed page. Because of this, books that are plot-driven (that is, most mysteries, westerns, and romances, some science fiction/fantasy novels, and many mainstream novels) often don't make good choices for discussion. In these books, the author spells out everything for the reader, the plot predicaments are neatly tied up, and character development is subordinate to the story. There's little to say except, "I loved (or hated) the book," or "Wasn't that interesting?"

The best books for discussion are those with three-dimensional characters who are forced to make difficult choices, under difficult situations. Why a character behaved as he or she did is often a fruitful question to raise with the group. For example, in Ward Just's *A Dangerous Friend*, why was Sydney so determined to rescue the captured American pilot? In Graham Greene's *The End of the Affair*, why didn't Sarah leave her husband? In Edith Wharton's *The Age of Innocence*, why, at the end of the novel, does Archer refuse to see Ellen? In Eudora Welty's *The Optimist's Daughter*, why did Judge McKelva marry Fay, a woman as different from his first wife as anyone could be?

Other good choices are books with ambiguous endings, where the outcome of the novel is not crystal clear. There is certainly no general consensus about what happens at the end of Tim O'Brien's *In the Lake of the Woods*, James McManus's *Going to the Sun*, Wallace Stegner's *The Angle of Repose*, James Buchan's *The Persian Bride*, Tim Winton's *The Riders*, and Jon Cohen's *The Man in the Window*.

In addition, books that relate to the readers' own experiences (a mothers-and-daughters group might enjoy discussing Amy Tan's *The Joy Luck Club*) and books that contain controversial ideas are generally good springboards for discussion.

There are also several pairs of books that make good discussions. Although some groups discuss these books in the same meeting, the busy schedules of most book group participants may make it better to read and discuss these in successive months. Good pairs include

- Molly Gloss's *Wild Life* and Robert Michael Pyle's *Where Bigfoot Walks: Crossing the Dark Divide*

- Michael Cunningham's *The Hours* and Virginia Woolf's *Mrs. Dalloway*

- Ward Just's *A Dangerous Friend* and Graham Greene's *The Quiet American*

- E. Annie Proulx's *Close Range*, Kent Haruf's *Plainsong*, and Tim Egan's *Lasso the Wind*—a good triple-header.

A five-month Africa reading blitz consisting of Barbara Kingsolver's *The Poisonwood Bible*, Joseph Conrad's *Heart of Darkness*, Ronan Bennett's *The Catastrophist*, Adam Hochchild's *King Leopold's Ghost*, and Ann Jones's *Looking for Lovedu* is also a way to ensure good discussions, as each month's conversation will build on the books read in the previous months. Mixing nonfiction and fiction together in these groups of books can result in wonderful discussions.

There are some books that seem as though they were written for the benefit of book groups. These are the books that you just can't stop talking about, books that raise so many issues that conversation is nonstop. It's hard to see how a discussion about Andre Dubus III's *House of Sand and Fog*, Ernest Gaines's *A Lesson Before Dying*, Russell Banks's *The Sweet Hereafter*, Barbara Kingsolver's *The Poisonwood Bible*, or Tim O'Brien's *In the Lake of the Woods* can help but be successful. No duds here, I promise you!

# Discussing the Book

Although many groups don't see the necessity for a group leader (either a member of the group or a paid facilitator), my experience has been that someone needs to take responsibility for keeping the discussion flowing and on track and for making sure that everyone who wants to has a chance to offer his or her opinion. One way to make this happen is to designate a leader (perhaps rotating with each meeting) whose job it is to come up with some questions to get the discussion started and keep it going. Another option is for each group member to take the responsibility of coming to the meeting with one discussion question about the book. Some groups find it useful to have the leader also bring information about the author along with reviews or articles about the book.

The Internet has made a huge difference in the ease with which book group members can access information about specific books and authors. Most publishers, as well as other institutions and organizations who regularly do reading group discussion guides, have made them available on their Web sites. Those book group members who lack access to the Internet can frequently find these materials in paper format at their local bookstores or library. Simon & Schuster (www.simonsays.com), HarperCollins (www.harpercollins.com/hc/readers/index.asp), and Random House (www.randomhouse.com/vintage/read/) are particularly active in producing reader's guides for their books. Ballantine Books binds in a reader's guide in their most popular book club books.

Although there are questions specific to particular books, there are also some general questions that can be asked of any work of fiction.

- How does the title relate to the book?

- What is the theme of the book?

- Are the characters believable? Did you understand why they behaved as they did?

- Were all the characters equally well developed?

- Consider the structure of the book. Did the author make use of flashbacks? Was the book written in the first person? From multiple points of view? Why did the author choose to present the plot this way?

- Can you imagine a different ending than the one the author wrote?
- What if the book were written from another character's point of view—what would be different and what would be the same?

## Book Group Guides

Some of my favorite guides to book groups are included in the following list. Although there is, of course, some duplication in the discussions of the nuts and bolts of successful book groups, each of these books offers valuable insights and suggestions for choosing books and ensuring positive experiences for everyone in the group.

- Shireen Dodson's *The Mother-Daughter Book Club: How Ten Busy Mothers and Their Daughters Came Together to Talk, Laugh, and Learn Through Their Love of Reading* (HarperPerennial, 1997)
- Monique Greenwood, Lynda Johnson, and Tracy Mitchell-Brown's *The Go On Girl! Book Club Guide for Reading Groups* (Hyperion, 1999)
- Rachel Jacobsohn's *The Reading Group Handbook: Everything You Need to Know to Start Your Own Bookclub* (Hyperion, 1998)
- David Laskin and Holly Hughes's *The Reading Group Book* (Plume, 1995)
- Pat Neblett's *Circles of Sisterhood: A Book Discussion Group Guide for Women of Color* (Harlem River Press, 1996)
- Mickey Pearlman's *What to Read: The Essential Guide for Reading Group Members and Other Book Lovers* (HarperPerennial, 1999)
- Rollene Saal's *The New York Public Library Guide to Reading Groups* (Crown, 1995)
- Patrick Sauer's *The Complete Idiot's Guide to Starting a Reading Group* (Alpha Books, 2000)
- Ellen Slezak's *The Book Group Book*, 3d edition (Chicago Review Press, 2000)

# Appendix B: Book Awards

## American Library Association Notable Books
(50 E. Huron St., Chicago, IL 60611-2765)

Selected annually by a 12-member Notable Books Council of the American Library Association. Books are chosen for their exceptional literary merit.

## Betty Trask Prize/Awards
(The Society of Authors, 84 Drayton Gardens, London SW 10 9SB, England)

Begun in 1983, the prize and awards are given by the Society of Authors in the United Kingdom for best first novels by a Commonwealth citizen under the age of 35.

## The Booker Prize
(Book Trust (England), Book House, 5 East Hill, London SW 18 2QZ, England)

Founded in 1969 by Booker McConnell, Ltd., and administered by the National Book League in the United Kingdom. Awarded to the best novel written in English by a citizen of the United Kingdom, the Commonwealth, Eire, Pakistan, or South Africa.

## The Boston Book Review/Fisk Fiction Prize
(Boston Book Review, 30 Brattle St., 4th Flr., Cambridge, MA 02138)

Established in 1994 to recognize the finest literary fiction.

## The Giller Prize
(Kelly Duffin, Administrator, 21 Steepleview Crescent, Richmond Hill, ONT, Canada L4C9R1)

Established in 1994 to highlight excellence in creative writing. It is awarded to the author of a Canadian novel or short story collection published in English.

## The Governor General's Literary Awards
(Canada Council, 350 Albert St., P.O. Box 1047, Ottawa, ONT, Canada K1P5V8)

Presented annually by the Canada Council for outstanding English and French language works of fiction.

## The Guardian Fiction Prize

Sponsored by the Guardian newspaper, on the recommendation of a panel of five judges. The award winner must be a work of fiction by a British or Commonwealth writer that has been published in the United Kingdom.

## The International IMPAC/Dublin Literary Award
(Cumberland House, Fenian St., Dublin 2, Ireland)

Created in 1995 as a joint initiative of the Municipal Government of Dublin, Ireland, the Dublin Corporation, and IMPAC, a productivity improvement company. It is administered by Dublin City Public Libraries.

## The James Tait Black Memorial Prize
(University of Edinburgh Center, 7-11 Nicolson St., Edinburgh, Scotland EH89BE)

Presented annually to a work written in English originating with a British publisher.

## The Kiriyama Pacific Rim Book Prize
(USF Center for the Pacific Rim, 2130 Fulton St., San Francisco, CA 94117-1080)

Co-sponsored by the Kiriyama Pacific Rim Foundation and the Center for the Pacific Rim at the University of San Francisco, the award is given to the book that best contributes to greater understanding among nations and peoples of the Pacific Rim.

## The Miles Franklin Award
(Administered by the Permanent Trustee Co., Ltd., of Sydney, Australia)

Given annually since 1957 to an Australian novel or play of the highest literary merit that presents aspects of Australian life. It is adminsitered by the Permanent Trustee Co., Ltd., of Sydney, Australia.

## The National Book Award
(260 Fifth Ave., Rm. 904, New York, NY 10001)

Given annually by the National Book Foundation to honor American books of the highest literary merit.

## The National Book Critics Circle Award
(c/o Art Winslow, The Nation, 72 Fifth Ave., New York, NY 10011)

Chosen by the National Book Critics Circle, a group of professional book review editors and critics.

## The Orange Prize
(Administered by Orange Telecommunications Co.)

Established in 1996, the prize is open to women writing in English worldwide. It is given by Orange.

## The PEN/Faulkner Award
(Folger Shakespeare Library, 201 E. Capital St. SE, Washington, DC 20003)

Created by writers in 1980 to honor their peers. It is awarded annually by the PEN/Faulkner Foundation.

## The Prix Goncourt
(Academie Goncourt, Place Gaillon, 75002 Paris, France)

Given to recognize an author for an outstanding work of French prose.

## The Pulitzer Prize
(Columbia University, 702 Journalism, New York, NY 10027)

Given annually by Columbia University since 1917, on the recommendation of a Pulitzer Prize Board.

## The Whitbread Award
(Booksellers Association of Great Britain & Ireland, Minister House, 272 Vauxhall Bridge Rd., London SW1V 1BA, England)

Given to a novel and a first novel; authors must have lived in Great Britain or Ireland for more than three years.

# Appendix C: Bridges to Genre Fiction

As discussed in the introduction, many mainstream novels contain strong elements of genre fiction. Fans of genre fiction may wish to explore mainstream titles that include elements of their favorite genres. And likewise, mainstream readers who wish to venture into genre fiction may want to start with these genre bridges.

## Romance

Ansa, Tina McElroy. *The Hand I Fan With.*

Bailey, Paul. *Kitty and Virgil.*

Buchan, James. *The Persian Bride.*

Davenport, Kiana. *Song of the Exile.*

Dimmick, Barbara. *In the Presence of Horses.*

Hendricks, Judith Ryan. *Bread Alone.*

Johnson, Diane. *Le Mariage.*

Kay, Terry. *Taking Lottie Home.*

Kingsolver, Barbara. *Animal Dreams.*

Kirchner, Bharti. *Sharmila's Book.*

Landvik, Lorn. *The Tall Pine Polka.*

Lennox, Judith. *Some Old Lover's Ghost.*

Lipman, Elinor. *The Inn at Lake Devine.*

Mapson, Jo-Ann. *The Wilder Sisters.*

McNamer, Deirdre. *My Russian.*

Morris, Mary. *Acts of God.*

Ray, Jeanne. *Julie and Romeo.*

Salamanca, J. R. *That Summer's Trance.*

Shreve, Anita. *The Pilot's Wife.*

Shreve, Anita. *Where or When.*

St. John, Madeleine. *A Stairway to Heaven.*

Trollope, Joanna. *A Passionate Man.*

Weber, Katherine. *The Music Lesson.*

Wolfe, Swain. *The Lake Dreams the Sky.*

Wolk, Lauren. *Those Who Favor Fire.*

# Mystery and Detection

Amis, Martin. *Night Train.*

Atwood, Margaret. *The Blind Assassin.*

Berne, Suzanne. *A Crime in the Neighborhood.*

Bohjalian, Chris. *Midwives.*

Bradley, James. *Wrack.*

Bromell, Henry. *Little America.*

Clark, Robert. *Mr. White's Confession.*

Davis, Kathryn. *The Walking Tour.*

Dexter, Pete. *The Paperboy.*

Ishiguro, Kazuo. *When We Were Orphans.*

Johnson, Wayne. *Don't Think Twice.*

Kohler, Sheila. *Cracks.*

Lethem, Jonathan. *Motherless Brooklyn.*

Long, David. *The Daughters of Simon Lamoreaux.*

Maitland, Sara. *Ancestral Truths.*

Miller, Sue. *While I Was Gone.*

Murakami, Haruki. *The Wind-Up Bird Chronicle.*

O'Brien, Tim. *In the Lake of the Woods.*

Sakamoto, Kerri. *The Electrical Field.*

Whitehead, Colson. *The Intuitionist.*

Winton, Tim. *The Riders.*

# Historical

Alvarez, Julia. *In the Time of the Butterflies.*

Bainbridge, Beryl. *The Birthday Boys.*

Baker, Kevin. *Dreamland.*

Barry, Sebastian. *The Whereabouts of Eneas McNulty.*

Bennett, Ronan. *The Catastrophist.*

Binding, Tim. *Lying with the Enemy.*

Bradley, James. *Wrack.*

Brown, Carrie. *The Hatbox Baby.*

Buchan, James. *The Persian Bride.*

Chabon, Michael. *The Amazing Adventures of Kavalier & Clay.*

Davenport, Kiana. *Song of the Exile.*

DeLillo, Don. *Underworld.*

Faulks, Sebastian. *Charlotte Gray.*

Foden, Giles. *The Last King of Scotland.*

Ghosh, Amitav. *The Glass Palace.*

Giardina, Denise. *Saints and Villains.*

Johnston, Wayne. *The Colony of Unrequited Dreams.*

Marcom, Micheline Aharonian. *Three Apples Fell from Heaven.*

Millhauser, Steven. *Martin Dressler: The Tale of an American Dreamer.*

Morrison, Toni. *Jazz.*

Unsworth, Barry. *Losing Nelson.*

# Fantasy

Carey, Lisa. *In the Country of the Young.*

Chamoiseau, Patrick. *Chronicle of the Seven Sorrows.*

Clark, Martin. *The Many Aspects of Mobile Home Living.*

Frucht, Abby. *Polly's Ghost.*

Golding, Michael. *Benjamin's Gift.*

Gutcheon, Beth. *More Than You Know.*

Nahai, Gina B. *Moonlight on the Avenue of Faith.*

Orlock, Carol. *The Hedge, the Ribbon.*

Robinson, Eden. *Monkey Beach.*

Sherrill, Steven. *The Minotaur Takes a Cigarette Break.*

Thornton, Lawrence. *Naming the Spirits.*

Zabor, Rafi. *The Bear Comes Home.*

# Gentle Reads

Berry, Wendell. *Jayber Crow.*

Brookner, Anita. *Falling Slowly.*

Brown, Carrie. *Lamb in Love.*

Burnard, Bonnie. *A Good House.*

Chiaverini, Jennifer. *The Quilter's Apprentice.*

Earley, Tony. *Jim the Boy.*

Kay, Terry. *Taking Lottie Home.*

Landvik, Lorn. *The Tall Pine Polka.*

Ross, Ann B. *Miss Julia Speaks Her Mind.*

## Suspense Thriller

Bromell, Henry. *Little America.*

Buchan, James. *The Persian Bride.*

Emerson, Gloria. *Loving Graham Greene.*

Just, Ward. *A Dangerous Friend.*

Koch, Christopher. *Highways to a War.*

Lamar, Jake. *The Last Integrationist.*

Lethem, Jonathan. *Motherless Brooklyn.*

McCabe, Patrick. *The Butcher.*

O'Brien, Tim. *In the Lake of the Woods.*

## Horror (Dark Fantasy)

Barker, Pat. *Another World.*

Gutcheon, Beth. *More Than You Know.*

# Author/Title Index

The author/title index is arranged as follows:

Titles in **_boldface italic_** are main entries, with page numbers in **boldface** indicating the main entry and those in regular typeface referring to the "Now try" sections. Main entries for authors are in **boldface** type. Authors in regular typeface and titles in _italics_ are listed in the "Now try" sections.

**_@expectations_, 53**
Abbey, Edward, 14, 54
_Abide with Me,_ 38
**_About a Boy_, 102**
**Abraham, Pearl, 47**
_Absalom, Absalom,_ 14
_Absolution,_ 122
_According to Mark,_ 111
_Accordion Crimes,_ 15
Achebe, Chinua, 7
**Ackerman, Karl, 23**
**Ackerman, Marianne, 1**
_The Act of the Damned,_ 69
**_Acts of God_, 48**
_Acts of Revision,_ 114
Adams, Alice, 64
Adams, Douglas, 63
**Adams, Glenda, 67**
**Adams, Richard, 14**
**Adler, Warren, 58**
**_Adrian Mole: The Cappuccino Years_, 61**
_Adrian Mole: The Lost Years,_ 61
_Affliction,_ 150
_After Life,_ 83, 127
_Against All Hope: A Memoir of Life in Castro's Prisons,_ 75
_Agassiz: A Novel in Stories,_ 83
_The Age of Grief,_ 17, 131
**_Age of Iron_, 148**
_The Age of Longing,_ 9
Agee, James, 119
**Agee, Jonis, 23**
_The Aguero Sisters,_ 63, 75, 100
**_Ahab's Wife_, 105**
**_Ain't Nobody's Business If I Do_, 64**
Akins, Ellen, 52
_The Albany Cycle,_ 3
Alberts, Laurie, 44
**Alcalá, Kathleen, 1, 22**

Alexie, Sherman, 31, 43, 51, 106, 110
_Alice in Wonderland,_ 104
**_Alice Springs_, 8**
_All American Dream Dolls,_ 100
**_All Quiet on the Orient Express_, 117,** 118, 134
_All Quiet on the Western Front,_ 73, 103
_All Stories Are True,_ 119
_All Summer Long,_ 133
_All the Nice Girls,_ 68
**_All the Pretty Horses_,** 79, **157**
_All We Need of Hell,_ 149
**_All-Bright Court_,** 109, **124,** 141, 159
_The All-True Travels and Adventures of Lidie Newton,_ 17
Allende, Isabel, 7, 22, 95, 118, 119, 143
Allison, Dorothy, 25, 70, 97, 118
_Almighty Me,_ 70
_Almost Heaven,_ 112, 140
**_Almost Home_, 116**
Al-Shayk, Hanan, 18
**Alvarez, Julia, 2,** 50, 52, 67, 119, 134
**_Always Outnumbered, Always Outgunned_,** **119,** 139
_Amanda/Miranda,_ 50
**_The Amazing Adventures of Kavalier & Clay_,** 38, **82,** 110
_The Ambassadors,_ 10
_The American Ambassador,_ 26, 131, 155
_American Chica: Two Worlds, One Childhood,_ 24
_American Dad,_ 105
_American Heaven,_ 28, 68
_American Knees,_ 60
_American Owned Love,_ 98
_Americn Pastoral,_ 126, 131
Ames, Jonathan, 57, 75, 114
**Amidon, Stephen, 2**
Amis, Kingsley, 123, 134

**Amis, Martin**, 73, 80, **145**, 148
*Amnesia Moon*, 156
*Amsterdam*, **115**, 156, 157
*Amy and Isabelle*, 35, 59, 75, 81, 114, **133**
Anaya, Rudolfo, 68
*Ancestral Truths*, 50, **112**
**Anderson, Barbara, 68**
Anderson, Jessica, 136, 145
**Anderson, Scott, 68**
**Anderson-Dargatz, Gail**, **2**, 96
*Angel City*, 14
*Angel Landing*, 152
*Angel of Light*, 142
*Angela's Ashes*, 146
*Angels*, 154
*The Angels Will Not Care*, 41
*Angle of Repose*, 11, 20, 94
*Anil's Ghost*, 15, 16, 17, 148, 151, **160**
*Animal Dreams*, **106**
*Animal Husbandry*, 33, 65
*Anita and Me*, 103
*Anna Karenina*, 158
*The Anna Papers*, 90, 145
*Another Roadside Attraction*, 70
*Another World*, **72**
**Ansa, Tina McElroy, 24**
Anshaw, Carol, 121
*The Answer Is Yes*, **44**
*Antarctic Navigation*, 3, 16
Anthony, Patricia, 73
Antrim, Donald, 90
**Antunes, Antonio Lobo**, **69** ·
*Anywhere But Here*, 35, 59
*Apologizing to Dogs*, 29, 64, **84**
**Appachana, Anjana, 69**
Appelfeld, Aharon, 148
Arana, Maria, 24
*Arcadia*, 122, 148
*Are You Mine?*, 93, 138
*Arithmetic*, **115**
*Armadillo*, **77**
Arnold, Janis, 37
*Arranged Marriage*, 87
*Arrogance*, 129, 137
*Artemisia*, 68
Arthur, Elizabeth, 3, 16
*An Artist of the Floating World*, 104
*The Artist's Widow*, **68**, 112
*As I Lay Dying*, 14, 93
*As Max Saw It*, 120
*As She Climbed Across the Table*, 79, 138
Askew, Rilla, 159

*Asking for Love and Other Stories*, 55
**Astley, Thea**, 67, **69**, 70
*Asya: A Novel*, 153
*At Home in Mitford*, 55
*At Risk*, 39, 76
*At the Jerusalem*, 72
*At the Sign of the Naked Waiter*, 102
*At War As Children, 53*
*At Weddings and Wakes*, 157
**Atkinson, Kate**, 69, **70**, 85, 115, 130, 145, 146
**Atwood, Margaret**, **145**, 147
*Audrey Hepburn's Neck*, 80, 108
**Auerbach, Jessica**, **14**, 70
*Aunt Julia and the Scriptwriter*, 137
**Auster, Paul**, **70**, **71**, 145
*The Autobiography of Miss Jane Pitman*, 93
*Autobiography of My Mother*, 27
**Averill, Thomas Fox, 24**
*The Awakening*, 94, 151
*Away*, 136
*An Awfully Big Adventure, 3*
**Azzopardi, Trezza**, **146**

Babcock, Richard, 33, 116
*Babel Tower*, 79
Babel, Isaac, 149
*Baby of the Family*, 24
*Back When We Were Grownups*, **126**
**Bacon, Charlotte, 71**
*Bad Haircut: Stories of the 70s*, **50**
*Bad Land: An American Romance*, **6**
**Badami, Anita Rau, 130**
*Badenheim, 1939*, **148**
**Bail, Murray, 2**
**Bailey, Paul**, **71**, 72
*Baileys Café*, **126**
**Bainbridge, Beryl**, **3**, 125, 136
Baker, Dorothy, 64, 105
**Baker, Kevin, 3**
Baker, Larry, 108
Baker, Nicholson, 137
Balakian, Peter, 156
Baldwin, James, 119
**Baldwin, William**, **72**, 159
*Ballad of Another Time*, 7
*The Ballad of the Sad Café, 120*
Ballantyne, Sheila, 85
Ballard, J. G., 48, 104
*Balls*, 46
*Baltimore's Mansion*, 10
*Bang the Drum Slowly*, 108

**Banks, Russell**, 42, 50, 54, **72**, 76, 82, 102, 150
Banti, Anna, 68
Baraka, Amiri, 154
Baricco, Alexander, 3, 147
Barker, Nicola, 12
**Barker, Pat**, 53, **72**, 73
**Barkley, Brad**, 73
*Barn Blind*, 131
**Barnes, Julian**, 73, **132**
Barolini, Helen, 52
*The Baron in the Trees*, 15
Barr, Nevada, 41
Barrett, Andrea, 3
**Barry, Lynda**, **73**, 140
**Barry, Nicholas**, **146**
Barth, John, 130
Barthelme, Frederick, 99
Basso, Hamilton, 62
*Bastard Out of Carolina*, 25, 70, 97
*Bat Out of Hell*, 149
*Battle Creek*, **108**
*Battlefields and Playgrounds*, 22
**Bausch, Richard**, **74**, 99
**Baxter, Charles**, 51, **74**
Bayer, Valerie Townsend, 80
Bazan, Emilia Pardo, 124
*Beach Boy*, 125
*Beachcombing for a Shipwrecked God*, **29**, 84
*Beaming Sunny Home*, 123
*The Bean Trees*, 107
*The Bear Comes Home*, **64**, 105
*The Bear Went Over the Mountain*, 64
**Beard, Richard**, 74
Beattie, Ann, 67
Beattie, Geoffrey, 8
*Beautiful Wasps Having Sex*, **81**
*Bebe's by Golly Wow!*, 40
**Becker, Laney Katz**, **24**, 53
Bedford, Martyn, 114
**Bedford, Simi**, **4**
*Bee Season*, **36**
Beerbohm, Max, 49
*Before and After*, **27**, 39, 72
*Beggars and Choosers*, 41
*Begin to Exit Here*, 63
Begley, Louis, 120, 148
*Behind the Scenes at the Museum*, 69, **70**, 85, 115, 130, 146
*Being Brett*, 101
*Being Dead*, 63, **148**

*Bel Canto*, 123
*Believers*, 74
**Bell, Christine**, 63, **75**
Bell, Madison Smartt, 123
Beller, Miles, 78
**Beller, Thomas**, **75**
*Bellwether*, 74
*Beloved*, 158, 159
*The Bend for Home*, 8
**Bender, Aimee**, **75**, 76
**Bender, Karen**, 75, **76**
Benitez, Sandra, 119
*Benjamin's Gift*, **95**
**Bennett, Ronan**, **4**, 107
Beresford-Howe, Constance, 2
**Berg, Elizabeth**, 24, **25**, 35, 46, 65, 143
Bergen, David, 79, 83
Berger, John, 71
*Berlin Game*, 140
Bernays, Anne, 47, 52, 134
**Berne, Suzanne**, **16**
**Berry, Wendell**, **4**
*The Best of Jackson Payne*, 64
*The Best There Ever Was*, 46
**Betts, Doris**, **76**, 94
*Big Babies*, 44
*Big Bad Love*, 14
*Big Cherry Holler*, 61
*Big Fish*, 63
*The Big Money*, 3
*The Big Rock Candy Mountain*, 10, 136
*Big Stone Gap*, **61**
*A Big Storm Knocked It Over*, 83
*Bigfoot Dreams*, 52, 115
*Biggest Elvis*, 97
*Billy Bathgate*, 92
*Billy Dead*, 53
*Billy Phelan's Greatest Game*, 3
Binchy, Maeve, 62
*The Binding Chair: A Visit from the Foot Emancipation Society*, 99
**Binding, Tim**, **76**, 77
Bingham, Kate, 25
*The Biographer's Tale*, 79
*The Bird Artist*, 3, 13, 15, **160**
*Birds of the Air*, 143
Birdsell, Sandra, 79, 83
*Birdsong*, 32, 103
*Birth Mother*, 56
*The Birthday Boys*, **3**
*Bisbee '17*, 6
*Bitter Grounds*, 119

*The Black Brook*, 89
*Black Cherry Blues*, 20
*Black Dog of Fate: A Memoir*, 158
*Black Dogs*, 115
*The Black Envelope*, 11, 72
*Black, White and Jewish: Autobiography of a Shifting Self*, 27
*Blackberry Wine*, 98
**The Blackwater Lightship**, **135**
**Blameless**, **53**
Blanco, Evangeline, 7
*Bleak House*, 103, 151
**Bledsoe, Lucy Jane**, **25**
*Bleeding London*, 120
*Bless Me, Ultima*, 68
**The Blind Assassin**, **145**
*The Blindfold*, 71
*Blindness*, 69
*The Blood Brother*, 20
*Blood Meridian*, 79, 157
*Blow Your House Down*, 73
*Blown Away*, 70
*Blue Afternoon*, 77
**Blue Angel**, 46, **52**
**Blue Diary**, **39**, 153
*The Blue Flower*, 92
*The Blue Hour*, 91
*Blue Italian*, 82
*Blue Rodeo*, 113, 153
*Blue Skin of the Sea*, 40, 125
*Blue Spruce*, 44, 110
*Blueback*, 141
*Blues Dancing*, 116
*Bluesman*, 89
*The Bluest Eye*, 138, 159, 159
**Blu's Hanging**, **142**
Bly, Carol, 49
*Boat People*, 9, 80, 94
*Bob the Gambler*, 99
Bodsworth, Fred, 32
*Body*, 79, **149**
**The Body Is Water**, 38, 59, **128**
*Body of Knowledge*, 31
**Bohjalian, Chris**, **26**, 27, 72, 105
**Bokat, Nicole**, **26**
*The Bold Vegetarian: 150 Innovative Recipes*, 40
*Bone*, 60
*The Bone People*, 68
**The Bonesetter's Daughter**, **60**
*The Bonfire of the Vanities*, 43, 105, 112
*Book*, 76, 145
*The Book and the Brotherhood*, 102

**The Book Borrower**, **156**
*The Book of Eve*, 2
*The Book of Laughter and Forgetting*, 107
*Book of Medicines: Poems*, 153
*The Book of Ruth*, 98
*The Book of Sand*, 22
*The Bookshop*, 26, 92
*Boomfell*, 101
*Bop*, 28
**Bordeaux**, **124**
*Border Crossing*, 53, 73
Borges, Jorge Luis, 22
*Born Brothers*, 90
Boswell, Robert, 55, 90, 98
Bouldrey, Brian, 97
*Bourgeois Blues*, 43
Bowen, Elizabeth, 90
Bowering, George, 137
*A Bowl of Cherries*, 112
*The Box Garden*, 162
*Boy Blue*, 85
**The Boy in the Lake**, **59**
**A Boy in Winter**, **28**, 34, 60, 93
*Boy with Loaded Gun: A Memoir*, 121
*Boy's Life*, 20, 142, 153
**Boyd, William**, 7, **77**, 90, 156
Boylan, James Finney, 21
**Boyle, T. Coraghessan**, 1, 3, **77**, 89, 92, 149
Bradbury, Malcolm, 70, 72
Bradford, Scott, 114
**Bradley, James**, **146**
Bradley, John Ed, 46
*The Brass Dolphin*, 54, 62
*Brazil-Maru*, 21
*Brazzaville Beach*, 77, 156
**Bread Alone**, 24, **39**, 48
*The Bread of Time to Come*, 103
*Breakfast in Babylon*, 45
**Breakfast on Pluto**, 8, 45, 47, 105, **113**, 114, 146
**Breakfast with Scot**, **87**, 102
*Breaking and Entering*, 140
Brenner, Leslie, 83
*The Bride Price*, 4
*The Bridegroom: Stories*, 14, 154
*A Bridge Between Us*, 143
*Bridge Fall Down*, 54
*Bridget Jones: The Edge of Reason*, 40, 105
*Bridget Jones's Diary*, 24, 29, 32, 40, 114
*Brief Lives*, 125
*Bright Angel Time*, 7, 103
*Brightness Falls*, 112

Brink, Andre, 148
Brizzi, Enrico, 124, 125, 140
**Bromell, Henry**, **26**
Broner, E. M., 30
**Brookner, Anita**, **77**, 78, 111, 125
Brooks, Geraldine, 18
*Brother Frank's Gospel Hour*, 49
*Brotherly Love*, 150
*Brothers and Keepers*, 119
*The Brothers K*, 34, 50, 82, **89**, 103, 104, 108, 116, 130
Brown, Alan, 80, 108
**Brown, Carrie**, 63, **78**
Brown, John Gregory, 118
**Brown, Larry**, 14, 20, **78**, 142
**Brown Rosellen**, **27**, 39, 72, 129
Brownmiller, Susan 88
Brownrigg, Sylvia, 53
***Bruna and Her Sisters in the Sleeping City***, 7, **21**
*Bruno's Dream,* 133, 148
Bryers, Paul, 81
***The Bubble Reputation***, 59, 90, **123**
**Buchan, James**, 2, 4, **5**, 34, 96, 147
*Bucking the Sun*, 6
*Budding Prospects*, 77
**Budhos, Marina**, **79**
*Bullet Park,* 145
Bullosa, Carmen, 126
"Bullpen: A Late Inning Comedy," 107
Burgess, Anthony, 114, 140
Burke, James Lee, 20
**Burnard, Bonnie**, **79**, 90
Busch, Frederick, 29, 44, 52, 72, 76, 89, 117, 136
**Bush, Catherine**, **147**
Bushnell, Candce, 55, 105
*Buster Midnight's Café*, 120
*But I Love You Anyway*, 44
***The Butcher Boy***, 91, **114**
Butler, Robert Olen, 9, 80
*The Butte Pola*, 6
*Butterfly Lovers*, 7
*By the Shore*, 30
**Byatt, A. S.**, **79**, 85

***A Cab Called Reliable***, **105**
***The Cage***, 3, **16**, 41
*The Cage Keeper and Other Stories*, 89
**Cahill, Michael**, **27**
*Cakewalk*, 94
*Cal*, 156

*The Calcutta Chromosome: A Novel of Fevers, Delirium, and Discovery*, 35
Calvino, Italo, 15
*Camellia Street*, 124
Cameron, Carey, 81
**Cameron, Peter**, **80**, 135
**Camus, Albert**, **5**, 9, 116, 150
*A Cannibal in Manhattan*, 105
Cantor, Jay, 3, 75
*Cantora*, 7, 32
**Cao, Lan**, **80**
*The Cape Ann*, 133
*Cape Breton Road*, 6
Capote, Truman, 49
Caputo, Philip, 69
**Carey, Lisa**, 3, 24, 81, 93, **147**
Carey, Peter, 15, 137
*Caribe*, 7
Carkeet, David, 109
Carlson, Lori Marie, 30
Carpenter, William, 135
*Carpenter's Gothic*, 151
Carr, J. L., 122
**Carrington, Roslyn**, **80**, 147
Carroll, Lewis, 104
***Carter Clay***, **91**
Carter, Angela, 132, 145
**Carter, Dori**, **81**
**Cartwright, Justin**, **81**
Cary, Joyce, 4, 112
Cary, Lorene, 76
*Casanova's Chinese Restaurant*, 130
*A Case of Curiosities*, 155
**Casey, John**, 29, **81**, 90
*Casino & Other Stories*, 79
**Castillo, Ana**, **28**, 119
Catala, Victor, 124
*The Catastrophist*, 4, 107
*Catch 22*, 63
***Catch Your Breath***, **24**, 70
*The Catcher in the Rye,* 27, 42
***Catching Heaven***, **97**, 113
*Catching the Light*, 123
*Catherine Cormier*, 20
*Cat's Cradle*, 54
*Cat's Eye,* 145, 147
***Caucasia***, 27, **129**
Caudwell, Sarah, 141
*Cavedweller*, 118
*Celebration*, 55
"Celeste," 1
***A Celibate Season***, **131**

*The Cement Garden*, 157
**Cereus Blooms at Night**, **118**
*A Certain Age*, **104**
**Chabon, Michael**, 38, 46, **82**, 110, 134
**Chamoiseau, Patrick**, **5**
*A Change of Climate,* 19
*The Changeling*, 140
*Changing Heaven*, 80, 136
*Changing Places*, 84, 132, 134
Chappell, Fred, 72, 90
**Charlotte Gray**, **32**
**Charming Billy**, **157**
*Charms for the Easy Life*, 71, 143
*The Chatham School Affair*, 102
Chavez, Denise, 28, 32
**Cheever, Benjamin**, **28**
Cheever, John, 28, 145
Cheever, Susan, 28
**Chernoff, Maxine**, **28**, 34, 60, 68, 93
Chevalier, Tracy, 138
Chiaverini, Jennifer, 28
*Chicken Inspector No. 23*, 63
*The Children of Dynmouth*, 163
Childress, Mark, 93
Childs, Craig, 14
*Child's Play*, 131
*Chilly Scenes of Winter*, 67
*Chimera*, 130
**The Chin Kiss King**, **62**, 78, 119
*China Boy*, 6, 60, 119, 141
*China Wakes: The Struggle for the Soul of a Rising Power*, 13
*The Chip-Chip Gatherers,* 81
*The Chisellers*, 88
**Chocolat**, 26, **98**
*The Chocolate War*, 102
Choi, Susan, 56
Chong, Denise, 6
Chopin, Kate, 94, 151
*The Chosen*, 38, 132
**Choy, Wayson**, **5**
*The Chrome Suite*, 79
*Chronicle of a Death Foretold*, 162
**Chronicle of the Seven Sorrows**, **5**
*The Chymical Wedding*, 80
*The Cider House Rules*, 26, 95, 103
*Cimarron Rose*, 20
**Cinnamon Gardens**, **16**, 151
*Circle of Friends*, 62
*The Circus Fire*, 122
**Ciresi, Rita**, **82**
Cisneros, Sandra, 68, 139

*Cities of the Plain*, 157
*A City in Winter*, 152
*City of Childhood*, 80
*City of the Mind*, 13, 120
*Civil Rights*, 27
**The Civil Wars of Jonah Moran**, **53**
**Clark, Martin**, **82**
**Clark, Robert**, **29**
Clarke, Lindsay, 80
*Claudine at School*, 4
*Clear Light of Day*, 86
*Clearwater Summer*, 42, 125
*The Clock Winder*, 133
*Clockers*, 141
*A Clockwork Orange*, 114, 140
*Close Range: Wyoming Stories*, 15
*Close to the Bone*, 43
*Closer to the Sun,* 34
*The Cloud Sketcher*, 13, 120
*Cloudstreet*, 67, 70, 96, 141
*The Club Dumas*, 124
**Cobbold, Marika**, **29**, 103
Cody, Robin, 110
**Coetzee, J. M.**, 52, 126, **148**
*Coffee Will Make You Black*, 139
Cohen, Jon, 78, 86, 97, 107, 121
**Cohen, Matt**, **83**
*Cold Comfort Farm*, 84
*A Cold Day for Murder*, 41
*Cold Harbour*, 77
*The Coldest Winter Ever*, 73
Colette, 4
**The Collapsible World**, **44**
*The Collected Stories* (Babel), 149
*Collected Stories* (Trevor), 163
Collignon, Rick, 98, 100
**The Colony of Unrequited Dreams**, **10**
*The Color Purple,* 97, 154, 155
**Colwin, Laurie**, **83**
**Combs, Maxine**, **83**
*Come and Go, Molly Snow*, 156
*Come Together,* 23
*The Comedians*, 131
**Comfort and Joy**, **97**
*Comfort Woman*, 30, 80, 108, 142
*Coming Through Slaughter*, 160
*The Commitments*, 45, 88, 124
*The Company Store*, 6
Compton-Burnett, Ivy, 67
*Compulsive*, 99
*The Concubine's Children*, 6
Condon, Richard, 43

*A Confederacy of Dunces*, 49
*The Confession of Jack Straw*, 22
*The Confessions of Mycroft Holmes: A
    Paper Chase*, 134
*The Confessions of Nat Turner*, 136
*The Congressman Who Loved Flaubert, and
    Other Stories*, 155
**Conrad, James, 84**
Conrad, Pam, 29
Conroy, Pat, 89, 121
*The Constant Gardener*, 140
Constantini, Humberto, 134
*The Constellations*, 21
*Continental Drift*, 50, 82
Cook, Karin, 76, 85, 115, 124, 140
Cook, Thomas H., 102
**Coomer, Joe, 29**, 50, 64, **84**, 101
Coover, Robert, 63 108, 130
*Copper Crown*, 130
*Corelli's Mandolin*, 54, 77, 122
Cormier, Robert, 102
*Corner Boys*, 8
*The Corner of Rife and Pacific*, 6
*Corregidora*, 154
**The Counterlife, 127**
*Country Dying*, 88
**The Country Life**, 32, **84**, 106
Courtenay, Bryce, 6, 119
Cox, Susan Soon-Keum, 56
**Coyle, Beverly, 30**, 153
**Crace, Jim**, 63, 122, **148**
*Cracking India*, 14
*Cracks*, 42
*Crane Spreads Wings: A Bigamist's Story*, 51,
    83
Craven, Margaret, 137
**Craze, Galaxy, 30**
**Crazy for Cordelia, 36**
*Crazy in Alabama*, 93
*Crazy in Love*, 51
*Creek Walk and Other Stories*, 95
**Crews, Harry**, 3, 79, **148**
 *A Crime in the Neighborhood*, **76**
*Criminals*, 89, 111, 129
**Crocodile Soup, 52, 84**
**Crooked River Burning**, 10, 26, **140**, 150
*The Cross-Country Quilters*, 29
*The Crossing*, 157
*Crossing Paths: Encounters with Animals in
    the Wild*, 14
*Crossing to Safety*, 12, 74
*Crows Over a Wheatfield*, 130

**Cruddy, 73**, 140
*Cry of the Peacock*, 119
*The Crying Heart Tattoo*, 152
**Cunningham, Michael**, 98, 122, **149**, 158
*A Cure for Death By Lightning*, 2
*Cured By Fire*, 12
*The Curious Eat Themselves*, 41
Currey, Richard, 58
**Currie, Sheldon, 6**, 21
**Cusk, Rachel**, 32, **84**, 106
*Customs*, 143

*D'Arconville's Cat*, 162
**D'Erasmo, Stacy, 85**
*Daddy Boy*, 81, 87
*Daisy Miller*, 10
Dallas, Sandra, 120
*Dalva*, 98
*Damascus*, 74
*Damascus Gate*, 21
*Dance for the Dead*, 81
*Dance Me Outside*, 49
*Dance Real Slow*, 104
*Dancers in the Scalp House*, 54
*Dancing at the Rascal Fair*, 110
*Dancing on Coral*, 67
*Danger Tree*, 12
*A Dangerous Friend*, 2, 19, 96, 111, 150, **155**
*The Dangerous Husband*, 33
**A Dangerous Woman, 118**
*The Danish Girl*, 118
Dann, Patty, 111, 115
*A Dark-Adapted Eye*, 29
Darling, Julia, 52 , **84**
**Dating Big Bird**, 36, **65**
*Daughter of Fortune*, 105
*Daughter of Jerusalem*, 112
*Daughters of Memory*, 37
**The Daughters of Simon Lamoreaux, 44**
*Daughters of the New World*, 105
**Davenport, Kiana, 30**, 98, 108
*David Copperfield*, 10
Davidson, Catherine Temma, 98
Davies, Robertson, 77, 92, 102, 136
**Davies, Stevie, 85**
**Davis, Claire, 6**
**Davis, Kathryn, 85**
Davis, Thulani, 100
Davis-Gardner, Angela, 6
*Davita's Harp*, 127
**Dawson, Carol, 30**
Dawson, George 26

*The Day*, 101
*A Day Late and a Dollar Short,* 24, 40
*The Day of the Locust,* 3, 81, 137
de Bernieres, Louis, 54, 77, 122
*Dead Babies,* 73
*Dead Languages,* 116
*Deadwood,* 150
**Deane, Seamus,** 80, **149**
*The Dean's List,* 72
***Dear Stranger, Dearest Friend,* 24**, 53
***Dear Will,* 23**
*The Dearly Departed,* 111
*Death in Summer,* 148
*Death of a River Guide,* 33
*The Death of Che Guevara,* 3, 75
*The Death of Ivan Illych,* 148
*The Death of the Heart,* 90
***The Death of Vishnu,* 133**
*Death Takes Passage,* 41
*The Debt to Pleasure,* 29
*The Debut,* 111
*Decatur Road,* 29
*Decorations in a Ruined Cemetery,* 118
*The Deep End of the Ocean,* 34, 126
***Deep in the Heart,* 137**
*Deep South,* 41
DeHaven, Tom, 82
Deighton, Len, 140
*DelCorso's Gallery,* 69
**DeLillo, Don,** 3, 71, **150**, 160, 161
*The Delinquent Virgin,* 41
*Derby Dugan's Depression Funnies,* 82
**Derbyshire, John, 86**
**Desai, Anita, 86**
*Desert Images,* 14
*A Desert in Bohemia,* 107
*Desert Solitaire,* 14
*Deserted Cities of the Heart,* 58
**DeWitt, Helen,** 70, **86**
**Dexter, Pete,** 20, 78, 142, **150**
*The Diamond Lane,* 98
*The Diaries of Jane Somers,* 142
Dickens, Charles, 10, 103, 151
Dickey, Eric Jerome, 38
Dickinson, Peter, 77
*Dietrich, Bonhoeffer: A Spoke in the Wheel,* 36
**Dillen, Frederick, 86**
**Dimmick, Barbara, 31**, 38
*Dingley Falls,* 89, 113
*Dinner at the Homesick Restaurant,* 120
*Director of the World,* 114

*Dirty Work,* 78
*Disappearing Moon Café,* 1
*The Disenchanted,* 137
***Disgrace,* 52, 126, 148**
*Disobedience,* 129
*Distant View of a Minaret,* 18
*The Distinguished Guest,* 117
*Disturbances in the Field,* 79, 117, 128, 153
**Divakaruni, Chitra Banerjee,** 35, 42, **87**
*The Divine Ryans,* 10
*Divine Secrets of the Ya-Ya Sisterhood,* 26
Dixon, Stephen, 102
Djebar, Assia, 116
*Do Lord Remember Me,* 139
*A Do Right Man,* 64
*Do Try to Speak As We Do,* 106
***Do Unto Others,* 43**
Doctorow, E. L., 3, 12, 78, 92, 115, 150
Dodd, Susan M., 4, 56
*Dogeaters,* 125
*Doggy Bag,* 70
Doig, Ivan, 6, 8, 90, 110
*Domestic Pleasures,* 37
***Don't Think Twice,* 40**
Donaldson, Scott, 28
Donleavy, J. P., 45
Donnelly, Nisa, 135
Donoghue, Emma, 26, 52, 87
Donoso, Jose, 22
Dooling, Richard, 7
*The Dork of Cork,* 78
Dorris, Michael, 6, 20, 31, 135
Dos Passos, John, 3, 141
Doty, Mark, 161
*Double Negative,* 109
Douglas, Ann, 158
Douglas, Lloyd, 39
*Down by the River,* 53
**Downing, Michael, 87**, 102, 126
**Downs, Robert C. S., 87**, 88
Doxiados, Apostolos, 75
**Doyle, Roddy,** 8, 45, 47, 53, **88**, 91, 124, 156, 163
*The Dragon Can't Dance,* 81
Drabble, Margaret, 79
*Dragon Bones: The Story of Peking Man,* 13
*Dream Boy,* 97
*Dream of the Walled City,* 104
*Dream of Venus,* 78
*DreamEden,* 125
*Dreaming in Cuban,* 63, 75
***Dreamland,* 3**

*Dreams of the Centaur*, 2
*The Dressmaker*, 125
*The Dreyfus Affair: A Love Story*, 97
*A Drinking Life*, 38
*The Drowning Season*, 152
**Drury, Tom**, **88**, 89
*Dry Rain*, 34
*Duane's Depressed*, 37, **46**
**Dubus, Andre**, III, 41, **89**
Duffy, Bruce, 76
Dufresne, John, 127, 131
**Duncan, David James**, 34, 50, 82, **89**, 103,
    104, 110, 116, 130
Duncker, Patricia, 80
*Dunedin*, 12
**Dunmore, Helen**, **90**
*Duplicate Keys*, 17, 132
*Durable Goods* **(Berg)**, **25**
*Durable Goods* (Matson), 45
**Dwyer, Kelly**, 85, **90**, 123
Dylan, Bob, 132

*The Eagle Has Landed*, 77
**Earley, Tony**, **90**
*Earthquake Weather*, 39
*Easier to Kill*, 64
*East Bay Grease*, **140**
*East Is East*, **77**
*East of the Mountains*, **151**
Eastlake, William, 54
*The Easy Way Out*, 23, 47, 111, 114
*Eating Pavlova*, 3
*Eating People Is Wrong*, 70, 72
Ebershoff, David, 118
Eberstadt, Fernanda, 112
*Eccentric Neighborhoods*, 7
Echewa, T. Obinkaram, 4
*Echo House*, 155
Eco, Umberto, 155
*Eddie's Bastard*, **198**
Edelman, Hope, 85
*Eden Close*, 58
*The Edge of the Crazies*, 19
Edgerton, Clyde, 55, 61
*Edwin Mullhouse: The Life and Death of an
    American Writer, 1943-1954*, 13, 64, 86
Egan, Jennifer, 45
**Egawa, Keith**, **31**
Ehle, John, 91
Ehrlich, Gretel, 46
Eighner, Lars, 12, 71

*Eight Months on Ghazzah Street*, 18, 19
*Einstein's Dreams*, 74, 79
*Election*, 50
*The Electrical Field*, 54, **56**, 62
*Elizabeth and After*, **83**
*Elizabeth Appleton*, 12
Elkin, Stanley, 136
*Ellen Foster*, 25, 33
**Ellis, Alice Thomas**, **91**, 143
Ellis, Rhian, 83, 1217
*Elsie de Wolfe: A Life in the High Style*, 18
Emecheta, Buchi, 4
**Emerson, Gloria**, **150**
*Emotionally Weird*, **70**, 145
*Empire Falls*, 21, **127**, 139
*Empire of the Sun*, 48, 104
*The Empress of One*, 133
*Empress of the Splendid Season*, **100**
**Emshwiller, Carol**, **31**
*The Enchantment of Lily Dahl*, 71
*The End of the Hunt*, 8
*The End of Vandalism*, **88**
*End Zone*, 150
*Endgame: A Journal of the Seventy-Ninth
    Year*, 142
*Endless Love*, 58, 116, 132
*Enduring Love*, 115
*England, England*, **73**
*English Creek*, 90
*English Passengers*, 33, 98
*The English Patient*, 32, 54, 77, **122**, 146
*The Englishman's Boy*, **137**
*Enormous Changes at the Last Minute:
    Stories*, 156
*Erasure*, 43, 73, 134
*Errands*, 126
**Escandón, María**, **31**
*Esperanza's Book of Saints*, **31**
Esquivel, Laura, 22, 39, 98
*The Essence of the Thing*, 132
Estaver, Paul, 55
*Eternal Curse on the Reader of These Pages*, 103
*Eucalyptus*, **2**
**Eugenides, Jeffrey**, 42, **150**
*Eva Luna*, 95, 118
*Eva Moves the Furniture*, 24, 111
*Eva's Man*, 155
**Evans, Elizabeth**, **91**
**Evans, Nicholas**, 31, **32**
*Eveless Eden*, 5, 11, 47, 69, 72, **139**, 147
*Even Cowgirls Get the Blues*, 96

*Evening*, 149, **157**
*Evening News*, 28, 34, **60**
*Evensong*, **36**
Everett, Percival, 43, 73, 134
*Every Day*, 126
*Every Day Is Mother's Day*, 95
*Everyday People*, 122
*Everything You Know*, **100**
*Excellent Women*, 78, 111, 125
*Excursions in the Real World: Memoirs*, 163
*Exodus*, 22
*Expensive Habits*, 102
*Expensive People*, 67
*An Explanation for Chaos*, 128
*Exposure*, 99, 128
*Extra Innings: A Memoir*, 142
*The Extra Man*, 57, 75, 114
*The Eye in the Door*, 73

*Face of an Angel*, 28, 32
*Face-Time: A Novel*, 144
*Facing the Tank*, 93
Fadiman, Anne, 26
*Fading, My Parmacheene Belle*, 129
*Fair and Tender Ladies*, 31
*A Fairly Honorable Defeat*, 132
*The Fall*, 5
*The Fall of a Sparrow*, 131
*Fall On Your Knees*, 6, 69, 99, 118
Fallaci, Oriana, 120
*Falling*, 128
*Falling Bodies*, **45**
*The Falling Boy*, 44
*Falling Slowly*, 77
*Families and Survivors*, 64
*Family Feeling*, 142
*Family Happiness*, 83
*Family Life*, 72
*Family Pictures*, **117**
*Family Planning*, 123
*Family Terrorists*, 120
*Famous Last Words*, 91
*A Far Cry from Kensington*, 92
*The Far Euphrates*, **132**
*A Farewell to Arms*, 48
Farr, Judith, 3
Farrell, J. G., 35
Fast, Howard, 127
*Fasting, Feasting*, **86**
*The Fat Man in History: Stories*, 15
*Fata Morgana* (Kotzwinkle), 49
*Fata Morgana* (Stegner), 59

*Father and Son*, 78, 142
*Father Melancholy's Daughter*, 36, 110, 125
Faulkner, William, 14, 93, 151, 163
**Faulks, Sebastian**, **32**, 103
Faust, Ron, 34
*Fay*, 14, 20, 79
*The Feast of Love*, **74**
*A Feast of Snakes*, 79, 149
*Feels Like Far: A Rancher's Life on the Great Plains*, 6
*Felice*, 6
*Felicia's Journey*, 29, 114, 148, **162**
*Female Ruins*, **120**
*Fencing the Sky*, **7**
Fenkl, Heinz Insu, 56
*The Fennel Family Papers*, **72**
Ferber, Edna, 10
**Ferre, Rosario**, **6**
*Fever Pitch*, 102
**Fforde, Katie**, **32**, 44
*Ficciones,* 22
*Fidelity: Five Stories*, 4
Fielding, Helen, 24, 29, 32, 40, 105, 114
Fielding, Henry, 134
*Fierce Invalids Home from Hot Climates*, **54**
*The Fifth Season*, **87**
**Findley, Timothy**, 67, **91**, **92**
*A Fine Balance*, 14, 17, 133, **158**
**Finnamore, Suzanne**, **33**, 128
*Fiona Range*, **118**
*Fire in Beulah*, 159
*Fireflies*, 81
*The First Book of Eppe*, 92
*First Lady*, 113
*First Light*, 51
*The First Man*, **5**, 9, 116, 150
Fischer, Tibor, 17
Fisher, Carrie, 111
*Fisher's Hornpipe*, 115
*Fiskadoro*, 154
**Fitch, Janet**, **33**, 116, 121
Fitzgerald, F. Scott, 80, 112, 137
**Fitzgerald, Penelope**, 26, **92**, 138
Fitzpatrick, Nina, 11
*Five Fortunes*, 35
Flagg, Fannie, 37, 57, 120, 130
*The Flamingo Rising*, 108, 120
**Flanagan, Richard**, 8, **33**, 152
Flanagan, Thomas, 8
*Flanders*, 73
*The Flanders Panel*, 124

*Flander's Point*, 102
*Flaubert's Parrot*, 73
Fleischman, Lisa Huang, 104
*Flesh and Blood*, 149
*Flesh Guitar*, 120
*Fleur de Leigh's Life of Crime*, 110
*Floating in My Mother's Palm*, 38
*The Floatplane Notebooks*, 55
*Flower Boy*, **15**, 16
*The Flower in the Skull*, **1**
*Flowers for Algernon*, 93
*The Fly-Truffler*, 18
*The Foam of Perilous Seas*, 83
Foden, Giles, **7**, 107
*The Following Story*, 112
*Folly*, 158
Fontes, Montserrat, 2
*Fool*, **86**
*Fool's Crow*, 31
*Fool's Gold*, **18**
*Fools of Fortune*, 163
*Foolscap*, 72, **113**
*For Love*, 116
*For the Love of Money*, 38
*For Whom the Bell Tolls*, 48
**Foran, Charles, 7**
Ford, Marjorie Leet, 106
**Ford, Richard, 92**, 94, 101, 130
*The Foreign Student*, 56
*Forrest Gump*, 40
*Forever and Ever*, 35
Forster, E. M., 80
*Fortune's Rocks*, 58
*The 42nd Parallel*, 3
*The Fountainhead*, 13, 120
*Four Blondes*, 55, 104
*Four Dreamers and Emily*, **85**
*Four Letters of Love*, 147
*The Fourteen Sisters of Emilio Montez O'Brien*, 63
*The Fourth Hand*, 103
Fowler, Karen Joy, 123
Fowles, John, 79
Foxell, Nigel, 136
Frame, Janet, 68
Franklin, Miles, 10
Frayn, Michael, 33, 52
Fredriksson, Marianne, 64
Freedman, Benedict, 137
**Freeman, Charlotte McGuinn, 34**
Freud, Esther, 103, 115, 122
*Friday Night at Silver Star*, 9

*Fried Green Tomatoes at the Whistle-Stop Café*, 120, 130
*A Friend of the Earth*, 77
***Friends for Life*, 64**
***A Frolic of His Own*, 151**
***From the Black Hills*, 135**
**Fromm, Pete, 34**, 89
***Frozen Music*, 29**
**Frucht, Abby, 35, 37, 74, 93**, 95, 138
Fuentes, Carlos, 92
*Fugitive Moon*, 34
*Fugitive Pieces*, 122, 156
Fuller, Jack, 64
***The Fundamentals of Play*, 19, 75, 112**
*The Funeral Makers*, 15, 72, 95
*Funerals for Horses*, 39
***The Funnies*, 52, 82, 109, 128**
***Funny Boy*, 15, 16**, 151
*Fury*, 161
Furst, Alan, 32

*Gabriel's Lament*, 72
Gaddis, Sarah, 28
**Gaddis, William, 151**
**Gadol, Peter, 34**, 152
*Gaff Topsails*, 15
**Gaffney, Patricia, 24, 34**
*Gain*, 18, 160
**Gaines, Ernest, 20, 93**
*Galatea 2.2*, 160
**Gale, Patrick, 93**
Gallico, Paul, 100
**Galvin, James, 7, 8**
***Gambler's Rose*, 74, 99**
*Games of the Strong*, 67
**Ganesan, Indira, 35**
*Gap Creek*, 91
Garcia, Cristina, 63, 75, 100
Garcia Marquez, Gabriel, 15, 69, 100, 162
*Garden in the Dunes*, 51
Gardner, John, 21, 130, 142
Gardner, Mary 9, 80, 94
*Gate of Angels*, 138
**Gates, David, 82, 94**, 101, 130
*A Gathering of Old Men*, 20, 93
*A Gay and Melancholy Sound*, 136
*Gaza: A Year in the Intifada*, 150
**Gemmell, Nikki, 8**
*Genius of Desire*, 97
***Geographies of Home*, 50**
**George, Anne Carroll, 94**
Gertler, Stephanie, 8

*A Gesture Life*, 13, 20, **108**, 154
*Getting Over Homer*, 87, 114
*Getting Over It*, 40, 55
**Ghosh, Amitav, 35**
*Ghost Dancing*, 110
*The Ghost Road*, 73
Ghost Town, 63
*The Ghost Writer*, 127
*Giant*, 10
**Giardina, Denise**, 6, 20, **35**
Gibbons, Kaye, 25, 33, 34, 71, 91, 143
Gibbons, Stella, 84
*The Gift of Stones*, 148
**Gilbert, Elizabeth, 94**, 95, 147
Gilchrist, Ellen, 90, 95, 147
Giles, Molly, 53, 88, 95
Gilling, Tom, 15
Gillison, Samantha, 13, 151
**Gilson, Chris, 36**
*The Ginger Man*, 45
*The Girl at the Lion d'Or*, 32
*Girl in Hyacinth Blue*, 138
*The Girl in the Flammable Skirt*, 75
*The Girl Who Trod on a Loaf*, 85
*Girl with a Pearl Earring*, 138
*Girls* (Busch), 29. 72, 76, 117, 136
*The Girls* (Yglesias), **142**
Givon, Thomas, 5
*The Glacé Bay Miners' Museum*, **6**, 20
Glancy, Diane, 20
*The Glass Palace*, **35**
*The Glass-Sided Ants' Nest*, 77
Glaubman, Richard, 26
*Glimmer*, 27
*Glimpses*, 58
*Gloria*, **12**, 48
Gloss, Molly, 8, 11
Glück, Louise, 36
*A Goat's Song*, 8, 11
*The God of Small Things*, 15, 70, 151, 158
*The Goddess Letters*, 49
*God's Pocket*, 150
**Godwin, Gail, 36**, 94, 110, 125, 128, 135
*Going After Cacciato*, 121
*Going Back to Bisbee*, 14, 106
*Going to Chicago*, 78
*Going to Pot*, **43**
*Going to the Sun*, 1, 121, 143
**Goldberg, Myla, 36**
*The Gold Bug Variations,* 160
*The Goldberg Variations,* 9
*Golden Days*, 57

Golden, Arthur, 143
**Golding, Michael, 95**
**Goldman, Francisco, 95**
**Goldman, Judy, 37**, 47
Goldstein, Rebecca, 51, 79
Gonzalez, Jose Luis, 7
*Good as Gold*, 63
*A Good House*, **79**, 90
*Good in Bed*, 36, 55, 128
*Good King Harry*, 36
*A Good Man in Africa*, 7, 77
*A Good Scent from a Strange Mountain*, 9, 80
*The Good Mother*, 51, 60, 116, 129
*The Good Times Are Killing Me*, 73
*Goodbye Without Leaving*, **83**
Goodman, Allegra, 47
*Goodness*, 76, **123**
*Goodnight, Nebraska*, 121
Gordimer, Nadine, 27
Gordon, Jacquie, 102
Gordon, Mary, 157
**Govrin, Michal, 96**
**Gowdy, Barbara**, 85, **96**
*Grace Notes*, 115, **156**
*Graced Land*, 41
*The Grand Complication*, **155**
*The Granny,* 88
Grant, Linda, 22
*The Grass Dancer*, **51**, 63, 106, 153
*The Grass Harp*, 49
**Graver, Elizabeth, 96**
*Graveyard of the Atlantic*, 38
*Gravity's Rainbow*, 151
*The Great Divorce*, 113
*The Great Gatsby*, 80, 112
*Great Jones Street*, 161
*Green Grass, Running Water*, 20, 106
Greene, Bob, 133
Greene, Graham, 4, 11, 26, 96, 131, 155
*The Greenhouse Effect*, 59
*Greenlanders*, 132
Greer, Andrew Sean, 12
*Greetings from the Golden State*, 83
*Grendel*, 130
**Griesemer, John, 97**
**Griffith, Patricia Browning, 37**
*The Grifters*, 79
Grimes, Martha, 122
**Grimsley, Jim, 97**
Grisham, John, 106
Groom, Winston, 40
*The Ground Beneath Her Feet*, 5, **161**

*The Group*, 12
*The Groves of Academe*, 84
Grudin, Robert, 70, 145
Grumbach, Doris, 142
Gu Hua, 60
Guest, Judith, 126
*Guided Tours of Hell*, 52
**Gunesekera, Romesh**, 16, **151**
*Guppies for Tea*, 29, 103
Gurganus, Alan, 161
**Gutcheon, Beth, 37**
**Guterson, David**, 54, **151**, 152

Hagedorn, Jessica, 125
**Hagy, Alyson, 37**, 131
Hahn, Emily, 68
*The Hairstons: An American Family in Black
    and White*, 62
*Half a Heart*, **27**, 129
*Half Asleep in Frog Pajamas*, 54
*The Half-Life of Happiness*, **81**, 90
Hall, Brian, 30, 36, 49
**Hall, Sands, 97**, 113
*The Hallelujah Side,* **103**, 120
*Hallucinating Foucault*, 80
**Hamill, Pete, 38**
*Hamilton Stark*, 72
**Hamilton, Jane**, 18, 24, 60, **98**, 129
*The Hand I Fan With*, **24**
*Hand to Mouth*, 71
*Handbook of the Strange*, 83
Handler, David, 38
Handler, Lowell, 56
*Handling Sin*, 73, 82, 127
*The Handmaid of Desire*, 76
*The Handyman*, **57**
*Hangman's Beach*, 6
*Hank and Chloe*, 113
Hannah, Barry, 149
Hansen, Ron, 51
*Happenstance*, 29, 58, 127, 131
*The Hard to Catch Mercy*, 72, 159
*Hard-Boiled Wonderland and the End of the
    World*, 159
*The Harder They Fall*, 119
*Hardware River Stories*, 38
*Harmony of the World*, 74
*Haroun and the Sea of Stories*, 161
**Harris, E. Lynn, 38**
**Harris, Joanne**, 26, **98**
Harris, MacDonald, 145
Harris, Mark, 108

Harrison, Jamie, 19
**Harrison, Jim**, **98**, 152
**Harrison, Kathryn**, **99**, 128
*Harry and Catherine*, 52, 74, 89
**Haruf, Kent**, 11, 39, 90, 94, **99**, 110
*The Harvest*, 22
Harvey, Caroline, 54, 62
Hasselstrom, Linda, 6
Hassler, Jon, 72
*The Hatbox Baby*, 63, **78**
*Have You Seen Me?*, 96
**Hawkes, G. W.**, 74, **99**
Hay, Elizabeth, 2, 78, 114
**Haynes, David**, 40, **99**, 100, 139
*Hazard Zone*, 12
*He Say, She Say*, 40
*He, She and It*, 82
*Headhunter*, 92
*Heading West*, 76
*Headlong*, 33, 52
*The Healing*, **159**
**Healy, Dermot**, **8**, 11
*Heart Conditions*, 44
*Heart's Journey in Winter*, 5
*The Hearts of Soldiers*, **56**
*The Heartsong of Charging Elk*, 31
*Heat and Dust*, 20
*The Heather Blazing*, 135
*Heaven's Coast*, 161
*The Hedge, The Ribbon*, 22, **49**
Hedges, Peter, 89, 115, 122, 125
**Hegi, Ursula**, **38**, 135
*Hell*, 85
Hellenga, Robert 131
Heller, Jane, 36
Heller, Joseph, 63
**Heller, Zoe, 100**
**Helprin, Mark**, 92, 100, **152**
Hemingway, Ernest, 48
*Hemingway's Chair*, 44
*Hemingway's Suitcase*, 145
**Hendricks, Judith Ryan**, 24, **39**, 98
**Hendrie, Laura**, 11, 23, **100**
**Henley, Patricia**, **9**, 96, 134, 160
*Henry of Atlantic City*, 97, 107, **125**, 135
Henry, Sue, 41
*Her First American*, 68
*Here We Are in Paradise*, 90
*Hero*, 87
*The Hero's Walk*, 130
Herrick, Amy, 102
Hessler, Peter, 7

*Hey, Joe*, 98, 141
*Hidden Pictures*, 64
*Hideous Kinky*, 103, 115, 122
**The Hiding Place**, **146**
*Hie to the Hunters*, 91
Higgins, Jack, 77
*High Cotton*, 43
*High Fidelity*, 102
*High Latitudes*, 5
Highbridge, Dianne, 152
**Highways to a War**, **11**, 60
**Hijuelos, Oscar**, 63, **100**
*Hilda and Pearl*, 156
Hill, Ernest, 92
Hill, Richard, 105, 140
Hillenbrand, Laura, 38
Hillmer, Timothy, 101
*His Third, Her Second*, 55
*The History of Luminous Motion*, 114
*The History of the Siege of Lisbon*, 69
*The Hitchhiker's Guide to the Galaxy*, 63
Hjortesberg, William, 92
Hobbes, Thomas, 71
Hobbett, Anastasia, 32
**Hobbie, Douglas**, **101**
Hochschild, Adam, 4, 107
Hoeg, Peter, 161
**Hoffman, Alice**, **39**, 49, 76, **101**, 102, 120,
     **152**, 153
Hoffman, Eva, 68, 109
**Hogan, Linda**, 147, **153**
*Holden's Performance*, 3
*A Hole in the Earth*, 74, 99
*Home Across the Road*, 62
*A Home At the End of the World*, 98, 149
*Home Before Dark*, 28
*Home Cooking*, 83
**Home to India**, **17**
*Homebodies*, 129
*Homesick*, 137
*Homesickness*, 3
*The Homesman*, 8
*Hometown Brew*, 52
*Homework* (Livesey), 111
*Homework* (Peres da Costa), 86
**The Honey Thief**, **96**
**Honeymoon: A Romantic Rampage**, **40**
*The Honk and Holler Opening Soon*, 24
*The Honorary Consul*, 96
**Hood**, 26, 52, **87**
**Hood, Ann**, **39**, 80
**The Hookmen**, **101**

*Hoopi Shoopi Donna*, 57
*Horace Afoot*, 78, 84, 97, 125
**Hornby, Nick**, **102**
**Horse Heaven**, 31, 38, **131**
*The Horse Whisperer*, 31, 32
*The Horse's Mouth*, 112
Hospital, Janette Turner, 8
*Host Family*, 45
**The Hotel Alleluia**, **55**
*Hotel du Lac*, 78, 125
*The Hotel New Hampshire*, 103
*Hotel of the Saints*, 38
*Hotel Paradise*, 122
Hotel Pastis, 18
**The Hours**, 122, **149**, 158
*House Arrest*, 48
*The House Gun*, 27
*A House in the Country*, 22
*A House Named Brazil*, 16
**House of Sand and Fog**, 41, **89**
*The House of the Spirits*, 7, 22, 95, 119, 143
*The House of Ulloa*, 124
*The House of Waiting*, 79
*The House on Mango Street*, 68, 139
*The House on R Street*, 42
**The House on the Lagoon**, **6**
*The House Tibet*, 33, 118
*Housekeeping*, 85
*The Housekeeping Book,* 68
Houston, Robert, 6
**How All This Started**, **34**, 89
*How Green Was My Valley*, 90
*How I Became Hettie Jones*, 129
*How It Was For Me*, 12
*How She Died*, 142
**How the Garcia Girls Lost Their Accents**, 50,
     52, **67**, 68, 119
*How to Be Good*, 102
*How to Make an American Quilt*, 29
**Howard, Blanche**, **131**
**Howard, Maureen**, **102**
*Howards End*, 80
**Huddle, David**, **102**
**Huffey, Rhoda**, **103**, 130
*Hula*, 103
**Hull, Jonathan**, 32, **103**
Hulme, Keri, 68
*Human Croquet*, 70
*The Human Factor*, 4, 26
**The Human Stain,** **126**
**Human Voices**, **92**
**Hummingbird House**, **9**, 96, 134, 160

*The Hundred Brothers*, 90
*The Hundred Secret Senses*, 60
**The Hunger Moon**, **45**, 46
Hunnicutt, Ellen, 156
*The Hunters: Two Short Novels*, 116
*Hunter's Moon*, 41
*Hunters and Gatherers*, 52, 161
*Hunts in Dreams*, 89
**Huo, T. C.**, **9**
Hurston, Zora Neale, 158
**Huston, Nancy**, **9**
Hustved, Siri, 71
**Hyde, Catherine**, **39**
Hynes, James, 72, 138

*I Am One of You Forever*, 72, 90
*I Been in Sorrow's Kitchen and Licked Out All
   the Pots*, 154
*I Heard the Owl Call My Name*, 137
**I Loved You All**, **130**
**I Married a Communist**, **126**
*I Never Came to You in White*, 3
*I Saw the Sky Catch Fire*, 4
*I Want to Buy a Vowel*, 63, 86
*I Was Amelia Earhart*, 3
*I Wish This War Were Over*, 25
Ibsen, Henrik, 120
*An Ice Cream War*, 90
*The Ice Storm*, 70
*Icefields*, 137
**Icy Sparks**, **55**, 156
*If Beale Street Could Talk*, 119
*If I Die in a Combat Zone*, 49
*If This World Were Mine*, 38
**Ignatieff, Michael**, 30, 60, 88, 124, **153**
**Iida, Deborah**, 21, **40**
Ikeda, Stewart, 54, 56
**Illumination Night**, **49**
*The Illusionist*, 118
*Illywacker*, 15
**Imaginary Crimes**, **85**
**An Imaginative Experience**, **138**
*Imagining Argentina*, 2, 95, 134, 160
*Imaginings of Sand*, 148
*An Immaculate Mistake*, 72
*In Another Country*, 91
*In Country*, 4, 44, 48
*In Custody*, 86
*In Praise of the Stepmother*, 137
**In the Country of the Young**, 3, 24, 93, **147**
*In the Cut*, 128
*In the Deep Midwinter*, 29

*In the Eye of the Sun*, 18
**In the Family Way: An Urban Comedy**, 41,
   57, **128**
*In the Footsteps of Mr. Kurtz: Living on the
   Brink of Disaster in Mobutu's Congo*, 4
*In the Heart of the Country*, 148
*In the Kingdom of Air*, 77
**In the Lake of the Woods**, 49, 109, **121**
*In the Place of Fallen Leaves*, 149
*In the Pond*, 154
**In the Presence of Horses**, **31**, 38
*In the Skin of a Lion*, 160
**In the Time of the Butterflies**, **2**, 68, 134
*In the Walled City*, 122
**In Troubled Waters**, **30**, 153
*Incantations and Other Stories*, 69
**Independence Day**, **92**, 94, 101, 130
*Indian Creek Chronicles*, 34
*Indian Killer*, 31, 43
*Infinite Jest*, 161
Ingalls, Rachel, 130
**Inheritance**, **35**
**The Inn at Lake Devine**, 23, 64, **111**, 114
**The Inner Life of Objects**, **83**
*The Innocent*, 115
*Innocent Erendira and Other Stories*, 15
*An Instance of the Fingerpost*, 155
*Instruments of Darkness*, 9
*Interstate*, 102
*Interviewing Matisse or The Woman Who
   Died Standing Up*, 19
*Intimates*, 102
*Into Thin Air: A Personal Account of the
   Mt. Everest Disaster*, 16
**The Intuitionist**, **138**, 139
*Inventing the Abbotts, and Other  Stories*, 27
*The Invisible Circus*, 45
**An Invisible Sign of My Own**, **75**, 76
*Iron and Silk*, 16
**Iron Shoes**, 53, 88, **95**
*Ironweed*, 3
**Irving, John**, 10, 26, 40, 70, 95, **103**, 108,
   121, 161
Irwin, Robert, 9
Isaacs, Susan, 25
*Isabel's Bed*, 47, 111, 114
*Isaiah Berlin: A Life*, 153
**Ishiguro, Kazuo**, 13, 15, 16, **104**, 108, 151,
   159
*Island*, 129
*The Island of the Day Before*, 155

Isler, Alan, 70
*It's Raining in Mango*, 67
***Italian Fever*, 113**
*The Italian Girl*, 80
*The Itch*, 43

*J. Eden*, 53
*Jack Frusciante Has Left the Band*, 124, 125, 140
***Jackie by Josie*, 51**, 87
*Jackson's Dilemma*, 102
***The Jade Peony*, 5**
**Jaffe, Michael Grant, 102, 104**
*Jailbird*, 63
James, Darius, 43, 154
James, Henry, 10, 37
Jamison, Kay Redfield, 90
*Jane and Prudence*, 78, 125
**Janowitz, Tama, 104**, 105
*Japanese By Spring*, 63
Japrisot, Sebastien, 32, 103
Jarrell, Randall, 132
***Jayber Crow*, 4**
*Jazz*, 124, **158**,159
**Jenkins, Amy, 40**
**Jennings, Kate, 10**
*Jernigan*, 94
*Jesus' Son*, 154
*The Jew Store*, 37
*Jewel*, 76
Jhabvala, Ruth Prawer, 20
***Jim the Boy*, 90**
*Jimmy's Girl*, 8
**Jin, Ha, 14, 153**, 154
*Jitterbug Perfume*, 54
*Joe*, 20, **78**
***Joe College*, 50**
**Joe, Yolanda, 40**
*John Cheever*, 28
*John Dollar*, 140
***John Henry Days*, 139**
**Johnson, Denis, 154**
**Johnson, Diane, 10**, 18, 106, 113, 128
**Johnson, Wayne, 40**, 41`
**Johnston, Wayne, 10**
*Jonah's Gourd Vine*, 158
**Jones, Gayl, 154**, 155
Jones, Hettie, 129
Jones, Thom, 119
*Joshua Then and Now*, 132
*The Journals of John Cheever*, 28

*The Journey*, 35
***The Journey Home*, 110, 122**
*The Journey of August King*, 91
*Joy in Our Cause*, 31
*The Joy Luck Club,* 60
*Joy School*, 25
Joyce, James, 151
*JR*, 151
***Judge on Trial*, 17, 107**
***The Jukebox Queen of Malta*, 54**
**Julavits, Heidi, 11**
***Julie and Romeo*, 52**
*Julip*, 98
***Jump*, 1**
*The Jump-Off Creek*, 8, 11
***Jumping the Green*, 45, 128**
*Jumping the Queue*, 138
**Just, Ward**, 2, 11, 19, 26, 96, 111, 131, 150, **155**
*Justice*, 19

*Kaaterskill Falls*, 47
Kafka, Franz, 104, 135
Kafka, Kimberly, 41
**Kalpakian, Laura, 41**, 57, 128
Kanon, Joseph 19. 92
*Kansas in August*, 93
Kaplan, James, 84
Karbo, Karen, 98
Karon, Jan, 55
*Karoo*, 100, 121
Kasischke, Laura, 118
*Kate Vaiden,* 162
Kavanagh, Patrick, 15
**Kay, Jackie, 105**
Kay, Rosemary, 63
**Kay, Terry, 41**
Keady, Walter, 147
Keegan, John, 42, 125
***Keeneland*, 37**, 131
*A Keeper of Sheep*, 135
***Keeping Faith*, 51**
*Keeping Warm*, 94
Keillor, Garrison, 43, 49
Keller, Nora Okja, 30, 80, 108, 142
Keneally, Thomas, 36
Kennedy, Pagan, 136
Kennedy, William, 3
Kenney, Susan, 29, 91
Kerr, Philip, 145
Kesey, Ken, 20, 89
*Keystone*, 137

**Kim, Patti, 105**
Kincaid, Nanci, 46
*Kinfolks*, 43
*King*, 71
*King Leopold's Ghost: A Story of Greed, Terror and Heroism in Colonial Africa*, 4, 107
**King, Lily**, 10, **106**, 113
**King, Thomas**, 20, 51, **106**
**Kingsolver, Barbara**, 4, 7, 9, 39, 55, **106**, **107**, 160
Kingston, Maxine Hong, 80
Kinsella, W. P., 44
Kiraly, Sherwood, 44
**Kirchner, Bharti, 42**, 86
**Kirn, Walter**, 27, **42**, 138
*The Kiss*, 99
*The Kitchen God's Wife*, **60**, 135
*Kitty and Virgil*, **71**
**Klima, Ivan**, **17**, 107
Kluge, P. F., 97
**Kluger, Steve**, 38, 89, 101, **107**, 108
Kneale, Matthew, 33, 98
*The Kneeling Bus*, 30
*The Knife Thrower and Other Stories*, 13
*The Knockout Artist*, 149
**Koch, Christopher**, **11**, 69
Koestler, Arthur, 9
Kogawa, Joy, 21
**Kohler, Sheila, 42**
Kotzwinkle, William, 49, 64
**Kowalski, William, 108**
Krakauer, Jon, 16
*Kraven Images*, 70
Krentz, Jayne Ann, 39
Kristoff, Nicholas D., 14
Kuban, Karla, 39, 99
Kundera, Milan, 107, 137
**Kurzweil, Allen, 155**

"L'Affaire Tartuffe," 1
L'Engle, Madeleine, 4
L'Heureux, John, 70
Lachmet, Djanet, 9
*Ladder of Years*, 46, 136
*The Ladies Auxiliary*, 37, 42, **47**
*The Ladies' Man*, 111
*Lady Moses*, 55
*Lady Oracle*, 145
*Ladysmith*, 7
*The Lake Dreams the Sky*, **20**
*Lake Wobegon Days*, 43, 49

*Lallia*, 9
Lamar, Jake, 43
*Lamb in Love*, **78**
Lanchester, John, 29, 148
*The Land of Green Plums*, 11, 17, 72
*Land of Smiles*, 9
*A Landing on the Sun*, 34
**Landvik, Lorna, 43**, 61, 84
*The Language of Threads*, **62**
Lapin, Mark, 127
*Larry's Party*, 79, 82, 127, **130**, 163
Lasser, Scott, 108
*Last Comes the Egg*, 76
*The Last Days of Disco with Cocktails at Petrossian Afterwards*, 19
*Last Days of Summer*, 38, 89, 102, **107**, 108
*The Last Integrationist*, **43**
*The Last King of Scotland*, **7**, 107
*The Last Life*, 5, 9, **116**, 140
*Last of the Curlews*, 32
*Last Orders*, **133**
*The Last Picture Show*, 34, 46
*The Last Samurai*, **70**, 86
*Last Things*, 25, 59, **121**
*The Last Time They Met*, 58
*The Last Tycoon*, 137
*Later the Same Day*, 150
**Lattany, Kristin Hunter, 43**
*Laurence, Margaret*, 2, 145
**Laurimore, Jill, 43**
*The Law of Similars*, 26
Lawson, Robert, 14
*Layover*, **143**
Le Carré, John, 140
*Le Divorce*, 10, 106, 113, 128
*Le Mariage*, 10, 113, 128
Leacock, Stephen, 49
*Leading the Cheers*, **81**
*Leaf Storm and Other Stories*, 15
*Leap Year*, 80
*Leaping Man Hill*, **31**
*Learning to Swim and Other Stories*, 133
*Leave a Light On for Me*, 87
*Leaving Tabasco*, 126
Leavitt, David, 97
*The Lecturer's Tale*, 72
*Ledoyt*, 31
**Lee, Chang-rae**, 13, 30, **108, 109**, 154
Lee, Gus, 6, 60, 119, 141
**Lee, Helen Elaine**, **109**, 120
Lee, Sky, 1
Leebron, Fred, 109

Lefcourt, Peter, 97
*Legacy of Love*, 62
*Legends of the Fall*, 98
*Legs*, 3
*Lempriere's Dictionary*, 145
**Lennon, J. Robert**, 8, 52, 82, 88, **109**, 110, 128
**Lennox, Judith**, **110**
**Lesley, Craig**, 8, 9, **110**
**Leslie, Diane**, **110**
Lessing, Doris, 142
*A Lesson Before Dying*, **93**
Lester, Julius, 139
*Let No Man Write My Epitaph*, 140
*Let Us Now Praise Famous Men*, 119
**Lethem, Jonathan**, 56, 79, 131, 138, 145, **155**
*Letter to a Child Never Born*, 120
Letts, Billie, 24
Levandoski, Robert, 78
*Leviathan* **(Auster)**, **70**
Leviathan (Hobbes), 70
Levin, Meyer, 22
Lewis, David, 158
**Lewis, Sara**, **44**
*Liar's Game*, 38
**Libera, Antoni**, **11**, 17, 61
*Liberty Falling*, 41
*Libra*, 3, 150, 160
*Life & Times of Michael K*, 148
*Life Before Death*, 35
*Life Before Man*, 93, 147
*A Life for a Life*, 93
*Life is So Good*, 26
*Life Skills*, **32**
*Light at Dusk*, **34**
*Light in August*, 163
*Light in the Company of Women*, 12
*The Light of Falling Stars*, 110
Lightman, Alan, 74, 79
*Lightning Song*, 121
*Like Normal People*, 75, **76**
*Like Water for Chocolate*, 22, 39, 98
*Lilith*, 127
*Lily of the Valley*, **57**
*Lily White*, 25
*Limited Partnerships*, 143
Lindbergh, Reeve, 7
*Linden Hills*, 120
Lindsay, Joan, 42
Linzer, Anna, 110
**Lipman, Elinor**, 23, 26, 44, 47, 52, 64, 82, **111**, 114
*Listening Now*, **69**

*Little America*, **26**
Little, Benilde, 43
*Little Bits of Baby*, 93
*Live at Five*, 40, 100, 139
Lively, Penelope, 13, 111, 120, 122, 125, 145
*Lives of Girls and Women*, 83
*The Lives of Riley Chance*, 74
*Lives of the Saints*, 45, 154
**Livesey, Margot**, 24, 89, **111**, 129
*Living to Tell*, **120**
*Living Together*, 88
Llewellyn, Richard, 90
Lloyd, Josie, 23
*Locas*, 119
Lodge, David, 72, 84, 85, 132, 134
Lofton, Ramnoa (Sapphire), 73, 141
*Loitering with Intent*, 70, 138
*London Fields*, 145
*London Holiday*, **50**
*The Lone Ranger and Tonto Fistfight in Heaven*, 106, 110
*The Loneliness of the Long Distance Runner*, 114
**Long, David**, **44**, 110
*The Long Falling*, **53**, 146
*Long Hot Summer*, 68
*Long Way from Home*, 44
*The Long Night of Francisco Sanctis*, 134
*The Long Night of White Chickens*, 95
*Longleg*, **67**
*Look at It This Way*, 81
The Loop (Coomer), 50, 84, 101
*The Loop* **(Evans)**, 29, **32**
Lopez, Medina, Sylvia, 7, 32
*Los Alamos*, 29, 92
*Losing Julia*, 32, **103**
*Losing Nelson*, **136**
*Lost*, 117, **135**
*The Lost Boy*, 78
*Lost Daughters*, 44
*The Lost Father*, 49
*Lost Geography*, **71**
*The Lost Glass Plates of Wilfred Eng*, **49**
*Lost Highway*, 58
*Lost in Place*, 16
*Lost in Translation*, **13**
*Lost in Translation: A Life in a New Language*, 68, 109
*The Lost Language of Cranes*, 97
*The Lost Legends of New Jersey*, **125**
Lott, Bret, 76
Louis, Adrian, 150

*Louisa*, **22**, 96
*Louisiana Power and Light*, 131
*Love Among the Ruins*, 29
*Love and Garbage*, 107
*Love, Etc.*, 73
*Love in the Middle Ages*, 52
*Love in the Time of Cholera*, 69, 100
**Love Like Gumbo**, **52**
*The Love Songs of Phoenix Bay*, 135
**A Lover's Almanac**, **102**
*The Loves of Faustyna*, 11
*Love Warps the Mind a Little*, 127
Lovelace, Earl, 81
*Loverboys: Stories*, 28
Lovesey, Peter, 137
*Loving Chloe*, 113
*Loving Emma*, 136
**Loving Graham Greene**, **150**
*Loving Hands at Home*, 10
*Loving Roger*, 123
*Loving Women: A Novel of the Fifties*, 38
*Low Flying Aircraft*, 116
**The Lucky Gourd Shop**, **56**
*Lucky Jim*, 123
*Lucy Crocker 2.0*, 51
*Lying Awake*, 16, 51
**Lying with the Enemy**, **76**
*The Lyre of Orpheus*, 77

Macaulay, Rose, 141
MacDonald, Ann-Marie, 6, 69, 99, 118
MacDonald, D. R., 6
**Macfarlane, David**, **12**
*Machine Dreams*, 124
**Mackay, Shena**, 12, 15, 68, **112**, 122
**MacLaverty, Bernard**, 115, **156**
Maclean, Norman, 19, 101, 110
MacLeish, Roderick, 92
**Macy, Caitlin**, 19, 75, **112**
*Madame*, **11**, 17, 61, 75
*Madame Sousatzka*, 86
**Madchild Running**, **31**
Madden, David
Madden, Deirdre, 8
*Madonna on Her Back*, 38
*The Magician's Assistant*, 101
*The Magician's Wife*, 9
The Magus, 79
*Magnificent Obsession*, 39
Mahfouz, Naguib, 18
*Mail*, 37, 47
**Mailer, Norris Church**, **44**

**Maillard, Keith**, **12**, 48
**Make Believe**, **129**
*Making History*, 57
**Making Love to the Minor Poets of Chicago**,
   **84**
*Making Minty Malone*, 40
Malamud, Bernard, 198
*Malcolm*, 49
*The Male Cross-Dresser Support Group*, 105
**Malone, Michael**, 72, 73, 82, 89, **113**, 127
Malouf, David, 103, 131
*The Mambo Kings Play Songs of Love*, 100
*The Mammy*, 88
*A Man*, 120
*The Man in the Box*, 47
*The Man in the Window*, 78, 86, 97, 107, 121
**The Man of the House**, **114**
**The Man Who Ate the 747**, **57**, 61
*The Man Who Tried to Save the World*, 69
**The Man Who Wrote the Book**, **139**
*The Manchurian Candidate*, 43
Manea, Norman, 11, 72
*The Manikin*, 129
Mantel, Hilary, 18, 19, 95
*The Manticore*, 92
**The Many Aspects of Mobile Home Living**, **82**
**The Map of Love**, **18**
*A Map of the World*, 18, 24, 60,98
**Mapson, Jo-Ann**, 76, 98, **113**, 153
*Marchlands*, 39, 99
Marciano, Francesca, 14
**Marcom, Micheline Aharonian**, **156**
*Mariette in Ecstasy*, 51
**Marino, Anne N.**, **44**
*Marjorie Morningstar*, 12
**Mark, Andrew**, **45**
*The Mark of the Angel*, 9
*Marrying the Mistress*, 50
Marshall, Paule, 5
*Marshland Brace*, 20
*Martha Calhoun*, 33, 116
**Martin Dressler: The Tale of an American
   Dreamer**, 3, **13**
Martin, David, 152
**Martin, Emer**, **45**
**Martin, Valerie**, **113**
Martinez, Tomas Eloy, 3
*Mary McGreevy*, 147
*Mary Reilly*, 113
*Masai Dreaming*, 81
Mason, Bobbie Ann, 4, 44, 48
*Master Georgie*, 3, 136

"The Masterbuilder," 120
Masters, Edgar Lee, 4
*A Match to the Heart*, 46
*Mating*, 156, **161**
*The Matisse Stories*, 85
**Matson, Suzanne, 45, 46**
**Mattison, Alice, 156**
Maupin, Armistread, 93
*Maurice*, 80
Maxted, Anna, 40, 55
Maxwell, William, 122
*Maybe in Missoula*, 56
Mayle, Peter, 18
**McCabe, Patrick,** 8, 45, 47, 91, 105, **113,**
   **114,** 146
**McCafferty, Jane, 114**
McCaig, Donald, 6
McCammon, Robert, 20, 142, 153
**McCann, Colum, 12**
**McCarthy, Cormac,** 79, **157**
McCarthy, Mary, 12, 84
**McCauley, Stephen,** 23, 25, 47, 111, **114,** 146
McCloud, Scott, 82
McCloy, Kristin, 26
McCourt, Frank, 146
McCullers, Carson, 14, 25, 120
McCullough, Colleen, 76, 152
**McDermott, Alice, 151**
**McEwan, Ian, 115,** 156, 157
**McEwen, Todd, 115**
**McGhee, Alison, 115**
McInerney, Jay, 112
**McKinney-Whetsone, Diane, 116,** 120, 139
McLaurin, Tim, 12
McManus, James 1, 121, 143
McMillan, Terry, 24, 40
**McMurtry, Larry,** 34, 37, **46**
**McNally, T. M., 116**
**McNamer, Deirdre,** 6, **46,** 71, 119
McNeal, Tom, 121
McPhee, Martha, 7, 103
McPherson, William, 14
*McX: A Romance of the Dour*, 115
*The Meadow*, **8**
*Mean Spirit*, 153
**Medwed, Mameve,** 36, **46,** 47
*Meely LaBauve*, **19**
*Meeting the Minotaur*, 31
Mehta, Gita, 120
*A Member of the Family*, **47**
*The Member of the Wedding*, 14, 25
*Memoir from Antproof Case*, 92, 100, **152**

*Memoirs of a Geisha*, 143
*Memories of My Ghost Brother*, 56
*The Men and the Girls*, 62
*Men Giving Money, Women Yelling: Stories*,
   156
*Men in Black*, 132
Mendelsohn, Jane, 3
*Mercy*, 56
*Mermaids*, 111, 115
*The Mermaids Singing*, 81, **147**
**Merrell, Susan, 47**
**Messud, Claire,** 5, 9, **116,** 150
*The Metaphysical Touch*, 53
*Metroland*, 73
Michaels, Anne, 122, 156
*Middle Son*, 21, **40**
Middlebrook, Diane Wood, 105
*Midnight Sandwiches at the Mariposa*
   *Express*, 20, 120
*Midnight's Children*, 13, 14, 120, 158, 161
"A Midsummer Night's Dream," 74
*Midwives*, **26,** 27
*Milk in My Coffee*, 38
*Milkweed*, **94**
Miller, Karen E. Quinones, 40
Miller, Merle, 136
**Miller, Sue,** 27, 46, 51, 60, **117,** 129
**Millhauser, Steven,** 3, **13,** 64, 86
**Mills, Magnus, 117,** 134
Minatoya, Lydia, 21, 135
*The Mind-Body Problem*, 51, 79
*The Mineral Palace*, **11**
**Minot, Eliza, 157**
**Minot, Susan,** 149, **157**
*The Minotaur Takes a Cigarette Break*, **130**
*Minus Time*, 147
Mirayama, Milton, 21
**Mirvis, Tova,** 37, 42, **47**
*The Miserables*, 68
Mishima, Yukio, 13, 14, 130
*Miss Julia Speaks Her Mind*, **55**
*Miss Julia Takes Over*, 55
*The Missing World*, **111**
*Mississippi History*, 142
*Mister Johnson*, 4
*Mister Sandman*, 85, **96**
*Mistler's Exit*, 148
*Mistress of Spices*, 42, 87
**Mistry, Rohinton,** 14, 17, 133, **158**
Mitchard, Jacquelyn, 34, 126, 129
Mitchell, W. O., 83
*A Model World and Other Stories*, 82

*Modern Baptists*, 72
*Mohawk*, 127
**Mones, Nicole, 13**
*Money*, 145
***Money, Love*, 73**
***Monkey Beach*, 126**
***Monkey Bridge*, 80**
*The Monkey Wrench Gang*, 54
*Monkeys*, 157, 158
*Monkfish Moon*, 16, 151
***Montana 1948*, 19,** 20, 110
*A Month in the Country*, 122
***Moo*, 17,** 72, 84, 85, **131**
*Mood Indigo*, 9
Moody, Rick, 70
*Moon Tiger*, 111, 122, 125, 145
***Moonlight on the Avenue of Faith*, 119**
*The Moons of Jupiter*, 133
Moore, Brian, 9
Moore, Susanna, 25, 91, 1128, 142
***The Moor's Last Sigh*, 13,** 69, 112, 152, 156, 158, **162**
**Mootoo, Shani, 118**
*Morality Play*, 136
**Moran, Thomas, 47**
***More Bread or I'll Appear*, 45**
*More Home Cooking: A Writer Returns to the Kitchen*, 83
***More Than You Know*, 37**
Morgan, Robert, 91
**Morris, Mary, 48**
**Morris, Mary McGarry, 118**
Morris, Wright, 8
**Morrison, Toni, 124, 138, 158, 159**
**Mort, John, 48**
**Mosley, Walter, 119,** 139
***Mosquito*, 154**
*The Mosquito Coast*, 21
*Mother and Son*, 67
*A Mother and Two Daughters*, 36, 128, 135
***The Mother-in-Law Diaries*, 30**
*Mother Rocket: Stories*, 82
***MotherKind*, 74, 124**
***Motherless Brooklyn*, 56,** 131, 138, 145, **155**
*Motherless Daughters: The Legacy of Loss*, 85
Motley, Willard, 140
*Mourning Doves: Stories*, 136
*The Mouse That Roared*, 63
*The Moviegoer*, 92
Mowat, Farley, 41
*Mr. Phillips*, 148
*Mr. Vertigo*, 71

***Mr. White's Confession*, 29**
*Mrs. 'Arris Goes to Paris*, 100
*Mrs. Caliban*, 130
*Mrs. Dalloway*, 149, 158
*Mrs. Mike*, 137
*Mrs. Palfrey at the Claremont*, 142
*Mrs. Ted Bliss*, 136
*Mrs. Vargas and the Dead Naturalist*, 1, 22
*A Much Younger Man*, 152
*The Mulching of America*, 3
Müller, Herta, 11, 17, 72
*Mumbo Jumbo*, 155
***Mummy's Legs*, 25**
Munro, Alice, 83, 133
**Murakami, Haruki, 159**
*Murder Makes Waves*, 94
*Murder on the Iditarod Trail*, 41
*Murder Runs in the Family*, 94
Murdoch, Iris, 80, 102, 132, 133, 148
**Murphy, Yannick, 48**
**Murray, Yxta Maya, 119**
*The Museum Guard*, 6, 160
*The Music of Chance*, 71
***The Music Lesson*, 47, 138**
***Music of the Swamp*, 14,** 20, 159
Muske-Dukes, Carol, 51, 86, 117, 129
***My Drowning*, 97**
*My Golden Trades*, 107
*My Hard Bargain*, 42
*My Life as a Man*, 126
*My Name Is Asher Lev*, 38, 136
*My Old Sweetheart*, 25, 91, 142
*My Present Danger*, 137
***My Russian*, 46**
*Mysteries of Algiers*, 9
*The Mysteries of Pittsburgh*, 82
*Mystery Ride*, 55, 90
*The Mystery Roast*, 34, 152

**Nahai, Gina B., 119**
Naipaul, V. S., 81
***The Name*, 96**
*The Name of the Rose*, 155
***The Name of the World*, 154**
*The Names*, 71
*The Names of the Mountains*, 7
***Naming the Spirits*, 134**
*A Narrow Time*, 87
Naslund, Sara Jeter, 105
*Nathan Coulter*, 4
***Native Speaker*, 108, 109**
*The Natural*, 108

*Natural History*, 102
*The Natural Order of Things*, **69**
**Naylor, Gloria**, 30, **120**, 139
*The Needle's Eye*, 80
*Negrophobia: An Urban Parable*, 43, 154
Neihart, Ben, 98, 141
**Nelson, Antonya**, 100, **120**
Nelson, Jim, 99
**Nelson, Liza**, 30, **48**
*Never Change*, 25
*Never Cry Wolf*, 41
*Nevermore*, 92
*The New City*, **2**
*The New York Trilogy*, 71, 145
Ng, Fae Myenne, 60
*Nice Work*, 72
**Nicholson, Geoff, 120**
*Nickel Mountain*, 21
*Night Falls Fast: Understanding Suicide*, 90
*Night of Many Dreams*, 62
*Night of the Avenging Blowfish*, **63**
*The Night Sky*, 48
*Night Swimming*, 34
*Night Train*, *145*, 148
*Nine Parts of Desire: The Hidden World of
    Islamic Women*, 18
*1919*, 3
*1959*, 100
*A Nixon Man*, **27**
*No Earthly Notion*, 4, 56
*No Fond Return of Love*, 91
*No Hiding Place*, 64
*No One Thinks of Greenland*, **97**
*No Saints or Angels*, 107
*Nobody's Fool*, 50, 127
*Nobody's Girl*, 100, 120
"Noises Off," 34
Nooteboom, Cees, 112
**Nordan, Lewis, 14**, 15, 20, 95, **121**, 142, 158, **159**
Norfolk, Lawrence, 145
**Norman, Howard**, 3, 6, 13, 15, **160**
*North Galdiola*, 72
*Northern Edge*, 16
*The Northern Lights*, 160
*Not a Day Goes By*, **38**
*Not Wanted on the Voyage*, 92
*Not Where I Started From*, 20
*Notches*, 20
*The Notebooks of Don Rigoberto*, **137**
*Nothing Is Terrible*, **57**
*The Nuclear Age*, 121
Nyiri, Janos, 22

O'Brien, Edna, 53
**O'Brien, Tim**, 48, **49**, 109, **121**
O'Carroll, Brendan, 88
**O'Dell, Tawni, 121**
O'Donnell, Mark, 87, 114
O'Hara, John, 12
O'Hehir, Diana, 25
**O'Nan, Stewart**, 76, **122**
Oates, Joyce Carol, 67, 114, 119, 142, 163
*Obasan*, 21
*An Obedient Father*, **129**
*The Object of My Affection*, 25, 111, 114
*Objects in Mirror Are Closer Than They
    Appear*, 10, 138
*An Ocean in Iowa*, 89, 115, 122, 125
*Ocean of Words: Army Stories*, 154
*Ocean Sea*, 3, 147
*October Light*, 142
*The Odd Sea*, 44, 125
*The Odd Woman*, 36
*Off Keck Road*, 12
**Offill, Jenny**, 25, 59, **121**
*Offshore*, 92
Offutt, Chris, 20
Okri, Ben, 4
**Olafsson, Olaf**, 110, **122**
*The Old Gringo*, 92
"Oleanna," 109
*On Gold Mountain: The Hundred-Year
    Odyssey of a Chinese-American Family*,
    60
*On the Night Plain*, 8, 99, 110
*Once Upon a Time on the Banks*, 21, 95
**Ondaatje, Michael**, 15, 16, 17, 32, 54, 77,
    **122**, 146, 148, 151, **160**
*One by One in the Darkness*, 8
*One Flew Over the Cuckoo's Nest*, 20
*One Girl: A Novel in Stories*, 42
*One Heart*, **114**
*One Hundred and One Ways*, **143**
*The 158-Pound Marriage*, 10
*One Hundred Years of Solitude*, 69
*One Sweet Quarrel*, 6, 46, 71, 119
*The Only Piece of Furniture in the House*, 20
*Only the Little Bone*, 102
*The Optimist's Daughter*, 93
*Oral History*, 91
*Oranges Are Not the Only Fruit*, 85, 141
*The Orchard on Fire*, 15, 112, 122
*The Orchid Thief*, 44
*Ordinary Love and Good Will*, 131
*Ordinary People*, 126

*The Ordinary Seaman*, **95**
Orlean, Susan, 44
**Orlock, Carol**, 22, **49**
**Orton, Thomas**, **49**
*The Other Side*, 68, 157
*Otherwise Engaged*, **33**, 128
Otto, Whitney, 29
*Our House in the Last World*, 100
"Our Lady of Sligo," 146
"Our Town," 4
*Outerbridge Reach*, 29
Owens, Louis, 51
*Owls Do Cry*, 68
*The Oxygen Man*, **142**
*Oyster*, 8
Oz, Amos, 22

*The Pact*, 51
*Paddy Clarke Ha-Ha-Ha*, 88
*A Painted House*, 106
*Painting on Glass*, 24
*Palace Walk*, 18
*A Pale View of the Hills*, 104
Paley, Grace, 156
Palin, Michael, 44
*Panther in the Basement*, 22
*Paper Wings*, 35, 59, 60
*The Paperboy*, 20, 78, 142, **150**
*Paradise*, 124, **159**
*A Parish of Rich Women*, 5
Parks, Suzan-Lori, 154
**Parks, Tim**, 76, **123**
*Part of the Furniture*, 92, 138
*The Partisan*, 28
*Passage*, 70
*The Passion*, 118, 141
*A Passionate Man*, **62**
*Past the Bleachers*, 72
**Patchett, Ann**, 45, 52, 101, **123**
*Patenting the Sun: Polio and the Salk Vaccine*, 18
*The Patron Saint of Liars*, 45, 52, 101, **123**
*The Patron Saint of Unmarried Women*, 23
*Patty Jane's House of Curl*, 43, 56, 61, 84
*Pay It Forward*, **39**
**Payne, Peggy**, **14**, 133
Peacock, Nancy, 62
*Pearl's Progress*, 84
Pears, Iain, 155
Pears, Tim 149
**Peck, Richard**, **50**
*The Peculiar Memories of Thomas Penman*, 27

*Peel My Love Like an Onion*, **28**
**Pelletier, Cathie**, 15, 21, 59, 72, 90, 95, **123**
*Peoples*, 88
Percy, Walker, 92
*Perdido*, 98, 100
Perelman, S. J., 63
Peres da Costa, Suneeta, 86
*The Perez Family*, 63, **75**
**Perez, Loida Maritza**, **50**
Perez-Reverte, Arturo, 124
*Perfect Agreement*, 87, 126
*The Perfect Elizabeth: A Tale of Two Sisters*, 98, **128**
*A Perfect Execution*, 77
*Perfect Happiness*, 125
*The Perfect Place*, 42
**Perrotta, Tom**, **50**, 124
Perry, Thomas, 81
*The Persian Bride*, 2, 4, **5**, 34, 96, 147
*Persian Brides*, 120
*Persian Nights*, 18
Petry, Ann, 139
*Philadelphia Fire*, 119, 139
**Phillips, Jayne Anne**, 74, **124**
Phillips, Max, 11, 61
*A Philosophical Investigation*, 145
*The Piano Man's Daughter*, 67, **91**
*Picnic at Hanging Rock*, 42
**Picoult, Jody**, 51, 56, 88
*Picture Bride*, 21
*Picture Perfect*, 51, 88
*Pictures from an Institution*, 132
Pierce, Julian, 55, 107
Percy, Marge, 82, 155
*Pigs in Heaven*, 106, 107
*Pilgrim*, **92**
*Pilgrims*, 95
*The Pilot's Wife*, **58**
Pinckney, Darryl, 43
*Pink Slip*, **82**
*Pinocchio in Venice*, 130
*Pipers at the Gates of Dawn: A Triptych*, 59
*Place Last Seen*, **34**
*The Plagiarist*, **28**
*The Plague*, 5
*Plains Song, for Female Voices*, 8
*Plainsong* **(Haruf)**, 11, 39, 90, **99**, 110
*Plainsong* (Huston), 9
*Plantation Boy*, 21
*Player Piano*, 54
*Playing Botticelli*, 30, **48**
*Plays Well with Others*, 161

*The Pleasing Hour*, 10, **106**, 113
*The Pleasure of Believing*, 32
*The Pledge*, 127
*Pledge of Allegiance*, 127
*Plowing the Dark*, **160**
*Plum & Jaggers*, **131**
*Pobby and Dingan*, **15**
*Points of Light*, 76
*Poison*, 99
*The Poisonwood Bible*, 4, 7, 9, 55, 106, **107**, 160
*Polly's Ghost*, 37, 74, **93**, 95
*Polonaise*, 9
Pope, Susan, 123
**Popham, Melinda Worth, 14**, 32
**Porter, Connie**, 109, **124**, 141, 159
*Portnoy's Complaint*, 134
*Portrait of a Lady*, 10
*Portrait of the Artist's Wife*, **68**
*Possession*, **79**, 85
*Postcards*, 15
*Postcards from the Edge*, 111
*The Potato Baron*, 8
Potok, Chaim, 38, 127, 132, 136
Powell, Anthony, 130
*Power*, 153
*The Power and the Glory*, 96
*The Power of One*, 6, 119
**Power, Susan**, **51**, 63, 106, 153
*The Powerbook*, 141
**Powers, Richard**, 18, 140, **160**
*Practical Magic*, 49, 102, 152
*The Prague Orgy*, 127
*Praise Jerusalem!*, 62
*Praisesong for the Widow*, 5
*The Prayer of the Bone*, 81
*A Prayer for Owen Meany*, 40
*A Prayer for the Dying*, 122
**Preston, Caroline**, **51**, 87
*Preston Falls*, 82, **94**, 101, 130
**Price, Reynolds**, **160**, 161, 162
Price, Richard, 141
*The Priest Fainted*, 98
*The Prime of Miss Jean Brodie*, 4, 42
*The Primitive*, 2
*The Prince of Tides*, 89, 121
*Princess Charming*, 36
*A Private State: Stories*, 71
*Prodigal Summer*, 39
*The Professor of Light*, **79**
*Professor Romeo*, 47, 52, 134
*The Promise*, 132

*The Promise of Rest*, **160**
**Prose, Francine**, 46, **52**, 115, 161
**Proulx, E. Annie**, 3, 13, **15**, 160
**Puertolas, Soledad**, **124**
*The Pugilist at Rest*, 119
Puig, Manuel, 103
*The Pull of the Moon*, 25, 46, 143
*Pumpkin Moon*, 29
Purdy, James, 49
*A Pure Clear Light*, 132
*Purple Passage: A Novel About a Lady Both Famous and Infamous*, 68
*The Purveyor of Enchantment*, 29
*Push*, 73, 141
Pym, Barbara, 78, 91, 111, 125
Pynchon, Thomas, 151

*Quarantine*, 148
Quarrington, Paul, 149
*Quartet in Autumn*, 111
*The Queen and I*, 62
*The Quick & the Dead*, **140**
Quick, Barbara, 16
*The Quiet American*, 11, 155
*A Quiet Life*, 125
*The Quilter's Apprentice*, **28**

Raban, Jonathan, 6
*Rabbit at Rest*, **163**
*Rabbit Hill*, 14
*Rabbit Is Rich*, 163
*Rabbit Redux*, 163
*Rabbit Run*, 92, 94, 163
Rabinyan, Dorit, 120
Raddall, Thomas H., 6
*Ragtime*, 3, 12, 92, 150
*Rain of Gold*, 68
*Rainlight*, 115
*The Raj Quartet*, 35
*Rally Round the Flag, Boys!*, 63
*Rameau's Niece*, 51, 80
Rand, Ayn, 13, 120
*Random Hearts*, 58
*Range of Motion*, 25
*The Rapure of Canaan*, 103
*Ratner's Star*, 71
Raucher, Herman, 61
**Rawles, Nancy**, **52**
*Ray in Reverse*, **63**, 148
**Ray, Jeanne**, **52**
Raymo, Chet, 78
Raymond, Linda, 63, 78

Rayner, Richard, 13, 120
*Reaching Tin River*, 70
Read, Piers Paul, 9
*The Reader*, 61, 127, 135
***Reading in the Dark*, 80, 149**
*The Real Life of Alejandro Mayta*, 137
*Reality and Dreams*, 70
**Realuyo, Bino A., 125**
**Reardon, Lisa, 53**
*The Rebel Angels*, 77, 102
*Rebuilding Coventry*, 93
***A Recipe for Bees*, 2, 96**
*The Recognitions*, 151
*The Rector's Wife*, 62, 110
***Redeeming Eve*, 26**
Reed, Ishmael, 63, 155
**Reed, Kit, 53**
***The Reef*, 151**
Rees, Emlyn, 33
*Refuge: An Unnatural History of Family and*
    *Place*, 153
*Regeneration*, 73
Reidy, Sue
**Reiken, Frederick, 44, 125**
*The Reivers*, 14
*The Remains of the Day*, 13, 15, 16, 104, 108,
    151
Remarque, Erich Maria, 73, 103
***Remember Me*, 23, 100**
*Remix: Conversations with Immigrant*
    *Teenagers*, 79
*The Republic of Love*, 74
*Requiem for a Woman's Soul*, 2
***Rescue*, 126**
*Reservation Blues*, 106
*Reservation Road*, 72, 102
***Resting in the Bosom of the Lamb*, 62**
*Resistance*, 58
*Restoration*, 61
***The Restraint of Beasts*, 117, 134**
*Resurrection Update: Collected Poems*
    *1975-1997*, 8
**Reuss, Frederick, 78, 84, 97, 107, 125, 135**
**Reynolds, Marjorie, 53**
**Rice, Ben, 15**
Rice, Luanne, 51
*Rich Like Us*, 17
***The Rich Man's Table*, 132**
**Richards, Elizabeth, 126**
Richler, Mordecai, 132
*Ricochet River*, 110
***The Riders*, 141**

**Ridgway, Keith, 53, 146**
*Riding Solo with the Golden Horde*, 105, 140
Rifaat, Alifa, 18
***Right By My Side*, 99**
*Rima in the Weeds*, 46
**Rinaldi, Nicholas, 54**
*The Risk Pool*, 127
Rivabella, Omar, 2
*A Rival Creation*, 29
*Riven Rock*, 77, 92
*The River Is Home*, 14
***The River King*, 39, 101, 153**
*A River Runs Through It, and Other Stories*,
    19, 101, 110
*River Song*, 110
*A River Sutra*, 120
*River Teeth: Stories and Writing*, 89
*River Town: Two Years on the Yangtze*, 7
*The River Why*, 89, 110
Rivera, Beatriz, 21, 120
**Rizzuto, Rahna Reiko, 54, 105**
*RL's Dream*, 119, 139
***The Road Home*, 98, 152**
*The Road to Wellville*, 149
*The Robber Bride*, 145
**Robbins, Tom, 54, 70, 96**
**Roberts, Karen, 15, 16**
Robinson Bruce, 27
**Robinson, Eden, 126**
Robinson, Marilynne, 85
**Robinson, Roxanna, 54**
*Rocking the Babies*, 63, 78
Rodoreda, Merce, 124
*The Romance Reader*, 47
***The Romantics*, 13, 14, 130**
*Rookery Blues*, 72
*Rose's Garden*, 78
**Rosenfield, Lucinda, 55**
**Ross, Ann B., 55**
Rossi, Agnes, 45
**Roth, Philip, 126, 127, 131, 134**
Rouaud, Jean, 32
*Rough Strife*, 128
*Rough Translations*, 95
*Round Robin*, 29
*Rowing in Eden*, 91
*Roxanna Slade*, 162
Roy, Arundhati, 15, 70, 151, 158
**Roy, Lucinda, 55**
Rubens, Bernice, 86
**Rubio, Gwyn Hyman, 55, 156**
**Ruby, 38, 80**

*Rule of the Bone*, 42
**The Rules of Engagement**, **147**
*Rules of the Wild*, 14
*Run with the Horsemen*, 42
*The Runaway*, 42
*Running in the Family*, 122
*Running Through the Tall Grass*, 5
**Rush, Norman**, 156, **161**
**Rushdie, Salman**, 5, 13, 14, 69, 112, 120,
    152, 156, **161**, **162**
Russell, Mary Doria, 2, 36, 91, 132, 150
*The Russian Album*, 153
*The Russian Girl*, 134
Russo, Richard, 21, 46, 50, 72, 81, 84, 87,
    101, 110, 113, 124, 127, 139
Ryman, Geoff, 135

*S*, 21
*Sabbath's Theater*, 126
*Sacred Country*, 61, 105, 118
*Sacred Hunger*, 136
Sahgal, Nayantara, 17
*Sailing*, 29
*Sailing in a Spoonful of Water*, 29
*Saint*, 75
*Saint Maybe*, 136
**Saints and Villains**, **35**
**Sakamoto, Kerri**, 54, **56**, 62
**Salamanca, J. R.**, **127**
Salinger, J. D. 27, 42
Salisbury, Graham, 40, 125
**The Salt Dancers**, **38**, 135
**Salzman, Mark**, **16**, 51, 156
Sams, Ferrol, 42
*The Samurai's Garden*, 62
*Sandman*, 32
*Santa Evita*, 3
Saramago, Jose, 69, 162
Sarton, May, 142
Sartre, Jean-Paul, 32
*The Saskiad*, 30, 36, 49
*Satin Doll*, 40
*Saul*, 63
Savage, Georgia, 33, 118
Savage, Thomas, 6, 31
*Saving Agnes*, 84
**The Saving Graces**, 24, **34**
*Saving St. Germ*, 51, 86, 117, 129
*Say Goodbye*, 58
*Saying Grace*, 37
*The Scapegoat*, 6
*Scar Tissue*, 30, 60, 88, 124, **153**

*Schindler's List*, 36
Schine, Cathleen, 51, 80
Schlink, Bernhard, 61, 127, 135
**Schmais, Libby**, 98, **128**
**Schroeder, Joan Vannorsdall**, **56**
Schulberg, Budd, 81, 119, 137
**Schulman, Audrey**, 3, **16**, 41
**Schumacher, Julie**, 38, 59, **128**
Schwartz, John Burnham, 72, 102
**Schwartz, Lynne Sharon**, 41, 57, 79, 117,
    **128**, 153
**Schwartz, Leslie**, 45, **128**
**Schweighardt, Joan**, **129**
**Scott, Joanna**, **129**, 137
**Scott, Joanna C.**, **56**
Scott, Paul, 35
*The Sculptress*, 29
*A Sea Change*, 127
*Sea Level*, 45
**The Sea of Trees**, **48**
*Seabiscuit: An American Legend*, 38
*Searching for Caleb*, 120, 152
**Second Hand**, **64**
*The Secret Diaries of Adrian Mole*, 62
*The Secret of Cartwheels*, 9
*The Secret Years,* 110
**Secrets of the Tsil Café**, **24**
*Seduction Theory*, 75
**See, Carolyn**, **57**
See, Lisa, 60
**Seeing Calvin Coolidge in a Dream**, **86**
Segal, Lore, 68
Segura, Chris, 20
**Self-Portrait with Ghosts**, **90**, 123
*Selling Ben Cheever: Back to Square One in a*
    *Service Economy*, 28
*Selling the Lite of Heaven*, 57
**Selvadurai, Shyam**, 15, **16**, 151
*Semaphore*, 99
**Senna, Danzy**, 27, **129**
*Sent for You Yesterday*, 139
*The Serpent's Gift*, 109, 120
Seth. Vikram, 130
Settle, Mary Lee, 6, 55
*Seven for the Apocalypse*, 53
*Seven Moves*, 121
*The Seven Year Atomic Make-Over Guide*
    *and Other Stories*, 75
**Seventh Heaven**, **152**
*Sexing the Cherry*, 141
Sexton, Linda Gray, 76
**Shadow Baby**, **115**

*The Shadow Knows*, 10
*The Shadow Lines*, 25
*Shadow Ranch*, 76, 113
*Shadow Song*, 42
Shakespeare, William, 74
*Shame*, 161
Shapiro, Jane, 33
*Shark Dialogues*, 30, 98
**Sharma, Akhil, 129**
*Sharmila's Book*, **42**, 86
**Sharp, Paula, 130**
*The Sharp Teeth of Love*, 76
**Sharpe, Matthew, 57**
*The Sharpest Sight*, 51
*The Sharpshooter Blues*, 15, 20, 95, **121**, 142, 158
*She Needed Me*, 42, 138
Shea, Lisa, 103
**Shea, Suzanne Strempek, 52**
*Shelter*, 124
Shelton, Richard, 14, 106
**Sherrill, Steven, 130**
**Sherwood, Ben, 57**, 61
**Shields, Carol**, 29, 58, 68, 70, 71, 74, 79, 82, 94, 127, **130, 131**, 145, 162, **163**
Shikeguni, Julie, 143
**Shiner, Lewis, 58**
*The Shipping News*, 3, 13, **15**, 160
*Shiva Dancing*, 42
*Shiver*, 8
*Shoot an Arrow to Stop the Wind*, 20
*Shoot!*, 137
*The Short History of a Prince*, **98**
**Shreve, Anita**, 37, **58**, 131
**Shreve, Susan Richards**, 105, **131**
Shulman, 63
*Shy Girl*, 26
*Siam: Or the Woman Who Shot a Man*, **19**, 155
Siddons, Anne Rivers, 101
Sidhwa, Bapsi, 14
*Sights Unseen*, 34, 91
Silko, Leslie Marmon, 51
Sillitoe, Alan, 114
**Simecka, Martin, 17**
*A Simple Plan*, 34
*Simple Prayers*, 95
Simpson, Mona, 12, 35, 49, 59
**Singer, Katie, 58**, 133
*The Singapore Grip*, 35
**Singh, Jacquelin, 17**
*Single Man*, 38
*Sister India*, **14**, 133

*Sister of My Heart*, 35, 42, **87**
*Sister Water*, 74
Sivanandan, Ambalavaner, 16
*Six Crooked Highways*, 41
*Six Figures*, **109**
*6 Persons*, 154
*Skateaway*, 102, **104**
*Sketches in Winter*, 7
*Skinny Legs and All*, 70
*Skins*, 150
*The Sky Fisherman*, 90, **110**
*Skywater*, **14**, 32
*Slam*, 58
*Slammerkin*, 87
**Slater, Dashka, 59**
*Slaves of New York*, 105
Slavitt, David R., 45, 154
*Sleep, Baby, Sleep*, 24
*The Sleep-Over Artist*, **75**
The Slightest Distance, 26
*The Slow Natives*, **69**
*The Slow Way Back*, **37**, 47
*Slowness*, 137
*Small Ceremonies*, 162
*The Small Rain*, 4
*Small World*, 72, 84, 85, 134
**Smiley, Jane**, **17**, 31, 38, 41, 72, 84, 85, 99, **131**
*Smilla's Sense of Snow*, 161
Smith, Dinitia, 118
**Smith, Jane S., 18**
Smith, Lee, 31, 91, 94
Smith, Patrick D., 14
Smith, Scott, 34
**Smith, Zadie**, 130, **162**
*Snake*, **10**
*Snakebite Sonnet*, 11, 61
*The Snapper*, 45, 88, 163
*Snow Angels*, 76, **122**
*Snow Falling on Cedars*, 54, 152
*Snow in August*, **38**
*So Far from God*, 28, 119
*So Long, See You Tomorrow*, 122
*So Vast the Prison*, 116
Sobin, Gustaf, 18
*Solar Storms*, 147, **153**
*Soldier in Paradise*, **48**
*A Soldier of the Great War*, 152
*Solitary Lives*, 56
*Solitude*, 124
*The Soloist*, 16, 156
Solomon, Andrew, 153
*Some Girls*, 26

*Some Old Lover's Ghost*, **110**
*Some Tame Gazelle*, 91
*Something to Declare*, 2
*Some Things that Stay*, **140**
*Something Blue*, 39
*Sometimes a Great Notion*, 89
*Sometimes I Dream in Italian*, 82
*Somewhere Off the Coast of Maine*, 39
*Somewhere South of Here*, 108
*A Son of the Circus*, 161
*Song of Enchantment*, 4
*Song of the Exile*, **30**, 108
*Songdogs*, 12
*Songs in Ordinary Time*, 118
Sontag, Susan, 136
*The Sooterkin*, 15
**Soueif, Ahdaf, 18**
*Soul Kiss*, 141
Souljah, Sister, 73
*Souls Raised from the Dead*, **76**, 94
*The Sound and the Fury*, 151
*The Sound of One Hand Clapping*, 8,  **33**, 152
*The Source of Light*, 161
*The South*, 135
*South of Resurrection*, 23
*South of the Border, West of the Sun*, 159
*A Southern Family*, 94
*Southern Light*, 127
*A Spanish Lover*, 62
Spark, Muriel, 4, 42, 70, 92, 138
*The Sparrow*, 2, 36, 81, 132, 150
*Spartina*, 29, 81
*Speak Rwanda*, 55, 107
*A Spell of Winter*, 90
**Spencer, Scott**, 44, 58, 116, **132**, 141
*Spiderweb*, **111**
*Spinsters*, 136
*The Spirit Cabinet*, 149
*The Spirit Catches You and You Fall Down*, 26
*Spirits of the Ordinary*, 1
*Split Skirt*, 45
*Spoon River Anthology*, 4
*The Sportswriter*, 92, 101, 130
*Spring Snow*, 151
**St. John, Madeleine, 132**
Stabenow, Dana, 41
*A Stairway to Paradise*, **132**
*A Star Called Henry*, 8, 47, **88**, 91, 146
Stark, Elizabeth, 26
*The Starlite Drive-In*, 53
*The Start of the End of It All*, 31
*State of Grace*, 140

*Stately Pursuits*, 32, 44
**Stegner, Lynn, 59**
Stegner, Wallace, 10, 11, 12, 20, 74, 94, 137
*Steps and Exes*, **41**, 57, 128
*Stern Men*, **94**, 147
"The Steward of Christendom," 146
*Still Life*, 79
**Stillman, Whit, 18**
*Stir-fry*, 87
**Stollman, Aryeh, 132**
Stolz, Karen, 24
*The Stone Angel*, 2, 145
*A Stone Boat*, 153
*The Stone Diaries*, 71, 79, 94, **162**
*The Stone Raft*, 162
Stone, Robert, 21, 29
Stonich, Sarah, 158
*Stones from the River*, 38
*Stories from the Tube*, 57
*Storming Heaven*, 6, 20, 36
*The Story of a Million Years*, **102**
*The Story of the Night*, 134, 135
*Straight Man*, 46, 72, 82, 84, 87, 101, 110, 113, 124, 127
Straight, Susan, 154
Straley, John, 41
*Strange Fits of Passion*, 58
*The Strangeness of Beauty*, 21, 135
*The Stranger*, 5
*A Stranger in the Earth*, **134**
*The Street*, 139
**Strout, Elizabeth**, 35, 59, 75, 81, 114, **133**
Stuart, Colin, 20
*A Student of Weather*, 2, 78, 114
*Stygo*, 11
Styron, William, 100, 136
Suberman, Stella, 37
*Success*, 90
*Such a Long Journey*, 17, **158**
*Sudden Times*, 8
*The Suicide's Wife*, 59
*A Suitable Boy*, 130
*Suite for Calliope*, 156
*Suits Me: The Double Life of Billy Tipton*, 105
Sukenick, Ronald, 70
*Sula*, 158
**Sullivan, Faith, 133**
Sullivan, Walter, 153
*Summer Gone*, **12**
*The Summer House: A Trilogy*, 91
*Summer Light*, 55
*Summer of '42*, 61

*The Sunday Tertulia*, 30
**Sunday You Learn How to Box**, **141**
*Sunshine Sketches of a Little Town*, 49
*Supporting the Sky*, 37
*The Surface of the Earth*, 161
**Suri, Manil**, **133**
*Surveyor*, 99
*Suspicious River*, 118
*Suttree*, 157
*Swallow Hard*, 28
Swallow, Jean, 87
*Swann*, 68, 70, 145, 162
**Swanson, Eric**, **59**
Swarthout, Glendon, 8
*Sweat*, 25
*Sweet Diamond Dust*, 7
**Swick, Marly**, 28, 34, 35, 59, **60**
**The Sweet Hereafter**, 54, **72**, 76, 102
*The Sweetheart Season*, 123
**Swift, Graham**, 111, **133**
*Swimming Lessons & Other Stories*, 158
*Swimming Out of the Collective Unconscious*, 83
*Swimming with Jonah*, 16
Syal, Meera, 103

*Taft*, 101, 123
*Taken In*, 30
**Taking Lottie Home**, **41**
*Taking the Wall: Stories*, 23
*Tales from Firozsha Baag*, 158
*Tales from the Blue Archives*, 134
*Tales of the City*, 93
*Talk Before Sleep*, 24, 25, 35
*Talking in Bed*, 120
*Talking It Over*, 73, 132
*Talking to the Dead*, 90
**The Tall Pine Polka**, **43**, 61, 84
**Tan, Amy**, **60**, 135
*Tanks*, 48
*Tara Road*, 62
*Tarantula*, 132
**Tarloff, Erik**, **134**
Taylor, Elizabeth, 142
Taylor-Hall, Mary Ann, 156
*Tea*, 85, 87
*The Tempest of Clemenza*, 67
**Tempest Rising**, **116**
*The Temple of My Familiar*, 154
*Tender Mercies*, 27
*The Tennis Handsome*, 149
*Tenorman*, 102

*Terrible Honesty: Mongrel Manhattan in the 1920s*, 159
*The Terrible Twos*, 63
*Territorial Rights*, 138
Tesich, Steve, 100, 121
*Testing the Current*, 14
*Texaco*, 5
*Texasville*, 46
Thane, Elswyth, 24
*That Eye, The Sky*, 141
*That Night*, 151, 157
**That Summer's Trance**, **127**
Thayer, Nancy, 30
*Then She Found Me*, 26, 44, 111
*Theophilus North*, 57
*A Theory of Relativity*, 126, 129
Theroux, Alexander, 162
**Theroux, Marcel**, **134**
Theroux, Paul, 21
*These Granite Islands*, 158
**Thicker Than Water**, **99**
*Things Fall Apart*, 7
*Things Invisible to See*, 59, 74, 89, 108, 126
*The Things They Carried*, 48, 49
*Thirst*, 2
**A Thirst for Rain**, **80**, 147
*This Boy's Life*, 42
*This Family of Women*, 50
*This House of Sky*, 8, 110
**This Is My Daughter**, **54**
**This Is Your Life**, 64
**This Just In...**, **40**
**This One and Magic Life**, **94**
**This Side of Brightness**, **112**
**This Time Last Year**, **101**
Thomas, D. M., 3
Thompson, Jim, 79
Thorndike, John, 8
Thornton, Lawrence, 2, 95, 160
**Those Who Favor Fire**, **20**
**A Thousand Acres**, **17**, 41, 90
*A Thousand Wings*, 9
**Three Apples Fell from Heaven**, **156**
*Three Farmers On Their Way to a Dance*, 140, 160
*Three Times Table*, 112
*Three to See the King*, 118
*Three Women at the Water's Edge*, 30
*Through the Arc of the Rain Forest*, 21
*Through the Green Valley*, 96
*Through the Safety Net*, 74
**Thumbsucker**, 27, **42**

*Thus Was Adonis Murdered*, 141
*The Tie That Binds*, 94, 99
*Till the Day Goes Down*, 110
*Tim*, 76, 152
**Timbuktu, 71**
*The Time of the Doves*, 124
*A Time to Dance*, 153
*Time's Witness*, 113
*The Tin Can Tree*, 76
*The Tiny One*, **157**
*Tirra Lirra by the River*, 136, 145
*To Dance with the White Dog*, 42
*To Have and To Hold*, 35
*To the Lighthouse*, 158
*Toby's Lie*, 141
**Toibin, Colm**, 134, **135**
Tolstoy, Leo, 148, 158
*Tom Jones*, 134
**Tomcat in Love, 49**
*The Tomcat's Wife and Other Stories*, 49
*Tongues of Flame*, 123
Toole, John Kennedy, 49
*The Tortilla Curtain*, 1, 89
*The Toughest Indian in the World*, 51
*The Towers of Trebizond*, 141
**Townsend, Sue**, 27, **61**, 93
*The Tracks of Angels*, 85, 90
*The Train Home*, 131
*Trans-Sister Radio*, 26, 105
*Traplines*, 126
*Travels with Lizbeth*, 12, 71
*Treasures in Heaven*, 1
*The Tree of Man*, 10, 67
**Tree Surgery for Beginners, 93**
**Treichel, Hans-Ulrich**, 117, **135**
**Tremain, Rose**, 11, **61**, 105, 118
**Trevor, William**, 29, 114, 148, **162**, 163
**Triage, 68**
*Trials of Tiffany Trot*, 40
*The Trick of It*, 34
**A Trick of Nature**, 45, **46**
**Trigiani, Adriana, 61**
**Trobaugh, August, 62**
**Trollope, Joanna**, 50, **62**, 110
*Tropic of Orange*, 21
Trott, Susan, 51, 83
*Troubled Sleep*, 32
**Troy, Judy**, **135**, 136
*True and False Romances*, 7
*True History of the Kelly Gang*, 137
**True North, 41**
**Trumpet, 105**

**Truth and Bright Water**, 51, **106**
*Trust Me*, 39
*Trying to Smile and Other Stories*, 44
*Tryst*, 24
**Tsukiyama, Gail, 62**
**Tuck, Lily**, **19**, 155
**Tempest Rising**, **116**, 120, 139
*Tunnel of Love*, 50
*The Turn of the Screw*, 37
**Turtle Moon**, 102, 120, **152**
*The 27th Kingdom*, 91
*Twitch and Shout: A Touretter's Tale*, 56
**Two Cities, 139**
*Two Women*, 64
Ty-Casper, Linda, 125
**Tyler, Anne**, 46, 76, 120, 133, **136**, 152
Tyree, Omar, 38, 64

Uchida, Yoshiko, 21
*Ultimate Intimacy*, 107
*The Ultraviolet Sky*, 68
*Ulysses*, 151
**The Umbrella Country, 125**
*Uncivil Seasons*, 113
*Uncle Petros and Goldbach's Conjecture*, 75
**The Unconsoled**, **109**, 159
*Under the Frog*, 17
*Under the Net*, 80
*Under the Red Flag: Stories*, 154
**The Underpainter**, 112, **136**
*Understanding Comics*, 82
**Undertow, 59**
**Underworld**, **150**, 160
*The Undiscovered Country*, 13, 151
*Undue Influence*, 111
*The Unfastened Heart*, 22, 32, 57
*Union Street*, 73
*The Universal Baseball Association, Inc., J. Henry Waugh, Prop.*, 63, 108
*The Unknown Errors of Their Lives*, 87
*The Unquiet Earth*, 36
*An Unquiet Mind*, 90
*The Unravelling*, 96
**Unsworth, Barry, 136**
*Until the Real Thing Comes Along*, 25, 65
*Until Your Heart Stops*, 116
*Unto the Soul*, 148
*Up in the Air*, 42
*Up Island*, 101
*Up the Country*, 10
**Updike, John**, 21, 92, 94, **163**
Uris, Leon, 22

**Urquhart, Jane**, 80, 112, **136**
*USA Trilogy*, 3, 141

Vakil, Ardashir, 125
Valladeres, Armando, 75
*The Van*, 45, **88**
Van Oosterzee, Penny, 13
**Vanderhaeghe, Guy**, **137**
*Vanished*, 118
*Vanishing Act*, 81
*Vanishing Points*, 70
**Vargas Llosa, Mario**, **137**
*Various Miracles*, 162
**Veciana-Suarez, Ana**, **62**, 78, 119
Vega, Ana Lydia, 7
"Venus," 154
"Venus of Dublin," 1
*Veneer*, 142
*The Veracruz Blues*, 141
*A Very Long Engagement*, 32, 103
Vian, Boris, 9
*Vida*, 155
*The View from Pompey's Head*, 62
Villanueva, Alma Luz, 62
Villasenor, Victor, 68
Vilmure, Daniel, 141
Vine, Barbara, 29
*The Vine of Desire*, 87
*Vinegar Puss*, 63
*Violet Clay*, 36
*The Virgin Suicides*, 42, 60, **150**
*Virtual Silence*, **129**
*The Visitation*, 68
*The Visiting Physician*, 131
*The Vision of Emma Blau*, 87
*Vita Nova*, 36
*Voices from Another Place: A Collection of
    Works from a Generation Born in Korea
    and Adopted to Other Countries*, 56
*The Volcano Lover*, 136
Volk, Toni, 56
Von Herzen, Lane, 22, 32, 57, 130
Vonnegut, Kurt, 54, 63
*Vox*, 137
*The Voyage of the Narwhal*, 3
Vreeland, Susan, 138

*Waiting*, 14, **153**
*Waiting for the Barbarians*, 148
*The Waking Spell*, 31
*Waking the Dead*, 44, 132, 141
Walker, Alice, 97, 154, 155

Walker, Mildred, 10
Walker, Rebecca, 27
*Walkin' the Dog*, 119
*Walking Across Egypt*, 91
*The Walking Tour*, **85**
**Wallace, Daniel**, **63**, 148
Wallace, David Foster, 161
*The Walnut King and Other Stories*, 48
Walsh, Jill Paton, 107
Walters, Minette, 29
*War and Peace*, 158
**Warner, Sharon Oard**, **137**
*The Wars*, 91
*Was*, 135
*Watch Your Mouth*, 38
*Water, Carry Me*, **47**
*Water Marked*, **109**
*The Water-Method Man*, 70
*Water Music*, 77
*Waterland*, 111, 1133
Waters, Annie, 27
*Watership Down*, 14
*The Waterworks*, 3, 115
**Watson, Larry**, **19**, 20, 110
*Waverly Place*, 88
*The Way I Found Her*, 11, **61**
*The Way Men Act*, 52, 82, 111, 114
*A Weave of Women*, 30
**Weber, Katherine**, 10, 47, **138**
*The Wedding*, 101, 105, 109
*The Weekend*, **80**, 135
*The Weight of Dreams*, **23**
*The Weight of Water*, 21, 37, 58
*The Weight of Winter*, 123
Weiner, Jennifer, 36, 55, 128
Welch, James, 20, 31
*Welcome to the Great Mysterious*, 43
*Welcome to the World, Baby Girl!*, 37, 57
**Wells, Ken**, **19**
Wells, Rebecca, 26
Welter, John, 63, 86
Welty, Eudora, 93
*Werewolves in Their Youth*, 82
**Wesley, Mary**, **92**, **138**
**Wesley, Valerie Wilson**, **64**
*West of Venus*, 136
West, Dorothy, 101, 105, 109
West, Nathanael, 3, 81, 137
Wharton, Thomas, 137
*What a Woman Must Do*, **133**
*What Are People For?*, 4
*What Girls Learn*, 76, 85, 115, 124, 140

*What It Takes to Get to Vegas*, **119**
*What Makes Sammy Run*, 81, 137
*What She Saw…*, **55**
*What the Scarecrow Said*, 54, 56
*What's Bred in the Bone*, 77, 136
**Wheeler, Kate**, 11, **20**
*When Harlem Was in Vogue*, 158
*When I Lived in Modern Times*, 22
*When Memory Dies*, 16
*When Mountains Walked*, 11, **20**
*When the Sons of Heaven Meet the Daughters of the Earth*, 112
*When the World Was Steady*, 116
*When We Were Orphans*, 104
*Where or When*, **58**, 131
*The Whereabouts of Eneas McNulty*, **146**
*While I Was Gone*, **46**, **117**
*The Whisper of the River*, 42
*The White Bone*, 85, 96
*White Crosses*, 19
*White Man's Grave*, 7
*White Noise*, 150, 160
*White Oleander*, **33**, 116, 121
White, Patrick, 10, 67
*The White Rooster & Other Stories*, 74
*White Teeth*, 130, **162**
**Whitehead, Colson**, 138, **139**
*Whites*, 161
*Who Has Seen the Wind*, 83
*The Wholeness of a Broken Heart*, **58**, 133
*Why She Left Us*, **54**, 105
Wibberly, Leonard, 63
*Wide Open*, 12
Wideman, John Edgar, 119, 139
*A Widow for One Year*, **103**, 121
Wiencek, Henry, 62
**Wiggins, Marianne**, 5, 11, 47, 69, 72, 112, **139**, 140, 147
Wilcox, James, 72
*The Wild Birds: Six Stories of the Port William Membership*, 4
*The Wild Colonial Boy*, 138
*The Wild Iris*, 36
*Wild Life*, 11
*Wild Meat and the Bully Burgers*. 40, 141, 142
*A Wild Sheep Chase*, 159
*The Wilder Sisters*, 98, **113**
Wilder, Thornton, 4, 57
*Wildfire*, 92
Wilkins, Damien, 68
Willard, Nancy, 59, 74, 89, 108, 126
**Williams, Joy**, **140**

Williams, Niall, 147
Williams, Terry Tempest, 153
**Williamson, Eric Miles**, **140**
Willis, Connie, 70, 74
**Willis, Sarah**, **140**
Wind, Renate, 36
*Windchill Summer*, **44**
*The Wind-Up Bird Chronicle*, **159**
**Winegardner, Mark**, 10, 26, **140**, 150
*Winners & Losers*, 150
*The Winter Birds*, 97
*Winter in the Blood*, 20
*Winter Range*, **6**
*Winter Wheat*, 10
*Winterkill*, 8, 110
**Winterson, Jeanette**, 85, 118, **141**
**Winton, Tim**, 67, 70, 96, **141**
*Wise Children*, 132, 145
*The Wishbones*, 50, **124**
*The Wishing Box*, **59**
*With Your Crooked Heart*, **90**
*Without a Hero*, 3
Woiwode, Larry, 90
*Wolf, No Wolf*, 20
*Wolf Whistle*, 15, 158, **159**
**Wolfe, Swain**, **20**
Wolfe, Thomas, 78
Wolfe, Tom, 43, 105, 112
Wolff, Isabel, 40
Wolff, Tobias, 42
Wilitzer, Hilm, 50
**Wolitzer, Meg**, **64**
**Wolk, Lauren**, **20**
*Woman at the Edge of Time*, 155
*The Woman Warrior*, 80
*The Woman Who Lives in the Earth*, 20
*The Woman Walked into Doors*, 8, 53, **88**, 156
*The Woman Who Walked on Water*, 19
*Woman Who Watches Over the World: A Native Memoir*, 153
*Women Falling Down in the Street*, 10
*The Women in Black*, 132
*The Women of Brewster Place*, 30, 120, 139
*Women of Influence*, 79
*Women of Sand and Myrrh*, 18
*Women of the Silk*, 62
*Women with Men: Three Long Short Stories*, 92
*Wonder Boys*, 46, 82, 134
*The Wonders of the Invisible World*, 94
Wong, Shawn, 60
Woolf, Virginia, 149, 158

*Working Parts*, **25**
Works Well with Others, 161
The World According to Garp, 95, 103, 108
**The World Around Midnight**, **37**
The World at Night, 32
The World Below, 117
The World I Made for Her, 47
A World Lost, 4
The World, More or Less, 32
World of Pies, 24
World's End, 3, 77
World's Fair, 78
Wouk, Herman, 12
***Wrack***, **146**
**Wright, Bil**, **141**
***Written on the Body***, 118, **141**
Wrong, Michela, 4
WuDunn, Sheryl, 14

*X20: A Novel of (Not) Smoking*, 74

**Yamanaka, Lois-Ann**, 40, 141, **142**
**Yamashita, Karen Tei**, **21**
**Yánez Cossío, Alicia**, 7, **21**
*Yank, the Army Weekly: World War II from
   the Guys Who Brought You Victory*, 107
**Yarbrough, Steve**, **142**

*A Year in Provence*, 18
*A Year of Lesser*, 79, 83
*The Year of Living Dangerously*, 11
*The Year of Silence*, 1123
*The Year of the Frog*, 17
*A Yellow Raft in Blue Water*, 6, 20, 31, 135
*The Yellow Room Conspiracy*, 77
**Yglesias, Helen**, **142**
*Yo!*, 50, 52, **68**, 119
***Yoruba Girl Dancing***, **4**
**Yoshikawa, Mako**, **143**
*You Must Remember This*, 119
*Young Man with a Horn*, 64, 105
Youngblood, Shay, 141
*The Youngest Doll*, 7
*Your Blue-Eyed Boy*, 90
*Your Oasis on Flame Lake*, 43, 61, 84

**Zabor, Rafi**, **64**, 105
Zadoorian, Michael, 64
**Zeidner, Lisa**, **143**
**Zelitch, Simone**, **22**, 96
**Zigman, Laura**, 33, 36, **65**
*Zombie*, 114, 163
*Zuckerman Unbound*, 127
*Zuleika Dobson*, 49
*The Zygote Chronicles*, 33

# Subject Index

1900s
Taking Lottie Home, 72
1910s
Dreamland, 3
Leaping Man Hill, 31
1920s
Cinnamon Gardens, 16
The Englishman's Boy, 137
Jazz, 158
1930s
All the Pretty Horses, 157
The Hatbox Baby, 78
Jim the Boy, 90
The Language of Threads, 62
The Mineral Palace, 11
Mr. White's Confession, 29
When We Were Orphans, 104
1940s
The Amazing Adventures of Kavalier &
    Clay, 82
Bailey's Café, 120
Charlotte Gray, 32
The Jukebox Queen of Malta, 54
Last Days of Summer, 107
A Lesson Before Dying, 93
Louisa, 22
Snow in August, 38
1950s
Acts of God, 48
The Catastrophist, 4
Fleur de Leigh's Life of Crime, 110
Gloria, 12
The Hallelujah Side, 103
I Married a Communist, 126
Little America, 26
The Mark of the Angel, 9
Seventh Heaven, 152
The Sky Fisherman, 110
Some Things That Stay, 140
Trumpet, 105
What a Woman Must Do, 133
1960s
Arithmetic, 115
The Brothers K, 89
The Butcher Boy, 114

Durable Goods, 25
The Hiding Place, 146
Lamb in Love, 78
A Nixon Man, 27
Soldier in Paradise, 48
Tempest Rising, 116
Windchill Summer, 44
1970s
Almost Home, 116
Big Stone Gap, 61
Breakfast on Pluto, 113
The Brothers K, 89
By the Shore, 30
Caucasia, 129
A Crime in the Neighborhood, 76
Emotionally Weird, 70
A Fine Balance, 158
Funny Boy, 16
Land of Smiles, 9
The Last King of Scotland, 7
Money, Love, 73
Naming the Spirits, 134
The New City, 2
A Nixon Man, 27
The Oxygen Man, 142
The Umbrella Country, 125
Highways to a War, 11
1980s
Acts of God, 48
The Englishman's Boy, 137
Friends for Life, 64
Funny Boy, 16
The Fundamentals of Play, 112
Joe College, 50
The Last Days of Disco with Cocktails at
    Petrossian's Afterwards, 18
The Lost Legends of New Jersey, 125
The Year of the Frog, 17
1990s
A Certain Age, 104
Friends for Life, 64
Loving Graham Greene, 150
The Wishbones, 124

Abandoned Children
    *The End of Vandalism*, 88
    *The Hatbox Baby*, 78
Aboriginals
    *Alice Springs*, 8
Abortion
    *Deep in the Heart*, 137
    *I Loved You All*, 130
    *The Long Falling*, 53
    *Skateaway*, 104
Abusive Relationships
    *Ancestral Truths*, 112
    *Beachcombing for a Shipwrecked God*, 29
    *Keeneland*, 37
    *Leaping Man Hill*, 31
    *The Long Falling*, 53
    *The Sound of One Hand Clapping*, 33
    *Truth and Bright Water*, 106
    *The Woman Who Walked into Doors*, 88
Academia (See also College Professors,
        Teachers)
    *Emotionally Weird*, 70
    *The Fennel Family Papers*, 72
    *Making Love to the Minor Poets of
        Chicago,* 84
    *Foolscap*, 113
    *Four Dreamers and Emily*, 85
    *The Human Stain*, 126
    *The Man Who Wrote the Book*, 134
    *Moo*, 131
    *The Name of the World*, 154
Accidental Death
    *A Boy in Winter*, 28
    *Evening News*, 60
Acculturation (See also Culture Clash)
    *How the Garcia Girls Lost Their Accents*,
        67
Actors and Acting
    *The Answer Is Yes, 44*
    *Catching Heaven*, 97
    *The Missing World*, 111
    *Not a Day Goes By*, 38
    *The Perfect Elizabeth: A Tale of Two
        Sisters*, 128
    *Plum & Jaggers*, 131
    *That Summer's Trance*, 127
Adoption
    *The Answer Is Yes*, 44
    *Breakfast with Scot*, 87
    *A Gesture Life*, 100
    *Henry of Atlantic City*, 125
    *The Lucky Gourd Shop*, 56

*A Member of the Family*, 47
*The Road Home*, 98
*Ruby*, 39
Adultery (see also Love Affairs, Love Stories,
        Male/Female Relationships)
    *Ain't Nobody's Business If I Do*, 64
    *The Bird Artist*, 160
    *Blameless*, 53
    *A Boy in Winter*, 28
    *Brazil-Maru*, 21
    *A Certain Age*, 104
    *A Crime in the Neighborhood*, 76
    *The Daughters of Simon Lamoreaux*, 44
    *The Feast of Love*, 74
    *Fiona Range*, 118
    *Goodbye Without Leaving*, 83
    *Goodness*, 123
    *Honeymoon: A Romantic Rampage*, 40
    *Host Family*, 46
    *House of Sand and Fog*, 89
    *Keeping Faith*, 51
    *Layover*, 143
    *Le Mariage*, 10
    *The Lost Legends of New Jersey*, 125
    *The Mark of the Angel*, 9
    *My Russian*, 46
    *A Passionate Man*, 62
    *The Pilot's Wife*, 58
    *The Pleasing Hour*, 106
    *Portrait of the Artist's Wife*, 68
    *Ray in Reverse*, 63
    *Slow Natives*, 69
    *Snake,* 10
    *A Stairway to Paradise*, 132
    *The Story of a Million Years*, 102
    *That Summer's Trance*, 127
    *Tomcat in Love*, 49
    *Tree Surgery for Beginners*, 93
    *A Trick of Nature*, 46
    *Undertow*, 59
    *When Mountains Walked*, 20
    *Where or When*, 58
    *While I Was Gone*, 117
    *A Widow for One Year*, 103
    *With Your Crooked Heart*, 90
    *The World Around Midnight*, 37
    *Written on the Body*, 141
Africa
    *Age of Iron*, 148
    *The Catastrophist*, 4
    *Disgrace*, 148
    *The First Man*, 5

*The Hotel Alleluia*, 55
*The Last King of Scotland*, 7
*Mating*, 161
*The Poisonwood Bible*, 107
African American Authors
   *Ain't Nobody's Business If I Do*, 64
   *All-Bright Court*, 124
   *Always Outnumbered, Always Outgunned*,
     119
   *Bailey's Café*, 120
   *Do Unto Others*, 43
   *The Hand I Fan With*, 38
   *The Healing*, 154
   *The Intuitionist*, 138
   *Jazz*, 158
   *John Henry Days*, 139
   *The Last Integrationist*, 43
   *A Lesson Before Dying*, 93
   *Mosquito*, 154
   *Not a Day Goes By*, 38
   *Paradise*, 158
   *Right By My Side*, 99
   *Sunday You Learn How to Box*, 141
   *This Just In...*, 40
   *Tempest Rising*, 116
   *Two Cities*, 139
   *Water Marked*, 109
African Americans
   *Ain't Nobody's Business If I Do*, 63
   *All-Bright Court*, 124
   *Always Outnumbered, Always Outgunned*,
     119
   *Bailey's Café*, 120
   *Do Unto Others*, 43
   *The Hand I Fan With*, 24
   *The Human Stain*, 126
   *The Intuitionist*, 138
   *Jazz*, 158
   *John Henry Days*, 139
   *The Last Integrationist*, 42
   *A Lesson Before Dying*, 93
   *Not a Day Goes By*, 38
   *Paradise*, 159
   *Resting in the Bosom of the Lamb*, 63
   *Right By My Side*, 99
   *This Just In...*, 40
   *Sunday You Learn How to Box*, 141
   *This Side of Brightness*, 12
   *Tempest Rising*, 116
   *Two Cities*, 139
   *Water Marked*, 109

Africans
   *Do Unto Others*, 43
Aging
   *Back When We Were Grownups*, 136
   *The Fifth Season*, 87
   *The Girls*, 142
   *Losing Julia*, 103
   *The Meadow*, 8
   *A Recipe for Bees*, 2
   *Skywater*, 14
Agoraphobia
   *Damascus*, 74
AIDS
   *The Blackwater Lightship*, 135
   *Butterfly Lovers*, 7
   *The Promise of Rest*, 160
   *The Weekend*, 80
ALA Notable Books
   *About a Boy*, 102
   *Age of Iron*, 148
   *All the Pretty Horses*, 157
   *All-Bright Court*, 124
   *The Amazing Adventures of Kavalier &*
     *Clay*, 82
   *Ancestral Truths*, 111
   *Anil's Ghost*, 160
   *Animal Dreams*, 106
   *Bailey's Café*, 120
   *Before and After*, 27
   *Behind the Scenes at the Museum*, 70
   *Being Dead*, 149
   *The Bird Artist*, 160
   *The Birthday Boys*, 3
   *The Blind Assassin*, 145
   *Blu's Hanging*, 142
   *The Body Is Water*, 128
   *The Brothers K*, 89
   *The Cage*, 16
   *Charming Billy*, 157
   *The Colony of Unrequited Dreams*, 10
   *The Country Life*, 84
   *A Dangerous Friend*, 155
   *A Dangerous Woman*, 118
   *Disgrace*, 148
   *East Is East*, 77
   *The End of Vandalism*, 88
   *The English Patient*, 122
   *Eveless Eden*, 139
   *Family Pictures*, 117
   *The Far Euphrates*, 132
   *A Fine Balance*, 158
   *The First Man*, 5

ALA Notable Books (*cont.*)
*Foolscap*, 113
*Funny Boy*, 16
*A Gesture Life*, 108
*Goodness*, 123
*The Grass Dancer*, 51
*Henry of Atlantic City*, 125
*The Hours*, 149
*House of Sand and Fog*, 89
*How the Garcia Girls Lost Their Accents*,
   67
*I Married a Communist*, 126
*Illumination Night*, 101
*In the Lake of the Woods*, 121
*In the Time of the Butterflies*, 2
*In Troubled Waters*, 30
*The Jade Peony*, 5
*Jazz*, 158
*Joe*, 78
*Judge on Trial*, 108
*Last Orders*, 133
*The Last Samurai*, 86
*A Lesson Before Dying*, 93
*Leviathan*, 70
*Living to Tell*, 120
*The Meadow*, 8
*The Middle Son*, 40
*Montana 1948*, 19
*Motherless Brooklyn*, 155
*Music of the Swamp*, 14
*Native Speaker*, 109
*Nobody's Fool*, 127
*The Paperboy*, 150
*The Patron Saint of Liars*, 123
*The Perez Family*, 75
*Possession*, 79
*The Quick and the Dead*, 140
*Reading in the Dark*, 149
*The Reef*, 151
*Scar Tissue*, 153
*Seventh Heaven*, 152
*The Sharpshooter Blues*, 121
*The Shipping News*, 15
*Skywater*, 14
*Snow Angels*, 122
*Solar Storms*, 153
*Souls Raised from the Dead*, 76
*A Star Called Henry*, 88
*The Sweet Hereafter*, 72
*A Thousand Acres*, 17
*Triage*, 68
*Truth and Bright Water*, 106

*Turtle Moon*, 152
*The Unconsoled*, 103
*The Virgin Suicides*, 150
*Waiting*, 153
*White Teeth*, 162
*The Wind-Up Bird Chronicle*, 159
*Wolf Whistle*, 159
*The Wishbones*, 124
*The Woman Who Walked into Doors*, 88
*The World Around Midnight*, 37
*Yo!*, 68
Alabama
*This One and Magic Life*, 94
Alaska
*True North*, 41
Alcoholics and Alcoholism
*Almost Home*, 116
*Carter Clay*, 91
*Charming Billy*, 157
*Falling Bodies*, 45
*A Goat's Song*, 8
*Grace Notes*, 156
*The Hookmen*, 101
*I Loved You All*, 130
*Joe*, 78
*Meely LaBauve*, 19
*Music of the Swamp*, 14
*My Drowning*, 97
*The Plagiarist*, 28
*Right by My Side*, 99
*The Sound of One Hand Clapping*, 33
*The Wilder Sisters*, 113
*With Your Crooked Heart*, 90
*The Woman Who Walked into Doors*, 88
Algeria
*The First Man*, 5
*The Last Life*, 116
*Loving Graham Greene*, 150
*The Mark of the Angel*, 9
Alzheimer's Disease
*Animal Dreams*, 106
*The Bonesetter's Daughter*, 60
*Falling Bodies*, 45
*The Fifth Season*, 87
*In Troubled Waters*, 30
*Remember Me*, 100
*Scar Tissue*, 153
Amazon
*Fierce Invalids Home from Hot Climates*, 54
American Indian Authors
*The Grass Dancer*, 51
*Madchild Running*, 31

*Solar Storms*, 153
*Truth and Bright Water*, 106
American Indians
    *Don't Think Twice*, 40
    *The Englishman's Boy,* 137
    *The Grass Dancer,* 51
    *The Lake Dreams the Sky*, 20
    *Leading the Cheers*, 81
    *Madchild Running*, 31
    *The Road Home,* 98
    *The Sky Fisherman*, 110
    *Solar Storms, 153*
    *True North,* 41
    *Truth and Bright Water,* 106
American Midwest
    *Crooked River Burning*, 140
    *The End of Vandalism*, 88
    *The Feast of Love*, 74
    *Peel My Love Like an Onion*, 28
    *The Hallelujah Side*, 103
    *Second Hand*, 65
    *Skateaway*, 104
    *The Tall Pine Polka*, 43
    *This Just In...*, 40
    *The Weight of Dreams*, 23
American Northeast (See also New
   England, individual states)
    *Illumination Night*, 101
    *The River King*, 101
    *Those Who Favor Fire*, 20
American South (See also individual states)
    *Evensong*, 36
    *The Fennel Family Papers*, 72
    *The Hand I Fan With*, 24
    *In Troubled Waters*, 30
    *Jim the Boy*, 90
    *Joe*, 78
    *A Lesson Before Dying*, 93
    *The Many Aspects of Mobile Home Living*, 82
    *Meely LaBauve*, 19
    *Miss Julia Speaks Her Mind,* 55
    *Money, Love*, 73
    *Music of the Swamp*, 14
    *My Drowning*, 97
    *The Oxygen Man*, 142
    *The Paperboy*, 150
    *The Sharpshooter Blues*, 121
    *Six Figures*, 109
    *The Slow Way Back*, 37
    *Souls Raised from the Dead*, 76
    *Taking Lottie Home*, 41
    *That Summer's Trance*, 127

*This One and Magic Life*, 94
*Wolf Whistle*, 154
American Southwest (See also individual states)
    *Catching Heaven*, 97
    *Deep in the Heart*, 137
    *Mosquito*, 154
    *Remember Me*, 100
    *Skywater*, 14
    *The Wilder Sisters*, 113
American West (See also individual states)
    *The Answer Is Yes*, 44
    *The Collapsible World*, 44
    *Duane's Depressed*, 46
    *Fencing the Sky*, 7
    *The Hookmen*, 101
    *The Lake Dreams the Sky*, 20
    *Leaping Man Hill*, 31
    *The Loop*, 32
    *The Meadow*, 8
    *The Mineral Palace*, 11
    *Montana 1948*, 19
    *Place Last Seen*, 34
    *Plainsong*, 99
    *The World Around Midnight*, 37
Amin, Idi
    *The Last King of Scotland*, 7
Amnesia
    *Ancestral Truths*, 112
    *The Missing World*, 111
    *Six Figures,* 109
Amusement Parks
    *Dreamland*, 3
Anarchists
    *The Book Borrower*, 156
Animals
    *Skywater*, 14
    *Second Hand*, 64
Ann Arbor, Michigan (See also American
   Midwest)
    *The Feast of Love*, 74
Antarctica
    *The Birthday Boys*, 3
Anthropologists and Anthropology (See also
   Science and Scientists)
    *Spiderweb*, 111
Anti-Semitism
    *The Inn at Lake Devine*, 111
    *Snow in August*, 38
Antiques
    *Apologizing to Dogs*, 84
    *London Holiday*, 50
    *Second Hand*, 64

Apartheid
  *Age of Iron*, 148
Appalachia
  *Icy Sparks*, 55
Arab Authors
  *The Map of Love*, 18
Archaeologists and Archaeology
  *Beachcombing for a Shipwrecked God*, 29
  *Lost in Translation*, 13
  *Wrack*, 146
Architects and Architecture
  *A Celibate Season*, 131
  *Female Ruins*, 120
  *Frozen Music*, 29
  *Martin Dressler: The Tale of an American
      Dreamer*, 13
  *Salt Dancers*, 38
Arctic
  *The Cage*, 16
Argentina
  *Naming the Spirits*, 134
Arizona
  *Almost Home*, 116
  *Animal Dreams*, 106
  *The Quick & the Dead*, 140
Arkansas
  *Windchill Summer*, 44
Armenia
  *Three Apples Fell from Heaven*, 156
Arson
  *Armadillo*, 77
  *The Civil Wars of Jonah Moran*, 53
Art and Artists
  *Alice Springs*, 8
  *The Artist's Widow*, 112
  *Beachcombing for a Shipwrecked God*, 29
  *The Bird Artist*, 160
  *The Book Borrower*, 156
  *The Bubble Reputation*, 123
  *Catching Heaven*, 97
  *Charlotte Gray*, 32
  *The Handyman*, 57
  *Headlong*, 33
  *The Hedge, The Ribbon*, 49
  *An Imaginative Experience*, 64
  *In the Country of the Young*, 147
  *Jumping the Green*, 128
  *The Lake Dreams the Sky*, 20
  *The Last Integrationist*, 43
  *Lily of the Valley*, 57
  *The Lost Glass Plates of Wilfred Eng*, 49
  *A Lover's Almanac*, 102

  *The Moor's Last Sigh*, 163
  *The Music Lesson*, 138
  *The Notebooks of Don Rigoberto*, 137
  *Playing Botticelli*, 48
  *Plowing the Dark*, 160
  *Portrait of the Artist's Wife*, 68
  *Some Things That Stay*, 140
  *This One and Magic Life*, 94
  *The Underpainter*, 136
  *The Walking Tour*, 85
Art History
  *Fool's God*, 18
Asia
  *Highways to a War*, 11
  *Land of Smiles*, 9
  *The Wind-Up Bird Chronicle*, 159
Asian American Authors
  *Blu's Hanging*, 42
  *The Bonesetter's Daughter*, 60
  *Brazil-Maru*
  *A Cab Called Reliable*, 105
  *A Gesture Life*, 108
  *The Kitchen God's Wife*, 60
  *The Language of Threads*, 62
  *Monkey Bridge*, 80
  *Native Speaker*, 109
  *One Hundred and One Ways*, 143
  *The Umbrella Country*, 125
  *Why She Left Us*, 54
Asian Americans
  *Blu's Hanging*, 42
  *The Bonesetter's Daughter*, 60
  *A Cab Called Reliable*, 105
  *East Is East*, 77
  *A Gesture Life*, 108
  *The Kitchen God's Wife*, 60
  *Middle Son*, 40
  *Monkey Bridge*, 80
  *Native Speaker*, 109
  *One Hundred and One Ways*, 143
  *Why She Left Us*, 54
Asian Authors
  *Waiting*, 153
  *The Wind-Up Bird Chronicle*, 159
Asian Canadians
  *The Jade Peony*, 5
Asians
  *Waiting*, 153
Asians in America
  *The Bonesetter's Daughter*, 60
  *A Cab Called Reliable*, 105
  *East Is East*, 77

*A Gesture Life*, 108
*The Kitchen God's Wife*, 60
*Land of Smiles*, 40
*Middle Son*, 40
*Monkey Bridge*, 80
*Native Speaker*, 109
*Why She Left Us*, 54
Asperger's Syndrome
   *The Civil Wars of Jonah Moran*, 53
Asthma
   *Catch Your Breath*, 24
Au Pairs
   *The Pleasing Hour*
Aunts
   *Dating Big Bird*, 65
   *What a Woman Must Do*, 133
Austen, Jane
   *Redeeming Eve*, 26
Austin, Texas (see also Texas)
   *Deep in the Heart*, 137
Australia
   *Alice Springs*, 8
   *Eucalyptus*, 2
   *Longleg*, 67
   *Pobby and Dingan*, 15
   *The Slow Natives*, 69
   *Snake*, 10
   *The Sound of One Hand Clapping*, 33
   *Wrack*, 146
Australian Authors
   *Alice Springs*, 8
   *Eucalyptus*, 2
   *Highways to a War*, 11
   *Longleg*, 67
   *The Riders*, 141
   *The Slow Natives*, 69
   *Snake*, 10
   *The Sound of One Hand Clapping*, 33
   *Wrack*, 146
Autism
   *Family Pictures*, 117

Bachelors
   *Plainsong*, 99
   *Remember Me*, 11
Bakeries
   *Bread Alone*, 39
Ballet Dancers
   *The Hunger Moon*, 45
   *The Short History of a Prince*, 98

Baltimore, Maryland
   *Back When We Were Grownups*, 136
Baseball
   *Battle Creek*, 108
   *Brazil-Maru*, 21
   *The Brothers K*, 89
   *How All This Started*, 34
   *Last Days of Summer*, 107
   *Taking Lottie Home*, 41
   *Underworld*, 150
Beckett, Samuel
   *Jump*, 1
Bees and Beekeeping
   *The Honey Thief*, 96
   *A Recipe for Bees*, 2
Belgian Congo
   *The Catastrophist*, 4
Benares, India (See also India)
   *The Romantics*, 13
   *Sister India*, 14
Bibliophiles
   *The Grand Complication*, 155
Bigamy
   *Home to India*, 17
   *The Perez Family*, 75
   *The Pilot's Wife*, 58
Biographical Fiction
   *The Birthday Boys*, 3
   *The Colony of Unrequited Dreams*, 10
   *Saints and Villains*, 35
Biologists (See also Science and Scientists,
      Women Scientists)
   *The Loop*, 32
Biracial Characters
   *Caucasia*, 129
   *Half a Heart*, 27
   *The Hotel Alleluia*, 55
   *White Teeth*, 162
Birds
   *The Bird Artist*, 160
Birth Defects
   *The Chin Kiss King*, 62
Black Humor
   *All Quiet on the Orient Express*, 117
   *Body*, 149
   *Goodness*, 123
   *Lost*, 135
   *The Restraint of Beasts, 117*
   *The Sharpshooter Blues*, 121
   *Wolf Whistle*, 159
Boarding Houses
   *Sister India*, 14

Boats and Boating
   *Beachcombing for a Shipwrecked God*, 29
   *Gambler's Rose*, 99
   *Life Skills*, 32
   *The Ordinary Seaman*, 95
Body Image
   *Body*, 149
Bodybuilding
   *Body*, 149
Bombay, India
   *The Death of Vishnu*, 133
Bonhoeffer, Dietrich
   *Saints and Villains*, 35
Booker Prize Winners
   *Amsterdam*, 115
   *The Blind Assassin*, 145
   *The English Patient*, 122
   *Last Orders*, 133
   *Possession*, 79
Boston, Massachusetts (See also
   Massachusetts)
   *The Hunger Moon*, 45
Botany (See also Science and Scientists,
   Trees)
   *Eucalyptus*, 2
Botswana
   *Mating*, 161
Boxing
   *The Jade Peony*, 5
   *What It Takes to Get to Vegas*, 119
Boys' Lives
   *Arithmetic*, 115
   *Jim the Boy*, 90
   *Longleg*, 67
Brazil
   *Brazil-Maru*, 21
British Authors
   *Adrian Mole: The Cappuccino Years*, 61
   *Amsterdam*, 115
   *Ancestral Truths*, 112
   *Another World*, 72
   *Armadillo*, 77
   *Behind the Scenes at the Museum*, 70
   *Being Dead*, 148
   *The Birthday Boys*, 3
   *By the Shore*, 30
   *Charlotte Gray*, 32
   *The Country Life*, 84
   *Crocodile Soup*, 85
   *Damascus*, 74
   *Emotionally Weird*, 70
   *England, England*, 73

   *Falling Slowly*, 77
   *Female Ruins*, 120
   *Four Dreamers and Emily*, 85
   *Frozen Music*, 29
   *Going to Pot*, 43
   *Goodness*, 123
   *Headlong*, 33
   *Honeymoon: A Romantic Rampage*, 40
   *Human Voices*, 92
   *An Imaginative Experience*, 138
   *The Last King of Scotland*, 7
   *Last Orders*, 133
   *Leading the Cheers*, 81
   *Life Skills*, 32
   *Losing Nelson*, 136
   *A Lover's Almanac*, 102
   *Lying with the Enemy*, 76
   *Mummy's Legs*, 25
   *Night Train*, 156
   *A Passionate Man*, 62
   *The Persian Bride*, 5
   *Pobby and Dingan*, 15
   *Possession*, 79
   *Seeing Calvin Coolidge in a Dream*, 86
   *Sister India*, 14
   *Some Old Lover's Ghost*, 115
   *A Stairway to Paradise*, 132
   *Spiderweb*, 11
   *Tree Surgery for Beginners*, 91
   *The 27th Kingdom*, 91
   *The Unconsoled*, 103
   *The Way I Found Her*, 61
   *When We Were Orphans*, 103
   *White Teeth*, 162
   *With Your Crooked Heart*, 90
   *Written on the Body*, 141
British Columbia, Canada (See also Canada)
   *Monkey Beach*, 126
   *A Recipe for Bees*, 2
Bronte, Emily
   *Four Dreamers and Emily*, 85
Brooklyn, New York (See also New York)
   *The Amazing Adventures of Kavalier &
      Clay*, 82
   *Dreamland*, 3
   *Last Days of Summer*, 107
   *Motherless Brooklyn,* 155
   *Snow in August*, 38
Brothers (See also Brothers and Sisters,
   Family Relationships)
   *Anil's Ghost*, 160
   *The Brothers K*, 89

*East of the Mountains*, 151
*The Fifth Season*, 87
*Gambler's Rose*, 99
*Lost*, 135
*Middle Son, 40*
*Montana 1948*, 19
*The Paperboy*, 150
*Plainsong*, 99
*Scar Tissue*, 153
*The Short History of a Prince*, 98
*The Weekend*, 80
*With Your Crooked Heart*, 90
Brothers and Sisters
   *Almost Home*, 116
   *Bee Season*, 36
   *The Blackwater Lightship*, 135
   *Blu's Hanging*, 142
   *The Brothers K*, 89
   *The Civil Wars of Johan Moran*, 53
   *The Electrical Field*, 56
   *Empire Falls*, 127
   *Family Pictures*, 117
   *Fasting, Feasting*, 86
   *Fool's Gold*, 18
   *The Funnies*, 109
   *The Geographies of Home*, 50
   *A Good House*, 79
   *How All This Started*, 34
   *In the Country of the Young*, 147
   *The Jade Peony*, 15
   *Jumping the Green*, 128
   *Living to Tell*, 120
   *Lost Geography*, 71
   *Monkey Beach*, 126
   *More Bread or I'll Appear*, 45
   *My Drowning*, 97
   *A Nixon Man*, 27
   *The Oxygen Man*, 142
   *Plum & Jaggers*, 131
   *Pobby and Dingan*, 15
   *Self-Portrait with Ghosts*, 90
   *Some Things That Stay*, 140
   *The Tiny One*, 157
Brueghel, Pieter
   *Headlong*, 33
Buffalo, New York (See also New York)
   *All-Bright Court*, 124
Burma
   *The Glass Palace*, 35
Business and Businessmen
   *Acts of God*, 48
   *Armadillo*, 77

*Crazy for Cornelia*, 36
*The Fundamentals of Play*, 112
*Independence Day*, 92
*Martin Dressler: Tale of an American
   Dreamer*, 13
*Memoir from Antproof Case*, 152
*The New City*, 2
*The Plagiarist*, 28
*Seeing Calvin Coolidge in a Dream*, 86
*The Van*, 88
*Where or When*, 58
*With Your Crooked Heart*, 90

Cafés and Restaurants
   *Bailey's Café*, 120
   *Empire Falls*, 127
   *The Minotaur Takes a Cigarette Break*,
     130
   *Secrets of the Tsil Café*
Cajuns
   *Meely LaBauve*, 19
Calcutta, India (See also India)
   *Sister of My Heart*, 87
California
   *Arithmetic*, 115
   *East Bay Grease*, 140
   *Evening News*, 60
   *Fleur de Leigh's Life of Crime*, 110
   *House of Sand and Fog*, 89
   *Iron Shoes*, 95
   *The Kitchen God's Wife*, 60
   *Land of Smiles*, 9
   *Leaping Man Hill*, 31
   *Otherwise Engaged*, 33
   *Tree Surgery for Beginners*, 93
Cambodia
   *Highways to a War*, 11
Cambridge, Massachusetts (See also New
   England, American Northeast,
   Massachusetts)
   *Host Family*, 46
   *The Man of the House*, 114
Canada (See also individual provinces)
   *The Bird Artist*, 160
   *The Blind Assassin*, 145
   *The Englishman's Boy*, 137
   *The Rules of Engagement*, 147
   *The Shipping News*, 15
   *The Stone Diaries*,162
Canadian Authors
   *Anil's Ghost*, 160
   *The Blind Assassin*, 145

Canadian Authors (*cont.*)
  *Butterfly Lovers*, 7
  *Cereus Blooms at Night*, 118
  *The Colony of Unrequited Dreams*, 10
  *The Electrical Field*, 56
  *Elizabeth and After*, 83
  *The English Patient*, 122
  *The Englishman's Boy*, 137
  *A Fine Balance*, 158
  *The Glace Bay Miners' Museum*, 6
  *Gloria*, 12
  *A Good House*, 79
  *The Jade Peony*, 5
  *Jump*, 1
  *The Mark of the Angel*, 9
  *Mister Sandman*, 96
  *Monkey Beach*, 126
  *The Piano Man's Daughter*, 91
  *Pilgrim*, 92
  *A Recipe for Bees*, 2
  *Such a Long Journey*, 158
  *Summer Gone*, 12
  *The Underpainter*, 136
Canadian Indians
  *Monkey Beach*, 126
Cancer (See also Terminal Illness)
  *Age of Iron*, 148
  *Blue Diary*, 39
  *Dear Stranger, Dearest Friend*, 24
  *East of the Mountains*, 151
  *Evening*, 5
  *The Fifth Season*, 6
  *The Inner Life of Objects*, 83
  *Living to Tell*, 8
  *MotherKind*, 124
  *The Saving Graces*, 34
  *A Thousand Acres*, 17
  *Written on the Body*, 12
Canoeing
  *Summer Gone*, 12
Cape Breton Island, Canada (See also Canada)
  *The Glace Bay Miners' Museum*, 6
Car Accidents
  *Carter Clay*, 91
  *An Imaginative Experience*, 138
  *Living to Tell*, 120
Career Women
  *Beautiful Wasps Having Sex*, 81
  *Bordeaux*, 124
  *Dating Big Bird*, 65
  *England, England*, 73
  *Friends for Life*, 64

  *Pink Slip*, 82
  *The Salt Dancers*, 38
Caribbean
  *Chronicle of the Seven Sorrows*, 5
  *The House on the Lagoon*, 6
  *A Thirst for Rain*, 80
Caribbean Authors
  *Chronicle of the Seven Sorrows*, 5
  *The House on the Lagoon*, 6
  *A Thirst for Rain*, 80
Carmelites
  *Lying Awake*, 16
Cartoons (See also Comics)
  *The Funnies*, 109
Central America
  *Hummingbird House*, 9
  *The Ordinary Seaman*, 95
Ceylon (See also Sri Lanka)
  *Cinnamon Gardens*, 16
  *The Flower Boy*, 15
Charlotte, North Carolina (See also North
    Carolina, American South, Southern
    Authors)
  *Six Figures*, 109
Chicago, Illinois (See also Illinois, American
    Midwest)
  *The Hatbox Baby*, 78
  *Making Love to the Minor Poets of
    Chicago*, 84
  *Peel My Love Like an Onion*, 28
  *This Just In...*, 40
Child Abuse
  *Blameless*, 53
  *Catch Your Breath*, 24
  *Cereus Blooms at Night*, 118
  *Durable Goods*, 4
  *In Troubled Waters*, 5
  *The Long Falling*, 6
  *My Drowning*, 97
  *The Slow Natives*, 69
  *The Sound of One Hand Clapping*, 33
  *Sunday You Learn How to Box*, 141
  *Truth and Bright Water*, 106
  *Tempest Rising*, 116
  *Undertow*, 116
  *The Weight of Dreams*, 23
Child Prodigies (See also Geniuses, Gifted
    Children)
  *In the Country of the Young*, 147
  *The Last Samurai*, 86
Childhood (See also Boys' Lives)
  *Pobby and Dingan*, 15

China (See also Asia)
  *The Bonesetter's Daughter*, 60
  *Butterfly Lovers*, 7
  *The Kitchen God's Wife*, 60
  *Blu's Hanging*, 42
  *The Bonesetter's Daughter*, 60
  *A Cab Called Reliable*, 105
  *Lost in Translation*, 13
  *The Sea of Trees*, 48
  *Seeing Calvin Coolidge in a Dream*, 86
  *Waiting*, 153
  *When We Were Orphans*, 104
Chinese American Authors
  *The Bonesetter's Daughter*, 60
  *The Kitchen God's Wife*, 60
  *The Language of Threads*, 62
Chinese Americans
  *The Bonesetter's Daughter*, 60
  *The Kitchen God's Wife*, 60
Chinese Authors
  *Waiting*, 153
Chinese Canadians
  *The Jade Peony*, 5
Chocolate
  *Chocolat*, 98
CIA
  *Fierce Invalids Home from Hot Climates*, 54
  *Little America*, 26
Civil Rights
  *Half a Heart*, 27
Cleveland, Ohio (See also Ohio, American
    Midwest)
  *Crooked River Burning*, 140
Cocaine (See also Drugs and Drug Abuse)
  *Preston Falls*, 94
Coffee
  *Memoir from Antproof Case*, 152
Cold War
  *Little America*, 26
  *Underworld*, 150
College Professors (See also Academia,
    Teachers)
  *Age of Iron*, 148
  *Blue Angel*, 52
  *Disgrace*, 148
  *The Human Stain*, 126
  *Making Love to the Minor Poets of
    Chicago*, 84
  *The Man Who Wrote the Book*, 134
  *Moo*, 131
  *The Name of the World*, 154
  *Tomcat in Love*, 54

College Students
  *Emotionally Weird*, 70
  *Joe College*, 50
  *Possession*, 79
Colonialism
  *Chronicle of the Seven Sorrows*, 5
  *The Glass Palace*, 35
  *The House on the Lagoon*, 6
  *The Map of Love*, 18
  *The Mark of the Angel*, 18
Colorado (See also American West)
  *Fencing the Sky*, 7
  *The Hookmen*, 101
  *The Meadow*, 8
  *The Mineral Palace*, 11
  *Plainsong*, 99
Comedy of Manners
  *Dear Will*, 23
  *Human Voices*, 23
  *Le Mariage*, 10
Comfort Women
  *A Gesture Life*, 108
Comic Books (See also Comics, Cartoons)
  *The Amazing Adventures of Kavalier &
    Clay,* 82
Comics
  *The Funnies*, 109
Coming-of-Age
  *All the Pretty Horses*, 157
  *Arithmetic*, 115
  *Bee Season*, 36
  *Benjamin's Gift*, 115
  *The Butcher Boy*, 114
  *Caucasia*, 129
  *A Crime in the Neighborhood*, 76
  *Durable Goods*, 25
  *East Bay Grease*, 140
  *Eddie's Bastard*, 108
  *The Far Euphrates*, 132
  *The Flower Boy*, 15
  *Funny Boy*, 16
  *Gloria*, 12
  *The Grass Dancer*, 51
  *The Hallelujah Side*, 103
  *Henry of Atlantic City*
  *The Hookmen*, 101
  *Iron Shoes*, 95
  *Jim the Boy*, 90
  *Larry's Party*, 130
  *Playing Botticelli*, 48
  *Madame*, 11
  *Meely LaBauve*, 19

Coming-of-Age (*cont.*)
*Money, Love*, 73
*Monkey Beach*, 126
*Montana 1948*, 19
*Music of the Swamp*, 14
*A Nixon Man*, 27
*Nothing Is Terrible*, 57
*The Rich Man's Table*, 132
*Right by My Side*, 99
*The Romantics*, 13
*Secrets of the Tsil Café*, 25
*The Sea of Trees*, 48
*Shadow Baby*, 115
*The Sky Fisherman*, 110
*Some Things That Stay*, 140
*A Star Called Henry*, 88
*Sunday You Learn How to Box*, 141
*Thicker Than Water*, 99
*Thumbsucker*, 42
*Truth and Bright Water*, 106
*The Umbrella Country*, 125
*Virtual Silence*, 129
*The Way I Found Her*, 61
*What She Saw*, 55
*Windchill Summer*, 44
*The Year of the Frog*, 17
*Yoruba Girl Dancing*, 4
Coming Out (See also Gay Men, Gay
    Teenagers, Lesbians)
*Comfort and Joy*, 97
*The Short History of a Prince*, 98
Communal Living
*Brazil-Maru*, 21
Communism
*Butterfly Lovers*, 7
*I Married a Communist*, 126
*Judge on Trial*, 107
*Madame*, 11
*The Year of the Frog*, 17
Composers (See also Music and Musicians)
*Amsterdam*, 115
*Grace Notes*, 156
Computers
*@expectations*, 53
Concentration Camps (See also Internment Camps)
*Judge on Trial*, 107
*Saints and Villains*, 35
Coney Island
*Dreamland*, 3
Congo
*The Catastrophist*, 4
*The Poisonwood Bible*, 107

Connecticut (See also American Northeast,
    New England)
*Sunday You Learn How to Box*, 141
Conservation
*The Loop*, 32
Construction Accidents
*This Side of Brightness*, 12
Convents
*Fierce Invalids Home from Hot Climates*,
    54
*Lying Awake*, 16
Cooking
*Bread Alone*, 39
*Secrets of the Tsil Café*, 24
Cooks
*The Journey Home*, 122
*The Minotaur Takes a Cigarette Break*, 130
Coolidge, Calvin
*Seeing Calvin Coolidge in a Dream*, 86
Cousins
*The Amazing Adventures of Kavalier &
    Clay*, 82
*Fiona Range*, 118
*Sister of My Heart*, 87
*What a Woman Must Do*, 133
Cowboys
*The Englishman's Boy*, 137
*Fencing the Sky*, 7
*Leaping Man Hill*, 31
*The Meadow*, 8
Creole Culture
*Chronicle of the Seven Sorrows*, 5
Creoles
*Love Like Gumbo*, 52
Crime (See also Murder, Mystery)
*Cruddy*, 73
*Night Train*, 145
Cuba
*The Chin Kiss King*, 62
*Empress of the Splendid Season*, 100
*The Perez Family*, 75
Cuban Americans
*Empress of the Splendid Season*, 100
Culinary Arts (See also Cooking,
    Cooks)
*Adrian Mole: The Cappuccino Years*, 61
*Chocolat*, 98
*The Journey Home*, 130
*The Minotaur Takes a Cigarette Break*, 130
*The Reef*, 151
Cultural Identity
*The Romantics*, 13

Curses
*Fierce Invalids Home from Hot Climates*, 54
Custody Battles
*Keeping Faith*, 51
*Make Believe*, 1219
Czechoslovakia
*Judge on Trial*, 107
*The Year of the Frog*, 17
Czechoslovakian Authors
*Judge on Trial*, 107
*The Year of the Frog*, 17

Dancers and Dancing
*Peel My Love Like an Onion*, 28
*The Short History of a Prince*, 98
Daughters-in-Law
*Louisa*, 22
Deafness
*Ancestral Truths*, 112
Death and Dying (See also Cancer, Death of a Parent, Death of a Spouse, Death of a Child, Death of a Sibling, Suicide, Terminal Illness)
*Age of Iron*, 148
*Being Dead*, 148
*The Birthday Boys*, 3
*The Book Borrower*, 156
*The Death of Vishnu*, 133
*Evening*, 157
*The Girls*, 142
*Hood*, 87
*Losing Julia*, 103
*Night Train*, 145
*Pay It Forward*, 39
*The Promise of Rest*, 160
*The Road Home*, 13
*The Saving Graces*, 35
*This Time Next Year*, 101
Death of a Child
*Before and After*, 27
*A Boy in Winter*, 28
*Catch Your Breath*, 24
*A Crime in the Neighborhood*, 76
*Don't Think Twice*, 40
*Esperanza's Box of Saints*, 31
*Evening News*, 60
*Falling Bodies*, 45
*The Hearts of Soldiers*, 56
*Layover*, 143
*The Long Falling*, 53
*Middle Son*, 40

*The Name of the World*, 154
*Native Speaker*, 109
*One Heart*, 114
*The Poisonwood Bible*, 107
*The Quick & the Dead*, 140
*Some Old Lovers Ghost*, 110
*Souls Raised from the Dead*, 76
*The Sweet Hereafter*, 72
*This Time Last Year*, 101
*Two Cities*, 139
Death of a Parent
*Almost Home*, 116
*Blu's Hanging*, 142
*Carter Clay*, 91
*Durable Goods*, 25
*Elizabeth and After*, 83
*Everything You Know*, 100
*A Good House*, 79
*Land of Smiles*, 9
*Lost Geography*, 71
*Memoir from Antproof Case*, 152
*A Passionate Man*, 62
*Plum & Jaggers*, 131
*Polly's Ghost*, 93
*Scar Tissue*, 153
*Tea*, 85
*The Tiny One*, 157
*The Walking Tour*, 85
Death of a Sibling (See also Death and Dying)
*A Good House*, 79
*The Hearts of Soldiers*, 56
*In the Presence of Horses*, 31
*Jumping the Green*, 128
*Monkey Beach*, 126
*The Short History of a Prince*, 98
Death of a Spouse (See also Death and Dying)
*The Artist's Widow*, 112
*Elizabeth and After*, 83
*Everything You Know*, 100
*Falling Bodies*, 45
*The Long Falling*, 53
*The Name of the World*, 154
*The Pilot's Wife*, 58
*Ruby*, 39
*Two Cities*, 139
Delhi, India (See also India)
*Listening Now*, 69
Depression
*About a Boy*, 102
*Duane's Depressed*, 46
*Mummy's Legs*, 25
*Self-Portrait with Ghosts*, 90

Detectives
    *Motherless Brooklyn*, 155
    *When We Were Orphans*, 103
Detroit, Michigan (See also Michigan)
    *Second Hand*, 64
Developmental Disabilities
    *Like Normal People*, 76
    *A Nixon Man*, 17
Diaries
    *Adrian Mole: The Cappuccino Years*, 61
Diplomacy
    *Light at Dusk*, 34
Disco
    *The Last Days of Disco, With Cocktails at
        Petrossian Afterwards*, 18
Disfigurement
    *Pay It Forward*, 39
Divorce
    *Fool*, 86
    *In the Family Way*, 128
    *Keeping Faith*, 51
    *Souls Raised from the Dead*, 76
    *Snow Angels*, 122
    *Summer Gone*, 12
    *Turtle Moon*, 152
    *With Your Crooked Heart*, 90
Doctors and Patients
    *Anil's Ghost*, 160
    *The Hatbox Baby*, 78
    *The Last King of Scotland*, 7
    *A Passionate Man*, 62
    *Skateaway*, 104
    *Waiting*, 153
Dogs
    *Apologizing to Dogs*, 84
    *East of the Mountains*, 151
    *The Man of the House*, 114
    *Timbuktu*, 71
    *Truth and Bright Water*, 106
Domestic Violence (See also Abusive
        Relationships)
    *The Woman Who Walked into Doors*, 88
Dominican Authors
    *Geographies of Home*, 50
    *How the Garcia Girls Lost Their Accents*,
        67
    *In the Time of the Butterflies*, 2
    *Yo!*, 68
Dominican Republic
    *In the Time of the Butterflies*, 2
Down Syndrome
    *Place Last Seen*, 34

Drugs and Drug Abuse
    *Almost Home*, 116
    *The Collapsible World*, 44
    *Cruddy*, 73
    *House of Sand and Fog*, 89
    *The Many Aspects of Mobile Home Living*, 82
    *Preston Falls*, 94
    *Rabbit at Rest*, 163
    *A Trick of Nature*, 46
Drunk Driving
    *Carter Clay*, 91
    *Living to Tell*, 120
Duels
    *The Rules of Engagement*, 147
Dublin, Ireland (See also Ireland)
    *The Long Falling*, 53
    *A Star Called Henry*, 88
    *The Van*, 88
Dwarfs
    *Dreamland*, 3
    *The Hatbox Baby*, 78
Dysfunctional Families
    *Back Roads*, 121
    *Crocodile Soup*, 84
    *East Bay Grease*, 140
    *Emotionally Weird*, 70
    *Family Pictures*, 117
    *Fleur de Leigh's Life of Crime*, 110
    *The Funnies*, 109
    *The Hiding Place*, 146
    *I Loved You All*, 130
    *Joe*, 78
    *The Last Life*, 116
    *The Oxygen Man*, 142
    *The Professor of Light*, 79
    *Self-Portrait with Ghosts*, 90
    *The Slow Natives*, 69
    *The Sound of One Hand Clapping*, 33
    *The Weight of Water*, 23

Eastern Europe (See also individual countries)
    *Eveless Eden*, 139
    *Judge on Trial*, 107
    *Madame*, 11
    *The Year of the Frog*, 17
Eastern European Authors
    *Judge on Trial*, 107
    *Madame*, 11
    *The Year of the Frog*, 17
Eastern Europeans
    *Madame*, 11
    *The Year of the Frog*, 17

Eating Disorders
*The Hunger Moon*, 45
*More Bread or I'll Appear*, 45
*Thicker Than Water*, 99
Eccentrics and Eccentricities
*Apologizing to Dogs*, 84
*The Artist's Widow*, 112
*Big Stone Gap*, 61
*Bruna and Her Sisters in the Sleeping City*, 21
*The Bubble Reputation*, 123
*The Fennel Family Papers*, 72
*The Hedge, The Ribbon*, 49
*Lamb in Love*, 78
*Milkweed*, 94
*Mister Sandman*, 96
*Moo*, 131
*Sister India*, 14
*Stern Men*, 94
*A Stranger in the Earth*, 134
*Timbuktu*, 71
*The Wind-Up Bird Chronicle*, 159
Ecofiction
*Animal Dreams*, 106
*Skywater*, 14
Ecuadorian Authors
*Bruna and Her Sisters in the Sleeping City*, 21
Egypt
*The Map of Love*, 18
Egyptian Authors
*The Map of Love*, 18
Elderly Men (See also Aging, Seniors)
*The Englishman's Boy*, 137
*The Fifth Season*, 87
*Losing Julia*, 103
*A Lover's Almanac*, 102
*Memoir from Antproof Case*, 152
*The Underpainter*, 136
*Wrack*, 146
Elderly Women (See also Aging, Seniors)
*The Blind Assassin*, 145
*Bordeaux*, 124
*Cereus Blooms at Night*, 118
*The Fifth Season*, 87
*Fool*, 86
*The Girls*, 142
*The Hedge, The Ribbon*, 49
*In the Family Way*, 128
*A Lover's Almanac*, 102
*The Quilter's Apprentice*, 28

*Resting in the Bosom of the Lamb*, 62
Elevators
*The Intuitionist*, 138
Embroidery
*Remember Me*, 100
England
*All Quiet on the Orient Express*, 117
*Armadillo*, 77
*Another Country*, 72
*Being Dead*, 148
*Charlotte Gray*, 32
*England, England*, 73
*Four Dreamers and Emily*, 85
*Going to Pot*, 43
*The Journey Home*, 122
*Lamb in Love*, 78
*Life Skills*, 32
*London Holiday*, 50
*Losing Nelson*, 136
*Some Old Lover's Ghost*, 110
*Spiderweb*, 111
*A Stranger in the Earth*, 134
*Trumpet*, 105
*When We Were Orphans*, 103
*Yoruba Girl Dancing*, 4
Entrepreneurs
*The Van*, 88
Epilepsy
*Butterfly Lovers*, 7
*The Piano Man's Daughter*, 91
Epistolary Novels
*Age of Iron*, 148
*A Celibate Season*, 131
*Dear Stranger, Dearest Friend*, 24
Equestrians
*Horse Heaven*, 131
*Keeneland*, 37
Erotica (See also Sex and Sexuality)
*The Notebooks of Don Rigoberto*, 137
Euthanasia
*Second Hand*, 64
Expatriates
*The Catastrophist*, 4
*Hummingbird House*, 9
*Lost in Translation*, 13
*More Bread or I'll Appear*, 45
*The Persian Bride*, 5
*The Romantics*, 13
Explorers and Explorations
*The Birthday Boys*, 3

Faith Healing
    *The Healing*, 153
Family Feuds
    *Julie and Romeo*, 52
Family Relationships
    *Alice Springs*, 8
    *All-Bright Court*, 124
    *Ancestral Truths*, 112
    *Back When We Were Grownups*, 136
    *Before and After*, 27
    *Behind the Scenes at the Museum*, 72
    *The Blackwater Lightship*, 135
    *Blue Diary*, 39
    *Brazil-Maru*, 21
    *The Bonesetter's Daughter*, 60
    *The Brothers K*, 89
    *The Bubble Reputation*, 123
    *Caucasia*, 129
    *The Chin Kiss King*, 62
    *Comfort and Joy*, 97
    *Do Unto Others*, 43
    *East of the Mountains*, 151
    *Elizabeth and After*, 83
    *The Empress of the Splendid Season*, 100
    *Fasting, Feasting*, 86
    *Felicia's Journey*, 162
    *A Fine Balance*, 158
    *The Flower in the Skull*, 1
    *The Funnies*, 109
    *Geographies of Home*, 50
    *The Glass Palace*, 35
    *A Good House*, 79
    *The Half-Life of Happiness*, 81
    *The Hearts of Soldiers*, 56
    *The Hedge, The Ribbon*, 49
    *Home to India*, 17
    *The House on the Lagoon*, 6
    *How the Garcia Girls Lost Their Accents*, 67
    *Icy Sparks*, 55
    *In the Time of the Butterflies*, 2
    *In Troubled Waters*, 30
    *The Jade Peony*, 5
    *Jim the Boy*, 90
    *Jumping the Green*, 128
    *The Kitchen God's Wife*, 60
    *Leaping Man Hill*, 31
    *Like Normal People*, 76
    *Lily of the Valley*, 57
    *Living to Tell*, 120
    *Longleg*, 67
    *The Lost Legends of New Jersey*, 125
    *Love Like Gumbo*, 52

    *A Member of the Family*, 47
    *Mister Sandman*, 96
    *Montana 1948*, 19
    *Money, Love*, 73
    *Monkey Beach*, 126
    *Montana 1948*, 19
    *The Moor's Last Sigh*, 162
    *More Bread or I'll Appear*, 45
    *Nobody's Fool*, 127
    *The Natural Order of Things*, 69
    *A Nixon Man*, 27
    *An Obedient Father*, 129
    *Place Last Seen*, 34
    *The Poisonwood Bible*, 107
    *Portrait of the Artist's Wife*, 68
    *The Promise of Rest*, 160
    *Rabbit at Rest*, 163
    *Reading in the Dark*, 149
    *A Recipe for Bees*, 2
    *Rescue*, 126
    *The Road Home*, 98
    *The Salt Dancers*, 38
    *Secrets of the Tsil Café*, 24
    *Self-Portrait with Ghosts*, 90
    *Sharmila's Book*, 42
    *The Shipping News*, 15
    *Skateaway*, 104
    *The Slow Natives*, 69
    *Solar Storms*, 153
    *Steps and Exes*, 41
    *The Stone Diaries*, 162
    *Such a Long Journey*, 158
    *Tempest Rising*, 116
    *Thicker Than Water*, 99
    *A Thirst for Rain*, 80
    *This One and Magic Life*, 94
    *A Thousand Acres*, 17
    *A Trick of Nature*, 46
    *The Umbrella Country*, 125
    *The Van*, 88
    *Water Marked*, 109
    *The Weekend*, 80
    *What a Woman Must Do*, 133
    *While I Was Gone*, 117
    *The Wholeness of a Broken Heart*, 58
    *With Your Crooked Heart*, 90
    *Yo!*, 68

Family Secrets
    *Animal Dreams*, 106
    *Behind the Scenes at the Museum*, 70
    *Blue Diary*, 39

*The Bonesetter's Daughter*, 60
*A Dangerous Woman*, 118
*The Far Euphrates*, 132
*The Fennel Family Papers*, 72
*The House on the Lagoon*, 6
*Inheritance*, 35
*The Kitchen God's Wife*, 60
*Listening Now*, 69
*Mister Sandman*, 96
*Monkey Bridge, 80*
*A Nixon Man*, 39
*Reading in the Dark*, 149
*Resting in the Bosom of the Lamb*, 62
*Sister of My Heart*, 87
*The Slow Way Back*, 37
Farms and Farm Life
*Brazil-Maru*, 21
*Disgrace*, 148
*Lost Geography*, 71
*A Recipe for Bees*, 2
*Snake*, 10
*A Thousand Acres*, 17
*Winter Range*, 6
Fathers and Daughters
*Alice Springs*, 8
*Animal Dreams*, 106
*Bee Season*, 36
*The Body Is Water*, 128
*By the Shore*, 30
*A Cab Called Reliable*, 105
*Charlotte Gray*, 32
*The Collapsible World*, 44
*Cruddy*, 73
*The Daughters of Simon Lamoreaux*, 44
*Dear Will*, 23
*Disgrace*, 148
*Durable Goods*, 25
*The Electrical Field*, 56
*Empire Falls*, 127
*Eucalyptus*, 2
*Female Ruins*, 120
*The Half-Life of Happiness*, 81
*The Hiding Place*, 146
*A Hole in the Earth*, 74
*Host Family*, 46
*An Invisible Sign of My Own*, 75
*Iron Shoes*, 95
*Lost in Translation*, 13
*Lying with the Enemy, 76*
*Montana 1948*, 19
*An Obedient Family*, 129
*The Poisonwood Bible*, 107

*The Salt Dancers*, 38
*Souls Raised from the Dead*, 76
*The Sound of One Hand Clapping*, 33
*This Is My Daughter*, 54
*A Thousand Acres*, 17
*The Weight of Water*, 23
*A Widow for One Year*
*Written on the Body*, 141
Fathers and Sons
*Adrian Mole: The Cappuccino Years*, 61
*Battle Creek*, 108
*Charlotte Gray*, 32
*Crooked River Burning*, 140
*East Bay Grease*, 140
*Empire Falls*, 1127
*The Fifth Season*, 87
*Fool*, 86
*From the Black Hills*, 135
*Gambler's Rose*, 99
*Henry of Atlantic City*, 125
*The Hookmen*, 101
*Independence Day*, 92
*Joe College*, 50
*Land of Smiles*, 9
*Little America*, 26
*Meely LaBauve*, 19
*A Member of the Family*, 47
*Native Speaker*, 109
*The New City*, 2
*The Paperboy*, 150
*A Passionate Man*, 62
*The Plagiarist*, 28
*The Promise of Rest*, 160
*Ray in Reverse*, 63
*The Rich Man's Table*, 132
*Right by My Side*, 99
*The Slow Natives*, 69
*The Sharpshooter Blues*, 121
*Summer Gone*, 12
*Thumbsucker*, 42
*Truth and Bright Water*, 106
*The Umbrella Country*, 125
*The Weight of Dreams*, 23
Fathers Deserting Their Families
*Henry of Atlantic City*, 125
*Preston Falls*, 94
*Water Marked*, 109
*The Wishing Box*, 59
Feminism
*Mosquito*, 154
Filipino Authors
*The Umbrella Country*, 125

Filipino American Authors
  *The Umbrella Country*, 125
First Novels
  *All-Bright Court*, 124
  *Almost Home*, 116
  *Amy and Isabelle*, 133
  *Back Roads*, 121
  *Battle Creek*, 108
  *The Bear Comes Home*, 64
  *Beautiful Wasps Having Sex*, 81
  *Bee Season*, 37
  *Behind the Scenes at the Museum*, 70
  *The Body Is Water*, 128
  *Big Stone Gap*, 61
  *Bread Alone*, 39
  *Butterfly Lovers*, 7
  *By the Shore*, 30
  *A Cab Called Reliable*, 105
  *The Cage*, 16
  *Caucasia*, 29
  *Cereus Blooms at Night*, 118
  *The Chin Kiss King*, 62
  *The Collapsible World*, 44
  *Crazy for Cornelia*, 36
  *A Crime in the Neighborhood*, 76
  *Crocodile Soup*, 84
  *Dear Stranger, Dearest Friend*, 24
  *The Death of Vishnu*, 133
  *Deep in the Heart*, 137
  *Dreamland*, 3
  *Durable Goods*, 25
  *East Bay Grease*, 140
  *Eddie's Bastard*, 108
  *The Electrical Field*, 56
  *Esperanza's Box of Saints*, 31
  *Everything You Know*, 100
  *Falling Bodies*, 45
  *The Far Euphrates*, 132
  *Fleur de Leigh's Life of Crime*, 110
  *The Flower Boy*, 15
  *Fool's Gold*, 18
  *The Fundamentals of Play*, 112
  *Funny Boy*, 16
  *Geographies of Home*, 50
  *Going to Pot*, 41
  *A Good House*, 79
  *The Grass Dancer*, 51
  *The Hallelujah Side*, 103
  *The Hiding Place*, 146
  *Home to India*, 17
  *Honeymoon: A Romantic Rampage*, 40
  *The Hookmen, 101*

  *How All This Started*, 34
  *How the Garcia Girls Lost Their Accents*, 67
  *Hummingbird House*, 9
  *The Hunger Moon*, 45
  *Icy Sparks*, 55
  *In the Presence of Horses*, 31
  *The Intuitionist*, 138
  *An Invisible Sign of My Own*, 75
  *Jackie by Josie*, 51
  *The Jade Peony*, 5
  *Jim the Boy*, 90
  *Julie and Romeo*, 52
  *Jump*, 1
  *Jumping the Green*, 128
  *Keeneland*, 37
  *The Ladies Auxiliary*, 47
  *The Last Days of Disco with Cocktails at Petrossian Afterwards*, 19
  *Last Days of Summer*, 107
  *The Last Integrationist*, 43
  *The Last King of Scotland*, 7
  *Last Things*, 121
  *Like Normal People Listening Now*, 69
  *The Long Falling*, 53
  *Losing Julia*, 103
  *Lost*, 135
  *Lost Geography*, 71
  *The Lost Glass Plates of Wilfred Eng*, 49
  *Lost in Translation*, 13
  *Love Like Gumbo*, 52
  *Loving Graham Greene*, 150
  *The Lucky Gourd Shop*, 56
  *Madame*, 11
  *Madchild Running*, 31
  *The Man Who Ate the 747*, 57
  *The Many Aspects of Mobile Home Living*, 82
  *Making Love to the Minor Poets of Chicago*, 84
  *Mating, 161*
  *The Meadow*, 8
  *Meely LaBauve*, 19
  *A Member of the Family*, 47
  *The Mermaids Singing*, 147
  *Middle Son*, 40
  *The Mineral Palace*, 11
  *The Minotaur Takes a Cigarette Break*, 130
  *Miss Julia Speaks Her Mind*, 55
  *Money, Love*, 73
  *Monkey Beach*, 126

*Monkey Bridge*, 80
*Mummy's Legs*, 25
*The Name*, 96
*Native Speaker*, 109
*A Nixon Man*, 27
*No One Thinks of Greenland*, 97
*Nothing Is Terrible*, 57
*An Obedient Father*, 129
*One Heart*, 114
*One Hundred and One Ways*, 143
*Otherwise Engaged*, 33
*The Oxygen Man*, 132
*The Perfect Elizabeth*, 128
*Place Last Seen*, 34
*The Plagiarist*, 28
*Playing Botticelli*, 48
*The Pleasing Hour*, 106
*Pobby and Dingan*, 15
*The Quilter's Apprentice*, 28
*Reading in the Dark*, 149
*Redeeming Eve*, 26
*The Reef*, 151
*The Restraint of Beasts*, 117
*Right by My Side*, 99
*The Romantics*, 13
*The Sea of Trees*, 48
*Second Hand*, 64
*Secrets of the Tsil Café*, 24
*Sister India*, 14
*Six Figures*, 109
*Skywater*, 14
*The Slow Way Back*, 37
*Snake*, 10
*Snow Angels*, 122
*Soldier in Paradise*, 48
*Some Things That Stay*, 140
*Stern Men*, 94
*The Story of a Million Years*, 102
*A Stranger in the Earth*, 134
*Such a Long Journey*, 158
*Summer Gone*, 12
*Sunday You Learn How to* Box, 140
*Tea*, 85
*Thicker Than Water*, 99
*A Thirst for Rain*, 80
*Those Who Favor Fire*, 20
*Three Apples Fell from Heaven*, 156
*The Tiny One*, 157
*Triage*, 68
*True North*, 41
*Trumpet*, 105
*The Umbrella Country*, 125

*Undertow*, 59
*The Virgin Suicides*, 150
*What She Saw...*, 55
*When Mountains Walked*, 20
*White Oleander*, 33
*White Teeth*, 162
*The Wholeness of a Broken Heart*, 58
*Why She Left Us*, 54
*Windchill Summer*, 44
*Winter Range*, 6
*The Wishbones*, 124
*The Wishing Box*, 59
*Working Parts*, 25
*The World Around Midnight*, 37
*The Year of the Frog*, 17
*Yoruba Girl Dancing*, 4
First Peoples
　*Monkey Beach*, 126
Fish Farming
　*The Oxygen Man*, 142
Fishing
　*The Sky Fisherman*, 110
　*Stern Men*, 94
Florida
　*The Chin Kiss King*, 62
　*The Fifth Season*, 87
　*The Girls*, 142
　*In Troubled Waters*, 30
　*The Paperboy*, 150
　*Soldier in Paradise*, 48
　*Turtle Moon*, 152
Florists
　*Julie and Romeo*, 52
Folk Tales
　*Chronicle of the Seven Sorrows*, 5
Football Coaches
　*A Trick of Nature*, 46
Foreign Correspondents
　*Eveless Eden*, 139
Forensics
　*Anil's Ghost*, 160
Fort Worth, Texas (See also Texas)
　*Apologizing to Dogs*, 84
Foster Children
　*Tempest Rising*, 116
　*White Oleander*, 33
France
　*Bordeaux*, 124
　*Charlotte Gray*, 32
　*Chocolat*, 98
　*Fool's Gold*, 18
　*The Last Life*, 116

France (*cont.*)
  *Le Mariage*, 100
  *Losing Julia*, 103
  *Lost Geography*, 71
  *The Mark of the Angel*, 9
  *The Pleasing Hour*, 106
French Authors
  *The First Man*, 5
  *The Mark of the Angel*, 9
Freud, Sigmund
  *Dreamland*, 3
Friendship (See also Men's Friendships,
    Women's Friendships)
  *The Boy in the Lake*, 59
  *Cracks*, 42
  *A Dangerous Friend*, 155
  *A Fine Balance*, 158
  *Jayber Crow*, 4
  *The Language of Threads*, 62
  *Last Days of Summer*, 107
  *A Lesson Before Dying*, 93
  *The Man of the House*, 114
  *The Meadow*, 8
  *The Quick & the Dead*, 140
  *Snow in August*, 38
  *Such a Long Journey*, 158
  *Virtual Silence*, 129
  *The Weekend*, 80
  *The Whereabouts of Eneas McNulty*, 146

Gamblers and Gambling
  *Gambler's Rose*, 99
  *The Hiding Place*, 146
  *A Hole in the Earth*, 74
Gangs
  *The Ordinary Seaman*, 95
Gangsters
  *Dreamland*, 3
Gardens and Gardening
  *Larry's Party*, 130
Gay Men
  *The Amazing Adventures of Kavalier &
    Clay*, 83
  *The Blackwater Lightship*, 135
  *The Boy in the Lake*, 53
  *Breakfast with Scot*, 87
  *The Bubble Reputation*, 123
  *Cereus Blooms at Night*, 118
  *Cinnamon Gardens*, 16
  *Comfort and Joy*, 97
  *An Imaginative Experience*, 64
  *Light at Dusk*, 35

  *The Long Falling*, 53
  *The Man of the House*, 114
  *Mister Sandman*, 96
  *The Promise of Rest*, 160
  *The Short History of a Prince*, 98
  *Until the Real Thing Comes* Along, 25
  *The Weekend*, 80
Gay Teenagers
  *Funny Boy*, 16
  *The Short History of a Prince*, 98
  *The Umbrella Country*, 125
Gender Roles
  *Cereus Blooms at Night*, 118
  *Trumpet*, 105
Geniuses
  *In the Country of the Young*, 147
  *The Last Samurai*, 86
Genocide
  *Naming the Spirits*, 134
  *Three Apples Fell from Heaven*, 156
Georgia
  *East Is East*, 77
  *The Hand I Fan With*, 24
  *My Drowning*, 97
German Authors
  *Lost*, 135
Germany
  *Lost*, 135
  *Saints and Villains*, 35
Gettysburg, Pennsylvania (See also
    Pennsylvania)
  *The Hearts of Soldiers*, 56
Ghetto Life
  *Always Outnumbered, Always Outgunned*,
    119
  *Moonlight on the Avenue of Faith*, 119
  *Sunday You Learn How to Box*, 141
  *Two Cities*, 139
Ghosts
  *The Hand I Fan With*, 24
  *In the Country of the Young*, 147
  *Italian Fever*, 113
  *More Than You Know*, 37
  *One Hundred and One Ways*, 143
  *Polly's Ghost*, 93
  *The Quick & the Dead*, 140
  *The River King*, 110
Gifted Children (See also Geniuses)
  *Bee Season*, 36
  *In the Country of the Young*, 147
  *The Last Samurai*, 86

Gnosticism
   *Henry of Atlantic City*, 125
Golems
   *The Amazing Adventures of Kavalier &
      Clay*, 82
   *Snow in August*, 38
Good vs. Evil
   *The 27th Kingdom*, 91
Grandparents
   *Another World*, 72
   *The Boy in the Lake*, 59
   *Eddie's Bastard*, 108
   *The Lost Legends of New Jersey*, 125
   *Make Believe*, 129
   *Monkey Beach*, 126
   *Rabbit at Rest*, 163
   *The Road Home*, 99
   *Triage*, 68
   *Water, Carry Me*, 47
   *Yoruba Girl Dancing*, 4
Greene, Graham
   *Loving Graham Greene*, 150
Greenland
   *No One Thinks of Greenland*, 97
Grief
   *In the Presence of Horses*, 31
   *Layover*, 143
   *Lying with the Enemy*, 76
   *The Sweet Hereafter*, 72
   *Two Cities*, 139
Guatemala
   *Hummingbird House*, 9
Guernsey, England
   *Lying with the Enemy*, 76
Guyana
   *The Professor Light*, 79
Gypsies
   *Armadillo*, 77
   *Chocolat*, 98
   *Peel My Love Like an Onion*, 28

Haisla Indians
   *Monkey Beach*, 126
Harlem
   *Jazz*, 158
Hawaii
   *Blu's Hanging*, 142
   *Middle Son*, 40
   *Song of the Exile*, 30
Hebrides
   *Emotionally Weird*, 70

Henry, John
   *John Henry Days*, 139
Hindus
   *The Death of Vishnu*, 133
Hippies
   *By the Shore*, 30
Historical Setting
   *The Birthday Boys*, 3
   *The Catastrophist*, 4
   *Charlotte Gray*, 32
   *The Colony of Unrequited Dreams*, 10
   *Dreamland*, 3
   *The Glass Palace*, 35
   *The Hatbox Baby*, 78
   *In the Time of the Butterflies*, 2
   *The Last King of Scotland*, 7
   *Leaping Man Hill*, 31
   *Losing Julia*, 103
   *Lying with the Enemy*, 76
   *Martin Dressler: Portrait of an American
      Dreamer*, 13
   *The Piano Man's Daughter*, 91
   *Pilgrim*, 92
   *Saints and Villains*, 35
   *Song of the Exile*, 30
   *The Whereabouts of Eneas McNulty*, 146
Hockey
   *The Lost Legends of New Jersey*, 125
   *Skateaway*, 104
Hollywood
   *Beautiful Wasps Having Sex*, 81
   *The Englishman's Boy*, 137
   *Fleur de Leigh's Life of Crime*, 110
Holocaust
   *The Amazing Adventures of Kavalier &
      Clay*, 82
   *The Far Euphrates*, 132
   *Louisa*, 22
   *The Name*, 96
Homelessness
   *Always Outnumbered, Always Outgunned*, 119
   *A Certain Age*, 104
   *This Side of Brightness*, 12
Hong Kong
   *The Language of Threads*, 62
Horse Racing
   *Horse Heaven*, 131
   *Keeneland*, 37
Horses
   *Horse Heaven*, 131
   *In the Presence of Horses*, 31
   *Keeneland*, 37

Housing Projects (See also Ghetto Life)
  *All-Bright Court*, 124
  *Sunday You Learn How to Box*
Humorous Fiction
  *About a Boy*, 102
  *Adrian Mole: The Cappuccino Years*, 61
  *All Quiet on the Orient Express*, 117
  *The Answer Is Yes*, 44
  *Arithmetic*, 115
  *Behind the Scenes at the Museum*, 70
  *Big Stone Gap*, 61
  *Body,* 149
  *The Country Life*, 84
  *Crazy for Cornelia*, 36
  *Damascus*, 74
  *Duane's Depressed*, 49
  *Emotionally Weird*, 70
  *England, England*, 73
  *Fierce Invalids Home from Hot Climates*, 54
  *Fleur de Leigh's Life of Crime*, 110
  *Fool's Gold*, 18
  *Foolscap*, 113
  *Four Dreamers and Emily*, 85
  *A Frolic of His Own*, 151
  *Going to Pot*, 43
  *The Hallelujah Side*, 103
  *Horse Heaven*, 131
  *Human Voices*, 92
  *An Imaginative Experience*, 138
  *Joe College*, 124
  *The Last Days of Disco with Cocktails at
    Petrossian Afterwards*, 19
  *Life Skills*, 32
  *Lost*, 135
  *The Man Who Ate the 747*, 57
  *The Man Who Wrote the Book*, 134
  *The Many Aspects of Mobile Home Living*,
    82
  *Miss Julia Speaks Her Mind*, 55
  *Money, Love*, 74
  *Moo*, 131
  *Night of the Avenging Blowfish*, 63
  *Nobody's Fool*, 127
  *Nothing Is Terrible*, 57
  *Otherwise Engaged*, 32
  *Ray in Reverse*, 63
  *The Restraint of Beasts*, 117
  *A Stranger in the Earth*, 134
  *Thumbsucker*, 42
  *Tomcat in Love*, 49
  *The 27th Kingdom*, 91
  *The Van*, 88

  *The Wishbones*, 124
  *The World Around Midnight*, 37
  *Yoruba Girl Dancing*, 4
Hungary
  *Louisa*, 22
Husbands and Wives (See also Marriage)
  *@expectations*, 53
  *Another World*, 72
  *The Answer Is Yes, 44*
  *Bee Season*, 36
  *Blue Diary*, 39
  *A Celibate Season*, 131
  *Deep in the Heart*, 137
  *Elizabeth and After*, 83
  *Empire Falls*, 127
  *Evening News*, 60
  *Evensong*, 36
  *Goodbye Without Leaving*, 83
  *Goodness*, 123
  *Headlong*, 33
  *Home to India*, 17
  *The House on the Lagoon*, 6
  *I Married a Communist*, 126
  *An Imaginative Experience*, 64
  *In the Family Way*, 128
  *The Inner Life of Objects*, 83
  *Iron Shoes*, 95
  *Keeneland*, 37
  *Layover*, 143
  *The Mineral Palace*, 11
  *More Than You Know*, 37
  *My Russian*, 46
  *Native Speaker*, 109
  *A Passionate Man*, 62
  *Seeing Calvin Coolidge in a Dream*, 86
  *Siam: Or The Woman Who Shot a Man*, 19
  *Six Figures*, 109
  *Snake*, 10
  *That Summer's Trance*, 127
  *This Is My Daughter*, 54
  *A Trick of Nature*, 46
  *The Walking Tour*, 85
  *When Mountains Walked*, 20
  *Where or When*, 58
  *While I Was Gone*, 117
  *White Teeth*, 162
  *The Wind-Up Bird Chronicle*, 159
  *The Woman Who Walked Into Doors*, 88
  *The World Around Midnight*, 37

Iceland
  *The Journey Home*, 122

Icelandic Authors
   *The Journey Home*, 122
Illegitimate Children
   *Amy and Isabelle*, 133
Illiteracy
   *Working Parts*, 25
Illness (See also Cancer, Terminal Illness)
   *Dear Stranger, Dearest Friend*, 24
   *East of the Mountains*, 151
   *An Invisible Sign of My Own*, 75
   *Iron Shoes*, 95
   *Lying Awake*, 16
   *The Promise of Rest*, 160
Imaginary Friends
   *Pobby and Dingan*, 15
Immigrants and Refugees
   *Armadillo*, 77
   *Brazil-Maru*, 21
   *Dreamland*, 3
   *The Flower in the Skull*, 1
   *The Hiding Place*, 146
   *The Jade Peony*, 5
   *Land of Smiles*, 9
   *Light at Dusk,* 34
   *The Mark of the Angel*, 9
   *Monkey Bridge*, 80
   *Moonlight on the Avenue of Faith*, 119
   *Mosquito*, 154
   *The Ordinary Seaman*, 95
   *The Perez Family*, 75
   *The Professor of Light*, 79
   *The Rules of Engagement*, 147
   *The Sea of Trees*, 48
   *The Sound of One Hand Clapping*, 33
   *Yoruba Girl Dancing*, 4
Immortality
   *Pilgrim*, 92
Incest
   *Cereus Blooms at Night*, 118
   *An Obedient Father*, 129
   *Thicker Than Water*, 99
India
   *Cereus Blooms at Night*, 118
   *The Death of Vishnu*, 133
   *Fasting, Feasting*, 86
   *A Fine Balance*, 158
   *The Glass Palace*, 35
   *The Ground Beneath Her Feet*, 161
   *Home to India*, 17
   *Inheritance*, 35
   *Listening Now*, 69
   *The Moor's Last Sigh*, 162

   *An Obedient Father*, 129
   *The Romantics*, 13
   *Sharmila's Book*, 42
   *Sister India*, 14
   *Sister of My Heart*, 87
   *Such a Long Journey*, 158
Indian Authors
   *Cinnamon Gardens*, 16
   *The Death of Vishnu*, 133
   *Fasting, Feasting*, 86
   *Funny Boy*, 16
   *The Glass Palace*, 35
   *The Ground Beneath Her Feet*, 161
   *Inheritance*, 35
   *Listening Now*, 69
   *The Moor's Last Sigh*, 162
   *An Obedient Father*, 129
   *The Romantics*, 13
   *Sister of My Heart*, 87
Indochina
   *The Sea of Trees*, 48
Infertility
   *Redeeming Eve*, 26
   *Rescue*, 126
   *The Saving Graces*, 34
Insomnia
   *East Is East*, 77
Insurance Agents
   *Acts of God*, 48
Insurance Investigations
   *East Is East*, 77
Intermarriage
   *Home to India*, 17
   *The Map of Love*, 18
   *The Professor of Light*, 79
   *The Slow Way Back*, 37
Internet
   *@expectations*, 53
Internment Camps
   *The Electrical Field*, 56
   *The Language of Threads*, 62
   *Why She Left Us*, 54
Interracial Relationships
   *Caucasia*, 129
   *East Is East*, 77
   *The Flower Boy*, 15
   *Half a Heart*, 27
   *Meely LaBauve*, 19
   *The Lake Dreams the Sky*, 20
   *The Last Integrationist*, 43
   *Love Like Gumbo*, 52
   *Make Believe*, 129

Interracial Relationships (*cont.*)
    *The Many Aspects of Mobile Home Living*,
       82
    *One Hundred and One Ways*, 143
    *This Side of Brightness*, 12
    *True North*, 41
    *Trumpet*, 105
Investment Advisors
    *Fool*, 86
Iowa
    *The End of Vandalism*, 88
    *The Hallelujah Side*, 103
    *A Thousand Acres*, 17
Iran
    *House of Sand and Fog*, 89
    *Moonlight on the Avenue of Faith*, 119
    *The Persian Bride*, 5
    *The Rules of Engagement*, 147
Ireland
    *The Blackwater Lightship*, 135
    *Breakfast on Pluto*, 113
    *The Butcher Boy*, 114
    *Felicia's Journey*, 162
    *A Goat's Song*, 8
    *Grace Notes*, 156
    *Hood*, 87
    *In the Country of the Young*, 147
    *The Long Falling*, 53
    *The Mermaids Singing*, 147
    *More Bread or I'll Appear*, 45
    *The Music Lesson*, 138
    *Reading in the Dark*, 149
    *A Star Called Henry*, 88
    *The Van*, 88
    *The Woman Who Walked into Doors*, 88
    *Water, Carry Me*, 47
    *The Whereabouts of Eneas McNulty*, 146
Irish Americans
    *Charming Billy*, 157
Irish Authors
    *The Blackwater Lightship*, 135
    *Breakfast on Pluto*, 113
    *The Butcher Boy*, 114
    *The Catastrophist*, 4
    *Felicia's Journey*, 162
    *A Goat's Song*, 8
    *Grace Notes*, 156
    *Hood*, 87
    *In the Country of the Young*, 147
    *The Long Falling*, 53
    *The Mermaids Singing*, 147
    *More Bread or I'll Appear*, 45

*The Music Lesson*, 138
    *Reading in the Dark*, 149
    *A Star Called Henry*, 88
    *This Side of Brightness*, 12
    *The Van*, 88
    *The Woman Who Walked into Doors*, 88
    *Water, Carry Me*, 47
    *The Whereabouts of Eneas McNulty*, 146
Irish Mythology
    *The Mermaids Singing*, 147
Irish Republican Army
    *The Music Lesson*, 138
    *A Star Called Henry*, 88
    *The Whereabouts of Eneas McNulty*, 146
Isle of Wight
    *England, England*, 73
Israel
    *Louisa*, 22
    *The Name*, 96
Israeli Authors
    *The Name*, 96
Italian Americans
    *Pink Slip*, 82
Italy
    *The English Patient*, 122
    *Italian Fever*, 113

Japan
    *Brazil-Maru*, 21
    *Middle Son*, 40
    *The Wind-Up Bird Chronicle*, 159
Japanese American Authors
    *Blu's Hanging*, 142
    *Brazil-Maru*, 21
    *The Language of Threads*, 62
    *One Hundred and One Ways*, 143
Japanese Americans
    *East Is East*, 77
    *Middle Son*, 40
    *One Hundred and One Ways*, 143
    *Why She Left Us*, 54
Japanese Authors
    *The Unconsoled*, 103
    *When We Were Orphans*, 103
    *The Wind-Up Bird Chronicle*, 159
Japanese Canadians
    *The Electrical Field*, 56
Jazz
    *The Bear Comes Home*, 64
    *East Bay Grease*, 140
    *Jazz*, 158
    *Trumpet*, 105

Jerusalem, Israel
  *The Name*, 96
Jews and Judaism
  *The Amazing Adventures of Kavalier &
    Clay*, 82
  *Beautiful Wasps Having Sex*, 81
  *Bee Season*, 36
  *Dreamland*, 3
  *The Far Euphrates*, 132
  *The Inn at Lake Devine*, 111
  *Judge on Trial*, 107
  *The Ladies Auxiliary*, 47
  *Louisa*, 22
  *Moonlight on the Avenue of Faith*, 119
  *The Name*, 96
  *Redeeming Eve*, 26
  *The Slow Way Back*, 37
  *Snow in August*, 38
  *Tea*, 85
  *The Wholeness of a Broken Heart*, 58
Journalists
  *Amsterdam*, 115
  *The Catastrophist*, 4
  *Eveless Eden*, 139
  *Frozen Music*, 29
  *Highways to a War*, 11
  *John Henry Days*, 139
  *Jump*, 1
  *The Shipping News*, 15
  *A Stranger in the Earth*, 134
  *The World Around Midnight*, 115
Jung, Carl
  *Pilgrim*, 92
Juvenile Delinquents
  *East Bay Grease*, 140
  *Rescue*, 126
  *Turtle Moon*, 152
  *The Weight of Dreams*, 23

Kansas
  *Living to Tell*, 120
  *The Weight of Dreams*, 23
Kentucky
  *Icy Sparks*, 55
  *Jayber Crow*, 4
  *Keeneland*, 37
  *The Patron Saints of Liars*, 123
Kidnapping
  *House of Sand and Fog*, 89
  *Light at Dusk*, 34
  *Plowing the Dark*, 160
  *The Way I Found Her*, 61

Kleptomania
  *Bee Season*, 36
  *The Honey Thief*, 96
Korea
  *The Lucky Gourd Shop*, 56
Korean American Authors
  *A Cab Called Reliable*, 105
  *A Gesture Life*, 108
  *Native Speaker*, 109
Korean Americans
  *A Cab Called Reliable*, 105
  *The Lucky Gourd Shop*, 56
  *Native Speaker*, 109
Korean Japanese Relations
  *A Gesture Life*, 108
Korean War
  *No One Thinks of Greenland*, 97
Kurdistan
  *Triage*, 68

Labor Unions
  *The Glace Bay Miners' Museum*, 6
Laborers
  *The Restraint of Beasts*, 117
Lagos, Nigeria
  *Yoruba Girl Dancing*, 4
Lakota Sioux Indians
  *The Road Home*, 98
Laos
  *Land of Smiles*, 9
Laotian Authors
  *Land of Smiles*, 9
Latino Authors
  *Bordeaux*, 124
  *Bruna and Her Sisters in the Sleeping City*,
    21
  *The Chin Kiss King*, 62
  *Empress of the Splendid Season*, 100
  *Esperanza's Box of Saints*, 31
  *The Flower in the Skull*, 1
  *Geographies of Home*, 50
  *The House on the Lagoon*, 6
  *How the Garcia Girls Lost Their Accents*,
    67
  *In the Time of the Butterflies*, 2
  *Peel My Love Like an Onion*, 28
  *Yo!*, 68
Latinos
  *Bordeaux*, 124
  *Bruna and Her Sisters in the Sleeping City*,
    21
  *The Chin Kiss King*, 62

Latinos (*cont.*)
  *Empress of the Splendid Season*, 100
  *Esperanza's Box of Saints*, 31
  *The Flower in the Skull*, 1
  *Geographies of Home*, 50
  *The House on the Lagoon*, 6
  *How the Garcia Girls Lost Their Accents*,
      67
  *In the Time of the Butterflies*, 2
  *Peel My Love Like an Onion*, 28
  *The Perez Family*, 75
  *What It Takes to Get to Vegas*, 119
  *Yo!*, 68
Latinos in America
  *The Chin Kiss King*, 62
  *Empress of the Splendid Season*, 100
  *Esperanza's Box of Saints*, 31
  *The Flower in the Skull*, 1
  *Geographies of Home*, 50
  *How the Garcia Girls Lost Their Accents*,
      67
  *The Ordinary Seaman*, 95
  *Peel My Love Like an Onion*, 28
  *The Perez Family*, 75
  *What It Takes to Get to Vegas*, 119
  *Yo!*, 68
Law and Lawyers
  *A Celibate Season*, 131
  *A Frolic of His Own*, 151
  *The Last Integrationist*, 43
  *The Many Aspects of Mobile Home Living*,
      82
Lesbians
  *Cereus Blooms at Night*, 118
  *Crocodile Soup*, 84
  *The Half-Life of Happiness*, 81
  *Hood*, 87
  *Love Like Gumbo*, 52
  *Mister Sandman*, 96
  *Nothing is Terrible*, 57
  *Tea*, 85
  *Working Parts*, 25
Librarians
  *The Grand Complication*, 155
Life Choices
  *The Lost Glass Plates of Wilfred Eng*, 49
Lighthouses
  *The Fennel Family Papers*, 72
Literacy
  *Working Parts*, 25
Literary Agents
  *Dear Will*, 23

London, England (See also England)
  *About a Boy*, 102
  *Armadillo*, 77
  *By the Shore*, 30
  *Damascus*, 74
  *Female Ruins*, 120
  *Human Voices*, 92
  *An Imaginative Experience*, 138
  *Kitty and Virgil*, 74
  *The Last Samurai*, 86
  *London Holiday*, 50
  *The Missing World*, 111
  *The Rules of Engagement*, 147
  *A Stranger in the Earth*, 134
  *The 27th Kingdom*, 91
  *White Teeth*, 162
Loneliness
  *Bordeaux*, 124
  *Falling Slowly*, 77
  *Night of the Avenging Blowfish*, 63
Long Island, New York (See also New York)
  *Seventh Heaven*, 152
Los Angeles, California (See also
  California)
  *Always Outnumbered, Always Outgunned*,
      119
  *The Flower in the Skull*, 1
  *The Handyman*, 57
  *Like Normal People*, 76
  *Love Like Gumbo*, 52
  *Moonlight on the Avenue of Faith*, 119
  *What It Takes to Get to Vegas*, 119
Loss of a Parent (See also Death of a Parent)
  *When We Were Orphans*, 103
Love Affairs (See also Adultery, Love Stories,
  Male/Female Relationships)
  *@expectations*, 53
  *Acts of God*, 48
  *The Blind Assassin*, 145
  *A Boy in Winter*, 28
  *The Catastrophist*, 4
  *Catching Heaven*, 97
  *Damascus*, 74
  *Evening*, 157
  *Falling Slowly*, 77
  *Female Ruins*, 120
  *The Ground Beneath Her Feet*, 161
  *The Hearts of Soldiers*, 56
  *The Healing*, 154
  *In the Family Way*, 128
  *Inheritance*, 35
  *Jumping the Green*, 128

*Kitty and Virgil*, 71
*Le Mariage*, 10
*Lost in Translation*, 13
*A Lover's Almanac*, 102
*Lying with Enemy*, 76
*Money, Love*, 146
*The Music Lesson*, 138
*Not a Day Goes By*, 38
*The Notebooks of Don Rigoberto*, 137
*One Heart*, 114
*A Passionate Man*, 62
*Peel My Love Like an Onion*, 28
*Pink Slip*, 82
*The Rules of Engagement*, 147
*Say Goodbye*, 58
*Song of the Exile*, 30
*A Stairway to Paradise*, 132
*Steps and Exes*, 41
*The Story of a Million Years*, 102
*That Summer's Trance*, 1127
*A Trick of Nature*, 46
*Undertow*, 59
*What a Woman Must*, 133
*When Mountains Walked*, 20
*Where or When*, 58
*The Wishbones*, 124
*Written on the Body*, 141
Love Stories (See also Love Affairs,
    Male/Female Relationships)
*Animal Dreams*, 106
*Apologizing to Dogs*, 84
*The Bird Artist*, 160
*Charlotte Gray*, 32
*Comfort and Joy*, 97
*Crazy for Cornelia*, 36
*Dear Will*, 23
*East of the Mountains*, 151
*Eveless Eden*, 139
*Falling Bodies*, 45
*The Feast of Love*, 74
*Frozen Music*, 29
*Gambler's Rose*, 99
*The Glass Palace*, 35
*A Goat's Song*, 8
*In the Presence of Horses*, 31
*The Inn at Lake Devine*, 11
*An Invisible Sign of My Own*, 75
*Jazz*, 158
*The Jukebox Queen of Malta*, 54
*Julie and Romeo*, 52
*Kitty and Virgil*, 71
*The Lake Dreams the Sky*, 20

*Lamb in Love*, 78
*Leaping Man Hill*, 31
*Life Skills*, 32
*Losing Julia*, 103
*The Man Who Ate the 747*, 57
*The Map of Love*, 18
*Mating*, 161
*More Than You Know*, 37
*No One Thinks of Greenland*, 97
*Pay It Forward*, 37
*The Persian Bridge*, 5
*Possession*, 79
*The River King*, 101
*Second Hand*, 64
*Sister of My Heart*, 87
*The Shipping News*, 15
*Some Old Lover's Ghost*, 110
*The Tall Pine Polka*, 43
*Those Who Favor Fire*, 20
*Turtle Moon*, 152
Lower Classes
*The Fundamentals of Play*, 112
*A Star Called Henry*, 88
Lumumba, Patrice
*The Catastrophist*, 4

Magic Realism
*Bailey's Café*, 120
*The Bear Comes Home*, 64
*Benjamin's Gift*, 95
*Bruna and Her Sisters in the Sleeping City*,
    21
*The Chin Kiss King*, 62
*The Chronicle of the Seven Sorrows*, 5
*Esperanza's Box of Saints*, 31
*The Grass Dancer*, 51
*The Hedge, The Ribbon*, 49
*Illumination Night*, 101
*In the Country of the Young*, 147
*The Many Aspects of Mobile Home Living*,
    82
*Moonlight on the Avenue of Faith*, 119
*The Notebooks of Don Rigoberto*, 137
*The Quick & the Dead*, 140
*Turtle Moon*, 152
*The 27th Kingdom*, 91
*The Wishing Box*, 59
*Wolf Whistle*, 159
Maine (See also American Northeast, New
    England)
*The Bubble Reputation*, 123
*Falling Bodies*, 45

Maine (*cont.*)
   *In the Country of the Young*, 147
   *More Than You Know*, 37
   *Stern Men*, 94
Malaya
   *The Glass Palace*, 35
Male/Female Relationships
   *Alice Springs*, 8
   *Back When We Were Grownups*, 136
   *Big Stone Gap*, 61
   *A Certain Age*, 104
   *Cinnamon Gardens*, 16
   *The Colony of Unrequited Dreams*, 10
   *Crooked River Burning*, 140
   *Dear Will*, 23
   *East Is East*, 77
   *The English Patient*, 122
   *Eucalyptus*, 2
   *Falling Slowly*, 77
   *The Feast of Love*, 74
   *Foolscap*, 113
   *Four Dreamers and Emily*, 85
   *The Fundamentals of Play*, 112
   *The Hand I Fan With*, 24
   *A Hole in the Earth*, 74
   *Honeymoon: A Romantic Rampage*, 40
   *An Imaginative Experience*, 138
   *The Inn at Lake Devine*, 111
   *Jazz*, 158
   *Larry's Party*, 130
   *The Last Days of Disco with Cocktails at
      Petrossian Afterwards*, 19
   *Leading the Cheers*, 81
   *The Loop*, 32
   *The Lost Glass Plates of Wilfred Eng*, 49
   *Louisa*, 22
   *Making Love to the Minor Poets of
      Chicago*, 84
   *The Man Who Ate the 747*, 57
   *Mating*, 161
   *The Mermaids Singing*, 147
   *The Missing World*, 111
   *Moo*, 131
   *The Mother-in-Law Diaries*, 30
   *My Drowning*, 97
   *Not a Day Goes By*, 38
   *Night of the Avenging Blowfish*, 63
   *One Hundred and One Ways*, 143
   *Otherwise Engaged*, 33
   *The Patron Saint of Liars*, 123
   *The Persian Bride*, 5
   *The Pilot's Wife*, 58

   *Pink Slip*, 82
   *Rabbit at Rest*, 163
   *A Recipe for Bees*, 2
   *Redeeming Eve*, 26
   *Say Goodbye*, 58
   *Seventh Heaven*, 152
   *Sharmila's Book*, 42
   *The Sleep-Over Artist*, 75
   *Souls Raised from the Dead*, 76
   *Steps and Exes*, 41
   *Those Who Favor Fire*, 20
   *A Thirst for Rain*, 80
   *Tomcat in Love*, 49
   *Trumpet*, 41
   *The Unconsoled*, 103
   *Underworld*, 150
   *Undertow*, 59
   *Waiting*, 153
   *Water, Carry Me*, 47
   *What She Saw...*, 55
   *A Widow for One Year*, 103
   *Winter Range*, 6
   *The Wishbones*, 124
   *The World Around Midnight*, 37
Malta
   *The Jukebox Queen of Malta*, 54
Manic Depression
   *How All This Started*, 334
Manila, Philippines
   *The Umbrella Country*, 125
Maps
   *The Collapsible World*, 44
Marriage
   *Back When We Were Grownups,* 136
   *Being Dead*, 148
   *Blue Diary*, 39
   *A Celibate Season*, 131
   *Deep in the Heart*, 137
   *East of the Mountains*, 151
   *The End of Vandalism*, 88
   *Evensong*, 36
   *Family Pictures*, 117
   *The Half-Life of Happiness*, 81
   *Honeymoon: A Romantic Rampage*, 40
   *Host Family*, 46
   *Illumination Night*, 101
   *In the Lake of the Woods*, 121
   *Jackie by Josie*, 51
   *Larry's Party*, 130
   *Le Mariage,* 10
   *The Mother-in-Law Diaries*, 30
   *My Russian*, 46

*The Perez Family*, 75
*The Pilot's Wife*, 58
*Portrait of the Artist's Wife*, 68
*Preston Falls*, 94
*Ray in Reverse*, 63
*Sharmila's Book*, 42
*Snake*, 10
*That Summer's Trance*, 127
*When Mountains Walked*, 20
*While I Was Gone*, 117
*Winter Range*, 6
Martinique
   *Chronicle of the Seven Sorrows*, 5
Martha's Vineyard, Massachusetts (See also
      Massachusetts)
   *Illumination Night*, 101
Maryland
   *The New City*, 2
Massachusetts (See also American Northeast,
      Boston, Massachusetts, New England)
   *Julie and Romeo*, 52
   *The River King*, 101
   *The Tiny One*, 157
Massacres
   *The Englishman's Boy*, 137
Mathematics
   *Gambler's Rose*, 99
   *An Invisible Sign of My Own*, 75
Mazes
   *Larry's Party*, 130
Memory
   *When We Were Orphans*, 103
Memphis, Tennessee (See also Tennessee)
   *The Ladies Auxiliary*, 47
Men's Friendships
   *Amsterdam*, 115
   *Battle Creek*, 108
   *The Birthday Boys*, 3
   *Breakfast with Scot*, 87
   *Butterfly Lovers*, 7
   *Fencing the Sky*, 7
   *The Fundamentals of Play*, 112
   *Highways to a War*, 11
   *Joe*, 78
   *Last Orders*, 133
   *A Lesson Before Dying*, 93
   *Leviathan*, 70
   *Light at Dusk*, 34
   *Lying with the Enemy*, 77
   *Nobody's Fool*, 127
   *Soldier in Paradise*, 48
   *The Underpainter*, 136

*The Van*, 88
*The Virgin Suicides*, 150
*White Teeth*, 162
Men's Lives
   *Butterfly Lovers*, 7
   *Duane's Depressed*, 46
   *Jayber Crow*, 4
   *Larry's Party*, 130
   *Last Orders*, 133
   *Memoir from Antproof Case*, 152
   *The Moor's Last Sigh*, 162
   *Tomcat in Love*, 49
   *The Underpainter*, 136
Mental Illness
   *Damascus*, 74
   *The Glace Bay Miners' Museum*, 6
   *The Honey Thief*, 96
   *How All This Started*, 34
   *The Lake Dreams The Sky*, 20
   *Last Things*, 121
   *Leaping Man Hill*, 31
   *Longleg*, 67
   *More Bread or I'll Appear*, 45
   *The Piano Man's Daughter*, 91
   *Pilgrim*, 92
   *Self-Portrait with Ghosts*, 90
   *Skateaway*, 104
   *Timbuktu*, 71
Mental Retardation
   *Lamb in Love*, 78
   *Like Normal People*, 76
   *True North*, 41
Mexican American Authors
   *The Flower in the Skull*, 1
   *Peel My Love Like an Onion*, 28
Mexican Americans
   *Peel My Love Like an Onion*, 28
   *What It Takes to Get to Vegas*, 119
Mexican Authors
   *Esperanza's Box of Saints*, 31
Mexico
   *All the Pretty Horses*, 157
   *Everything You Know*, 100
   *The Flower in the Skull*, 1
Miami, Florida (See also Florida)
   *The Girls*, 142
   *The Perez Family*, 75
Michigan
   *Battle Creek*, 108
   *Blameless*, 53
   *The Feast of Love*, 74

Middle-Aged Men
  *Butterfly Lovers*, 7
  *Duane's Depressed*, 46
  *Fool*, 86
  *Independence Day*, 92
  *Larry's Party*, 130
  *Preston Falls*, 94
  *Rabbit at Rest*, 163
  *This Time Last Year*, 101
Middle East (See also individual countries)
  *Little America*, 26
  *Louisa*, 22
  *The Map of Love*, 18
  *The Persian Bride*, 5
Middle-Aged Women
  *Ancestral Truths*, 112
  *London Holiday*, 50
Midlife Crisis
  *Duane's Depressed*, 46
  *Fool*, 86
  *In the Lake of the Woods*, 121
  *Independence Day*, 92
  *My Russian*, 46
  *Preston Falls*, 94
Midwives
  *Midwives*, 26
Military Hospitals
  *No One Thinks of Greenland*, 97
Millenium
  *A Lover's Almanac*, 102
Mines and Mining
  *The Glace Bay Miners' Museum*, 6
  *Those Who Favor Fire*, 20
Ministers, Priests, Rabbis
  *Evensong*, 36
  *Hummingbird House*, 9
  *The Poisonwood Bible*, 107
  *Snow in August*, 38
Minnesota
  *Don't Think Twice*, 40
  *In the Lake of the Woods*, 121
  *Milkweed*, 94
  *Mr. White's Confession*, 29
  *Solar Storms*, 153
  *The Tall Pine Polka*, 43
  *Tomcat in Love*, 49
  *What a Woman Must Do*, 133
Mississippi
  *Joe*, 78
  *The Music of the Swamp*, 14
  *The Oxygen Man*, 142
  *The Sharpshooter Blues*, 121

  *Wolf Whistle*, 159
Montana
  *The Lake Dreams the Sky*, 20
  *The Loop*, 32
  *Montana 1948*, 19
  *Truth and Bright Water*, 106
  *Winter Range*, 6
Montreal, Canada (See also Canada)
  *Jump*, 1
Moral/Ethical Dilemmas
  *Always Outnumbered, Always Outgunned*, 119
  *Leviathan*, 70
  *Saints and Villains*, 35
Mormons
  *Thumbsucker*, 41
Mothers and Daughters
  *Age of Iron*, 148
  *Alice Springs*, 8
  *Amy and Isabelle*, 133
  *Back When We Were Grownups*, 136
  *The Blackwater Lightship*, 135
  *The Bonesetter's Daughter*, 60
  *The Bubble Reputation*, 123
  *By the Shore*, 30
  *The Chin Kiss King*, 62
  *The Civil Wars of Jonah Moran*, 53
  *Emotionally Weird*, 70
  *Esperanza's Box of Saints*, 31
  *Evening News*, 51
  *Gloria*, 12
  *Grace Notes*, 156
  *Half a Heart*, 27
  *The Hiding Place*, 146
  *The Honey Thief*, 96
  *I Loved You All*, 130
  *Inheritance*, 35
  *Iron Shoes*, 95
  *The Kitchen God's Wife*, 60
  *Listening Now*, 69
  *Lost Geography*, 71
  *The Mermaids Singing*, 147
  *Midwives*, 26
  *Milkweed*, 94
  *Monkey Bridge*, 80
  *Moonlight on the Avenue of Faith*, 119
  *More Bread or I'll Appear*, 45
  *More Than You Know*, 45
  *Mummy's Legs*, 25
  *The Piano Man's Daughter*, 119
  *Place Last Seen*, 34
  *Playing Botticelli*, 48

*The Poisonwood Bible*, 107
*Portrait of the Artist's Wife*, 68
*Redeeming Eve*, 26
*The Sea of Trees*, 48
*Shadow Baby*, 115
*Souls Raised from the Dead*, 76
*Tempest Rising*, 116
*A Thirst for Rain*, 80
*This Is My Daughter*, 54
*The Walking Tour*, 85
*The Wholeness of a Broken Heart*, 58
*White Oleander*, 33
Mothers and Sons
*Adrian Mole: The Cappuccino Years*, 61
*The Bird Artist*, 160
*Blue Diary*, 39
*A Boy in Winter*, 28
*Butterfly Lovers*, 7
*Elizabeth and After*, 83
*Evening News*, 60
*Family Pictures*, 117
*The Fifth Season*, 87
*Host Family*, 46
*The Hours*, 149
*Jim the Boy*, 90
*The Last Samurai*, 86
*The Long Falling*, 53
*Longleg*, 67
*A Member of the Family*, 47
*The Mother-in-Law Diaries*, 30
*Pay It Forward*, 39
*The Piano Man's Daughter*, 91
*Polly's Ghost*, 93
*The Promise of Rest*, 160
*Right by My Side*, 99
*The Road Home*, 98
*Scar Tissue*, 153
*The Sky Fisherman*, 110
*The Sleep-Over Artist*, 75
*Sunday You Learn How to Box* , 141
*The 27th Kingdom*, 91
*Two Cities*, 139
*The Way I Found Her*, 61
*Why She Left Us*, 54
Mothers Deserting Their Families
*The Body Is Water*, 128
*Cereus Blooms at Night*, 118
*Fiona Range*, 118
*Inheritance*, 35
*Losing Nelson*, 136
*The Lost Legends of New Jersey*, 125
*Moonlight on the Avenue of Faith*, 119

*My Russian*, 46
*Plainsong*, 99
*The Riders*, 141
*Right by My Side*, 99
*The Sound of One Hand Clapping*, 33
*Thicker Than Water*, 99
*Thumbsucker*, 105
*A Trick of Nature*, 46
*Why She Left Us*, 54
Mothers-in-Law
*Louisa*, 22
*The Mother-in-Law Diaries*, 30
Motion Picture Industry
*Beautiful Wasps Having Sex*, 81
*The Tall Pine Polka*, 43
Movies
*The Last Samurai*, 86
Multigenerational Novels
*Behind the Scenes at the Museum*, 70
*Bruna and Her Sisters in the Sleeping City*, 21
*The Chin Kiss King*, 62
*The Flower in the Skull*, 1
*The Glass Palace*, 35
*A Good House*, 79
*The House on the Lagoon*, 6
*Lost Geography*, 71
*The Moor's Last Sigh*, 162
*The Natural Order of Things*, 69
*One Hundred and One Ways*, 143
*The Piano Man's Daughter*, 91
*The Road Home*, 98
*Solar Storms*, 153
*White Teeth*, 162
Murder
*Always Outnumbered, Always Outgunned*, 119
*Anil's Ghost*, 160
*Back Roads*, 121
*Before and After*, 27
*Being Dead*, 148
*The Bird Artist*, 160
*Blameless*, 53
*A Boy in Winter*, 28
*The Butcher Boy*, 114
*A Crime in the Neighborhood*, 76
*The Electrical Field*, 56
*The English Patient*, 122
*Evening News*, 60
*Fencing the Sky*, 7
*From the Black Hills*, 135
*House of Sand and Fog*, 89

Murder (*cont.*)
  *The Long Falling*, 53
  *Lying with the Enemy*, 76
  *More Than You Know*, 37
  *Motherless Brooklyn*, 155
  *Mr. White's Confession*, 29
  *The Music Lesson*, 138
  *The Oxygen Man*, 142
  *The Sharpshooter Blues*, 121
  *Siam: Or The Woman Who Shot a Man*, 19
  *A Star Called Henry*, 88
  *Tree Surgery for Beginners*, 93
  *Turtle Moon*, 152
  *While I Was Gone*, 117
  *White Oleander*, 33
  *Wolf Whistle*, 159
Museums
  *Crocodile Soup*, 84
Music and Musicians (See also Composers,
    Rock and Roll)
  *Amsterdam*, 115
  *The Bear Comes Home*, 64
  *A Cab Called Reliable*, 105
  *East Bay Grease*, 40
  *Goodbye Without Leaving*, 83
  *Grace Notes*, 156
  *The Ground Beneath Her Feet*, 161
  *The Healing*, 154
  *The Mark of the Angel*
  *Mister Sandman*, 96
  *The Rich Man's Table*, 132
  *Say Goodbye*, 58
  *The Song of the Exile*, 30
  *The Unconsoled*, 103
  *The Wishbones*, 123
Muslim/Christian Marriage
  *The Map of Love*, 18
Muslims
  *The Death of Vishnu*, 133
  *The Map of Love*, 18
Mystery (See also Murder)
  *Ancestral Truths*, 145
  *The Daughters of Simon Lamoreaux*, 44
  *Don't Think Twice,* 40
  *The Grand Complication*, 155
  *In the Lake of the Woods*, 121
  *Motherless Brooklyn*, 155
  *Mr. White's Confession*, 29
  *Night Train*, 145
  *Turtle Moon*, 152
  *When We Were Orphans*, 103
  *Winter Range*, 85

Mythological Creatures
  *The Minotaur Takes a Cigarette Break*, 130
Mythology (See also Irish Mythology)
  *The Ground Beneath Her Feet*, 161

National Book Award Winners
  *All the Pretty Horses*, 157
  *Charming Billy*, 157
  *A Frolic of His Own*, 151
  *Mating*, 161
  *The Shipping News*, 15
  *Waiting*, 153
National Book Critics Circle Award Winners
  *All the Pretty Horses*, 157
  *Being Dead*, 148
  *A Lesson Before Dying*, 93
  *Rabbit at Rest*, 163
  *The Stone Diaries*, 162
  *A Thousand Acres*, 17
Nazis
  *Lying with the Enemy*, 76
  *Saints and Villains*, 35
Nebraska
  *The Man Who Ate the 747*, 57
  *The Weight of Dreams*, 23
Nelson, Horatio
  *Losing Nelson*, 136
New England (See also American Northeast,
    individual states)
  *Amy and Isabelle*, 133
  *Beachcombing for a Shipwrecked God*, 29
  *Before and After*, 27
  *Host Family*, 46
  *The Hunger Moon*, 45
  *Illumination Night*, 101
  *Midwives*, 26
  *More Than You Know*, 37
  *The River King*, 101
New Hampshire (See also American
    Northeast, New England)
  *Beachcombing for a Shipwrecked God*, 27
  *Before and After*, 29
New Jersey
  *The Body Is Water*, 128
  *Henry of Atlantic City*, 125
  *The Lost Legends of New Jersey*, 125
  *Virtual Silence*, 129
New Mexico
  *Catching Heaven*, 97
  *Playing Botticelli*, 48
  *Remember Me*, 100
  *The Wilder Sisters*, 113

New South Wales, Australia (See
    also Australia)
    *Eucalyptus*, 2
New York
    *A Certain Age*, 104
    *Crazy for Cornelia*, 36
    *Dating Big Bird*, 65
    *Eddie's Bastard*
    *Empire Falls*, 127
    *Empress of the Splendid Season*, 100
    *The Fundamentals of Play*, 112
    *Geographies of Home*, 50
    *Goodbye Without Leaving*, 83
    *In the Family Way*, 128
    *Jazz*, 158
    *The Last Days of Disco with Cocktails at
        Petrossian Afterwards*, 19
    *A Lover's Almanac*, 102
    *Martin Dressler: Portrait of an American
        Dreamer*, 13
    *Nobody's Fool*, 127
    *Nothing Is Terrible*, 57
    *The Perfect Elizabeth*, 128
    *Preston Falls*, 94
    *Shadow Baby*, 115
    *The Sleep-Over Artist*, 75
    *The Sweet Hereafter*
    *This Side of Brightness*, 12
    *Triage*, 68
    *What She Saw...*, 55
New Zealand
    *Portrait of the Artist's Wife*, 68
New Zealand Authors
    *Portrait of the Artist's Wife*, 68
Newfoundland, Canada (See also Canada)
    *The Bird Artist*, 160
    *The Colony of Unrequited Dreams*, 10
    *The Shipping News*, 15
Newspapers
    *A Stranger in the Earth*, 134
Nigeria
    *Yoruba Girl Dancing*, 4
Nigerian Authors
    *Yoruba Girl Dancing*, 4
North Africa
    *The English Patient*, 122
North Carolina (See also American South)
    *Evensong*, 36
    *Foolscap*, 113
    *The Half-Life of Happiness*, 81
    *Jim the Boy*, 90

*The Many Aspects of Mobile Home Living*,
    82
*The Minotaur Takes a Cigarette Break*, 130
*Miss Julia Speaks Her Mind*, 55
*Money, Love*, 72
*My Drowning*, 97
*Six Figures*, 109
*The Slow Way Back*, 37
*Souls Raised from the Dead*, 76
*That Summer's Trance*, 127
North Dakota
    *The Grass Dancer*, 51
    *Milkweed*, 94
Nova Scotia, Canada
    *The Glace Bay Miners' Museum*, 6
Novels in Translation
    *Bordeaux*, 124
    *Bruna and Her Sisters in the Sleeping City*,
        21
    *Chronicle of the Seven Sorrows*, 5
    *The First Man*, 5
    *Judge on Trial*, 107
    *Lost*, 135
    *Madame*, 11
    *The Name*, 96
    *The Natural Order of Things*, 69
    *The Notebooks of Don Rigoberto*, 137
    *The Wind-Up Bird Chronicle*, 159
    *The Year of the Frog*, 17
Novels with Multiple Viewpoints
    *A Boy in Winter*, 28
    *The Colony of Unrequited Dreams*, 10
    *House of Sand and Fog*, 89
    *Make Believe*, 129
    *The Poisonwood Bible*, 107
    *Self-Portrait with Ghosts*, 90
    *The Road Home*, 98
    *The Story of a Million Years*, 102
    *The Sweet Hereafter*, 72
    *Three Apples Fell from Heaven*, 156
    *Why She Left Us*, 54
Nuns
    *Fierce Invalids Home from Hot Climates*, 54
    *Lying Awake*, 16
    *The Patron Saint of Liars*, 123
    *The 27th Kingdom*, 91
Nurses
    *Cereus Blooms at Night*, 118
    *Hummingbird House*, 9
    *Waiting*, 153
Nursing Homes
    *Losing Julia*, 103

Oakland, California
    *East Bay Grease*, 140
Obsession (See also Obsessive Love)
    *Crocodile Soup*, 84
    *Damascus*, 74
    *The Professor of Light*, 79
    *Seeing Calvin Coolidge in a Dream*, 86
Obsessive-Compulsive Disorder
    *Thumbsucker*, 42
Obsessive Love (See also Obsession)
    *Illumination Night*, 101
    *Losing Nelson*, 136
    *The Riders*, 141
    *The Way I Found Her*, 61
Ohio
    *The Boy in the Lake*, 59
    *Crooked River Burning*, 140
    *Skateaway*, 104
Ojibwa Indians
    *Don't Think Twice*, 40
Oklahoma
    *Paradise*, 159
Older Men/Younger Women
    *Amy and Isabelle*, 133
    *Disgrace*, 148
    *Gloria*, 12
    *Illumination Night*, 101
    *Inheritance*, 35
    *Mr. White's Confession*, 129
    *The Name of the World*, 154
    *The Story of a Million Years*, 154
Older Women/Younger Men
    *Back Roads*, 121
    *Beautiful Wasps Having Sex*, 81
    *Benjamin's Gift*, 95
    *From the Black Hills*, 135
    *Madame*, 11
    *Seventh Heaven*, 152
    *The Sleep-Over Artist*, 75
    *Tree Surgery for Beginners*, 93
    *Two Cities*, 139
    *The Way I Found Her*, 61
    *A Widow for One Year*, 103
Onassis, Jacqueline Kennedy
    *Jackie by Josie*, 51
Ontario, Canada
    *The Far Euphrates*, 132
    *The Piano Man's Daughter*, 91
    *Summer Gone*, 12
Oprah Winfrey Selection
    *Back Roads*, 121
    *A Fine Balance*, 158

*Midwives*, 26
    *The Pilot's Wife*, 58
    *White Oleander*, 33
Organized Crime
    *Dreamland*, 3
Ornithologists (See also Science and Scientists)
    *Last Things*, 121
Orphans
    *Benjamin's Gift*, 95
    *Blu's Hanging*, 142
    *Breakfast with Scot*, 87
    *Eddie's Bastard*, 108
    *A Lover's Almanac*, 102
    *A Member of the Family*, 47
    *Milkweed*, 94
    *Motherless Brooklyn*, 155
    *Nothing Is Terrible*, 57
    *Plum & Jaggers*, 131
    *Some Old Lover's Ghost*, 110
    *Water, Carry Me*, 47
    *What a Woman Must Do*, 133
Overweight Women
    *Beachcombing for a Shipwrecked God*, 29

Pacific Northwest (See also individual states)
    *The Brothers K*, 89
    *The Civil Wars of Jonah Moran*, 53
    *East of the Mountains*, 151
    *Fierce Invalids Home from Hot Climates*, 54
    *Madchild Running*, 31
    *The Sky Fisherman*, 110
Palestine (See also Middle East)
    *Louisa*, 22
Paranormal Phenomena
    *The Inner Life of Objects*, 83
Paris, France (See also France)
    *Le Mariage*, 10
    *Light at Dusk*, 34
    *The Way I Found Her*, 61
Park Rangers
    *The Hookmen*, 101
Parrots
    *Fierce Invalids Home from Hot Climates*, 54
Pedophilia
    *An Obedient Father*, 129
Pennsylvania
    *In the Presence of Horses*, 31
    *The Quilter's Apprentice*, 28
    *Snow Angels*, 122
    *Those Who Favor Fire*, 20
    *Two Cities*, 139

Peru
    *The Notebooks of Don Rigoberto*, 137
    *When Mountains Walked*, 20
Peruvian Authors
    *The Notebooks of Don Rigoberto*, 137
Pharmacists
    *Big Stone Gap*, 61
Philadelphia, Pennsylvania (See also
    Pennsylvania)
    *Tempest Rising*, 116
    *Two Cities*, 139
Philippines
    *The Umbrella Country*, 125
Philosophy
    *The Professor of Light*, 79
    *Scar Tissue*, 153
Photography and Photographers
    *The Cage*, 16
    *Eveless Eden*, 139
    *Highways to a War*, 11
    *Fool's Gold*, 18
    *The Name*, 96
    *Triage*, 68
Physical Disabilities
    *Ancestral Truths*, 112
    *Carter Clay*, 91
    *The Country Life*, 84
    *Goodness*, 123
    *Peel My Love Like an Onion*, 28
Physics
    *The Professor of Light*, 79
Pilots
    *The Pilot's Wife*, 58
    *True North*, 41
Pittsburgh, Pennsylvania (See also
    Pennsylvania)
    *Two Cities*, 139
Poets and Poetry
    *Kitty and Virgil*, 71
    *Leviathan*, 70
    *Lying Awake*, 16
    *Making Love to the Minor Poets of
        Chicago*, 84
    *Possession*, 79
    *Timbuktu*, 71
    *White Oleander*, 33
Poland (See also Eastern Europe)
    *Madame*, 11
Policemen
    *Mr. White's Confession*, 29
    *The River King*, 101
    *Winter Range*, 6

Policewomen
    *Night Train*, 145
Polio
    *Peel My Love Like an Onion*, 28
Political Fiction
    *Anil's Ghost*, 160
    *A Dangerous Friend*, 155
    *The Flower in the Skull*, 1
    *A Goat's Song*, 8
    *The Hotel Alleluia*, 55
    *Hummingbird House*, 9
    *In the Time of the Butterflies*, 2
    *Judge on Trial*, 107
    *The Last Integrationist*, 43
    *Kitty and Virgil*, 71
    *Little America*, 26
    *Loving Graham Greene*, 150
    *Madame*, 11
    *Naming the Spirits*, 134
    *Night of the Avenging Blowfish*, 63
    *An Obedient Father*, 129
    *The Ordinary Seaman*, 95
    *The Poisonwood Bible*, 107
    *The Rules of Engagement*, 147
    *Underworld*, 150
    *Water, Carry Me*, 47
    *The Wind-Up Bird Chronicle*, 159
    *The Year of the Frog*, 17
Political Prisoners
    *Hummingbird* House, 9
    *Saints and Villains*, 35
Political Unrest
    *Hummingbird House*, 9
    *In the Time of the Butterflies*, 2
    *Naming the Spirits*, 134
Politics
    *Adrian Mole: The Cappuccino Years*, 61
    *The Half-Life of Happiness*, 81
    *Lost in Translation*, 13
Pornography
    *The Man Who Wrote the Book*, 134
Portugal
    *The Natural Order of Things*, 69
Portuguese Authors
    *The Natural Order of Things*, 69
Postmodern Fiction
    *Emotionally Weird*, 70
    *A Frolic of His Own*, 151
    *Plowing the Dark*, 160
    *Underworld*, 150
Postpartum Depression
    *Grace Notes*, 156

Poverty
   *Always Outnumbered, Always Outgunned,*
      119
   *The Hiding Place,* 146
   *Joe,* 78
   *My Drowning,* 97
   *A Star Called Henry,* 88
Pregnancy
   *Felicia's Journey,* 162
   *Ruby,* 39
Premature Babies
   *The Chin Kiss King,* 62
   *The Hatbox Baby,* 78
Prisoners of War
   *Song of the Exile,* 30
Private Schools
   *Cracks,* 42
   *The River King,* 101
   *Yoruba Girl Dancing,* 4
Property Disputes
   *House of Sand and Fog,* 89
   *True North,* 41
Prophecy
   *Fierce Invalids Home from Hot Climates,* 54
Prostitutes
   *Breakfast on Pluto,* 113
   *The Mineral Palace,* 11
Provence
   *Fool's Gold,* 18
Psychiatric Hospitals
   *Crazy for Cornelia,* 36
   *The Lake Dreams the Sky,* 20
   *Memoir from Antproof Case,* 152
   *Pilgrim,* 92
Psychiatrists, Psychoanalysts,
      Psychotherapists
   *The Boy in the Lake,* 59
   *In the Family Way,* 128
   *Pilgrim,* 92
Psychics
   *The Inner Life of Objects,* 83
Psychological Fiction
   *Longleg,* 67
   *Mr. White's Confession,* 29
   *Tree Surgery for Beginners,* 93
Puerto Rican Authors
   *The House on the Lagoon,* 6
Puerto Rico
   *The House on the Lagoon,* 6
Pulitzer Prize Winners
   *The Amazing Adventures of Kavalier &
      Clay,* 82

*The Hours,* 149
*Independence Day,* 92
*Martin Dressler: The Tale of an American
   Dreamer,* 13
*Rabbit at Rest,* 163
*The Shipping News,* 15
*The Stone Diaries,* 162
*A Thousand Acres,* 17

Quebec, Canada (See also Canada)
   *Jump,* 1
Quilting
   *The Quilter's Apprentice,* 28

Race Relations (See also Racism)
   *Funny Boy,* 16
   *The Intuitionist,* 138
   *John Henry Days,* 139
   *The Last Integrationist,* 43
   *The New City,* 2
   *Right by My Side,* 99
   *This Side of Brightness,* 12
Racism
   *East Is East,* 77
   *The Healing,* 154
   *The Human Stain,* 126
   *In Troubled Waters,* 30
   *The Intuitionist,* 138
   *John Henry Days,* 139
   *A Lesson Before Dying,* 93
   *The New City,* 2
   *This Just In...,* 40
   *Trumpet,* 105
   *Wolf Whistle,* 159
Radio Stations
   *Human Voices,* 92
Rags-to-Riches Story
   *The Colony of Unrequited Dreams, 10*
   *Dreamland,* 3
   *The Glass Palace,* 35
   *Martin Dressler: The Tale of an American
      Dreamer,* 13
Ranches
   *The Loop,* 32
Rape
   *Disgrace,* 148
   *Geographies of Home,* 50
Red Guards
   *Seeing Calvin Coolidge in a Dream,* 86
Religion (See also Religious Extremism)
   *The Brothers K,* 89
   *The Hallelujah Side,* 103

*Keeping Faith*, 51
*The Name*, 96
*Some Things That Stay*, 140
Religious Extremism (See also Religion)
  *Breakfast on* Pluto, 113
  *The Brothers K*, 89
  *The Hallelujah Side*, 103
  *I Loved You All, 130*
  *The Music Lesson*, 138
  *Plowing the Dark*, 160
  *The Whereabouts of Eneas McNulty*, 146
Remarriage
  *This Is My Daughter*, 54
Research Novels
  *Foolscap*, 113
  *Possession*, 79
  *Some Old Lover's Ghost*, 110
Resorts
  *Don't Think Twice*, 40
  *The Inn at Lake Devine*, 111
Reunions
  *Acts of God*, 48
  *Leading the Cheers*, 81
Revenge
  *Winter Range*, 6
Revolution
  *When Mountains Walked*, 20
Road Novels
  *Last Things*, 121
Rock and Roll
  *Goodbye Without Leaving*, 83
  *The Ground Beneath Her Feet*, 161
  *Say Goodbye*, 58
  *The Wishbones*, 124
Romance
  *The Hand I Fan With*, 24
Romania
  *Eveless Eden*, 139
  *Kitty and Virgil*, 71
  *A Member of the Family*, 47
Runaways
  *Playing Botticelli*, 48

Sailors and Sailing
  *East Is East*, 77
San Diego, California (See also California)
  *The Answer Is Yes*, 44
San Francisco, California (See also California)
  *The Collapsible World*, 44
  *Jumping the Green*, 128
Saskatchewan, Canada
  *The Englishman's Boy*, 137

*Lost Geography*, 71
Satirical Fiction
  *Body*, 149
  *A Certain Age*, 104
  *The Country Life*, 84
  *England, England*, 73
  *Fool's Gold*, 18
  *A Frolic of His Own*, 151
  *Headlong*, 33
  *Horse Heaven*, 131
  *Leading the Cheers*, 81
  *Moo*, 131
  *Night of the Avenging Blowfish*, 63
Schiele, Egon
  *The Notebooks of Don Rigoberto*, 137
Science and Scientists (See also individual
    sciences)
  *The Answer Is Yes*, 44
  *Being Dead*, 148
  *Falling Bodies*, 45
  *Host Family*, 46
  *Mating*, 161
  *The Professor of Light*, 79
  *Last Things*, 121
  *Undertow*, 59
Scotland
  *Emotionally Weird*, 70
  *The Last King of Scotland*, 7
  *The Restraint of Beasts*, 117
Scottish Authors
  *All Quiet on the Orient Express*, 117
  *The Artist's Widow*, 112
  *Grace Notes*, 156
  *The Missing World*, 111
  *The Restraint of Beasts*, 117
  *Trumpet*, 105
Search and Rescue Teams
  *Place Last Seen*, 34
Seattle, Washington (See also Washington)
  *Bread Alone*, 39
  *Fierce Invalids Home from Hot Climates*, 49
  *The Lost Glass Plates of Wilfred Eng*, 49
  *Madchild Running*, 31
  *Plowing the Dark*, 160
Seniors (See also Aging, Elderly  Men,
    Elderly Women)
  *Julie and Romeo*, 52
Serial Killers
  *Felicia's Journey*, 162
Seventh Day Adventists (See also Religion,
    Religious Extremism)
  *Geographies of Home*, 50

Sex and Sexuality (See also Erotica)
  *Body*, 149
  *The Man Who Wrote the Book*, 134
Sex Crimes
  *Mr. White's Confession*, 29
Sexism
  *The Human Stain*, 126
  *This Just In...*, 40
Sexual Abuse (See also Child Abuse)
  *A Dangerous Woman*, 118
  *Felicia's Journey*, 162
  *Montana 1948*, 19
  *The Sweet Hereafter*, 72
  *A Thousand Acres*, 17
  *Undertow*, 59
  *The Wholeness of a Broken Heart*, 58
Sexual Adventures
  *Layover*, 143
Sexual Harassment
  *Blue Angel*, 52
Sexual Identity
  *Breakfast on Pluto*, 113
  *Cereus Blooms at Night*, 118
  *Sunday You Learn How to Box*, 141
Shanghai, China (See also China)
  *When We Were Orphans*, 103
Sheriffs
  *The End of Vandalism*, 88
  *Winter Range*, 6
Sierra Leone (See also Africa)
  *The Hotel Alleluia*, 55
Sikhs
  *Home to India*, 17
Single Fathers (See also Single Men)
  *Adrian Mole: The Cappuccino Years*, 61
  *A Hole in the Earth*, 74
Single Men
  *Bordeaux*, 124
  *Dear Will*, 23
  *Falling Slowly*, 77
  *The Handyman*, 57
  *The Honey Thief*, 96
  *Lamb in Love*, 78
  *Night of the Avenging Blowfish*, 63
  *Nobody's Fool*, 127
  *The Sleep-Over Artist*, 75
Single Mothers
  *About a Boy*, 102
  *Acts of God*, 48
  *All Quiet on the Orient Express*, 117
  *By the Shore*, 30
  *Catch Your Breath*, 24

*Dating Big Bird*, 65
*The First Man*, 5
*A Gesture Life*, 108
*The Honey Thief*, 96
*The Hunger Moon*, 45
*The Inner Life of Objects*, 83
*Jump*, 1
*The Last Samurai*, 86
*Living to Tell*, 48
*The Man of the House*, 114
*Milkweed*, 94
*MotherKind*, 123
*The Patron Saint of Liars*, 123
*Ruby*, 39
*Shadow Baby*, 115
*Turtle Moon*, 152
*Until the Real Thing Comes Along*, 25
*Windchill Summer*, 44
*The Wishing Box*, 59
Single Women
  *About a Boy*, 102
  *The Body Is Water*, 128
  *A Certain Age*, 104
  *Dating Big Bird*, 65
  *Falling Slowly*, 77
  *Fiona Range*, 118
  *Four Dreamers and Emily*, 85
  *Honeymoon: A Romantic Rampage*, 40
  *Italian Fever*, 113
  *The Ladies Auxiliary*, 47
  *Lamb in Love*, 78
  *Life Skills*, 32
  *Pink Slip*, 82
  *The Pleasing Hour*, 106
  *The Salt Dancers*, 38
  *Spiderweb*, 111
  *Truth North*, 41
  *Until the Real Thing Comes Along*, 25
  *What She Saw...*, 54
  *The Wholeness of a Broken Heart*, 58
Sioux Indians
  *The Grass Dancer*, 51
Sisters (See also Brothers and Sisters, Family
    Relationships)
  *Animal Dreams*, 106
  *Blameless*, 53
  *The Blind Assassin*, 145
  *Blue Diary*, 39
  *The Body Is Water*, 128
  *The Bubble Reputation*, 123
  *Catching Heaven*, 97
  *Caucasia*, 129

*The Collapsible World*, 44
*Dating Big Bird*, 65
*The Daughters of Simon Lamoreaux*, 44
*Durable Goods*, 25
*Falling Slowly*, 77
*The Girls*, 142
*The Hiding Place*, 146
*The Hotel Alleluia*, 55
*How the Garcia Girls Lost Their Accents*,
    67
*I Loved You All*, 130
*In the Presence of Horses*, 31
*In the Time of the Butterflies*, 2
*Jumping the Green*, 128
*Like Normal People*, 76
*One Heart*, 114
*The Perfect Elizabeth*, 128
*The Pleasing Hour*, 106
*The Poisonwood Bible*, 107
*The Slow Way Back*, 37
*Tea*, 85
*Tempest Rising*, 116
*This Is My Daughter*, 54
*A Thousand* Acres, 17
*True North*, 41
*Water Marked*, 109
*What It Takes to Get to Vegas*, 119
*The Wilder Sisters*, 113
*The Wishing Box*, 59
*Yo!*, 68
Small-Town Life
    *All Quiet on the Orient Express*, 117
    *Amy and Isabelle*, 133
    *Animal Dreams*, 106
    *Big Stone Gap*, 61
    *The Bird Artist*, 160
    *Blameless*, 53
    *Bruna and Her Sisters in the Sleeping City*,
        21
    *Chocolat*, 98
    *The Civil Wars of Jonah Moran*, 53
    *A Dangerous Woman*, 118
    *Elizabeth and After*, 83
    *Empire Falls*, 127
    *The End of Vandalism*, 88
    *Evensong*, 36
    *From the Black Hills*, 135
    *A Good House*, 79
    *The Hand I Fan With*, 24
    *The Hedge, The Ribbon*, 49
    *Icy Sparks*, 55
    *Jayber Crow*, 4

*Jim the Boy*, 90
*Lamb in Love*, 78
*The Mineral Palace*, 6
*Miss Julia Speaks Her Mind*, 55
*The Music of the Swamp*, 14
*Nobody's Fool*, 127
*Paradise*, 159
*Plainsong*, 99
*Remember Me*, 100
*The River King*, 101
*The Sharpshooter Blues*, 121
*The Shipping News*, 15
*The Sky Fisherman*, 110
*The Sweet Hereafter*, 72
*The Tall Pine Polka*, 43
*Those Who Favor Fire*, 20
*Trumpet*, 41
*Truth and Bright Water*, 106
*Water Marked*, 109
*Windchill Summer*, 44
*Winter Range*, 6
*The World Around Midnight*, 37
Sociopaths
    *The Butcher Boy*, 114
Soldiers
    *No One Thinks of Greenland*, 7
    *Soldier in Paradise*, 48
South Africa (See also Africa)
    *Age of Iron*, 148
    *Cracks*, 42
    *Disgrace*, 148
South African Authors
    *Age of Iron*, 148
    *Cracks*, 42
    *Disgrace*, 148
South America (See also individual Countries)
    *Fierce Invalids Home from Hot Climates*, 54
    *Naming the Spirits*, 134
    *The Notebooks of Don Rigoberto*, 137
South American Authors
    *The Notebooks of Don Rigoberto*, 137
South Carolina (See also American South)
    *The Fennel Family Papers*, 72
South Dakota
    *From the Black Hills*, 135
South Korea (See also Korea)
    *The Lucky Gourd Shop*, 56
South Pole
    *The Birthday Boys*, 3
South Vietnam (See also Southeast Asia,
    Vietnam)
    *Monkey Bridge*, 80

Southeast Asia
  *A Dangerous Friend*, 155
  *Highways to a War*, 11
  *Land of Smiles*, 9
  *Siam: Or the Woman Who Shot a Man*, 19
Southern Authors
  *Body*, 149
  *In Troubled Waters*, 30
  *Jim the Boy*, 90
  *Joe*, 78
  *The Many Aspects of Mobile Home Living*,
      82
  *Meely LaBauve*, 19
  *The Minotaur Takes a Cigarette Break*,
      130
  *Money, Love*, 73
  *Music of the Swamp*, 14
  *The Oxygen Man*, 142
  *Resting in the Bosom of the Lamb*, 62
  *Souls Raised from the Dead*, 76
  *The Sharpshooter Blues*, 121
  *This One and Magic Life*, 94
  *Trumpet*, 41
  *Wolf Whistle*, 159
Spain
  *Triage*, 68
Spanish Authors
  *Bordeaux*, 124
Spanish Civil War
  *Triage*, 68
Sports
  *Not a Day Goes By*, 38
Sri Lanka (See also Ceylon)
  *Anil's Ghost*, 160
  *Cinnamon Gardens*, 16
  *The Flower Boy*, 15
  *Funny Boy*, 16
  *The Reef*, 151
Sri Lankan Authors
  *The Flower Boy*, 15
St. Louis, Missouri (See also Missouri)
  *Right by My Side*, 99
St. Paul, Minnesota (See also Minnesota)
  *Mr. White's Confession*, 29
Stepfamilies (See also Stepmothers)
  *@expectations*, 53
  *Another World*, 72
  *Lily of the Valley*, 57
  *Rescue*, 126
  *Sunday You Learn How to Box*, 141
  *This Is My Daughter*, 54
  *With Your Crooked Heart*, 90

Stepmothers
  *Back When We Were Grownups*, 136
  *Rescue*, 126
Stroke Patients
  *Beachcombing for a Shipwrecked God*, 29
  *Remember Me*, 100
Suburbia
  *A Crime in the Neighborhood*, 76
  *A Gesture Life*, 108
  *Seventh Heaven*, 152
Suicide
  *The Boy in the Lake*, 59
  *The Bubble Reputation*, 123
  *Cruddy*, 73
  *Everything You Know*, 100
  *The Half-Life of Happiness*, 81
  *The Last Life*, 116
  *The Lost Legends of New Jersey*, 125
  *Madchild Running*, 31
  *My Drowning*, 97
  *Night Train*, 145
  *The River King*, 101
  *Self-Portrait with Ghosts*, 90
  *Tea*, 85
  *The Virgin Suicides*, 150
Sussex, England
  *The Country Life*, 84
Sweden
  *Frozen Music*, 29
Sydney, Australia (See also Australia)
  *Longleg*, 67
Syria
  *Fierce Invalids Home from Hot Climates*, 54

Tasmania
  *The Sound of One Hand Clapping*, 33
Teachers
  *Butterfly Lovers*, 7
  *An Invisible Sign of My Own*, 75
  *The Man of the House*, 114
  *Nothing Is Terrible*, 57
  *Plainsong*, 99
  *Plowing the Dark*, 160
  *The River King*, 101
Teenage Boys (See also Teenage Girls,
      Teenagers)
  *About a Boy*, 102
  *All the Pretty Horses*, 157
  *Almost Home*, 116
  *Back Roads*, 121
  *Before and After*, 27
  *The Boy in the Lake*, 59

*The Butcher Boy*, 114
*East Bay Grease*, 140
*Empire Falls*, 127
*Evensong*, 36
*From the Black Hills*, 135
*The Lost Legends of New Jersey*, 125
*Madame*, 11
*Meely LaBauve*, 19
*The Music of the Swamp*, 14
*The New City*, 2
*Rescue*, 126
*Right by My Side*, 99
*The River King*, 101
*The Slow Natives*, 69
*Snow Angels*, 122
*Snow in August*, 38
*Thumbsucker*, 42
*Truth and Bright Water*, 106
*Turtle Moon*, 152
*The Umbrella Country*, 125
*The Virgin Suicides*, 150
Teenage Girls (See also Teenage Boys, Teenagers)
*Almost Home*, 116
*Amy and Isabelle*, 133
*Carter Clay*, 91
*Cracks*, 42
*Cruddy*, 73
*Deep in the Heart*, 137
*Empire Falls*, 127
*The Hallelujah Side*, 103
*Illumination Night*, 101
*The Last Life*, 116
*The Lost Legends of New Jersey*, 125
*Madchild Running*, 31
*Plainsong*, 99
*The Quick & the Dead*, 140
*The Reef*, 35
*Ruby*, 39
*Some Things That Stay*, 140
*Stern Men*, 94
*A Thirst for Rain*, 80
*The Virgin Suicides*, 150
*Virtual Silence*, 129
Teenage Love (See also Teenage Boys, Teenage Girls, Teenagers)
*Almost Home*, 116
*The Feast of Love*, 74
Teenage Pregnancy
*Plainsong*, 99
*A Thirst for Rain*, 80

Teenagers
*Almost Home*, 116
*The Boy in the Lake*, 59
*Carter Clay*, 91
*Empire Falls*, 127
*The Feast of Love*, 74
*The Hallelujah Side*, 103
*Jump*, 1
*The Lost Legends of New Jersey*, 125
*The New City*, 2
*Right by My Side*, 99
*The River King*, 101
*The Slow Natives*, 69
*Truth and Bright Water*, 106
*The Virgin Suicides*, 150
*Virtual Silence*, 129
Television
*Plum & Jaggers*, 131
*This Just In...*, 40
Tennessee
*The Ladies Auxiliary*, 47
Terminal Illness (See also Cancer, Illness)
*Dear Stranger, Dearest Friend*, 24
*East of the Mountains*, 151
*Iron Shoes*, 95
*The Journey Home*, 122
*MotherKind*, 124
*The Promise of Rest*, 160
*The Saving Graces*, 34
*Souls Raised from the Dead*, 76
Terrorists and Terrorism (See also Violence)
*Leviathan*, 70
*Plum & Jaggers*, 131
*A Star Called Henry,* 88
Tesla, Nikola
*Crazy for Cornelia*, 36
Texas
*Apologizing to Dogs*, 84
*Deep in the Heart*, 137
*Duane's Depressed*, 46
*How All This Started*, 34
*Mosquito*, 154
*The World Around Midnight*, 37
Thailand
*Land of Smiles*, 9
*Siam: Or the Woman Who Shot a Man*, 19
Theater (See also Actors and Acting)
*The Answer is Yes*, 44
*Jump*, 1
Theologians and Theology
*Saints and Villains*, 35

Thumb Sucking
  *Thumbsucker*, 42
Tijuana, Mexico (See also Mexico)
  *Esperanza's Box of Saints*, 31
Toronto, Canada (See also Canada)
  *The Rules of Engagement*, 147
Tourette's Syndrome
  *Icy Sparks*, 55
  *Motherless Brooklyn*, 155
Transvestites
  *Breakfast on Pluto*, 113
Tree Surgeons
  *Tree Surgery for Beginners*, 93
Trees
  *Eucalyptus*, 2
  *Tree Surgery for Beginners*, 93
Trials
  *Midwives*, 26
Triangle Shirtwaist Factory Fire
  *Dreamland*, 3
Triangles
  *The End of Violence*, 88
  *Home to India*, 17
  *A Stairway to Paradise*, 132
Trinidad (See also Caribbean)
  *A Thirst for Rain*, 80
Trinidadian Authors
  *A Thirst for Rain*, 80
Truck Drivers
  *Mosquito*, 154
Tuberculosis (See also Illness, Terminal
    Illness
  *Some Things That Stay*, 140
Tucson, Arizona (See also Arizona)
  *The Flower in the Skull*, 1
Tunnels
  *This Side of Brightness*, 12
Twins
  *Crocodile Soup*, 84
  *In the Country of the Young*, 147
  *Shadow Baby*, 115
  *This One and Magic Life*, 94
  *A Trick of Nature*, 46
  *White Teeth*, 162

Uganda (See also Africa)
  *The Last King of Scotland*, 7
Uncles
  *Self-Portrait with Ghosts*, 90
  *Jim the Boy*, 90
Unsolved Crimes
  *The Daughters of Simon Lamoreaux*, 44

Upper Classes
  *Cinnamon Gardens*, 16
  *Crazy for Cornelia*, 36
  *Crooked River Burning*
  *Evening*, 157
  *The Fundamentals of Play*, 112
  *Gloria*, 12
  *Half a Heart*, 27
  *The Last Days of Disco with Cocktails at
    Petrossian Afterwards*, 19
  *Loving Graham Greene*, 150
  *The Weekend*, 80
U.S. Army
  *No One Thinks of Greenland*, 97
Utopian Novels
  *Mating*, 161

Vancouver, Canada (See also British
    Columbia, Canada, Canada)
  *The Jade Peony*
Vermeer, Johannes
  *The Music Lesson*, 138
Vermont (See American Northeast, New
    England)
  *Blue Angel*, 52
  *A Dangerous Woman*, 118
  *Last Things*, 121
  *Midwives*, 26
  *This Time Last Year*, 101
Veterinarians
  *Disgrace*, 148
  *While I Was Gone*, 117
Vietnam
  *A Dangerous Friend*, 155
  *The Sea of Trees*, 48
Vietnam Veterans
  *Carter Clay*, 91
  *In the Lake of the Woods*, 121
  *The New City*, 2
Vietnam War (See also Vietnam, Vietnam
    Veterans)
  *The Brothers K*, 89
  *Highways to a War*, 11
  *In the Lake of the Woods*, 121
  *Land of Smiles*, 9
  *Monkey Bridge*, 80
  *Pay It Forward*, 39
  *Soldier in Paradise*, 48
  *Windchill Summer*, 44
Vietnamese Authors
  *Monkey Bridge*, 80

Violence (See also Terrorists)
   *Anil's Ghost*, 160
   *Being Dead*, 148
   *The Butcher Boy*, 114
   *Cracks*, 42
   *Disgrace*, 148
   *A Fine Balance*, 158
   *Funny Boy*, 15
   *The Paperboy*, 150
   *Pay It Forward*, 39
   *Paradise*, 159
   *The Persian Bride*, 5
   *Plowing the Dark*, 160
   *Six Figures*, 109
   *True North*, 41
   *Virtual Silence*, 129
   *Water, Carry Me*, 47
   *The Weight of Dreams*, 23
   *The Whereabouts of Eneas McNulty*, 146
Virginia
   *Big Stone Gap*, 61
Virtual Reality
   *Plowing the Dark*, 160

Waitresses
   *The Hunger Moon*, 45
Wales
   *The Walking Tour*, 85
   *The Hiding Place*, 146
War (See also specific wars)
   *The Persian Bride*, 5
Washington (See also Seattle, Washington)
   *The Civil Wars of Jonah Moran*, 53
   *East of the Mountains*, 151
   *Plowing the Dark*, 160
   *Undertow*, 59
Washington, D.C.
   *A Crime in the Neighborhood*, 76
   *Monkey Bridge*, 80
   *Night of the Avenging Blowfish*, 63
Watches
   *The Grand Complication*, 155
West Africa
   *The Hotel Alleluia*, 55
West Indians
   *The 27th Kingdom*, 91
West Virginia
   *Gloria*, 12
Wichita, Kansas
   *Living to Tell*, 120
Widowers
   *East of the Mountains*, 151

Widows
   *The Artist's Widow*, 112
   *Back When We Were Grownups*, 136
   *Empress of the Splendid Season*, 100
   *An Imaginative Experience*, 138
   *Jim the Boy*, 90
   *Miss Julia Speaks Her Mind*, 55
   *Ruby*, 39
   *The 27th Kingdom*, 91
   *The Wilder Sisters,* 136
Wilderness
   *Summer Gone*, 12
Wildlife
   *Skywater*, 14
Winnipeg, Canada (See also Canada)
   *Larry's Party*, 130
Wolves
   *The Loop*, 32
Women Artists
   *The Artist's Widow*, 112
   *Portrait of the Artist's Wife*, 68
Women in Prison
   *White Oleander*, 33
Women Scientists (See also Science and
   Scientists, individual sciences)
   *Undertow*, 59
Women's Friendships
   *Beachcombing for a Shipwrecked God*, 29
   *The Book Borrower*, 156
   *Blue Diary*, 39
   *Bread Alone*, 39
   *Dear Stranger, Dearest Friend,* 24
   *Friends for Life*, 64
   *Hood*, 87
   *The Hunger Moon*, 45
   *Listening Now*, 69
   *London Holiday*, 50
   *Mosquito*, 154
   *The Quilter's Apprentice*, 28
   *Resting in the Bosom of the Lamb*, 62
   *Ruby*, 39
   *The Saving Graces*, 34
   *Solar Storms*, 153
   *The Tall Pine Polka*, 43
   *This Just In...*, 40
   *Working Parts*, 25
   *Yoruba Girl Dancing,* 4
Women's Lives
   *The Blind Assassin*, 145
   *The Hiding Place*, 146
   *The Hours*, 149
   *The Journey Home*, 122

Women's Lives (*cont.*)
*Milkweed*,
*Spiderweb*, 11
*The Stone Diaries*, 162
*When Mountains Walked*, 20
*A Widow for One Year*, 103
Woolf, Virginia
*The Hours*, 149
Working Classes
*Crooked River Burning*, 140
*Empire Falls*, 127
*Joe College*, 50
*The Ordinary Seaman*, 95
*The Restraint of Beasts*, 117
*The Sound of One Hand Clapping*, 33
*Windchill Summer*, 44
World War I
*Another Country*, 72
*Leaping Man Hill*, 31
World War II
*Charlotte Gray*, 32
*The English Patient*, 122
*The Far Euphrates*, 132
*A Gesture Life*, 108
*Human Voices*, 92
*The Jade Peony*, 5
*The Journey Home*, 122
*The Jukebox Queen of Malta*, 48
*The Kitchen God's Wife*, 60
*Last Days of Summer*, 107
*Last Orders*, 133
*Louisa*, 22
*Lying with Enemy*, 76
*The Mark of the Angel*, 9
*Saints and Villains*, 35
*Some Old Lover's Ghost*, 110
*The Sea of Trees*, 48
*The Song of the Exile*, 30

World's Fairs
*The Hatbox Baby*, 78
Writers and Writing
*Beautiful Wasps Having Sex*, 81
*Blue Angel,* 52
*Dangerous Woman*, 118
*East is East*, 77
*Everything You Know*, 100
*The Feast of Love*, 74
*Foolscap*, 113
*Frozen Music*, 29
*The Hours*, 149
*Italian Fever*, 113
*Jackie by Josie*, 51
*Kitty and Virgil*, 71
*Leviathan*, 70
*Making Love to the Minor Poets of Chicago*, 84
*The Man Who Wrote the Book*, 134
*The Paperboy*, 150
*Pink Slip*, 82
*The Plagiarists*, 28
*Portrait of the Artist's Wife*, 68
*Possession*, 79
*Some Old Lover's Ghost*, 110
*Timbuktu*, 71
*The Way I Found Her*, 61
*A Widow for One Year*, 103
Wyoming
*Fencing the Sky*, 7

Zionism
*Louisa*, 22
Zoology and Zoologists (See also Science and Scientists, Women Scientists, individual sciences)
*Being Dead*, 148

# Author/Title Index from *Now Read This*

The author/title index is arranged as follows:

Titles in **boldface italic** are main entries, with page numbers in **boldface** indicating the main entry and those in regular typeface referring to the "Now try" sections. Main entries for authors are in **boldface** type. Authors in regular typeface and titles in *italics* are listed in the "Now try" sections.

*. . . and Ladies of the Club*, 3
***The 13th Valley*, 49**
***1959*, 49**, 52, 155
***1988*, 16**
***21 Sugar Street*, 76,** 128
*The 26th Man: One Minor League Pitcher's Pursuit of A Dream*, 111
*The Abbess of Crewe*, 36
Abbey, Edward, 19–20
***Abbreviating Ernie*, 67, 76,** 140
Abe, Kobo, 286
**Abeel, Erica, 29**, 110
*About A Boy*, 171
*Abra*, 122
**Abraham, Pearl, 1**, 12, 57, 161, 210
*Absalom, Absalom*, 19, 25
*Absent Friends*, 132
***Absolute Truths*, 172**
**Abu-Jaber, Diana, 29**
***The Acacia*, 294**
*The Accident*, 10
*An Accidental Man*, 198
***The Accidental Tourist*, 50, 64, 139, 157, 234,** 235
*According to Mark*, 275
*Accordion Crimes*, 20
Achebe, Chinua, 2, 52, 287, 298
*The Acid House*, 272
**Ackerman, Karl, 30**, 90
Ackroyd, Peter, 257
*The Acorn Plan*, 194
***Act of the Damned*, 249**
*An Act of Treason*, 176
*The Activist's Daughter*, 34
*Actors*, 87
*Acts of Fear*, 273
***Acts of Love*, 78**
*Ada*, 284

*Adaku & Other Stories*, 287
Adam, Ruth, 86
**Adams, Alice**, 112, **115**, 190
Adams, Richard, 19
**Adebayo, Diran, 115**
**Adler, Renata, 247**, 279, 298
*The Adrian Mole Diaries*, 149, 156
*The Advent Calendar*, 276
*The Aerodynamics of Pork*, 159
*Affliction*, 34, 88, 122, 179, 260
*African Passions and Other Stories*, 94
*African Visas: A Novella and Stories*, 26
***After Moondog*, 90, 221**
***After Roy*, 77, 88, 93, 129, 231**
***After the War*, 174, 189**
***Afterlife*, 164, 196**
*Against All Hope*, 125
***Against Gravity*, 54**
*Agassiz: A Novel in Stories*, 128
*The Age of Grief*, 25
*The Age of Innocence*, 1, 3
***Age of Iron*, 256**
*The Age of Wonders*, 271
Agee, James, 198, 209
**Agee, Jonis**, 38, 79, **116**, 195, 234
*The Agony and the Ecstasy*, 166, 174, 219
***The Aguero Sisters*, 125, 264**
Aikath-Gyaltsen, Indrani, 11
*Ain't Gonna Be the Same Fool Twice: A Novel*, 102
*Akenfield*, 139
**Akins, Ellen, 30**, 206
***Alamo House: Women Without Men, Men Without Brains*, 39**
*Alaska*, 20
**Albert, Mimi**, 14, **30**, 117
**Alberts, Laurie, 30**
***Alburquerque*, 3**

*The Alchemist*, 6
Alder, Ken, 45
Alexander, Karl, 63, 90
**Alexander, Lynne**, 72, **116**
**Alexander, Meena, 2**
*The Alexandria Quartet*, 5, 26
**Alexie, Sherman**, 14, 109, **116**, 144
Algren, Nelson, 209
*Alias Grace*, 219
*Alice at 80*, 294
*Alice in Bed*, 98
*Alice in Wonderland*, 272
*Alice: A Novel*, 55
*Aliens of Affection: Stories*, 210
*All the Days and Nights*, 280
*All the Little Live Things*, 227
*All My Friends Are Going to Be Strangers*,
        117
*All My Relations: An Anthology of
        Contemporary Native Fiction*, 14
*The All of It*, 62
*All the Pretty Horses*, 3, 107, 193, **280**
*All Quiet on the Western Front*, 174, 251, 294
*All Souls*, **279**
*All Souls' Day*, 84
*All Souls' Rising*, 24, 125
*All Summer Long*, **60**, 230
*All-Bright Court*, **209**, 241, 282
**Allende, Isabel**, 6, **31**, 65, 169, **247, 248**
*Alligator Dance*, 205
**Allison, Dorothy**, 121, 124, 146, 153, 166,
        182, 197, 238, **248**
Allison, Karen Hubert, 94
*Almanac of the Dead*, 137, **223**
*AlmA Mater: A College Homecoming*, 15
*Almost Famous*, 224
*Almost Heaven*, 277, 300
*Almost Innocent*, 21, **40**, 185, 240
*Alone*, 224
**Alpert, Cathryn**, 35, **117**
*Already Dead*, 272
**al-Shaykh, Hanan, 1**, 133, 203
**Alther, Lisa**, 74, **117**, 132
**Alvarez, Julia, 2**, 11, 21, 29, **117, 118**, 169,
        296
*Always and Forever*, 15
**Amado, Jorge, 2**, 24, 25
*The American Ambassador*, 24, **176**
*Americana*, 259
*An American Brat*, 23
*American Dad*, 67
*American Heaven*, 46, 117

*American Knees*, 184, **244**
*American Owned Love*, 5, 142
*American Pastoral*, **290**
*American Pie*, **110**
Ames, Jonathan, 67, 100, **118**
**Amis, Kingsley, 118**, 204, 239
**Amis, Martin, 31**, 74, 127, 137, 209, 239, 263
*Amnesia*, **144**, 276
*Among Birches*, 170
*Among the Ginzburgs*, 203
*Amongst Women*, **193**
*Amsterdam*, 281
*Anagrams: A Novel*, 83
Anand, Valerie, 79
*The Anatomy Lesson*, **290**
*Anatomy of Restlessness: Selected Writings*,
        139
**Anaya, Rudolfo, 3**, 11, 107, 118, 136, 139
*Ancestral Truths*, 34, 208, 237, **277**
*The Ancient Child*, **196**
*Ancient Evenings*, 188
*And All Our Wounds Forgiven*, 274
*And the Band Played On*, 164
*And Venus Is Blue: Stories*, 66
Anderson, Alison, 83
**Anderson, Jessica**, 72, **118**, 262, 271, 275
**Anderson, Jim, 3, 31**
**Anderson-Dargatz, Gail, 119**
*Andorra*, 130
*Angel Angel*, **227**
*Angel City*, 19
*Angela's Ashes*, 36
Angelou, Maya, 274
*Angels and Insects*, 149
*Angie, I Says*, 37, **242**
*The Angle of Repose*, 180, 227, 261
*Animal Acts*, **77**
*Animal Dreams*, 47, **179**
*Animal Husbandry*, **113**
*Anita and Me*, **230**
*Aniyunwiya, Real Human Beings: An
        Anthology of Contemporary Prose*, 45
*Anna Delaney's Child*, 26
*Annie John*, **72**, 258
*Anna Karenina*, 282
*The Anna Papers*, **58**, 153
*Another Roadside Attraction*, 95
*Another Way Home: A Single Father's Story*, 26
**Ansa, Tina McElroy, 31**
**Ansay, A. Manette, 32**
**Anshaw, Carol, 248**, 286

*An Answer in the Tide*, 98
*Answers to Lucky*, 89
*Antarctic Navigation*, 22, 121
*The Antelope Wife*, 154
Anthony, Patricia, 59, 250
***Antonia Saw the Oryx First*, 26**
Antrim, Donald, 209
**Antunes, Antonio Lobo, 249**
***Any Old Iron*, 253**
***Anywhere But Here*, 202, 224**
***Apes and Angels*, 32**
**Appel, Allan, 32**
Appelfeld, Aharon, 167, 271, 287
*The Apple in the Dark*, 92
**Appleman, Philip, 32**
**Appleton, Janet, 33**
*Appointment in Samarra*, 159
*The Apprenticeship of Duddy Kravitz*, 21
*Aquamarine*, 248
***Arabian Jazz*, 29**
*The Arabian Nightmare*, 174
***Arcadia*, 257, 287**
***The Archivist*, 257**
*Are We Not Men: Stories*, 226
***Are You Mine?*, 158, 180**
*Arkansas: Three Novellas*, 274
*Armadillo in the Grass*, 49
*Armadillo*, 129
Arnold, Bruce, 166
**Arnold, Janis, 18, 33, 60**
*Arranged Marriage*, 86
***Arrogance*, 166, 219**
*Art and Ardor*, 287
***The Art Fair*, 130, 186**
*The Art Lover*, 280
*The Art of the Knock*, 266
*The Art of Starvation: A Story of Anorexia and
   Survival*, 214
**Arthur, Elizabeth, 22, 33, 121, 142**
***An Artist of the Floating World*, 69, 189, 271**
*Arts and Sciences*, 16
Arvin, Reed, 231
*As I Lay Dying*, 19, 25, 251
*As Max Saw It*, 38, 251, 253
***As She Climbed Across the Table*, 68, 77, 289**
Ascher, Carol, 212
Ashour, Linda, 72
Asinof, Eliot, 73
**Aslam, Nadeem, 249**
*The Aspern Papers*, 68
*The Assassins: A Book of Hours*, 202
***The Assault*, 283, 299**

**Astley, Thea, 40, 119**
*Asya: A Novel*, 270
*At the Bottom of the River*, 72
*At Home in Mitford*, 64, 69
*At Home with the Glynns*, 75
*At Play in the Fields of the Lord*, 84
*At Risk*, 74, 220, 252
*At Seventy*, 78, 216
***At the Sign of the Naked Waiter*, 169**
*At Weddings and Wakes*, 100, 162, 280
*Athletes and Artists: Stories*, 96
**Atkinson, Kate, 84, 119, 178**
*Atlas Shrugged*, 108
**Atlas, James, 33**
*Attachments*, 96
***Atticus*, 166, 167**
**Atwood, Margaret, 61, 83, 101, 110, 120,
   128, 164, 183, 217, 219, 279**
**Atxaga, Bernardo, 249**
**Auchincloss, Louis, 3, 251**
***Audrey Hepburn's Neck*, 5, 135, 171, 178**
Auerbach, Jessica, 63
***August*, 96**
***Augusta Cotton*, 52**
***Aunt Julia and the Scriptwriter*, 236, 288**
*Auntie Mame*, 214
*AurorA* 7, 16
Austen, Jane, 94, 191
**Auster, Paul, 34, 150, 270**
***Author from a Savage People*, 207**
*The Autobiography of Miss Jane Pittman*, 164,
   264, 274
*The Autobiography of My Mother*, 132, 147
*Autumn of the Patriarch*, 265
*Ava*, 280
*The Awakening*, 164, 199, 255, 262
*Away*, 299
*An Awfully Big Adventure*, 121

*B. F.'s Daughter*, 251
**Ba, Mariama, 120, 293**
**Babcock, Richard, 34**
*Babel Tower*, 195, 254
Babel, Isaac, 259
*Babette's Feast*, 53, 75
*The Baby Boat: A Memoir of Adoption*, 145
*Baby Doctor*, 74
***Baby of the Family*, 31**
*Babycakes*, 191
**Bache, Ellyn, 34, 108**
*Bachelor Brothers' Bed & Breakfast*, 179
*Bachelorhood: Tales of the Metropolis*, 187

*Back East*, 203
*The Back of the Tiger*, 259
*The Bacon Fancier*, 67
***Bad Angel*, 37**
*Bad Haircut: Stories of the 70s*, 207
*Bad Land: An American Romance*, 22
Badami, Anita Rau, 159
*Badenheim, 1939*, 256
***Bailey's Café*, 94, 156, 200**
**Bainbridge, Beryl**, 19, 22, 56, 83, **121**
Baker, Calvin, 184
Baker, Dorothy, 65, 112
**Baker, Larry, 35**
Baker, Nicholson, 133, 157, 261
**Baker, Sharlene, 35**, 117
Bakis, Kirstin, 70
Baldwin, James, 208
**Baldwin, William, 35**, 285
*The Ballad of the Sad Café*, 200
**Ballantyne, Sheila**, 70, **121**
**Ballard, J. G., 3**, 31, 32, 85
*Balls: A Novel*, 73
Banbury, Jen, 172
*Bang the Drum Slowly*, 73, 111
**Banks, Lynne Reid**, 13, **121**
**Banks, Russell**, 34, 50, 88, **122**, 124, 179,
    191, 210, **250**, 252, 260
Bantock, Nick, 51
Bao, Ninh, 268
***Baotown*, 238**
*Bar Stories: A Novel After All*, 147
**Barfoot, Joan, 122**, 139, 264
Barich, Bill, 108
**Barker, Pat, 250**, **251**, 254, 300
*Barking Man and Other Stories*, 125
**Barnard, Josie, 35**
**Barnes, Julian**, 133, **251**, 265
Barnes, Kim, 162, 243
**Barnhardt, Wilton**, 46, **122**
*The Barracks Thief*, **243**
*Barrayar*, 160
**Barrett, Andrea**, 12, **123**
Barry, Lynda, 230
Barth, John, 123, 232
**Barthelme, Donald, 123**
**Barthelme, Frederick**, 34, **123**
**Bartolomeo, Christina, 36**, 113, 234
Basso, Hamilton, 89, 131
*Bastard Out of Carolina*, 121, 141, 146, 153,
    166, 182, 238, **248**
**Bauer, Douglas, 36**, 280

*Baumgartner's Bombay*, **146**
**Bausch, Richard**, 50, 78, **124**
**Bawden, Nina, 36**, 44
**Baxter, Charles, 37**, 93
Bayer, Valerie Townsend, 254
***Beach Boy*, 102, 149, 168, 236, 261**
*Beach Music*, 257
*The Beach*, 9, **12**, 232
*Beachcombing for a Shipwrecked God*, 67
*Beaches*, 91
*Beachmasters*, 119
Beagle, Peter, 102
Beals, Melba Patillo, 49
*Beaming Sonny Home*, 140
***The Beans of Egypt, Maine*, 141**, 151, 206, 248
***The Bear Comes Home*, 74, 112**
***The Bear Went Over the Mountain*, 31, 74,**
    112, 137, 226
*Bear*, 67, 77, 129
**Beattie, Ann**, 101, 123, **124**, 207, 267
*Beautiful Girl*, 115
*A Beautiful Mind*, 162
***The Beautiful Mrs. Seidenman*, 104**, 262
*The Beautiful Room Is Empty*, 241
*Bech at Bay: A Quasi Novel*, 236
***Bech Is Back*, 236**
*Bech: A Book*, 236
Beckerman, Ilene, 36
*Becoming a Man: Half a Life Story*, 196
***Bed Rest*, 53, *69***
*Beecher*, 192
***The Beet Queen*, 154**, 155
*Before and After Zachariah*, 75
***Before and After*, 42**, 78, 218, 250
*Before Women Had Wings*, 72
*The Beginner's Book of Dreams*, 126, 212
***Beginning the World Again*, 24**, 176
**Begley, Louis**, 38, **251**, 253
***Behind the Scenes at the Museum*, 79, 84,**
    **119**, 120, 178
**Behr, Mark, 4**, 7
*Being There*, 74, 135, 181
*Beirut Blues*, 203
***Beka Lamb*, 153**
*The Bell Jar*, 61, 100, 238
**Bell, Betty Louise, 124**, 155
**Bell, Christine, 124**
**Bell, Madison Smartt**, 24, **125**
**Bellow, Saul**, **125**, 278, 291
***Bellwether*, 176, 242, 246, 283**
***Belonging*, 105**

*Beloved*, 282
**Ben Jelloun, Tahar, 252**
Benchley, Peter, 281
Benedict, Elizabeth, 126, 211
**Benedict, Helen, 37**
**Benedict, Pinckney, 4**
*Benediction at the Savoia*, **88**
Benitez, Sandra, **4**, 6, 19, 168, 261
**Bennett, James Gordon, 37**, 168
Benski, Stanislaw, 287
Benson, E. F., 10
**Beresford-Howe, Constance**, 72, **126**
**Berg, Elizabeth**, 51, 91, **126**, 135, 182, 221
**Bergen, David, 37**
**Berger, John, 38**
**Berger, Thomas, 38**, 146, 281
**Bergland, Martha, 38**, 159
*Berlin Game*, 300
Berne, Suzanne, 61
Berriault, Gina, 41
Berry, Wendell, 111
*The Best Little Girl in the World*, 77, 214
*Best Nightmare on Earth*, 160
*The Best There Ever Was*, 40
*The Bestseller*, 17
*Betrayed by Rita Hayworth*, 289
***The Bean Trees*, 179**
**Betts, Doris**, 50, 65, 160, 220, **252**
*Between Earth and Sky*, 89
*Beyond the Bedroom Wall*, 155
*Beyond Deserving*, 219
**Bhabra, H. S., 4**
**Bhattacharya, Keron, 5**
*Bicycle Days*, 218
***Big Babies*, 79, 179**
*Big Bad Love*, 19
***The Big Ballad Jamboree*, 48**
*The Big Rock Candy Mountain*, 227
*The Big Sleep*, 283
*The Bigamist's Daughter*, 280
*Bigfoot Dreams*, 211, 294
***Biggest Elvis***, 2, **15**, 80, 176
*Bilgewater*, 39, 52, 145, 159, 184
***Billarooby***, 3, **31**
**Billington, Rachel, 127**, 210
**Bills, Greg, 127**
*Billy Bathgate*, 177, 260, 261
*Billy Dead*, 248
*Billy Phelan's Greatest Game*, 273
Binchy, Maeve, 51
***Binding Spell*, 33**, 142
**Binding, Tim, 127**

*Binstead's Safari*, 67
***The Bird Artist*, 19**, 20, 121, 201, 206, 276
**Bird, Sarah, 39**
*Birds of America*, 83
*Birds of the Innocent Land*, 16
**Birdsell, Sandra**, 120, **128**
*Birdsong*, 59
***The Birthday Boys***, 19, 22, 56, 83, **121**
*Bitter Grounds*, 4, 6
*Bitteroot Landing*, 213
*Black and Blue*, 212
*Black Box*, 203, 222
*The Black Brook*, 150, 289
*Black Cherry Blues*, 18
***Black Dogs*, 281**
***The Black Envelope***, 199, **278**
*Black Gold*, 43
*Black Idol*, 25
*Black Mountain Breakdown*, 89, 295
*The Black Prince*, 284
*Black Swan*, 269
*Black Tickets*, 207
*The Black Velvet Girl*, 210
**Black, Baxter, 39**
**Blackaby, Mark, 39**
*Blackbird Days*, 140
*Blacker Than a Thousand Midnights*, 229
**Blanchard, Stephen, 39**
*Bleak House*, 264
*The Bleeding Heart*, 101
*Bleeding London*, 242
*Bless Me, Ultima*, 3, 11, 118, 136
***A Blessing On the Moon*, 102**, 296
*Blind Date*, 181
***The Blindfold***, 34, 250, **270**
*Blindness*, 265, 293
***Bliss*, 135**
*Blood and Orchids*, 178
*Blood Lines*, 89
*Blood Meridian*, 4, 253
*Blood of Requited Love*, 289
*Blood Red, Sister Rose*, 71
*Blood Tie*, 220
*Bloodline: Odyssey of a Native Daughter*, 165
**Bloom, Amy, 128**
**Bloom, Steven**, 116, **128**
*Blow the House Down*, 250
***Blu's Hanging***, 37, **245**
*Blue Calhoun*, 170, 210
*The Blue Flower*, 263
***The Blue Hour*, 155**
***Blue Italian*, 141**

*The Blue Mountain*, **23**
*The Blue Nature*, **56**
*Blue Rise*, **170**
*Blue River*, **134**
*Blue Rodeo*, 80, 171
*Blue Ruin*, 73
*Blue Skin of the Sea*, **22**, 173
*Blue Spruce*, 276
*Blue Windows*, 121
*Bluebird Canyon*, **192**
*Blueprints*, **107**
*Blues for An Alabama Sky*, 46
*Blues for the Buffalo*, 3
*The Bluest Eye*, 186, 238, 282
Blythe, Ronald, 139
*Boat People*, **57**, 135
*Bob the Gambler*, 123
*Bobby Rex's Greatest Hit*, **59**
*Bodily Harm*, 217
*Body and Soul*, 281
*The Body Is Water*, 103, 197, **218**
*Body of Knowledge*, 25, **49**, 225, 232
*Body of Water*, 57
**Bohjalian, Chris, 40**, 42, 53, 66, 88, 89, 146,
   199, 250
Boissard, Janine, 72
*The Bone People*, **270**
*Bone*, 104, **200**
*The Bonfire of the Vanities*, 17
*Bonneville Blue*, 139
*The Book Class*, **3**
*The Book of Candy*, **152**
*The Book of Famous Iowans*, **36**, 280
*The Book of Jamaica*, 122
*The Book of Knowledge*, 285
*The Book of Laughter and Forgetting*, 180, 273
*The Book of Marvels*, 77
*Book of Medicines: Poems*, 269
*The Book of Mercy*, 256
*A Book of One's Own*, 16
*The Book of Phoebe*, 102
*The Book of Reuben*, **73**
*The Book of Ruth*, 63, **166**
*The Book of Saints*, **21**
*The Book of Secrets*, **27**, 249, 294
*The Book of Uncommon Prayer*, 199
*The Bookshop*, **10**, 271
*Bop*, 46
*Borrowed Time: An AIDS Memoir*, 196
**Boswell, Robert, 5**, **129**, 142
**Bosworth, Sheila**, 21, **40**, 240

Bouldrey, Brian, 274
*Bound for Glory*, 48
*Bound to Violence*, 298
*Boundaries*, 24
Bourjaily, Vance, 197
Bowen, Elizabeth, 191, 250, 267
**Bowen, John, 40**
*The Box Garden*, 222
*Box Socials*, 73
*The Boy Who Went Away*, 42, **162**, 210
*The Boy Without a Flag: Tales of the South
   Bronx*, 95
*Boy's Life*, 35, 61, **80**, 171, 208
*A Boy's Own Story*, 18, **241**
**Boyd, Blanche McCrary, 129**, 211
Boyd, Brendan, 73
**Boyd, William, 77**, 88, 93, **129**, 161, 231
*The Boyfriend School*, 39
*Boyhood: Scenes from Provincial Life*, 256
Boyle, T. Coraghessan, 68, 76, 81, 107, **130**,
   240, **252**
Bracewell, Michael, **130**
**Bradbury, Malcolm**, 34, **130**, 177, 276
**Bradley, John Ed, 41**
**Brady, Maureen**, 99, **130**
*Braided Lives*, 92, 300
*Brain Fever*, **216**
*Brain Storm*, 51
**Brainard, Cecilia Manguerra, 41**, 53, 72
Brand, Dionne, 190
Brandt, Nat, 40
*The Brass Bed*, 190
*Brazil*, 298
*Brazzaville Beach*, 77, 88, 93, **129**, 161, 231
*Break and Enter*, 276
*Break Point*, 101
*Breakfast on Pluto*, 14
*Breaking Point*, 101
**Breasted, Mary, 41**, 54
*Breath, Eyes, Memory*, 72, **258**
*Breathing Lessons*, **234**
*A Breed of Heroes*, 68
*A Breeze Called the Freemantle Doctor:
   Poems/Tales*, 58
*Briarpatch*, 15
*The Bride Price*, 52
*The Bride Who Ran Away*, 202
*The Bride*, 23
*Brideshead Revisited*, 271
*A Bridge Between Us*, **100**
*Bridget Jones's Diary*, **156**
*Brief Lives*, 58

*Bright Angel Time*, **82**, 135, 165
*Bright Lights, Big City*, 17, 67, 100, 228
*Brightness Falls*, **17**
Brin, David, 99
*Bring Larks and Heroes*, 71
*Bring Us the Old People*, 10, 67, **103**, 121,
    282, 283
**Bringle, Mary, 41**, 57, 295
**Brink, Andre, 42**, 157, 176, 255
Brittain, Vera, 300
**Brizzi, Enrico**, 65, **131**, 207
**Brook, Rhidian, 42**
*The Brooklyn Book of the Dead*, 162
**Brookner, Anita**, 42, 251, **253**, 263
*The Broom of the System*, 299
*Brotherly Love*, 260
*Brothers and Keepers*, 241
*Brothers and Sisters*, **45**
*The Brothers K*, 31, 34, 52, 95, 134, 136, **150**,
    183, 207, 209, 257, 295
*Brothers*, 34, 123
*Brown Girl, Brownstones*, 190
**Brown, Alan, 5**, 135, 171, 178
**Brown, John Gregory**, 18, **131**
**Brown, Larry**, 19, **253**
Brown, Linda Beatrice, 184
**Brown, Rebecca**, 38, 46, **131**
**Brown, Rita Mae, 132**
**Brown, Rosellen, 42**, 78, 117, **132**, 147, 210,
    216, 218, 250
Brownmiller, Susan, 32, 99, 149, 155
Bruchac, Joseph, 45
*Bruno's Dream*, 131, 284
*The Bubble Reputation*, 125
**Buchan, James, 42**
*Bucking the Sun*, **9**
*The Buddha of Suburbia*, 83, 115, **181**, 182
*Budding Prospects*, 130
*Buffalo Afternoon*, 89, **217**, 286
Buffong, Jean, 190
Bujold, Lois McMaster, 160
Bulgakov, Michael, 68
*The Bungalow*, 157
*Bunker Man*, 272
**Bunkley, Anita, 43**
*Burger's Daughter*, 256, 266
**Burgess, Anthony, 253**
Burke, James Lee, 18
*Burning the Days: Recollections*, 222
*Burning Down the House: Essays of Fiction*,
    37
*The Burning House*, 124

*Burning Patience*, 9, **24**, 90
*Burning*, 175
**Burns, Olive Ann**, 35, **43**, 97, 132, 240, 296
*Burr*, 166
**Burroway, Janet, 43**, 82
**Busch, Frederick**, 13, 53, 64, 70, **132**, **133**,
    140, 142, 150, 160, 167, 234, 250, 252
**Bushell, Agnes, 44**
*The Bushwhacked Piano*, 193
**Busia, Akosua, 133**
*The Business of Fancydancing*, 116, 144
**Buss, Louis**, 36, **44**, 249, 258
*Busted Scotch: Selected Stories*, 272
*Buster Midnight's Café*, 17, **48**, 156, 200
**Butler, Robert Olen**, 58, **133**, 135, 267
**Buttenwieser, Paul**, 44, 100
*By the River Piedra I Sat Down and Wept*, **6**
**Byatt, A. S.**, 13, 85, 149, 151, 173, 179, 195,
    **254**, 256

**Cady, Jack, 44**, 62, 174
*Caetana's Sweet Song*, **92**
*The Cage*, 12, 20, **22**, 121
Cain, Chelsea, 143
*Cal*, **188**
Caldwell, Erskine, 206
*California's Over*, 68
*California Rush*, 179
*California Time*, 54
*Call It Sleep*, 124
Callahan, John, 216
Cambor, Kathleen, 256
*Camelot*, 94
**Cameron, Peter**, 56, 130, **134**
**Campbell, Bebe Moore, 45**
Campbell, Helen, 72
**Camus, Albert, 6**, 261
*Can't Quit You, Baby*, **148**, 163, 205
*Candide*, 54
**Canin, Ethan, 134**
*The Cannibal Galaxy*, **287**
*A Cannibal in Manhattan*, 67
Cantor, Jay, 26, 121, 125
*Cantora*, **78**
**Canty, Kevin, 134**
**Cao, Lan**, 106, **134**
Capote, Truman, 188
*Captain Pantoja and the Special Service*, 236
*The Cardboard Crown*, 232
*The Caretaker*, 73
**Carey, Jacqueline, 135**

**Carey, Peter, 135**, 243
**Carillo, Charles, 136**
**Carkeet, David, 45**, 130, 183, 219
*Carnival Wolves*, 213
**Carpenter, William, 45**, 123
*Carpenter's Gothic*, 264
**Carr, J. L., 254**, 287
Carroll, James, 88, 250
Carroll, Jonathan, 133
Carroll, Lewis, 272
*Carry Me Back*, 48, 231
*Carry Me Home*, 49
*Carson Valley: A Novel*, 108
**Carter, Angela, 136**, 151, 229, 233, 240, 243, 295
Cary, Lorene, 252
*The Case of the Gilded Fly*, 82
*A Case of Knives*, 82
**Casey, John, 254**
*Cast a Spell*, 207
**Castedo, Elena, 6**
**Castillo, Ana, 136**
*Casualties*, 13, **121**
*Cat's Eye*, 83, **120**, 128
*Catch 22*, 147, 260
*Catch Your Breath*, 63
*The Catcher in the Rye*, 122, 131, 150, 243, 261
***Catching the Light*, 92**, 103, 204
**Cates, David, 137**
Cather, Willa, 22, 195, 198
*Caucasia*, 76, 197, 238, 295
*Caveat*, 176
*Cavedweller*, 124, 197, 248
*The Caveman's Valentine*, 162
*The Caves of Guernica*, 249
*The Cay*, 12
*The Cazelet Chronicle*, 51, 79
*Cecile*, 72
**Cela, Camilo Jose, 137**
*Celebration*, 71, 72, 181, 211, **220**
*Celestial Navigation*, 60, 234
*The Cement Garden*, 281
*Ceremony in Lone Tree*, 198
*Ceremony*, 223
**Chabon, Michael, 31**, 74, **137**, 189, 215, 226
**Chace, Susan, 46**, 230
**Chai, May-Lee, 138**
Chamberlin, Ann, 220
**Chamoiseau, Patrick, 2**, 8, **255**
*The Champion*, 159
*A Chance to See Egypt*, **70**, 218

*A Chancer*, 272
Chandler, Raymond, 283
**Chandra, Vikram, 8**, 9, **138**, 196
Chang, Jung, 138
*A Change of Climate*, 159, 275, 279
*Changing Heaven*, 254, 299
*Changing Places*, 34, 182, 276, 279
*The Chant of Jimmie Blacksmith*, 71
**Chappell, Fred, 138**
*Charades*, 167, **269**
*Charlie Chan Is Dead: An Anthology of Contemporary Asian-American Literature*, 244
*Charlotte's Web*, 7
*Charming Billy*, 280
***Charms for the Easy Life*, 122**, 139, **160**, 192, 200, 205, 264
Charters, Samuel, 211
**Chase, Joan, 78**, **138**, 198, 290
*Chasing Shadows*, 8
*Chatterton*, 257
**Chatwin, Bruce, 139**
**Chavez, Denise, 78**, 79, **139**
***Cheap Ticket to Heaven*, 224**, 260
**Cheek, Mavis, 139**
*The Cheerleader* (MacDougall), 59, 83, 91, 131
*The Cheerleader* (McCorkle), 192
***Cheerleaders Can't Afford to Be Nice*, 97**
Cheever, Benjamin, 90
Cheever, John, 236
**Chernoff, Maxine, 46**, 117
Cheuse, Alan, 32
*Chevrolet Summers, Dairy Queen Nights*, 60
***Chez Chance*, 164**, 177
*Chicano in China*, 3
*The Child in Time*, 64
*Child of Darkness: Yoko and Other Stories*, 286
*Child of the Holy Ghost*, 249
*The Children in the Woods*, 132
*The Children of Dynmouth*, 222, 297
***Children of Light*, 228**, 272
*The Children's Crusade*, 131
**Childress, Mark, 43**, 80, **140**, 176, 206
Childs, Craig, 20, 66
*Chilly Scenes of Winter*, 124, 207
*Chimney Rock*, 225
*The Chin Kiss King*, 6
*Chin Music*, 81
**Chin, Frank, 140**
*Chinaman's Chance*, 15

*China Boy*, 7, 140, 141, **183**
*Chinchilla Farm*, **57**
*The Chinese Western: Short Fiction from Today's China*, 238
*The Chocolate War*, 71
**Choi, Susan**, 189, **255**
Chong, Denise, 141, 184
Chopin, Kate, 164, 199, 254, 262
*The Chosen*, 96, 228
**Chowder, Ken**, 133, **140**
**Choy, Wayson, 141**, 184, 200
*The Christie Caper*, 98
Christman, Rick, 244
*The Chrome Suite*, 120, **128**
*Chronicle of a Death Foretold*, 238, **265**
**Chute, Carolyn, 141**, 151, 206, 248
*The Chymical Wedding*, 254, **256**
*The Cider House Rules*, **173**, 180
Ciment, Jill, 224
*The Circle of Reason*, 265
*Circles of Deceit*, **36**, 44
*Circles on the Water*, 92
**Ciresi, Rita, 141**
Cisneros, Sandra, 107, 118, 136
*Cities of the Plain*, 193
*Cities of Salt*, 249
*A City in Winter*, 268
*City of Childhood*, 254
*City of Glass*, 34, 270
*City of the Mind*, 18
*City*, 70
*Civil Wars*, 117, **132**
*The Clairvoyant*, 183, 232
**Clark, Robert**, 36, 62, **255**
**Clarke, Lindsay**, 254, **256**
*Claudine and Annie*, 212
*Clay Walls*, **213**
**Cleage, Pearl, 46**
*Clear Light of Day*, 2, **8**, 291
*Clearwater Summer*, **70**
Clewlow, Carol, 239
*The Cliff*, 294
*The Clock Winder*, 108, 227, 234, 237
*Clockers* (Ford), 122
*Clockers* (Price), 95, **211**, 239
*The Cloning of JoannA May*, 68, 239
*Close Quarters*, 268
*Closed Circle*, 59
*Closely Akin to Murder*, 98
*Closer to the Sun*, 158
*Closet Case*, 241
*Closing Arguments*, 133

*Cloud Chamber*, 88, 148
*Cloudsplitter*, 122
*Cloudstreet*, 120, 163, **243**, 253, 300
*Clover*, 215
Cobb, Thomas, 281
**Cobbold, Marika, 142**
Coccioli, Carlo, 288
*Cockpit*, 181
*The Cockroaches of Stay More*, 109
*Coda*, 119
**Coelho, Paulo, 6**
**Coetzee, J. M.**, 157, 189, **255**
*Coffee Will Make You Black*, **102**
**Cohen, Jon**, 33, 49, **142**, 144, 208, 212, 255, 286
**Cohen, Leah Hager, 47**
*A Cold Day for Murder*, 20
*Cold Mountain*, 290
*Cold Sassy Tree*, 35, **43**, 97, 132, 240, 296
*Cold Spring Harbor*, **300**
*Cold Times*, 166
Colette, 212
*Collaborators*, **178**
*Collected Stories* (Babel), 259
*Collected Stories* (McGahern), 41; 193
*The Collected Stories* (Paley), 207
*The Collected Stories* (Trevor), 297
*Collected Stories, 1948-1986*, 198
*The Collector Collector: A Novel*, 263
Collier, John, 138
Collier, Zena, 67
**Collignon, Rick**, 5, 107, 139, **142**
Collins, Larry, 5
*The Colonel's Daughter and Other Stories*, 297
*The Colony*, 61
*The Color Purple*, 163, **237**, 248
*Colored People*, 182
**Colwin, Laurie**, 57, 108, **143**, 232, 251, 276
*Come and Go, Molly Snow*, 48, 59, **231**
*Come Back, Dr Caligari*, 123
*Come to AfricA and Save Your Marriage*, 26, 129
*Come to Me*, 128
*Comedians*, 182
*The Comfort of Strangers*, 281
*Comfort Woman*, 6, 8, 58, 135, **178**, 189, 197, 245
*The Comforts of Madness*, **216**
*Coming Attractions*, 140, 156
*The Coming of Rain*, 189
*The Commitments*, 149, 207

*Common Ground*, 7
*The Company of Women*, 162
*The Complete Stories*, 271
*Compromising Positions*, 152
*Compulsory Happiness: Four Novellas*, 278
Conan, Allan, 63
*The Conclave*, 130
*The Concubine's Children*, 141, 184
*A Confederacy of Dunces*, 152, 189, **233**
*Confederates*, 71
*Confessions of a Failed Southern Lady*, 59
*The Confessions of Nat Turner*, 296
*Confessions of Summer*, 187
**Connaughton, Shane, 7**
Connell, Evan, 222
Conrad, Joseph, 12
Conrad, Pamela, 34
Conroy, Frank, 281
**Conroy, Pat**, 19, 131, 150, 200, 201, 116,
    232, **257**
*The Conservationist*, 284
*Consider This Home*, **127**
*Consider This, Senora*, 261
*Constancia and Other Stories for Virgins*, 158
**Constantini, Humberto, 143**, 146
*Continent*, 257
*Continental Drift*, **122**, 124, 191, 260
*Conundrum*, 297
*The Conversations at Curlew Creek*, 278
*The Conversion of Chaplain Cohen*, 32
**Cook, Karin**, 47, **143**, 225
**Cook-Lynn, Elizabeth, 144**
Cookson, Catherine, 50, 58
*A Cooler Climate*, 67
**Cooley, Martha, 257**
**Coomer, Joe**, 67, **144**, 212, 255
Cooper, Bernard, 163
**Cooper, Douglas, 144**, 276
Cooper, Michael H., 77
*Copper Crown*, 237
Corbin, Steven, 43
*Corelli's Mandolin*, 236, **258**, 282, 287
**Corey, Deborah Joy, 47**
**Corman, Avery, 47**
Cormier, Robert, 71
*The Corner of Rife and Pacific*, **22**
*Coronation*, 9
Cortazar, Julio, 48
*The Cost of Living*, 84
*The Counterlife*, **290**
*Counting Coup: A Novel*, 58

*The Country Ahead of Us, the Country
    Behind*, 62
*The Country Girl*, 285
*The Country Road*, 119
*The Country*, **209**
*The Coup*, **298**
**Coupland, Douglas, 47**
*The Court Jesters*, 287
**Courtenay, Bryce**, 4, **7**, 141, 184
Covington, Dennis, 52, 194
**Covington, Vicki, 144**
**Cowan, Andrew, 7**
*Cowboys Are My Weakness*, 117, 181, 226
**Coyle, Beverly**, 131, **145**, 270
**Crace, Jim, 257**, 287
*Cracking India*, **23**
*Crane Spreads Wings: A Bigamist's Story*,
    93, 113, 186, **234**
*Crash Diet*, 33, 192
*Crazy Heart*, 281
*Crazy in Alabama*, 43, **140**, 206
*Crazy in Love*, 93, **94**
*Crazy Ladies*, 110
*Crescendo*, 176
Crews, Harry, 18, 253
*Crime and Punishment*, 288
*A Crime in the Neighborhood*, 61
*Criminals*, 36, 84, 150, **275**
Crispin, Edmund, 82
*Critical Care*, 51
*The Crook Factory*, 90
*Crooked Hearts*, 5
*Crooked Little Heart*, 101
*Cross Channel*, 251
Cross, Amanda, 96
*Crossing Blood*, **73**, 128
*Crossing Over Jordan*, 184
*Crossing Paths: Encounters with Animals in
    the Wild*, 20, 66
*Crossing to Safety*, 75, 78, 118, 160, **227**, 229
*The Crossing*, 193
*The Crow Eaters*, 23
*Crows Over A Wheatfield*, **99**
*Crows*, 50
*Crucial Conversations*, 251
*Cry, the Beloved Country*, 287
*The Crying Heart Tattoo*, 171
*The Crystal Cave*, 253
*The Crystal World*, 3
Cunningham, Laura, 81
**Cunningham, Michael, 257**
*Cupid & Diana*, **36**, 113, 234

*The Cure for Death by Lightning*, **119**
*A Cure for Dreams*, 160
*Cured by Fire*, 194
**Currey, Richard, 48**, 84

*D'Arconville's Cat*, 292
Dagan, Avigdor, 287
Dailey, Janet, 30
*Daisy Fay and the Miracle Man*, 140, 156
*Daisy Miller*, 175
***Dale Loves Sophie to Death***, 26, **146**
**Dallas, Sandra**, 17, **48**, 156, 200, 203
*Dalva*, 133, 160, 165, **167**, 195
*Damage*, 133, **167**
*Damascus Gate*, 228, 260, 273
*Damballah*, 241
*Dance Dance Dance*, 283
*Dance Me Outside: More Tales from the
      Erminesken Reserve*, 73
*The Dancer Upstairs*, 23
***Dancer with Bruised Knees*, 81**
*Dancing After Hours*, 213
*Dancing at the Rascal Fair*, 9
*Dancing at the Victory Café*, 73
*Dancing in the Movies*, 5
**Dangarembgo, Tsitsi, 145**
*A Dangerous Woman*, **197**
**Dann, Patty**, 42, 131, **145**, 157
**Danticat, Edwidge**, 72, 190, **258**
*The Dark*, 193
*Darkest England*, 51, **269**
*Darkness Visible*, 161
*Darkness Visible: A Memoir of Madness*, 296
**Darling, Diana, 8**, 138, 196
Dart, Iris, 91
*Darwin's Ark*, 32
*Daughter of Jerusalem*, 277
*Daughters of the House*, 11
*Daughters of Memory*, 18, 33, 60
*Daughters of the New World*, 101
*Daughters*, **190**
**Davenport, Kiana, 8**, 106, 178
Davidson, Catherine Temma, 53, 156, 226
**Davidson, Donald, 48**
Davidson, Leif, 249
**Davies, Robertson**, 173, 223, 241, **258**, 299
Davis, Kathryn, 101
**Davis, Thulani, 49**, 52, 102, 155, 237
**Davis-Gardner, Angela, 146**
Davis-Goff, Annabel, 70
*Davita's Harp*, 1, 15, 209
**Dawkins, Louisa, 8**

*Dawn*, 10
**Dawson, Carol**, 25, **49**, 225, 232
Dawson, Janet, 74
*A Day No Pigs Would Die*, 7
*The Day of the Locust*, 177
*The Day of the Scorpion*, 23
*Days and Nights on the Grand Trunk Road*,
      110
**de Bernieres, Louis**, 236, **258**, 287
**De Botton, Alain, 259**
de LaClos, Choderlos, 133
*Dead Babies*, 253
*The Dead Father*, 123
***Dead Languages***, 34, 37, **223**
*Deadwood*, 260
***The Dean's December*, 125**, 126
**Deane, Seamus**, 14, 16, 42, 135, **259**, 286
*Dear Digby*, 92
***Dear James*, 64**, 71
*Dear Once*, 15
*A Death in the Family*, 198
*Death in Venice*, 5
*Death of An Alaskan Princess*, 30
*The Death of Artemio Cruz*, 158
*The Death of Che Guevara*, 26, 121, 125
*The Death of the Heart*, 191, 267
***Debatable Land*, 82**
*The Debt to Pleasure*, 53, 75
*The Debut*, 253, 263
*The Decatur Road*, 144
***Decorations in a Ruined Cemetery*, 131**
**Dee, Jonathan**, 40, 143, **146**, 217, 258
***The Deep End of the Ocean***, 108, **196**, 218,
      248
*Defending Civilization*, 88
*Defiance*, 280
Deighton, Len, 300
Del Castillo, Michel, 137
**Del Vecchio, John, 49**
*Delicate Geometry*, 140
**DeLillo, Don**, 56, 83, 121, **259, 260**
*Delmore Schwartz: the Life of An American
      Poet*, 34
*Delta Wedding*, 110
***Deluge***, 148, 229
Denker, Henry, 179, 230, 250
Dennis, Patrick, 214
*Depth Takes a Holiday*, 187
**Desai, Anita**, 2, **8**, **146**, 291
**Desai, Kieran, 9**, 146
*Desert Images*, 20
*Desert Solitaire*, 20

*The Destiny of Nathalie "X" and Other Stories*, 129
*The Devil's Dream*, 48
***The Devil's Own Work***, **68**
**Dew, Robb Forman, 146**
***Dewey Defeats Truman***, **16**, 21
**Dexter, Pete**, 34, 88, 130, 179, 191, 225, 253, **260**
*Dexterity*, 36
*The Dharma Bums*, 14
*Dharma Girl*, 143
*Di and I*, 76
***the Diamond Lane***, 164, **177**, 187
*The Diaries of Jane Somers*, 119, 122
*The Diary of Emily Dickinson*, 179
*Diary of a Mad Housewife*, 70
*The Diary of a Magus*, 6
Dickens, Charles, 173, 264
**Dickinson, Charles**, 18, **50**, 57, 72
Dickinson, Peter, 88, 231
*Did You Love Daddy When I Was Born?*, 78
Didion, Joan, 247
*Difficult Women: A Memoir of Three*, 209
*A Difficult Young Man*, 232
Dillard, Annie, 185
*Diminished Capacity*, 179
Dinesen, Isak, 53, 75, 279, 284
*Dingley Falls*, 56, 150, 165, 188, 257
***Dinner at the Homesick Restaurant***, **235**
*Dinosaurs in the Attic: An Excursion into the American Museum of Natural History*, 93
*The Dirty Duck*, 61
*Dirty Work*, 253
*A Disaffection*, 272
*Disappearing Acts*, 64, 194
***Disappearing Moon Café***, **184**
*The Discovery of Heaven*, 283
*The Disinherited*, 137
*Dispatches*, 268
***The Distance from the Heart of Things***, **108**
*The Distinguished Guest*, 195
***Disturbances in the Field***, 161, **218**, 270
Divakaruni, ChitrA Banerjee, 53, 86
***Divine Concepts of Physical Beauty***, **130**
***Divine Secrets of the Ya-Ya Sisterhood***, 40, 228, **239**
*Divining Blood*, 80
*Division of the Spoils*, 23
*Divorcing Daddy*, 234
*Dixie City Jam*, 18
**Dixon, Melvin, 50**

**Dixon, Stephen, 50**
***Do Lord Remember Me***, **274**
*Do the Windows Open?*, 22, 145, 150, 172
*Do With Me What You Will*, 202
**Doane, Michael, 147**
**Dobyns, Stephen**, 97, 132, **147**
*Doctor Criminale*, 130
*Doctor Faustus*, 68
*Doctor Rat*, 109
**Doctorow, E. L.**, 16, 81, 177, 219, **260**, **261**, 268
**Dodd, Susan M.**, **50**, 168
**Doerr, Harriet**, 38, 219, **261**
***Dog Days***, **139**
*Dog Soldiers*, 228
***Dogeaters***, 23, **164**
***Dogs of God***, **4**
*The Dogs of March*, 101
***Dogs, Dreams, and Men***, **70**
**Doig, Ivan**, **9**, 11, 185
*Doing Battle: the Making of A Skeptic*, 222
*The Dollmaker*, 111
*Domestic Pleasures*, 62
Dominick, Andre, 81
*Don't Call It Night*, 203
*Don't Tell Alfred*, 211
*Don't Worry, He Won't Get Far on Foot*, 216
***Donald Duk***, **140**
*Dona Flor and Her Two Husbands*, 2
Donleavy, J. P., 189
**Donnelly, Frances**, **51**
**Donnelly, Nisa**, **147**
**Donoso, Jose**, **9**
**Dooling, Richard**, **51**, 129, 269
***The Dork of Cork***, 37, 40, 142, 144, 151, **212**, 216
**Dorris, Michael**, 88, 116, **148**, 155
Dostoyevsky, Fyodor, 288
***Double Fault***, **101**
*Double Negative*, 45, 130, 183, 219
*Double Yoke*, 52
**Douglas, Ellen**, **148**, 163, 205
**Dove, Rita**, **148**
*The Dower House*, 70
***Down by the River***, **285**
*Down these Mean Streets*, 95
**Doyle, Roddy**, 7, 32, 99, **149**, 155, 207, 221, 227, 236, 297
*Dr. Neruda's Cure for Evil*, 112
**Drabble, Margaret**, 44, 66, 103, **149**, 254, 284
*Dream Boy*, 163

*DreamEden*, **26**
*Dreamers*, 165
*Dreaming in Cuban*, 125, 265
*Dreaming: A Novel*, 160
***Dreams of the Centaur***, 2, **11**
*Dreams of Dead Women's Handbags:
    Collected Stories*, 276
***Dreams of My Russian Summers***, **277**
*Dreams of Sleep*, 49, **172**
*The Dreyfus Affair*, 76
*A Drinking Life: A Memoir*, 106, 166
*Drinking: A Love Story*, 66, 106, 161
***The Drowning Season***, **170**
*Drugstore Cowboy*, 209
*Drunk with Love*, 58
*The Drunkard*, 159
**Drury, Tom**, 38, 133, **149**, 234, 275, 289
*A Dry White Season*, 42
Duane, Daniel, 201
*Duane's Depressed*, 60
***Dubin's Lives***, **278**
Dubus, Andre, 213
*Due East*, 216
*Dues: A Novel of War and After*, 77
***Duet for Three***, **122**, 139, 264
*Duet*, 55
Duff, Alan, 270
**Duffy, Bruce, 150**
**Dufresne, John**, **150**, 213, 215
*The Duke of Deception*, 81
DuMaurier, Daphne, 59
**Duncan, David James**, 31, 34, 52, 95, 134,
    136, **150**, 183, 207, 209, 257, 295
**Duncker, Patricia**, **151**, 181, 254
**Dundon, Susan**, **51**
Dunkel, Elizabeth, 96
**Dunmore, Helen**, **151**
**Dunn, Katherine**, 117, **151**, 211
**Duong, Thu Hong**, **152**
*Duplicate Keys*, 25
*Durable Goods*, 126, 221
**Duras, Marguerite**, 44, 133, **261**
Durenmatt, Frederick, 143
***During the Reign of the Queen of Persia***,
    **138**, 198, 290
Durrell, Lawrence, 5, 26
*A Dutiful Daughter*, 178
**Dworkin, Susan**, 141, **152**
Dwyer, Kelly, 33
*The Dying Art*, 273
***Dying Young***, 76, 232
***The Dylanist***, **198**

*Early Disorder*, 63, 214
*Early from the Dance*, 19
*Earthly Possessions*, 50, 234, 267
*Ease*, 159
***East Is East***, **130**
*The Easter Parade*, 300
*Easy Keeper*, 231
***Easy Travel to Other Planets***, **83**
***The Easy Way Out***, 39, 158, 176, **192**, 202
**Eberstadt, Fernanda**, 130, **152**, 186
*Echo House*, 146, 273
***An Echo of Heaven***, **286**
*Eden's Close*, 101
**Edgarian, Carol**, **152**
*The Edge of the Crazies*, 27, 193
*The Edge of Paradise: America in Micronesia*,
    15
*The Edge of Time*, 22
**Edgell, Zee**, **153**
**Edgerton, Clyde**, 43, 104, 138, 142, **153**
*The Edible Woman*, 101, 120, 279
*Edisto Revisited*, 210
***Edisto***, **210**
***Edson***, 48, **84**
*The Education of
    H\*Y\*M\*A\*N\*K\*A\*P\*L\*A\*N*, 219
Edwards, Samuel, 249
*Edwin Mullhouse: the Life and Death of an
    American Writer, 1943–1954*, 18, 112,
    236
**Egan, Jennifer**, 58, **153**
**Ehrlich, Gretel**, **10**, 180
*Eight Men Out*, 73
*Eight Months on Ghazzah Street*, 1, 159, 279
***Einstein's Dreams***, 68, 87, **274**
*Eleanor*, 77
*Election: A Novel*, 207
*The Electric Kool-Aid Acid Test*, 82
*The Electrical Field*, 13, 228
*Elementary Education*, 202
*Eleni*, 13
*The Elephant Vanishes: Stories*, 283
*Eleven Hours*, 224
**Elkin, Stanley**, 32, 103, 119, **154**, **262**, 285
*Ellen Foster*, 97, 160
**Ellis, Erika**, 32, **51**, 64
**Ellison, Emily**, **52**
**Ellmann, Lucy**, 53, **154**
*Elvis Presley Calls His Mother After the Ed
    Sullivan Show*, 210
**Emecheta, Buchi**, **52**, 287
*Emerald City*, 153

*Emily L.*, 261
*Emma*, 191
**Emma Who Saved My Life**, 46, **122**
*Emperor of the Air*, 134
**Empire of the Sun**, **3**, 31, 32, 85
*The Empty Book*, 237
*The Enchantment of Lily Dahl*, 250, 270
Enchi, Fumiko, 59
*Encore: A Journal of the Eightieth Year*, 216, 227
*The End of the Hunt*, 14
*The End of Tragedy: Four Novellas*, 67
**The End of Vandalism**, 38, 116, 133, **149**, 234, 275
*End Zone*, 260
Ende, Michael, 275
*Endgame: A Journal of the Seventy-Ninth Year*, 216, 227
**Endless Love**, 134, 144, **295**
*Endurance: Shackleton's Incredible Voyage*, 121
*Enduring Love*, 192, 275, 281
Engel, Marian, 67, 77, 129
**Engel, Monroe**, **154**
**The English Patient**, 257, 258, 275, **287**
Ephron, Delia, 78
**Epstein, Leslie, 10**
*Equal Affections*, 274
*Equal Distance*, 274
Erdman, Loula Grace, 22
**Erdrich, Louise**, 116, 124, 148, **154**, **155**
**Erhart, Margaret, 52**
*Eric*, 65
**Errands**, **62**
**The Error of Our Ways**, **45**, 130
*Esau*, 23
**Espinosa, Maria, 155**
**Esquivel, Laura, 52**, 75, 154, 171, 247
**Estaver, Paul, 53**, 183, 222, 230
*Eternal Curse on the Reader of these Pages*, 289
**Eugenides, Jeffrey**, 55, 200, **262**, 280
*EurekA Street: A Novel of Ireland Like No Other*, 242
**Evans, Elizabeth, 155**
*Eve's Apple*, 63, **214**
*Eveless Eden*, 74, 126, 147, 278, **300**
*Even Cowgirls Get the Blues*, 95, 117, 163
*The Evening of the Holiday*, 267
*The Evening Wolves*, 78, 139
*Evening*, 196
*Evensong*, 160

*Ever After*, 118
*The Everlasting Story of Nory*, 157, 261
*Every Day Gets A Little Closer: A Twice-Told therapy*, 112
*Every Man for Himself*, 56
*Every Woman Loves A Russian Poet*, 96
**Eva Luna**, **247**
*The Evolution of Jane*, 36, 98
*Excellent Women*, 94
*Excursions in the Real World: Memoirs*, 297
**Excuse Me for Asking**, **33**
**The Executioner's Song**, **188**
*The Exes*, 72
Exley, Frederick, 159
*Exodus*, 17
**An Experiment in Love**, 159, **278**
*An Explanation for Chaos*, 218
*An Explanation of the Birds*, 249
**Exposure**, 133, **267**
**Exquisite Corpse**, **174**
*Extra Innings: A Memoir*, 61, 227
**The Extra Man**, 67, 100, **118**
*The Eye in the Door*, 250, 251

*Fables of the Irish Intelligentsia*, 54
*A Face at the Window*, 281
**Face of an Angel**, 78, 79, **139**
**Face of a Stranger**, **112**
**Face**, 142, **208**
**Faces in the Moon**, **124**, 155
*Fading, My Parmacheene Belle*, 219
**Failure to Zigzag**, **106**
**Fair and Tender Ladies**, **294**
*Fair Augusto and Other Stories*, 267
*Fair Game*, 175
Fairbairn, Ann, 73
*A Fairly Honorable Defeat*, 38
*Faith Fox*, 142
**Fakinou, Eugenia, 156**
*Falconer*, 170
*The Fall of the Sparrow*, 13
**Fall on Your Knees**, 8, 66, **79**
*The Fall*, 6
**The Falling Boy**, 108, 110, **276**
*Falling in Love at the End of the World*, 244
**Falling in Place**, **124**
*Falling Towards England*, 174
**False Starts**, 92, ***103***
**False Years**, 215, **237**
*Fame and Folly*, 287
**Familiar Heat**, **66**, 68, 80, 90, 224
*Families and Survivors*, 112, 115

*Family Happiness*, 57, **143**, 232, 251
*The Family Heart: A Memoir of When Our Son Came Out*, 147
*Family Life*, 250
*Family Linen*, 89, **225**, 295
*The Family Markowitz*, 12, 15, 22, 85, 172
*Family Matters*, 55
*Family Matters: Why Homeschooling Makes Sense*, 62
*Family Money*, 36
*Family Night*, **55**
*Family Pictures*, **195**, 199, 281
*Family Planning*, 204
*Family Resemblances*, 30, 34, **206**, 290
*The Family*, 209
*Family*, 265
*The Family*, 52
*The Famished Road*, **287**
*Famous Last Words*, 54
*A Fan's Notes*, 159
*A Far Cry from Kensington*, 27, 94, 98, 207, **295**
*The Far Euphrates*, **228**
*Faraway Places*, 145, 226
*The Farewell Symphony*, 241
*Farewell, I'm Bound to Leave You*, 138
*A Farm Under a Lake*, **38**
*The Farming of Bones*, 190, 258
Farr, Judith, 257
Farrell, J. G., 16
Fast, Howard, 32
*Fat Lightning*, 89
*The Fat Woman's Joke*, 68
*Fatal Light*, 48
*Father and Son*, 253
*Father Melancholy's Daughter*, 160, 197
*Fathers*, 265
*The Fatigue Artist*, 218
*FatA Morgana*, 103
Faulkner, William, 19, 25, 43, 251, 262, 297
Faulks, Sebastian, 59
*Fault Lines*, 2
*Fear of Flying*, 29, 300
*Fear*, 226
*Fearful Symmetry*, 127
*Feast in the Garden*, 263
*A Feast of Snakes*, 253
*Feather Crowns*, 111
*A Feather on the Breath of God*, **87**
**Feldman, Ellen, 53**, 55
*Felice*, 146
*Felicia's Journey*, 239, **297**

**Fenkl, Heinz Insu**, 41, **53**
*The Fennel Family Papers*, 35
Ferrandino, Joseph, 243
**Ferriss, Lucy, 54**
*The Feud*, 38
*Fidelity: Five Stories*, 111
*The Field of Vision*, 198
**Fielding, Helen, 156**
*Fields of Glory*, **214**
*The Fiery Pantheon*, 185
*Fifth Business*, 173, 223, 241, 258
*The Fifth Child*, **185**
*Fifty Days of Solitude*, 61, 227
Files, Meg, 99
*Fima*, 203
*Final Payments*, 162
Finch, Phillip, 225
*Finding Brendan*, 88
*Finding Makeba*, **90**
*Finding Signs*, **35**, 117
**Findley, Timothy, 54**, 56, 226, 299
*A Fine and Private Place*, 102
*A Fine Balance*, 220, 266, 277, **282**
*Fine*, 44, 100
**Fink, Ida**, 104, **262**
**Finney, Ernest, 54**
*Fire on the Mountain*, 9
*Firefight*, 243
*The Fireman's Fair*, 107, 172
*The Fire-Raiser*, 159
*First Confession*, 11
*First Light* (Baxter), **37**, 93
*First Light* (Ellison), **52**
*The First Man*, **6**
**Fischer, Tibor**, 24, 31, 199, **262**
Fitzgerald, F. Scott, 134, 228
**Fitzgerald, Penelope, 10**, 13, **263**, 271
Fitzhugh, Louise, 162
**Fitzpatrick, Nina**, 41, **54**
*Five Fortunes*, 62
*Five Seasons*, 111, **245**
*Five Smooth Stones*, 73
*The Fixer*, 278
*A Flag for Sunrise*, 260, 272
**Flagg, Fannie**, 39, 48, 71, 94, 131, 139, **156**, 200, 140
*The Flamingo Rising*, **35**
Flanagan, Thomas, 14
*The Flanders Road*, 294
*Flanders*, 59, 250
**Flanigan, Sara, 55**
*Flashman in the Great Game*, 11

Flaubert, Gustave, 123
*Flaubert's Parrot*, 251
*Flesh and Blood*, 258
*Floating in My Mother's Palm*, 178, 267
*The Floating Opera*, 123
**The Floating World, 69**
*The Floatplane Notebooks*, 138
**Flokos, Nicholas, 55**, 258
*The Flood*, 212
**Flook, Maria, 55**, 153, 190
**Florey, Kitty Burns, 55**
*Florry of Washington Heights*, 128, **177**
*Flowers and Shadows*, 287
*Flowers for Algernon*, 264
*Flying Hero Class*, 178
*Flying in Place*, 98
*Flying in to Love*, 259
*Flying West*, 46
Flynn, Robert, 244
*The Fan Man*, 74, 213
Fogle, James, 209
**Follow Your Heart, 104**
**The Following Story, 87**, 208, 275, 277
*Folly*, 196
**Fontes, Montserrat, 2, 11**
*Fool's Sanctuary*, 14
*Fools Crow*, 109, 116
*Fools of Fortune*, 84, 297
**Foolscap, *188*, 276**
**Footprints, *64*, 65**
*For Colored Girls Who've Considered Suicide
  When the Rainbow Is Enuf*, 194
*For Every Sin*, 267, 287
*For I Have Sinned*, 101
*For Kings and Planets*, 134
*For Love*, 195
*For the Sake of All Living Things*, 49
*For Whom the Bells Toll*, 137
**Ford, Elaine, 156**
Ford, Ford Madox, 250
**Ford, Richard, 73**, 77, 122, **263**, 285, 299
**Foreign Affairs, *187*, 188**, 190, 275
*The Foreign Legion: Stories and Chronicles*,
  92
**The Foreign Student, 189, 255**
*Foreigner*, 20
**Forgiving, 78**
**Forms of Shelter, 146**
**The Forms of Water, 123**
Forrester, Helen, 36
Forster, E. M., 134, 233, 267
*Fortress in the Plaza*, 26

*Fortunate Lives*, 147
*Fortune Catcher*, 20
*Fortune's Daughter*, 204, 264
*The Fountainhead*, 18, 108
**Four Letters of Love, 242**
*The Four of Us: the Story of A Family*, 97
**Fowler, Connie May, 72**, 204, **263**
**Fowler, Karen Joy, 157**, 230
Fowles, John, 59, 110, 254, 284
Fox, Laurie, 210
*Foxfire: Confessions of a Girl Gang*, 153
**Foxybaby, 68**
*The Franchiser*, 154
Franklin, Miles, 119, 145
*Franny and Zooey*, 299
**Franzen, Jonathan, 54, 56**, 299
Fraser, George MacDonald, 11
*Fraud*, 251
Frayn, Michael, 44
Frazier, Charles, 290
**Free Association, 44**, 100
**Free, Suzanne, 56**
**Freed, Lynn, 42, 157**
Freedman, Samuel G., 194
*Freedom at Midnight*, 5
*Freedomland*, 211, 239
**Freeman, David, 56**
**Freeman, Judith, 57**
*The French Lieutenant's Woman*, 59
French, Albert, 73, 241
**French, Marilyn, 29, 57**, 117, 300
**The Frequency of Souls, 246**
**Freud, Esther, 145, 157**
**Fried Green Tomatoes at the Whistle-Stop
  Café**, 39, 48, 71, 94, **156**, 200, 240
**Friends for Life, 112**
**The Friends of Freeland, 274**
*Frieze*, 208
*Frog*, 50
**A Frolic of His Own, 264**
**From the River's Edge, 144**
*From the Terrace*, 255
*Frozen Desire: the Meaning of Money*, 43
**Frucht, Abby, 126, 158**, 180
*Fruit of the Month*, 158
**Fuentes, Carlos, 158**, 174
Fugard, Athol, 4, 256
**Fugitive Blue, 99**, 131, 228
**Fugitive Pieces**, 13, 58, 116, 121, 199, 257,
  258, **282**, 287, 296
*The Full Catastrophe*, 45
Fuller, Jamie, 179

*The Funeral Makers*, 20, 111, **206**
*Funny Boy*, 18, 163, **220**
**Furman, Laura**, **57**
*Further Tales of the City*, 191
Furui, Yoshikichi, 286
Fussell, Paul, 222, 251, 254

*Gabriela, Clove and Cinnamon*, 2
**Gaddis, William, 264**
**Gadol, Peter**, 108, **158**, 211, 268
*Gaff Topsails*, 20
*Gagarin & I*, **39**
Gage, Nicholas, 13
*Gain*, 25, 289
**Gaines, Ernest**, 50, 164, **264**, 274
Gaitskill, Mary, 280
*Galatea 2.2*, **288**
**Gale, Patrick, 158**
*The Galton Case*, 283
**Galvin, James**, **11**, 26, 58, 198
*The Game in Reverse: Poems*, 86
*The Game of Thirty*, 74
**Ganesan, Indira, 11**
**Garcia, Cristina**, 125, **264**
**Garcia Marquez, Gabriel**, 83, 92, 169, 238, 248, 251, **265**, 292, 293
**Gardam, Jane**, 39, 52, 142, 145, **159**, 184, 210
*The Garden of the Peacocks*, **110**
*The Garden Path*, 55
*Gardens of Stone*, 268
**Gardner, John**, 262, **265**
**Gardner, Mary**, **57**, 135
*The Garish Day*, 127, 210
**Garland, Alex**, 9, **12**, 232
*The Garlic Ballads*, 238
*The Garrick Year*, 44, 149
Gass, William, 123
*The Gate of Angels*, 10
*The Gated River*, 54
*The Gates of Ivory*, 67
**Gates, David**, 127, **159**, 222, 226, 291
Gates, Henry Louis, 182
*Gathering Home*, 145
*A Gathering of Old Men*, 264
*A Gay and Melancholy Sound*, 231, 247, 299
**Gearino, G. D.**, **58**
**Gee, Maurice, 159**
*Geek Love*, **151**, 211, 233
*The General in His Labyrinth*, 83
*Generation X*, 48
*The Genius of Desire*, 163, 274

*Gentleman's Agreement*, 229
**George Mills**, **154**
Gerber, Merrill Joan, 1
**Gernes, Sonia**, **58**
*Gerontius*, 158, **166**
Gerson, Jack, 259
*Gestures*, **4**
*The Gettin Place*, 229
*Getting Over Homer*, 158, 192, **202**
*Geyser Life*, **167**, 269, 281
Ghosh, Amitav, 265
*Ghost Dance*, **279**, 280
*A Ghost in the Music*, **201**
*The Ghost Road*, **250**, 251
*The Ghost Writer*, 137, 290, **291**
*The Giant's House*, 64, 67, 144, 151, **193**
**Gibbons, Kaye**, 97, 122, 139, **160**, 192, 200, 205, 264
Gibson, William, 83
*The Gifts of the Body*, 38, 46, 131
Gilbert, Sarah, 216
**Gilchrist, Ellen**, **58**, 153
**Gillison, Samantha**, **12**, 122
Gilmore, Mikal, 188
*The Ginger Man*, 189
**Gingher, Marianne**, **59**
Girardi, Robert, 268
*Girl in Landscape*, 77, 165
*A Girl of Forty*, **160**
*Girl with Curious Hair*, 299
*Girlfriend in A Coma*, 48
*Girls Forever Brave and True*, 94
*The Girls From the Five Great Valleys*, 17, 48, 98
*Girls in the Grass: Stories*, 106
*Girls in their Married Bliss*, 285
*The Girls of Slender Means*, 136, 279
*Girls*, 13, 64, 70, **132**, 142, 218, 234, 250, 252
*The Girls: A Story of Village Life*, **40**
Gironella, Jose Maria
*Give Me Your Good Ear*, 99, **130**
Givon, Thomas, 6
*Glad Rags*, 63
*The Glass House*, 57
*A Glass of Blessings*, **93**, 94
*Glass, Paper, Beans*, 47
*Glimmer*, 168, **238**
*Glittering Images*, 172
Gloss, Molly, 11
*Go Tell It on the Mountain*, 208
*God Bless the Child*, 53, 55
*God Bless You, Mr. Rosewater*, 108

*The God of Small Things*, 9, 25, 46, 120, 123, 151, 152, 249, 282, **291**, 292, 293
*God on the Rocks*, 142
*God's Ear*, 32, 77
*God's Grace*, 278
*God's Little Acre*, 206
*God's Pocket*, 260
*God's Snake*, **226**
**Goddard, Robert, 59**
**Godwin, Gail**, 52, 53, **160**, 197, 216, 218, 261
**Goethe, Ann, 59**
*Going After Cacciato*, 49, **285**
*Going Back to Bisbee*, 20, 179
*Going Native: A Novel*, 244
*Going to the Sun*, **81**, 86, 267, 286
*The Gold Bug Variations*, 289
**Gold, Herbert, 160**, 265
**Gold, Ivan, 161**
*Golden Days*, **98**, 175
*The Golden Gate: A Novel in Verse*, 23, 160, 191
*The Golden Notebook*, 185
*Golden States*, 258
Golden, Marita, 184
**Golding, William**, 9, 12, **161**, 180, 232
Goldsmith, Olivia, 17
**Goldstein, Rebecca**, 1, 93, **161**, 218
*Gone South*, 80
*The Good Apprentice*, 105, **284**
*Good Behavior*, 70
*The Good Brother*, **88**
*A Good Day to Die*, 193
*Good Fences*, 32, **51**, 64
*The Good Husband*, 126, **160**, 216, 261
*The Good Mother*, 63, **195**, 199
*The Good Negress*, **237**
*The Good Old Boys*, 65
*A Good Scent from A Strange Mountain*, 58, 133, 135
*The Good Times Are Killing Me*, 230
*Goodbye, Columbus, and Five Short Stories*, 290
**Goodman, Allegra**, 1, **12**, 15, 22, 85, 172
*Goodness*, **204**
*Goodnight Silky Sullivan*, 30
*Goodnight, Nebraska*, 34, **195**, 224
Goran, Lester, 88
**Gordimer, Nadine**, 4, 42, 52, 256, **266**, 284
**Gordon, Mary, 161, 162**, 222
*The Gospel According to Jesus Christ*, 293
*Gospel*, 123

**Gottlieb, Eli**, 42, **162**, 210
Gould, Lois, 36
**Gowdy, Barbara, 162**
*The Grab*, 249
*Graced Land*, 80, **176**
*The Graceful Exit*, 70
*A Gracious Plenty*, 213
**Graham, Philip, 266**
*The Grandmother's Club*, 32
*Granite Lady; Poems*, 217
**Grant, Stephanie, 60**
*The Grapes of Wrath*, 65, 122
*The Grass Dancer*, 37, **93**, 116, 148, 155, 223, 269
Grass, Gunter, 212, 267
**Grau, Shirley Ann, 163**
*Gravity's Rainbow*, 264, 289, 297
Gray, Alasdair, 297
Gray, Francine du Plessix, 247
*The Great Alone*, 30
*The Great Divide*, 109
*The Great Divorce*, **190**
*The Great Gatsby*, 134
*Great Jones Street*, 259
*The Great Pretender*, **33**
*The Great Railway Bazaar*, 232
*The Great Santini*, 226, 232, 257
*The Great War and Modern Memory*, 251, 254
*The Great World and Timothy Colt*, 251
*The Great World*, **278**
*Green Grass, Running Water*, **14**, 116, 148, 155
Green, George Dawes, 162
Green, Tim, 168
**Greenberg, Joanne, 60**, 77, 100, 162, 210
**Greene, Bob, 60**, 230
Greene, Graham, 74
**Greene, Harlan, 163**
*Greensleeves*, 33
*Griffin and Sabine, An Extraordinary Correspondence*, 51
**Griffith, Patricia Browning, 60**, 109
*The Grifters*, 253
**Grimes, Martha, 61**, 203
**Grimsley, Jim, 163**, 248, 266
*The Grisly Wife*, 165
**Grossman, Judith, 61**
*Group Therapy*, 64
*The Group*, 29, 110, 115, 279
*Growing Through the Ugly*, 102
*The Growth of the Soil*, 238
**Grumbach, Doris, 61**, 227, 285

**Grunwald, Lisa**, 18, **61**
**Gu Hua, 163**
Guare, John, 276
**Guest, Judith, 62**, 64, 170, 220
*Guided Tours of Hell*, 211
**Gummerman, Jay, 164**, 177
*Gun, with Occasional Music*, 77
*The Gunny Sack*, 27
**Guppies for Tea, 142**
Gupta, Sunetra, 79
**Gurganus, Allan**, 131, **164**
*Gus in Bronze*, 126, **190**, 225, 261
**Gustafsson, Lars**, 87, **266**
**Gutcheon, Beth, 62**, 63, 101, 196, 248
**Guterson, David**, 10, 45, **62**, 89, 146, 288
Guthrie, Woody, 48

*H*, 199, **222**
*The Hacienda*, 25, 155
*Hacks at Lunch: A Novel of the Literary Life*, 42, 295
**Hagedorn, Jessica**, 23, **164**, 244
**Haien, Jeannette, 62**, 168, 255
**Hailey, Elizabeth Forsythe**, 51, **63**, 222, 273
*Hairdo*, 216
Haldeman, Joe, 63
**Hale, Janet Campbell, 165**, 229
*The Half-Life of Happiness*, 254
*Halfway Home*, 196
**Hall, Brian**, 52, 82, 135, **165**, 198
**Hall, Rodney, 165**
*Halloran's World War*, 79
*Hallucinating Foucault*, **151**, 181, 254
**Hamill, Pete**, 106, **166**
*Hamilton Stark*, 250
**Hamilton, Jane**, 15, 18, 25, 38, 62, **63**, 95, 163, **166**
**Hamilton-Paterson, James, 166**
Hamsun, Knut, 238
**Hanauer, Cathi**, 60, **63**, 101
*The Hand I Fan With*, 32
*Hand in Glove*, 59
*A Handbook for Visitors from Outer Space*, 181
**Handling Sin**, 43, 65, **189**, 201, 206, 215, 216
**The Handmaid of Desire**, 77, 137, 148, **182**, 190, 202
*The Handmaid's Tale*, 164
*Hanging Up*, 78
*Hank & Chloe*, 80, 133
*Hannah's House*, 64
Hansen, Erik Fosnes, 97

**Hansen, Ron, 166**
*Happenstance*, 147, 158, 203, 215, **222**
*The Happy Isles of Oceania*, 232
**The Hard to Catch Mercy**, **35**, 285
*Hard-boiled Wonderland and the End of the World*, 283
**Hardy, Edward, 167**, 269, 281
Hardy, Thomas, 139
Harington, Donald, 109
*Harlot's Ghost*, 188
*Haroun and the Sea of Stories*, 292, 297
*Harriet the Spy*, 162
**Harris, MacDonald, 63**
Harris, Mark, 73, 111
Harrison, Colin, 276
Harrison, Jamie, 27, 193
**Harrison, Jim**, 133, 165, **167**, 193, 195
**Harrison, Kathryn**, 133, **267**
**Harry and Catherine**, 53, **133**, 140, 150, 160, 167
Hart, Carolyn, 98
**Hart, Josephine, 167**
**Haruf, Kent, 168**
*Harvesting the Heart*, 91
**Hassler, Jon**, 55, **64**, 69, 71, 97
*The Haunted Bookshop*, 98
**Haviaras, Stratis, 13**, 226
*Hawaii*, 8
Hawthorne, Nathaniel, 85
**Haynes, David, 64**
**Hazzard, Shirley, 267**
**Headhunter**, **54**, 56, 299
*Heading West*, 50, 252
**Hearon, Shelby**, 33, 49, **64**, 65
*Heart Failure*, 91
*The Heart Is a Lonely Hunter*, 137
**Heart Mountain**, **10**, 62, 181
*The Heart of Darkness*, 12
*A Heart So White*, 279
*Heartbreak Tango*, 289
*Hearts*, 103
*Heat and Dust*, 175, 179, 273
**Heat Lightning, 47**
*The Heat of the Day*, 251
Heath, Roy, 195
*The Heather Blazing*, 233
*Heaven and Earth*, 288
Hebert, Ernest, 101
Hecht, Julie, 22, 145, 150
**Hedges, Peter**, 37, 91, 102, 150, **168**, 236, 281
**Hegi, Ursula**, 178, 212, 238, 258, **267**, 283

**Heinemann, Larry**, 89, 244, **268**, 286
*Hell Bent Men and Their Cities*, 50
*Hell on Wheels, 109*
**Hellenga, Robert, 13**
Heller, Joseph, 147, 260
*Hello Down There*, **204**, 206
Helprin, Mark, 21, 67, 104, 158, 169, 173, 187, **268**
*The Hemingway Hoax*, 63
*The Hemingway Sabbatical*, 63
*Hemingway's Chair*, 9, **90**
*Hemingway's Suitcase*, **63**
**Hemphill, Paul, 65**
*Henderson the Rain King*, 278
Henderson, William McCranor, 15, 90
**Hendrie, Laura, 168**
**Henkin, Joshua**, 127, **168**, 179, 229
*Henry and Clara*, 16
*Henry in Love*, 232
*Her First American*, **117**, 218
*Her Native Colors*, **67**
*Her Own Place*, **215**
*Her Own Terms*, **61**
*Her Side of It*, 22
*Herb 'n' Lorna*, 75
*Here's Your Hat, What's Your Hurry*, 193
*Herma*, 63
Herman, Michelle, 15
*The Heroic Age*, 13, 226
Herr, Michael, 268
**Herrick, Amy, 169**
*Herzog*, 126
Hess, Joan, 98
**Hewat, Alan V., 268**
*Hey, Cowboy, Wanna Get Lucky?*, **39**
*Hey, Joe*, **18**
**Hickman, Martha Whitmore**, 64, **65**
*Hidden Latitudes*, 83
*Hidden Pictures*, 112
*Hideous Kinky*, 145, **157**
*The Hiding Place*, 241
*High Cotton*, **208**
*High Fidelity*, 16, 48, **171**
*High Holiday Sutra: A Novel*, 32
*High Latitudes*, 43
*High Tide in Tucson: Essays from Now or Never*, 179
**Highbridge, Dianne**, 132, **169**, 171, 193
Highsmith, Patricia, 38
*Highways to War*, 74
**Hijuelos, Oscar**, 50, **169**
*HildA and Pearl*, 210

**Hill, David, 65**, 142
**Hill, Rebecca, 170**
**Hill, Richard, 65**
Hillerman, Tony, 144
Hinton, S. E., 177
*His Monkey Wife*, 138
*His Third, Her Second*, **53**, 183, 222, 230
*The History Man*, 34, 177, 276
*The History of the Siege of Lisbon*, 94, 274, **293**
Hoban, Russell, 88, 99, 190
Hobbes, Thomas, 250
**Hobbet, Anastasia, 66**
Hobson, Laura, 229
Hockenberry, John, 216
Hoeg, Peter, 292
**Hoffman, Alice**, 47, 74, 80, 138, **170, 171**, 200, 204, 220, 252, 264, 265
Hoffman, Eva, 29, 117, 183
**Hogan, Linda**, 205, **269**
*The Holder of the World*, **85**
Holland, Isabelle, 208
Hollis, Tom, 102
*Holly*, 73
Holt, Victoria, 172
*Homage to Catalonia*, 137
*Home Again*, 69
*A Home at the End of the World*, **257**
*Home Fires*, 94
*Home Free*, 202
*Home Free*, **63**, 273
*Home Ground*, 42, **157**
*Home Movie*, **30**, 206
*Homebase*, 140, 244
*Homebodies*, **218**
*Homecoming*, 117
*Homefires*, 47
*The Homesman*, 11
*Hometown Brew*, 30
*Homework*, 275
Hong, Zhu, 238
*Honky Tonk Logic*, 102
*Honor & Duty*, 184
**Hood, Ann, 66**, 126, 186
**Hood, Mary, 66**, 68, 80, 90, 224
*Hoopi, Shoopi Donna*, 100
*Hope Mills*, **91**
**Hope, Christopher**, 51, **269**
*Hopscotch*, 48, 265
*Horace Afoot*, 150, **212**
Hornbacher, Marya, 214
**Hornby, Nick**, 16, 48, **171**

*Horowitz and Mrs. Washington*, 230
**Horowitz, Eve, 172**
**Hospital, Janette Turner,** 11, 32, 109, 167, 269
*Hot Properties*, 17
*Hotel du Lac*, 42, **253**
*The Hotel New Hampshire*, 151
*Hotel Paradise*, **61**, 203
*The Hour of the Star*, 136
*The Hours*, 258
*The House Gun*, 42
*A House in the Country*, **9**
*House Made of Dawn*, 196
*The House of Mirth*, 3
*The House of the Spirits*, 6, **248**
*The House on Mango Street*, 4, 107, 118, 136
*The House Tibet*, **98**, 285
*The House with the Blind Glass Windows*, **238**
*The Houseguest*, 38
*Household Saints*, 141, 157
*The Housekeeping Book*, 117
*Housekeeping*, 23, 38, 47, 55, 206, 256, **290**
Houston, Pam, 117, 181, 226
*How Close We Come*, 33
*How the Garcia Girls Lost their Accents*, 29, **117**, 118, 169
*How I Gave My Heart to the Restaurant*, 94
*How I Got Him Back, or, Under the Cold Moon's Shine*, 216
*How Late It Was, How Late*, **272**
*How Many Miles to Babylon?*, 14
*How Proust Can Change Your Life: Not A Novel*, 259
*How StellA Got Her Groove Back*, 194
*How to Make An American Quilt*, **203**
*How to Read An Unwritten Language*, **266**
Howard, Elizabeth Jane, 51, 79
*Howards End*, 134, 167
**Howatch, Susan, 172,** 245
*Huckleberry Finn*, 150, 261
*Hula*, **221**
*Hullabaloo in the Guava Orchard*, **9**, 146
**Hulme, Keri, 270**
*Humboldt's Gift*, 126, 291
*Human Croquet*, 120
**Humphreys, Josephine,** 49, 107, **172**
*The Hundred Brothers*, 209
*The Hundred Secret Senses*, 104
**Huneven, Michelle, 66**
*Hunger in America*, **137**
*Hunger Point*, 60, 63, 101

*Hunters and Gatherers*, 95, 129, **211**, 292
Hurston, ZorA Neale, 145, 213, 282
*The Hustler*, 105
**Huston, Nancy, 172**
**Hustvedt, Siri,** 34, 250, **270**
**Hyde, Elisabeth, 67**
Hynes, James, 193, 215

*I Am One of You Forever*, **138**
*I Been in Sorrow's Kitchen and Licked out All the Pots*, 187, **229**, 237
*I Can't Wait on God*, 241
*I Cannot Get You Close Enough*, 58
*I Capture the Castle*, 221
*I Dreamt the Snow Was Burning*, 24
*I Had Seen Castles*, 184
*I Killed Hemingway*, 90
*I Know This Much Is True*, 201
*I Know Why the Caged Bird Sings*, 274
*I Never Came to You in White*, 121, 257
*I Never Promised You A Rose Garden*, 60, 77, 100, 162, 210
*I Pass Like Night*, 118
*I Shouldn't Be Telling You This*, 41
*I Want to Buy a Vowel*, 33, 55, 221, **240**, 252
*I Was Amelia Earhart*, 12, **82**, 121
*I Wish This War Were Over*, **202**
*I'll Take It*, 75, **214**
*I'm Losing You*, 228
*I'm Not Complaining*, 86
*The Ice Storm*, 91, 123, 124, 132
*Icy Sparks*, 223, 295
*Idle Curiosity*, 159
*If Ever I Return, Pretty Peggy-O*, 295
*If Morning Ever Comes*, 204, 235
*If the River Were Whiskey*, 252
*If You Lived Here, You'd Be Home Now*, 164, 177, **187**
**Ignatieff, Michael,** 145, 225, 229, **270**
**Iida, Deborah, 173**
**Ikeda, Stewart David, 13**
*Illumination Night*, **170**
*The Illusionist*, **225**, 252
*Imaginary Crimes*, **121**
*An Imaginative Experience*, 240
*Imagining Argentina*, 2, 21, 143, 233, 241, 248, **296**
*Imagining Robert: My Brother, Madness, and Survival*, 162
*Imaginings of Sand*, **42**, 157, 256
*Immortality*, 273
*The Impossible Country*, 165

*In Another Country*, **72**
*In Another Place, Not Here*, 190
*In the Beauty of the Lilies*, 298
*In the City of Fear*, 176
*In Cold Blood*, 188
*In the Country of Last Things*, 34, 270
*In Country*, 89, 111, 181, **191**, 207
*In Coyoacan*, 187
*In Custody*, 146
*In the Cut*, 197
*In the Deep Midwinter*, 36, 62, **255**
*In A Father's Place*, 232
*In the Flesh*, 111
*In A Glass House*, 21
*In the Heart of the Country*, 256
*In the Heart of the Valley of Love*, 69
*In the Kingdom of Air*, **127**
*In the Lake of the Woods*, 34, 81, 86, 212,
    217, 248, **286**
*In the Land of Plenty*, 205
*In the Language of Love*, 103, 120, 128, **217**
*In the Last Analysis*, 96
*In the Lion's Den*, 21
*In the Memory of the Forest*, **288**
*In Memory of Junior*, 138
*In the Miro District and Other Stories*, 296
*In the Night Café*, **14**
*In Pale Battalions*, **59**
*In the Palomar Arms*, 46, 103, 111
*In Pharoah's Army: Memories of the Lost
    War*, 243
*In the Place of Fallen Leaves*, **205**, 259
*In the Pond*, 238
*In Praise of the Stepmother*, 236
*In the Season of Daisies*, 188
*In Shelly's Leg*, 107
*In the Tennessee Country*, 296
*In the Time of the Butterflies*, **2**, 11, 21, 296
*In Troubled Waters*, 108, 125, 131, **145**, 270
*In the Twelfth Year of the War*, 32
*In the Wilderness: Coming of Age in Unknown
    Country*, 162, 243
*Inagehi*, **44**, 62, 174
*Incline Our Hearts*, 233
*Independence Day*, 73, **263**, 285, 299
*The India Fan*, 172
*The Indian in the Cupboard*, 121
*Indian Killer*, 14, 116, 144
*The Indian Lawyer*, **109**
*India Song*, 294
*Infinite Jest*, 66, 289, **299**
*The Infinite Plan*, **31**, 169

*The Information*, **31**, 74, 127, 137
**Ingalls, Rachel, 67**, 193
*Inheritance*, 11
*The Ink Truck*, 273
*The Inn at Lake Devine*, 186, 192, 234
*Innocence*, 13
*Innocent Erendira, and Other Stories*, 265
*Inspector Ghote Breaks an Egg*, 11
*An Instance of the Fingerpost*, 256
*Instruments of Darkness*, **172**
*The Insurrection*, 24
*Interstate*, **50**
*Interviewing Matisse; or, the Woman Who
    Died Standing Up*, 298
*Intimacy*, **46**, 230
*Intimate Enemies*, **94**
*Into the Forest*, 99
*Into the Great Wide Open*, **134**
*Into their Labors*, 38
*Into Thin Air: A Personal Account of the Mt.
    Everest Disaster*, 22
*Into the Wild*, 20, 56
*Inventing the Abbotts, and Other Stories*, 42
*The Invisible Circus*, 58, **153**
*Iona Moon*, **105**
*The Iowa Baseball Confederacy*, 73
*Iron and Silk*, 97
*Ironweed*, 92, **273**
**Irving, John**, 35, 102, 123, 135, 137, 147,
    151, **173**, 180, 241
**Irwin, Robert, 174**
*Isaac and His Devils*, **152**
*Isabel's Bed*, 152, 186
**Ishiguro, Kazuo**, 10, 69, 87, 189, 266, **271**,
    **272**, 274, 283
*Island*, 219
**Isler, Alan, 67**
*The Italian Girl*, 254, 284
*Itsuka*, 181
*Ivory Bright*, **156**
*The Ivory Swing*, 11
*The Ivory Tower: Soviet Artists in a Time of
    Glasnost*, 225
Iwago, Mitsuaki, 21

*Jack Frusciante Has Left the Band*, 65, **131**,
    207
*Jack Gance*, 176
*Jackie by Josie*, 36, **93**, 94, 186
*Jackson's Dilemma*, 284
Jacobs, Mark, 221
*The Jade Peony*, **141**, 184, 200

*Jadis*, 133, **140**
*Jailbird*, **108**
*The Jailing of Cecelia Capture*, **165**, 229
**James, Clive**, **174**, 290
James, Henry, 1, 3, 68, 175, 239
*Jane and Prudence*, 94, 263
**Janowitz, Tama**, **67**, 76
*Japanese by Spring*, 174, 182, **289**
**Japrisot, Sebastien**, 59, **174**, 294
Jarrell, Randall, 182, 276
*Jasmine*, 85, 86
*Jazz*, 148, 209, **282**
**Jen, Gish**, **175**, 184
Jenkins, Dan, 39
*Jennie*, **93**, 129
*Jernigan*, **159**, 226
*The Jewel in the Crown*, 5, 23, 293
*Jewel*, **187**, 229
Jezer, Marty, 223
**Jhabvala, Ruth Prawer**, **175**, 179, 273
Jin, Ha, 238
*Jitterbug Perfume*, 95
*Joe*, 170, **253**
*John Dollar*, 300
Johnson, Angela, 215
**Johnson, Denis**, **272**
**Johnson, Diane**, 1, 20, 69, 127, 148, **175**, **176**, 188, 239, 294
**Johnson, Joyce**, **14**, 30
**Johnson, Nora**, **68**, 198, 201
**Johnston, Jennifer**, **14**
**Jolley, Elizabeth**, **68**, 72
*Jonah's Gourd Vine*, 282
Jones, Gayl, 99
**Jones, Louis B.**, **68**, 77
Jong, Erica, 29, 300
Josephs, Rebecca, 63, 214
*Joshua Then and Now*, 21, 228
*The Journal of Antonio Montoya*, 107, 139, 142
*The Journey* (Fink), 104, **262**
*The Journey* (Ganesan), **11**
*The Joy Luck Club*, 100, 105, 200, **230**
Joyce, James, 162, 208, 245, 264
*JR*, 264
**Judd, Alan**, **68**
*Judge on Trial*, **180**
*July's People*, 52, **266**
*Jumping the Queue*, 40, **240**
*The Jump-Off Creek*, 11
Junger, Sebastian, 82, 254

*The Jungle*, 90
*Just Relations*, **165**
**Just, Ward**, 24, 146, **176**, 273
*Justice*, 27

*Kaaterskill Falls*, 1, **12**
**Kadohata, Cynthia**, **69**
Kafka, Franz, 109, 271, 272
**Kafka, Paul**, **69**
**Kalpakian, Laura**, 80, **176**, 267
Kanon, Joseph, 24, 281
*Kansas in August*, **158**
**Kaplan, James**, **177**, 182
**Karbo, Karen**, 164, **177**, 187
**Karon, Jan**, 64, **69**, 71
*Karoo*, 80, 145, 150, 168, 177, 201, 228, **231**
Karr, Mary, 123, 237
**Kashner, Rita**, 53, **69**
Kasischke, Laura, 197
*Kate Vaiden*, **210**, 294
*Katherine*, 138, 231
Katkov, Norman, 178
**Katz, Steve**, 128, **177**
Katzenbach, Maria, 249
**Kauffman, Janet**, **178**
**Kaufman, Joan**, **70**
Kaufman, Sue, 70
Kavanagh, Patrick, 20
**Kay, Terry**, **70**
Kazantzakis, Nikos, 258
**Keane, Molly**, **70**
Keating, H. R. F., 11
**Keegan, John**, **70**
*Keeper of the Moon: A Southern Boyhood*, 194
*A Keeper of Sheep*, **45**, 123
*The Keepers of the House*, 163
*Keepers of the House*, 2, 25
*Keeping Warm*, 58
**Keillor, Garrison**, 69, **71**, 156, 236
**Keller, Nora Okja**, 6, 8, 58, 135, **178**, 189, 196, 245
Kellerman, Faye, 1
Kelly, Susan, 33
**Kelman, James**, **272**
**Keneally, Thomas**, **71**, 98, 104, 158, **178**
**Kennedy, Pagan**, 50, 57, **72**, 119
**Kennedy, William**, 92, **273**
**Kenney, Susan**, **72**
*Kentucky Love*, 144
*Kentucky Straight*, 88

**Kercheval, Jesse Lee, 72**
**Kernan, Michael**, 8, 100, **178**
Kerouac, Jack, 14
Kesey, Ken, 95, 150, 185
Keyes, Daniel, 264
*Killer Instinct*, 101
*The Killing Ground*, 220
**Killing Mister Watson**, **191**
*Killing Time in St. Cloud*, 170
**Kincaid, Jamaica, 72**
**Kincaid, Nanci, 73**, 128, 258
*Kinflicks*, 74, 117
*Kinfolks*, **182**, 215
*King of the Jews*, **10**
*King of the Mountain*, 40
*King of the Road*, **65**
King, Florence, 59
King, Francis, 273
**King, Tabitha, 73**
**King, Thomas, 14**, 116, 148, 155
**Kingsolver, Barbara**, 12, 47, 162, **179**, 205, 279
Kingston, Maxine Hong, 41, 53, 135
**Kinsella, W. P.**, **73**, 97, 116
**Kiraly, Sherwood**, 79, **179**
Kirchner, Bhart, 86
**Kirn, Walter**, 158, **180**, 192
Kisor, Henry, 58
*Kiss of the Spider Woman*, 233, **289**
*The Kiss*, 267
*The Kitchen God's Wife*, **104**, 138
**Klass, Perri, 73**
**Klein, Elizabeth, 15**
Klein, Joe, 274
**Klima, Ivan, 180**
**Kline, Christina Baker, 74**
**Kluge, P. F.**, 2, **15**, 80, 176
Knapp, Caroline, 66, 106
*The Kneeling Bus*, 145
*The Knife Thrower and Other Stories*, 18
*The Knight Has Died*, 87
*The Knight, Death, and the Devil*, 184
Knight, Kathryn Lasky, 57
*The Knockout Artist*, 18
*Know Nothing*, 220
**Knowles, John**, 3, 71, **180**
**Koch, Christopher, 74**
**Kogawa, Joy**, 146, **180**
Konrad, George, 263
**Kosinski, Jerzy**, 53, 74, 135, 151, **181**
Kotlowitz, Alex, 186

**Kotzwinkle, William**, 31, **74**, 109, 112, 137, 213, 226
**Kraft, Eric, 75**
Krakauer, Jon, 20, 22, 55
*Kramer vs. Kramer*, 47
**Kramer, Kathryn**, **181**, 194
*Kraven Images*, 67
*Krik? Krak!*, 258
Kristin, Berji, 220
**Kuban, Karla, 181**
**Kundera, Milan**, 180, **273**
**Kupfer, Fern**, 66, **75**
**Kureishi, Hanif**, 83, 115, **181**
**Kurtz, Don, 15**
Kusz, Natalie, 56

**L'Heureux, John**, 77, 148, **182**, 190, 202
*Labrador*, 101
*Ladder of Years*, 135
*Lady Oracle*, 61, 83, 120
*The Lady with the Alligator Purse*, **54**
*Lady's Time*, **268**
LaFarge, Oliver, 109
*Lake Wobegon Days*, 69, 71, 156
*Lamb*, 188
**Lamb, Wally**, 46, 97, **182**, 201, 248
*Lament for a Silver-Eyed Woman*, 102
Lamott, Anne, 101, 161
*Lancelot*, 206
**Lanchester, John**, 53, **75**
*Land Kills*, 40
*The Land of Green Plums*, 21, 24, **199**, 278
*The Land of Laughs*, 133
*Landscapes of the Heart*, 295
**Landvik, Lorna**, 71, **75**, 156, 252
**Langley, Lee**, 27, **273**
Lansing, Alfred, 121
Lapierre, Dominique, 5
*Lapse of Time*, 238
*Larry's Party*, 150, 215, 294, 298
*The Last Bongo Sunset*, **209**
*Last Comes the Egg*, **150**
*The Last Duty*, 298
*The Last Gentleman*, 206
*The Last Good Night*, 78
*The Last Great Snake Show*, 181, **194**
*The Last Hotel for Women*, **144**
*The Last Klick*, 244
*Last Letters from Hav*, 130
*Last Night at the Brain Thieves Ball*, 226
*The Last Night at the Ritz*, 98
*The Last of the Menu Girls*, 139

*Last Orders*, 60, **230**
*The Last Resort: A Novel*, 188
*The Last Tycoon*, 228
*The Last World*, 87
*Late Bloomers—The Coming of Age in America*, 186
*A Late Divorce*, **245**, 252
*The Late George Apley*, 236
*The Late-Summer Passion of a Woman of Mind*, 218
Lathen, Emma, 84, 156
**Lattany, Kristin Hunter, 182**, 215
**Lauber, Lynn, 76**, 128
*Laughing Boy*, 109
*The Laughing Sutra*, 97
Laughlin, James, 119
**The Law of Enclosures, 205**
*Law of Falling Bodies*, 224
**Lawrence, Karen, 183**
**The Laws of Return, 229**
Lawson, Robert, 19
Laxalt, Robert, 249
le Carre, John, 43, 96, 126, 176, 300
*Le Divorce*, 69, **175**, 188, 239, 295
*Leap Year Day: New and Selected Poems*, 46
*Leap Year*, 134
*Learning to Swim and Other Stories*, 230
Least-Heat Moon, William, 11
*Leave It to Me*, 85
*The Leavetaking*, 193
*Leaving Barney*, **85**, 103
*Leaving Cold Sassy*, 43
**Leaving the Land, 26, 235**
**Leavitt, Caroline, 183**
**Leavitt, David, 274**
**Lee, Chang-Rae, 183**, 213, 244
**Lee, Gus, 7**, 140, 141, **183**
Lee, Harper, 43, 55, 61, 157, 167
**Lee, Helen Elaine, 184**, 200, 241
**Lee, Sky, 184**
**Lefcourt, Peter, 67, 76**, 139
**Leffland, Ella, 31**, 32, 119, 143, **184**
**The Legend of Olivia Cosmos Montevideo, 108**
*The Legends of Jesse Dark*, 147
*Legs*, 273
**Leimbach, Marti, 76**, 232
**Leithauser, Brad, 274**
**Leland, Christopher, 76**
**Lemann, Nancy, 40, 185**, 204
**Lerman, Rhoda, 32, 77**

*Les Liaisons Dangereuses*, 133
**Lesley, Craig, 9**, 11, 148, 168, **185**
*Less Than Angels*, 211
**Lessing, Doris, 119**, 122, **185**
**A Lesson Before Dying, 50, 264**
**Lester, Julius, 274**
*Let Nothing You Dismay*, 118, 202
*Let there Be Light*, 32
**Lethem, Jonathan, 68, 77**, 165, 289
*Letourneau's Used Auto Parts*, 141
*Letters Home: Correspondence 1950–1963*, 61
**Letting Loose, 76**
**Levenkron, Steven, 77**, 214
Levi, Primo, 10
**Leviathan** (Auster), **250**
*Leviathan* (Hobbes)*, 250
Levin, Meyer, 17
Lewis, David, 282
*The Liars' Club*, 123, 237
**The Liberty Campaign, 40, 143, 146**, 217
**Libra, 56, 121, 259**
*Licorice*, 158
Lidz, Franz, 138
*Lie Down in Darkness*, 296
*Lies of Silence*, 193
*The Lies That Bind*, 3
**Life & Times of Michael K, 157, 189, 256**
*Life After God*, 48
*The Life and Loves of a She-Devil*, 61, 136, 239
*Life Before Death*, 126, 158
**Life Before Man, 120**, 217
*Life Designs*, 157
*Life Estates*, 64
*Life for Me Ain't Been No Crystal Stair*, 186
**Life Force, 36, 239**, 240, 295
*The Life of Helen Alone*, 183
*Life on Earth: Stories*, 121
*Lifelines*, 183
**Life-Size, 60, 101**
*Light in August*, 297
*The Light in the Piazza*, 295
*A Light in the Window*, 69
*Light a Penny Candle*, 51
*The Light Thickens*, 82
**Lightman, Alan, 68, 87, 274**
*Lightning Song*, 201
*Like a Hole in the Head*, 172
*Like Life: Stories*, 83
**Like Water for Chocolate, 4, 52**, 53, 75, 154, 171, 247
*Lily White*, 152

*The Limits of Vision*, 174
**Lindbergh, Reeve, 78**
*Linden Hills*, 200
Linett, Deena, 79
Linklater, Eric, 279
*The Lion in the Lei Shop*, 106, 202
**Lipman, Elinor**, 55, 116, 127, 169, 176, **185**, 192, 234, 246
**Lipsky, David**, 130, **186**
Lispector, Clarice, 92, 136
**List, Shelley, 78**
**Listfield, Emily, 78**
*Little Altars Everywhere*, 40, 240
*Little Drummer Girl*, 43, 96, 176
*Little Follies*, 75
*Little Miss Strange*, 135, 153, 165
*The Little People*, 63
*A Little Stranger*, 82
*Little Woman*, 30
*Littlejohn*, 89
*Live at Five*, **64**
**Lively, Penelope**, 18, 58, 68, **275**, 287
*The Lives of Girls and Women*, 120
*Lives of the Monster Dogs*, 70
*Lives of the Saints* (Lemann), 40, 41, **185**, 204
*Lives of the Saints* (Slavitt), **294**
**Livesey, Margot**, 36, 84, 150, **275**
*Living Arrangements*, 81
*The Living End*, 154
*The Living Is Easy*, 110
*Living Other Lives*, **183**
*Living Out Loud*, 212
*The Living*, 185
*LA Maravilla*, **107**
*Local Deities*, **44**
**Lodge, David**, 34, 127, 130, 177, 182, **186**, **276**, 279
**Loewinsohn, Ron, 276**
**Lofton, Ramona (Sapphire), 186**
**Loh, Sandra Tsing**, 164, 177, **187**
*Lolita*, 128, 261
*The Lone Man*, 249
*The Lone Pilgrim*, 143
*The Lone Ranger and Tonto Fistfight in Heaven*, 116
*The Lonely Girl*, 285
*A Long and Happy Life*, 210
*Long Distance Life*, 184
*The Long Night of Francisco Sanctis*, **143**, 146
*The Long Rain*, 108, 158
*A Long Way from Verona*, 39, 52, 159, 210

*The Long Way Home*, **25**
**Long, David**, 108, 110, **276**
*Longing*, **155**
*The Longings of Women*, **92**, 242, 273
*Look How the Fish Live*, 288
*Looking for Love*, **53**
*Looking for Mo*, 201
*Looking for Mr. Goodbar*, 96
*The Looking Glass Lover*, 91
*Loon Lake*, 261
*The Loop*, **144**, 212, 255
*Loose Woman: Poems*, 136
**Lopate, Phillip, 187**
**Lopez-Medina, Sylvia, 78**
*The Lord of the Flies*, 9, 12, 161, 232
*The Lords of Discipline*, 257
*Los Alamos*, 24, 281
*Losing Absalom*, 90
*Losing Eddie*, **47**
*Losing Isaiah*, 87, 195, 199
*Loss of Flight*, 107
*The Lost Diaries of Frans Hals*, 85, 100, **178**
*The Lost Father*, 55, 167, 224
*Lost Highway*, **48**, 84
*Lost in Jersey City*, 99
*Lost in Place*, 97
*Lost in Translation: A Life in a New Language*, 29, 117, 183
*The Lost Language of Cranes*, **274**
*Lost Man's River*, 191
*The Lost Son*, **226**
**Lott, Bret**, 89, **187**, 229
*The Lottery*, 65
Louis, Adrian, 260
*Louisiana Power and Light*, 150
*Love and Friendship*, 188
*Love and Garbage*, 180
*Love and Houses*, 76
*Love and Longing in Bombay*, 138
*Love and Obits*, 41
*Love Enter*, **69**
*Love in a Cold Climate*, 211
*Love in the Ruins*, 206
*Love in a Small Town*, 238
*Love in the Time of Cholera*, 92, 169, 248, 251, **265**, 293
*Love Invents Us*, **128**
*The Love Letter*, **98**, 249, 295
*Love Medicine*, 116, 124, **154**, 155
*Love on a Barren Mountain*, 238
*The Love Queen of the Amazon*, 208
*The Love Songs of Phoenix Bay*, **147**

*Love Story*, 76, 141
**Love Warps the Mind a Little**, **150**, 213, 215
*Love, Loss and What I Wore*, 36
**Love, Stars, and All That**, **86**
*Love's Executioner and Other Tales of*
    *Psychotherapy*, 112
**Love's Mansion**, **300**
*The Lover of History*, 146, 258
**The Lover**, 44, 133, **261**
*Loverboys: Stories*, 136
*Lovers and Tyrants*, 247
**The Loves of Faustyna**, 41, **54**
*Lovesick*, 23
**Loving Attitudes**, **127**
*Loving Chloe*, 80
*Loving Edith*, 169, 231
*Loving Hands at Home*, 127
**Loving Little Egypt**, **81**
*Loving Roger*, 204
**Loving Women: A Novel of the Fifties**, **166**
**Lovingkindness**, **96**
Lowry, Malcolm, 161
*The L-Shaped Room*, 121
*Lucid Stars*, 123
*Lucinella: A Novel*, 219
**The Luckiest Girl in the World**, **77**
*Lucky Jim*, 204
Lund, Doris, 65
**Lurie, Alison**, 99, 177, 182, **187**, 190, 275
*Lust for Life*, 166, 174
**The Luxury of Exile**, 36, **44**, 249, 258
**Lying Low**, **176**
**Lying on the Couch**, **112**
*The Lyre of Orpheus*, 258

*M31: A Family Romance*, 244
**MacDonald, Ann-Marie**, 8, 66, **79**
Macdonald, Malcolm, 101
MacDougall, Ruth Doan, 29, 59, 83, 84, 91,
    126, 131
*The MacGuffin*, 285
**Machine Dreams**, **207**, 208
**Macho!**, **107**
**Mackay, Shena**, 19, 20, **276**
**MacLaverty, Bernard**, **188**
Maclean, Norman, 27
MacLeod, Sheila, 214
*Madame Bovary*, 123
*Madame Sousatska*, 97
Madden, David, 125
**Madden, Deirdre**, 14, **16**, 188
*Madeleine's Ghost*, 268

*Madeleine's World*, 165
**The Magician's Assistant**, 170, **204**
**The Magician's Girl**, **61**
**Magnetic Field(s)**, **276**
*The Magus*, 59, 110, 254, 284
**Mahfouz, Naguib**, 249, **277**
**Mahoney, Tim**, **79**, 116
*Mail*, 141
**Mailer, Norman**, **188**
*Mainland*, 217
**Maitland, Sara**, 34, 208, 237, **277**
*Maker of Saints*, 49
**Makine, Andrei**, **277**
*Making History*, 99
**Malamud, Bernard**, 73, 111, **278**
**The Male Cross-Dresser Support Group**, **67**,
    76, 118
"Malgudi" novels, 86
**Mallon, Thomas**, **16**, 21
**Malone, Michael**, 43, 56, 65, 150, 165, **188**,
    **189**, 192, 201, 206, 216, 257, 276
**Malouf, David**, **278**
*Mamaw*, 50
**The Mambo Kings Play Songs of Love**, **169**
**Mama Day**, **200**
Mamet, David, 183
*Mama Makes Up Her Mind*, 240
*Man's Hope*, 137
*Managing Ignatius: the Lunacy of Lucky Dogs*
    *and Life in the Quarter*, 233
*A Man and His Mother*, 168
**Manderino, John**, **79**, 179
**Manea, Norman**, 199, **278**
*The Manikin*, 219
Mann, Thomas, 5, 68
Manning, Olivia, 8
Manning, Victor, 7
**Mantel, Hilary**, 1, 159, 275, **278**
*The Manticore*, 258
**A Map of the World**, 15, 25, 38, 62, **63**, 80
*Mapp and Lucia*, 10
**Mapson, Jo-Ann**, **79**, 108, 133, 252, 265
**Maraire, J. Nozipo**, **189**
*Marchlands*, 181
**Marciano, Francesca**, 221, **279**
Margolis, Seth, 87, 195, 199
**Marias, Javier**, **279**
*Mariette in Ecstacy*, 167
**Marine Life**, **230**
**Marius, Richard**, 174, **189**
*Marjorie Morningstar*, 288

Mark, Jan, **189**
Markham, Beryl, 83
Marquand, J. P., 236, 251
*The Marriage Bed*, **126**
*A Marriage Made at Woodstock*, 30, **90**, 104,
   221
*A Married Man*, 186
*Married to a Stranger*, **20**
*Marry Me*, 276
Marshall, Alexandra, 80, 126, **190**, 225, 261
Marshall, Paule, **190**
*Martha Calhoun*, **34**
*Martha Quest*, 185
*Martin and John*, 164, 205
*Martin Dressler: the Tale of An American
   Dreamer*, **18**, 21
Martin, Betty, 8
Martin, David, 171
Martin, Valerie, **190**
Martinez, Demetria, 78, 205
Martinez, Tomas Eloy, 121
*Mary Reilly*, 190
*A Mask for Arras*, 104
Maso, Carole, **279**
*Mason and Dixon*, 289
Mason, Bobbie Ann, 111, 181, **191**, 207, 225
*Mason's Retreat*, 49, 101, **232**
*Massacre of the Dreamers: Essays on
   Xicanisma*, 136
*The Master and Margarita*, 68
*Master Georgie*, 121
*The Master of Petersburg*, 256
*Masters of Illusion: A Novel of the
   Connecticut Circus Fire*, **102**
Masters, Edgar Lee, 102
Mastretta, Angeles, 23
*A Match to the Heart*, 10
*Mating*, 129, 258, **292**
*A Matter of Time*, 190
*Matters of Chance*, **62**, 168, 255
Matthiessen, Peter, 84, **191**
Mattison, Alice, 210
Maupin, Armistead, 147, 159, 160, **191**, 212
*Maurice*, 134, 233
Mawer, Simon, 35, 60, 117, 151, **191**, 212
*Max Lakeman and the Beautiful Stranger*, 142
Maxwell, William, 203, **280**, 296
*Maybe I'll Call Anna*, **227**
*Maybe in Missoula*, **108**
*Maybe the Moon*, 212
*Mazel*, 161
*Mazurka for Two Dead Men*, **137**

McCall, Dan, 192
McCammon, Robert, 35, 61, **80**, 208
McCarry, Charles, 259
McCarthy, Cormac, 3, 4, 74, 107, 193, 253,
   **280**
McCarthy, Mary, 29, 110, 115, 279
McCauley, Stephen, 39, 123, 158, 176, **192**,
   202, 258
McCorkle, Jill, 33, 160, 170, **192**
McCormick, Ann du Mais, **80**
McCourt, Frank, 36
McCoy, Maureen, **80**
McCracken, Elizabeth, 64, 67, 144, 151, **193**
McCrum, Robert, 178
McCrumb, Sharyn, 48
McCullers, Carson, 19, 49, 137, 200
McCullough, Colleen, 27, 169, 171
McCunn, Ruthanne Lum, 230
McDermott, Alice, 100, 134, 155, 162, 206,
   262, **280**, 296
McEwan, Ian, 64, 192, 275, 280, **281**
McFall, Lynne, **81**
McFarland, Dennis, 120, 167, **281**
McGahan, Andrew, **16**, 48
McGahern, John, 41, **193**
McGarry, Jean, 33
McGrail, Anna, 275
McGraw, Eloise, 33
McGuane, Thomas, **193**
McInerney, Jay, **17**, 67, 100, 228
*McKay's Bees*, 81
McKinney-Whetstone, Diane, 32, **194**, 200
McLaurin, Tim, 181, **194**
McLean, Duncan, 272
McMahon, Thomas, **81**
McManus, James, **81**, 86, 267, 286
McMillan, Terry, 64, **194**
McMurtry, Larry, 39, 60, 117, 126
McNamer, Deirdre, **17**, 48, 235, 276
McNeal, Tom, 34, **195**, 224
McPhee, Martha, **82**, 135, 165
McPherson, William, 19, 102, **281**
McVeigh, Alice, **82**
McWilliam, Candia, **82**
*Me and My Baby View the Eclipse*, 295
*The Meadow*, **11**, 26, 58, 198
*The Measured Man*, **89**
*Medicine Men*, 190
*Medicine River*, 14
*Meditations in Green*, **244**, 268
Medoff, Jillian, 63, 101

Medwed, Mameve, 141
*Meeting Evil*, **38**, 146
*Meeting the Minotaur*, 49
*Meeting Rozzy Halfway*, 183
*Meg*, **159**
Mehta, Gita, 200, 249
**Mekler, Eva, 17**
**Melville, Pauline, 195**
*The Member of the Wedding*, 19, 49
*Memoir from Antproof Case*, 21, 67, 104, 158, 169, 173, 187, **268**
*Memories of the Ford Administration*, 236
*Memories of My Ghost Brother*, 41, **53**
*Memories of Rain*, 79
*Memory Mambo*, 87
*Men and Angels*, **161**
*The Men and the Girls*, 136, **233**
*Men at Arms*, 239
*Men in Black*, 137, **226**
*Men in Trouble*, 104
*The Men of Brewster Place*, 200
*The Men's Club*, 218
Menaker, Daniel, 96, 112
*Mendel's Dwarf*, 35, 60, 117, 151, **191**, 212
**Mendelsohn, Jane, 12, 82, 121**
*Mercy*, **91**
*Meridian 144*, 99
*Meridian*, 132
Merkin, Robert, 268
*Mermaids*, 42, 131, **145**, 157
*Merry Men*, 141
*Meshugah*, 17
*Mean Spirit*, 269
*The Message to the Planet*, 284
*Messenger Bird*, 192
**Messud, Claire, 18**
*Metamorphoses*, 87
*Metamorphosis*, 109
*Meteors in August: A Novel*, 106
*Metroland*, 251
Metz, Don, 40
*The Man from Japan*, **174**, 290
**Michaels, Anne, 13, 58, 116, 121, 199, 257, 258, 282, 287, 296**
Michaels, Leonard, 218
Michaels, Lisa, 165
Michener, James, 8, 20
*Mickelsson's Ghosts*, **265**
*Microserfs*, **47**
*The Middle Ground*, **149**
*Middle Son*, **173**
*The Middleman and Other Stories*, 85

*Midnight Lemonade*, **59**
*Midnight Sandwiches at the Mariposa Express*, **94**, 156, 200
*Midnight Sweets*, 207
*Midnight's Children*, 5, 154, 249, **292**, 293
*Midwives*, 40, 42, 54
*Miles from Nowhere: A Round the World Bicycle Adventure*, 81
Miller, Lucien, 238
Miller, Merle, 231, 247
**Miller, Sue, 42, 63, 195, 199, 281**
**Millhauser, Steven, 18, 21, 112, 236**
*Millroy the Magician*, 204
*The Millstone*, 103, 149
*The Man in the Grey Flannel Suit*, 47, 84
*The Man in the Window*, 33, 49, **142**, 144, 208, 212, 255, 286
Min, Anchee, 138, 231
*The Mind-Body Problem*, 1, 93, **161**
*Minor Characters*, 14, 30
**Minot, Susan, 196**
*Miracle at Carville*, 8
*Mirror Images*, 220
*The Mirror*, 157
Mishima, Yukio, 262
*The Miss Hereford Stories*, 119
*Miss Lizzie*, 83
*Miss Lonelyhearts*, 92
*Miss Ophelia*, **102**
*Miss Peabody's Inheritance*, 68, 72
*Miss Undine's Livingroom*, 111
*Missed Connections*, 157
*Missing Pieces*, 287
*Missing*, 15
*Mistaken Identity*, 293
*Mister Sandman*, **162**
*Mistler's Exit*, 251
*The Mistress of Spices*, 53
**Mistry, Rohinton, 220, 266, 277, 282**
**Mitchard, Jacquelyn, 108, 196, 219, 248**
Mitford, Nancy, 211
*Mitz: The Marmoset of Bloomsbury*, 87
*Mixquiahuala Letters*, 136
**Mo, Timothy, 83, 182**
Mo, Yan, 238
*The Modern American Novel*, 130
*Modern Baptists*, 111
*The Man of the House*, 39, 192
*The Man of My Dreams*, 217
*Man of the People*, 298
*Mohawk*, 124, 215
*Moira's Way*, 97

**Momaday, N. Scott, 196**
*The Mommy Club*, 39
*Mommy Dressing*, 36
*Momo*, 275
*Monday's Warriors*, 159
*Mondays on the Dark Night*, 86
**Monette, Paul**, 164, **196**
***Mona in the Promised Land*, 175**
*Monkey Bay*, 157
***The Monkey Bridge*, 106, 134**
*The Monkey King*, 83
***Monkeys*, 196**
Monninger, Joseph, 269
*Monosook Valley*, 67
***Montana 1948*, 27**, 78, 91, 151, 276
*Montana Women*, 108
***A Month in the Country*, 254**, 287
*Moo*, 25, 177, 182, 266
Moody, Rick, 91, 123, 124, 132
*Moon Palace*, 34
***Moon Tiger*, 275**, 287
**Mooney, Ted, 83**
*The Moons of Jupiter*, 120
***The Moor's Last Sigh*, 9**, 175, 268, 291, **292**, 293
Moore, Brian, 193
Moore, Elizabeth Jordan, 166
**Moore, Lorrie**, 30, 54, **83**, 102
**Moore, Susanna**, 8, 106, 178, 196, **197**, 202, 245
*Man or Mango? A Lament*, 154
*Morality Play*, 236
*More Tales of the City*, 191
Morehead, Ann, 9
Morehead, Don, 9
**Morgan, Clay, 84**
*Morgan's Passing*, 40, 234
Mori, Kyoko, 6
Morley, Christopher, 98
**Morris, Bill, 84**
Morris, Jan, 130, 297
**Morris, Mary McGarry, 197**
**Morris, Mary, 197**
**Morris, Wright**, 11, **198**
**Morrison, Toni**, 46, 130, 132, 186, 209, 213, 238, 274, **282**
**Morrissey, Bill**, 48, **84**
**Morrissy, Mary, 84**
*Mortal Friends*, 88
*Morte d'Urban*, 288
**Mortimer, John, 198**
Mortimer, Penelope, 96

**Morton, Brian**, 161, **198**, 223, 228, 291
**Mosby, Katherine**, 59, **198**
**Mosher, Howard Frank**, 23, **199**
**Moskowitz, Bette Ann**, **85**, 103
***The Mosquito Coast*, 22**, 122, **232**
*Mosquito*, 99
*The Most Wanted*, 196
*A Mother and Two Daughters*, 52, 53, 160, 218
*Mother Less Child: the Love Story of A Family*, 196
***Mother of Pearl*, 84**
*Mother Tongue*, 78, 205
***A Mother's Love*, 197**
***Motor City*, 84**
***Mount Misery*, 44, 100**
*The Mourners Bench*, 50
*Mourning Doves: Stories*, 234
*The Moviegoer*, 172, 185, 206, 263, 291
*Moving On*, 39
*Moving Parts*, 177
*Moving Violations: War Zones, Wheelchairs, and Declarations of Independence*, 216
*Mr. Bridge*, 222
***Mr. Field's Daughter*, 78, 124**
*Mr. Ives' Christmas*, 50, 169
*Mr. Mani*, 245
*Mr. Vertigo*, 250
*Mr. White's Confession*, 255
*Mrs. Bridge*, 222, 262
***Mrs. Caliban*, 67**, 193
*Mrs. Dalloway*, 266
*Mrs. Einstein*, 275
*Mrs. Munck*, 184
*Mrs. Palfrey at the Claremont*, 119, 208
*Mrs. Randall*, 77
*Mrs. Stevens Hears the Mermaids Singing*, 216
***Mrs. Ted Bliss*, 103**, 119, **262**
***A Much Younger Man*, 132, 169**, 171, 193
**Mukherjee, Bharati**, **85**, 86
**Mulisch, Harry, 283**, 299
**Muller, Herta**, 21, 24, **199**, 278
*Mumbo Jumbo*, 290
Munif, Abdal Rahman, 249
Munro, Alice, 120
**Murakami, Haruki, 283**
*Murder Makes the Wheels Go Round*, 84
*Murder, She Meowed*, 132
**Murdoch, Iris**, 105, 131, 167, 198, 254, **284**, 294
**Murphy, Yannick, 85**

*The Museum Guard*, 19
**The Museum of Happiness, 72**
*Museum Pieces*, 175
*Museum: Poems*, 148
*Music in the Hills*, 205
*The Music Lesson*, 239
**The Music of Chance, 34**
*Music of the Swamp*, **18**, 19, 80, 97, 285
*The Music Room*, 120, 167, **281**
*The Music School*, 298
*The Music*, 166
**Muske-Dukes, Carol,** 92, 195, **199**, 222
**The Man Who Fell in Love with the Moon,
226**
*The Man Who Once Played Catch with Nellie
Fox*, 79
**The Man Who Was Late, 251**
*The Man with the Golden Arm*, 209
*The Man Without a Face*, 208
*My Antonia*, 22, 195, 198
*My Beautiful Laundrette*, 182
*My Brilliant Career*, 119, 145
*My Brother*, 72
**My Drowning, 163**, 248, 266
**My Father's Geisha, 37**, 168
*My Father's Glory*, 214
*My Golden Trades*, 180
*My Hard Bargain*, 180
*My Life as a Man*, 148, 190, 290
**My Life as a Whale, 100**
*My Life, Starring Dara Falcon*, 101
**My Lucky Face, 138**
*My Mother's Castle*, 214
*My Name Is Asher Lev*, 96, 210, 299
**My Old Sweetheart,** 8, 106, 178, 196, **197,**
202, 245
*My Ride With Gus*, 136
*My Sister from the Black Lagoon*, 210
*My Sister Life*, 55, 153
**My Sister's Bones,** 60, **63**, 101
**My Summer with George, 57**
**My Year of Meats,** 6, 68, **90**, 174
*My Year Off: Recovering Life After a Stroke*, 178
**Myerson, Julie, 85**
*The Mysteries of Pittsburgh*, 137
**Mystery Ride, 129**
**The Mystery Roast, 158**, 211, 268

Nabokov, Vladimir, 128, 244, 261, 284, 299
*The Naked and the Dead*, 188
*Naked Sleeper*, 87

*The Name of the Rose*, 256
**The Names of the Dead,** 49, **89**, 191, 217, 268
**The Names of the Mountains, 78**
**The Names,** 250, **259**
*Naming the New World*, 184
*Naming the Spirits*, 296
**Nampally Road, 2**
**Narayan, Kirin, 86**
Narayan, R. K., 9
*The Narrowing Circle*, 21
Nasar, Sylvia, 162
*The Nashville Sound*, 65
**Nasrin, Taslima, 86**
Nastase, Ilie, 101
**Native Speaker, 183**, 213, 244
**Natives and Strangers, 8**
*The Natural*, 73, 111
**Naumoff, Lawrence,** 27, **86**, 199, 205
Navratilova, Martina, 101
**Naylor, Gloria,** 94, 156, 194, **200**
*The Needle's Eye*, 254, 284
*Needles*, 81
*Neighbors*, 38
**Neihart, Ben, 18**
Nelson, Antonya, 5, 139, 142, 169
**Nervous Conditions, 145**
*The Net*, 101
Neugeboren, Jay, 162
*Neuromancer*, 83
*The New Girls*, 62
*New Jersey*, 269
**New Year's Eve,** 18, **61**
*Next to Nature, Art*, 68, 275
**Ng, Fae Myenne,** 104, **200**
*Nice Work*, 130, 186
**Nichols, John,** 42, **201**
**Nicholson, Joy,** 106, **201**, 291
Niemienen, Raija, 58
*Night of the Avenging Blowfish*, 240
*Night of Many Dreams*, 106
*The Night of the Weeping Women*, 27, 86, 199,
205
*Night Over Day Over Night*, 217
*Night Ride Home*, 145
**The Night Travellers, 295**
*Night*, 10
*Nights at the Circus*, 136, 253
**Nike,** 55, 258
*Nine Months in the Life of An Old Maid*, 96,
203, 238
*Nisei Daughter*, 10
**No Country for Young Men, 286**

*No Earthly Notion*, **50**, 168
*No Easy Place to Be*, 43
*No Fond Return of Love*, 61, 98, 211
*No New Jokes*, 116, **128**
*No New Land*, 27
*No Regrets*, 66, 75
*Nobody Make Me Cry*, 78
*Nobody's Angel*, 193
*Nobody's Child*, 74
*Nobody's Fool*, 150, **214**
*Nobody's Girl*, 5, 139, 142, 169
*Noises Off: A Play in Three Acts*, 44
*None to Accompany Me*, 266
*No-No Boy*, 10
*The Noonday Devil*, 68
**Nooteboom, Cees, 87**, 208, 275, 277
**Nordan, Lewis, 18**, 19, 20, 35, 43, 80, 97, 151, 173, **201**, 282, **285**
**Norman, Howard, 19**, 20, 201, 206, 276
*Norma Jean the Termite Queen*, 70, 121
*North China Lover*, 261
*North Gladiola*, 111
*North of Hope*, 55, 64, 69
*Northern Borders*, 23, **199**
*Northern Edge*, **20**, 22
*Northern Exposure*, **80**
*The Northern Lights*, 19
*Not the End of the World*, 228
*The Notebooks of Don Rigoberto*, 236
*Nothing But Blue Skies*, **193**
*Novel Without a Name*, **152**
*Now I Know Everything*, **92**
*Now It's Time to Say Goodbye*, 205
*Now Molly Knows*, 1
*Now You See Her*, 203
*The Nowhere City*, 99, 177, 187, 188
*The Nuclear Age*, 286
**Nunez, Sigrid, 87**
Nunn, Kem, 201

*O Beulah Land*, 220
*O Come Ye Back to Ireland*, 242
**O'Brien, Edna, 285**
**O'Brien, Kevin, 87**, 212
**O'Brien, Tim, 34**, 49, 81, 86, 212, 217, 248, **285, 286**
**O'Connell, Sanjida, 87**
**O'Connor, Philip, 88**
**O'Donnell, Mark, 158**, 192, **202**
**O'Faolain, Julia, 286**
O'Flaherty, Liam, 251
**O'Hagan, Christine, 88**

O'Hara, John, 159, 255
**O'Hehir, Diana, 202**
**O'Nan, Stewart, 49**, 89, 191, **202**, 217, 268, 280
**Oates, Joyce Carol, 153**, 185, 188, **202**, **285**, 297
*Obabakoak*, **249**
*Obasan*, 146, **180**
*The Obedient Wife*, 286
Obejas, Achy, 87
*Object Lessons*, 100, **212**
*The Object of My Affection*, 39, 123, **192**, 246, 258
*Objects in Mirror Are Closer Than they Appear*, 175, **239**
*The Oblivion Seekers*, 252
*The Obscene Bird of Night*, 9
*Occasion for Loving*, 4
*An Ocean in Iowa*, 37, 91, 102, 150, **168**, 236, 261, 281
*Ocean Vu, Jog to Beach*, **244**
*October Light*, 262
*The Odd Sea*, 196, **212**
*The Odd Woman*, 52, 160
**Oe, Kenzaburo, 286**
*Of Illustrious Men*, 214
*Of Love and Shadows*, 248
*Of Mice and Men*, 137
*Of Such Small Differences*, **60**
*Officers and Gentlemen*, 239
*The Off-Seasons*, 45
*Offshore*, **263**
**Offutt, Chris, 88**
Ogilvie, Elisabeth, 98
*Oh, God!*, 47
Okada, John, 10
Okpewho, Isidore, 298
**Okri, Ben, 287**
*The Old Curiosity Shop*, 173
*The Old Devils*, **118**
*Old Devotions*, **91**
*The Old Forest and Other Stories*, 296
*The Old Gringo*, **158**, 174
*The Old Jest*, **14**
*Old Morals, Small Continents, Darker Times*, 88
*The Old Neighborhood*, **47**
*The Old Silent*, 61
*Old Soldier*, 197
*Old Wives' Tales*, 50
*Oldest Living Confederate Widow Tells All*, 164
*Oleander, Jacaranda: A Childhood Perceived, A Memo*, 275

*Oleanna*, 183
*On the Beach*, 99
**On the Black Hill**, **139**
*On Common Ground*, 79
*On Gold Mountain*, 104
**On Love**, **259**
*On Moral Fiction*, 266
*The Once and Future King*, 253
*Once Upon the River Love*, 277
*Once Upon a Time On the Banks*, 153, 206
*Once Were Warriors*, 270
**Ondaatje, Michael**, 257, 258, 275, **287**
*One Bird*, 6
**One by One in the Darkness**, 14, **16**, 188
*One Deadly Summer*, 174
*One Hundred Years of Solitude*, 265, 292, 293
*One Million Dead*, 137
*One Night Out Stealing*, 270
**One of Us**, **56**
*One on One*, 73
**One Sweet Quarrel**, **17**, 235, 276
*One Thousand Chestnut Trees*, 213
*The One True Story of the World*, 81
*One True Thing*, 91, 126, 131, 143, 212
*The Only Dark Spot in the Sky*, 148
*The Only Daughter*, 119
*Only Son*, 212
**The Only Son**, **87**
*Opal on Dry Ground*, 219
*The Open Heart*, 245
*Open Secrets*, 120
*Open Water*, 190
**Opening Nights**, **43**, 82
*Operation Wandering Soul*, 289
*The Optimist's Daughter*, 43, 145
*Oral History*, 89, 295
*The Orange Fish*, 222
**Oranges Are Not the Only Fruit**, 136, 213, **243**
*The Orchard Keeper*, 74
**The Orchard on Fire**, 19, 20, **276**
*An Ordinary Lunacy*, 119
*Ordinary Money*, 68
*Ordinary People*, 62, 64, 220
**Original Sins**, **117**, 132
*Orlando*, 225, 252
**Osborn, Karen**, **89**
*Oscar and Lucinda*, 135, 243
**The Other Family**, **135**
**The Other Garden**, **27**
*The Other Side* (Alvarez), 117
**The Other Side** (Gordon), **162**, 222

**Other Women's Children**, **73**
**Otto, Whitney**, **203**
Ouologuem, Yambo, 298
*Our House in the Last World*, 169
*Our John Willie*, 50, 58
"Our Town," 102
*Out of Africa*, 279
*Out of the Blue*, 81
*Out of This World*, 25
*Out to Canaan*, 69
*Outbreak of Love*, 232
*Outerbridge Reach*, 82, 228, 254
*Outside Passage: A Memoir of an Alaskan Childhood*, 137
*The Outsider*, 32
*The Outsiders*, 177
*Overnight to Many Distant Cities*, 123
Ovid, 87
**Owen, Howard**, **89**
*Oyster*, 32, 109, 269
**Oz, Amos**, **203**
**Ozeki, Ruth**, 6, 68, **90**, 174
**Ozick, Cynthia**, **287**

**Paco's Story**, 89, 244, **268**, 286
*The Pact*, 91, 218
**Paddy Clarke Ha Ha Ha**, 7, **149**, 221, 236
*The Page Turner*, 274
Pagnol, Marcell, 214
**The Painted Alphabet**, **8**, 138, 196
*The Painted Bird*, 53
*A Painted Devil*, 127
*Painting the Darkness*, 59
*Palace of Desire*, 277
*The Palace Thief*, 134
**Palace Walk**, 249, **277**
*Pale Fire*, 244, 299
**A Pale View of the Hills**, **271**
**Palin, Michael**, 9, **90**
**Pall, Ellen**, **203**
Palliser, Charles, 173
Palwick, Susan, 98
*Pandaemonium*, 10
*Panther in the Basement*, 203
*Papa and Fidel*, 63, 90
**The Paper Men**, **161**
*Paper Wings*, 259
**The Paperboy**, 34, 88, 179, 191, 225, 253, **260**
*Parades End*, 250
**Paradise** (Barthelme), **123**
**Paradise** (Castedo), **6**
*Paradise* (Morrison), 46, 132, 209, 282

*Paradise Fever: Growing Up in the Shadow of the New Age*, 82
*Paradise Junction*, 225
*Paradise News*, 130, 186
*Paradise of the Blind*, 152
*Paradise Postponed*, **198**
*Paris Trout*, 130, **260**
*A Parish of Rich Women*, **42**
*Park City*, 124
**Parker, Michael, 204**, 206
**Parks, Tim, 204**
*Parlor Games*, 139
Parri, Susanne, 20
*Parrot in the Oven: Mi Vida*, 7
*Particles and Luck*, **68**, 77
*The Partisan*, 90
*Passenger*, 158, **178**
*Passing On*, 58, **275**
*The Passion Dream Book*, 203
*The Passion of Alice*, **60**
*The Passion*, 243
*A Passionate Man*, 233
*Past the Bleachers*, 88, 250
**Patchett, Ann**, 92, 157, 170, **204**
*A Patchwork Planet*, 235
*Patchwork*, **89**
**Pate, Alexs, 90**
Paton, Alan, 287
*Patrimony: A True Story*, 291
*The Patron Saint of Liars*, 92, 157, 170, **204**
*The Patron Saint of Unmarried Women*, **30**, 90
Patterson, Richard North, 158
*Patty Jane's House of Curl*, 76, 156
*Paula*, 65, 248
*Pause Between Acts*, 139
*Payment in Full*, 179
**Payne, David, 19**, 257
*Peace Breaks Out*, 180
*Pearl*, 73
*Pearl's Progress*, **177**, 182
*The Pearlkillers: Four Novellas*, 67
*The Pearls of Coromandel*, **5**
Pears, Iain, 256
**Pears, Tim, 205**, 259
**Peck, Dale**, 164, **205**
Peck, Robert, 7
**Peery, Janet, 205**
**Pei, Lowry**, 30, 34, **206**, 290
Pei, Meg, 6
**Pelletier, Cathie**, 20, 30, **90**, 104, 125, 139, 153, **206**, 220

*Pen, Sword, Camisole: A Fable to Kindle a Hope*, 24
*Penmarric*, 172
**Percy, Walker**, 172, 185, **206**, 233, 263, 291
*Perdido*, 5, 65, 107, 139, **142**
*The Perez Family*, **124**
*A Perfect Execution*, 127
*A Perfect Spy*, 300
*The Perfect Storm*, 82, 254
*Perfect Together*, **68**
**Perrin, Ursula, 91**
**Perrotta, Tom**, 131, **207**
*Persian Nights*, 1, 20, 176
*The Persian Pickle Club*, 48, 203
*Persistent Rumours*, 27, **273**
*A Personal Matter*, 286
**Pesetsky, Bette, 207**
*Pete & Shirley: the Great Tar Heel Novel*, 138
Phelan, Tom, 188
*Philip's Girl*, 54
*Philippe at His Bath*, 91
**Phillips, Jayne Anne, 207**, **208**
**Phillips, Kate**, 103, 119, **208**, 266
**Phillips, Max, 288**
*The Philosopher's Pupil*, **284**
*The Piano Man's Daughter*, 54
**Picoult, Jodi, 91**, 149, 218
*Picture Bride*, 112, 184
*The Picture of Dorian Gray*, 68
*Picture Perfect*, 91, 149
*Pictures from an Institution*, 177, 182, 276
*Picturing Will*, 124, 267
**Pierce, Constance, 91**
**Piercy, Marge**, 44, 70, **92**, 94, 154, 176, 242, 273, 290, 295, 300
*Pig*, **7**
*Pigs in Heaven*, 179, 205
Pilcher, Rosamund, 51
*The Pilot's Wife*, 66, 101
*Pinball*, 151, **181**
*The Pinch Runner Memorandum*, 286
*Pincher Martin*, 180
**Pinckney, Darryl, 208**
**Pineda, Cecile**, 142, **208**
*Pink Slip*, 141
**Pinon, Nelida, 92**
*Pinto and Sons*, 10
*Pitch Dark*, **247**, 279, 298
*A Place on Earth*, 111
*A Place Where the Sea Remembers*, **4**, 19, 168, 261

*Places in the World a Woman Could Walk*, 178
*The Plague*, 6
***Plain Grief*, 46**
***Plain Jane*, 172**
***Plains Song, for Female Voices*, 11, 198**
*Plainsong*, 173
*Plans for Departure*, 293
**Plante, David, 209**
Plath, Sylvia, 61, 238
*The Player*, 177, 201, 228
*Playing with Fire*, 99
***Plays Well with Others*, 131, 164**
***Pleasure of Believing*, 66**
**Plesko, Les, 209**
*Pnin*, 244
*Points of Light*, 47, **220**, 231, 252
*The Poison Oracle*, 88, 231
*The Poisonwood Bible*, 12, 162, 179, 279
***Poker Face*, 35**, 36
*The Polish Lover*, 110
***Polite Sex*, 111**
*Poor Things: Episodes from the Early Life of Archibald McCandless, M.D.*, 297
**Pope, Susan, 92**, 103, 204
**Popham, Melinda Worth**, 14, **19**
Popkin, Zelda, 15
*A Population of One*, 72, 126
*The Porcupine*, 251
*The Port of Missing Men*, 102
**Porter, Connie, 209**, 241, 282
*Portnoy's Complaint*, 34, 291
*The Portrait of a Lady*, 175
*Portrait of My Body*, 187
*A Portrait of My Desire*, 63
*Possessing the Secret of Joy*, 120, 138, 238
*Possession*, 13, 85, 173, 179, **254**
*Postcards*, 20, 88
*The Postman*, 99
**Postman, Andrew, 92**
***The Potato Baron*, 11, 26**, 106, 129, 199, 235
**Potok, Chaim**, 1, 15, 96, **209**, 228, 299
**Poverman, C. E., 210**
**Powell, Padgett, 210**
*The Power of the Dog*, 22
*The Power of Horses and Other Stories*, 144
***The Power of One*, 4, 7**, 141, 184
*The Power to Change Geography*, 202
**Power, Susan**, 37, **93**, 116, 148, 155, 223, 269
**Powers, Charles T., 288**
Powers, J. F., 288
**Powers, Richard**, 25, **288**

*Practical Magic*, 47, 171, 200
*The Prague Orgy*, 290
*PrairyErth*, 11
*Praise*, 16
*Praisesong for the Widow*, 190
***A Prayer for Owen Meany*, 173**, 241
*The Presence of Grace*, 288
*Preservation Hall*, 226
*Preston Falls*, 127, 159, 222, 291
**Preston, Caroline, 93**, 94, 186
**Preston, Douglas, 93**
*Pretending the Bed Is a Raft: Stories*, 73
***Pretty Girls*, 29, 110**
*The Price of a Child*, 252
*The Price of Land in Shelby*, 30
**Price, Reynolds, 210**, 294
**Price, Richard**, 95, **211**, 239
*Pride and Prejudice*, 94
*The Priest Fainted*, 53, 156, 226
*Primary Colors*, 274
*The Prime of Miss Jean Brodie*, 279, 295
*Prince of Darkness and Other Stories*, 288
***The Prince of Tides*, 19, 131, 150, 200, 201, 257**
***The Prince of West End Avenue*, 67**
*Principles of American Nuclear Chemistry*, 81
*Prisoner's Dilemma*, 289
*Prisons*, 220
*Private Acts*, 220
***Private Altars*, 59, 198**
***The Private Life of Axie Reed*, 180**
Proffitt, Nicholas, 268
*The Promise of Light*, 193
*The Promise of Rest*, 210, 232
*The Promise*, 96, 210, 228
*Property Of*, 170
**Prose, Francine**, 95, 129, 141, 157, **211**, 292, 294
**Proulx, E. Annie**, 19, **20**, 88, 121, 206, 276
Proust, Marcel, 265, 277, 300
*Psalm at Journey's End*, 97
*Public Life*, 30
*Publish and Perish*, 215
**Puig, Manuel**, 233, **289**
*The Pull of the Moon*, 51, 135
*The Pumpkin Eater*, 96
*Pumpkin Moon*, 34
*Pursued the Crooked Man*, 234
*The Pursuit of Happiness*, 96
***Push*, 186**
**Pym, Barbara**, 61, **93**, 98, **211**, 253, 263
**Pynchon, Thomas**, 264, 272, **289**, 297

*Quarantine*, 257
*Quartet in Autumn*, 211
*Quartet*, 279
**Queen Lear**, **70**
**The Queen of the Tambourine**, **159**
**The Queen's Gambit**, **105**
**Quick, Barbara, 20**, 22
*The Quick: A Novella & Stories*, 96
*The Quiet American*, 74
*The Quiet Room: A Journey Out of the
    Torment of Madness*, 162
Quigley, Martin, 255
*The Quincunx*, 173
**Quindlen, Anna**, 91, 100, 126, 131, 143, **212**
**Quite a Year for Plums**, 69, **240**

Raban, Jonathan, 22
**The Rabbi of Casino Boulevard**, **32**
*The Rabbi of Lud*, 32
**Rabbit at Rest**, **298**
*Rabbit Hill*, 19
**Rabbit Is Rich**, 73, **298**
*Rabbit Redux*, 298
*Rabbit, Run*, 263, 298
*The Rachel Papers*, 31, 239, 263
**Rachlin, Nahid, 20**
**The Rage of the Vulture**, **235**, 236
*A Rage to Live*, 255
Ragen, Naomi, 1
*Ragtime*, 16, 81, 219, 261, 268
*Rain of Gold*, 107
**Rainy Lake**, **95**, 206
*Raise High the Roof Beam, Carpenters*, 203,
    299
*Rameau's Niece*, 93, 98, 173, 179, 254
Ramos, Manuel, 3
Rand, Ayn, 18, 108
*Raney*, 43, 104, 153
*Range of Motion*, 126
Ransmayr, Christoph, 87
**The Rape of Shavi**, **52**
**The Rapture of Canaan**, **213**, 243
**Rates of Exchange**, **130**
*Ratner's Star*, 260
**Rattlesnake Farming**, **181**, 194
Raucher, Herman, 206
*Raw Silk*, 44
**Raymo, Chet**, 37, 40, 142, 144, 151, **212**, 215
**Raymond, Linda, 94**, 96
**Reaching Tin River**, **119**
Read, Piers Paul, 186
**The Reader**, **217**

**Reading in the Dark**, 14, 16, 42, 135, **259**, 286
*The Real Life of Alejandro Mayta*, 236
**Real Life**, **55**
*Reality and Dreams*, 228
Reardon, Lisa, 248
*Rebecca*, 59
*The Rebel Angels*, 258
*Rebel Powers*, 124
*Rebound: the Odyssey of Michael Jordan*, 60
*Recipes from the Dump*, 62, 75
**A Reckoning**, **216**
*The Recognitions*, 264
*Recombinations*, 74
**Reconciliations**, **15**
*The Rector of Justin*, 3
*The Rector's Wife*, 56, 233
*The Red and the Green*, 284
*Red Azalea*, 138, 231
**Red Earth and Pouring Rain**, 8, 9, **138**, 196
*Red Leaves*, 224
*Red Roads*, 225
**Reed, Ishmael**, 174, 182, **289**
*Refuge*, 127, 269
**Regeneration**, 250, **251**, 254, 300
**Reiken, Frederick**, 196, **212**
*The Reivers*, 19, 43
*Relic*, 93
*Reliquary*, 93
**The Remains of the Day**, 10, 87, **271**
Remarque, Erich Maria, 174, 251, 294
*Rembrandt's Hat*, 278
*Remembering Babylon*, 278
*Remembering Light and Stone*, 16
*Remembrance of Things Past*, 265, 277, 300
*Remote*, 223
*The Republic of Dreams*, 92
**The Republic of Love**, 53, 57, **222**, 230, 242
**Requiem for a Woman's Soul**, 2, **21**, 199
**Reservation Blues**, 109, **116**, 144
**Reservation Road**, 50, 64, 212, **218**, 234, 250
**Reservations Recommended**, **75**
*Resistance*, 101
*The Rest of Us*, 196
*Restoration*, 297
*Resume with Monsters*, 227
*Resurrection Update: Collected Poems
    1975–1997*, 11
*The Retreat*, 271
*Return of the Brute*, 251
**Reuss, Frederick**, 150, **212**
*The Revolution of Little Girls*, 129
*Revolutionary Road*, 159

Reynolds, Sheri, **213**, 243
*Rhine Maidens*, 99
Rhys, Jean, 70, 209, 279
Ricci, Nino, **21**, 294
Rice, Luanne, 93, **94**
*Rich in Love*, 107, 172
*Rich Like Us*, 120, **293**
*The Rich Man's Table*, 296
Richardson, Bill, 179
*The Richer, the Poorer: Stories, Sketches, and Reminiscences*, 110
Richler, Mordecai, 16, **21**, 228, 261
*Riddley Walker*, 99
*Ride With Me, Mariah Montana*, 9, 185
*The Riders*, 243
*Riding Solo with the Golden Horde*, **65**
*Right by My Side*, 64
*Rima in the Weeds*, 17, 48
*Rio Grande Fall*, 139
*Ripley Bogle*, 92, **242**
*Ripley Under Ground*, 38
*Rise the Euphrates*, **152**
*The Risk Pool*, 124, 201, 215
*The Ritual Bath*, 1
*Rituals*, 87
Rivabella, Omar, 2, **21**, 199
*The River Beyond the World*, **205**
*The River in Winter*, **224**
*The River Is Home*, 19
*River of Hidden Dreams*, **263**
*A River Runs Through It*, 27
*A River Sutra*, 200, 249
*River Teeth: Stories and Writing*, 150
*A River Town*, 71
*The River Why*, 150
Rivera, Beatriz, **94**, 156, 200
*Rivers of the West; Stories from the Columbia*, 255
Rivers, Caryl, **94**
*Riversong*, 185
*The Roaches Have No King*, **109**
*The Road Home*, 167
*Road Song*, 56
*The Road to Wellville*, 68, 81
*Roadwalkers*, **163**
*The Robber Bride*, 83, 111, 120
Robbins, Tom, **95**, 117, 163
*Robert Crews*, 281
Robinson, Marilynne, 23, 38, 47, 55, 206, 256, **290**
Rock, Peter, **213**
Rockcastle, Mary Francois, **95**, 206

*Rocket City*, 35, **117**
*Rocking the Babies*, **94**, 96
Rodi, Robert, 241
Rodriguez, Jr., Abraham, **95**
Roiphe, Anne, **96**
*The Romance Reader*, **1**, 12, 57, 161, 210
*The Romantic Movement*, 259
Ronyoung, Kim, **213**
*Rookery Blues*, 97
*Rootie Kazootie*, 86
Rose, Joanna, 135, 153, 165
Rosen, Jonathan, 63, **214**
*Rosie*, 161
Rossi, Agnes, 94, **96**
Rossner, Judith, **96**, 203, 238
Rosten, Leo, 219
Roth, Henry, 124
Roth, Philip, 34, 137, 148, 169, 190, **290**, **291**
Rouaud, Jean, **214**
*Rough Strife*, 218
*Round Rock*, **66**
*Roxanna Slade*, 210, 294
Roy, Arundhati, 9, 25, 46, 120, 123, 151, 152, 249, 282, **291**, 292, 293
Rubens, Bernice, 97
Rubio, Gwyn Hyman, 223, 295
*Ruby*, 186
Rudnick, Paul, 75, **214**
*The Rug Merchant*, **187**
*Ruin Creek*, **19**, 257
*Rule of the Bone*, **122**, 260
*Rules of the Wild*, 221, **279**
*Rummies*, 281
*Rumors of Peace*, 31, 32, 119, 143, **184**
*Rumours of Rain*, 256
*Rumpole of the Bailey*, 198
*The Run of the Country*, **7**
*Run River*, 247
*Run with the Horsemen*, **97**
*Running Dog*, 259
*Running in the Family*, 287
*Running Through the Tall Grass*, 6
*Running to Paradise*, 166
*Running Wild*, 3
Rush, Norman, 129, 211, 258, **292**
Rushdie, Salman, 5, 86, 152, 154, 175, 249, 268, 291, **292**, **293**, 297
Russell, Mary Doria, 6, 172, 228, 288
*The Russian Album*, 270
Russo, Richard, 45, 124, 127, 150, 166, 182, 188, 201, **214**, **215**, 237, 266, 276, 278, 290, 299

Rylant, Cynthia, 184
**Ryman, Geoff**, 96, 224, 286

Sa'dawi, Nawal, 21
*Sabbath's Theater*, 169, **291**
*The Sacred and Profane Love Machine*, 167, 284
*Sacred Clowns*, 144
*Sacred Country*, 225, **297**
*Sacred Dust*, **65**, 142
*Sacred Hunger*, 236
*The Sacred Night*, 252
*The Sacrifice of Tamar*, 1
*Safe Conduct*, 126
*Safe Houses*, 71, **116**
*Safe Passage*, **34**, 108
**Sahgal, Nayantara**, 120, **293**
*Sailing in a Spoonful of Water*, 144
*Sailing*, 72
*Sailor Song*, 95
*Saint Maybe*, 123
*Saint Rachel*, 130
*Saint*, 125
*Saints and Strangers*, 233, 253
**Saiter, Susan Sullivan**, 97
Sakamato, Kerri, 13, 228
*Salaryman*, 6
Salinger, J. D., 122, 131, 150, 203, 243, 261, 299
**Salisbury, Graham**, **22**, 173
*The Salt Line*, 295
*Salvation on Sand Mountain: Snake Handling and Redemption in Southern Appalachia*, 52, 194
**Salzman, Mark**, 97, 281
*Sam and His Brother Len*, **79**, 179
*The Same River Twice*, 88
*Sams in a Dry Season*, **161**
Sams, Ferrol, 97
*The Samurai's Garden*, 8, **106**
*The Sand Child*, 252
**Sanders, Dori**, 215
**Sandlin, Tim**, 215
*SantA Evita*, 121
*Santiago and the Drinking Party*, **84**
Santmyer, Helen Hooven, 3
*Sarah Canary*, 140, 157, 230
**Saramago, Jose**, 94, 265, 274, 292, **293**
*Saratoga Backtalk*, 147
*Saratoga Bestiary*, 147
*The Sardine Deception*, 249
Saro-Wiwa, Ken, 287

**Sarton, May**, 78, **216**, 251
*The Saskiad*, 52, 82, 135, **165**, 198
*The Satanic Verses*, 86, 152, 154
Satterthwait, Walter, 83
*Savage Inequalities*, 125
Savage, Barbara, 81
**Savage, Elizabeth**, 17, **98**
**Savage, Georgia**, **98**, 285
**Savage, Thomas**, 22
*Saving St. Germ*, **199**, 222
*Saw*, 177
**Sayer, Paul**, 216
**Sayers, Valerie**, 216
*Saying Grace*, **62**, 63
*The Scapegoat*, 220
*Scar Tissue*, 145, 225, 229, **270**
*The Scarlet Letter*, 85
*Scarlet Song*, 120
*Scenes from the Homefront*, 107
**Schaeffer, Susan Fromberg**, 89, **217**, 286
Schecter, Martin, 241
Schiller, Lori, 162
*Schindler's List*, **71**, 104, 158
**Schine, Cathleen**, 36, 93, **98**, 173, 179, 254
**Schlink, Bernhard**, 217
**Schoemperlen, Diane**, 103, 120, 128, **217**
*The School Book*, 67
*School Days*, 255
*School for the Blind*, 281
Schulberg, Budd, 177, 201
**Schulman, Audrey**, 12, 20, **22**, 121
**Schumacher, Julie**, 103, 197, **218**
**Schwartz, John Burnham**, 50, 64, 212, **218**, 234, 250
**Schwartz, Lynne Sharon**, **218**, 270
Schwartz, Steven, 112
**Schweighardt, Joan**, **218**
**Scofield, Sandra**, 70, **219**
**Scott, Joanna**, 166, **219**
Scott, Paul, 5, 23, 293
*A Scrap of Time and Other Stories*, 262
Scully, Julia, 137
*The Sea, the Sea*, 167, **284**, 294
*Searching for Bobbie Fischer: the Father of A Prodigy Observes the World of Chess*, 105
*Searching for Caleb*, 57, 171, 183, 235
*Searching for Mercy Street*, 220
*Season of the Jew*, 159
*Season of the Rainbirds*, **249**
*The Seasons of Beento Blackbird*, **133**
*Seaward*, 274

*The Second Bridegroom*, 165
**The Second Coming**, **206**
*The Second Dune*, 33
**Second Marriage**, **123**
*Second Nature*, 138
*The Second Story Man*, 30
*Second-Class Citizen*, 287
*Secret Anniversaries*, 296
*Secret Harmonies*, 123
**The Secret History**, 5, **105**, 284
*Secrets and Surprises: Short Stories*, 123, 124
**See, Carolyn**, **98**, 175
See, Lisa, 104
Segal, Erich, 76, 141
**Segal, Lore**, 117, **219**
*Self-Help: Stories*, 83
**Selling the Lite of Heaven**, **99**
**Selvadurai, Shyam**, 18, 163, **220**
*Semi-Tough*, 39
Sencion, Viriato, 296
Senna, Danzy, 76, 197, 238
*Sense and Sensibility*, 94
**Sent for You Yesterday**, 235, **241**
**The Sea of Trees**, **85**
*A Separate Peace*, 3, 71, 180
*September*, 51
*Serenity House*, 269
**The Serpent's Gift**, **184**, 200, 241
*Set for Life*, 57
*Set This House on Fire*, 296
**Seth, Vikram**, **22**, 160, 191
*Setting Free the Bears*, 173
**Settle, Mary Lee**, 71, 72, 181, 211, **220**
*The Settlers*, 17
**Seven Moves**, **248**, 286
*The Seven Year Atomic Make-Over Guide*, 125
**The Seventh Garment**, **156**
**Seventh Heaven**, **170**
*Sex Crimes*, 101
*Sexing the Cherry*, 243
**Sexton, Linda Gray**, **220**, 231, 252
*Seymour: An Introduction*, 203, 299
**Shacochis, Bob**, **221**, 272
Shadbolt, Maurice, 159
*The Shadow Bride*, 195
*The Shadow Catcher*, 104, 282
*The Shadow Knows*, 148, 176
*The Shadow Line*, 57
*The Shadow Man*, 162
**The Shadow of Desire**, 99, 131, **228**
*Shadow Play*, 37

**Shadow Ranch**, **79**, 80, 108, 252, 265
*Shadow Song*, 70
*Shadows on Our Skin*, 14
**Shake Down the Stars**, **51**
**Shakespeare, Nicholas**, **23**
Shakespeare, William, 284
**Shalev, Meir**, **23**
*Shallows*, 243
**Shame** (Nasrin), **86**
**Shame** (Rushdie), **293**
*Shampoo Planet*, 48
Shange, Ntozake, 194
**Shapiro, Dani**, **99**, 131, 228
**Shapiro, Jane**, 90, **221**
**Shards of Memory**, **175**
**Shark Dialogues**, **8**, 106, 178
*The Sharp Teeth of Love*, 252
**Sharp, Paula**, **99**
**The Sharpshooter Blues**, 20, 151, 173, **201**, 282
*The Shawl*, 287
*She Flew the Coop*, 110
**She Needed Me**, 158, **180**, 192
*She Took My Arm as if She Loved Me*, 160
*She Walks these Hills*, 48
**She's Come Undone**, 46, 97, **182**, 248
**Shea, Lisa**, **221**
**Shea, Suzanne Strempek**, **99**
**Shearer, Cynthia**, **221**
Sheehan, Susan, 186
**Sheldon, Dyan**, **100**
**Shelter**, 207, **208**
Shelton, Richard, 179
**Shem, Samuel**, 44, **100**
**Shepard, Elizabeth**, 199, **222**
**Shepherd Avenue**, **136**
*Shepherds of the Night*, 2
**Shields, Carol**, 53, 57, 118, 147, 150, 158, 203, 211, 215, **222**, **223**, 228, 230, 242, **294**, 298
**Shields, David**, 34, 37, **223**
**Shigekuni, Julie**, **100**
*Shiloh and Other Stories*, 191, 225
Shilts, Randy, 164
*Shine Hawk*, 225
*Shine On, Bright and Dangerous Object*, 108, 143, 276
*Ship Fever*, 123
**The Shipping News**, 19, **20**, 121, 206, 276
*Shiva Dancing*, 86
**Shoeless Joe**, **73**, 97

*Shoot the Piper*, 65

*The Short History of a Prince*, 18, 47, 63, 95, 163

*Short of Glory*, 68

*A Short Season*, 9

*Shot in the Heart*, 188

**Show Down**, **2**, 25

*Show World*, 123

*The Shrapnel Academy*, 139, **300**

**Shreve, Anita**, 66, **101**

**Shreve, Susan Richard, 101**

*The Shrine at Altamira*, 182

**Shriver, Lionel, 101**

**Shute, Jenefer**, 60, **101**

Shute, Nevil, 31, 99, 109, 278

*Sick Friends*, 161

Siddons, Anne Rivers, 61, 105, 170

**Sidhwa, Bapsi, 23**

*Sights Unseen*, 97, 160

*Signals of Distress*, 257

*Significant Others*, 191

*Silas Marner*, 170

*The Silence in the Garden*, 84

*The Silence of the Ilano: Short Stories*, 107

*The Silent City*, 286

*Silent Witness*, 60

***Silk Hope, NC***, **86**

**Silko, Leslie Marmon**, 137, **223**, 226

**Silman, Roberta**, **24**, 176

*Silver Cloud Café*, 107

*Silver*, 62, **111**, 245

Simak, Clifford, 70

**Simecka, Martin M.**, **24**, 199

Simmons, Dan, 90

Simmons, Thomas, 121

**Simon, Claude, 294**

**Simons, Paullina, 224**

**Simpson, Mona**, 55, 167, 202, **224**

*Sin*, 167

**Sinclair, April, 102**

Sinclair, Upton, 90

Singer, Isaac Bashevis, 17

Singh, Khushwant, 86

*Singing in the Comeback Choir*, 45

*Singing into the Piano*, 83

*Single Mom*, 32, 51, 148, 194

*The Sirens of Titan*, 108

*Sister Water*, 241

*Sitting Opposite My Brother*, 38

*Six Degrees of Separation*, 276

*The Sixkiller Chronicles*, 65

***The Sixteen Pleasures***, **13**

**Skarmeta, Antonio**, 9, **24**, 90

**Skibell, Joseph, 102**, 296

***Skinny Legs and All***, **95**

*Skins*, 260

*Skipped Parts*, 216

*Skirts*, 14, **30**, 117

*Skywater*, 14, **19**

*The Slave Girl*, 287

**Slavitt, David R., 294**

*Sleeping at the Starlite Motel*, 240

*Sleeping Beauty*, 197

*The Sleeping Car Murders*, 174

*Sleepwalking*, 61

*Sleepwalking*, 86

*A Slipping-Down Life*, 40

***Slow Dancing on Dinosaur Bones***, **111**

***Slow Dancing***, **126**

*Slow Emergencies*, 173

*Slow Motion: A True Story*, 99

*Slow Poison*, 40

*The Slow Train to Milan*, 25

*Small Ceremonies*, 222

***Small Tales of a Town***, **109**

*Small World*, 182, 186

***Small World: An Academic Romance***, 177, **276**

**Small, David, 224**

***The Smell of Apples***, **4**, 7

**Smiley, Jane**, 15, **25**, 38, 80, 90, 177, 182, 238, 266

*Smilla's Sense of Snow*, 292

Smith, Betty, 191

Smith, Bridget A., 30

**Smith, Charlie, 224**, 260

**Smith, Dinitia, 225**, 252

Smith, Dodie, 221

**Smith, Lee**, 48, 89, **225**, **294**

Smith, Lillian, 55

**Smith, Mary Burnett, 102**

**Smith, Mary-Ann Tirone, 102**

Smith, Patrick D., 19

**Smith, Terri McFerrin**, 92, **103**

***Snakebite Sonnet***, **288**

*Snap*, 158

*The Snapper*, 149, 297

*The Snare of Serpents*, 172

***Snow Angels***, 61, **202**, 280

***Snow Falling on Cedars***, 10, 45, **62**, 89, 146, 288

*Snow in August*, 166

*Snowflakes in the Sun*, 190

***So Far from God***, **136**

*So Long a Letter*, **120**, 293
*So Long, See You Tomorrow*, 203, **280**
*Social Blunders*, **215**, 216
*Social Disease*, 214
*The Solace of Food*, 255
*The Solace of Open Spaces*, 10
*Solar Storms*, 205, **269**
*A Soldier of the Great War*, 174, 268
*Soldier's Joy*, 125
*Solibo Magnificent*, 255
*The Soloist*, **97**, 281
*Solomon Gursky Was Here*, 16, **21**, 261
**Solomon, Andrew, 225**, 270
*Solomon's Daughter*, **210**
*Some Kind of Black*, **115**
*Some Tame Gazelle*, 211, 253
*Somebody Else's Mama*, 64
*Something Blue*, **66**
*Something Borrowed*, 80, 190
*Sometimes A Great Notion*, 150, 185
*Somewhere Off the Coast of Maine*, 66, 126
*A Son of the Circus*, 102, 173
*Son of the Morning*, 202
*The Son*, 41
Sone, Monica, 10
*Song of Solomon*, 274
*The Songlines*, 139
*Songs in Ordinary Time*, 197
*Songs of Enchantment*, 287
*Songs of the Humpback Whale*, 91
*Sophie's Choice*, 103, **296**
*Sorrow Floats*, 216
*The Sorrow of War*, 268
*Sort of Rich*, 111
*Souls Raised from the Dead*, 65, 160, 220, **252**
*The Sound and the Fury*, 262
*Sour Sweet*, **83**, 182
*The Source of Light*, 232
*South of the Big Four*, **15**
*South of the Border, West of the Sun*, 283
*South of the Clouds: Tales from Yunnan*, 238
*South of Nowhere*, 249
*South of Resurrection*, 38, 116
*Southern Discomfort*, **132**
*Space*, 72
**Spanbauer, Tom**, 145, **226**
**Spanidou, Irini, 226**
**Spanier, Muriel, 103**
*Spanish Labyrinth*, 137
*A Spanish Lover*, 233

**Spark, Muriel**, 27, 36, 94, 98, 136, 207, 228, 279, **295**
*The Sparrow*, 6, 172, 288
*Spartina*, **254**
*Speaking in Tongues*, 72
*The Spectator Bird*, 227
*Speed Queen*, 89
*Speedboat*, 247, 298
*A Spell of Winter*, **151**
*Spence + Lila*, 191, 225
**Spencer, Brent, 226**
**Spencer, Elizabeth, 295**
**Spencer, Scott**, 134, 137, 144, **226**, 248, **295**
**Spencer, William Browning**, 133, **227**
*Spidertown*, **95**
*Spinsters*, 50, 57, **72**
*Split Skirt*, 94, **96**
*Split: A Counterculture Childhood*, 165
*Splitting*, 139
*Spokesong: Bicycle Adventures on Three Continents*, 81
*Spoon River Anthology*, 102
*The Sportswriter*, 263
*Spring Snow*, 262
*Springs of Living Water*, **183**
**St. Aubin de Teran, Lisa**, 2, **25**, 155
Stabenow, Dana, 20
*Staggerford*, 55
*Stanley and the Women*, 239
Starbird, Kaye, 106, 202
*Stark Raving Elvis*, 15
**Stark, Marisa Kantor**, 10, 67, **103**, 121, 282, 283
*The Starlight Passage*, 43
*Starting Out in the Evening*, 161, 198, 223, 228, 291
*Statutes of Limitations*, **154**
*Staying Afloat*, **103**
*Staying On*, 23
*Stealing Home*, **88**
**Stegner, Lynn, 103**
**Stegner, Wallace**, 75, 78, 118, 160, 180, **227**, 229, 261
Steinbeck, John, 122, 137
*A Step Beyond Innocence*, 68, 198
Stephens, Michael, 162
*The Sterile Cuckoo*, 201
**Stevens, April, 227**
Stevenson, D. E., 205
Stewart, Mary, 253
*Still Life with Woodpecker*, 95
*Still Life*, 254

*Still Missing*, 62, 101, 196, 248
*The Stillest Day*, 167
*Stolen Goods*, 141, 152
*Stolen Words*, 16
**Stollman, Aryeh, 228**
*A Stone Boat*, **225**, 270
*Stone Cowboy*, 221
*The Stone Diaries*, 211, **294**
*Stone Heart*, 94
*The Stone Raft*, 292
Stone, Abigail, 62, 75
Stone, Irving, 166, 174, 219
**Stone, Robert**, 82, **228**, 260, 272, 273
*Stones for Ibarra*, 38, 219, **261**
*Stones from the River*, 212, 238, 258, **267**, 283
*Stool Wives: A Fiction of Africa*, 298
*Stop-Time*, 281
*The Stories of Edith Wharton*, 3
*The Stories of John Cheever*, 236
*The Story of Annie D.*, 195
*The Story of the Night*, **233**, 289
*The Story of Zahra*, 133
*Storyteller*, 226
*The Storyteller*, 236
Stout, Mira, 213
**Stowe, Rebecca**, 99, 131, **228**
**Stracher, Cameron, 229**
Strahan, Jerry, 233
*Straight Cut*, 125
*Straight Man*, 45, 127, 137, 166, 188, 207, **215**, 237, 266, 276, 278, 290, 299
**Straight, Susan**, 187, **229**, 237
Straley, John, 20, 30
*Strands*, 270
*Strange Angels*, 195, 209
*Strange Attractors*, 161
*Strange Fruit*, 55
*Strange Pilgrims*, 265
*A Stranger in the Kingdom*, 199
*The Stranger*, 6, 261
*A Stranger's House*, 187
*Strangers on a Train*, 38
*Stringer*, 176
*Stripping, and Other Stories*, 72
*Strong Motion*, 56
**Strong, Albertine**, 148, **229**
**Stuart, Sarah Payne, 104**
*Stuttering: A Life Bound Up in Words*, 223
*Stygo*, 65, **168**
**Styron, William**, 103, **296**
*Success*, 209

**Such Good People**, 64, **65**
*Such a Long Journey*, 220, 282
**Sudie, 55**
*Sugar Cage*, 264
*Sugar Street*, 277
*The Suicide's Wife*, 125
**A Suitable Boy, 22**
*Sula*, 213, 282
**Sullivan, Walter,** 75, 119, 199, 227, **229**, 235, 270
*The Sultan's Daughter*, 220
*Summer at Gaglow*, 157
*Summer Crossing*, 231
*Summer of '42*, 206
*Summer of Black Widows*, 14
*Summer*, 61
*Summer's Lease*, 198
*A Summons to Memphis*, 74, **296**
*Sun Dial Street*, 76
**Sunrise Shows Late, 17**
**Superior Women, 115**
*Supply of Heroes*, 250
*Supporting the Sky*, 60
*A Supposedly Fun Thing I'll Never Do Again*, 299
*Sure of You*, 191
*The Surface of the Earth*, 232
*Surfacing*, 183
**The Surprise of Burning, 147**
*Survival in Auschwitz*, 10
**Surviving the Seasons**, 66, **75**
*Survivor's Medicine*, 14
*Susan*, 210
*Suspicious River*, 197
Sutcliff, Rosemary, 253
*Suttree*, 4
**Svendsen, Linda, 230**
Swados, Elizabeth, 97
**Swann**, **223**, 228
**Sweet Desserts**, 53, **154**
**The Sweet Dove Died, 211**
**Sweet Eyes**, 79, **116**, 234
**The Sweet Hereafter**, 50, 170, 210, **250**, 252
*Sweet Summer: Growing Up With and Without My Dad*, 45
**Sweet Water** (Kline), **74**
*Sweet Water* (Kramer), 181
**The Sweetheart Season**, **157**, 204
Swick, Marly, 259
**Swift, Graham,** 25, 60, 118, **230**, 256, 276
*Swimmer in the Secret Sea*, 74

*Swimming Across the Hudson*, 127, **168**, 179, 229
*Swimming in the Volcano*, **221**, 272
*The Swine's Wedding*, 109
*Swing Hammer Swing!*, **297**
*Sword at Sunset*, 253
**Syal, Meera, 230**
**Szczypiorski, Andrzej, 104**, 262, 282

*Taft*, 170, 204
*The Takeover*, 295
*Taking Care of Mrs Carroll*, 196
*Tales from the Blue Archives*, 296
*Tales from the Garbage Hills*, 220
*Tales from the Irish Club*, 88
*Tales of the City*, 147, 159, 160, **191**
*Talk Before Sleep*, 91, **126**, 182
*Talking It Over*, 133, **251**, 265
*Talking to the Dead: A Novel*, 151
Tallent, Elizabeth, 175
*Tamarind Men*, 159
**Tamaro, Susanna, 104**
**Tan, Amy, 104**, 105, 138, 200, **230**
**Tannen, Mary**, 77, 88, 93, 129, 168, **231**
*Tapping the Source*, 201
*Tar Baby*, 130
Tarr, Herbert, 15, 32
**Tartt, Donna, 5, 105**
Taylor, Elizabeth, 119, 208
**Taylor, Peter, 74, 296**
Taylor, Susan Chehak, 195
Taylor, theodore, 12
**Taylor-Hall, Mary Ann**, 48, 59, **231**
*The Tears of Autumn*, 259
*Teen Angel and Other Stories of Young Love*, 59
*Tempest Rising: A Novel*, 194
*"The Tempest,"* 284
*The Temple of My Familiar*, 238
*Temporary Shelter*, 162
**Tempting Fate, 30**
**Ten Indians, 125**
*Ten Poems*, 148
*The Tenants of Time*, 14
*Tender Mercies*, 42, 210, 216
*Tender Offer*, 190
*Tender*, 80, 140, 176
**Tending to Virginia**, 160, 170, **192**
*Tent of Miracles*, 2
**Terminal Velocity, 129**, 211
*Terms of Endearment*, 126
*The Terrible Girls*, 131

*Terrible Honesty: Mongrel Manhattan in the 1920s*, 282
*The Terrible Twos*, 290
**Tesich, Steve**, 80, 145, 150, 168, 176, 201, 228, **231**
*Tess of the d'Urbervilles*, 139
*A Test of Wills*, 59
*Testament of Friendship*, 300
**The Testimony of Taliesin Jones, 42**
**Testing the Current**, 19, 102, **281**
**Tevis, Walter, 105**
**Texaco**, 2, 8, **255**
*That Eye, That Sky*, 243
**That Night**, 134, 155, 206, 262, **280**, 296
**That Summer, 33**
**Thayer, Nancy, 105**
*Their Eyes Were Watching God*, 145, 213
*them*, 202
*Then She Found Me*, 55, 127, 169
*Theo and Matilda*, 127
*The Theory of Everything*, 61
**Theory of Mind, 87**
**Therapy** (Lodge), 127, **186**
*Therapy* (Schwartz), 112
*There Are No Children Here*, 186
Theroux, Alexander, 292
**Theroux, Paul**, 12, 122, 204, **232**
*These Demented Lands*, 272
**These High, Green Hills, 69**, 71
*They Came Like Swallows*, 280
*They Forged the Signature of God*, 296
**They Whisper, 133**, 267
*The Thief of Time*, 144
*Things Fall Apart*, 2, 52, 287
**Things Invisible to See**, 136, 150, 169, 171, **241**
*The Things They Carried*, 49, 286
*This Boy's Life*, 122, 243
*This House of Sky*, 9, 11
**This Is the Place, 213**
*This Is Your Life*, 112
*Thomas and Beulah*, 148
Thomas, D. M., 259
Thomas, Dylan, 238
**Thomas, Maria, 26**, 129
Thomas, Piri, 95
Thomas, Ross, 15
**Thon, Melanie Rae, 105**
**Thorndike, John**, 11, **26**, 106, 129, 199, 235
**Thornton, Lawrence**, 2, 21, 143, 233, 241, 248, **296**
*The Thought Gang*, 263
**A Thousand Acres**, 15, **25**, 38, 89, 90, 238

*Three Children*, **106**
*A Three Cornered Sun: A Historical Novel*, 26
*Three Farmers on Their Way to a Dance*, 289
*Three Lives*, 3
*Three Lovers*, 286
*Three Thousand Dollars*, 186
*Three Times Table*, 277
*Three Women at the Water's Edge*, 105
*Three-Legged Horse*, 66
*Through the Green Valley*, 163
*Through the Ivory Gate*, **148**
*Thunder and Lightnings*, 190
**Thurm, Marian**, 45, 76, 143, 183, **232**
*Tidewater Tales*, 232
*The Tie That Binds*, **168**
*The Tiger in the Tiger Pit*, 269
*The Tiger*, 25
*Tiger's Tail*, 184
*A Tiler's Afternoon*, 87, **266**
**Tilghman, Christopher**, 49, 101, **232**
*Tim*, 27, 169, 171
*Time in Its Flight*, 217
*A Time to Dance*, 75, 119, 199, 227, **229**, 235,
    270
*Time Will Darken It*, 296
*Time's Witness*, 188, 192
*The Tin Can Tree*, 47, 231, 235, 252
*The Tin Drum*, 212, 267
*Tinker, Tailor, Soldier, Spy*, 126
*Tirra Lirra by the River*, 72, **118**, 119, 262,
    271, 275
*Titmuss Regained*, 198
*To the Birdhouse*, 98
*To Dance with the White Dog*, **70**
*To Kill a Mockingbird*, 43, 55, 61, 157, 167
*To My Ex-Husband*, **51**
*To a Native Shore*, 79
*To Say Nothing of the Dog*, 242
*To See You Again*, 115
*To the Tenth Generation*, 70
*To the Wedding*, **38**
*Tobacco Road*, 206
Todd, Charles, 59
**Toibin, Colm, 233**, 289
Tolkin, Michael, 177, 201, 228
Tolstoy, Leo, 282
*Tongues of Flame*, 204
*Toning the Sweep*, 215
*Too Far to Go: the Maples Stories*, 221
**Toole, John Kennedy**, 152, 189, **233**
**Toppel, Lori, 106**
**Torrington, Jeff, 297**

*The Tortilla Curtain*, 76, 107, 240, **252**
*Tortoise by Candlelight*, 36
*Tortuga*, 3, 107
*Total Immersion*, 12
*The Total Zone*, 101
*The Touch*, **85**
*Toward the End of Time*, 68, 236
*Toward the End*, **98**
*The Towers of Silence*, 23
*A Town Like Alice*, 31, 109, 278
*Town Smokes*, 4
Townsend, Sue, 149, 156
*Traces*, 262
*The Tracks of Angels*, 33
*Tracks*, 148, 154, **155**
*Traffic and Laughter*, 83
*Train Go Sorry: Inside a Deaf World*, 47
*The Train Home*, 101
*Train to Pakistan*, 86
*Trainspotting*, 16, 272
*The Transit of Venus*, **267**
*The Trap*, 283, **299**
*Trash*, 248
*Treasures of Time*, 275
*The Treatment*, 96, 112
*A Tree Grows in Brooklyn*, 191
**Tremain, Rose**, 225, **297**
*Trespassers Welcome Here*, 177
**Trevor, William**, 222, 239, **297**
*The Trial*, 272
*The Tribes of Palos Verdes*, 106, **201**, 291
**Trollope, Joanna**, 56, 136, **233**
**Trott, Susan**, 93, 113, 186, **234**
*Trouble the Water*, **50**
*Trouble*, 239
*Troubles*, 16
**Troy, Judy**, 38, 116, **234**
*True Confessions: the Novel*, **41**, 57
*The True Detective*, 211, **239**
*Truth: Four Stories I Am Finally Old Enough
    to Tell*, 148
*Trying to Save Pinky Sneed*, 173
**Tsukiyama, Gail**, 8, **106**
**Tuck, Lily**, 247, **298**
*Tully*, **224**
*Tumbling*, 32, **194**, 200
*Tunnel of Love*, 53, 111
*The Tunnel*, 123
*Tupelo Nights*, **41**
*The Turkey War*, 235
*Turkish Delights*, 294
*Turkish Reflections*, 220

*Turnip Blues*, 72
*Turtle Diary*, 87, 190
**Turtle Moon**, 80, **171**, 200, 265
**Tuxedo Park, 57**
Twain, Mark, 150, 161
**The Twenty-Seventh City**, 54, **56**, 299
*Two Girls, Fat and Thin*, 280
*Two Guys from Verona*, 177
*Two Halves of New Haven*, 241
*The Two of Us*, 201
*The Two-Headed Calf*, 128
*Twopence to Cross the Mersey*, 36
Two-Rivers, E. Donald, 14
**Ty-Casper, Linda, 26**
**Tyler, Anne**, 50, 57, 60, 64, 108,123, 135,
    139, 157, 171, 183, 204, 227, 231, **234**,
    **235**, 237, 252, 267
*Typical American*, 175, 184
Tyree, Omar, 32, 51, 148, 194

Uchida, Yoshiko, 112, 184
*Ugly Ways*, 32
*Uhuru Street*, 27
*The Ultimate Good Luck*, 77
*Ulysses*, 162, 208, 245, 264, 289
**The Unbearable Lightness of Being**, 273
*Uncivil Seasons*, 188, 192
*Unconquered Countries: Four Novellas*, 97
**The Unconsoled**, 266, **272**, 274, 283
**Under the Frog: A Black Comedy**, 24, 31,
    199, **262**
*Under Milkwood*, 238
*Under the Net*, 198
*Under the Volcano*, 161
*Under A Wing: A Memoir*, 78
**The Underpainter**, 21, 174, **299**
**Undertow, 103**
*Underworld*, 260
**The Undiscovered Country**, **12**, 122
**The Unfastened Heart**, 143, **237**, 242, 265
**Unger, Douglas**, 26, **235**
**Unholy Loves, 202**
*Unreliable Memoirs*, 174
*The Unseen Shore*, 121
*Unstrung Heroes*, 138
*An Unsuitable Attachment*, 94
**Unsworth, Barry, 235**
*Unto the Soul*, 256
*The Untouchable*, 43
*Up Island*, 105, 170
*Up the Sandbox*, 70
**Updike, John**, 68, 73, 221, **236**, 263, 276, **298**

*Upon This Rock: the Miracles of the Black
    Church*, 194
Uris, Leon, 17
**Urquhart, Jane,** 21, 174, 254, 271, **299**
*Utz*, 139

**Vakil, Ardashir**, 102, 149, 168, **236**, 261
*The Value of Kindness: Stories*, 34
*The Van*, 149
**Vandenburgh, Jane, 106**
*Vanished*, 197
*Vanishing Points*, 40
*Vanishing Rooms*, 50
**Vargas Llosa, Mario**, **236**, 288
**Vassanji, M. G.**, **27**, 249
Vazquez, Jr., Diego, 102
**Van der Velde**, Rink, 283, **299**
**Vea, Alfredo, 107**
*A Vegetable Emergency*, 46
*Veils*, 20
*A Vein of Riches*, 180
**The Ventriloquist's Tale**, **195**
**The Veracruz Blues**, **111**
**Verdelle, A. J., 237**
*Vertigo Park*, 202
**A Very Long Engagement**, 59, **174**, 294
*Very Old Bones*, 273
*The Very Rich Hours*, 33
Van Gieson, Judith, 3
*Van Gogh's Room at Arles: Three Novellas*,
    262
**Vicens, Josefina**, 215, **237**
*Victim of the Aurora*, 178
*Victory Over Japan*, 58
*Vida*, 44, 94, 154, 176, 290, 295
Vidal, Gore, 166
*The View From Pompey's Head*, 89, 131
**Villasenor, Victor, 107**, 118, 252
**Vinegar Hill, 32**
**Vineland**, 272, **289**
*Violence*, 50, 124
*Violet Clay*, 160
*The Virgin in the Garden*, 149, 254, 284
*Virgin of the Rodeo*, 39
**The Virgin Suicides**, 55, 200, **262**, 280
**Virgin Widows, 163**
*Virgins*, 94
**The Vision of Elena Silves**, **23**
*The Visit*, 143
**The Visiting Physician**, **101**
**Vogan, Sara, 107**
*Voices from Silence*, 235

*The Voices of Eve*, 126
*The Volcano Lover*, 221
**Volk, Toni, 108**
Voltaire, 54
**Von Herzen, Lane,** 143, **237**, 342, 265
**Vonnegut, Kurt, 108**
*Vox*, 133
*The Voyage of the Narwhal*, 12, 123
*Voyage to the Island*, 58
Van Wert, William, 298

Wagner, Bruce, 228
*Waiting for the Barbarians*, 256
*Waiting for the End of the World*, 125
***Waiting to Exhale*, 194**
*Waiting to Vanish*, 66
*The Waiting Years*, 59
Waitzkin, Fred, 105
*Waking the Dead*, 248, 296
*The Waking Spell*, 49
*A Walk on the West Side*, 160
**Walker, Alice,** 120, 132, 138, 163, **237**, 248
Walker, Mildred, 145
***Walking Across Egypt*, 142, 153**
***Walking After Midnight*, 80**
***Walking Distance*,** 45, 76, 143, **232**
*Walking Dunes*, 219
**Wallace, David Foster,** 289, **299**
*Waltz in Marathon*, 50
*The Wanderers*, 211
**Wang, Anyi, 238**
*War and Peace*, 282
*War Babies*, 133
*The War Between the Tates*, 182, 188
*The War of Don Emmanuel's Nether Parts*, 258
**Warlick, Ashley, 108**
**Warloe, Constance, 108**
Warner, Alan, 272
*Warriors Don't Cry*, 49
*Was*, **96**, 224, 286
*Washington Square*, 1, 3
**Wassmo, Herbjorg, 238**
*Wasted: A Memoir of Anorexia and Bulimia,*
    214
*Watch Time Fly*, 57
*The Water Is Wide*, 257
*Water Music*, 130
*Water Witches*, **40**, 66, 89, 146
*Waterland*, **25**, 256, 276
**Waters, Annie,** 168, **238**
*Watership Down*, 19
Watkins, Paul, 193, 217

**Watson, Larry, 27**, 78, 91, 151, 276, 280
Watt, Laura, 48, 231
Waugh, Evelyn, 239, 271
*Waverly Place*, 32, 99, 149, 155
*The Way I Found Her*, 297
*The Way Men Act*, 116, 176, **185**, 246
***The Way to St. Ives*, 58**
*The Way Water Enters Stone: Stories*, 150
*The Way We Live Now*, 232
*We Are What We Ate; 24 Memories of Food*, 111
*We Find Ourselves in Moontown*, 164
*We Were the Mulvaneys*, 185
***We're Not Here*, 79**, 116
**Weber, Katherine,** 175, **239**
**Webster, Susan, 109**
***The Wedding*, 110**, 170, 208
***The Weekend*, 134**
**Weesner, Theodore,** 211, **239**
***The Weight of Water*, 101**
*The Weight of Winter*, 140, 206
Weir, Willie, 81
**Weiss, Daniel Evan, 109**
**Welch, James, 109**
*Welcome to the Club*, 244
*Welcome to Hard Times*, 261
*Welcome to the World, Baby Girl!*, 131, 156
**Weldon, Fay,** 36, 61, 68, 136, 139, **239**, 240,
    295, **300**
**Weller, Anthony, 110**
**Wells, Rebecca,** 40, 228, **239**
Welsh, Irvine, 16, 272
**Welter, John,** 33, 55, 221, **240**, 252
Welty, Eudora, 43, 110, 145
**Wesley, Mary, 240**
***West of Venus*,** 38, 116, **234**
*West with the Night*, 83
**West, Dorothy, 110**, 170, 208
West, Jessamyn, 190
**West, Michael Lee, 110**
West, Nathanael, 92, 177
**West, Paul, 300**
**Weyr, Garret,** 29, **110**
Wharton, Edith, 1, 3
*What Are Big Girls Made Of?: Poems*, 92
***What the Dead Remember*, 163**
***What the Deaf-Mute Heard*, 58**
***What Girls Learn*,** 47, **143**, 225, 290
***What I Lived For*, 285**
***What Looks Like Crazy on An Ordinary Day*,**
    **46**
*What Makes Sammy Run?*, 177, 201

*What Rough Beast*, 65
**What the Scarecrow Said**, **13**
**What's Bred in the Bone**, **258**, 299
*What's Eating Gilbert Grape?*, 168
*What's That Pig Outdoors? A Memoir of Deafness*, 58
**Wheat That Springeth Green**, **288**
*Wheels*, 84
*When All the World Was Young*, 97
*When Blackbirds Sing*, 232
*When Harlem Was in Vogue*, 282
*When in Greece*, 156
*When Nietzche Wept*, 112
**When the Rainbow Goddess Wept**, **41**, 53, 72
*When the Sons of Heaven Meet the Daughters of the Earth*, 130, 152, 186
*When Things Get Back to Normal*, 91
**When the Tree Sings**, **13**
**When the World Was Steady**, **18**
*Where All the Ladders Start*, 276
*Where the Bluebird Sings to the Lemonade Springs*, 227
*Where Do You Stop?*, 75
*Where or When*, 66
*Where the Rivers Flow North*, 199
*Where Shall We Go This Summer?*, 146
*Where You Once Belonged*, 168
**While the Music Lasts**, **82**
*The Whisper of the River*, 97
*The White Bus*, 45
*White Crosses*, 27
*White Girls*, 76
**White Horses**, **171**
**White Man's Grave**, **51**, 129, 269
**White Noise**, 83, **260**
*White People*, 164
**White Rabbit**, 103, 119, **208**, 266
**White, Bailey**, 69, **240**
White, E. B., 7
**White, Edmund**, 18, **241**
White, T. H., 253
*The Whiteness of Bones*, 197
*Whites*, 292
*Who Do You Love*, 216
**Who Will Run the Frog Hospital?**, 30, 54, **83**, 102
*A Whole New Life*, 210
**Why Should You Doubt Me Now?**, **41**, 54
*Why We Never Danced the Charleston*, 163
*Wickford Point*, 236
*Wide Sargasso Sea*, 70
**Wideman, John Edgar**, 235, **241**

*A Widow for One Year*, 35, 123, 137, 173
*The Widow of Oz*, 57
**The Widows' Adventures**, 18, **50**, 57, 72
*Wife and Mother*, 29, 126
Wiggin, Helene, 72
**Wiggins, Marianne**, 74, 126, 147, 277, 278, **300**
**Wilcox, James**, **111**
*The Wild Colonial Boy*, 193
**Wild Embers**, **43**
*Wild Meat and Bully Burgers*, 173, 245
**A Wild Sheep Chase**, **283**
*Wild Steps of Heaven*, 107
*Wild Swans: Three Daughters of China*, 138
Wilde, Oscar, 68
Wilder, Thornton, 102
*Wildfire*, 263
**Willard, Nancy**, 136, 150, 169, 171, **241**
**Williams, Niall**, **242**
Williams, Terry Tempest, 127, 269
**Willis, Connie**, 176, **242**, 246, 283
Wilson, A. N., 233
Wilson, Barbara, 121
**Wilson, Robert McLiam**, 92, **242**
Wilson, Sloan, 47, 84
*The Wind in the Wheat*, 231
*The Wind*, 294
*The Windeater*, 270
**The Wind-Up Bird Chronicle**, **283**
**Winegardner, Mark**, **111**
*Winesburg, Ohio*, 238
**Wing, Avra**, 37, **242**
*The Wings of the Dove*, 3, 239
*Wings of Fire*, 59
*Wings of Stone*, 26
*Winners and Losers*, 255
*The Winter Birds*, 163
*Winter Brothers*, 9
*Winter in the Blood*, 109
*Winter Tales*, 284
*Winter Wheat*, 145
**Winterkill**, 9, 11, 148, 168, **185**
**Winterson, Jeanette**, 136, 213, **243**, 259, 280
**Winton, Tim**, 120, 163, **243**, 253, 300
**Wise Children**, **136**, 229, 240, 243, 295
*Wise Virgin*, 233
**The Wishbones**, 131, **207**
*With or Without and Other Stories*, 50
**Witt, Lana**, **111**
*The Wizard of Loneliness*, 42, 201
**WLT: A Radio Romance**, **71**, 236
*Wobegon Boy*, 71

Woiwode, Larry, 155
*Wolf Whistle*, 20, 35, 43, 173, 201, 282, **285**
Wolfe, Tom, 17, 82
Wolff, Geoffrey, 81
**Wolff, Tobias**, 122, **243**
**Wolitzer, Hilma**, 46, 53, 63, 103, **111**, 245
**Wolitzer, Meg**, 61, **112**
*A Woman's Guide to Adultery*, 239
*The Woman and the Ape*, 129
*Woman at Point Zero*, 21
*Women at Forty*, 58
*Women Like Us*, **29**, 110
*The Women of Brewster Place*, 194
*Women of Sand and Myrrh*, **1**
*Women of the Silk*, 106
*Women with Men: Three Long Short Stories*, 263
*The Women's Room*, 29, 57, 117, 300
*Woman Hollering Creek*, 107
*The Woman in the Dunes*, 286
*Woman in A Lampshade*, 68
*A Woman Named Drown*, 210
*A Woman of Independent Means*, 51, 63, 222
*Woman of the Inner Sea*, **71**, 98, 109
*A Woman of Spirit*, 15
*Woman on the Edge of Time*, 70
*The Woman Warrior*, 41, 53, 135
*The Woman Who Married a Bear*, 20, 30
*The Woman Who Walked into Doors*, 32, 99, **149**, 155, 227
*The Woman Who Walked on Water*, 247, **298**
*The Woman Who Was Not All There*, 99
*The Wonder Book of the Air*, **221**
*Wonder Boys*, 31, 74, **137**, 189, 215, 226
*The Wonder Worker*, 245
*Wonderland*, 202
**Wong, Shawn**, 140, 184, **244**
**Wood, Clement Biddle, 244**
*Wooden Fish Songs*, 230
*The Woods*, 209
Woolf, Virginia, 225, 252, 266
*Words of My Roaring*, 54
*The World According to Garp*, 35, 135
*The World Around Midnight*, **60**, 109
*A World Away*, 89
*A World Like This*, 37
*The World More or Less*, 214
*The World of Henry Orient*, 68
*World's End*, 130
*World's Fair*, **261**

Wouk, Herman, 212, 288
*The Wrecked, Blessed Body of Shelton LaFleur*, 18, 131
*The Wrecking Yard*, 4
*The Wrestler's Cruel Study*, 97, 132, **147**
**Wright, Stephen, 244**, 268
*Written on the Body*, 243, 259, 280
**Wyndham, Francis, 27**

**Yalom, Irving, 112**
**Yamaguchi, Yoji, 112**
**Yamanaka, Lois-Ann**, 37, 173, **245**
**Yates, Richard, 300**
*A Year in the Dark: Journal of A Film Critic, 1968–69*, 247
*The Year of the French*, 14
*The Year of the Frog*, **24**, 199
*A Year of Lesser*, **37**
*The Year of Living Dangerously*, 74
*A Year of Rhymes*, 163
*The Year of Silence*, **125**
*The Year Roger Wasn't Well*, **104**
*The Year the Yankees Lost the Pennant*, 68
**Yehoshua, A. B.**, 111, **245**
*A Yellow Raft in Blue Water*, 116, **148**, 155
*Yellow Woman and A Beauty of the Spirit*, 223
Yglesias, Rafael, 17
*Yo!*, 117, **118**
*You Went Away*, 226
*You Will Learn to Love Me*, 46
*You'll Never Be Here Again*, **39**
*Young Hearts Crying*, 300
*Young Man with A Horn*, 65, 112
*Youngblood Hawke*, 212
*Your Blue-Eyed Boy: A Novel*, 151
*Your Blues Ain't Like Mine*, 45
*Your Oasis on Flame Lake*, 71, **75**, 252

**Zabor, Rafi**, 74, **112**
*Zeno Was Here*, **189**
*Zenzele: A Letter to My Daughter*, **189**
*Zero db and Other Stories*, 125
**Zigman, Laura, 113**
*Zod Wallop*, 133
Zola, Emile, 159
*Zombie Jamboree*, 268
*Zombie*, 188, 297
*Zorba the Greek*, 258
*Zuckerman Unbound*, 290
**Zuravleff, Mary Kay, 246**